Case Studies in Contemporary Criticism

# MARY SHELLEY

## *Frankenstein*

# Case Studies in Contemporary Criticism
SERIES EDITOR: Ross C Murfin

Jane Austen, *Emma*
EDITED BY Alistair M. Duckworth, University of Florida

Charlotte Brontë, *Jane Eyre*, Second Edition
EDITED BY Beth Newman, Southern Methodist University

Emily Brontë, *Wuthering Heights*, Second Edition
EDITED BY Linda H. Peterson, Yale University

Geoffrey Chaucer, *The Wife of Bath*
EDITED BY Peter G. Beidler, Lehigh University

Kate Chopin, *The Awakening*, Second Edition
EDITED BY Nancy A. Walker, Vanderbilt University

Samuel Taylor Coleridge, *The Rime of the Ancient Mariner*
EDITED BY Paul H. Fry, Yale University

Joseph Conrad, *Heart of Darkness*, Third Edition
EDITED BY Ross C Murfin, Southern Methodist University

Thomas Hardy, *Tess of the d'Urbervilles*
EDITED BY John Paul Riquelme, Boston University

Nathaniel Hawthorne, *The Scarlet Letter*, Second Edition
EDITED BY Ross C Murfin, Southern Methodist University

Henry James, *The Turn of the Screw*, Third Edition
EDITED BY Peter G. Beidler, Lehigh University

James Joyce, *The Dead*
EDITED BY Daniel R. Schwarz, Cornell University

James Joyce, *A Portrait of the Artist as a Young Man*, Second Edition
EDITED BY R. B. Kershner, University of Florida

Mary Shelley, *Frankenstein*, Third Edition
EDITED BY Johanna M. Smith, University of Texas at Arlington

Bram Stoker, *Dracula*, Second Edition
EDITED BY John Paul Riquelme, Boston University

Jonathan Swift, *Gulliver's Travels*
EDITED BY Christopher Fox, University of Notre Dame

Edith Wharton, *The House of Mirth*
EDITED BY Shari Benstock, University of Miami

# Case Studies in Contemporary Criticism

SERIES EDITOR: Ross C Murfin, *Southern Methodist University*

# MARY SHELLEY
# *Frankenstein*

Complete, Authoritative Text with
Biographical, Historical, and Cultural Contexts;
Critical History; and Essays from
Contemporary Critical Perspectives

## THIRD EDITION

EDITED BY

## Johanna M. Smith
*University of Texas at Arlington*

## Bedford/St. Martin's

A Macmillan Education Imprint

Boston • New York

For Bedford/St. Martin's

*Vice President, Editorial, Macmillan Higher Education Humanities:*
 Edwin Hill
*Editorial Director, English and Music:* Karen S. Henry
*Senior Executive Editor:* Stephen A. Scipione
*Publishing Services Manager:* Andrea Cava
*Production Supervisor:* Carolyn Quimby
*Marketing Manager:* Joy Fisher Williams
*Project Management:* DeMasi Design and Publishing Services
*Director of Rights and Permissions:* Hilary Newman
*Cover Design:* William Boardman
*Cover Art: A Snowstorm in Greenland* (engraving), English School,
 (19th century)/Private Collection/© Look and Learn/Bridgeman Images
*Composition:* Achorn International, Inc.
*Printing and Binding:* LSC Communications

Manufactured in the United States of America.

7  8  9  10     25  24  23  22  21
f

*For information, write:* Bedford/St. Martin's, 75 Arlington Street,
Boston, MA 02116   (617-399-4000)

ISBN 978-0-312-46318-2

**Acknowledgments**

"Victor's Secret: Queer Gothic in Lynd Ward's Illustrations to *Frankenstein*
(1934)" by Grant F. Scott. From *Word & Image*, Volume 28, Issue 2, 2012. Copyright © 2012 Taylor & Francis Ltd. Reprinted by permission of Taylor & Francis
Ltd (http://www.tandfonline.com).

 "'This Thing of Darkness': Racial Discourse in Mary Shelley's *Frankenstein*"
by Allan Lloyd Smith from *Gothic Studies* 6.2 (November 2004). Copyright ©
2004 The University of Manchester Press. Reprinted by permission.

 "Crusades Against Frost: Frankenstein, Polar Ice, and Climate Change in
1818" by Siobhan Carroll. From *European Romantic Review*, Volume 24, Issue 2,
April 1, 2013. Copyright © 2013 Taylor & Francis Ltd. Reprinted by permission
of Taylor & Francis Ltd (http://www.tandfoline.com).

Distributed outside North America by PALGRAVE MACMILLAN
Houndmills, Basingstoke, Hampshire RG21 6XS

# About the Series

Volumes in the *Case Studies in Contemporary Criticism* series introduce college students to the current critical and theoretical ferment in literary studies. Each volume reprints the complete text of a significant literary work, together with critical essays that approach the work from different theoretical perspectives and editorial matter that introduces both the literary work and the critics' theoretical perspectives.

The volume editor of each *Case Study* has selected and prepared an authoritative text of a classic work, written introductions (sometimes supplemented by cultural documents) that place the work in biographical and historical context, and surveyed the critical responses to the work since its original publication. Thus situated biographically, historically, and critically, the work is subsequently examined in several critical essays that have been prepared especially for students. The essays show theory in practice; whether written by established scholars or exceptional young critics, they demonstrate how current theoretical approaches can generate compelling readings of great literature.

As series editor, I have prepared introductions to the critical essays and to the theoretical approaches they entail. The introductions, accompanied by bibliographies, explain and historicize the principal concepts, major figures, and key works of particular theoretical approaches as a prelude to discussing how they pertain to the critical essays that follow. It is my hope that the introductions will reveal to students that effective criticism—including their own—is informed by a set of coherent assumptions that can be not only articulated but also modified and extended through comparison of different theoretical approaches. Finally, I have included a glossary of key terms that recur in these volumes and in the discourse of contemporary theory and criticism. I hope that the *Case Studies in Contemporary Criticism* series will reaffirm the richness of its literary works, even as it presents invigorating new ways to mine their apparently inexhaustible wealth.

I would like to thank Supryia M. Ray, with whom I wrote *The Bedford Glossary of Critical and Literary Terms,* for her invaluable help in revising the introductions to the critical approaches represented in this volume.

Ross C Murfin
*Southern Methodist University*
Series Editor

# About This Volume

Part One of this volume consists of the complete text of Mary Shelley's *Frankenstein* and two sections of contextual material: a "Biographical and Historical Contexts" essay on the author, and a section of cultural documents, both print and visual, about the novel. The text of *Frankenstein* reprinted is based on the third edition of 1831, the last version overseen and approved by Mary Shelley. I have retained this edition's spelling and punctuation, correcting only glaring errors and misprints; where appropriate, I have made these corrections in accordance with the 1818 text as edited by James Rieger. Charles Robinson's magisterial edition of *The* Frankenstein *Notebooks* (1996) now makes it possible for interested teachers and students to compare the published texts with the manuscript versions.

Part Two consists of a history of *Frankenstein* criticism and essays that read *Frankenstein* from the perspective of specific critical methodologies — psychoanalytic, Marxist, feminist, gender studies and Queer theory, cultural studies, and postcolonial studies. In choosing the critical modes to be represented, I was sometimes guided by existing work. For example, the three essays retained from the 2000 edition of this volume, Warren Montag's in Marxist criticism, David Collings's in psychoanalytic criticism, and mine in feminist criticism, represent critical methodologies with a continuing history of attention to *Frankenstein*. In my other choices I was guided by the opportunity to represent newer critical methods that have been directed to Mary Shelley's novel.

## New to This Edition

In Part One, an updated selection of documents and artifacts edited by Christopher Stampone indicates the wide range of the novel's cultural contexts. In Part Two, I retained the category of cultural studies but used a new essay. I removed the "Combining Critical Perspectives" category and added essays in the two new categories of gender criticism/queer theory and postcolonial criticism.

## Acknowledgments

My first debt of gratitude is to the scholars who contributed to this volume, for the professionalism and good humor with which they responded to my editorial nudgings. I thank all the scholars and teachers who took the time to respond to a publisher's questionnaire about the second edition: Timothy Croft, University of Alabama; Deborah Pollak, Quinnipiac University; I. (Lamar) Adam Mekler, Morgan State University; Deborah Montuori, Shippensburg University; John Pagano, Barnard College, Columbia University; Ronald Eugene Miller, Jr., University of South Carolina; Joanna Tardoni, Western Wyoming Community College; Ashton Nichols, Dickinson College; Thomas R. Irish, Sauk Valley Community College; and David K. Sauer, Spring Hill College.

I am grateful to Joan Feinberg and Denise Wydra of Bedford/ St. Martin's for the continuing opportunity to revise this volume, the continuing counsel of Karen Henry, and especially for the guidance and patience of Steve Scipione. Of the numerous editorial assistants who lent a hand, I would like to especially thank Marisa Feinstein, who ran the review program, and Eliza Kritz, who handled manuscript preparation and turnover. At Bedford/St. Martin's I also thank Andrea Cava for overseeing the production of the book, performed by DeMasi Design and Publishing Services. I am pleased to thank Chris Stampone for his timely and energetic work on the "Cultural Documents and Illustrations" section. I am particularly grateful for collegial support from past and present co-laborers C. Jan Swearingen, Martin Danahay, Neill Matheson, and Stacy Alaimo. Thanks go to the University of Texas at Arlington library staff—my burden would have been heavy indeed without their efficient interlibrary loan service. I also thank the many colleagues who not only used the first and second editions of this book but made a point of telling me so; such feedback is cheering when so much academic work seems to disappear into the void. Finally, but first in time, it is a pleasure to thank Ross Murfin, model colleague and editor, for many years of *Frankenstein*-fueled support and friendship.

Johanna M. Smith
*University of Texas at Arlington*

# Contents

**About the Series**  v

**About This Volume**  vii

---

## PART ONE
### Frankenstein:
### The Complete Text

Introduction: Biographical and Historical Contexts  3

The Complete Text  19

---

## PART TWO
### Frankenstein in Cultural Context

RICHARD ROTHWELL, Portrait of Mary Shelley (c.1840)  194

JOHN MILTON, *from* Paradise Lost, A Poem in Twelve Books (1673)  195

WILLIAM GODWIN, *from* Things as They Are; or, the Adventures of Caleb Williams (1794)  199

MARY WOLLSTONECRAFT, *from* Maria: or, the Wrongs of Woman (1798)  202

PARACELSUS, Writings on creation (1531–1538)  206

The Execution of William Burke (1829) [Broadside]  211

HUMPHRY DAVY, A Discourse, Introductory to a Course of Lectures on Chemistry (1802)  215

LUIGI GALVANI, *from* De viribus electricitatis (1791)   226

HENRY R. ROBINSON, "A Galvanized Corpse" (1836)   227

Frankenstein's Laboratory (James Whale's *Frankenstein*, 1931)   228

ERASMUS DARWIN, *from* The Temple of Nature; or, The Origin
of Society—A poem, with philosophical notes (1803)   229

SAMUEL TAYLOR COLERIDGE, *from* The Rime of the Ancyent Marinere,
In Seven Parts (1798)   235

JOHANN WOLFGANG VON GOETHE, *from* The Sorrows of Young
Werther (1774)   246

## *Frankenstein* and Political Cartoons   248

JOHN TENNIEL, "The Brummagem Frankenstein" (1866)   249

JOHN TENNIEL, "The Irish Frankenstein" (1882)   250

CLIFFORD K. BERRYMAN, "Are WE Frankensteins?" (1940)   251

STEVE GREENBERG, "Frankenfish" (2009)   252

## *Frankenstein* on the Big Screen   253

Charles Ogle as the Creature in Thomas Edison's Kinetogram
Film (1910)   253

Boris Karloff as the Creature in James Whale's *Frankenstein*
(1931)   254

Christopher Lee as the Creature in Terence Fischer's *The Curse of
Frankenstein* (1957)   255

Aaron Eckhart as the Creature in *I, Frankenstein* (2014)   256

The Creature and his Bride-to-be from James Whale's *The Bride of
Frankenstein* (1935)   257

Teri Garr, Gene Wilder, and Marty Feldman with Peter Boyle as the
Creature in Mel Brooks's *Young Frankenstein* (1974)   258

Poster for *Lady Frankenstein* (1971)   259

Poster for *Andy Warhol's Flesh for Frankenstein* (1973)   260

## *Frankenstein* Toys, Video Games, and Children's Books   261

MATTEL, Create-a-Monster Toy Package (2010)   261

STORM CITY GAMES, The Island of Dr. Frankenstein (2009)   262

R. L. STINE, Frankenstein's Dog (2013)   263

# PART THREE

# *Frankenstein*:

# A Case Study in Contemporary Criticism

**A Critical History of *Frankenstein***    267

**Psychoanalytic Criticism and *Frankenstein***    300

What Is Psychoanalytic Criticism?    300
Psychoanalytic Criticism: A Selected Bibliography    312
A Psychoanalytic Perspective:
> **DAVID COLLINGS, The Monster and the Maternal Thing:**
> **Mary Shelley's Critique of Ideology**    323

**Feminist Criticism and *Frankenstein***    340

What Is Feminist Criticism?    340
Feminist Criticism: A Selected Bibliography    349
A Feminist Perspective:
> **JOHANNA M. SMITH, "Cooped Up" with "Sad Trash":**
> **Domesticity and the Sciences in *Frankenstein***    360

**Gender Criticism, Queer Theory, and *Frankenstein***    381

What Are Gender Criticism and Queer Theory?    381
Gender Criticism and Queer Theory: A Selected Bibliography    394
A Gender/Queer Perspective:
> **GRANT F. SCOTT, Victor's Secret: Queer Gothic in Lynd Ward's**
> **Illustrations to *Frankenstein* (1934)**    400

**Marxist Criticism and *Frankenstein***    446

What Is Marxist Criticism?    446
Marxist Criticism: A Selected Bibliography    458
A Marxist Perspective:
> **WARREN MONTAG, The "Workshop of Filthy Creation": A**
> **Marxist Reading of *Frankenstein***    469

## Cultural Criticism and *Frankenstein*    481

What Is Cultural Criticism?    481
Cultural Criticism: A Selected Bibliography    496
A Cultural Critic's Perspective:
>    SIOBHAN CARROLL, Crusades Against Frost: *Frankenstein*,
>    Polar Ice, and Climate Change in 1818    502

## Postcolonial Criticism and *Frankenstein*    530

What Is Postcolonial Criticism?    530
Postcolonial Criticism: A Selected Bibliography    539
A Postcolonial Perspective:
>    ALLAN LLOYD SMITH, "This Thing of Darkness": Racial
>    Discourse in Mary Shelley's *Frankenstein*    547

## Glossary of Critical and Theoretical Terms    569

## About the Contributors    595

# PART ONE

# *Frankenstein*:
# The Complete Text

# Introduction:
# Biographical and
# Historical Contexts

"July 24: Write my story." This laconic entry in Mary Shelley's 1816 journal is her first reference to what would be a fifteen-year process of writing and rewriting *Frankenstein*. She began it in mid-June of 1815 as a short ghost story and gradually expanded it over the next year; in January 1818 *Frankenstein; or, The Modern Prometheus* was published anonymously in a three-volume edition. In 1823, to capitalize on the success of Richard Brinsley Peake's stage adaptation, *Presumption; or, The Fate of Frankenstein*, Mary's father, William Godwin, arranged for a new two-volume edition of her novel. This edition incorporates over one hundred editorial emendations by Godwin (Robinson c), and a copy of the book which Mary Shelley gave to a friend contains her handwritten notes for possible revision, but no substantial changes were made until the edition of 1831, published by Colburn and Bentley in their Standard Novels series. In her introduction to this revised *Frankenstein*, Mary looked back on her own history as well as the novel's, in order to answer a "very frequently asked" question: " 'How I, then a young girl, came to think of, and to dilate upon, so very hideous an idea' " (p. 19 in this volume). My introduction too will look back on this dual history of author and novel, to answer that question in a somewhat larger context. Mary's conflicted heritage from her radical parents plays out in *Frankenstein*, and in that form it can also serve as a microcosm of a conflicted period in British politics: the years between

1789, the onset of the French Revolution, and 1832, the passage of the Reform Bill that enfranchised portions of the English middle classes for the first time.

Both Mary Shelley and *Frankenstein* in many ways figure a revolutionary age. Mary accepted much of the radical sexual and political philosophy of her parents, Mary Wollstonecraft and William Godwin; her elopement with the married Percy Shelley attests to this radicalism, as do the sections of *Frankenstein* that critique Britain's political and social order. Yet other elements of Mary's life and novel are quite orthodox. She eventually married Percy Shelley, she came to accept an ideology of dependent femininity, and portions of *Frankenstein* suggest that a society produces monsters less by systematic oppression than by inept parenting. These latter, more conventional elements indicate the reformer rather than the revolutionary, a Mary Shelley concerned to change certain *aspects* of her culture's social and political structures rather than the structures themselves. Such oscillations between revolution and reform are equally apparent in the lives of her parents, in the course of her culture from 1789 to 1832, and in *Frankenstein*. Beginning with the often contradictory relation between theory and practice in the lives and works of Mary Shelley's parents, we can move through her equally conflicted sense of this heritage to an understanding of *Frankenstein* as revolutionary yet reformist text.

Mary Shelley was born on August 30, 1797, to radical feminist Mary Wollstonecraft and radical philosopher William Godwin. Both of her parents were prominent in revolutionary movements that peaked in the late eighteenth century, both experienced difficulties in practicing their revolutionary principles, and in these ways both profoundly influenced their daughter.

Now best known for *A Vindication of the Rights of Woman* (1792), during her lifetime Mary Wollstonecraft had already achieved notoriety with *A Vindication of the Rights of Men* (1790). This work, which preceded Thomas Paine's revolutionary *The Rights of Man* by a year, was the first full-length response to Edmund Burke's conservative *Reflections on the Revolution in France* (1790). In it and in her later *Historical and Moral View of the Origin and Progress of the French Revolution* (1795), Wollstonecraft countered Burkean attacks on the Revolution and on its British sympathizers the Jacobins, in part by enumerating the "continual miseries" that impelled the poor toward revolution (*Rights of Men* 62). Wollstonecraft's feeling for the working poor came from personal experience as well as political conviction. Although her father rose from master weaver to gentleman farmer, his drunkenness and general fecklessness impoverished his family, and before she turned to writing Wollstonecraft had worked variously as lady's companion, seamstress, director of a girls' school, and governess. This hand-to-mouth existence doubtless influenced her view that more professions should be open to "honest, independent women" (*Rights of Woman* 239). Moreover, as a working woman Wollstonecraft recognized that women and workers were equally disadvantaged under the current political order. While the 1760s and 1780s had seen movements for political reform, in the 1790s voting eligibility was still restricted to men and dependent on property ownership, so that a population of 8.5 million was represented in Parliament only by the votes of propertied men. Under this "convenient handle for despotism" (237), Wollstonecraft writes with ironic admiration, women are fully "as well represented as a numerous class of hard-working mechanics, who pay for the support of royalty when they can scarcely stop [i.e., fill] their children's mouths with bread."

*Rights of Woman* consistently links arguments for women's rights with critiques of political oppression. Here Wollstonecraft joins a long tradition of feminism that not only demanded education and other rights for women but did so in political terms. That tradition, as Anna Clark shows, includes generations of women who engaged in riots and strikes, sometimes with but sometimes against male coworkers, for labor as well as gender equity. In its written form, this tradition extends from the Puritan women revolutionaries of the 1650s, to Mary Astell's question in 1700 as to why, "if absolute sovereignty be not necessary in a state, how comes it to be so in a family?" (39), to Mary Collier's claim in her 1739 poem "The Woman's Labour" not only that laboring women worked more than did men of their class but also that all workers were robbed of the fruits of their industry. By the 1780s and 1790s such feminist writers as Catherine Macaulay Graham were making women's claims more vociferously, in part because two rebellions against political tyranny—the American Revolution and the French Revolution—seemed to promise new liberties for women. In *Rights of Woman*, then, Wollstonecraft argues that "the pernicious effects which arise from the unnatural distinctions established in society" must be displaced by a "virtuous equality," and that women cannot achieve the necessary virtue unless they are, "in some degree, independent of men" (230–31).

But *Rights of Woman* supports this position with contradictory arguments that suggest the difficulties of conceiving a revolutionary feminism. On the one hand, Wollstonecraft represents women as "human creatures, who, in common with men, are placed on this earth to unfold their faculties" (76–77), not to display the "gentleness, docility, and . . . spaniel-like affection" (106) commonly "supposed to be the sexual characteristics of the weaker vessel" (78). Thus she criticizes "tyrants" (71) who "*force* all women, by denying them civil and political rights, to remain immured in their families"; instead, women must be educated to foster the "strength, both of mind and body" (77), that will make them "respectable members of society" (78). On the other hand, Wollstonecraft makes this case for women's education by using an insistently domestic language: if women are "prepared by education to become the companion of man" (70), they will be "more observant daughters, more affectionate sisters, more faithful wives, more reasonable mothers—in a word, better citizens" (241). In other words, while Wollstonecraft is clearly concerned to improve women's position as "citizens," she also sees that position as rooted in their domestic roles. It is true that her idea of the companionate wife is a fairly revolutionary critique of other domestic roles available to women, such as "play-thing" (95), "humble dependent" (101), or "upper servant" (113); but it is also true that her language tends to define women less as "human creatures" and "members of society" than by their domestic relations to men.

Similar contradictions appeared in Wollstonecraft's life as a feminist. Although *Rights of Woman* warned readers that "love, from its very nature, must be transitory" (101) and that happiness "must arise from well regulated affections" (232), Wollstonecraft herself clung to her affair with the American adventurer Gilbert Imlay, and she twice attempted suicide in response to his affairs with other women. The passionate sensibility that in the 1790s signaled a political and sexual revolutionary, in other words, also undermined a feminist view that lovers should be "equally necessary [to] and independent of each other" (233); hence the paradox of the "exponent of the rights of women . . . driven to attempted suicide for the sake of her lover" (Spark 6). Later Wollstonecraft experienced other problems as she tried to live in the new world promised by revolution and feminism. When she married William Godwin she remained independent (they maintained separate households), but not without difficulty. In a note asking him to settle a business matter, for example, she wrote that "I am perhaps as unfit as yourself to do it, and my time appears to me as valuable as that of other persons accustomed to employ themselves" (qtd. in Grylls 4); her snappish tone hints at the stresses of practicing a theory of equality and shared responsibility in marriage. Perhaps the most poignant sign of such stresses is the fate of her reputation when it was left in her husband's care. After her death Godwin wrote his *Memoirs of the Author of A Vindication of the Rights of Woman* (1798), which included her sexual as well as her intellectual history; but the book he intended as a tribute to "this admirable woman" (*Memoirs* 123) instead called forth vituperation of her as "a philosophical wanton" (qtd. in Durant 340) and the like.

I have discussed the contradictions in Wollstonecraft's works and life at length because they profoundly affected her daughter. Mary knew her mother's history, if not from Godwin directly then from his *Memoirs*, which she and Percy Shelley often read. While she may not have known the day-to-day difficulties of her parents' marriage, she may well have known about the unfriendly reviews of the *Memoirs* and thus have had an inkling of the public reaction a revolutionary feminist with an unconventional sexual life could expect. And certainly Mary was steeped in her mother's literary history. She read Wollstonecraft's books in her teens, her later journal shows that she and Percy read them over and over, and Mary was in fact rereading *A Vindication of the Rights of Woman* as well as *Historical and Moral View of the French Revolution* while writing *Frankenstein*. We will see how the contradictions in Wollstonecraft's life and books reappear in Mary's novel and her own history.

The legacy from her father's works was perhaps less problematic, but it too suggested for Mary Shelley the difficulties, indeed dangers, of living out a political ideal. The son of a Sandemanian minister, Godwin was educated in this sect's strict principles of primitive Christianity and himself became a minister. Resigning his ministry in 1782, he became an atheist and a writer, and turned his attention from religion to ethics and politics. With his treatise *Enquiry concerning Political Justice* (1793) and his novel *Caleb Williams; or, Things as They Are* (1794), he surpassed even Tom Paine as a spokesperson for political radicalism; "No one was more talked of, more looked up to, more sought after," the radical essayist William Hazlitt later recalled (qtd. in St. Clair 91). Godwin was one of many in England who initially welcomed the French Revolution uncritically. Some thirty enthusiastic defenses of the Revolution followed Wollstonecraft's 1790 *Vindication of the Rights of Men*, and radicals formed Corresponding Societies to discuss how best to extend the French example into England. The phenomenal sale of Paine's *The Rights of Man Part II* (1792)—200,000 copies within a year, or approximately one for every thirty Britons (Thompson 117)—further testifies to the revolutionary fervor of those days when, as William Wordsworth later put it in his *Prelude*, "Reason seemed the most to assert her rights" (bk. IX, l. 113) against moribund political institutions.

But the year of *Rights of Man II* also began a period of repression that made it more dangerous for Britons to publicly support the French Republic. In December 1792 Paine was outlawed from Britain and his book banned as seditious libel; in February 1793 the British government declared war on France and moved no less harshly against Britain's Jacobins. Booksellers were prosecuted for selling Paine's *Rights of Man*; leaders of Corresponding Societies were arrested; habeas corpus was suspended in 1794, large public meetings lacking permits were banned in 1795, secret organizations were outlawed in 1797, and the Combination Acts against workers' associations were passed in 1799. And although the *Critical Review* had thought Godwin's *Enquiry concerning Political Justice* unlikely to "circulate among the inferior classes of society" (qtd. in Locke 60), in May of 1793 the government's Privy Council was considering a prosecution to suppress the book. While by no means as popular as *Rights of Man II*, Godwin's book sold four thousand copies in three licit and two pirated editions; the "inferior classes" often pooled their money to buy one copy which was then read aloud, so Godwin's revolutionary ideas circulated more widely than the sales figures might suggest.

In some ways, however, *Political Justice* is antirevolutionary, and a brief consideration of its political philosophy will prepare one for the contradictions of Mary Shelley's and *Frankenstein*'s politics. In 1800 Godwin recollected that in 1789 his heart had "beat high with sentiments of liberty," but he added that "I never for a moment ceased to disapprove of mob government and violence" (qtd. in Locke 40). *Political Justice* displays this same ambivalence about the process of political change. As a radical, Godwin considers all government pernicious; not only does it owe its existence "to the errors and perverseness of a few," but it is perpetuated by "the infantine and uninstructed confidence of the many" (125), who confuse the obedience enforced by a superior in *rank* with the reverence due a superior in *wisdom*. Furthermore, because the upper ranks have "usurped certain advantages . . . to which they can show no equitable claim" (123), revolutionaries "angry with corruption, and impatient at injustice," are motivated by "the excess of a virtuous feeling" (139). The key word here is *excess*, because it signals the radical Godwin's conservative fear of revolution: in its "excess," revolutionary disruption suspends the "patient speculations" that would otherwise gradually produce "uninterrupted progress" toward "political truth and social improvement" (137–38). Yet revolution and violence are not simply destructive, Godwin concludes, for often they have led to "important changes of the social system" (139). In one sense, then, Godwin *was* a revolutionary: his view that the gradual decay of government is a "euthanasia" devoutly to be wished (125), like his statement that revolutionary violence may be useful, was unlikely to cheer proponents of the status quo. Yet he was also antirevolutionary: what he desired was *gradual* progress toward the point at which government is unnecessary because, "the plain dictates of justice" having become evident to all, "the whole species [has] become reasonable and virtuous" (221).

Unavoidably, such a summary oversimplifies Godwin's position, and he underestimated neither the length of time required for progress toward political justice nor the difficulties in educating humans toward this goal. Yet he had moments of sunny optimism that his daughter, despite her agreement with some of his ideas, could not share. Mary was rereading *Political Justice* as she wrote *Frankenstein*, and her novel's politics are in part an answer to her father's. I turn now to Mary's life and her conflicted responses to her literary heritage.

Wollstonecraft died of a puerperal infection in 1797, ten days after Mary's birth. Godwin raised his new daughter and her half sister Fanny (Wollstonecraft's daughter by Imlay) alone until 1801, when he married Mary Jane Clairmont. Although an attentive and affectionate father, he felt "totally unfitted" to educate his daughters without Wollstonecraft's help (qtd. in Grylls 11), and he gave this "incompetence" as one motive for his remarriage (qtd. in Mellor 8). Godwin's second wife, however, was not fully committed to her predecessor's educational principles, and she seems, perhaps understandably, to have taken more interest in educating her own daughter, Jane (later Claire) Clairmont, than Wollstonecraft's. At this remove it is hard to know whether she was in fact a "wicked stepmother," but certainly Mary felt that the new Mrs. Godwin resented her, and she may also have felt rather neglected, for the Godwins were busy managing (and writing books for) their bookshop, and Godwin himself admitted to a "somewhat sententious and authoritative" manner with his children (qtd. in Spark 16). Despite her "excessive & romantic attachment" to her father (*Letters* 2: 215), then, Mary gradually came to spend more and more time reading her mother's books at Wollstonecraft's grave in St. Pancras churchyard. During the summer of 1814, when she was seventeen, this favorite spot also became the site of clandestine meetings with twenty-two-year-old poet Percy Shelley.

Long an admirer of Godwin's principles, Percy had introduced himself to Mary's father in 1812 and was soon dining regularly at the Godwins' home with his wife Harriet. With his usual quixotic impetuosity, in

1811 he had married sixteen-year-old Harriet in order, he said, to rescue her from her father's "most horrible" persecution (*PBS Letters* 1: 103) but also to "cultivat[e]" her latent talents (1: 402). Later he decided that this "rash & heartless union" had become "loathsome and horrible," and after meeting Mary he "speedily conceived an ardent passion" for the "genuine elevation and magnificence of [her] intellectual nature" (1: 402). He and Mary declared their love to each other but agreed that they must part; after a series of hullabaloos including Percy's threat before the entire Godwin family to commit suicide (Sunstein 75–78), however, they ran off to France on July 18, 1814, taking Mary's half-sister Jane/Claire Clairmont with them.

Mary Shelley later recalled the next eight years with Percy as "happy, though chequered" (*Journals* 430), and "checkered" seems a mild description of this turbulent time. As Percy's mistress she was subject to the same kind of censure visited on her mother's sexual history. Even though she married Percy in 1816, within a month of his wife Harriet's suicide, Mary never entirely escaped the social effects of her early indiscretion: as late as 1843 she records "impertinence" and "insult" when she ventured into society (*Letters* 3: 56–59). Her years with Percy were financially "chequered" as well. Although their financial position later improved, Percy was always strapped for cash; he was generous to the unemployed lace makers near their home at Marlow, and over the years Godwin wheedled the substantial sum of £4,700 from him. In addition to money troubles were intermittent domestic disturbances, for Claire's continued presence in the household was often an irritant and sometimes worse. She had an illegitimate daughter by the poet Lord Byron, and she often entangled the Shelleys in her schemes to get the child from him; furthermore, Mary was deeply distressed by repeated rumors that Percy and Claire had had a child and that Percy had bundled it off to a foundling hospital (*Letters* 1: 204–09). And finally there were the deaths of Mary's and Percy's children. One son survived, but two daughters died in infancy, and after the death of their three-and-a-half-year-old son William in 1819, Mary experienced a depression so deep that she felt she "ought to have died" too (*Letters* 1: 108); a miscarriage in mid-1822 caused another depression. It also caused an estrangement from Percy, or perhaps increased her sense of estrangement due to his recent infatuations with Emilia Viviana and Jane Williams. In any event, when Percy Shelley drowned on July 8, 1822, Mary's grief seems to have been heightened by guilt over their recent differences.

More enduring, however, was her sense that Percy had helped her to fulfill the promise of her literary heritage. Wollstonecraft's "greatness of soul" and Godwin's "high talents," Mary told a friend in 1827, "perpetually reminded me that I ought to degenerate as little as I could" from them, and Percy had "fostered this ambition" (*Letters* 2: 4). She makes the same point in her introduction to the 1831 *Franken-stein*: although she feels it natural that "the daughter of two persons of distinguished literary celebrity . . . should very early in life have thought of writing," Percy too was "very anxious that I should prove myself worthy of my parentage" (p. 21).

Yet one suspects that Percy Shelley's encouragement could be something of a burden. He appears not to have noticed that the time he urged Mary to spend writing would have taken away from time devoted to "the cares of a family" (p. 21), which of course fell on his wife and not him. Nor can it have been entirely bracing to have one's husband "for ever inciting me to obtain literary reputation. . . . not so much with the idea that I could produce any thing worthy of notice, but that he might himself judge how far I possessed the promise of better things" (p. 21). To be "incited" only to be judged, in other words, might reduce rather than heighten one's literary confidence. Mary herself records the sense of "incapacity & timidity" that prevented her from joining the conversations between Byron and her husband that contributed to *Frankenstein* (*Journals* 439), and even in 1831, after that novel had fulfilled "the promise of better things," her introduction suggests a continuing sense of incapacity: the sentence that begins with a testy assertion—"I certainly did not owe the suggestion of one incident, nor scarcely of one train of feeling, to my husband"—concludes, generously but also meekly, that she would not have developed the tale "but for his incitement" (pp. 24–25).

Understandably, this lack of confidence emerged with particular force for Mary after her husband's death. Although at one point she vows to pursue her "literary labors" (*Journals* 431), more characteristic are the entries in which she desires only to be "a faint continuation of *his* being, & as far as possible the revelation to the earth of what he was" (*Journals* 436). Of course such statements display the excess of first grief, but the sense of desolation recurs. In a particularly low-spirited letter of 1835, for instance, she laments that "I was always a dependant thing—wanting fosterage & support—I am left to myself—crushed by fortune—and I am nothing" (*Letters* 2: 246). Mary Shelley in fact produced an impressive body of work—five novels, several poems, a dozen articles and reviews, twenty short stories, a travel book, two books of biographies, and critical editions of Percy's poetry and prose—and it may be that her husband's early "inciting" helped sustain her after his death. Not only was she a widow trying to support herself and a young son by writing, when she began to publish she had to contend with her father-in-law, Sir Timothy Shelley, and his rigid ideas of feminine propriety: Sir Timothy forbade her planned biography of his son and repeatedly threatened to suspend the small income he had allowed her, so as to show his displeasure at her bringing his family name before the public (Sunstein 260–72). That Mary continued to write under these circumstances is testimony perhaps to Percy's encouragement and certainly to her own determination. Yet her sense of being "unable to put myself forward unless led, cherished & supported" (*Journals* 555) also testifies not just to her personal feeling of dependence on Percy but also to a conservative ideology of dependent femininity, a belief that women are "weaker" than men (*Letters* 2: 246) and have "a love of looking up & being guided" (*Journals* 555).

Such gender conservatism suggests that Mary Shelley failed to live up to her parents' sexual and political radicalism. Jennifer A. Wagner finds Mary's views radical but also "deeply" conservative (589), while Lee Sterrenburg sees a "gravitation" away from her "utopian and radical heritage" as early as *Frankenstein* (143). And there is some truth to these claims. Unlike feminist contemporaries such as her friends Caroline Norton and Fanny Wright or the French socialist Flora Tristan, for instance, Mary Shelley was never a public advocate of women's rights. From Betty Bennett's scholarship on Mary's friend Diana Dods, however, we now know some specifics of Mary's determination personally to "defend & support victims to the social system" (*Journals* 557). This delicate balance between radical and conservative, public and private, in matters of gender is equally apparent in Mary's politics. After her son had inherited his grandfather's title and estate, one hears neither Wollstonecraft nor Godwin in Mary's complaint about "the number of Maids one must keep in the country" or her comment that "giving work to the industrious" is "one of the best ways in the world of doing good" (*Letters* 3: 347). Yet there is her compassion for the poor: in 1845 she animadverts on Lord Norfolk's suggestion that starving Irish laborers drink hot water and curry ("very warm and comfortable to the stomachs of the people," he explained, "if it could be got cheap"), and in 1847 she notes the large sums she and her son are spending to relieve the "bitter want" near his estate (*Letters* 3: 267, 305). It is possible to fault such sympathy with the poor as the sort of Dickensian sentimentality that gives liberals a bad name, but the example of Lord Norfolk is a salutary reminder that there are worse attitudes than compassion. And it is Mary's *oscillation*—between fear of the revolutionary class and sympathy with the laboring poor — that is of interest, for it illuminates not only her own politics but those of early-nineteenth-century England and of *Frankenstein*. The contradictions in Mary Shelley's views, then, are best approached as symptomatic of England's uneven industrial development and its political consequences. Early in the eighteenth century, England's economy had begun to move jerkily from predominantly small-scale agriculture to "rationalized" or large-scale and mechanized agriculture, a movement accompanied by the gradual development of the mining and textile industries. Common lands, formerly cultivated collectively by small farmers, by midcentury were being bought up and enclosed by large landowners, and the Corn Laws of 1815 maintained subsidies on grain and thus further strengthened the landowning interests. But the enclosures increased an underclass of landless poor, for as they accelerated in the late eighteenth century — from 1760 to 1799, between two and three million acres were enclosed (Porter 209) — many small landowners, tenant farmers, and laborers were squeezed out of agriculture and began to migrate to the new textile and manufacturing centers. This influx of displaced agriculturalists, increased by the return of 300,000 soldiers discharged when the Napoleonic Wars ended in 1815, greatly enlarged the workforce and so kept wages down. In addition, the boom-slump cycle characteristic of early capitalism caused intermittent but chronic unemployment, further exacerbated in some textile industries by competition from more efficient Continental producers (Foster 18–20).

The political consequences of these changes were many and diverse. They ranged from workers' combinations (proto-unions) and friendly societies (proto-self-insurance groups) to strikes and riots (Langford 34–36), and some of these riots originated with issues more political than economic: the popular disturbances in the 1760s supporting John Wilkes's campaign for electoral rights and freedom of the press, the riots of 1753 and of 1780 against proposed extensions of civil rights to Jews and Catholics respectively. The efforts of the Association movement in 1779–80 and of 1780s reformers such as Major John Cartwright to extend the suffrage met with relatively sedate popular approval, but in the revolutionary 1790s an expanded electorate was perceived as a potential political problem. E. P. Thompson has located the formation of the working class and class consciousness in this decade, and the consequent ruling-class unease is clear in a 1797 comment that "in times of warm political debate, the Right of Suffrage communicated to an ignorant and ferocious Populace would lead to tumult" (qtd. in

Thompson 26). Certainly there was concern to relieve the suffering of the un- and underemployed (if only out of self-interest) as attested by the turn-of-the-century debate about how best to administer poor relief and by the substantial amounts of private philanthropy. But poor relief and private charity did not reach all the poor, and they were rejected by many workers who continued to seek redress for economic grievances through strikes and riots. Between 1790 and 1810 there were five hundred riots over the price of bread in textile districts such as Nottinghamshire, which was also the center of the Luddite risings of 1811 to 1813, when unemployed knitters broke up the machinery that had displaced them.

Percy Shelley was familiar with this district, and the desperate conditions he saw there helped inspire his revolutionary poem *Queen Mab* (1812). This is the book he gave Mary in 1814 as a pledge of love, and for a time she shared its radical vision. Still, she was not long a Jacobin: in 1814 she had enjoyed "frighten[ing]" away a bore by "talking of cutting off Kings['] heads" (*Journals* 23), but by 1817 she was herself "shudd[ering]" at the possibility of "a revolution in this country" and at the thought of "encourag[ing] in the multitude the worst possible human passion *revenge*" (*Letters* 1: 49). Another letter of the same year, however, expresses her compassion for an unemployed seaman who had died of starvation (*Letters* 1: 54). As I have shown, this alternation between fear of vengeful revolution and sympathy for the suffering poor was characteristic of Mary Shelley's culture, and it can also be found in the 1818 *Frankenstein*. One example would be the creature's burning the De Lacey cottage after being rejected by these quondam benefactors: as his " 'feelings of revenge and hatred' " (p. 123) and even " 'a kind of insanity' " issue in his screaming and " 'danc[ing] with fury' " (p. 123) around the cottage, he is fearsome indeed; yet the reader has also been encouraged to pity his " 'anguish' " and " 'despair' " (p. 121).

The historical context of the 1831 *Frankenstein* is an even richer mix of the "burnings," "alarms," and "absorbing politics of the day" (*Letters* 2: 120). As Tim Marshall has demonstrated, one set of "alarms" was the methods by which medical practitioners obtained dead bodies for dissection; the public commotion ran from the Burke and Hare murders in 1828 to the Anatomy Act of 1832 and is thus particularly pertinent to *Frankenstein* (p. 211). Probably the most "absorbing politics," however, were the increasing, and increasingly violent, public debates over a Reform Bill to extend the suffrage. These debates were in some ways the culmination of a decade of political disturbances over the popular franchise, and here as in the problem of revolution we can trace a disputed political issue through the reactions recorded in Mary Shelley's letters. The letters of 1820 comment on many contemporary events that contributed to the desire for reform. Mary's description of George IV as "good-for-nothing" (*Letters* 1: 131) and "bankrupt in character" shows her own "radicalism," but it is also in line with the popular dislike of this dissolute monarch; her repeated criticisms of the "despotism" of "our most detestable governors" (*Letters* 1: 124) echo such radical periodicals as *The Black Dwarf*. The letters of 1829 to 1831 are particularly telling as they follow the reform debate: in December 1829, "some change some terrible event is expected" when Parliament meets (*Letters* 2: 95); in November 1830, "our position is critical and dreadful," despite King William IV's willingness to accept "any measures" to aid the "suffering population" (*Letters* 2: 118); one month later, "we must be revolutionized" unless "the Aristocrats sacrifice enough to tranquillize" the people (*Letters* 2: 124). By March 1831, "We are all here on the *qui vive* about the Reform Bill," for "the Whigs triumphed gloriously in the boldness of their measure" and "England will be free if it is carried" (*Letters* 2: 133). At issue in these two-plus years of debate was the extent to which the franchise should be extended. Early versions of the bill would have enfranchised a portion of the working as well as the middle classes; the propertied class feared to lose its exclusive legislative power to the propertyless rabble, a fear exacerbated when working-class supporters of the early bill rioted each time it was voted down. In the event, the Reform Bill of 1832 extended the franchise only to segments of the middle classes. Mary Shelley's characteristically double view of this debate appears in a letter to the radical Robert Dale Owen.

> *Progressiveness* is certainly finely developed just now in Europe—together with a degree of *tyrant quellingtiveness* which is highly laudable—it is a pity that in our country this should be mingled with a *sick destructiveness*; yet the last gives action to the former—and without [it], would our Landholders be brought to reason? Yet it is very sad—the punishment of the poor men being not the least disaster attendant on it. (*Letters* 2: 122)

Clearly Mary favors "progress" and "tyrant quelling," but equally clearly she fears "sick destructiveness"; the latter seems a corollary to the former, and is perhaps necessary to force the propertied classes to cede their exclusive right to the vote; "yet it is very sad." If this passage waffles, it is also an effort, like Godwin's in *Political Justice*, to come to terms with a national revolutionary impulse.

As Glyn Williams and others have noted, *Frankenstein*'s creature and his creator may be read as figures for this impulse and the conflicted responses to it. In Victor's view, the creature is like the rebellious working class: he has no right and no claim to the recognition he demands from his superior. Yet when the creature asks nicely—for sympathy, for understanding, for a mate—Victor can recognize the justice of his claims, just as the more benevolent middle- and upper-class liberals might heed respectful requests for the vote from the respectable working class. But when Victor imagines the consequences of ceding control, of passing his power to create life to the creature and creaturette, he fears the "sick destructiveness" that they, and especially she, might then engender. (Here the danger of a female uncontrollably putting herself forward, like Mary Shelley did as a woman writer, heightens the perceived threat of a working class that might be equally uncontrollable if given the vote.) Victor then withdraws his concession and justifies himself by arguing the creature's " 'malignity' " (p. 187), just as opponents of working-class suffrage justified themselves by arguing that the lower orders were "helots" quite willing to "set London on fire" if balked (qtd. in Thompson 894). In Victor's self-justification, as in Mary's delight with the "boldness" of the Whig measures excluding the working classes from the franchise, is relief that revolutionary monsters are disempowered.

But *Frankenstein*'s representation of the creature can also be read as support for revolt against class oppression. The creature's analysis of the origins of poverty draws on Volney's *Ruins of Empire*, an extremely influential book in 1790s radical circles (Thompson 107–08), and the fact that Mary revised only a few words of this analysis for the 1831 edition indicates a continuing link with her early radicalism. Against Victor's belief that his creation is inherently monstrous, she places the creature's argument that his culture has made him monstrous, an argument in line with both elements of her radical heritage: Wollstonecraft's view that women's inherent capacities are stunted when they are treated only as "alluring objects of desire" (*Rights of Woman* 97), and Godwin's view that human character and behavior are the product not of "innate principles" but of "circumstances and events" (*Political Justice* 28). If Victor and his culture have created a monster, then there are clear grounds for two conclusions: that a society and not its outcasts creates revolutionary violence, and that the creature's rage is, as

Godwin might have put it, the revolutionary's "excess of a virtuous feeling."

These tensions and contradictions, between fear of revolution and sympathy with the revolutionary, reveal Mary Shelley's personal ambivalence and hence the novel's biographical context. But they do more than that. Along with *Frankenstein*'s chronology—set in the revolutionary 1790s, first published in 1818 at a time of postwar social and political instability, and published again in 1831 when revolution seemed imminent if the Reform Bill were not passed—they locate the novel in a historical context of oscillation between revolution and reform.

## WORKS CITED

Astell, Mary. "Appendix to *Some Reflections on Marriage*." *The Other Eighteenth Century: English Women of Letters 1660–1800*. Ed. Robert W. Uphaus and Gretchen M. Foster. East Lansing: Colleagues, 1991. 33–49. Print.

Bennett, Betty T. *Mary Diana Dods, A Gentleman and a Scholar*. New York: Morrow, 1991. Print.

Clark, Anna. *The Struggle for the Breeches: Gender and the Making of the British Working Class*. Berkeley: U of California P, 1995. Print.

Durant, W. Clark. "Supplement to *Memoirs of Mary Wollstonecraft*." Godwin, *Memoirs* 135–347. Print.

Foster, John. *Class Struggle and the Industrial Revolution: Early Industrial Capitalism in Three English Towns*. London: Methuen, 1974. Print.

Godwin, William. *Enquiry concerning Political Justice*. 1793. Ed. K. Codell Carter. Oxford: Clarendon, 1971. Print.

———. *Memoirs of Mary Wollstonecraft*. 1798. New York: Haskell House, 1969. 5–126. Print.

Grylls, R. Glynn. *Mary Shelley: A Biography*. London: Oxford UP, 1938. Print.

Langford, Paul. "The Eighteenth Century (1688–1789)." *The Eighteenth Century and the Age of Industry*. Oxford: Oxford UP, 1992. 1–71. Print.

Locke, Don. *A Fantasy of Reason: The Life and Thought of William Godwin*. London: Routledge, 1980. Print.

Marshall, Tim. *Murdering to Dissect: Graverobbing, Frankenstein and the anatomy literature*. Manchester: Manchester UP, 1995. Print.

Mellor, Anne K. *Mary Shelley: Her Life, Her Fiction, Her Monsters.* New York: Routledge, 1988. Print.

Porter, Roy. *English Society in the Eighteenth Century.* Rev. ed. London: Penguin, 1990. Print.

Robinson, Charles E., ed. Introduction. *The* Frankenstein *Notebooks: A Facsimile Edition of Mary Shelley's Novel, 1816–1817* (2 parts). Vol. IX of *The Manuscripts of the Younger Romantics.* General ed. Donald H. Reiman et al. 9 vols. New York: Garland, 1996. xxv–lxxv. Print.

Shelley, Mary. *The Journals of Mary Wollstonecraft Shelley.* Ed. Paula R. Feldman and Diana Kilvert-Scott. Baltimore: Johns Hopkins UP, 1987. Print.

———. *The Letters of Mary Wollstonecraft Shelley.* Ed. Betty T. Bennett. 3 vols. Baltimore: Johns Hopkins UP, 1980–88. Print.

Shelley, Percy Bysshe. *The Letters of Percy Bysshe Shelley.* Ed. Frederick L. Jones. 2 vols. Oxford: Clarendon, 1964. Print.

Spark, Muriel. *Mary Shelley.* Rev. ed. London: Sphere-Penguin, 1987. Print.

St. Clair, William. *The Godwins and the Shelleys: A Biography of a Family.* Baltimore: Johns Hopkins UP, 1989. Print.

Sterrenburg, Lee. "Mary Shelley's Monster: Politics and Psyche in *Frankenstein.*" *The Endurance of* Frankenstein: *Essays on Mary Shelley's Novel.* Ed. George Levine and U. C. Knoepflmacher. Berkeley: U of California P, 1979. 143–71. Print.

Sunstein, Emily W. *Mary Shelley: Romance and Reality.* Baltimore: Johns Hopkins UP, 1989. Print.

Thompson, E. P. *The Making of the English Working Class.* 1963. London: Penguin, 1988. Print.

Todd, Janet, ed. *Mary Wollstonecraft: Political Writings.* Toronto: U of Toronto P, 1993. Print.

Wagner, Jennifer A. "'I Am Cast as a Monster': Shelley's *Frankenstein* and the Haunting of Howard Brenton's *Bloody Poetry*" *Modern Drama* 37.4 (1994): 588–602. Print.

Williams, Glyn A. *Artisans and Sans-culottes: Popular Movements in France and Britain during the French Revolution.* 1968. London: Libris, 1989. Print.

Wordsworth, William. *The Prelude: 1799, 1805, 1850.* New York: Norton, 1979. Print.

Wollstonecraft, Mary. *A Vindication of the Rights of Men.* 1790. Todd 1–65. Print.

———. *A Vindication of the Rights of Woman.* 1792. Todd 67–296. Print.

# *Frankenstein*

## *or*

# *The Modern Prometheus*

Did I request thee, Maker, from my clay
To mould me man? Did I solicit thee
From darkness to promote me? —
*Paradise Lost* [X. 743–5]

TO

## WILLIAM GODWIN

*Author of Political Justice, Caleb Williams, & c.*

THESE VOLUMES

*Are respectfully inscribed*

BY

THE AUTHOR

## INTRODUCTION[1]

The Publishers of the Standard Novels, in selecting "Frankenstein" for one of their series, expressed a wish that I should furnish them with some account of the origin of the story. I am the more willing to comply, because I shall thus give a general answer to the question, so very frequently asked me—"How I, then a young girl, came to think of, and to dilate upon, so very hideous an idea?" It is true that I am very averse to bringing myself forward in print; but as my account will only appear as an appendage to a former production, and as it will be

---

[1] This Introduction by Mary Shelley appeared in 1831, when Henry Colburn and Richard Bentley published *Frankenstein* as number 9 in their Standard Novels series.

# FRANKENSTEIN;

## OR,

## THE MODERN PROMETHEUS.

◆

### IN THREE VOLUMES.

◆

Did I request thee, Maker, from my clay
To mould me man ? Did I solicit thee
From darkness to promote me ? —

PARADISE LOST.

## VOL. I.

### London:

#### PRINTED FOR
#### LACKINGTON, HUGHES, HARDING, MAVOR, & JONES,
#### FINSBURY SQUARE.

## 1818.

Facsimile of title page and dedication from the first edition of *Frankenstein*.

confined to such topics as have connection with my authorship alone, I can scarcely accuse myself of a personal intrusion.

It is not singular that, as the daughter of two persons of distinguished literary celebrity, I should very early in life have thought of writing. As a child I scribbled; and my favourite pastime, during the hours given me for recreation, was to "write stories." Still I had a dearer pleasure than this, which was the formation of castles in the air—the indulging in waking dreams—the following up trains of thought, which had for their subject the formation of a succession of imaginary incidents. My dreams were at once more fantastic and agreeable than my writings. In the latter I was a close imitator—rather doing as others had done, than putting down the suggestions of my own mind. What I wrote was intended at least for one other eye—my childhood's companion and friend; but my dreams were all my own; I accounted for them to nobody; they were my refuge when annoyed—my dearest pleasure when free.

I lived principally in the country as a girl, and passed a considerable time in Scotland. I made occasional visits to the more picturesque parts; but my habitual residence was on the blank and dreary northern shores of the Tay, near Dundee. Blank and dreary on retrospection I call them; they were not so to me then. They were the eyry of freedom, and the pleasant region where unheeded I could commune with the creatures of my fancy. I wrote then—but in a most common-place style. It was beneath the trees of the grounds belonging to our house, or on the bleak sides of the woodless mountains near, that my true compositions, the airy flights of my imagination, were born and fostered. I did not make myself the heroine of my tales. Life appeared to me too common-place an affair as regarded myself. I could not figure to myself that romantic woes or wonderful events would ever be my lot; but I was not confined to my own identity, and I could people the hours with creations far more interesting to me at that age, than my own sensations.

After this my life became busier, and reality stood in place of fiction. My husband, however, was, from the first, very anxious that I should prove myself worthy of my parentage, and enrol myself on the page of fame. He was for ever inciting me to obtain literary reputation, which even on my own part I cared for then, though since I have become infinitely indifferent to it. At this time he desired that I should write, not so much with the idea that I could produce any thing worthy of notice, but that he might himself judge how far I possessed the promise of better things hereafter. Still I did nothing. Travelling, and the cares of a family, occupied my time; and study, in the way of reading, or improving my ideas in communication with his far more cultivated mind, was all of literary employment that engaged my attention.

In the summer of 1816, we visited Switzerland, and became the neighbours of Lord Byron. At first we spent our pleasant hours on the lake, or wandering on its shores; and Lord Byron, who was writing the third canto of Childe Harold, was the only one among us who put his thoughts upon paper. These, as he brought them successively to us, clothed in all the light and harmony of poetry, seemed to stamp as divine the glories of heaven and earth, whose influences we partook with him.

But it proved a wet, ungenial summer, and incessant rain often confined us for days to the house. Some volumes of ghost stories, translated from the German into French, fell into our hands. There was the History of the Inconstant Lover, who, when he thought to clasp the bride to whom he had pledged his vows, found himself in the arms of the pale ghost of her whom he had deserted. There was the tale of the sinful founder of his race, whose miserable doom it was to bestow the kiss of death on all the younger sons of his fated house, just when they reached the age of promise. His gigantic, shadowy form, clothed like the ghost in Hamlet, in complete armour, but with the beaver up, was seen at midnight, by the moon's fitful beams, to advance slowly along the gloomy avenue. The shape was lost beneath the shadow of the castle walls; but soon a gate swung back, a step was heard, the door of the chamber opened, and he advanced to the couch of the blooming youths, cradled in healthy sleep. Eternal sorrow sat upon his face as he bent down and kissed the forehead of the boys, who from that hour withered like flowers snapt upon the stalk. I have not seen these stories since then; but their incidents are as fresh in my mind as if I had read them yesterday.

"We will each write a ghost story," said Lord Byron; and his proposition was acceded to. There were four of us. The noble author began a tale, a fragment of which he printed at the end of his poem of Mazeppa. Shelley, more apt to embody ideas and sentiments in the radiance of brilliant imagery, and in the music of the most melodious verse that adorns our language, than to invent the machinery of a story, commenced one founded on the experiences of his early life. Poor Polidori had some terrible idea about a skull-headed lady, who was so punished for peeping through a key-hole—what to see I forget—something very shocking and wrong of course; but when she was reduced to a worse condition than the renowned Tom of Coventry,° he did not know

*Tom of Coventry:* That is, Peeping Tom.

what to do with her, and was obliged to despatch her to the tomb of the Capulets, the only place for which she was fitted. The illustrious poets also, annoyed by the platitude of prose, speedily relinquished their uncongenial task.

I busied myself *to think of a story*, — a story to rival those which had excited us to this task. One which would speak to the mysterious fears of our nature, and awaken thrilling horror — one to make the reader dread to look round, to curdle the blood, and quicken the beatings of the heart. If I did not accomplish these things, my ghost story would be unworthy of its name. I thought and pondered — vainly. I felt that blank incapability of invention which is the greatest misery of authorship, when dull Nothing replies to our anxious invocations. *Have you thought of a story?* I was asked each morning, and each morning I was forced to reply with a mortifying negative.

Every thing must have a beginning, to speak in Sanchean° phrase, and that beginning must be linked to something that went before. The Hindoos give the world an elephant to support it, but they make the elephant stand upon a tortoise. Invention, it must be humbly admitted, does not consist in creating out of void, but out of chaos; the materials must, in the first place, be afforded: it can give form to dark, shapeless substances, but cannot bring into being the substance itself. In all matters of discovery and invention, even of those that appertain to the imagination, we are continually reminded of the story of Columbus and his egg. Invention consists in the capacity of seizing on the capabilities of a subject, and in the power of moulding and fashioning ideas suggested to it.

Many and long were the conversations between Lord Byron and Shelley, to which I was a devout but nearly silent listener. During one of these, various philosophical doctrines were discussed, and among others the nature of the principle of life, and whether there was any probability of its ever being discovered and communicated. They talked of the experiments of Dr. Darwin,° (I speak not of what the Doctor really did, or said that he did, but, as more to my purpose, of what was then spoken of as having been done by him,) who preserved a piece of vermicelli in a glass case, till by some extraordinary means it began to move with voluntary motion. Not thus, after all, would life be given.

---

**Sanchean:** Reference to Sancho Panza, the practical companion of the idealistic Don Quixote, in the Spanish novel *Don Quixote de la Mancha* (1605) by Miguel de Cervantes. **Dr. Darwin:** Erasmus Darwin (1731–1802), physician, poet, evolutionist, radical, and grandfather of the naturalist and theorist of natural selection Charles Darwin (1809–1882).

Perhaps a corpse would be re-animated; galvanism had given token of such things: perhaps the component parts of a creature might be manufactured, brought together, and endued with vital warmth.

Night waned upon this talk, and even the witching hour had gone by, before we retired to rest. When I placed my head on my pillow, I did not sleep, nor could I be said to think. My imagination, unbidden, possessed and guided me, gifting the successive images that arose in my mind with a vividness far beyond the usual bounds of reverie. I saw—with shut eyes, but acute mental vision,—I saw the pale student of unhallowed arts kneeling beside the thing he had put together. I saw the hideous phantasm of a man stretched out, and then, on the working of some powerful engine, show signs of life, and stir with an uneasy, half vital motion. Frightful must it be; for supremely frightful would be the effect of any human endeavour to mock the stupendous mechanism of the Creator of the world. His success would terrify the artist; he would rush away from his odious handywork, horror-stricken. He would hope that, left to itself, the slight spark of life which he had communicated would fade; that this thing, which had received such imperfect animation, would subside into dead matter; and he might sleep in the belief that the silence of the grave would quench for ever the transient existence of the hideous corpse which he had looked upon as the cradle of life. He sleeps; but he is awakened; he opens his eyes; behold the horrid thing stands at his bedside, opening his curtains, and looking on him with yellow, watery, but speculative eyes.

I opened mine in terror. The idea so possessed my mind, that a thrill of fear ran through me, and I wished to exchange the ghastly image of my fancy for the realities around. I see them still; the very room, the dark *parquet*, the closed shutters, with the moonlight struggling through, and the sense I had that the glassy lake and white high Alps were beyond. I could not so easily get rid of my hideous phantom; still it haunted me. I must try to think of something else. I recurred to my ghost story,—my tiresome unlucky ghost story! O! if I could only contrive one which would frighten my reader as I myself had been frightened that night!

Swift as light and as cheering was the idea that broke in upon me. "I have found it! What terrified me will terrify others; and I need only describe the spectre which had haunted my midnight pillow." On the morrow I announced that I had *thought of a story*. I began that day with the words, *It was on a dreary night of November*, making only a transcript of the grim terrors of my waking dream.

At first I thought but of a few pages—of a short tale; but Shelley urged me to develope the idea at greater length. I certainly did not owe the suggestion of one incident, nor scarcely of one train of feeling, to my husband, and yet but for his incitement, it would never have taken the form in which it was presented to the world. From this declaration I must except the preface. As far as I can recollect, it was entirely written by him.

And now, once again, I bid my hideous progeny go forth and prosper. I have an affection for it, for it was the offspring of happy days, when death and grief were but words, which found no true echo in my heart. Its several pages speak of many a walk, many a drive, and many a conversation, when I was not alone; and my companion was one who, in this world, I shall never see more. But this is for myself; my readers have nothing to do with these associations.

I will add but one word as to the alterations I have made. They are principally those of style. I have changed no portion of the story, nor introduced any new ideas or circumstances. I have mended the language where it was so bald as to interfere with the interest of the narrative; and these changes occur almost exclusively in the beginning of the first volume. Throughout they are entirely confined to such parts as are mere adjuncts to the story, leaving the core and substance of it untouched.

M. W. S.
*London, October* 15, 1831.

## PREFACE[2]

The event on which this fiction is founded, has been supposed, by Dr. Darwin, and some of the physiological writers of Germany, as not of impossible occurrence. I shall not be supposed as according the remotest degree of serious faith to such an imagination; yet, in assuming it as the basis of a work of fancy, I have not considered myself as merely weaving a series of supernatural terrors. The event on which the interest of the story depends is exempt from the disadvantages of a mere tale of spectres or enchantment. It was recommended by the novelty of the situations which it developes; and, however impossible as a physical fact, affords a point of view to the imagination for the delineating of human passions more comprehensive and commanding than any which the ordinary relations of existing events can yield.

---

[2]This Preface was written by Mary Shelley's husband Percy Shelley (1792–1822) for the 1818 first edition of *Frankenstein*.

I have thus endeavoured to preserve the truth of the elementary principles of human nature, while I have not scrupled to innovate upon their combinations. The Iliad, the tragic poetry of Greece—Shakespeare, in the Tempest and Midsummer Night's Dream,—and most especially Milton, in Paradise Lost, conform to this rule; and the most humble novelist, who seeks to confer or receive amusement from his labours, may, without presumption, apply to prose fiction a licence, or rather a rule, from the adoption of which so many exquisite combinations of human feeling have resulted in the highest specimens of poetry.

The circumstance on which my story rests was suggested in casual conversation. It was commenced partly as a source of amusement, and partly as an expedient for exercising any untried resources of mind. Other motives were mingled with these, as the work proceeded. I am by no means indifferent to the manner in which whatever moral tendencies exist in the sentiments or characters it contains shall affect the reader; yet my chief concern in this respect has been limited to the avoiding the enervating effects of the novels of the present day, and to the exhibition of the amiableness of domestic affection, and the excellence of universal virtue. The opinions which naturally spring from the character and situation of the hero are by no means to be conceived as existing always in my own conviction; nor is any inference justly to be drawn from the following pages as prejudicing any philosophical doctrine of whatever kind.

It is a subject also of additional interest to the author, that this story was begun in the majestic region where the scene is principally laid, and in society which cannot cease to be regretted. I passed the summer of 1816 in the environs of Geneva. The season was cold and rainy, and in the evenings we crowded around a blazing wood fire, and occasionally amused ourselves with some German stories of ghosts, which happened to fall into our hands. These tales excited in us a playful desire of imitation. Two other friends (a tale from the pen of one of whom would be far more acceptable to the public than any thing I can ever hope to produce) and myself agreed to write each a story, founded on some supernatural occurrence.

The weather, however, suddenly became serene; and my two friends left me on a journey among the Alps, and lost, in the magnificent scenes which they present, all memory of their ghostly visions. The following tale is the only one which has been completed.

*Marlow, September,* 1817.

## LETTER I

### To Mrs. Saville, England

St. Petersburgh, Dec. 11th, 17—.

You will rejoice to hear that no disaster has accompanied the commencement of an enterprise which you have regarded with such evil forebodings. I arrived here yesterday; and my first task is to assure my dear sister of my welfare, and increasing confidence in the success of my undertaking.

I am already far north of London; and as I walk in the streets of Petersburgh, I feel a cold northern breeze play upon my cheeks, which braces my nerves, and fills me with delight. Do you understand this feeling? This breeze, which has travelled from the regions towards which I am advancing, gives me a foretaste of those icy climes. Inspirited by this wind of promise, my day dreams become more fervent and vivid. I try in vain to be persuaded that the pole is the seat of frost and desolation; it ever presents itself to my imagination as the region of beauty and delight. There, Margaret, the sun is for ever visible; its broad disk just skirting the horizon, and diffusing a perpetual splendour. There—for with your leave, my sister, I will put some trust in preceding navigators—there snow and frost are banished; and, sailing over a calm sea, we may be wafted to a land surpassing in wonders and in beauty every region hitherto discovered on the habitable globe. Its productions and features may be without example, as the phenomena of the heavenly bodies undoubtedly are in those undiscovered solitudes. What may not be expected in a country of eternal light? I may there discover the wondrous power which attracts the needle; and may regulate a thousand celestial observations, that require only this voyage to render their seeming eccentricities consistent for ever. I shall satiate my ardent curiosity with the sight of a part of the world never before visited, and may tread a land never before imprinted by the foot of man. These are my enticements, and they are sufficient to conquer all fear of danger or death, and to induce me to commence this laborious voyage with the joy a child feels when he embarks in a little boat, with his holiday mates, on an expedition of discovery up his native river. But, supposing all these conjectures to be false, you cannot contest the inestimable benefit which I shall confer on all mankind to the last generation, by discovering a passage near the pole to those countries, to reach which at present so many months are requisite; or by ascertaining the secret of the magnet, which, if at all possible, can only be effected by an undertaking such as mine.

These reflections have dispelled the agitation with which I began my letter, and I feel my heart glow with an enthusiasm which elevates me to heaven; for nothing contributes so much to tranquillise the mind as a steady purpose,—a point on which the soul may fix its intellectual eye. This expedition has been the favourite dream of my early years. I have read with ardour the accounts of the various voyages which have been made in the prospect of arriving at the North Pacific Ocean through the seas which surround the pole. You may remember, that a history of all the voyages made for purposes of discovery composed the whole of our good uncle Thomas's library. My education was neglected, yet I was passionately fond of reading. These volumes were my study day and night, and my familiarity with them increased that regret which I had felt, as a child, on learning that my father's dying injunction had forbidden my uncle to allow me to embark in a seafaring life.

These visions faded when I perused, for the first time, those poets whose effusions entranced my soul, and lifted it to heaven. I also became a poet, and for one year lived in a Paradise of my own creation; I imagined that I also might obtain a niche in the temple where the names of Homer and Shakespeare are consecrated. You are well acquainted with my failure, and how heavily I bore the disappointment. But just at that time I inherited the fortune of my cousin, and my thoughts were turned into the channel of their earlier bent.

Six years have passed since I resolved on my present undertaking. I can, even now, remember the hour from which I dedicated myself to this great enterprise. I commenced by inuring my body to hardship. I accompanied the whale-fishers on several expeditions to the North Sea; I voluntarily endured cold, famine, thirst, and want of sleep; I often worked harder than the common sailors during the day, and devoted my nights to the study of mathematics, the theory of medicine, and those branches of physical science from which a naval adventurer might derive the greatest practical advantage. Twice I actually hired myself as an under-mate in a Greenland whaler, and acquitted myself to admiration. I must own I felt a little proud, when my captain offered me the second dignity in the vessel, and entreated me to remain with the greatest earnestness; so valuable did he consider my services.

And now, dear Margaret, do I not deserve to accomplish some great purpose? My life might have been passed in ease and luxury; but I preferred glory to every enticement that wealth placed in my path. Oh, that some encouraging voice would answer in the affirmative! My courage and my resolution is firm; but my hopes fluctuate, and my spirits are often depressed. I am about to proceed on a long and difficult voyage, the emergencies of which will demand all my fortitude: I am required not only to raise the spirits of others, but sometimes to sustain my own, when theirs are failing.

This is the most favourable period for travelling in Russia. They fly quickly over the snow in their sledges; the motion is pleasant, and, in my opinion, far more agreeable than that of an English stage-coach. The cold is not excessive, if you are wrapped in furs,—a dress which I have already adopted; for there is a great difference between walking the deck and remaining seated motionless for hours, when no exercise prevents the blood from actually freezing in your veins. I have no ambition to lose my life on the post-road between St. Petersburgh and Archangel.°

I shall depart for the latter town in a fortnight or three weeks; and my intention is to hire a ship there, which can easily be done by paying the insurance for the owner, and to engage as many sailors as I think necessary among those who are accustomed to the whale-fishing. I do not intend to sail until the month of June; and when shall I return? Ah, dear sister, how can I answer this question? If I succeed, many, many months, perhaps years, will pass before you and I may meet. If I fail, you will see me again soon, or never.

Farewell, my dear, excellent Margaret. Heaven shower down blessings on you, and save me, that I may again and again testify my gratitude for all your love and kindness.

Your affectionate brother,

R. Walton.

## LETTER II

### To Mrs. Saville, England

Archangel, 28th March, 17—.

How slowly the time passes here, encompassed as I am by frost and snow! yet a second step is taken towards my enterprise. I have hired a vessel, and am occupied in collecting my sailors; those whom I have already engaged appear to be men on whom I can depend, and are certainly possessed of dauntless courage.

---

*Archangel:* City in north of European Russia.

But I have one want which I have never yet been able to satisfy; and the absence of the object of which I now feel as a most severe evil. I have no friend, Margaret: when I am glowing with the enthusiasm of success, there will be none to participate my joy; if I am assailed by disappointment, no one will endeavour to sustain me in dejection. I shall commit my thoughts to paper, it is true; but that is a poor medium for the communication of feeling. I desire the company of a man who could sympathise with me; whose eyes would reply to mine. You may deem me romantic, my dear sister, but I bitterly feel the want of a friend. I have no one near me, gentle yet courageous, possessed of a cultivated as well as of a capacious mind, whose tastes are like my own, to approve or amend my plans. How would such a friend repair the faults of your poor brother! I am too ardent in execution, and too impatient of difficulties. But it is a still greater evil to me that I am self-educated: for the first fourteen years of my life I ran wild on a common, and read nothing but our uncle Thomas's books of voyages. At that age I became acquainted with the celebrated poets of our own country; but it was only when it had ceased to be in my power to derive its most important benefits from such a conviction, that I perceived the necessity of becoming acquainted with more languages than that of my native country. Now I am twenty-eight, and am in reality more illiterate than many schoolboys of fifteen. It is true that I have thought more, and that my day dreams are more extended and magnificent; but they want (as the painters call it) *keeping*; and I greatly need a friend who would have sense enough not to despise me as romantic, and affection enough for me to endeavour to regulate my mind.

Well, these are useless complaints; I shall certainly find no friend on the wide ocean, nor even here in Archangel, among merchants and seamen. Yet some feelings, unallied to the dross of human nature, beat even in these rugged bosoms. My lieutenant, for instance, is a man of wonderful courage and enterprise; he is madly desirous of glory: or rather, to word my phrase more characteristically, of advancement in his profession. He is an Englishman, and in the midst of national and professional prejudices, unsoftened by cultivation, retains some of the noblest endowments of humanity. I first became acquainted with him on board a whale vessel: finding that he was unemployed in this city, I easily engaged him to assist in my enterprise.

The master is a person of an excellent disposition, and is remarkable in the ship for his gentleness and the mildness of his discipline. This circumstance, added to his well known integrity and dauntless courage, made me very desirous to engage him. A youth passed in solitude, my best years spent under your gentle and feminine fosterage, has so refined the groundwork of my character, that I cannot overcome an intense distaste to the usual brutality exercised on board ship: I have never believed it to be necessary; and when I heard of a mariner equally noted for his kindliness of heart, and the respect and obedience paid to him by his crew, I felt myself peculiarly fortunate in being able to secure his services. I heard of him first in rather a romantic manner, from a lady who owes to him the happiness of her life. This, briefly, is his story. Some years ago, he loved a young Russian lady, of moderate fortune; and having amassed a considerable sum in prize-money, the father of the girl consented to the match. He saw his mistress once before the destined ceremony; but she was bathed in tears, and, throwing herself at his feet, entreated him to spare her, confessing at the same time that she loved another, but that he was poor, and that her father would never consent to the union. My generous friend reassured the suppliant, and on being informed of the name of her lover, instantly abandoned his pursuit. He had already bought a farm with his money, on which he had designed to pass the remainder of his life; but he bestowed the whole on his rival, together with the remains of his prize-money to purchase stock, and then himself solicited the young woman's father to consent to her marriage with her lover. But the old man decidedly refused, thinking himself bound in honour to my friend; who, when he found the father inexorable, quitted his country, nor returned until he heard that his former mistress was married according to her inclinations. "What a noble fellow!" you will exclaim. He is so; but then he is wholly uneducated: he is as silent as a Turk, and a kind of ignorant carelessness attends him, which, while it renders his conduct the more astonishing, detracts from the interest and sympathy which otherwise he would command.

Yet do not suppose, because I complain a little, or because I can conceive a consolation for my toils which I may never know, that I am wavering in my resolutions. Those are as fixed as fate; and my voyage is only now delayed until the weather shall permit my embarkation. The winter has been dreadfully severe; but the spring promises well, and it is considered as a remarkably early season; so that perhaps I may sail sooner than I expected. I shall do nothing rashly: you know me sufficiently to confide in my prudence and considerateness, whenever the safety of others is committed to my care.

I cannot describe to you my sensations on the near prospect of my undertaking. It is impossible to communicate to you a conception of the trembling sensation, half pleasurable and half fearful, with which I

am preparing to depart. I am going to unexplored regions, to "the land
of mist and snow;" but I shall kill no albatross, therefore do not be
alarmed for my safety, or if I should come back to you as worn and
woful as the "Ancient Mariner?"° You will smile at my allusion; but I
will disclose a secret. I have often attributed my attachment to, my passionate enthusiasm for, the dangerous mysteries of ocean, to that production of the most imaginative of modern poets. There is something
at work in my soul, which I do not understand. I am practically industrious—pains-taking;—a workman to execute with perseverance and
labour:—but besides this, there is a love for the marvellous, a belief in
the marvellous, intertwined in all my projects, which hurries me out of
the common pathways of men, even to the wild sea and unvisited
regions I am about to explore.

But to return to dearer considerations. Shall I meet you again, after
having traversed immense seas, and returned by the most southern cape
of Africa or America? I dare not expect such success, yet I cannot bear
to look on the reverse of the picture. Continue for the present to write
to me by every opportunity: I may receive your letters on some occasions when I need them most to support my spirits. I love you very tenderly. Remember me with affection, should you never hear from me
again.

Your affectionate brother,<br>
Robert Walton.

## LETTER III

### To Mrs. Saville, England

My dear Sister,                                                July 7th, 17——.
    I write a few lines in haste, to say that I am safe, and well advanced
on my voyage. This letter will reach England by a merchantman now
on its homeward voyage from Archangel; more fortunate than I, who
may not see my native land, perhaps, for many years. I am, however, in
good spirits; my men are bold, and apparently firm of purpose; nor do
the floating sheets of ice that continually pass us, indicating the dangers

---

"*the land of mist and snow*" . . . "*Ancient Mariner*": Reference to "The Rime of the
Ancient Mariner," written by Samuel Taylor Coleridge (1772–1834) and first published
in 1798.

of the region towards which we are advancing, appear to dismay them. We have already reached a very high latitude; but it is the height of summer, and although not so warm as in England, the southern gales, which blow us speedily towards those shores which I so ardently desire to attain, breathe a degree of renovating warmth which I had not expected.

No incidents have hitherto befallen us that would make a figure in a letter. One or two stiff gales, and the springing of a leak, are accidents which experienced navigators scarcely remember to record; and I shall be well content if nothing worse happen to us during our voyage.

Adieu, my dear Margaret. Be assured, that for my own sake, as well as yours, I will not rashly encounter danger. I will be cool, persevering, and prudent.

But success *shall* crown my endeavours. Wherefore not? Thus far I have gone, tracing a secure way over the pathless seas: the very stars themselves being witnesses and testimonies of my triumph. Why not still proceed over the untamed yet obedient element? What can stop the determined heart and resolved will of man?

My swelling heart involuntarily pours itself out thus. But I must finish. Heaven bless my beloved sister!

R. W.

## LETTER IV

### To Mrs. Saville, England

August 5th, 17—.

So strange an accident has happened to us, that I cannot forbear recording it, although it is very probable that you will see me before these papers can come into your possession.

Last Monday (July 31st), we were nearly surrounded by ice, which closed in the ship on all sides, scarcely leaving her the sea-room in which she floated. Our situation was somewhat dangerous, especially as we were compassed round by a very thick fog. We accordingly lay to, hoping that some change would take place in the atmosphere and weather.

About two o'clock the mist cleared away, and we beheld, stretched out in every direction, vast and irregular plains of ice, which seemed to have no end. Some of my comrades groaned, and my own mind began to grow watchful with anxious thoughts, when a strange sight suddenly attracted our attention, and diverted our solicitude from our own situation. We perceived a low carriage, fixed on a sledge and drawn by dogs, pass on towards the north, at the distance of half a mile: a being which had the shape of a man, but apparently of gigantic stature, sat in the sledge, and guided the dogs. We watched the rapid progress of the traveller with our telescopes, until he was lost among the distant inequalities of the ice.

This appearance excited our unqualified wonder. We were, as we believed, many hundred miles from any land; but this apparition seemed to denote that it was not, in reality, so distant as we had supposed. Shut in, however, by ice, it was impossible to follow his track, which we had observed with the greatest attention.

About two hours after this occurrence, we heard the ground sea; and before night the ice broke, and freed our ship. We, however, lay to until the morning, fearing to encounter in the dark those large loose masses which float about after the breaking up of the ice. I profited of this time to rest for a few hours.

In the morning, however, as soon as it was light, I went upon deck, and found all the sailors busy on one side of the vessel, apparently talking to some one in the sea. It was, in fact, a sledge, like that we had seen before, which had drifted towards us in the night, on a large fragment of ice. Only one dog remained alive; but there was a human being within it, whom the sailors were persuading to enter the vessel. He was not, as the other traveller seemed to be, a savage inhabitant of some undiscovered island, but an European. When I appeared on deck, the master said, "Here is our captain, and he will not allow you to perish on the open sea."

On perceiving me, the stranger addressed me in English, although with a foreign accent. "Before I come on board your vessel," said he, "will you have the kindness to inform me whither you are bound?"

You may conceive my astonishment on hearing such a question addressed to me from a man on the brink of destruction, and to whom I should have supposed that my vessel would have been a resource which he would not have exchanged for the most precious wealth the earth can afford. I replied, however, that we were on a voyage of discovery towards the northern pole.

Upon hearing this he appeared satisfied, and consented to come on board. Good God! Margaret, if you had seen the man who thus capitulated for his safety, your surprise would have been boundless. His limbs were nearly frozen, and his body dreadfully emaciated by fatigue and suffering. I never saw a man in so wretched a condition. We attempted to carry him into the cabin; but as soon as he had quitted the fresh air, he fainted. We accordingly brought him back to the deck, and restored him to animation by rubbing him with brandy, and forcing him to swallow a small quantity. As soon as he showed signs of life we wrapped him up in blankets, and placed him near the chimney of the kitchen stove. By slow degrees he recovered, and ate a little soup, which restored him wonderfully.

Two days passed in this manner before he was able to speak; and I often feared that his suffering had deprived him of understanding. When he had in some measure recovered, I removed him to my own cabin, and attended on him as much as my duty would permit. I never saw a more interesting creature: his eyes have generally an expression of wildness, and even madness; but there are moments when, if any one performs an act of kindness towards him, or does him any the most trifling service, his whole countenance is lighted up, as it were, with a beam of benevolence and sweetness that I never saw equalled. But he is generally melancholy and despairing; and sometimes he gnashes his teeth, as if impatient of the weight of woes that oppresses him.

When my guest was a little recovered, I had great trouble to keep off the men, who wished to ask him a thousand questions; but I would not allow him to be tormented by their idle curiosity, in a state of body and mind whose restoration evidently depended upon entire repose. Once, however, the lieutenant asked, Why he had come so far upon the ice in so strange a vehicle?

His countenance instantly assumed an aspect of the deepest gloom; and he replied, "To seek one who fled from me."

"And did the man whom you pursued travel in the same fashion?"

"Yes."

"Then I fancy we have seen him; for the day before we picked you up, we saw some dogs drawing a sledge, with a man in it, across the ice."

This aroused the stranger's attention; and he asked a multitude of questions concerning the route which the daemon, as he called him, had pursued. Soon after, when he was alone with me, he said, — "I have, doubtless, excited your curiosity, as well as that of these good people; but you are too considerate to make enquiries."

"Certainly; it would indeed be very impertinent and inhuman in me to trouble you with any inquisitiveness of mine."

"And yet you rescued me from a strange and perilous situation; you have benevolently restored me to life."

Soon after this he enquired if I thought that the breaking up of the ice had destroyed the other sledge? I replied, that I could not answer with any degree of certainty; for the ice had not broken until near midnight, and the traveller might have arrived at a place of safety before that time; but of this I could not judge.

From this time a new spirit of life animated the decaying frame of the stranger. He manifested the greatest eagerness to be upon deck, to watch for the sledge which had before appeared; but I have persuaded him to remain in the cabin, for he is far too weak to sustain the rawness of the atmosphere. I have promised that some one should watch for him, and give him instant notice if any new object should appear in sight.

Such is my journal of what relates to this strange occurrence up to the present day. The stranger has gradually improved in health, but is very silent, and appears uneasy when any one enters his cabin. Yet his manners are so conciliating and gentle, that the sailors are all interested in him, although they have had very little communication with him. For my own part, I begin to love him as a brother; and his constant and deep grief fills me with sympathy and compassion. He must have been a noble creature in his better days, being even now in wreck so attractive and amiable.

I said in one of my letters, my dear Margaret, that I should find no friend on the wide ocean; yet I have found a man who, before his spirit had been broken by misery, I should have been happy to have possessed as the brother of my heart.

I shall continue my journal concerning the stranger at intervals, should I have any fresh incidents to record.

August 13th, 17—.

My affection for my guest increases every day. He excites at once my admiration and my pity to an astonishing degree. How can I see so noble a creature destroyed by misery, without feeling the most poignant grief? He is so gentle, yet so wise; his mind is so cultivated; and when he speaks, although his words are culled with the choicest art, yet they flow with rapidity and unparalleled eloquence.

He is now much recovered from his illness, and is continually on the deck, apparently watching for the sledge that preceded his own. Yet, although unhappy, he is not so utterly occupied by his own misery, but that he interests himself deeply in the projects of others. He has frequently conversed with me on mine, which I have communicated to him without disguise. He entered attentively into all my arguments in favour of my eventual success, and into every minute detail of the measures I had taken to secure it. I was easily led by the sympathy which he evinced, to use the language of my heart; to give utterance to the burning ardour of my soul; and to say, with all the fervour that warmed me, how gladly I would sacrifice my fortune, my existence, my every hope, to the furtherance of my enterprise. One man's life or death were but a small price to pay for the acquirement of the knowledge which I sought; for the dominion I should acquire and transmit over the elemental foes of our race. As I spoke, a dark gloom spread over my listener's countenance. At first I perceived that he tried to suppress his emotion; he placed his hands before his eyes; and my voice quivered and failed me, as I beheld tears trickle fast from between his fingers,—a groan burst from his heaving breast. I paused;—at length he spoke, in broken accents:—"Unhappy man! Do you share my madness? Have you drank also of the intoxicating draught? Hear me,—let me reveal my tale, and you will dash the cup from your lips!"

Such words, you may imagine, strongly excited my curiosity; but the paroxysm of grief that had seized the stranger overcame his weakened powers, and many hours of repose and tranquil conversation were necessary to restore his composure.

Having conquered the violence of his feelings, he appeared to despise himself for being the slave of passion; and quelling the dark tyranny of despair, he led me again to converse concerning myself personally. He asked me the history of my earlier years. The tale was quickly told: but it awakened various trains of reflection. I spoke of my desire of finding a friend—of my thirst for a more intimate sympathy with a fellow mind than had ever fallen to my lot; and expressed my conviction that a man could boast of little happiness, who did not enjoy this blessing.

"I agree with you," replied the stranger; "we are unfashioned creatures, but half made up, if one wiser, better, dearer than ourselves—such a friend ought to be—do not lend his aid to perfectionate our weak and faulty natures. I once had a friend, the most noble of human creatures, and am entitled, therefore, to judge respecting friendship. You have hope, and the world before you, and have no cause for despair. But I—I have lost every thing, and cannot begin life anew."

As he said this, his countenance became expressive of a calm settled grief, that touched me to the heart. But he was silent, and presently retired to his cabin.

Even broken in spirit as he is, no once can feel more deeply than he does the beauties of nature. The starry sky, the sea, and every sight afforded by these wonderful regions, seems still to have the power of elevating his soul from earth. Such a man has a double existence: he may suffer misery, and be overwhelmed by disappointments; yet, when he has retired into himself, he will be like a celestial spirit, that has a halo around him, within whose circle no grief or folly ventures.

Will you smile at the enthusiasm I express concerning this divine wanderer? You would not, if you saw him. You have been tutored and refined by books and retirement from the world, and you are, therefore, somewhat fastidious; but this only renders you the more fit to appreciate the extraordinary merits of this wonderful man. Sometimes I have endeavoured to discover what quality it is which he possesses, that elevates him so immeasurably above any other person I ever knew. I believe it to be an intuitive discernment; a quick but never-failing power of judgment; a penetration into the causes of things, unequalled for clearness and precision; add to this a facility of expression, and a voice whose varied intonations are soul-subduing music.

                                                          August 19, 17——.
Yesterday the stranger said to me, "You may easily perceive, Captain Walton, that I have suffered great and unparalleled misfortunes. I had determined, at one time, that the memory of these evils should die with me; but you have won me to alter my determination. You seek for knowledge and wisdom, as I once did; and I ardently hope that the gratification of your wishes may not be a serpent to sting you, as mine has been. I do not know that the relation of my disasters will be useful to you; yet, when I reflect that you are pursuing the same course, exposing yourself to the same dangers which have rendered me what I am, I imagine that you may deduce an apt moral from my tale; one that may direct you if you succeed in your undertaking, and console you in case of failure. Prepare to hear of occurrences which are usually deemed marvellous. Were we among the tamer scenes of nature, I might fear to encounter your unbelief, perhaps your ridicule; but many things will appear possible in these wild and mysterious regions, which would provoke the laughter of those unacquainted with the ever-varied powers of nature:——nor can I doubt but that my tale conveys in its series internal evidence of the truth of the events of which it is composed."

You may easily imagine that I was much gratified by the offered communication; yet I could not endure that he should renew his grief by a recital of his misfortunes. I felt the greatest eagerness to hear the promised narrative, partly from curiosity, and partly from a strong desire to ameliorate his fate, if it were in my power. I expressed these feelings in my answer.

"I thank you," he replied, "for your sympathy, but it is useless; my fate is nearly fulfilled. I wait but for one event, and then I shall repose in peace. I understand your feeling," continued he, perceiving that I wished to interrupt him; "but you are mistaken, my friend, if thus you will allow me to name you; nothing can alter my destiny: listen to my history, and you will perceive how irrevocably it is determined."

He then told me, that he would commence his narrative the next day when I should be at leisure. This promise drew from me the warmest thanks. I have resolved every night, when I am not imperatively occupied by my duties, to record, as nearly as possible in his own words, what he has related during the day. If I should be engaged, I will at least make notes. This manuscript will doubtless afford you the greatest pleasure: but to me, who know him, and who hear it from his own lips, with what interest and sympathy shall I read it in some future day! Even now, as I commence my task, his full-toned voice swells in my ears; his lustrous eyes dwell on me with all their melancholy sweetness; I see his thin hand raised in animation, while the lineaments of his face are irradiated by the soul within. Strange and harrowing must be his story; frightful the storm which embraced the gallant vessel on its course, and wrecked it—thus!

## CHAPTER I

I am by birth a Genevese; and my family is one of the most distinguished of that republic. My ancestors had been for many years counsellors and syndics;° and my father had filled several public situations with honour and reputation. He was respected by all who knew him, for his integrity and indefatigable attention to public business. He passed his younger days perpetually occupied by the affairs of his country; a variety of circumstances had prevented his marrying early, nor was it until the decline of life that he became a husband and the father of a family.

As the circumstances of his marriage illustrate his character, I cannot refrain from relating them. One of his most intimate friends was a merchant, who, from a flourishing state, fell, through numerous mischances, into poverty. This man, whose name was Beaufort, was of a proud and unbending disposition, and could not bear to live in poverty and oblivion in the same country where he had formerly been distinguished for his rank and magnificence. Having paid his debts, therefore, in the most honourable manner, he retreated with his daughter to

*syndics:* Government officials.

the town of Lucerne, where he lived unknown and in wretchedness. My
father loved Beaufort with the truest friendship, and was deeply grieved
by his retreat in these unfortunate circumstances. He bitterly deplored
the false pride which led his friend to a conduct so little worthy of the
affection that united them. He lost no time in endeavouring to seek
him out, with the hope of persuading him to begin the world again
through his credit and assistance.

Beaufort had taken effectual measures to conceal himself; and it was
ten months before my father discovered his abode. Overjoyed at this
discovery, he hastened to the house, which was situated in a mean
street, near the Reuss. But when he entered, misery and despair alone
welcomed him. Beaufort had saved but a very small sum of money from
the wreck of his fortunes; but it was sufficient to provide him with sustenance for some months, and in the mean time he hoped to procure
some respectable employment in a merchant's house. The interval was,
consequently, spent in inaction; his grief only became more deep and
rankling, when he had leisure for reflection; and at length it took so fast
hold of his mind, that at the end of three months he lay on a bed of
sickness, incapable of any exertion.

His daughter attended him with the greatest tenderness; but she
saw with despair that their little fund was rapidly decreasing, and that
there was no other prospect of support. But Caroline Beaufort possessed a mind of an uncommon mould; and her courage rose to support
her in her adversity. She procured plain work; she plaited straw; and by
various means contrived to earn a pittance scarcely sufficient to support
life.

Several months passed in this manner. Her father grew worse; her
time was more entirely occupied in attending him; her means of subsistence decreased; and in the tenth month her father died in her arms,
leaving her an orphan and a beggar. This last blow overcame her; and
she knelt by Beaufort's coffin, weeping bitterly, when my father entered
the chamber. He came like a protecting spirit to the poor girl, who
committed herself to his care; and after the interment of his friend, he
conducted her to Geneva, and placed her under the protection of a
relation. Two years after this event Caroline became his wife.

There was a considerable difference between the ages of my parents, but this circumstance seemed to unite them only closer in bonds
of devoted affection. There was a sense of justice in my father's upright
mind, which rendered it necessary that he should approve highly to
love strongly. Perhaps during former years he had suffered from the
late-discovered unworthiness of one beloved, and so was disposed to

set a greater value on tried worth. There was a show of gratitude and worship in his attachment to my mother, differing wholly from the doting fondness of age, for it was inspired by reverence for her virtues, and a desire to be the means of, in some degree, recompensing her for the sorrows she had endured, but which gave inexpressible grace to his behaviour to her. Every thing was made to yield to her wishes and her convenience. He strove to shelter her, as a fair exotic is sheltered by the gardener, from every rougher wind, and to surround her with all that could tend to excite pleasurable emotion in her soft and benevolent mind. Her health, and even the tranquillity of her hitherto constant spirit, had been shaken by what she had gone through. During the two years that had elapsed previous to their marriage my father had gradually relinquished all his public functions; and immediately after their union they sought the pleasant climate of Italy, and the change of scene and interest attendant on a tour through that land of wonders, as a restorative for her weakened frame.

From Italy they visited Germany and France. I, their eldest child, was born at Naples, and as an infant accompanied them in their rambles. I remained for several years their only child. Much as they were attached to each other, they seemed to draw inexhaustible stores of affection from a very mine of love to bestow them upon me. My mother's tender caresses, and my father's smile of benevolent pleasure while regarding me, are my first recollections. I was their plaything and their idol, and something better—their child, the innocent and helpless creature bestowed on them by Heaven, whom to bring up to good, and whose future lot it was in their hands to direct to happiness or misery, according as they fulfilled their duties towards me. With this deep consciousness of what they owed towards the being to which they had given life, added to the active spirit of tenderness that animated both, it may be imagined that while during every hour of my infant life I received a lesson of patience, of charity, and of self-control, I was so guided by a silken cord, that all seemed but one train of enjoyment to me.

For a long time I was their only care. My mother had much desired to have a daughter, but I continued their single offspring. When I was about five years old, while making an excursion beyond the frontiers of Italy, they passed a week on the shores of the Lake of Como. Their benevolent disposition often made them enter the cottages of the poor. This, to my mother, was more than a duty; it was a necessity, a passion,—remembering what she had suffered, and how she had been relieved,—for her to act in her turn the guardian angel to the afflicted.

During one of their walks a poor cot in the foldings of a vale attracted their notice, as being singularly disconsolate, while the number of half-clothed children gathered about it, spoke of penury in its worst shape. One day, when my father had gone by himself to Milan, my mother, accompanied by me, visited this abode. She found a peasant and his wife, hard working, bent down by care and labour, distributing a scanty meal to five hungry babes. Among these there was one which attracted my mother far above all the rest. She appeared of a different stock. The four others were dark-eyed, hardy little vagrants; this child was thin, and very fair. Her hair was the brightest living gold, and, despite the poverty of her clothing, seemed to set a crown of distinction on her head. Her brow was clear and ample, her blue eyes cloudless, and her lips and the moulding of her face so expressive of sensibility and sweetness, that none could behold her without looking on her as of a distinct species, a being heaven-sent, and bearing a celestial stamp in all her features.

The peasant woman, perceiving that my mother fixed eyes of wonder and admiration on this lovely girl, eagerly communicated her history. She was not her child, but the daughter of a Milanese nobleman. Her mother was a German, and had died on giving her birth. The infant had been placed with these good people to nurse: they were better off then. They had not been long married, and their eldest child was but just born. The father of their charge was one of those Italians nursed in the memory of the antique glory of Italy,—one among the *schiavi ognor frementi*,° who exerted himself to obtain the liberty of his country. He became the victim of its weakness. Whether he had died, or still lingered in the dungeons of Austria, was not known. His property was confiscated, his child became an orphan and a beggar. She continued with her foster parents, and bloomed in their rude abode, fairer than a garden rose among dark-leaved brambles.

When my father returned from Milan, he found playing with me in the hall of our villa, a child fairer than pictured cherub—a creature who seemed to shed radiance from her looks, and whose form and motions were lighter than the chamois of the hills. The apparition was soon explained. With his permission my mother prevailed on her rustic guardians to yield their charge to her. They were fond of the sweet orphan. Her presence had seemed a blessing to them; but it would be unfair to her to

---

*schiavi ognor frementi:* "Slaves ever trembling"; reference to Italians under Austrian domination in the eighteenth and nineteenth centuries.

keep her in poverty and want, when Providence afforded her such powerful protection. They consulted their village priest, and the result was,
that Elizabeth Lavenza became the inmate of my parents' house—my
more than sister—the beautiful and adored companion of all my occupations and my pleasures.

Every one loved Elizabeth. The passionate and almost reverential
attachment with which all regarded her became, while I shared it, my
pride and my delight. On the evening previous to her being brought to
my home, my mother had said playfully,—"I have a pretty present for
my Victor—to-morrow he shall have it." And when, on the morrow,
she presented Elizabeth to me as her promised gift, I, with childish
seriousness, interpreted her words literally, and looked upon Elizabeth
as mine—mine to protect, love, and cherish. All praises bestowed on
her, I received as made to a possession of my own. We called each other
familiarly by the name of cousin. No word, no expression could body
forth the kind of relation in which she stood to me—my more than
sister, since till death she was to be mine only.

## CHAPTER II

We were brought up together; there was not quite a year difference
in our ages. I need not say that we were strangers to any species of disunion or dispute. Harmony was the soul of our companionship, and the
diversity and contrast that subsisted in our characters drew us nearer
together. Elizabeth was of a calmer and more concentrated disposition;
but, with all my ardour, I was capable of a more intense application, and
was more deeply smitten with the thirst for knowledge. She busied
herself with following the aerial creations of the poets; and in the
majestic and wondrous scenes which surrounded our Swiss home—
the sublime shapes of the mountains; the changes of the seasons; tempest and calm; the silence of winter, and the life and turbulence of our
Alpine summers,—she found ample scope for admiration and delight.
While my companion contemplated with a serious and satisfied spirit
the magnificent appearances of things, I delighted in investigating their
causes. The world was to me a secret which I desired to divine. Curiosity, earnest research to learn the hidden laws of nature, gladness akin to
rapture, as they were unfolded to me, are among the earliest sensations
I can remember.

On the birth of a second son, my junior by seven years, my parents
gave up entirely their wandering life, and fixed themselves in their

native country. We possessed a house in Geneva, and a *campagne*° on Belrive, the eastern shore of the lake, at the distance of rather more than a league from the city. We resided principally in the latter, and the lives of my parents were passed in considerable seclusion. It was my temper to avoid a crowd, and to attach myself fervently to a few. I was indifferent, therefore, to my schoolfellows in general; but I united myself in the bonds of the closest friendship to one among them. Henry Clerval was the son of a merchant of Geneva. He was a boy of singular talent and fancy. He loved enterprise, hardship, and even danger, for its own sake. He was deeply read in books of chivalry and romance. He composed heroic songs, and began to write many a tale of enchantment and knightly adventure. He tried to make us act plays, and to enter into masquerades, in which the characters were drawn from the heroes of Roncesvalles,° of the Round Table of King Arthur, and the chivalrous train who shed their blood to redeem the holy sepulchre from the hands of the infidels.

No human being could have passed a happier childhood than myself. My parents were possessed by the very spirit of kindness and indulgence. We felt that they were not the tyrants to rule our lot according to their caprice, but the agents and creators of all the many delights which we enjoyed. When I mingled with other families, I distinctly discerned how peculiarly fortunate my lot was, and gratitude assisted the developement of filial love.

My temper was sometimes violent, and my passions vehement; but by some law in my temperature they were turned, not towards childish pursuits, but to an eager desire to learn, and not to learn all things indiscriminately. I confess that neither the structure of languages, nor the code of governments, nor the politics of various states, possessed attractions for me. It was the secrets of heaven and earth that I desired to learn; and whether it was the outward substance of things, or the inner spirit of nature and the mysterious soul of man that occupied me, still my enquiries were directed to the metaphysical, or, in its highest sense, the physical secrets of the world.

Meanwhile Clerval occupied himself, so to speak, with the moral relations of things. The busy stage of life, the virtues of heroes, and the actions of men, were his theme; and his hope and his dream was to become one among those whose names are recorded in story, as the gallant and adventurous benefactors of our species. The saintly soul of

---

*campagne:* Countryside (Fr.).   ***Roncesvalles:*** Reference to a battle celebrated in the eleventh-century French heroic poem *The Song of Roland.*

Elizabeth shone like a shrine-dedicated lamp in our peaceful home. Her sympathy was ours; her smile, her soft voice, the sweet glance of her celestial eyes, were ever there to bless and animate us. She was the living spirit of love to soften and attract: I might have become sullen in my study, rough through the ardour of my nature, but that she was there to subdue me to a semblance of her own gentleness. And Clerval—could aught ill entrench on the noble spirit of Clerval?—yet he might not have been so perfectly humane, so thoughtful in his generosity—so full of kindness and tenderness amidst his passion for adventurous exploit, had she not unfolded to him the real loveliness of beneficence, and made the doing good the end and aim of his soaring ambition.

I feel exquisite pleasure in dwelling on the recollections of childhood, before misfortune had tainted my mind, and changed its bright visions of extensive usefulness into gloomy and narrow reflections upon self. Besides, in drawing the picture of my early days, I also record those events which led, by insensible steps, to my after tale of misery: for when I would account to myself for the birth of that passion, which afterwards ruled my destiny, I find it arise, like a mountain river, from ignoble and almost forgotten sources; but, swelling as it proceeded, it became the torrent which, in its course, has swept away all my hopes and joys.

Natural philosophy is the genius that has regulated my fate; I desire, therefore, in this narration, to state those facts which led to my predilection for that science. When I was thirteen years of age, we all went on a party of pleasure to the baths near Thonon; the inclemency of the weather obliged us to remain a day confined to the inn. In this house I chanced to find a volume of the works of Cornelius Agrippa.° I opened it with apathy; the theory which he attempts to demonstrate, and the wonderful facts which he relates, soon changed this feeling into enthusiasm. A new light seemed to dawn upon my mind; and, bounding with joy, I communicated my discovery to my father. My father looked carelessly at the titlepage of my book, and said, "Ah! Cornelius Agrippa! My dear Victor, do not waste your time upon this; it is sad trash."

If, instead of this remark, my father had taken the pains to explain to me, that the principles of Agrippa had been entirely exploded, and that a modern system of science had been introduced, which possessed much greater powers than the ancient, because the powers of the latter

---

*Cornelius Agrippa:* Heinrich Cornelius Agrippa (1486–1535), German physician and occultist.

were chimerical, while those of the former were real and practical; under such circumstances, I should certainly have thrown Agrippa aside, and have contented my imagination, warmed as it was, by returning with greater ardour to my former studies. It is even possible, that the train of my ideas would never have received the fatal impulse that led to my ruin. But the cursory glance my father had taken of my volume by no means assured me that he was acquainted with its contents; and I continued to read with the greatest avidity.

When I returned home, my first care was to procure the whole works of this author, and afterwards of Paracelsus and Albertus Magnus.° I read and studied the wild fancies of these writers with delight; they appeared to me treasures known to few beside myself. I have described myself as always having been embued with a fervent longing to penetrate the secrets of nature. In spite of the intense labour and wonderful discoveries of modern philosophers, I always came from my studies discontented and unsatisfied. Sir Isaac Newton is said to have avowed that he felt like a child picking up shells beside the great and unexplored ocean of truth. Those of his successors in each branch of natural philosophy with whom I was acquainted, appeared even to my boy's apprehensions, as tyros° engaged in the same pursuit.

The untaught peasant beheld the elements around him, and was acquainted with their practical uses. The most learned philosopher knew little more. He had partially unveiled the face of Nature, but her immortal lineaments were still a wonder and a mystery. He might dissect, anatomise, and give names; but, not to speak of a final cause, causes in their secondary and tertiary grades were utterly unknown to him. I had gazed upon the fortifications and impediments that seemed to keep human beings from entering the citadel of nature, and rashly and ignorantly I had repined.

But here were books, and here were men who had penetrated deeper and knew more. I took their word for all that they averred, and I became their disciple. It may appear strange that such should arise in the eighteenth century; but while I followed the routine of education in the schools of Geneva, I was, to a great degree, self taught with regard to my favourite studies. My father was not scientific, and I was left to struggle with a child's blindness, added to a student's thirst for knowledge. Under the guidance of my new preceptors, I entered with

---

**Paracelsus and Albertus Magnus:** Theophrastus Bombastus von Hohenheim (1493–1541), known as Paracelsus, Swiss physician who believed human beings could be produced alchemically. Albertus Magnus (1193–1280), theologian and Aristotelian who instructed St. Thomas Aquinas. **tyros:** Beginners.

the greatest diligence into the search of the philosopher's stone and the elixir of life; but the latter soon obtained my undivided attention. Wealth was an inferior object; but what glory would attend the discovery, if I could banish disease from the human frame, and render man invulnerable to any but a violent death!

Nor were these my only visions. The raising of ghosts or devils was a promise liberally accorded by my favourite authors, the fulfilment of which I most eagerly sought; and if my incantations were always unsuccessful, I attributed the failure rather to my own inexperience and mistake, than to a want of skill or fidelity in my instructors. And thus for a time I was occupied by exploded systems, mingling, like an unadept, a thousand contradictory theories, and floundering desperately in a very slough of multifarious knowledge, guided by an ardent imagination and childish reasoning, till an accident again changed the current of my ideas.

When I was about fifteen years old we had retired to our house near Belrive, when we witnessed a most violent and terrible thunder-storm. It advanced from behind the mountains of Jura; and the thunder burst at once with frightful loudness from various quarters of the heavens. I remained, while the storm lasted, watching its progress with curiosity and delight. As I stood at the door, on a sudden I beheld a stream of fire issue from an old and beautiful oak, which stood about twenty yards from our house; and so soon as the dazzling light vanished, the oak had disappeared, and nothing remained but a blasted stump. When we visited it the next morning, we found the tree shattered in a singular manner. It was not splintered by the shock, but entirely reduced to thin ribands of wood. I never beheld any thing so utterly destroyed.

Before this I was not unacquainted with the more obvious laws of electricity. On this occasion a man of great research in natural philosophy was with us, and, excited by this catastrophe, he entered on the explanation of a theory which he had formed on the subject of electricity and galvanism, which was at once new and astonishing to me. All that he said threw greatly into the shade Cornelius Agrippa, Albertus Magnus, and Paracelsus, the lords of my imagination; but by some fatality the overthrow of these men disinclined me to pursue my accustomed studies. It seemed to me as if nothing would or could ever be known. All that had so long engaged my attention suddenly grew despicable. By one of those caprices of the mind, which we are perhaps most subject to in early youth, I at once gave up my former occupations; set down natural history and all its progeny as a deformed and abortive creation; and entertained the greatest disdain for a would-be science, which could never even step within the threshold of real knowledge. In this mood of mind I betook myself to the mathematics, and the branches of study appertaining to that science, as being built upon secure foundations, and so worthy of my consideration.

Thus strangely are our souls constructed, and by such slight ligaments are we bound to prosperity or ruin. When I look back, it seems to me as if this almost miraculous change of inclination and will was the immediate suggestion of the guardian angel of my life—the last effort made by the spirit of preservation to avert the storm that was even then hanging in the stars, and ready to envelope me. Her victory was announced by an unusual tranquillity and gladness of soul, which followed the relinquishing of my ancient and latterly tormenting studies. It was thus that I was to be taught to associate evil with their prosecution, happiness with their disregard.

It was a strong effort of the spirit of good; but it was ineffectual. Destiny was too potent, and her immutable laws had decreed my utter and terrible destruction.

## CHAPTER III

When I had attained the age of seventeen, my parents resolved that I should become a student at the university of Ingolstadt.° I had hitherto attended the schools of Geneva; but my father thought it necessary, for the completion of my education, that I should be made acquainted with other customs than those of my native country. My departure was therefore fixed at an early date; but, before the day resolved upon could arrive, the first misfortune of my life occurred—an omen, as it were, of my future misery.

Elizabeth had caught the scarlet fever; her illness was severe, and she was in the greatest danger. During her illness, many arguments had been urged to persuade my mother to refrain from attending upon her. She had, at first, yielded to our entreaties; but when she heard that the life of her favourite was menaced, she could no longer control her anxiety. She attended her sick bed,—her watchful attentions triumphed over the malignity of the distemper,—Elizabeth was saved, but the consequences of this imprudence were fatal to her preserver. On the third day my mother sickened; her fever was accompanied by the most alarming symptoms, and the looks of her medical attendants prognos-

*Ingolstadt:* City in Germany.

ticated the worst event. On her death-bed the fortitude and benignity of this best of women did not desert her. She joined the hands of Elizabeth and myself:—"My children," she said, "my firmest hopes of future happiness were placed on the prospect of your union. This expectation will now be the consolation of your father. Elizabeth, my love, you must supply my place to my younger children. Alas! I regret that I am taken from you; and, happy and beloved as I have been, is it not hard to quit you all? But these are not thoughts befitting me; I will endeavour to resign myself cheerfully to death, and will indulge a hope of meeting you in another world."

She died calmly; and her countenance expressed affection even in death. I need not describe the feelings of those whose dearest ties are rent by that most irreparable evil; the void that presents itself to the soul; and the despair that is exhibited on the countenance. It is so long before the mind can persuade itself that she, whom we saw every day, and whose very existence appeared a part of our own, can have departed for ever—that the brightness of a beloved eye can have been extinguished, and the sound of a voice so familiar, and dear to the ear, can be hushed, never more to be heard. These are the reflections of the first days; but when the lapse of time proves the reality of the evil, then the actual bitterness of grief commences. Yet from whom has not that rude hand rent away some dear connection? and why should I describe a sorrow which all have felt, and must feel? The time at length arrives, when grief is rather an indulgence than a necessity; and the smile that plays upon the lips, although it may be deemed a sacrilege, is not banished. My mother was dead, but we had still duties which we ought to perform; we must continue our course with the rest, and learn to think ourselves fortunate, whilst one remains whom the spoiler has not seized.

My departure for Ingolstadt, which had been deferred by these events, was now again determined upon. I obtained from my father a respite of some weeks. It appeared to me sacrilege so soon to leave the repose, akin to death, of the house of mourning, and to rush into the thick of life. I was new to sorrow, but it did not the less alarm me. I was unwilling to quit the sight of those that remained to me; and, above all, I desired to see my sweet Elizabeth in some degree consoled.

She indeed veiled her grief, and strove to act the comforter to us all. She looked steadily on life, and assumed its duties with courage and zeal. She devoted herself to those whom she had been taught to call her uncle and cousins. Never was she so enchanting as at this time, when she recalled the sunshine of her smiles and spent them upon us. She forgot even her own regret in her endeavours to make us forget.

The day of my departure at length arrived. Clerval spent the last evening with us. He had endeavoured to persuade his father to permit him to accompany me, and to become my fellow student; but in vain. His father was a narrow-minded trader, and saw idleness and ruin in the aspirations and ambition of his son. Henry deeply felt the misfortune of being debarred from a liberal education. He said little; but when he spoke, I read in his kindling eye and in his animated glance a restrained but firm resolve, not to be chained to the miserable details of commerce.

We sat late. We could not tear ourselves away from each other, nor persuade ourselves to say the word "Farewell!" It was said; and we retired under the pretence of seeking repose, each fancying that the other was deceived: but when at morning's dawn I descended to the carriage which was to convey me away, they were all there — my father again to bless me, Clerval to press my hand once more, my Elizabeth to renew her entreaties that I would write often, and to bestow the last feminine attentions on her playmate and friend.

I threw myself into the chaise that was to convey me away, and indulged in the most melancholy reflections. I, who had ever been surrounded by amiable companions, continually engaged in endeavouring to bestow mutual pleasure, I was now alone. In the university, whither I was going, I must form my own friends, and be my own protector. My life had hitherto been remarkably secluded and domestic; and this had given me invincible repugnance to new countenances. I loved my brothers, Elizabeth, and Clerval; these were "old familiar faces;" but I believed myself totally unfitted for the company of strangers. Such were my reflections as I commenced my journey; but as I proceeded, my spirits and hopes rose. I ardently desired the acquisition of knowledge. I had often, when at home, thought it hard to remain during my youth cooped up in one place, and had longed to enter the world, and take my station among other human beings. Now my desires were complied with, and it would, indeed, have been folly to repent.

I had sufficient leisure for these and many other reflections during my journey to Ingolstadt, which was long and fatiguing. At length the high white steeple of the town met my eyes. I alighted, and was conducted to my solitary apartment, to spend the evening as I pleased.

The next morning I delivered my letters of introduction, and paid a visit to some of the principal professors. Chance — or rather the evil influence, the Angel of Destruction, which asserted omnipotent sway over me from the moment I turned my reluctant steps from my father's door — led me first to M. Krempe, professor of natural philosophy. He was an uncouth man, but deeply embued in the secrets of his science. He asked me several questions concerning my progress in the different branches of science appertaining to natural philosophy. I replied carelessly; and, partly in contempt, mentioned the names of my alchymists as the principal authors I had studied. The professor stared: "Have you," he said, "really spent your time in studying such nonsense?"

I replied in the affirmative. "Every minute," continued M. Krempe with warmth, "every instant that you have wasted on those books is utterly and entirely lost. You have burdened your memory with exploded systems and useless names. Good God! in what desert land have you lived, where no one was kind enough to inform you that these fancies, which you have so greedily imbibed, are a thousand years old, and as musty as they are ancient? I little expected, in this enlightened and scientific age, to find a disciple of Albertus Magnus and Paracelsus. My dear sir, you must begin your studies entirely anew."

So saying, he stept aside, and wrote down a list of several books treating of natural philosophy, which he desired me to procure; and dismissed me, after mentioning that in the beginning of the following week he intended to commence a course of lectures upon natural philosophy in its general relations, and that M. Waldman, a fellow-professor, would lecture upon chemistry the alternate days that he omitted.

I returned home, not disappointed, for I have said that I had long considered those authors useless whom the professor reprobated; but I returned, not at all the more inclined to recur to these studies in any shape. M. Krempe was a little, squat man, with a gruff voice and a repulsive countenance; the teacher, therefore, did not prepossess me in favour of his pursuits. In rather too philosophical and connected a strain, perhaps, I have given an account of the conclusions I had come to concerning them in my early years. As a child, I had not been content with the results promised by the modern professors of natural science. With a confusion of ideas only to be accounted for by my extreme youth, and my want of a guide on such matters, I had retrod the steps of knowledge along the paths of time, and exchanged the discoveries of recent enquirers for the dreams of forgotten alchymists. Besides, I had a contempt for the uses of modern natural philosophy. It was very different, when the masters of the science sought immortality and power; such views, although futile, were grand: but now the scene was changed. The ambition of the enquirer seemed to limit itself to the annihilation of those visions on which my interest in science was chiefly founded. I was required to exchange chimeras of boundless grandeur for realities of little worth.

Such were my reflections during the first two or three days of my residence at Ingolstadt, which were chiefly spent in becoming acquainted with the localities, and the principal residents in my new abode. But as the ensuing week commenced, I thought of the information which M. Krempe had given me concerning the lectures. And although I could not consent to go and hear that little conceited fellow deliver sentences out of a pulpit, I recollected what he had said of M. Waldman, whom I had never seen, as he had hitherto been out of town.

Partly from curiosity, and partly from idleness, I went into the lecturing room, which M. Waldman entered shortly after. This professor was very unlike his colleague. He appeared about fifty years of age, but with an aspect expressive of the greatest benevolence; a few grey hairs covered his temples, but those at the back of his head were nearly black. His person was short, but remarkably erect; and his voice the sweetest I had ever heard. He began his lecture by a recapitulation of the history of chemistry, and the various improvements made by different men of learning, pronouncing with fervour the names of the most distinguished discoverers. He then took a cursory view of the present state of the science, and explained many of its elementary terms. After having made a few preparatory experiments, he concluded with a panegyric upon modern chemistry, the terms of which I shall never forget:—

"The ancient teachers of this science," said he, "promised impossibilities, and performed nothing. The modern masters promise very little; they know that metals cannot be transmuted, and that the elixir of life is a chimera. But these philosophers, whose hands seem only made to dabble in dirt, and their eyes to pore over the microscope or crucible, have indeed performed miracles. They penetrate into the recesses of nature, and show how she works in her hiding places. They ascend into the heavens: they have discovered how the blood circulates, and the nature of the air we breathe. They have acquired new and almost unlimited powers; they can command the thunders of heaven, mimic the earthquake, and even mock the invisible world with its own shadows."

Such were the professor's words—rather let me say such the words of fate, enounced to destroy me. As he went on, I felt as if my soul were grappling with a palpable enemy; one by one the various keys were touched which formed the mechanism of my being: chord after chord was sounded, and soon my mind was filled with one thought, one conception, one purpose. So much has been done, exclaimed the soul of Frankenstein,—more, far more, will I achieve: treading in the steps already marked, I will pioneer a new way, explore unknown powers, and unfold to the world the deepest mysteries of creation.

I closed not my eyes that night. My internal being was in a state of insurrection and turmoil; I felt that order would thence arise, but I had no power to produce it. By degrees, after the morning's dawn, sleep came. I awoke, and my yesternight's thoughts were as a dream. There only remained a resolution to return to my ancient studies, and to devote myself to a science for which I believed myself to possess a natural talent. On the same day, I paid M. Waldman a visit. His manners in private were even more mild and attractive than in public; for there was a certain dignity in his mien during his lecture, which in his own house was replaced by the greatest affability and kindness. I gave him pretty nearly the same account of my former pursuits as I had given to his fellow-professor. He heard with attention the little narration concerning my studies, and smiled at the names of Cornelius Agrippa and Paracelsus, but without the contempt that M. Krempe had exhibited. He said, that "these were men to whose indefatigable zeal modern philosophers were indebted for most of the foundations of their knowledge. They had left to us, as an easier task, to give new names, and arrange in connected classifications, the facts which they in a great degree had been the instruments of bringing to light. The labours of men of genius, however erroneously directed, scarcely ever fail in ultimately turning to the solid advantage of mankind." I listened to his statement, which was delivered without any presumption or affectation; and then added, that his lecture had removed my prejudices against modern chemists; I expressed myself in measured terms, with the modesty and deference due from a youth to his instructor, without letting escape (inexperience in life would have made me ashamed) any of the enthusiasm which stimulated my intended labours. I requested his advice concerning the books I ought to procure.

"I am happy," said M. Waldman, "to have gained a disciple; and if your application equals your ability, I have no doubt of your success. Chemistry is that branch of natural philosophy in which the greatest improvements have been and may be made: it is on that account that I have made it my peculiar study; but at the same time I have not neglected the other branches of science. A man would make but a very sorry chemist if he attended to that department of human knowledge alone. If your wish is to become really a man of science, and not merely a petty experimentalist, I should advise you to apply to every branch of natural philosophy, including mathematics."

He then took me into his laboratory, and explained to me the uses of his various machines; instructing me as to what I ought to procure, and promising me the use of his own when I should have advanced far enough in the science not to derange their mechanism. He also gave me the list of books which I had requested; and I took my leave.

Thus ended a day memorable to me: it decided my future destiny.

## CHAPTER IV

From this day natural philosophy, and particularly chemistry, in the most comprehensive sense of the term, became nearly my sole occupation. I read with ardour those works, so full of genius and discrimination, which modern enquirers have written on these subjects. I attended the lectures, and cultivated the acquaintance, of the men of science of the university; and I found even in M. Krempe a great deal of sound sense and real information, combined, it is true, with a repulsive physiognomy and manners, but not on that account the less valuable. In M. Waldman I found a true friend. His gentleness was never tinged by dogmatism; and his instructions were given with an air of frankness and good nature, that banished every idea of pedantry. In a thousand ways he smoothed for me the path of knowledge, and made the most abstruse enquiries clear and facile to my apprehension. My application was at first fluctuating and uncertain; it gained strength as I proceeded, and soon became so ardent and eager, that the stars often disappeared in the light of morning whilst I was yet engaged in my laboratory.

As I applied so closely, it may be easily conceived that my progress was rapid. My ardour was indeed the astonishment of the students, and my proficiency that of the masters. Professor Krempe often asked me, with a sly smile, how Cornelius Agrippa went on? whilst M. Waldman expressed the most heartfelt exultation in my progress. Two years passed in this manner, during which I paid no visit to Geneva, but was engaged, heart and soul, in the pursuit of some discoveries, which I hoped to make. None but those who have experienced them can conceive of the enticements of science. In other studies you go as far as others have gone before you, and there is nothing more to know; but in a scientific pursuit there is continual food for discovery and wonder. A mind of moderate capacity, which closely pursues one study, must infallibly arrive at great proficiency in that study; and I, who continually sought the attainment of one object of pursuit, and was solely wrapt up in this, improved so rapidly, that, at the end of two years, I made some discoveries in the improvement of some chemical instruments, which procured me great esteem and admiration at the university. When I had arrived at this point, and had become as well acquainted with the theory and practice of natural philosophy as depended on the lessons of any of the professors at Ingolstadt, my residence there being no longer conducive to my improvements, I thought of returning to my friends and my native town, when an incident happened that protracted my stay.

One of the phenomena which had peculiarly attracted my attention was the structure of the human frame, and, indeed, any animal endued with life. Whence, I often asked myself, did the principle of life proceed? It was a bold question, and one which has ever been considered as a mystery; yet with how many things are we upon the brink of becoming acquainted, if cowardice or carelessness did not restrain our enquiries. I revolved these circumstances in my mind, and determined thenceforth to apply myself more particularly to those branches of natural philosophy which relate to physiology. Unless I had been animated by an almost supernatural enthusiasm, my application to this study would have been irksome, and almost intolerable. To examine the causes of life, we must first have recourse to death. I became acquainted with the science of anatomy: but this was not sufficient; I must also observe the natural decay and corruption of the human body. In my education my father had taken the greatest precautions that my mind should be impressed with no supernatural horrors. I do not ever remember to have trembled at a tale of superstition, or to have feared the apparition of a spirit. Darkness had no effect upon my fancy; and a churchyard was to me merely the receptacle of bodies deprived of life, which, from being the seat of beauty and strength, had become food for the worm. Now I was led to examine the cause and progress of this decay, and forced to spend days and nights in vaults and charnel-houses.° My attention was fixed upon every object the most insupportable to the delicacy of the human feelings. I saw how the fine form of man was degraded and wasted; I beheld the corruption of death succeed to the blooming cheek of life; I saw how the worm inherited the wonders of the eye and brain. I paused, examining and analysing all the minutiae of causation, as exemplified in the change from life to death, and death to life, until from the midst of this darkness a sudden light broke in upon me—a light so brilliant and wondrous, yet so simple, that while I became dizzy with the immensity of the prospect which it illustrated, I was surprised,

---

*charnel-houses:* Repositories for bones or corpses.

that among so many men of genius who had directed their enquiries towards the same science, that I alone should be reserved to discover so astonishing a secret.

Remember, I am not recording the vision of a madman. The sun does not more certainly shine in the heavens, than that which I now affirm is true. Some miracle might have produced it, yet the stages of the discovery were distinct and probable. After days and nights of incredible labour and fatigue, I succeeded in discovering the cause of generation and life; nay, more, I became myself capable of bestowing animation upon lifeless matter.

The astonishment which I had at first experienced on this discovery soon gave place to delight and rapture. After so much time spent in painful labour, to arrive at once at the summit of my desires, was the most gratifying consummation of my toils. But this discovery was so great and overwhelming, that all the steps by which I had been progressively led to it were obliterated, and I beheld only the result. What had been the study and desire of the wisest men since the creation of the world was now within my grasp. Not that, like a magic scene, it all opened upon me at once: the information I had obtained was of a nature rather to direct my endeavours so soon as I should point them towards the object of my search, than to exhibit that object already accomplished. I was like the Arabian° who had been buried with the dead, and found a passage to life, aided only by one glimmering, and seemingly ineffectual, light.

I see by your eagerness, and the wonder and hope which your eyes express, my friend, that you expect to be informed of the secret with which I am acquainted; that cannot be: listen patiently until the end of my story, and you will easily perceive why I am reserved upon that subject. I will not lead you on, unguarded and ardent as I then was, to your destruction and infallible misery. Learn from me, if not by my precepts, at least by my example, how dangerous is the acquirement of knowledge, and how much happier that man is who believes his native town to be the world, than he who aspires to become greater than his nature will allow.

When I found so astonishing a power placed within my hands, I hesitated a long time concerning the manner in which I should employ it. Although I possessed the capacity of bestowing animation, yet to prepare a frame for the reception of it, with all its intricacies of fibres, muscles, and veins, still remained a work of inconceivable difficulty and

---

*the Arabian:* Reference to the fourth voyage of Sinbad in *The Thousand and One Nights.*

labour. I doubted at first whether I should attempt the creation of a being like myself, or one of simpler organization; but my imagination was too much exalted by my first success to permit me to doubt of my ability to give life to an animal as complex and wonderful as man. The materials at present within my command hardly appeared adequate to so arduous an undertaking; but I doubted not that I should ultimately succeed. I prepared myself for a multitude of reverses; my operations might be incessantly baffled, and at last my work be imperfect: yet, when I considered the improvement which every day takes place in science and mechanics, I was encouraged to hope my present attempts would at least lay the foundations of future success. Nor could I consider the magnitude and complexity of my plan as any argument of its impracticability. It was with these feelings that I began the creation of a human being. As the minuteness of the parts formed a great hindrance to my speed, I resolved, contrary to my first intention, to make the being of a gigantic stature; that is to say, about eight feet in height, and proportionably large. After having formed this determination, and having spent some months in successfully collecting and arranging my materials, I began.

No one can conceive the variety of feelings which bore me onwards, like a hurricane, in the first enthusiasm of success. Life and death appeared to me ideal bounds, which I should first break through, and pour a torrent of light into our dark world. A new species would bless me as its creator and source; many happy and excellent natures would owe their being to me. No father could claim the gratitude of his child so completely as I should deserve theirs. Pursuing these reflections, I thought, that if I could bestow animation upon lifeless matter, I might in process of time (although I now found it impossible) renew life where death had apparently devoted the body to corruption.

These thoughts supported my spirits, while I pursued my undertaking with unremitting ardour. My cheek had grown pale with study, and my person had become emaciated with confinement. Sometimes, on the very brink of certainty, I failed; yet still I clung to the hope which the next day or the next hour might realise. One secret which I alone possessed was the hope to which I had dedicated myself; and the moon gazed on my midnight labours, while, with unrelaxed and breathless eagerness, I pursued nature to her hiding-places. Who shall conceive the horrors of my secret toil, as I dabbled among the unhallowed damps of the grave, or tortured the living animal to animate the lifeless clay? My limbs now tremble, and my eyes swim with the remembrance; but then a resistless, and almost frantic, impulse, urged me forward; I seemed to have lost all soul or sensation but for this one pursuit. It was indeed but a passing trance, that only made me feel with renewed acuteness so soon as, the unnatural stimulus ceasing to operate, I had returned to my old habits. I collected bones from charnel-houses; and disturbed, with profane fingers, the tremendous secrets of the human frame. In a solitary chamber, or rather cell, at the top of the house, and separated from all the other apartments by a gallery and staircase, I kept my workshop of filthy creation: my eye-balls were starting from their sockets in attending to the details of my employment. The dissecting room and the slaughter-house furnished many of my materials; and often did my human nature turn with loathing from my occupation, whilst, still urged on by an eagerness which perpetually increased, I brought my work near to a conclusion.

The summer months passed while I was thus engaged, heart and soul, in one pursuit. It was a most beautiful season; never did the fields bestow a more plentiful harvest, or the vines yield a more luxuriant vintage: but my eyes were insensible to the charms of nature. And the same feelings which made me neglect the scenes around me caused me also to forget those friends who were so many miles absent, and whom I had not seen for so long a time. I knew my silence disquieted them; and I well remembered the words of my father: "I know that while you are pleased with yourself, you will think of us with affection, and we shall hear regularly from you. You must pardon me if I regard any interruption in your correspondence as a proof that your other duties are equally neglected."

I knew well therefore what would be my father's feelings; but I could not tear my thoughts from my employment, loathsome in itself, but which had taken an irresistible hold of my imagination. I wished, as it were, to procrastinate all that related to my feelings of affection until the great object, which swallowed up every habit of my nature, should be completed.

I then thought that my father would be unjust if he ascribed my neglect to vice, or faultiness on my part; but I am now convinced that he was justified in conceiving that I should not be altogether free from blame. A human being in perfection ought always to preserve a calm and peaceful mind, and never to allow passion or a transitory desire to disturb his tranquillity. I do not think that the pursuit of knowledge is an exception to this rule. If the study to which you apply yourself has a tendency to weaken your affections, and to destroy your taste for those simple pleasures in which no alloy can possibly mix, then that study is certainly unlawful, that is to say, not befitting the human mind. If this rule were always observed; if no man allowed any pursuit whatsoever to interfere with the tranquillity of his domestic affections, Greece had not been enslaved; Caesar would have spared his country; America would have been discovered more gradually; and the empires of Mexico and Peru had not been destroyed.

But I forget that I am moralising in the most interesting part of my tale; and your looks remind me to proceed.

My father made no reproach in his letters, and only took notice of my silence by enquiring into my occupations more particularly than before. Winter, spring, and summer passed away during my labours; but I did not watch the blossom or the expanding leaves—sights which before always yielded me supreme delight—so deeply was I engrossed in my occupation. The leaves of that year had withered before my work drew near to a close; and now every day showed me more plainly how well I had succeeded. But my enthusiasm was checked by my anxiety, and I appeared rather like one doomed by slavery to toil in the mines, or any other unwholesome trade, than an artist occupied by his favourite employment. Every night I was oppressed by a slow fever, and I became nervous to a most painful degree; the fall of a leaf startled me, and I shunned my fellow-creatures as if I had been guilty of a crime. Sometimes I grew alarmed at the wreck I perceived that I had become; the energy of my purpose alone sustained me: my labours would soon end, and I believed that exercise and amusement would then drive away incipient disease; and I promised myself both of these when my creation should be complete.

## CHAPTER V

It was on a dreary night of November, that I beheld the accomplishment of my toils. With an anxiety that almost amounted to agony, I collected the instruments of life around me, that I might infuse a spark of being into the lifeless thing that lay at my feet. It was already one in the morning; the rain pattered dismally against the panes, and my candle was nearly burnt out, when, by the glimmer of the half-extinguished light, I saw the dull yellow eye of the creature open; it breathed hard, and a convulsive motion agitated its limbs.

How can I describe my emotions at this catastrophe, or how delineate the wretch whom with such infinite pains and care I had endeavoured to form? His limbs were in proportion, and I had selected his features as beautiful. Beautiful!—Great God! His yellow skin scarcely covered the work of muscles and arteries beneath; his hair was of a lustrous black, and flowing; his teeth of a pearly whiteness; but these luxuriances only formed a more horrid contrast with his watery eyes, that seemed almost of the same colour as the dun white sockets in which they were set, his shriveled complexion and straight black lips.

The different accidents of life are not so changeable as the feelings of human nature. I had worked hard for nearly two years, for the sole purpose of infusing life into an inanimate body. For this I had deprived myself of rest and health. I had desired it with an ardour that far exceeded moderation; but now that I had finished, the beauty of the dream vanished, and breathless horror and disgust filled my heart. Unable to endure the aspect of the being I had created, I rushed out of the room, and continued a long time traversing my bedchamber, unable to compose my mind to sleep. At length lassitude succeeded to the tumult I had before endured; and I threw myself on the bed in my clothes, endeavouring to seek a few moments of forgetfulness. But it was in vain; I slept, indeed, but I was disturbed by the wildest dreams. I thought I saw Elizabeth, in the bloom of health, walking in the streets of Ingolstadt. Delighted and surprised, I embraced her; but as I imprinted the first kiss on her lips, they became livid with the hue of death; her features appeared to change, and I thought that I held the corpse of my dead mother in my arms; a shroud enveloped her form, and I saw the graveworms crawling in the folds of the flannel. I started from my sleep with horror; a cold dew covered my forehead, my teeth chattered, and every limb became convulsed; when, by the dim and yellow light of the moon, as it forced its way through the window shutters, I beheld the wretch—the miserable monster whom I had created. He held up the curtain of the bed; and his eyes, if eyes they may be called, were fixed on me. His jaws opened, and he muttered some inarticulate sounds, while a grin wrinkled his cheeks. He might have spoken, but I did not hear; one hand was stretched out, seemingly to detain me, but I escaped, and rushed down stairs. I took refuge in the courtyard belonging to the house which I inhabited; where I remained during the rest of the night, walking up and down in the greatest agitation, listening attentively, catching and fearing each sound as if it were to announce the approach of the demoniacal corpse to which I had so miserably given life.

Oh! no mortal could support the horror of that countenance. A mummy again endued with animation could not be so hideous as that wretch. I had gazed on him while unfinished; he was ugly then; but when those muscles and joints were rendered capable of motion, it became a thing such as even Dante° could not have conceived.

I passed the night wretchedly. Sometimes my pulse beat so quickly and hardly, that I felt the palpitation of every artery; at others, I nearly sank to the ground through languor and extreme weakness. Mingled with this horror, I felt the bitterness of disappointment; dreams that had been my food and pleasant rest for so long a space were now become a hell to me; and the change was so rapid, the overthrow so complete!

Morning, dismal and wet, at length dawned, and discovered to my sleepless and aching eyes the church of Ingolstadt, its white steeple and clock, which indicated the sixth hour. The porter opened the gates of the court, which had that night been my asylum, and I issued into the streets, pacing them with quick steps, as if I sought to avoid the wretch whom I feared every turning of the street would present to my view. I did not dare return to the apartment which I inhabited, but felt impelled to hurry on, although drenched by the rain which poured from a black and comfortless sky.

I continued walking in this manner for some time, endeavouring, by bodily exercise, to ease the load that weighed upon my mind. I traversed the streets, without any clear conception of where I was, or what I was doing. My heart palpitated in the sickness of fear; and I hurried on with irregular steps, not daring to look about me:—

> Like one who, on a lonely road,
>   Doth walk in fear and dread,
> And, having once turned round, walks on,
>   And turns no more his head;
> Because he knows a frightful fiend
>   Doth close behind him tread.[3]

Continuing thus, I came at length opposite to the inn at which the various diligences and carriages usually stopped. Here I paused, I knew not why; but I remained some minutes with my eyes fixed on a coach that was coming towards me from the other end of the street. As it drew nearer, I observed that it was the Swiss diligence: it stopped just where I was standing; and, on the door being opened, I perceived Henry Clerval, who, on seeing me, instantly sprung out. "My

---

**Dante:** Reference to *The Inferno*, the first part of the three-part fourteenth-century epic poem *The Divine Comedy* by Dante Alighieri.
[3]Coleridge's "Ancient Mariner." [Mary Shelley's note.]

dear Frankenstein," exclaimed he, "how glad I am to see you! how fortunate that you should be here at the very moment of my alighting!"

Nothing could equal my delight on seeing Clerval; his presence
brought back to my thoughts my father, Elizabeth, and all those scenes
of home so dear to my recollection. I grasped his hand, and in a moment
forgot my horror and misfortune; I felt suddenly, and for the first time
during many months, calm and serene joy. I welcomed my friend,
therefore, in the most cordial manner, and we walked towards my college. Clerval continued talking for some time about our mutual friends,
and his own good fortune in being permitted to come to Ingolstadt.
"You may easily believe," said he, "how great was the difficulty to persuade my father that all necessary knowledge was not comprised in the
noble art of book-keeping; and, indeed, I believe I left him incredulous
to the last, for his constant answer to my unwearied entreaties was the
same as that of the Dutch schoolmaster° in the Vicar of Wakefield:—'I
have ten thousand florins a year without Greek, I eat heartily without
Greek.' But his affection for me at length overcame his dislike of learning, and he has permitted me to undertake a voyage of discovery to the
land of knowledge."

"It gives me the greatest delight to see you; but tell me how you left
my father, brothers, and Elizabeth."

"Very well, and very happy, only a little uneasy that they hear from
you so seldom. By the by, I mean to lecture you a little upon their
account myself.—But, my dear Frankenstein," continued he, stopping
short, and gazing full in my face, "I did not before remark how very ill
you appear; so thin and pale; you look as if you had been watching for
several nights."

"You have guessed right; I have lately been so deeply engaged in
one occupation, that I have not allowed myself sufficient rest, as you
see; but I hope, I sincerely hope, that all these employments are now at
an end, and that I am at length free."

I trembled excessively; I could not endure to think of, and far less
to allude to, the occurrences of the preceding night. I walked with a
quick pace, and we soon arrived at my college. I then reflected, and the
thought made me shiver, that the creature whom I had left in my apartment might still be there, alive, and walking about. I dreaded to behold
this monster; but I feared still more that Henry should see him. Entreating him, therefore, to remain a few minutes at the bottom of the stairs,

---

**Dutch schoolmaster:** The reference is to chapter 20 of *The Vicar of Wakefield* (1766) by
Oliver Goldsmith (1730–1774).

I darted up towards my own room. My hand was already on the lock of the door before I recollected myself. I then paused; and a cold shivering came over me. I threw the door forcibly open, as children are accustomed to do when they expect a spectre to stand in waiting for them on the other side; but nothing appeared. I stepped fearfully in: the apartment was empty; and my bedroom was also freed from its hideous guest. I could hardly believe that so great a good fortune could have befallen me; but when I became assured that my enemy had indeed fled, I clapped my hands for joy, and ran down to Clerval.

We ascended into my room, and the servant presently brought breakfast; but I was unable to contain myself. It was not joy only that possessed me; I felt my flesh tingle with excess of sensitiveness, and my pulse beat rapidly. I was unable to remain for a single instant in the same place; I jumped over the chairs, clapped my hands, and laughed aloud. Clerval at first attributed my unusual spirits to joy on his arrival; but when he observed me more attentively, he saw a wildness in my eyes for which he could not account; and my loud, unrestrained, heartless laughter, frightened and astonished him.

"My dear Victor," cried he, "what, for God's sake, is the matter? Do not laugh in that manner. How ill you are! What is the cause of all this?"

"Do not ask me," cried I, putting my hands before my eyes, for I thought I saw the dreaded spectre glide into the room; "*he* can tell. — Oh, save me! save me!" I imagined that the monster seized me; I struggled furiously, and fell down in a fit.

Poor Clerval! what must have been his feelings? A meeting, which he anticipated with such joy, so strangely turned to bitterness. But I was not the witness of his grief; for I was lifeless, and did not recover my senses for a long, long time.

This was the commencement of a nervous fever, which confined me for several months. During all that time Henry was my only nurse. I afterwards learned that, knowing my father's advanced age, and unfitness for so long a journey, and how wretched my sickness would make Elizabeth, he spared them this grief by concealing the extent of my disorder. He knew that I could not have a more kind and attentive nurse than himself; and, firm in the hope he felt of my recovery, he did not doubt that, instead of doing harm, he performed the kindest action that he could towards them.

But I was in reality very ill; and surely nothing but the unbounded and unremitting attentions of my friend could have restored me to life. The form of the monster on whom I had bestowed existence was for ever before my eyes, and I raved incessantly concerning him. Doubtless

my words surprised Henry: he at first believed them to be the wanderings of my disturbed imagination; but the pertinacity with which I continually recurred to the same subject persuaded him that my disorder
indeed owed its origin to some uncommon and terrible event.

By very slow degrees, and with frequent relapses, that alarmed
and grieved my friend, I recovered. I remember the first time I became
capable of observing outward objects with any kind of pleasure, I perceived that the fallen leaves had disappeared, and that the young buds
were shooting forth from the trees that shaded my window. It was a
divine spring; and the season contributed greatly to my convalescence.
I felt also sentiments of joy and affection revive in my bosom; my gloom
disappeared, and in a short time I became as cheerful as before I was
attacked by the fatal passion.

"Dearest Clerval," exclaimed I, "how kind, how very good you are
to me. This whole winter, instead of being spent in study, as you promised yourself, has been consumed in my sick room. How shall I ever repay
you? I feel the greatest remorse for the disappointment of which I have
been the occasion; but you will forgive me."

"You will repay me entirely, if you do not discompose yourself, but
get well as fast as you can; and since you appear in such good spirits, I
may speak to you on one subject, may I not?"

I trembled. One subject! what could it be? Could he allude to an
object on whom I dared not even think?

"Compose yourself," said Clerval, who observed my change of
colour, "I will not mention it, if it agitates you; but your father and
cousin would be very happy if they received a letter from you in your
own hand-writing. They hardly know how ill you have been, and are
uneasy at your long silence."

"Is that all, my dear Henry? How could you suppose that my first
thought would not fly towards those dear, dear friends whom I love,
and who are so deserving of my love."

"If this is your present temper, my friend, you will perhaps be glad
to see a letter that has been lying here some days for you: it is from your
cousin, I believe."

## CHAPTER VI

Clerval then put the following letter into my hands. It was from my
own Elizabeth:—

"My dearest Cousin,

"You have been ill, very ill, and even the constant letters of dear kind Henry are not sufficient to reassure me on your account. You are forbidden to write — to hold a pen; yet one word from you, dear Victor, is necessary to calm our apprehensions. For a long time I have thought that each post would bring this line, and my persuasions have restrained my uncle from undertaking a journey to Ingolstadt. I have prevented his encountering the inconveniences and perhaps dangers of so long a journey; yet how often have I regretted not being able to perform it myself! I figure to myself that the task of attending on your sick bed has devolved on some mercenary old nurse, who could never guess your wishes, nor minister to them with the care and affection of your poor cousin. Yet that is over now: Clerval writes that indeed you are getting better. I eagerly hope that you will confirm this intelligence soon in your own handwriting.

"Get well — and return to us. You will find a happy, cheerful home, and friends who love you dearly. Your father's health is vigorous, and he asks but to see you, — but to be assured that you are well; and not a care will ever cloud his benevolent countenance. How pleased you would be to remark the improvement of our Ernest! He is now sixteen, and full of activity and spirit. He is desirous to be a true Swiss, and to enter into foreign service; but we cannot part with him, at least until his elder brother returns to us. My uncle is not pleased with the idea of a military career in a distant country; but Ernest never had your powers of application. He looks upon study as an odious fetter; — his time is spent in the open air, climbing the hills or rowing on the lake. I fear that he will become an idler, unless we yield the point, and permit him to enter on the profession which he has selected.

"Little alteration, except the growth of our dear children, has taken place since you left us. The blue lake, and snow-clad mountains, they never change; — and I think our placid home, and our contented hearts are regulated by the same immutable laws. My trifling occupations take up my time and amuse me, and I am rewarded for any exertions by seeing none but happy, kind faces around me. Since you left us, but one change has taken place in our little household. Do you remember on what occasion Justine Moritz entered our family? Probably you do not; I will relate her history, therefore, in a few words. Madame Moritz, her mother, was a widow with four children, of whom Justine was the third. This girl had always been the favourite of her father; but, through a strange perversity, her mother could not endure her, and, after the death of M. Moritz, treated her very ill. My aunt observed this; and, when Justine was twelve years of age, prevailed on her mother to allow her to live at our house. The republican institutions of our country have produced simpler and happier manners than those which prevail in the great monarchies that surround it. Hence there is less distinction between the several classes of its inhabitants; and the lower orders, being neither so poor nor so despised, their manners are more refined and moral. A servant in Geneva does not mean the same thing as a servant in France and England. Justine, thus received in our family, learned the duties of a servant; a condition which, in our fortunate country, does not include the idea of ignorance, and a sacrifice of the dignity of a human being.

"Justine, you may remember, was a great favourite of yours; and I recollect you once remarked, that if you were in an ill-humour, one glance from Justine could dissipate it, for the same reason that Ariosto gives concerning the beauty of Angelica°—she looked so frank-hearted and happy. My aunt conceived a great attachment for her, by which she was induced to give her an education superior to that which she had at first intended. This benefit was fully repaid; Justine was the most grateful little creature in the world; I do not mean that she made any professions; I never heard one pass her lips; but you could see by her eyes that she almost adored her protectress. Although her disposition was gay, and in many respects inconsiderate, yet she paid the greatest attention to every gesture of my aunt. She thought her the model of all excellence, and endeavoured to imitate her phraseology and manners, so that even now she often reminds me of her.

"When my dearest aunt died, every one was too much occupied in their own grief to notice poor Justine, who had attended her during her illness with the most anxious affection. Poor Justine was very ill; but other trials were reserved for her.

"One by one, her brothers and sister died; and her mother, with the exception of her neglected daughter, was left childless. The conscience of the woman was troubled; she began to think that the deaths of her favourites was a judgment from heaven to chastise her partiality. She was a Roman Catholic; and I believe her confessor confirmed the idea which she had conceived. Accordingly, a few months after your departure for Ingolstadt, Justine was called home by her repentant mother. Poor girl! she wept when she quitted our house; she was much altered since the death of my aunt; grief had given softness and a winning mildness to her manners, which had before been remarkable for vivacity. Nor

*Angelica:* Heroine of the epic romance *Orlando Furioso* (1532) by Lodovico Ariosto (1474–1535).

was her residence at her mother's house of a nature to restore her gaiety. The poor woman was very vacillating in her repentance. She sometimes begged Justine to forgive her unkindness, but much oftener accused her of having caused the deaths of her brothers and sister. Perpetual fretting at length threw Madame Moritz into a decline, which at first increased her irritability, but she is now at peace for ever. She died on the first approach of cold weather, at the beginning of this last winter. Justine has returned to us; and I assure you I love her tenderly. She is very clever and gentle, and extremely pretty; as I mentioned before, her mien and her expressions continually remind me of my dear aunt.

"I must say also a few words to you, my dear cousin, of little darling William. I wish you could see him; he is very tall of his age, with sweet laughing blue eyes, dark eyelashes, and curling hair. When he smiles, two little dimples appear on each cheek, which are rosy with health. He has already had one or two little *wives*, but Louisa Biron is his favourite, a pretty little girl of five years of age.

"Now, dear Victor, I dare say you wish to be indulged in a little gossip concerning the good people of Geneva. The pretty Miss Mansfield has already received the congratulatory visits on her approaching marriage with a young Englishman, John Melbourne, Esq. Her ugly sister, Manon, married M. Duvillard, the rich banker, last autumn. Your favourite schoolfellow, Louis Manoir, has suffered several misfortunes since the departure of Clerval from Geneva. But he has already recovered his spirits, and is reported to be on the point of marrying a very lively pretty Frenchwoman, Madame Tavernier. She is a widow, and much older than Manoir; but she is very much admired, and a favourite with everybody.

"I have written myself into better spirits, dear cousin; but my anxiety returns upon me as I conclude. Write, dearest Victor,—one line—one word will be a blessing to us. Ten thousand thanks to Henry for his kindness, his affection, and his many letters: we are sincerely grateful. Adieu! my cousin; take care of your self; and, I entreat you, write!

"ELIZABETH LAVENZA.

"Geneva, March 18th, 17—."

"Dear, dear Elizabeth!" I exclaimed, when I had read her letter: "I will write instantly, and relieve them from the anxiety they must feel." I wrote, and this exertion greatly fatigued me; but my convalescence had commenced, and proceeded regularly. In another fortnight I was able to leave my chamber.

One of my first duties on my recovery was to introduce Clerval to the several professors of the university. In doing this, I underwent a kind of rough usage, ill befitting the wounds that my mind had sustained. Ever since the fatal night, the end of my labours, and the beginning of my misfortunes, I had conceived a violent antipathy even to the name of natural philosophy. When I was otherwise quite restored to health, the sight of a chemical instrument would renew all the agony of my nervous symptoms. Henry saw this, and had removed all my apparatus from my view. He had also changed my apartment; for he perceived that I had acquired a dislike for the room which had previously been my laboratory. But these cares of Clerval were made of no avail when I visited the professors. M. Waldman inflicted torture when he praised, with kindness and warmth, the astonishing progress I had made in the sciences. He soon perceived that I disliked the subject; but not guessing the real cause, he attributed my feelings to modesty, and changed the subject from my improvement, to the science itself, with a desire, as I evidently saw, of drawing me out. What could I do? He meant to please, and he tormented me. I felt as if he had placed carefully, one by one, in my view those instruments which were to be afterwards used in putting me to a slow and cruel death. I writhed under his words, yet dared not exhibit the pain I felt. Clerval, whose eyes and feelings were always quick in discerning the sensations of others, declined the subject, alleging, in excuse, his total ignorance; and the conversation took a more general turn. I thanked my friend from my heart, but I did not speak. I saw plainly that he was surprised, but he never attempted to draw my secret from me; and although I loved him with a mixture of affection and reverence that knew no bounds, yet I could never persuade myself to confide to him that event which was so often present to my recollection, but which I feared to detail to another would only impress more deeply.

M. Krempe was not equally docile; and in my condition at that time, of almost insupportable sensitiveness, his harsh blunt encomiums gave me even more pain than the benevolent approbation of M. Waldman. "D——n the fellow!" cried he; "why, M. Clerval, I assure you he has outstript us all. Ay, stare if you please; but it is nevertheless true. A youngster who, but a few years ago, believed in Cornelius Agrippa as firmly as in the gospel, has now set himself at the head of the university; and if he is not soon pulled down, we shall all be out of countenance.——Ay, ay," continued he, observing my face expressive of suffering, "M. Frankenstein is modest; an excellent quality in a young man.

Young men should be diffident of themselves, you know, M. Clerval: I was myself when young; but that wears out in a very short time." M. Krempe had now commenced an eulogy on himself, which happily turned the conversation from a subject that was so annoying to me.

Clerval had never sympathized in my tastes for natural science; and his literary pursuits differed wholly from those which had occupied me. He came to the university with the design of making himself complete master of the oriental languages, as thus he should open a field for the plan of life he had marked out for himself. Resolved to pursue no inglorious career, he turned his eyes toward the East, as affording scope for his spirit of enterprise. The Persian, Arabic, and Sanscrit languages engaged his attention, and I was easily induced to enter on the same studies. Idleness had ever been irksome to me, and now that I wished to fly from reflection, and hated my former studies, I felt great relief in being the fellow-pupil with my friend, and found not only instruction but consolation in the works of the orientalists. I did not, like him, attempt a critical knowledge of their dialects, for I did not contemplate making any other use of them than temporary amusement. I read merely to understand their meaning, and they well repaid my labours. Their melancholy is soothing, and their joy elevating, to a degree I never experienced in studying the authors of any other country. When you read their writings, life appears to consist in a warm sun and a garden of roses,—in the smiles and frowns of a fair enemy, and the fire that consumes your own heart. How different from the manly and heroical poetry of Greece and Rome!

Summer passed away in these occupations, and my return to Geneva was fixed for the latter end of autumn; but being delayed by several accidents, winter and snow arrived, the roads were deemed impassable, and my journey was retarded until the ensuing spring. I felt this delay very bitterly; for I longed to see my native town and my beloved friends. My return had only been delayed so long, from an unwillingness to leave Clerval in a strange place, before he had become acquainted with any of its inhabitants. The winter, however, was spent cheerfully; and although the spring was uncommonly late, when it came its beauty compensated for its dilatoriness.

The month of May had already commenced, and I expected the letter daily which was to fix the date of my departure, when Henry proposed a pedestrian tour in the environs of Ingolstadt, that I might bid a personal farewell to the country I had so long inhabited. I acceded with pleasure to this proposition: I was fond of exercise, and Clerval had always been my favourite companion in the rambles of this nature that I had taken among the scenes of my native country.

We passed a fortnight in these perambulations: my health and spirits had long been restored, and they gained additional strength from the salubrious air I breathed, the natural incidents of our progress, and the conversation of my friend. Study had before secluded me from the intercourse of my fellow-creatures, and rendered me unsocial; but Clerval called forth the better feelings of my heart; he again taught me to love the aspect of nature, and the cheerful faces of children. Excellent friend! how sincerely did you love me, and endeavour to elevate my mind until it was on a level with your own! A selfish pursuit had cramped and narrowed me, until your gentleness and affection warmed and opened my senses; I became the same happy creature who, a few years ago, loved and beloved by all, had no sorrow or care. When happy, inanimate nature had the power of bestowing on me the most delightful sensations. A serene sky and verdant fields filled me with ecstasy. The present season was indeed divine; the flowers of spring bloomed in the hedges, while those of summer were already in bud. I was undisturbed by thoughts which during the preceding year had pressed upon me, notwithstanding my endeavours to throw them off, with an invincible burden.

Henry rejoiced in my gaiety, and sincerely sympathised in my feelings: he exerted himself to amuse me, while he expressed the sensations that filled his soul. The resources of his mind on this occasion were truly astonishing: his conversation was full of imagination; and very often, in imitation of the Persian and Arabic writers, he invented tales of wonderful fancy and passion. At other times he repeated my favourite poems, or drew me out into arguments, which he supported with great ingenuity.

We returned to our college on a Sunday afternoon: the peasants were dancing, and every one we met appeared gay and happy. My own spirits were high, and I bounded along with feelings of unbridled joy and hilarity.

## CHAPTER VII

On my return, I found the following letter from my father: —

"My dear Victor,

"You have probably waited impatiently for a letter to fix the date of your return to us; and I was at first tempted to write only a few lines, merely mentioning the day on which I should expect you. But that would be a cruel kindness, and I dare not do it. What would be your surprise, my son, when you expected a happy and glad welcome, to behold, on the contrary, tears and wretchedness? And how, Victor, can I relate our misfortune? Absence cannot have rendered you callous to our joys and griefs; and how shall I inflict pain on my long absent son? I wish to prepare you for the woful news, but I know it is impossible; even now your eye skims over the page, to seek the words which are to convey to you the horrible tidings.

"William is dead!—that sweet child, whose smiles delighted and warmed my heart, who was so gentle, yet so gay! Victor, he is murdered!

"I will not attempt to console you; but will simply relate the circumstances of the transaction.

"Last Thursday (May 7th), I, my niece, and your two brothers, went to walk in Plainpalais. The evening was warm and serene, and we prolonged our walk farther than usual. It was already dusk before we thought of returning; and then we discovered that William and Ernest, who had gone on before, were not to be found. We accordingly rested on a seat until they should return. Presently Ernest came, and enquired if we had seen his brother: he said, that he had been playing with him, that William had run away to hide himself, and that he vainly sought for him, and afterwards waited for him a long time, but that he did not return.

"This account rather alarmed us, and we continued to search for him until night fell, when Elizabeth conjectured that he might have returned to the house. He was not there. We returned again, with torches; for I could not rest, when I thought that my sweet boy had lost himself, and was exposed to all the damps and dews of night; Elizabeth also suffered extreme anguish. About five in the morning I discovered my lovely boy, whom the night before I had seen blooming and active in health, stretched on the grass livid and motionless: the print of the murderer's finger was on his neck.

"He was conveyed home, and the anguish that was visible in my countenance betrayed the secret to Elizabeth. She was very earnest to see the corpse. At first I attempted to prevent her; but she persisted, and entering the room where it lay, hastily examined the neck of the victim, and clasping her hands exclaimed, 'O God! I have murdered my darling child!'

"She fainted, and was restored with extreme difficulty. When she again lived, it was only to weep and sigh. She told me, that that same

evening William had teased her to let him wear a very valuable miniature that she possessed of your mother. This picture is gone, and was
doubtless the temptation which urged the murderer to the deed. We
have no trace of him at present, although our exertions to discover him
are unremitted; but they will not restore my beloved William!

"Come, dearest Victor; you alone can console Elizabeth. She weeps
continually, and accuses herself unjustly as the cause of his death; her
words pierce my heart. We are all unhappy; but will not that be an additional motive for you, my son, to return and be our comforter? Your
dear mother! Alas, Victor! I now say, Thank God she did not live to
witness the cruel, miserable death of her youngest darling!

"Come, Victor; not brooding thoughts of vengeance against the
assassin, but with feelings of peace and gentleness, that will heal, instead
of festering, the wounds of our minds. Enter the house of mourning,
my friend, but with kindness and affection for those who love you, and
not with hatred for your enemies.

                         "Your affectionate and afflicted father,
                                    "ALPHONSE FRANKENSTEIN.
"Geneva, May 12th, 17—."

Clerval, who had watched my countenance as I read this letter, was
surprised to observe the despair that succeeded to the joy I at first
expressed on receiving news from my friends. I threw the letter on the
table, and covered my face with my hands.

"My dear Frankenstein," exclaimed Henry, when he perceived me
weep with bitterness, "are you always to be unhappy? My dear friend,
what has happened?"

I motioned to him to take up the letter, while I walked up and
down the room in the extremest agitation. Tears also gushed from the
eyes of Clerval, as he read the account of my misfortune.

"I can offer you no consolation, my friend," said he; "your disaster
is irreparable. What do you intend to do?"

"To go instantly to Geneva: come with me, Henry, to order the
horses."

During our walk, Clerval endeavoured to say a few words of consolation; he could only express his heartfelt sympathy. "Poor William!"
said he, "dear lovely child, he now sleeps with his angel mother! Who
that had seen him bright and joyous in his young beauty, but must
weep over his untimely loss! To die so miserably; to feel the murderer's
grasp! How much more a murderer, that could destroy such radiant

innocence! Poor little fellow! one only consolation have we; his friends mourn and weep, but he is at rest. The pang is over, his sufferings are at an end for ever. A sod covers his gentle form, and he knows no pain. He can no longer be a subject for pity; we must reserve that for his miserable survivors."

Clerval spoke thus as we hurried through the streets; the words impressed themselves on my mind, and I remembered them afterwards in solitude. But now, as soon as the horses arrived, I hurried into a cabriolet, and bade farewell to my friend.

My journey was very melancholy. At first I wished to hurry on, for I longed to console and sympathise with my loved and sorrowing friends; but when I drew near my native town, I slackened my progress. I could hardly sustain the multitude of feelings that crowded into my mind. I passed through scenes familiar to my youth, but which I had not seen for nearly six years. How altered every thing might be during that time! One sudden and desolating change had taken place; but a thousand little circumstances might have by degrees worked other alterations, which, although they were done more tranquilly, might not be the less decisive. Fear overcame me; I dared not advance, dreading a thousand nameless evils that made me tremble, although I was unable to define them.

I remained two days at Lausanne, in this painful state of mind. I contemplated the lake: the waters were placid; all around was calm; and the snowy mountains, "the palaces of nature," were not changed. By degrees the calm and heavenly scene restored me, and I continued my journey towards Geneva.

The road ran by the side of the lake, which became narrower as I approached my native town. I discovered more distinctly the black sides of Jura, and the bright summit of Mont Blanc. I wept like a child. "Dear mountains! my own beautiful lake! how do you welcome your wanderer? Your summits are clear; the sky and lake are blue and placid. Is this to prognosticate peace, or to mock at my unhappiness?"

I fear, my friend, that I shall render myself tedious by dwelling on these preliminary circumstances; but they were days of comparative happiness, and I think of them with pleasure. My country, my beloved country! who but a native can tell the delight I took in again beholding thy streams, thy mountains, and, more than all, thy lovely lake!

Yet, as I drew nearer home, grief and fear again overcame me. Night also closed around; and when I could hardly see the dark mountains, I felt still more gloomily. The picture appeared a vast and dim scene of evil, and I foresaw obscurely that I was destined to become the most wretched of human beings. Alas! I prophesied truly, and failed only in one single circumstance, that in all the misery I imagined and dreaded, I did not conceive the hundredth part of the anguish I was destined to endure.

It was completely dark when I arrived in the environs of Geneva; the gates of the town were already shut; and I was obliged to pass the night at Secheron, a village at the distance of half a league from the city. The sky was serene; and, as I was unable to rest, I resolved to visit the spot where my poor William had been murdered. As I could not pass through the town, I was obliged to cross the lake in a boat to arrive at Plainpalais. During this short voyage I saw the lightnings playing on the summit of Mont Blanc in the most beautiful figures. The storm appeared to approach rapidly; and, on landing, I ascended a low hill, that I might observe its progress. It advanced; the heavens were clouded, and I soon felt the rain coming slowly in large drops, but its violence quickly increased.

I quitted my seat, and walked on, although the darkness and storm increased every minute, and the thunder burst with a terrific crash over my head. It was echoed from Salêve, the Juras, and the Alps of Savoy; vivid flashes of lightning dazzled my eyes, illuminating the lake, making it appear like a vast sheet of fire; then for an instant every thing seemed of a pitchy darkness, until the eye recovered itself from the preceding flash. The storm, as is often the case in Switzerland, appeared at once in various parts of the heavens. The most violent storm hung exactly north of the town, over that part of the lake which lies between the promontory of Belrive and the village of Copêt. Another storm enlightened Jura with faint flashes; and another darkened and sometimes disclosed the Môle, a peaked mountain to the east of the lake.

While I watched the tempest, so beautiful yet terrific, I wandered on with a hasty step. This noble war in the sky elevated my spirits; I clasped my hands, and exclaimed aloud, "William, dear angel! this is thy funeral, this thy dirge!" As I said these words, I perceived in the gloom a figure which stole from behind a clump of trees near me; I stood fixed, gazing intently; I could not be mistaken. A flash of lightning illuminated the object, and discovered its shape plainly to me: its gigantic stature, and the deformity of its aspect, more hideous than belongs to humanity, instantly informed me that it was the wretch, the filthy daemon, to whom I had given life. What did he there? Could he be (I shuddered at the conception) the murderer of my brother? No sooner did that idea cross my imagination, than I became convinced of its truth; my teeth chattered, and I was forced to lean against a tree for support. The figure passed me quickly, and I lost it in the gloom. Nothing in human shape could have destroyed that fair child. *He* was the murderer! I could not doubt it. The mere presence of the idea was an irresistible proof of the fact. I thought of pursuing the devil; but it would have been in vain, for another flash discovered him to me hanging among the rocks of the nearly perpendicular ascent of Mont Salêve, a hill that bounds Plainpalais on the south. He soon reached the summit, and disappeared.

I remained motionless. The thunder ceased; but the rain still continued, and the scene was enveloped in an impenetrable darkness. I revolved in my mind the events which I had until now sought to forget: the whole train of my progress towards the creation; the appearance of the work of my own hands alive at my bedside; its departure. Two years had now nearly elapsed since the night on which he first received life; and was this his first crime? Alas! I had turned loose into the world a depraved wretch, whose delight was in carnage and misery; had he not murdered my brother?

No one can conceive the anguish I suffered during the remainder of the night, which I spent, cold and wet, in the open air. But I did not feel the inconvenience of the weather; my imagination was busy in scenes of evil and despair. I considered the being whom I had cast among mankind, and endowed with the will and power to effect purposes of horror, such as the deed which he had now done, nearly in the light of my own vampire, my own spirit let loose from the grave, and forced to destroy all that was dear to me.

Day dawned; and I directed my steps towards the town. The gates were open, and I hastened to my father's house. My first thought was to discover what I knew of the murderer, and cause instant pursuit to be made. But I paused when I reflected on the story that I had to tell. A being whom I myself had formed, and endued with life, had met me at midnight among the precipices of an inaccessible mountain. I remembered also the nervous fever with which I had been seized just at the time that I dated my creation, and which would give an air of delirium to a tale otherwise so utterly improbable. I well knew that if any other had communicated such a relation to me, I should have looked upon it as the ravings of insanity. Besides, the strange nature of the animal would elude all pursuit, even if I were so far credited as to persuade my relatives to commence it. And then of what use would be pursuit? Who could arrest a creature capable of scaling the overhanging sides of Mont Salêve? These reflections determined me, and I resolved to remain silent.

It was about five in the morning when I entered my father's house. I told the servants not to disturb the family, and went into the library to attend their usual hour of rising.

Six years had elapsed, passed as a dream but for one indelible trace, and I stood in the same place where I had last embraced my father before my departure for Ingolstadt. Beloved and venerable parent! He still remained to me. I gazed on the picture of my mother, which stood over the mantel-piece. It was an historical subject, painted at my father's desire, and represented Caroline Beaufort in an agony of despair, kneeling by the coffin of her dead father. Her garb was rustic, and her cheek pale; but there was an air of dignity and beauty, that hardly permitted the sentiment of pity. Below this picture was a miniature of William; and my tears flowed when I looked upon it. While I was thus engaged, Ernest entered; he had heard me arrive, and hastened to welcome me. He expressed a sorrowful delight to see me: "Welcome, my dearest Victor," said he. "Ah! I wish you had come three months ago, and then you would have found us all joyous and delighted. You come to us now to share a misery which nothing can alleviate; yet your presence will, I hope, revive our father, who seems sinking under his misfortune; and your persuasions will induce poor Elizabeth to cease her vain and tormenting self-accusations.—Poor William! he was our darling and our pride!"

Tears, unrestrained, fell from my brother's eyes; a sense of mortal agony crept over my frame. Before, I had only imagined the wretchedness of my desolated home; the reality came on me as a new, and a not less terrible, disaster. I tried to calm Ernest; I enquired more minutely concerning my father, and her I named my cousin.

"She most of all," said Ernest, "requires consolation; she accused herself of having caused the death of my brother, and that made her very wretched. But since the murderer has been discovered—"

"The murderer discovered! Good God! how can that be? who could attempt to pursue him? It is impossible; one might as well try to overtake the winds, or confine a mountain-stream with a straw. I saw him too; he was free last night!"

"I do not know what you mean," replied my brother, in accents of wonder, "but to us the discovery we have made completes our misery. No one would believe it at first; and even now Elizabeth will not be convinced, notwithstanding all the evidence. Indeed, who would credit that Justine Moritz, who was so amiable, and fond of all the family, could suddenly become capable of so frightful, so appalling a crime?"

"Justine Moritz! Poor, poor girl, is she the accused? But it is wrongfully; every one knows that; no one believes it, surely, Ernest?"

"No one did at first; but several circumstances came out, that have almost forced conviction upon us; and her own behaviour has been so confused, as to add to the evidence of facts a weight that, I fear, leaves no hope for doubt. But she will be tried to-day, and you will then hear all."

He related that, the morning on which the murder of poor William had been discovered, Justine had been taken ill, and confined to her bed for several days. During this interval, one of the servants, happening to examine the apparel she had worn on the night of the murder, had discovered in her pocket the picture of my mother, which had been judged to be the temptation of the murderer. The servant instantly showed it to one of the others, who, without saying a word to any of the family, went to a magistrate; and, upon their deposition, Justine was apprehended. On being charged with the fact, the poor girl confirmed the suspicion in a great measure by her extreme confusion of manner.

This was a strange tale, but it did not shake my faith; and I replied earnestly, "You are all mistaken; I know the murderer. Justine, poor, good Justine, is innocent."

At that instant my father entered. I saw unhappiness deeply impressed on his countenance, but he endeavoured to welcome me cheerfully; and, after we had exchanged our mournful greeting, would have introduced some other topic than that of our disaster, had not Ernest exclaimed, "Good God, papa! Victor says that he knows who was the murderer of poor William."

"We do also, unfortunately," replied my father; "for indeed I had rather have been for ever ignorant than have discovered so much depravity and ingratitude in one I valued so highly."

"My dear father, you are mistaken; Justine is innocent."

"If she is, God forbid that she should suffer as guilty. She is to be tried to-day, and I hope, I sincerely hope, that she will be acquitted."

This speech calmed me. I was firmly convinced in my own mind that Justine, and indeed every human being, was guiltless of this murder. I had no fear, therefore, that any circumstantial evidence could be brought forward strong enough to convict her. My tale was not one to announce publicly; its astounding horror would be looked upon as madness by the vulgar. Did any one indeed exist, except I, the creator, who would believe, unless his senses convinced him, in the existence of the living monument of presumption and rash ignorance which I had let loose upon the world? )

We were soon joined by Elizabeth. Time had altered her since I last beheld her; it had endowed her with loveliness surpassing the beauty of her childish years. There was the same candour, the same vivacity, but it was allied to an expression more full of sensibility and intellect. She welcomed me with the greatest affection. "Your arrival, my dear cousin," said she, "fills me with hope. You perhaps will find some means to justify my poor guiltless Justine. Alas! who is safe, if she be convicted of crime? I rely on her innocence as certainly as I do upon my own. Our misfortune is doubly hard to us; we have not only lost that lovely darling boy, but this poor girl, whom I sincerely love, is to be torn away by even a worse fate. If she is condemned, I never shall know joy more. But she will not, I am sure she will not; and then I shall be happy again, even after the sad death of my little William."

"She is innocent, my Elizabeth," said I, "and that shall be proved; fear nothing, but let your spirits be cheered by the assurance of her acquittal."

"How kind and generous you are! every one else believes in her guilt, and that made me wretched, for I knew that it was impossible: and to see every one else prejudiced in so deadly a manner rendered me hopeless and despairing." She wept.

"Dearest niece," said my father, "dry your tears. If she is, as you believe, innocent, rely on the justice of our laws, and the activity with which I shall prevent the slightest shadow of partiality."

## CHAPTER VIII

We passed a few sad hours, until eleven o'clock, when the trial was to commence. My father and the rest of the family being obliged to attend as witnesses, I accompanied them to the court. During the whole of this wretched mockery of justice I suffered living torture. It was to be decided, whether the result of my curiosity and lawless devices would cause the death of two of my fellow-beings: one a smiling babe, full of innocence and joy; the other far more dreadfully murdered, with every aggravation of infamy that could make the murder memorable in horror. Justine also was a girl of merit, and possessed qualities which promised to render her life happy: now all was to be obliterated in an ignominious grave; and I the cause! A thousand times rather would I have confessed myself guilty of the crime ascribed to Justine; but I was absent when it was committed, and such a declaration would have been considered as the ravings of a madman, and would not have exculpated her who suffered through me.

The appearance of Justine was calm. She was dressed in mourning; and her countenance, always engaging, was rendered, by the solemnity of her feelings, exquisitely beautiful. Yet she appeared confident in innocence, and did not tremble, although gazed on and execrated by thousands; for all the kindness which her beauty might otherwise have excited, was obliterated in the minds of the spectators by the imagination of the enormity she was supposed to have committed. She was tranquil, yet her tranquillity was evidently constrained; and as her confusion had before been adduced as a proof of her guilt, she worked up her mind to an appearance of courage. When she entered the court, she threw her eyes round it, and quickly discovered where we were seated. A tear seemed to dim her eye when she saw us; but she quickly recovered herself, and a look of sorrowful affection seemed to attest her utter guiltlessness.

The trial began; and, after the advocate against her had stated the charge, several witnesses were called. Several strange facts combined against her, which might have staggered any one who had not such proof of her innocence as I had. She had been out the whole of the night on which the murder had been committed, and towards morning had been perceived by a market-woman not far from the spot where the body of the murdered child had been afterwards found. The woman asked her what she did there; but she looked very strangely, and only returned a confused and unintelligible answer. She returned to the house about eight o'clock; and, when one enquired where she had passed the night, she replied that she had been looking for the child, and demanded earnestly if any thing had been heard concerning him. When shown the body, she fell into violent hysterics, and kept her bed for several days. The picture was then produced, which the servant had found in her pocket; and when Elizabeth, in a faltering voice, proved that it was the same which, an hour before the child had been missed, she had placed round his neck, a murmur of horror and indignation filled the court.

Justine was called on for her defence. As the trial had proceeded, her countenance had altered. Surprise, horror, and misery were strongly expressed. Sometimes she struggled with her tears; but, when she was desired to plead, she collected her powers, and spoke, in an audible although variable voice.

"God knows," she said, "how entirely I am innocent. But I do not pretend that my protestations should acquit me: I rest my innocence on a plain and simple explanation of the facts which have been adduced against me; and I hope the character I have always borne will incline my judges to a favourable interpretation, where any circumstance appears doubtful or suspicious."

She then related that, by the permission of Elizabeth, she had passed the evening of the night on which the murder had been committed at the house of an aunt at Chêne, a village situated at about a league from Geneva. On her return, at about nine o'clock, she met a man, who asked her if she had seen any thing of the child who was lost. She was alarmed by this account, and passed several hours in looking for him, when the gates of Geneva were shut, and she was forced to remain several hours of the night in a barn belonging to a cottage, being unwilling to call up the inhabitants, to whom she was well known. Most of the night she spent here watching; towards morning she believed that she slept for a few minutes; some steps disturbed her, and she awoke. It was dawn, and she quitted her asylum, that she might again endeavour to find my brother. If she had gone near the spot where his body lay, it was without her knowledge. That she had been bewildered when questioned by the market-woman was not surprising, since she had passed a sleepless night, and the fate of poor William was yet uncertain. Concerning the picture she could give no account.

"I know," continued the unhappy victim, "how heavily and fatally this one circumstance weighs against me, but I have no power of explaining it; and when I have expressed my utter ignorance, I am only left to conjecture concerning the probabilities by which it might have been placed in my pocket. But here also I am checked. I believe that I have no enemy on earth, and none surely would have been so wicked as to destroy me wantonly. Did the murderer place it there? I know of no opportunity afforded him for so doing; or, if I had, why should he have stolen the jewel, to part with it again so soon?

"I commit my cause to the justice of my judges, yet I see no room for hope. I beg permission to have a few witnesses examined concerning my character; and if their testimony shall not overweigh my supposed guilt, I must be condemned, although I would pledge my salvation on my innocence."

Several witnesses were called, who had known her for many years, and they spoke well of her; but fear, and hatred of the crime of which they supposed her guilty, rendered them timorous, and unwilling to come forward. Elizabeth saw even this last resource, her excellent dispositions and irreproachable conduct, about to fail the accused, when, although violently agitated, she desired permission to address the court.

"I am," said she, "the cousin of the unhappy child who was murdered, or rather his sister, for I was educated by and have lived with his parents ever since and even long before his birth. It may therefore be judged indecent in me to come forward on this occasion; but when I see a fellow-creature about to perish through the cowardice of her pretended friends, I wish to be allowed to speak, that I may say what I know of her character. I am well acquainted with the accused. I have lived in the same house with her, at one time for five, and at another for nearly two years. During all that period she appeared to me the most amiable and benevolent of human creatures. She nursed Madame Frankenstein, my aunt, in her last illness, with the greatest affection and care; and afterwards attended her own mother during a tedious illness, in a manner that excited the admiration of all who knew her; after which she again lived in my uncle's house, where she was beloved by all the family. She was warmly attached to the child who is now dead, and acted towards him like a most affectionate mother. For my own part, I do not hesitate to say, that, notwithstanding all the evidence produced against her, I believe and rely on her perfect innocence. She had no temptation for such an action: as to the bauble on which the chief proof rests, if she had earnestly desired it, I should have willingly given it to her; so much do I esteem and value her."

A murmur of approbation followed Elizabeth's simple and powerful appeal; but it was excited by her generous interference, and not in favour of poor Justine, on whom the public indignation was turned with renewed violence, charging her with the blackest ingratitude. She herself wept as Elizabeth spoke, but she did not answer. My own agitation and anguish was extreme during the whole trial. I believed in her innocence; I knew it. Could the daemon, who had (I did not for a minute doubt) murdered my brother, also in his hellish sport have betrayed the innocent to death and ignominy? I could not sustain the horror of my situation; and when I perceived that the popular voice, and the countenances of the judges, had already condemned my unhappy victim, I rushed out of the court in agony. The tortures of the accused did not equal mine; she was sustained by innocence, but the fangs of remorse tore my bosom, and would not forego their hold.

I passed a night of unmingled wretchedness. In the morning I went to the court; my lips and throat were parched. I dared not ask the fatal question; but I was known, and the officer guessed the cause of my visit. The ballots had been thrown; they were all black, and Justine was condemned)

I cannot pretend to describe what I then felt. I had before experienced sensations of horror; and I have endeavoured to bestow upon them adequate expressions, but words cannot convey an idea of the heart-sickening despair that I then endured. The person to whom I addressed myself added, that Justine had already confessed her guilt. "That evidence," he observed, "was hardly required in so glaring a case, but I am glad of it; and, indeed, none of our judges like to condemn a criminal upon circumstantial evidence, be it ever so decisive."

This was strange and unexpected intelligence; what could it mean? Had my eyes deceived me? and was I really as mad as the whole world would believe me to be, if I disclosed the object of my suspicions? I hastened to return home, and Elizabeth eagerly demanded the result.

"My cousin," replied I, "it is decided as you may have expected; all judges had rather that ten innocent should suffer, than that one guilty should escape. But she has confessed."

This was a dire blow to poor Elizabeth, who had relied with firmness upon Justine's innocence. "Alas!" said she, "how shall I ever again believe in human goodness? Justine, whom I loved and esteemed as my sister, how could she put on those smiles of innocence only to betray? her mild eyes seemed incapable of any severity or guile, and yet she has committed a murder."

Soon after we heard that the poor victim had expressed a desire to see my cousin. My father wished her not to go; but said, that he left it to her own judgment and feelings to decide. "Yes," said Elizabeth, "I will go, although she is guilty; and you, Victor, shall accompany me: I cannot go alone." The idea of this visit was torture to me, yet I could not refuse.

We entered the gloomy prison-chamber, and beheld Justine sitting on some straw at the farther end; her hands were manacled, and her head rested on her knees. She rose on seeing us enter; and when we were left alone with her, she threw herself at the feet of Elizabeth, weeping bitterly. My cousin wept also.

"Oh, Justine!" said she, "why did you rob me of my last consolation? I relied on your innocence; and although I was then very wretched, I was not so miserable as I am now."

"And do you also believe that I am so very, very wicked? Do you also join with my enemies to crush me, to condemn me as a murderer?" Her voice was suffocated with sobs.

"Rise, my poor girl," said Elizabeth, "why do you kneel, if you are innocent? I am not one of your enemies; I believed you guiltless, notwithstanding every evidence, until I heard that you had yourself declared your guilt. That report, you say, is false; and be assured, dear Justine, that nothing can shake my confidence in you for a moment, but your own confession."

"I did confess; but I confessed a lie. I confessed, that I might obtain absolution; but now that falsehood lies heavier at my heart than all my other sins. The God of heaven forgive me! Ever since I was condemned, my confessor has besieged me; he threatened and menaced, until I almost began to think that I was the monster that he said I was. He threatened excommunication and hell fire in my last moments, if I continued obdurate. Dear lady, I had none to support me; all looked on me as a wretch doomed to ignominy and perdition. What could I do? In an evil hour I subscribed to a lie; and now only am I truly miserable."

She paused, weeping, and then continued—"I thought with horror, my sweet lady, that you should believe your Justine, whom your blessed aunt had so highly honoured, and whom you loved, was a creature capable of a crime which none but the devil himself could have perpetrated. Dear William! dearest blessed child! I soon shall see you again in heaven, where we shall all be happy; and that consoles me, going as I am to suffer ignominy and death."

"Oh, Justine! forgive me for having for one moment distrusted you. Why did you confess? But do not mourn, dear girl. Do not fear. I will proclaim, I will prove your innocence. I will melt the stony hearts of your enemies by my tears and prayers. You shall not die!—You, my play-fellow, my companion, my sister, perish on the scaffold! No! no! I never could survive so horrible a misfortune."

Justine shook her head mournfully. "I do not fear to die," she said; "that pang is past. God raises my weakness, and gives me courage to endure the worst. I leave a sad and bitter world; and if you remember me, and think of me as of one unjustly condemned, I am resigned to the fate awaiting me. Learn from me, dear lady, to submit in patience to the will of Heaven!"

During this conversation I had retired to a corner of the prison-room, where I could conceal the horrid anguish that possessed me. Despair! Who dared talk of that? The poor victim, who on the morrow was to pass the awful boundary between life and death, felt not as I did, such deep and bitter agony. I gnashed my teeth, and ground them together, uttering a groan that came from my inmost soul. Justine started. When she saw who it was, she approached me, and said, "Dear sir, you are very kind to visit me; you, I hope, do not believe that I am guilty?"

I could not answer. "No, Justine," said Elizabeth; "he is more convinced of your innocence than I was; for even when he heard that you had confessed, he did not credit it."

"I truly thank him. In these last moments I feel the sincerest gratitude towards those who think of me with kindness. How sweet is the affection of others to such a wretch as I am! It removes more than half my misfortune; and I feel as if I could die in peace, now that my innocence is acknowledged by you, dear lady, and your cousin."

Thus the poor sufferer tried to comfort others and herself. She indeed gained the resignation she desired. But I, the true murderer, felt the never-dying worm alive in my bosom, which allowed of no hope or consolation. Elizabeth also wept, and was unhappy; but hers also was the misery of innocence, which, like a cloud that passes over the fair moon, for a while hides but cannot tarnish its brightness. Anguish and despair had penetrated into the core of my heart; I bore a hell within me, which nothing could extinguish. We stayed several hours with Justine; and it was with great difficulty that Elizabeth could tear herself away. "I wish," cried she, "that I were to die with you; I cannot live in this world of misery."

Justine assumed an air of cheerfulness, while she with difficulty repressed her bitter tears. She embraced Elizabeth, and said, in a voice of half-suppressed emotion, "Farewell, sweet lady, dearest Elizabeth, my beloved and only friend; may Heaven, in its bounty, bless and preserve you; may this be the last misfortune that you will ever suffer! Live, and be happy, and make others so."

And on the morrow Justine died. Elizabeth's heartrending eloquence failed to move the judges from their settled conviction in the criminality of the saintly sufferer. My passionate and indignant appeals were lost upon them. And when I received their cold answers, and heard the harsh unfeeling reasoning of these men, my purposed avowal died away on my lips. Thus I might proclaim myself a madman, but not revoke the sentence passed upon my wretched victim. She perished on the scaffold as a murderess!

From the tortures of my own heart, I turned to contemplate the deep and voiceless grief of my Elizabeth. This also was my doing! And my father's woe, and the desolation of that late so smiling home—all was the work of my thrice-accursed hands! Ye weep, unhappy ones; but these are not your last tears! Again shall you raise the funeral wail, and the sound of your lamentations shall again and again be heard! Frankenstein, your son, your kinsman, your early, much-loved friend; he who would spend each vital drop of blood for your sakes—who has no thought nor sense of joy, except as it is mirrored also in your dear countenances—who would fill the air with blessings, and spend his life in serving you—he bids you weep—to shed countless tears; happy beyond his hopes, if thus inexorable fate be satisfied, and if the destruction pause before the peace of the grave have succeeded to your sad torments!

Thus spoke my prophetic soul, as, torn by remorse, horror, and despair, I beheld those I loved spend vain sorrow upon the graves of William and Justine, the first hapless victims to my unhallowed arts.

## CHAPTER IX

Nothing is more painful to the human mind, than, after the feelings have been worked up by a quick succession of events, the dead calmness of inaction and certainty which follows, and deprives the soul both of hope and fear. Justine died; she rested; and I was alive. The blood flowed freely in my veins, but a weight of despair and remorse pressed on my heart, which nothing could remove. Sleep fled from my eyes; I wandered like an evil spirit, for I had committed deeds of mischief beyond description horrible, and more, much more (I persuaded myself), was yet behind. Yet my heart overflowed with kindness, and the love of virtue. I had begun life with benevolent intentions, and thirsted for the moment when I should put them in practice, and make myself useful to my fellow-beings. Now all was blasted: instead of that serenity of conscience, which allowed me to look back upon the past with self-satisfaction, and from thence to gather promise of new hopes, I was seized by remorse and the sense of guilt, which hurried me away to a hell of intense tortures, such as no language can describe.

This state of mind preyed upon my health, which had perhaps never entirely recovered from the first shock it had sustained. I shunned the face of man; all sound of joy or complacency was torture to me; solitude was my only consolation—deep, dark, deathlike solitude.

My father observed with pain the alteration perceptible in my disposition and habits, and endeavoured by arguments deduced from the feelings of his serene conscience and guiltless life, to inspire me with fortitude, and awaken in me the courage to dispel the dark cloud which brooded over me. "Do you think, Victor," said he, "that I do not suffer also? No one could love a child more than I loved your brother;" (tears came into his eyes as he spoke;) "but is it not a duty to the survivors, that we should refrain from augmenting their unhappiness by an appearance of immoderate grief? It is also a duty owed to yourself; (for excessive sorrow prevents improvement or enjoyment, or even the discharge of daily usefulness, without which no man is fit for society.")

This advice, although good, was totally inapplicable to my case; I should have been the first to hide my grief, and console my friends, if remorse had not mingled its bitterness, and terror its alarm with my other sensations. Now I could only answer my father with a look of despair, and endeavour to hide myself from his view.

About this time we retired to our house at Belrive. This change was particularly agreeable to me. The shutting of the gates regularly at ten o'clock, and the impossibility of remaining on the lake after that hour, had rendered our residence within the walls of Geneva very irksome to me. I was now free. Often, after the rest of the family had retired for the night, I took the boat, and passed many hours upon the water. Sometimes, with my sails set, I was carried by the wind; and sometimes, after rowing into the middle of the lake, I left the boat to pursue its own course, and gave way to my own miserable reflections. I was often tempted, when all was at peace around me, and I the only unquiet thing that wandered restless in a scene so beautiful and heavenly—if I except some bat, or the frogs, whose harsh and interrupted croaking was heard only when I approached the shore—(often, I say, (I was tempted to plunge into the silent lake, that the waters might close over me and my calamities for ever.) But I was restrained, when I thought of the heroic and suffering Elizabeth, whom I tenderly loved, and whose existence was bound up in mine] I thought also of my father, and surviving brother: should I by my base desertion leave them (exposed and unprotected to the malice of the fiend whom I had let loose among them?)

At these moments I wept bitterly, and wished that peace would revisit my mind only that I might afford them consolation and happiness. But that could not be. Remorse extinguished every hope. (I had been the author of unalterable evils; and I lived in daily fear, lest the monster whom I had created should perpetrate some new wickedness.) I had an obscure feeling that all was not over, and that he would still commit some signal crime, which by its enormity should almost efface the recollection of the past. There was always scope for fear, so long as any thing I loved remained behind. (My abhorrence of this fiend cannot be conceived] When I thought of him, I gnashed my teeth, my eyes became inflamed, and(I ardently wished to extinguish that life which I had so thoughtlessly bestowed) When I reflected on his crimes and malice, my hatred and revenge burst all bounds of moderation. I would have made a pilgrimage to the highest peak of the Andes, could I, when there, have precipitated him to their base. I wished to see him again, that I might wreak the utmost extent of abhorrence on his head, and avenge the deaths of William and Justine.

Our house was the house of mourning. My father's health was deeply shaken by the horror of the recent events. Elizabeth was sad and desponding; she no longer took delight in her ordinary occupations; all pleasure seemed to her sacrilege toward the dead; eternal woe and tears she then thought was the just tribute she should pay to innocence so blasted and destroyed. She was no longer that happy creature, who in earlier youth wandered with me on the banks of the lake, and talked with ecstasy of our future prospects.(The first of those sorrows which are sent to wean us from the earth, had visited her, and its dimming influence quenched her dearest smiles.)

"When I reflect, my dear cousin," said she, "on the miserable death of Justine Moritz,(I no longer see the world and its works as they before appeared to me.) Before, I looked upon the accounts of vice and injustice, that I read in books or heard from others, as tales of ancient days, or imaginary evils; at least they were remote, and more familiar to reason than to the imagination;(but now misery has come home, and men *whit?* *men?* appear to me as monsters thirsting for each other's blood.)Yet I am certainly unjust. Every body believed that poor girl to be guilty; and if she could have committed the crime for which she suffered, assuredly she would have been the most depraved of human creatures. For the sake of a few jewels, to have murdered the son of her benefactor and friend, a child whom she had nursed from its birth, and appeared to love as if it had been her own! I could not consent to the death of any human being; but certainly I should have thought such a creature unfit to remain in the society of men. But she was innocent. I know, I feel she was innocent; you are of the same opinion, and that confirms me. Alas! Victor, when falsehood can look so like the truth, who can assure themselves of certain happiness? I feel as if I were walking on the edge of a precipice, towards which thousands are crowding, and endeavouring to plunge me into the abyss. William and Justine were assassinated, and the murderer escapes; he walks about the world free, and perhaps respected. But even if I were condemned to suffer on the scaffold for the same crimes, I would not change places with such a wretch."

I listened to this discourse with the extremest agony. (I, not in deed, but in effect, was the true murderer.) Elizabeth read my anguish in my countenance, and kindly taking my hand, said, "My dearest friend, you must calm yourself. These events have affected me, God knows how deeply; but I am not so wretched as you are. There is an expression of despair, and sometimes of revenge, in your countenance, that makes me tremble. Dear Victor, banish these dark passions. Remember the friends around you, who centre all their hopes in you. Have we lost the power of rendering you happy? Ah! while we love—while we are true to each other, here in this land of peace and beauty, your native country, we may reap every tranquil blessing,—what can disturb our peace?"

And could not such words from her whom I fondly prized before every other gift of fortune, suffice to chase away the fiend that lurked in my heart? Even as she spoke I drew near to her, as if in terror; lest at that very moment the destroyer had been near to rob me of her.

Thus not the tenderness of friendship, nor the beauty of earth, nor of heaven, could redeem my soul from woe: the very accents of love were ineffectual. I was encompassed by a cloud which no beneficial influence could penetrate. The wounded deer dragging its fainting limbs to some untrodden brake, there to gaze upon the arrow which had pierced it, and to die—was but a type of me.

Sometimes I could cope with the sullen despair that overwhelmed me: but sometimes the whirlwind passions of my soul drove me to seek, by bodily exercise and by change of place, some relief from my intolerable sensations. It was during an access of this kind that I suddenly left my home, and bending my steps towards the near Alpine valleys, sought in the magnificence, the eternity of such scenes, to forget myself and my ephemeral, because human, sorrows. My wanderings were directed towards the valley of Chamounix. I had visited it frequently during my boyhood. Six years had passed since then: I was a wreck—but nought had changed in those savage and enduring scenes.

I performed the first part of my journey on horseback. I afterwards hired a mule, as the more sure-footed, and least liable to receive injury on these rugged roads. The weather was fine: it was about the middle of the month of August, nearly two months after the death of Justine; that miserable epoch from which I dated all my woe. The weight upon my spirit was sensibly lightened as I plunged yet deeper in the ravine of Arve. The immense mountains and precipices that overhung me on every side—the sound of the river raging among the rocks, and the dashing of the waterfalls around, spoke of a power mighty as Omnipotence—and I ceased to fear, or to bend before any being less almighty than that which had created and ruled the elements, here displayed in their most terrific guise. Still, as I ascended higher, the valley assumed a more magnificent and astonishing character. Ruined castles hanging on the precipices of piny mountains; the impetuous Arve, and cottages every here and there peeping forth from among the trees, formed a scene of singular beauty. But it was augmented and rendered sublime by the mighty Alps, whose white and shining pyramids and domes towered above all, as belonging to another earth, the habitations of another race of beings. heaven

I passed the bridge of Pélissier, where the ravine, which the river forms, opened before me, and I began to ascend the mountain that overhangs it. Soon after I entered the valley of Chamounix. This valley is more wonderful and sublime, but not so beautiful and picturesque, as that of Servox, through which I had just passed. The high and snowy mountains were its immediate boundaries; but I saw no more ruined castles and fertile fields. Immense glaciers approached the road; I heard the rumbling thunder of the falling avalanche, and marked the smoke of its passage. Mont Blanc, the supreme and magnificent Mont Blanc, raised itself from the surrounding *aiguilles,*° and its tremendous *dôme* overlooked the valley.

A tingling long-lost sense of pleasure often came across me during this journey. Some turn in the road, some new object suddenly perceived and recognized, reminded me of days gone by, and were associated with the light-hearted gaiety of boyhood. The very winds whispered in soothing accents, and maternal nature bade me weep no more. Then again the kindly influence ceased to act—I found myself fettered again to grief, and indulging in all the misery of reflection. Then I spurred on my animal, striving so to forget the world, my fears, and, more than all, myself—or, in a more desperate fashion, I alighted, and threw myself on the grass, weighed down by horror and despair.

At length I arrived at the village of Chamounix. Exhaustion succeeded to the extreme fatigue both of body and of mind which I had endured. For a short space of time I remained at the window, watching the pallid lightnings that played above Mont Blanc, and listening to the rushing of the Arve, which pursued its noisy way beneath. The same lulling sounds acted as a lullaby to my too keen sensations: when I

---

*aiguilles:* Fr. for peaks (literally, needles).

placed my head upon my pillow, sleep crept over me; I felt it as it came, and blest the giver of oblivion.


## CHAPTER X

I spent the following day roaming through the valley. I stood beside the sources of the Arveiron, which take their rise in a glacier, that with slow pace is advancing down from the summit of the hills, to barricade the valley. The abrupt sides of vast mountains were before me; the icy wall of the glacier overhung me; a few shattered pines were scattered around; and the solemn silence of this glorious presence-chamber of imperial Nature was broken only by the brawling waves, or the fall of some vast fragment, the thunder sound of the avalanche, or the cracking, reverberated along the mountains, of the accumulated ice, which, through the silent working of immutable laws, was ever and anon rent and torn, as if it had been but a plaything in their hands. These sublime and magnificent scenes afforded me the greatest consolation that I was capable of receiving. They elevated me from all littleness of feeling; and although they did not remove my grief, they subdued and tranquillised it. In some degree, also, they diverted my mind from the thoughts over which it had brooded for the last month. I retired to rest at night; my slumbers, as it were, waited on and ministered to by the assemblance of grand shapes which I had contemplated during the day. They congregated round me; the unstained snowy mountain-top, the glittering pinnacle, the pine woods, and ragged bare ravine; the eagle, soaring amidst the clouds—they all gathered round me, and bade me be at peace.

Where had they fled when the next morning I awoke? All of soul-inspiriting fled with sleep, and dark melancholy clouded every thought. The rain was pouring in torrents, and thick mists hid the summits of the mountains, so that I even saw not the faces of those mighty friends. Still I would penetrate their misty veil, and seek them in their cloudy retreats. What were rain and storm to me? My mule was brought to the door, and I resolved to ascend to the summit of Montanvert. I remembered the effect that the view of the tremendous and ever-moving glacier had produced upon my mind when I first saw it. It had then filled me with a sublime ecstasy, that gave wings to the soul, and allowed it to soar from the obscure world to light and joy. The sight of the awful and majestic in nature had indeed always the effect of solemnising my mind, and causing me to forget the passing cares of life. I determined to go without a guide, for I was well acquainted with the path, and the presence of another would destroy the solitary grandeur of the scene.

The ascent is precipitous, but the path is cut into continual and short windings, which enable you to surmount the perpendicularity of the mountain. It is a scene terrifically desolate. In a thousand spots the traces of the winter avalanche may be perceived, where trees lie broken and strewed on the ground; some entirely destroyed, others bent, leaning upon the jutting rocks of the mountain, or transversely upon other trees. The path, as you ascend higher, is intersected by ravines of snow, down which stones continually roll from above; one of them is particularly dangerous, as the slightest sound, such as even speaking in a loud voice, produces a concussion of air sufficient to draw destruction upon the head of the speaker. The pines are not tall or luxuriant, but they are sombre, and add an air of severity to the scene. I looked on the valley beneath; vast mists were rising from the rivers which ran through it, and curling in thick wreaths around the opposite mountains, whose summits were hid in the uniform clouds, while rain poured from the dark sky, and added to the melancholy impression I received from the objects around me. (Alas! why does man boast of sensibilities superior to those apparent in the brute; it only renders them more necessary beings. If our impulses were confined to hunger, thirst, and desire, we might be nearly free; but now we are moved by every wind that blows, and a chance word or scene that that word may convey to us.) ? we are not free

> We rest; a dream has power to poison sleep.
>   We rise; one wand'ring thought pollutes the day.
> We feel, conceive, or reason; laugh or weep,
>   Embrace fond woe, or cast our cares away;
> It is the same: for, be it joy or sorrow,
>   The path of its departure still is free.
> Man's yesterday may ne'er be like his morrow;
>   Nought may endure but mutability!°

It was nearly noon when I arrived at the top of the ascent. For some time I sat upon the rock that overlooks the sea of ice. A mist covered both that and the surrounding mountains. Presently a breeze dissipated the cloud, and I descended upon the glacier. The surface is very uneven, rising like the waves of a troubled sea, descending low, and interspersed by rifts that sink deep. The field of ice is almost a league in width, but I spent nearly two hours in crossing it. The opposite mountain is a bare

*We rest . . . mutability:* Last section of Percy Shelley's poem "Mutability" (1816).

perpendicular rock. From the side where I now stood Montanvert was exactly opposite, at the distance of a league; and above it rose Mont Blanc, in awful majesty. I remained in a recess of the rock, gazing on this wonderful and stupendous scene. The sea, or rather the vast river of ice, wound among its dependent mountains, whose aerial summits hung over its recesses. Their icy and glittering peaks shone in the sunlight over the clouds. My heart, which was before sorrowful, now swelled with something like joy; I exclaimed—"Wandering spirits, if indeed ye wander, and do not rest in your narrow beds, allow me this faint happiness, or take me, as your companion, away from the joys of life." want to die

As I said this, I suddenly beheld the figure of a man, at some distance, advancing towards me with superhuman speed. He bounded over the crevices in the ice, among which I had walked with caution; his stature, also, as he approached, seemed to exceed that of man. I was troubled: a mist came over my eyes, and I felt a faintness seize me; but I was quickly restored by the cold gale of the mountains. I perceived, as the shape came nearer (sight tremendous and abhorred!) that it was the wretch whom I had created. I trembled with rage and horror, resolving to wait his approach, and then close with him in mortal combat. He approached; his countenance bespoke bitter anguish, combined with disdain and malignity, while its unearthly ugliness rendered it almost too horrible for human eyes. But I scarcely observed this; rage and hatred had at first deprived me of utterance, and I recovered only to overwhelm him with words expressive of furious detestation and contempt.

"Devil," I exclaimed, "do you dare approach me? and do not you fear the fierce vengeance of my arm wreaked on your miserable head? Begone, vile insect! or rather, stay, that I may trample you to dust! and, oh! that I could, with the extinction of your miserable existence, restore those victims whom you have so diabolically murdered!"

"I expected this reception," said the daemon. "All men hate the wretched; how, then, must I be hated, who am miserable beyond all living things! Yet you, my creator, detest and spurn me, thy creature, to whom thou art bound by ties only dissoluble by the annihilation of one of us. You purpose to kill me. How dare you sport thus with life? Do your duty towards me, and I will do mine towards you and the rest of mankind. If you will comply with my conditions, I will leave them and you at peace; but if you refuse, I will glut the maw of death, until it be satiated with the blood of your remaining friends."

"Abhorred monster! fiend that thou art! the tortures of hell are too mild a vengeance for thy crimes. Wretched devil! you reproach me with your creation; come on, then, that I may extinguish the spark which I so negligently bestowed.")

My rage was without bounds; I sprang on him, impelled by all the feelings which can arm one being against the existence of another.

He easily eluded me, and said—

"Be calm! I entreat you to hear me, before you give vent to your hatred on my devoted head. Have I not suffered enough, that you seek to increase my misery? Life, although it may only be an accumulation of anguish, is dear to me, and I will defend it. Remember, thou hast made me more powerful than thyself; my height is superior to thine; my joints more supple. But I will not be tempted to set myself in opposition to thee. I am thy creature, and I will be even mild and docile to my natural lord and king, if thou wilt also perform thy part, the which thou owest me. Oh, Frankenstein, be not equitable to every other, and trample upon me alone, to whom thy justice, and even thy clemency and affection, is most due. Remember, that I am thy creature; I ought to be thy Adam; but I am rather the fallen angel, whom thou drivest from joy for no misdeed. Every where I see bliss, from which I alone am irrevocably excluded. I was benevolent and good; misery made me a fiend. Make me happy, and I shall again be virtuous."

"Begone! I will not hear you. There can be no community between you and me; we are enemies. Begone, or let us try our strength in a fight, in which one must fall."

"How can I move thee? Will no entreaties cause thee to turn a favourable eye upon thy creature, who implores thy goodness and compassion? Believe me, Frankenstein: I was benevolent; my soul glowed with love and humanity: but am I not alone, miserably alone? You, my creator, abhor me; what hope can I gather from your fellow-creatures, who owe me nothing? they spurn and hate me. The desert mountains and dreary glaciers are my refuge. I have wandered here many days; the caves of ice, which I only do not fear, are a dwelling to me, and the only one which man does not grudge. These bleak skies I hail, for they are kinder to me than your fellow-beings. If the multitude of mankind knew of my existence, they would do as you do, and arm themselves for my destruction. Shall I not then hate them who abhor me? I will keep no terms with my enemies. I am miserable, and they shall share my wretchedness. Yet it is in your power to recompense me, and deliver them from an evil which it only remains for you to make so great, that not only you and your family, but thousands of others, shall be swallowed up in the whirlwinds of its rage. Let your compassion be moved, and do not disdain me. Listen to my tale: when you have heard that, abandon or commiserate me, as you shall judge that I deserve. But hear me. The guilty are allowed, by human laws, bloody as they are, to speak in their own defence before they are condemned. Listen to me, Frankenstein. You accuse me of murder; and yet you would, with a satisfied conscience, destroy your own creature. Oh, praise the eternal justice of man! Yet I ask you not to spare me: listen to me; and then, if you can, and if you will, destroy the work of your hands."

"Why do you call to my remembrance," I rejoined, "circumstances, of which I shudder to reflect, that I have been the miserable origin and author? Cursed be the day, abhorred devil, in which you first saw light! Cursed (although I curse myself) be the hands that formed you! You have made me wretched beyond expression. You have left me no power to consider whether I am just to you, or not. Begone! relieve me from the sight of your detested form."

"Thus I relieve thee, my creator," he said, and placed his hated hands before my eyes, which I flung from me with violence; "thus I take from thee a sight which you abhor. Still thou canst listen to me, and grant me thy compassion. By the virtues that I once possessed, I demand this from you. Hear my tale; it is long and strange, and the temperature of this place is not fitting to your fine sensations; come to the hut upon the mountain. The sun is yet high in the heavens; before it descends to hide itself behind yon snowy precipices, and illuminate another world, you will have heard my story, and can decide. On you it rests, whether I quit for ever the neighbourhood of man, and lead a harmless life, or become the scourge of your fellow-creatures, and the author of your own speedy ruin."

As he said this, he led the way across the ice: I followed. My heart was full, and I did not answer him; but, as I proceeded, I weighed the various arguments that he had used, and determined at least to listen to his tale. I was partly urged by curiosity, and compassion confirmed my resolution. I had hitherto supposed him to be the murderer of my brother, and I eagerly sought a confirmation or denial of this opinion. For the first time, also, I felt what the duties of a creator towards his creature were, and that I ought to render him happy before I complained of his wickedness. These motives urged me to comply with his demand. We crossed the ice, therefore, and ascended the opposite rock. The air was cold, and the rain again began to descend: we entered the hut, the fiend with an air of exultation, I with a heavy heart, and depressed spirits. But I consented to listen; and, seating myself by the fire which my odious companion had lighted, he thus began his tale.

# CHAPTER XI

"It is with considerable difficulty that I remember the original era of my being: all the events of that period appear confused and indistinct. A strange multiplicity of sensations seized me, and I saw, felt, heard, and smelt, at the same time; and it was, indeed, a long time before I learned to distinguish between the operations of my various senses. By degrees, I remember, a stronger light pressed upon my nerves, so that I was obliged to shut my eyes. Darkness then came over me, and troubled me; but hardly had I felt this, when, by opening my eyes, as I now suppose, the light poured in upon me again. I walked, and, I believe, descended; but I presently found a great alteration in my sensations. Before, dark and opaque bodies had surrounded me, impervious to my touch or sight, but I now found that I could wander on at liberty, with no obstacles which I could not either surmount or avoid. The light became more and more oppressive to me; and, the heat wearying me as I walked, I sought a place where I could receive shade. This was the forest near Ingolstadt, and here I lay by the side of a brook resting from my fatigue, until I felt tormented by hunger and thirst. This roused me from my nearly dormant state, and I ate some berries which I found hanging on the trees, or lying on the ground. I slaked my thirst at the brook; and then lying down, was overcome by sleep.

"It was dark when I awoke; I felt cold also, and half-frightened, as it were instinctively, finding myself so desolate. Before I had quitted your apartment, on a sensation of cold, I had covered myself with some clothes; but these were insufficient to secure me from the dews of night. I was a poor, helpless, miserable wretch; I knew, and could distinguish, nothing; but feeling pain invade me on all sides, I sat down and wept.

"Soon a gentle light stole over the heavens, and gave me a sensation of pleasure. I started up, and beheld a radiant form rise from among the trees. I gazed with a kind of wonder. It moved slowly, but it enlightened my path; and I again went out in search of berries. I was still cold, when under one of the trees I found a huge cloak, with which I covered myself, and sat down upon the ground. No distinct ideas occupied my mind; all was confused. I felt light, and hunger, and thirst, and darkness; innumerable sounds rung in my ears, and on all sides various scents saluted me: the only object that I could distinguish was the bright moon, and I fixed my eyes on that with pleasure.

"Several changes of day and night passed, and the orb of night had greatly lessened, when I began to distinguish my sensations from each other. I gradually saw plainly the clear stream that supplied me with

drink, and the trees that shaded me with their foliage. I was delighted
when I first discovered that a pleasant sound, which often saluted my
ears, proceeded from the throats of the little winged animals who had
often intercepted the light from my eyes. I began also to observe, with
greater accuracy, the forms that surrounded me, and to perceive the
boundaries of the radiant roof of light which canopied me. Sometimes
I tried to imitate the pleasant songs of the birds, but was unable. Sometimes I wished to express my sensations in my own mode, but the
uncouth and inarticulate sounds which broke from me frightened me
into silence again.

"The moon had disappeared from the night, and again, with a lessened form, showed itself, while I still remained in the forest. My sensations had, by this time, become distinct, and my mind received every
day additional ideas. My eyes became accustomed to the light, and to
perceive objects in their right forms; I distinguished the insect from the
herb, and, by degrees, one herb from another. I found that the sparrow
uttered none but harsh notes, whilst those of the blackbird and thrush
were sweet and enticing.

"One day, when I was oppressed by cold, I found a fire which had
been left by some wandering beggars, and was overcome with delight
at the warmth I experienced from it. In my joy I thrust my hand into
the live embers, but quickly drew it out again with a cry of pain. How
strange, I thought, that the same cause should produce such opposite
effects! I examined the materials of the fire, and to my joy found it to
be composed of wood. I quickly collected some branches; but they
were wet, and would not burn. I was pained at this, and sat still watching the operation of the fire. The wet wood which I had placed near the
heat dried, and itself became inflamed. I reflected on this; and, by touching the various branches, I discovered the cause, and busied myself in
collecting a great quantity of wood, that I might dry it, and have a plentiful supply of fire. When night came on, and brought sleep with it, I was
in the greatest fear lest my fire should be extinguished. I covered it carefully with dry wood and leaves, and placed wet branches upon it; and
then, spreading my cloak, I lay on the ground, and sunk into sleep.

"It was morning when I awoke, and my first care was to visit the
fire. I uncovered it, and a gentle breeze quickly fanned it into a flame.
I observed this also, and contrived a fan of branches, which roused the
embers when they were nearly extinguished. When night came again, I
found, with pleasure, that the fire gave light as well as heat; and that the
discovery of this element was useful to me in my food; for I found some

of the offals that the travellers had left had been roasted, and tasted much more savoury than the berries I gathered from the trees. I tried, therefore, to dress my food in the same manner, placing it on the live embers. I found that the berries were spoiled by this operation, and the nuts and roots much improved.

"Food, however, became scarce; and I often spent the whole day searching in vain for a few acorns to assuage the pangs of hunger. When I found this, I resolved to quit the place that I had hitherto inhabited, to seek for one where the few wants I experienced would be more easily satisfied. In this emigration, I exceedingly lamented the loss of the fire which I had obtained through accident, and knew not how to reproduce it. I gave several hours to the serious consideration of this difficulty; but I was obliged to relinquish all attempt to supply it; and, wrapping myself up in my cloak, I struck across the wood towards the setting sun. I passed three days in these rambles, and at length discovered the open country. A great fall of snow had taken place the night before, and the fields were of one uniform white; the appearance was disconsolate, and I found my feet chilled by the cold damp substance that covered the ground.

"It was about seven in the morning, and I longed to obtain food and shelter; at length I perceived a small hut, on a rising ground, which had doubtless been built for the convenience of some shepherd. This was a new sight to me; and I examined the structure with great curiosity. Finding the door open, I entered. An old man sat in it, near a fire, over which he was preparing his breakfast. He turned on hearing a noise; and, perceiving me, shrieked loudly, and, quitting the hut, ran across the fields with a speed of which his debilitated form hardly appeared capable. His appearance, different from any I had ever before seen, and his flight, somewhat surprised me. But I was enchanted by the appearance of the hut: here the snow and rain could not penetrate; the ground was dry; and it presented to me then as exquisite and divine a retreat as Pandaemonium appeared to the daemons of hell° after their sufferings in the lake of fire. I greedily devoured the remnants of the shepherd's breakfast, which consisted of bread, cheese, milk, and wine; *doesn't like wine* the latter, however, I did not like. Then, overcome by fatigue, I lay down among some straw, and fell asleep.

---

*as Pandæmonium appeared to the dæmons of hell:* Reference to Book I, lines 670 ff. of the epic poem *Paradise Lost* (1667) by John Milton.

"It was noon when I awoke; and, allured by the warmth of the sun, which shone brightly on the white ground, I determined to recommence my travels; and, depositing the remains of the peasant's breakfast in a wallet I found, I proceeded across the fields for several hours, until at sunset I arrived at a village. How miraculous did this appear! the huts, the neater cottages, and stately houses, engaged my admiration by turns. The vegetables in the gardens, the milk and cheese that I saw placed at the windows of some of the cottages, allured my appetite. One of the best of these I entered; but I had hardly placed my foot within the door, before the children shrieked, and one of the women fainted. The whole village was roused; some fled, some attacked me, until, grievously bruised by stones and many other kinds of missile weapons, I escaped to the open country, and fearfully took refuge in a low hovel, quite bare, and making a wretched appearance after the palaces I had beheld in the village. This hovel, however, joined a cottage of a neat and pleasant appearance; but, after my late dearly bought experience, I dared not enter it. My place of refuge was constructed of wood, but so low, that I could with difficulty sit upright in it. No wood, however, was placed on the earth, which formed the floor, but it was dry; and although the wind entered it by innumerable chinks, I found it an agreeable asylum from the snow and rain.

"Here then I retreated, and lay down happy to have found a shelter, however miserable, from the inclemency of the season, and still more from the barbarity of man.

"As soon as morning dawned, I crept from my kennel, that I might view the adjacent cottage, and discover if I could remain in the habitation I had found. It was situated against the back of the cottage, and surrounded on the sides which were exposed by a pig-sty and a clear pool of water. One part was open, and by that I had crept in; but now I covered every crevice by which I might be perceived with stones and wood, yet in such a manner that I might move them on occasion to pass out: all the light I enjoyed came through the sty, and that was sufficient for me.

"Having thus arranged my dwelling, and carpeted it with clean straw, I retired; for I saw the figure of a man at a distance, and I remembered too well my treatment the night before, to trust myself in his power. I had first, however, provided for my sustenance for that day, by a loaf of coarse bread, which I purloined, and a cup with which I could drink, more conveniently than from my hand, of the pure water which flowed by my retreat. The floor was a little raised, so that it was kept perfectly dry, and by its vicinity to the chimney of the cottage it was tolerably warm.

"Being thus provided, I resolved to reside in this hovel, until something should occur which might alter my determination. It was indeed a paradise, compared to the bleak forest, my former residence, the rain-dropping branches, and dank earth. I ate my breakfast with pleasure, and was about to remove a plank to procure myself a little water, when I heard a step, and looking through a small chink, I beheld a young creature, with a pail on her head, passing before my hovel. The girl was young, and of gentle demeanour, unlike what I have since found cottagers and farm-house servants to be. Yet she was meanly dressed, a coarse blue petticoat and a linen jacket being her only garb; her fair hair was plaited, but not adorned: she looked patient, yet sad. I lost sight of her; and in about a quarter of an hour she returned, bearing the pail, which was now partly filled with milk. As she walked along, seemingly incommoded by the burden, a young man met her, whose countenance expressed a deeper despondence. Uttering a few sounds with an air of melancholy, he took the pail from her head, and bore it to the cottage himself. She followed, and they disappeared. Presently I saw the young man again, with some tools in his hand, cross the field behind the cottage; and the girl was also busied, sometimes in the house, and sometimes in the yard.

"On examining my dwelling, I found that one of the windows of the cottage had formerly occupied a part of it, but the panes had been filled up with wood. In one of these was a small and almost imperceptible chink, through which the eye could just penetrate. Through this crevice a small room was visible, whitewashed and clean, but very bare of furniture. In one corner, near a small fire, sat an old man, leaning his head on his hands in a disconsolate attitude. The young girl was occupied in arranging the cottage; but presently she took something out of a drawer, which employed her hands, and she sat down beside the old man, who, taking up an instrument, began to play, and to produce sounds sweeter than the voice of the thrush or the nightingale. It was a lovely sight, even to me, poor wretch! who had never beheld aught beautiful before. The silver hair and benevolent countenance of the aged cottager won my reverence, while the gentle manners of the girl enticed my love. He played a sweet mournful air, which I perceived drew tears from the eyes of his amiable companion, of which the old man took no notice, until she sobbed audibly; he then pronounced a few sounds, and the fair creature, leaving her work, knelt at his feet. He

raised her, and smiled with such kindness and affection, that I felt sensations of a peculiar and overpowering nature: they were a mixture of
pain and pleasure, such as I had never before experienced, either from
hunger or cold, warmth or food; and I withdrew from the window,
unable to bear these emotions.

"Soon after this the young man returned, bearing on his shoulders
a load of wood. The girl met him at the door, helped to relieve him of
his burden, and, taking some of the fuel into the cottage, placed it on
the fire; then she and the youth went apart into a nook of the cottage,
and he showed her a large loaf and a piece of cheese. She seemed
pleased, and went into the garden for some roots and plants, which she
placed in water, and then upon the fire. She afterwards continued her
work, whilst the young man went into the garden, and appeared busily
employed in digging and pulling up roots. After he had been employed
thus about an hour, the young woman joined him, and they entered the
cottage together.

"The old man had, in the mean time, been pensive; but, on the
appearance of his companions, he assumed a more cheerful air, and they
sat down to eat. The meal was quickly despatched. The young woman
was again occupied in arranging the cottage; the old man walked before
the cottage in the sun for a few minutes, leaning on the arm of the
youth. Nothing could exceed in beauty the contrast between these
two excellent creatures. One was old, with silver hairs and a countenance beaming with benevolence and love: the younger was slight and
graceful in his figure, and his features were moulded with the finest
symmetry; yet his eyes and attitude expressed the utmost sadness and
despondency. The old man returned to the cottage; and the youth, with
tools different from those he had used in the morning, directed his
steps across the fields.

"Night quickly shut in; but, to my extreme wonder, I found that
the cottagers had a means of prolonging light by the use of tapers, and
was delighted to find that the setting of the sun did not put an end to
the pleasure I experienced in watching my human neighbours. In the
evening, the young girl and her companion were employed in various
occupations which I did not understand; and the old man again took
up the instrument which produced the divine sounds that had enchanted
me in the morning. So soon as he had finished, the youth began, not to
play, but to utter sounds that were monotonous, and neither resembling the harmony of the old man's instrument nor the songs of the
birds: I since found that he read aloud, but at that time I knew nothing
of the science of words or letters.

"The family, after having been thus occupied for a short time, extinguished their lights, and retired, as I conjectured, to rest.

## CHAPTER XII

"I lay on my straw, but I could not sleep. I thought of the occurrences of the day. What chiefly struck me was the gentle manners of these people; and I longed to join them, but dared not. I remembered too well the treatment I had suffered the night before from the barbarous villagers, and resolved, whatever course of conduct I might hereafter think it right to pursue, that for the present I would remain quietly in my hovel, watching, and endeavouring to discover the motives which influenced their actions.

"The cottagers arose the next morning before the sun. The young woman arranged the cottage, and prepared the food; and the youth departed after the first meal.

"This day was passed in the same routine as that which preceded it. The young man was constantly employed out of doors, and the girl in various laborious occupations within. The old man, whom I soon perceived to be blind, employed his leisure hours on his instrument or in (contemplation.) Nothing could exceed the love and respect which the younger cottagers exhibited towards their venerable companion. They performed towards him every little office of affection and duty with gentleness; and he rewarded them by his benevolent smiles.

"They were not entirely happy. The young man and his companion often went apart, and appeared to weep. I saw no cause for their unhappiness; but I was deeply affected by it. (If such lovely creatures were miserable, it was less strange that I, an imperfect and solitary being, should be wretched.) Yet why were these gentle beings unhappy? They possessed a delightful house (for such it was in my eyes) and every luxury; they had a fire to warm them when chill, and delicious viands when hungry; they were dressed in excellent clothes; and, (still more, they enjoyed one another's company and speech, interchanging each day looks of affection and kindness.) What did their tears imply? Did they really express pain? I was at first unable to solve these questions; but perpetual attention and time explained to me many appearances which were at first enigmatic.

"A considerable period elapsed before I discovered one of the causes of the uneasiness of this amiable family: it was poverty; and they suffered that evil in a very distressing degree. Their nourishment

consisted entirely of the vegetables of their garden, and the milk of one
cow, which gave very little during the winter, when its masters could
scarcely procure food to support it. They often, I believe, suffered the
pangs of hunger very poignantly, especially the two younger cottagers;
for several times they placed food before the old man, when they
reserved none for themselves.

"This trait of kindness moved me sensibly. I had been accustomed,
during the night, to steal a part of their store for my own consumption;
but when I found that in doing this I inflicted pain on the cottagers, I
abstained, and satisfied myself with berries, nuts, and roots, which I
gathered from a neighbouring wood.

"I discovered also another means through which I was enabled to
assist their labours. I found that the youth spent a great part of each day
in collecting wood for the family fire; and, during the night, I often
took his tools, the use of which I quickly discovered, and brought home
firing sufficient for the consumption of several days.

"I remember, the first time that I did this, the young woman, when
she opened the door in the morning, appeared greatly astonished on
seeing a great pile of wood on the outside. She uttered some words in
a loud voice, and the youth joined her, who also expressed surprise. I
observed, with pleasure, that he did not go to the forest that day, but
spent it in repairing the cottage, and cultivating the garden.

"By degrees I made a discovery of still greater moment. I found
that these people possessed a method of communicating their experience and feelings to one another by articulate sounds. I perceived that
the words they spoke sometimes, produced pleasure or pain, smiles or
sadness, in the minds and countenances of the hearers. This was indeed
a godlike science, and I ardently desired to become acquainted with it.
But I was baffled in every attempt I made for this purpose. Their pronunciation was quick; and the words they uttered, not having any
apparent connection with visible objects, I was unable to discover any
clue by which I could unravel the mystery of their reference. By great
application, however, and after having remained during the space of
several revolutions of the moon in my hovel, I discovered the names
that were given to some of the most familiar objects of discourse; I
learned and applied the words, *fire, milk, bread,* and *wood.* I learned also
the names of the cottagers themselves. The youth and his companion
had each of them several names, but the old man had only one, which
was *father.* The girl was called *sister,* or *Agatha;* and the youth *Felix,
brother,* or *son.* I cannot describe the delight I felt when I learned the

ideas appropriated to each of these sounds, and was able to pronounce them. I distinguished several other words, without being able as yet to understand or apply them; such as *good, dearest, unhappy.*

"I spent the winter in this manner. The gentle manners and beauty of the cottagers greatly endeared them to me: when they were unhappy, I felt depressed; when they rejoiced, I sympathised in their joys. I saw few human beings beside them; and if any other happened to enter the cottage, their harsh manners and rude gait only enhanced to me the superior accomplishments of my friends. The old man, I could perceive, often endeavoured to encourage his children, as sometimes I found that he called them, to cast off their melancholy. He would talk in a cheerful accent, with an expression of goodness that bestowed pleasure even upon me. Agatha listened with respect, her eyes sometimes filled with tears, which she endeavoured to wipe away unperceived; but I generally found that her countenance and tone were more cheerful after having listened to the exhortations of her father. It was not thus with Felix. He was always the saddest of the group; and, even to my unpractised senses, he appeared to have suffered more deeply than his friends. But if his countenance was more sorrowful, his voice was more cheerful than that of his sister, especially when he addressed the old man.

"I could mention innumerable instances, which, although slight, marked the dispositions of these amiable cottagers. In the midst of poverty and want, Felix carried with pleasure to his sister the first little white flower that peeped out from beneath the snowy ground. Early in the morning, before she had risen, he cleared away the snow that obstructed her path to the milk-house, drew water from the well, and brought the wood from the out-house, where, to his perpetual astonishment, he found his store always replenished by an invisible hand. In the day, I believe, he worked sometimes for a neighbouring farmer, because he often went forth, and did not return until dinner, yet brought no wood with him. At other times he worked in the garden; but, as there was little to do in the frosty season, he read to the old man and Agatha.

"This reading had puzzled me extremely at first; but, by degrees, I discovered that he uttered many of the same sounds when he read, as when he talked. I conjectured, therefore, that he found on the paper signs for speech which he understood, and I ardently longed to comprehend these also; but how was that possible, when I did not even understand the sounds for which they stood as signs? I improved, however, sensibly in this science, but not sufficiently to follow up any kind of conversation, although I applied my whole mind to the endeavour: for I easily perceived that, although I eagerly longed to discover myself to the cottagers, I ought not to make the attempt until I had first become master of their language; which knowledge might enable me to make them overlook the deformity of my figure; for with this also the contrast perpetually presented to my eyes had made me acquainted.

("I had admired the perfect forms of my cottagers—their grace, beauty, and delicate complexions: but how was I terrified, when I viewed myself in a transparent pool! At first I started back, unable to believe that it was indeed I who was reflected in the mirror; and when I became fully convinced that I was in reality the monster that I am, I was filled with the bitterest sensations of despondence and mortification. Alas! I did not yet entirely know the fatal effects of this miserable deformity.)

"As the sun became warmer, and the light of day longer, the snow vanished, and I beheld the bare trees and the black earth. From this time Felix was more employed; and the heart-moving indications of impending famine disappeared. Their food, as I afterwards found, was coarse, but it was wholesome; and they procured a sufficiency of it. Several new kinds of plants sprung up in the garden, which they dressed; and these signs of comfort increased daily as the season advanced.

"The old man, leaning on his son, walked each day at noon, when it did not rain, as I found it was called when the heavens poured forth its waters. This frequently took place; but a high wind quickly dried the earth, and the season became far more pleasant than it had been.

"My mode of life in my hovel was uniform. During the morning, I attended the motions of the cottagers; and when they were dispersed in various occupations, I slept: the remainder of the day was spent in observing my friends. When they had retired to rest, if there was any moon, or the night was star-light, I went into the woods, and collected my own food and fuel for the cottage. When I returned, as often as it was necessary, I cleared their path from the snow, and performed those offices that I had seen done by Felix. I afterwards found that these labours, performed by an invisible hand, greatly astonished them; and once or twice I heard them, on these occasions, utter the words *good spirit, wonderful*; but I did not then understand the signification of these terms.

"My thoughts now became more active, and I longed to discover the motives and feelings of these lovely creatures; I was inquisitive to know why Felix appeared so miserable, and Agatha so sad. I thought (foolish wretch!) that it might be in my power to restore happiness to these deserving people. When I slept, or was absent, the forms of the venerable blind father, the gentle Agatha, and the excellent Felix, flitted before me. I looked upon them as superior beings, who would be the arbiters of my future destiny. I formed in my imagination a thousand pictures of presenting myself to them, and their reception of me. I imagined that they would be disgusted, until, by my gentle demeanour and conciliating words, I should first win their favour, and afterwards their love.

"These thoughts exhilarated me, and led me to apply with fresh ardour to the acquiring the art of language. My organs were indeed harsh, but supple; and although my voice was very unlike the soft music of their tones, yet I pronounced such words as I understood with tolerable ease. It was as the ass and the lap-dog;° yet surely the gentle ass whose intentions were affectionate, although his manners were rude, deserved better treatment than blows and execration.

"The pleasant showers and genial warmth of spring greatly altered the aspect of the earth. Men, who before this change seemed to have been hid in caves, dispersed themselves, and were employed in various arts of cultivation. The birds sang in more cheerful notes, and the leaves began to bud forth on the trees. Happy, happy earth! fit habitation for gods, which, so short a time before, was bleak, damp, and unwholesome. My spirits were elevated by the enchanting appearance of nature; the past was blotted from my memory, the present was tranquil, and the future gilded by bright rays of hope, and anticipations of joy. )

*likes nature*

### CHAPTER XIII

"I now hasten to the more moving part of my story. I shall relate events, that impressed me with feelings which, (from what I had been, have made me what I am.) *transformation*

"Spring advanced rapidly; the weather became fine, and the skies cloudless. It surprised me, that what before was desert and gloomy should now bloom with the most beautiful flowers and verdure. My senses were gratified and refreshed by a thousand scents of delight, and a thousand sights of beauty.

---

*the ass and the lap-dog:* In the *Fables* (IV, 5) of Jean de La Fontaine (1621–1695), the ass fawns on the dog's master, hoping to be rewarded with petting as the dog is; instead, he receives a beating.

"It was on one of these days, when my cottagers periodically rested from labour—the old man played on his guitar, and the children listened to him—that I observed the countenance of Felix was melancholy beyond expression; he sighed frequently; and once his father paused in his music, and I conjectured by his manner that he enquired the cause of his son's sorrow. Felix replied in a cheerful accent, and the old man was recommencing his music, when some one tapped at the door.

"It was a lady on horseback, accompanied by a countryman as a guide. The lady was dressed in a dark suit, and covered with a thick black veil. Agatha asked a question; to which the stranger only replied by pronouncing, in a sweet accent, the name of Felix. Her voice was musical, but unlike that of either of my friends. On hearing this word, Felix came up hastily to the lady; who, when she saw him, threw up her veil, and I beheld a countenance of angelic beauty and expression. Her hair of a shining raven black, and curiously braided; her eyes were dark, but gentle, although animated; her features of a regular proportion, and her complexion wondrously fair, each cheek tinged with a lovely pink.

"Felix seemed ravished with delight when he saw her, every trait of sorrow vanished from his face, and it instantly expressed a degree of ecstatic joy, of which I could hardly have believed it capable; his eyes sparkled, as his cheek flushed with pleasure; and at that moment I thought him as beautiful as the stranger. She appeared affected by different feelings; wiping a few tears from her lovely eyes, she held out her hand to Felix, who kissed it rapturously, and called her, as well as I could distinguish, his sweet Arabian. She did not appear to understand him, but smiled. He assisted her to dismount, and dismissing her guide, conducted her into the cottage. Some conversation took place between him and his father; and the young stranger knelt at the old man's feet, and would have kissed his hand, but he raised her, and embraced her affectionately.

"I soon perceived, that although the stranger uttered articulate sounds, and appeared to have a language of her own, she was neither understood by, nor herself understood, the cottagers. They made many signs which I did not comprehend; but I saw that her presence diffused gladness through the cottage, dispelling their sorrow as the sun dissipates the morning mists. Felix seemed peculiarly happy, and with smiles of delight welcomed his Arabian. Agatha, the ever-gentle Agatha, kissed the hands of the lovely stranger; and, pointing to her brother, made signs which appeared to me to mean that he had been sorrowful until she came. Some hours passed thus, while they, by their countenances, expressed joy, the cause of which I did not comprehend. Presently I found, by the frequent recurrence of some sound which the stranger repeated after them, that she was endeavouring to learn their language; and the idea instantly occurred to me, that I should make use of the same instructions to the same end. The stranger learned about twenty words at the first lesson, most of them, indeed, were those which I had before understood, but I profited by the others.

"As night came on, Agatha and the Arabian retired early. When they separated, Felix kissed the hand of the stranger, and said, 'Good night, sweet Safie.' He sat up much longer, conversing with his father; and, by the frequent repetition of her name, I conjectured that their lovely guest was the subject of their conversation. I ardently desired to understand them, and bent every faculty towards that purpose, but found it utterly impossible.

"The next morning Felix went out to his work; and, after the usual occupations of Agatha were finished, the Arabian sat at the feet of the old man, and, taking his guitar, played some airs so entrancingly beautiful, that they at once drew tears of sorrow and delight from my eyes. She sang, and her voice flowed in a rich cadence, swelling or dying away, like a nightingale of the woods.

"When she had finished, she gave the guitar to Agatha, who at first declined it. She played a simple air, and her voice accompanied it in sweet accents, but unlike the wondrous strain of the stranger. The old man appeared enraptured, and said some words, which Agatha endeavoured to explain to Safie, and by which he appeared to wish to express that she bestowed on him the greatest delight by her music.

"The days now passed as peaceably as before, with the sole alteration, that joy had taken place of sadness in the countenances of my friends. Safie was always gay and happy; she and I improved rapidly in the knowledge of language, so that in two months I began to comprehend most of the words uttered by my protectors.

"In the meanwhile also the black ground was covered with herbage, and the green banks interspersed with innumerable flowers, sweet to the scent and the eyes, stars of pale radiance among the moonlight woods; the sun became warmer, the nights clear and balmy; and my nocturnal rambles were an extreme pleasure to me, although they were considerably shortened by the late setting and early rising of the sun; for I never ventured abroad during daylight, fearful of meeting with the same treatment I had formerly endured in the first village which I entered.

"My days were spent in close attention, that I might more speedily master the language; and I may boast that I improved more rapidly than the Arabian, who understood very little, and conversed in broken accents, whilst I comprehended and could imitate almost every word that was spoken.

"While I improved in speech, I also learned the science of letters, as it was taught to the stranger; and this opened before me a wide field for wonder and delight.

"The book from which Felix instructed Safie was Volney's 'Ruins of Empires.'° I should not have understood the purport of this book, had not Felix, in reading it, given very minute explanations. He had chosen this work, he said, because the declamatory style was framed in imitation of the eastern authors. Through this work I obtained a cursory knowledge of history, and a view of the several empires at present existing in the world; it gave me an insight into the manners, governments, and religions of the different nations of the earth. I heard of the slothful Asiatics; of the stupendous genius and mental activity of the Grecians; of the wars and wonderful virtue of the early Romans—of their subsequent degenerating—of the decline of that mighty empire; of chivalry, Christianity, and kings. I heard of the discovery of the American hemisphere, and wept with Safie over the hapless fate of its original inhabitants.

"These wonderful narrations inspired me with strange feelings. Was man, indeed, at once so powerful, so virtuous, and magnificent, yet so vicious and base? He appeared at one time a mere scion of the evil principle, and at another, as all that can be conceived of noble and godlike. To be a great and virtuous man appeared the highest honour that can befall a sensitive being; to be base and vicious, as many on record have been, appeared the lowest degradation, a condition more abject than that of the blind mole or harmless worm. For a long time I could not conceive how one man could go forth to murder his fellow, or even why there were laws and governments; but when I heard details of vice and bloodshed, my wonder ceased, and I turned away with disgust and loathing.

"Every conversation of the cottagers now opened new wonders to me. While I listened to the instructions which Felix bestowed upon the

---

*Volney's 'Ruins of Empires': Les Ruines, ou Meditations sur les Revolutions des Empires* (1791) by Constantin Francois Chasseboeuf, comte de Volney (1757–1820), was an essay on the philosophy of history.

Arabian, the strange system of human society was explained to me. I heard of the division of property, of immense wealth and squalid poverty; of rank, descent, and noble blood.

"The words induced me to turn towards myself. I learned that (the possessions most esteemed by your fellow-creatures were high and unsullied descent united with riches) A man might be respected with only one of these advantages; but, without either, he was considered, except in very rare instances, as a vagabond and a slave, doomed to waste his powers for the profits of the chosen few! And what was I? Of my creation and creator I was absolutely ignorant; but I knew that I possessed no money, no friends, no kind of property. I was, besides, endued with a figure hideously deformed and loathsome; I was not even of the same nature as man. (I was more agile than they, and could subsist upon coarser diet; I bore the extremes of heat and cold with less injury to my frame; my stature far exceeded theirs. When I looked around, I saw and heard of none like me. Was I then a monster, a blot upon the earth, from which all men fled, and whom all men disowned?)

"I cannot describe to you the agony that these reflections inflicted upon me: I tried to dispel them, but sorrow only increased with knowledge. Oh, that I had for ever remained in my native wood, nor known nor felt beyond the sensations of hunger, thirst, and heat!

"Of what a strange nature is knowledge! It clings to the mind, when it has once seized on it, like a lichen on the rock. I wished sometimes to shake off all thought and feeling; but (I learned that there was but one means to overcome the sensation of pain, and that was death)—a state which I feared yet did not understand. I admired virtue and good feelings, and loved the gentle manners and amiable qualities of my cottagers; but I was shut out from intercourse with them, except through means which I obtained by stealth, when I was unseen and unknown, and which rather increased than satisfied the desire I had of becoming one among my fellows. The gentle words of Agatha, and the animated smiles of the charming Arabian, were not for me. The mild exhortations of the old man, and the lively conversation of the loved Felix, were not for me. Miserable, unhappy wretch!

"Other lessons were impressed upon me even more deeply. I heard of the difference of sexes; and the birth and growth of children; how the father doted on the smiles of the infant, and the lively sallies of the older child; how all the life and cares of the mother were wrapped up in the precious charge; how the mind of youth expanded and gained knowledge; of brother, sister, and all the various relationships which bind one human being to another in mutual bonds.

"But where were my friends and relations? No father had watched my infant days, no mother had blessed me with smiles and caresses; or if they had, all my past life was now a blot, a blind vacancy in which I distinguished nothing. From my earliest remembrance I had been as I then was in height and proportion. I had never yet seen a being resembling me, or who claimed any intercourse with me. What was I? The question again recurred, to be answered only with groans.

"I will soon explain to what these feelings tended; but allow me now to return to the cottagers, whose story excited in me such various feelings of indignation, delight, and wonder, but which all terminated in additional love and reverence for my protectors (for so I loved, in an innocent, half painful self-deceit, to call them).

## CHAPTER XIV

"Some time elapsed before I learned the history of my friends. It was one which could not fail to impress itself deeply on my mind, unfolding as it did a number of circumstances, each interesting and wonderful to one so utterly inexperienced as I was.

"The name of the old man was De Lacey. He was descended from a good family in France, where he had lived for many years in affluence, respected by his superiors, and beloved by his equals. His son was bred in the service of his country; and Agatha had ranked with ladies of the highest distinction. A few months before my arrival, they had lived in a large and luxurious city, called Paris, surrounded by friends, and possessed of every enjoyment which virtue, refinement of intellect, or taste, accompanied by a moderate fortune, could afford.

"The father of Safie had been the cause of their ruin. He was a Turkish merchant, and had inhabited Paris for many years, when, for some reason which I could not learn, he became obnoxious to the government. He was seized and cast into prison the very day that Safie arrived from Constantinople to join him. He was tried, and condemned to death. The injustice of his sentence was very flagrant; all Paris was indignant; and it was judged that his religion and wealth, rather than the crime alleged against him, had been the cause of his condemnation.

"Felix had accidentally been present at the trial; his horror and indignation were uncontrollable, when he heard the decision of the court. He made, at that moment, a solemn vow to deliver him, and then looked around for the means. After many fruitless attempts to gain admittance to the prison, he found a strongly grated window in an unguarded part of the building, which lighted the dungeon of the unfortunate Mahometan;° who, loaded with chains, waited in despair the execution of the barbarous sentence. Felix visited the grate at night, and made known to the prisoner his intentions in his favour. The Turk, amazed and delighted, endeavoured to kindle the zeal of his deliverer by promises of reward and wealth. Felix rejected his offers with contempt; yet when he saw the lovely Safie, who was allowed to visit her father, and who, by her gestures, expressed her lively gratitude, the youth could not help owning to his own mind, that the captive possessed a treasure which would fully reward his toil and hazard.

"The Turk quickly perceived the impression that his daughter had made on the heart of Felix, and endeavoured to secure him more entirely in his interests by the promise of her hand in marriage, so soon as he should be conveyed to a place of safety. Felix was too delicate to accept this offer; yet he looked forward to the probability of the event as to the consummation of his happiness.

"During the ensuing days, while the preparations were going forward for the escape of the merchant, the zeal of Felix was warmed by several letters that he received from this lovely girl, who found means to express her thoughts in the language of her lover by the aid of an old man, a servant of her father, who understood French. She thanked him in the most ardent terms for his intended services towards her parent; and at the same time she gently deplored her own fate.

"I have copies of these letters; for I found means, during my residence in the hovel, to procure the implements of writing; and the letters were often in the hands of Felix or Agatha. Before I depart, I will give them to you, they will prove the truth of my tale; but at present, as the sun is already far declined, I shall only have time to repeat the substance of them to you.

"Safie related, that her mother was a Christian Arab, seized and made a slave by the Turks; recommended by her beauty, she had won the heart of the father of Safie, who married her. The young girl spoke in high and enthusiastic terms of her mother, who, born in freedom, spurned the bondage to which she was now reduced. She instructed her daughter in the tenets of her religion, and taught her to aspire to higher powers of intellect, and an independence of spirit, forbidden to the female followers of Mahomet. This lady died; but her lessons were indelibly impressed on the mind of Safie, who sickened at the prospect of again returning to Asia, and being immured within the walls of a

*Mahometan:* A follower of the prophet Muhammad.

haram,° allowed only to occupy herself with infantile amusements, ill
suited to the temper of her soul, now accustomed to grand ideas and a
noble emulation for virtue. The prospect of marrying a Christian, and
remaining in a country where women were allowed to take a rank in
society, was enchanting to her.

"The day for the execution of the Turk was fixed; but, on the night
previous to it, he quitted his prison, and before morning was distant
many leagues from Paris. Felix had procured passports in the name of
his father, sister, and himself. He had previously communicated his plan
to the former, who aided the deceit by quitting his house, under the
pretence of a journey, and concealed himself, with his daughter, in an
obscure part of Paris.

"Felix conducted the fugitives through France to Lyons, and
across Mont Cenis to Leghorn, where the merchant had decided to
wait a favourable opportunity of passing into some part of the Turkish
dominions.

"Safie resolved to remain with her father until the moment of his
departure, before which time the Turk renewed his promise that she
should be united to his deliverer; and Felix remained with them in
expectation of that event; and in the mean time he enjoyed the society
of the Arabian, who exhibited towards him the simplest and tenderest
affection. They conversed with one another through the means of an
interpreter, and sometimes with the interpretation of looks; and Safie
sang to him the divine airs of her native country.

"The Turk allowed this intimacy to take place, and encouraged the
hopes of the youthful lovers, while in his heart he had formed far other
plans. He loathed the idea that his daughter should be united to a
Christian; but he feared the resentment of Felix, if he should appear
lukewarm; for he knew that he was still in the power of his deliverer, if
he should choose to betray him to the Italian state which they inhabited. He revolved a thousand plans by which he should be enabled to
prolong the deceit until it might be no longer necessary, and secretly to
take his daughter with him when he departed. His plans were facilitated
by the news which arrived from Paris.

"The government of France were greatly enraged at the escape of
their victim, and spared no pains to detect and punish his deliverer. The
plot of Felix was quickly discovered, and De Lacey and Agatha were
thrown into prison. The news reached Felix, and roused him from his
dream of pleasure. His blind and aged father, and his gentle sister, lay

_____

*haram:* Variant spelling of harem.

in a noisome dungeon, while he enjoyed the free air, and the society of her whom he loved. This idea was torture to him. He quickly arranged with the Turk, that if the latter should find a favourable opportunity for escape before Felix could return to Italy, Safie should remain as a boarder at a convent at Leghorn; and then, quitting the lovely Arabian, he hastened to Paris, and delivered himself up to the vengeance of the law, hoping to free De Lacey and Agatha by this proceeding.

"He did not succeed. They remained confined for five months before the trial took place; the result of which deprived them of their fortune, and condemned them to a perpetual exile from their native country.

"They found a miserable asylum in the cottage in Germany, where I discovered them. Felix soon learned that the treacherous Turk, for whom he and his family endured such unheard-of oppression, on discovering that his deliverer was thus reduced to poverty and ruin, became a traitor to good feeling and honour, and had quitted Italy with his daughter, insultingly sending Felix a pittance of money, to aid him, as he said, in some plan of future maintenance.

"Such were the events that preyed on the heart of Felix, and rendered him, when I first saw him, the most miserable of his family. He could have endured poverty; and while this distress had been the meed of his virtue, he gloried in it: but the ingratitude of the Turk, and the loss of his beloved Safie, were misfortunes more bitter and irreparable. The arrival of the Arabian now infused new life into his soul.

"When the news reached Leghorn, that Felix was deprived of his wealth and rank, the merchant commanded his daughter to think no more of her lover, but to prepare to return to her native country. The generous nature of Safie was outraged by this command; she attempted to expostulate with her father, but he left her angrily, reiterating his tyrannical mandate.

"A few days after, the Turk entered his daughter's apartment, and told her hastily, that he had reason to believe that his residence at Leghorn had been divulged, and that he should speedily be delivered up to the French government; he had, consequently, hired a vessel to convey him to Constantinople, for which city he should sail in a few hours. He intended to leave his daughter under the care of a confidential servant, to follow at her leisure with the greater part of his property, which had not yet arrived at Leghorn.

"When alone, Safie resolved in her own mind the plan of conduct that it would become her to pursue in this emergency. A residence in Turkey was abhorrent to her; her religion and her feelings were alike adverse to it. By some papers of her father, which fell into her hands, she heard of the exile of her lover, and learnt the name of the spot where he then resided. She hesitated some time, but at length she formed her determination. Taking with her some jewels that belonged to her, and a sum of money, she quitted Italy with an attendant, a native of Leghorn, but who understood the common language of Turkey, and departed for Germany.

"She arrived in safety at a town about twenty leagues from the cottage of De Lacey, when her attendant fell dangerously ill. Safie nursed her with the most devoted affection; but the poor girl died, and the Arabian was left alone, unacquainted with the language of the country, and utterly ignorant of the customs of the world. She fell, however, into good hands. The Italian had mentioned the name of the spot for which they were bound; and, after her death, the woman of the house in which they had lived took care that Safie should arrive in safety at the cottage of her lover.

## CHAPTER XV

"Such was the history of my beloved cottagers. It impressed me deeply. I learned, from the views of social life which it developed, to admire their virtues, and to deprecate the vices of mankind.

"As yet I looked upon crime as a distant evil; benevolence and generosity were ever present before me, inciting within me a desire to become an actor in the busy scene where so many admirable qualities were called forth and displayed. But, in giving an account of the progress of my intellect, I must not omit a circumstance which occurred in the beginning of the month of August of the same year.

"One night, during my accustomed visit to the neighbouring wood, where I collected my own food, and brought home firing for my protectors, I found on the ground a leathern portmanteau, containing several articles of dress and some books. I eagerly seized the prize, and returned with it to my hovel. Fortunately the books were written in the language, the elements of which I had acquired at the cottage; they consisted of 'Paradise Lost,' a volume of 'Plutarch's Lives,' and the 'Sorrows of Werter.'° The possession of these treasures gave me extreme delight; I

*Plutarch's Lives'. . .'Sorrows of Werter':* Plutarch (c. 46–119), a Greek biographer; *The Sorrows of Young Werther* (1774) by Johann Wolfgang von Goethe (1749–1832), a tragic novel about a romantic young artist.

now continually studied and exercised my mind upon these histories, whilst my friends were employed in their ordinary occupations.

"I can hardly describe to you the effect of these books. They produced in me an infinity of new images and feelings, that sometimes raised me to ecstasy, but more frequently sunk me into the lowest dejection. In the 'Sorrows of Werter,' besides the interest of its simple and affecting story, so many opinions are canvassed, and so many lights thrown upon what had hitherto been to me obscure subjects, that I found in it a never-ending source of speculation and astonishment. The gentle and domestic manners it described, combined with lofty sentiments and feelings, which had for their object something out of self, accorded well with my experience among my protectors, and with the wants which were for ever alive in my own bosom. But I thought Werter himself a more divine being than I had ever beheld or imagined; his character contained no pretension, but it sunk deep. The disquisitions upon death and suicide were calculated to fill me with wonder. I did not pretend to enter into the merits of the case, yet I inclined towards the opinions of the hero, whose extinction I wept, without precisely understanding it.

"As I read, however, I applied much personally to my own feelings and condition. I found myself similar, yet at the same time strangely unlike to the beings concerning whom I read, and to whose conversation I was a listener. I sympathised with, and partly understood them, but I was unformed in mind; I was dependent on none, and related to none. 'The path of my departure was free;'° and there was none to lament my annihilation. My person was hideous, and my stature gigantic: what did this mean? Who was I? What was I? Whence did I come? What was my destination? These questions continually recurred, but I was unable to solve them.

"The volume of 'Plutarch's Lives,' which I possessed, contained the histories of the first founders of the ancient republics. This book had a far different effect upon me from the 'Sorrows of Werter.' I learned from Werter's imaginations despondency and gloom: but Plutarch taught me high thoughts; he elevated me above the wretched sphere of my own reflections, to admire and love the heroes of past ages. Many things I read surpassed my understanding and experience. I had a very

---

'*The path of my departure was free*': Reference to Percy Shelley's "Mutability" (line 14): "The path of its departure still is free."

confused knowledge of kingdoms, wide extents of country, mighty rivers, and boundless seas. But I was perfectly unacquainted with towns, and large assemblages of men. The cottage of my protectors had been the only school in which I had studied human nature; but this book developed new and mightier scenes of action. I read of men concerned in public affairs, governing or massacring their species. I felt the greatest ardour for virtue rise within me, and abhorrence for vice, as far as I understood the significance of those terms, relative as they were, as I applied them, to pleasure and pain alone. Induced by these feelings, I was of course led to admire peaceable lawgivers, Numa, Solon, and Lycurgus, in preference to Romulus and Theseus. The patriarchal lives of my protectors caused these impressions to take a firm hold on my mind; perhaps, if my first introduction to humanity had been made by a young soldier, burning for glory and slaughter, I should have been imbued with different sensations.

"But 'Paradise Lost' excited different and far deeper emotions. I read it, as I had read the other volumes which had fallen into my hands, as a true history. It moved every feeling of wonder and awe, that the picture of an omnipotent God warring with his creatures was capable of exciting. I often referred the several situations, as their similarity struck me, to my own. Like Adam, I was apparently united by no link to any other being in existence; but his state was far different from mine in every other respect. He had come forth from the hands of God a perfect creature, happy and prosperous, guarded by the especial care of his Creator; he was allowed to converse with, and acquire knowledge from, beings of a superior nature: but I was wretched, helpless, and alone. Many times I considered Satan as the fitter emblem of my condition; for often, like him, when I viewed the bliss of my protectors, the bitter gall of envy rose within me.) *Envious, like SATAN*

"Another circumstance strengthened and confirmed these feelings. Soon after my arrival in the hovel, I discovered some papers in the pocket of the dress which I had taken from your laboratory. At first I had neglected them; but now that I was able to decipher the characters in which they were written, I began to study them with diligence. It was your journal of the four months that preceded my creation. You minutely described in these papers every step you took in the progress of your work; this history was mingled with accounts of domestic occurrences. You, doubtless, recollect these papers. Here they are. Every thing is related in them which bears reference to my accursed origin; the whole detail of that series of disgusting circumstances which produced it, is set in view; the minutest description of my odious and loathsome person is given, in language which painted your own horrors, and rendered mine indelible. I sickened as I read. ('Hateful day when I received life!' I exclaimed in agony. 'Accursed creator! Why did you form a monster so hideous that even *you* turned from me in disgust? God, in pity, made man beautiful and alluring, after his own image; but my form is a filthy type of yours, more horrid even from the very resemblance. Satan had his companions, fellow-devils, to admire and encourage him; but I am solitary and abhorred.)

"These were the reflections of my hours of despondency and solitude; but when I contemplated the virtues of the cottagers, their amiable and benevolent dispositions, I persuaded myself that when they should become acquainted with my admiration of their virtues, they would compassionate me, and overlook my personal deformity. Could they turn from their door one, however monstrous, who solicited their compassion and friendship? I resolved, at least, not to despair, but in every way to fit myself for an interview with them which would decide my fate. I postponed this attempt for some months longer; for the importance attached to its success inspired me with a dread lest I should fail. Besides, I found that my understanding improved so much with every day's experience, that I was unwilling to commence this undertaking until a few more months should have added to my sagacity.

"Several changes, in the mean time, took place in the cottage. The presence of Safie diffused happiness among its inhabitants; and I also found that a greater degree of plenty reigned there. Felix and Agatha spent more time in amusement and conversation, and were assisted in their labours by servants. They did not appear rich, but they were contented and happy; their feelings were serene and peaceful, (while mine became every day more tumultuous) Increase of knowledge only discovered to me more clearly what a wretched outcast I was. I cherished hope, it is true; but it vanished, when I beheld my person reflected in water, or my shadow in the moonshine, even as that frail image and that inconstant shade.

"I endeavoured to crush these fears, and to fortify myself for the trial which in a few months I resolved to undergo; and some times I allowed my thoughts, underlined by reason, to ramble in the fields of Paradise, and dared to fancy amiable and lovely creatures sympathising with my feelings, and cheering my gloom; their angelic countenances breathed smiles of consolation. (But it was all a dream; no Eve soothed my sorrows, nor shared my thoughts; I was alone.) I remembered

Adam's supplication° to his Creator. But where was mine? He had abandoned me; and, in the bitterness of my heart, I cursed him.

"Autumn passed thus. I saw, with surprise and grief, the leaves decay and fall, and nature again assume the barren and bleak appearance it had worn when I first beheld the woods and the lovely moon. Yet I did not heed the bleakness of the weather; I was better fitted by my conformation for the endurance of cold than heat. But my chief delights were the sight of the flowers, the birds, and all the gay apparel of summer; when those deserted me, I turned with more attention towards the cottagers. Their happiness was not decreased by the absence of summer. They loved, and sympathised with one another; and their joys, depending on each other, were not interrupted by the casualties that took place around them. The more I saw of them, the greater became my desire to claim their protection and kindness; my heart yearned to be known and loved by these amiable creatures: to see their sweet looks directed towards me with affection, was the utmost limit of my ambition. I dared not think that they would turn them from me with disdain and horror. The poor that stopped at their door were never driven away. I asked, it is true, for greater treasures than a little food or rest: I required kindness and sympathy; but I did not believe myself utterly unworthy of it.

"The winter advanced, and an entire revolution of the seasons had taken place since I awoke into life. My attention, at this time, was solely directed towards my plan of introducing myself into the cottage of my protectors. I revolved many projects; but that on which I finally fixed was, to enter the dwelling when the blind old man should be alone. I had sagacity enough to discover, that the unnatural hideousness of my person was the chief object of horror with those who had formerly beheld me. My voice, although harsh, had nothing terrible in it. I thought, therefore, that if, in the absence of his children, I could gain the goodwill and mediation of the old De Lacey, I might, by his means, be tolerated by my younger protectors.

"One day, when the sun shone on the red leaves that strewed the ground, and diffused cheerfulness, although it denied warmth, Safie, Agatha, and Felix departed on a long country walk, and the old man, at his own desire, was left alone in the cottage. When his children had departed, he took up his guitar, and played several mournful but sweet airs, more sweet and mournful than I had ever heard him play before.

---

**Adam's supplication:** In Book VIII, lines 377–97, of Milton's *Paradise Lost*, Adam requests a human companion.

At first his countenance was illuminated with pleasure, but, as he continued, thoughtfulness and sadness succeeded; at length, laying aside the instrument, he sat absorbed in reflection.

"My heart beat quick; this was the hour and moment of trial, which would decide my hopes, or realise my fears. The servants were gone to a neighbouring fair. All was silent in and around the cottage: it was an excellent opportunity; yet, when I proceeded to execute my plan, my limbs failed me, and I sank to the ground. Again I rose; and, exerting all the firmness of which I was master, removed the planks which I had placed before my hovel to conceal my retreat. The fresh air revived me, and, with renewed determination, I approached the door of their cottage.

"I knocked. 'Who is there?' said the old man—'Come in.'

"I entered; 'Pardon this intrusion,' said I: 'I am a traveller in want of a little rest; you would greatly oblige me, if you would allow me to remain a few minutes before the fire.'

" 'Enter,' said De Lacey; 'and I will try in what manner I can relieve your wants; but, unfortunately, my children are from home, and, as I am blind, I am afraid I shall find it difficult to procure food for you.'

" 'Do not trouble yourself, my kind host, I have food; it is warmth and rest only that I need.'

"I sat down, and a silence ensued. I knew that every minute was precious to me, yet I remained irresolute in what manner to commence the interview; when the old man addressed me—

" 'By your language, stranger, I suppose you are my countryman;—are you French?'

" 'No; but I was educated by a French family, and understand that language only. I am now going to claim the protection of some friends, whom I sincerely love, and of whose favour I have some hopes.'

" 'Are they Germans?'

" 'No, they are French. But let us change the subject. I am an unfortunate and deserted creature; I look around, and I have no relation or friend upon earth. These amiable people to whom I go have never seen me, and know little of me. I am full of fears; for if I fail there, I am an outcast in the world for ever.'

" 'Do not despair. To be friendless is indeed to be unfortunate; but the hearts of men, when unprejudiced by any obvious self-interest, are full of brotherly love and charity. Rely, therefore, on your hopes; and if these friends are good and amiable, do not despair.'

" 'They are kind—they are the most excellent creatures in the world; but, unfortunately, they are prejudiced against me. I have good dispositions; my life has been hitherto harmless, and in some degree beneficial; but a fatal prejudice clouds their eyes, and where they ought to see a feeling and kind friend, they behold only a detestable monster.

" 'That is indeed unfortunate; but if you are really blameless, cannot you undeceive them?'

" 'I am about to undertake that task; and it is on that account that I feel so many overwhelming terrors. I tenderly love these friends; I have, unknown to them, been for many months in the habits of daily kindness towards them; but they believe that I wish to injure them, and it is that prejudice which I wish to overcome.'

" 'Where do these friends reside?'

" 'Near this spot.'

"The old man paused, and then continued, 'If you will unreservedly confide to me the particulars of your tale, I perhaps may be of use in undeceiving them. I am blind, and cannot judge of your countenance, but there is something in your words, which persuades me that you are sincere. I am poor, and an exile; but it will afford me true pleasure to be in any way serviceable to a human creature.'

" 'Excellent man! I thank you, and accept your generous offer. You raise me from the dust by this kindness; and I trust that, by your aid, I shall not be driven from the society and sympathy of your fellow-creatures.'

" 'Heaven forbid! even if you were really criminal; for that can only drive you to desperation, and not instigate you to virtue. I also am unfortunate; I and my family have been condemned, although innocent: judge, therefore, if I do not feel for your misfortunes.'

" 'How can I thank you, my best and only benefactor? From your lips first have I heard the voice of kindness directed towards me; I shall be for ever grateful; and your present humanity assures me of success with those friends whom I am on the point of meeting.'

" 'May I know the names and residence of those friends?'

"I paused. This, I thought, was the moment of decision, which was to rob me of, or bestow happiness on me for ever. I struggled vainly for firmness sufficient to answer him, but the effort destroyed all my remaining strength; I sank on the chair, and sobbed aloud. At that moment I heard the steps of my younger protectors. I had not a moment to lose; but, seizing the hand of the old man I cried, 'Now is the time!—save and protect me! You and your family are the friends whom I seek. Do not you desert me in the hour of trial!'

" 'Great God!' exclaimed the old man, 'who are you?'

"At that instant the cottage door was opened, and Felix, Safie, and Agatha entered. Who can describe their horror and consternation on beholding me? Agatha fainted; and Safie, unable to attend to her friend, rushed out of the cottage. Felix darted forward, and with supernatural force tore me from his father, to whose knees I clung: in a transport of fury, he dashed me to the ground, and struck me violently with a stick. I could have torn him limb from limb, as the lion rends the antelope. But my heart sunk within me as with bitter sickness, and I refrained. I saw him on the point of repeating his blow, when, overcome by pain and anguish, I quitted the cottage, and in the general tumult escaped unperceived to my hovel.

*Safie = wisdom*
*Agatha = Good*
*Felix = happiness*

## CHAPTER XVI

"Cursed, cursed creator! Why did I live? Why, in that instant, did I not extinguish the spark of existence which you had so wantonly bestowed? I know not; despair had not yet taken possession of me; my feelings were those of rage and revenge. I could with pleasure have destroyed the cottage and its inhabitants, and have glutted myself with their shrieks and misery.

"When night came, I quitted my retreat, and wandered in the wood; and now, no longer restrained by the fear of discovery, I gave vent to my anguish in fearful howlings. I was like a wild beast that had broken the toils; destroying the objects that obstructed me, and ranging through the wood with a stag-like swiftness. O! what a miserable night I passed! the cold stars shone in mockery, and the bare trees waved their branches above me: now and then the sweet voice of a bird burst forth amidst the universal stillness. All, save I, were at rest or in enjoyment: I, like the arch-fiend, bore a hell within me; and, finding *Satan?* myself unsympathised with, wished to tear up the trees, spread havoc and destruction around me, and then to have sat down and enjoyed the ruin.

"But this was a luxury of sensation that could not endure; I became fatigued with excess of bodily exertion, and sank on the damp grass in the sick impotence of despair. There was none among the myriads of men that existed who would pity or assist me; and should I feel kindness towards my enemies? No: from that moment I declared everlasting war against the species, and, more than all, against him who had formed me, and sent me forth to this insupportable misery.

"The sun rose; I heard the voices of men, and knew that it was impossible to return to my retreat during that day. Accordingly I hid myself in some thick underwood, determining to devote the ensuing hours to reflection on my situation.

"The pleasant sunshine, and the pure air of day, restored me to some degree of tranquillity; and when I considered what had passed at the cottage, I could not help believing that I had been too hasty in my conclusions. I had certainly acted imprudently. It was apparent that my conversation had interested the father in my behalf, and I was a fool in having exposed my person to the horror of his children. I ought to have familiarised the old De Lacey to me, and by degrees to have discovered myself to the rest of his family, when they should have been prepared for my approach. But I did not believe my errors to be irretrievable; and, after much consideration, I resolved to return to the cottage, seek the old man, and by my representations win him to my party.

"These thoughts calmed me, and in the afternoon I sank into a profound sleep; but the fever of my blood did not allow me to be visited by peaceful dreams. The horrible scene of the preceding day was for ever acting before my eyes; the females were flying, and the enraged Felix tearing me from his father's feet. I awoke exhausted; and, finding that it was already night, I crept forth from my hiding-place, and went in search of food.

"When my hunger was appeased, I directed my steps towards the well-known path that conducted to the cottage. All there was at peace. I crept into my hovel, and remained in silent expectation of the accustomed hour when the family arose. That hour passed, the sun mounted high in the heavens, but the cottagers did not appear. I trembled violently, apprehending some dreadful misfortune. The inside of the cottage was dark, and I heard no motion; I cannot describe the agony of this suspense.

"Presently two countrymen passed by; but, pausing near the cottage, they entered into conversation, using violent gesticulations; but I did not understand what they said, as they spoke the language of the country, which differed from that of my protectors. Soon after, however, Felix approached with another man: I was surprised, as I knew that he had not quitted the cottage that morning, and waited anxiously to discover, from his discourse, the meaning of these unusual appearances.

" 'Do you consider,' said his companion to him, 'that you will be obliged to pay three months' rent, and to lose the produce of your garden? I do not wish to take any unfair advantage, and I beg therefore that you will take some days to consider of your determination.'

"'It is utterly useless,' replied Felix; 'we can never again inhabit your cottage. The life of my father is in the greatest danger, owing to the dreadful circumstance that I have related. My wife and my sister will never recover their horror. I entreat you not to reason with me any more. Take possession of your tenement, and let me fly from this place.'

"Felix trembled violently as he said this. He and his companion entered the cottage, in which they remained for a few minutes, and then departed. I never saw any of the family of De Lacey more.

"I continued for the remainder of the day in my hovel in a state of utter and stupid despair. My protectors had departed, and had broken the only link that held me to the world. For the first time the feelings of revenge and hatred filled my bosom, and I did not strive to control them; but, allowing myself to be borne away by the stream, I bent my mind towards injury and death. When I thought of my friends, of the mild voice of De Lacey, the gentle eyes of Agatha, and the exquisite beauty of the Arabian, these thoughts vanished, and a gush of tears somewhat soothed me. But again, when I reflected that they had spurned and deserted me, anger returned, a rage of anger; and, unable to injure any thing human, I turned my fury towards inanimate objects. As night advanced, I placed a variety of combustibles around the cottage; and, after having destroyed every vestige of cultivation in the garden, I waited with forced impatience until the moon had sunk to commence my operations.

"As the night advanced, a fierce wind arose from the woods, and quickly dispersed the clouds that had loitered in the heavens: the blast tore along like a mighty avalanche, and produced a kind of insanity in my spirits, that burst all bounds of reason and reflection. I lighted the dry branch of a tree, and danced with fury around the devoted cottage, my eyes still fixed on the western horizon, the edge of which the moon nearly touched. A part of its orb was at length hid, and I waved my brand; it sunk, and, with a loud scream, I fired the straw, and heath, and bushes, which I had collected. The wind fanned the fire, and the cottage was quickly enveloped by the flames, which clung to it, and licked it with their forked and destroying tongues.

"As soon as I was convinced that no assistance could save any part of the habitation, I quitted the scene, and sought for refuge in the woods.

"And now, with the world before me, whither should I bend my steps? I resolved to fly far from the scene of my misfortunes; but to me, hated and despised, every country must be equally horrible. At length the thought of you crossed my mind. I learned from your papers that you were my father, my creator; and to whom could I apply with more fitness than to him who had given me life? Among the lessons that Felix had bestowed upon Safie, geography had not been omitted: I had learned from these the relative situations of the different countries of the earth. You had mentioned Geneva as the name of your native town; and towards this place I resolved to proceed.

"But how was I to direct myself? I knew that I must travel in a south-westerly direction to reach my destination; but the sun was my only guide. I did not know the names of the towns that I was to pass through, nor could I ask information from a single human being; but I did not despair. From you only could I hope for succour, although towards you I felt no sentiment but that of hatred. Unfeeling, heartless creator! you had endowed me with perceptions and passions, and then cast me abroad an object for the scorn and horror of mankind. But on you only had I any claim for pity and redress, and from you I determined to seek that justice which I vainly attempted to gain from any other being that wore the human form.

"My travels were long, and the sufferings I endured intense. It was late in autumn when I quitted the district where I had so long resided. I travelled only at night, fearful of encountering the visage of a human being. Nature decayed around me, and the sun became heatless; rain and snow poured around me; mighty rivers were frozen; the surface of the earth was hard and chill, and bare, and I found no shelter. Oh, earth! how often did I imprecate curses on the cause of my being! The mildness of my nature had fled, and all within me was turned to gall and bitterness. The nearer I approached to your habitation, the more deeply did I feel the spirit of revenge enkindled in my heart. Snow fell, and the waters were hardened; but I rested not. A few incidents now and then directed me, and I possessed a map of the country; but I often wandered wide from my path. The agony of my feelings allowed me no respite: no incident occurred from which my rage and misery could not extract its food; but a circumstance that happened when I arrived on the confines of Switzerland, when the sun had recovered its warmth, and the earth again began to look green, confirmed in an especial manner the bitterness and horror of my feelings.

"I generally rested during the day, and travelled only when I was secured by night from the view of man. One morning, however, finding that my path lay through a deep wood, I ventured to continue my journey after the sun had risen; the day, which was one of the first of spring, cheered even me by the loveliness of its sunshine and the balminess of the air. I felt emotions of gentleness and pleasure, that had long appeared dead, revive within me. Half surprised by the novelty of these sensations, I allowed myself to be borne away by them; and, forgetting my solitude and deformity, dared to be happy. Soft tears again bedewed my cheeks, and I even raised my humid eyes with thankfulness towards the blessed sun which bestowed such joy upon me.

"I continued to wind among the paths of the wood, until I came to its boundary, which was skirted by a deep and rapid river, into which many of the trees bent their branches, now budding with the fresh spring. Here I paused, not exactly knowing what path to pursue, when I heard the sound of voices, that induced me to conceal myself under the shade of a cypress. I was scarcely hid, when a young girl came running towards the spot where I was concealed, laughing, as if she ran from some one in sport. She continued her course along the precipitous sides of the river, when suddenly her foot slipt, and she fell into the rapid stream. I rushed from my hiding-place; and, with extreme labour from the force of the current, saved her, and dragged her to shore. She was senseless; and I endeavoured, by every means in my power, to restore animation, when I was suddenly interrupted by the approach of a rustic, who was probably the person from whom she had playfully fled. On seeing me, he darted towards me, and tearing the girl from my arms, hastened towards the deeper parts of the wood. I followed speedily, I hardly knew why; but when the man saw me draw near, he aimed a gun, which he carried, at my body, and fired. I sunk to the ground, and my injurer, with increased swiftness, escaped into the wood.

"This was then the reward of my benevolence! I had saved a human being from destruction, and, as a recompense, I now writhed under the miserable pain of a wound, which shattered the flesh and bone. The feelings of kindness and gentleness, which I had entertained but a few moments before, gave place to hellish rage and gnashing of teeth. Inflamed by pain, I vowed eternal hatred and vengeance to all mankind. But the agony of my wound overcame me; my pulses paused, and I fainted.

"For some weeks I led a miserable life in the woods, endeavouring to cure the wound which I had received. The ball had entered my shoulder, and I knew not whether it had remained there or passed through; at any rate I had no means of extracting it. My sufferings were augmented also by the oppressive sense of the injustice and ingratitude of their infliction. My daily vows rose for revenge—a deep and deadly revenge, such as would alone compensate for the outrages and anguish I had endured.

"After some weeks my wound healed, and I continued my journey. The labours I endured were no longer to be alleviated by the bright sun or gentle breezes of spring; all joy was but a mockery, which insulted my desolate state, and made me feel more painfully that I was not made for the enjoyment of pleasure.

"But my toils now drew near a close; and, in two months from this time, I reached the environs of Geneva.

"It was evening when I arrived, and I retired to a hiding-place among the fields that surround it, to meditate in what manner I should apply to you. I was oppressed by fatigue and hunger, and far too unhappy to enjoy the gentle breezes of evening, or the prospect of the sun setting behind the stupendous mountains of Jura.

"At this time a slight sleep relieved me from the pain of reflection, which was disturbed by the approach of a beautiful child, who came running into the recess I had chosen, with all the sportiveness of infancy. Suddenly, as I gazed on him, an idea seized me, that this little creature was unprejudiced, and had lived too short a time to have imbibed a horror of deformity. If, therefore, I could seize him, and educate him as my companion and friend, I should not be so desolate in this peopled earth.

"Urged by this impulse, I seized on the boy as he passed, and drew him towards me. As soon as he beheld my form, he placed his hands before his eyes, and uttered a shrill scream: I drew his hand forcibly from his face, and said, 'Child, what is the meaning of this? I do not intend to hurt you; listen to me.'

"He struggled violently. 'Let me go,' he cried; 'monster! ugly wretch! you wish to eat me, and tear me to pieces—You are an ogre—Let me go, or I will tell my papa.'

"'Boy, you will never see your father again; you must come with me.'

"'Hideous monster! let me go. My papa is a Syndic—he is M. Frankenstein—he will punish you. You dare not keep me.'

"'Frankenstein! you belong then to my enemy—to him towards whom I have sworn eternal revenge; you shall be my first victim.'

"The child still struggled, and loaded me with epithets which carried despair to my heart; I grasped his throat to silence him, and in a moment he lay dead at my feet.

"I gazed on my victim, and my heart swelled with exultation and hellish triumph: clapping my hands, I exclaimed, 'I, too, can create desolation; my enemy is not invulnerable; this death will carry despair to him, and a thousand other miseries shall torment and destroy him.'

"As I fixed my eyes on the child, I saw something glittering on his breast. I took it; it was a portrait of a most lovely woman. In spite of my malignity, it softened and attracted me.) For a few moments I gazed with delight on her dark eyes, fringed by deep lashes, and her lovely lips; but presently my rage returned: (I remembered that I was for ever deprived of the delights that such beautiful creatures could bestow; and that she whose resemblance I contemplated would, in regarding me, have changed that air of divine benignity to one expressive of disgust and affright.)

"Can you wonder that such thoughts transported me with rage? (I only wonder that at that moment, instead of venting my sensations in exclamations and agony, I did not rush among mankind, and perish in the attempt to destroy them.)

"While I was overcome by these feelings, I left the spot where I had committed the murder, and seeking a more secluded hiding-place, I entered a barn which had appeared to me to be empty. A woman was sleeping on some straw; she was young: not indeed so beautiful as her whose portrait I held; but of an agreeable aspect, and blooming in the loveliness of youth and health. (Here, I thought, is one of those whose joy-imparting smiles are bestowed on all but me.) And then I bent over her, and whispered, (Awake, fairest, thy lover is near—he who would give his life but to obtain one look of affection from thine eyes: my beloved, awake!)

"The sleeper stirred; a thrill of terror ran through me. Should she indeed awake, and see me, and curse me, and denounce the murderer? Thus would she assuredly act, if her darkened eyes opened, and she beheld me. The thought was madness; it stirred the fiend within me— not I, but she shall suffer: the murder I have committed because I am for ever robbed of all that she could give me, she shall atone. The crime had its source in her: be hers the punishment! (Thanks to the lessons of Felix and the sanguinary laws of man, I had learned now to work mischief.) I bent over her, and placed the portrait securely in one of the folds of her dress. She moved again, and I fled.

"For some days I haunted the spot where these scenes had taken place; sometimes wishing to see you, sometimes resolved to quit the world and its miseries for ever. At length I wandered towards these mountains, and have ranged through their immense recesses, consumed by a burning passion which you alone can gratify. We may not part until you have promised to comply with my requisition. (I am alone, and miserable; man will not associate with me; but one as deformed and horrible as myself would not deny herself to me.) (My companion must be of the same species, and have the same defects. This being you must create.")  Wants a Companion

## CHAPTER XVII

The being finished speaking, and fixed his looks upon me in expectation of a reply. But I was bewildered, perplexed, and unable to arrange my ideas sufficiently to understand the full extent of his proposition. He continued—

"You must create a female for me, with whom I can live in the interchange of those sympathies necessary for my being. This you alone can do; and I demand it of you as a right which you must not refuse to concede."

The latter part of his tale had kindled anew in me the anger that had died away while he narrated his peaceful life among the cottagers, and, as he said this, I could no longer suppress the rage that burned within me.

"I do refuse it," I replied; "and no torture shall ever extort a consent from me. You may render me the most miserable of men, but you shall never make me base in my own eyes. Shall I create another like yourself, whose joint wickedness might desolate the world? Begone! I have answered you; you may torture me, but I will never consent."

"You are in the wrong," replied the fiend; "and, instead of threatening, I am content to reason with you. I am malicious because I am miserable. Am I not shunned and hated by all mankind? You, my creator, would tear me to pieces, and triumph; remember that, and tell me why I should pity man more than he pities me? You would not call it murder, if you could precipitate me into one of those ice-rifts, and destroy my frame, the work of your own hands. Shall I respect man, when he contemns me? Let him live with me in the interchange of kindness; and, instead of injury, I would bestow every benefit upon him with tears of gratitude at his acceptance. But that cannot be; the human senses are insurmountable barriers to our union. Yet mine shall not be the submission of abject slavery. I will revenge my injuries: if I cannot inspire love, I will cause fear; and chiefly towards you my arch-enemy, because my creator, do I swear inextinguishable hatred. Have a care: I will work at your destruction, nor finish until I desolate your heart, so that you shall curse the hour of your birth."

A fiendish rage animated him as he said this; his face was wrinkled into contortions too horrible for human eyes to behold; but presently he calmed himself and proceeded—

"I intended to reason. This passion is detrimental to me; for you do not reflect that _you_ are the cause of its excess. If any being felt emotions of benevolence towards me, I should return them an hundred and an hundred fold; for that one creature's sake, I would make peace with the whole kind! But I now indulge in dreams of bliss that cannot be realised. What I ask of you is reasonable and moderate; I demand a creature of another sex, but as hideous as myself; the gratification is small, but it is all that I can receive, and it shall content me. It is true, we shall be monsters, cut off from all the world; but on that account we shall be more attached to one another. Our lives will not be happy, but they will be harmless, and free from the misery I now feel. Oh! my creator, make me happy; let me feel gratitude towards you for one benefit! Let me see that I excite the sympathy of some existing thing; do not deny me my request!"

I was moved. I shuddered when I thought of the possible consequences of my consent; but I felt that there was some justice in his argument. His tale, and the feelings he now expressed, proved him to be a creature of fine sensations; and did I not, as his maker, owe him all the portion of happiness that it was in my power to bestow? He saw my change of feeling, and continued—

"If you consent, neither you nor any other human being shall ever see us again: I will go to the vast wilds of South America. My food is not that of man; I do not destroy the lamb and the kid to glut my appetite; acorns and berries afford me sufficient nourishment. My companion will be of the same nature as myself, and will be content with the same fare. We shall make our bed of dried leaves; the sun will shine on us as on man, and will ripen our food. The picture I present to you is peaceful and human, and you must feel that you could deny it only in the wantonness of power and cruelty. Pitiless as you have been towards me, I now see compassion in your eyes; let me seize the favourable moment, and persuade you to promise what I so ardently desire."

"You propose," replied I, "to fly from the habitations of man, to dwell in those wilds where the beasts of the field will be your only companions. How can you, who long for the love and sympathy of man, persevere in this exile? You will return, and again seek their kindness, and you will meet with their detestation; your evil passions will be renewed, and you will then have a companion to aid you in the task of destruction. This may not be: cease to argue the point, for I cannot consent."

"How inconstant are your feelings! but a moment ago you were moved by my representations, and why do you again harden yourself to my complaints? I swear to you, by the earth which I inhabit, and by you that made me, that, with the companion you bestow, I will quit the neighbourhood of man, and dwell as it may chance, in the most savage of places. My evil passions will have fled, for I shall meet with sympathy! my life will flow quietly away, and, in my dying moments, I shall not curse my maker."

His words had a strange effect upon me. I compassioned him, and sometimes felt a wish to console him; but when I looked upon him, when I saw the filthy mass that moved and talked, my heart sickened, and my feelings were altered to those of horror and hatred. I tried to stifle these sensations; I thought, that as I could not sympathise with him, I had no right to withhold from him the small portion of happiness which was yet in my power to bestow.

"You swear," I said, "to be harmless; but have you not already shown a degree of malice that should reasonably make me distrust you? May not even this be a feint that will increase your triumph by affording a wider scope for your revenge?"

"How is this? I must not be trifled with: and I demand an answer. If I have no ties and no affections, hatred and vice must be my portion; the love of another will destroy the cause of my crimes, and I shall become a thing, of whose existence every one will be ignorant. My vices are the children of a forced solitude that I abhor; and my virtues will necessarily arise when I live in communion with an equal. I shall feel the affections of a sensitive being, and become linked to the chain of existence and events, from which I am now excluded."

I paused some time to reflect on all he had related, and the various arguments which he had employed. I thought of the promise of virtues which he had displayed on the opening of his existence, and the subsequent blight of all kindly feeling by the loathing and scorn which his protectors had manifested towards him. His power and threats were not omitted in my calculations: a creature who could exist in the ice-caves of the glaciers, and hide himself from pursuit among the ridges of inaccessible precipices, was a being possessing faculties it would be vain to cope with. After a long pause of reflection, I concluded that the justice due both to him and my fellow-creatures demanded of me that I should comply with his request. Turning to him, therefore, I said—

"I consent to your demand, on your solemn oath to quit Europe for ever, and every other place in the neighbourhood of man, as soon as I shall deliver into your hands a female who will accompany you in your exile."

"I swear," he cried, "by the sun, and by the blue sky of Heaven, and by the fire of love that burns my heart, that if you grant my prayer, while they exist you shall never behold me again. Depart to your home, and commence your labours: I shall watch their progress with unutter-able anxiety; and fear not but that when you are ready I shall appear."

Saying this, he suddenly quitted me, fearful, perhaps, of any change in my sentiments. I saw him descend the mountain with greater speed than the flight of an eagle, and quickly lost him among the undulations of the sea of ice.

His tale had occupied the whole day; and the sun was upon the verge of the horizon when he departed. I knew that I ought to hasten my descent towards the valley, as I should soon be encompassed in dark-ness; but my heart was heavy, and my steps slow. The labour of winding among the little paths of the mountains, and fixing my feet firmly as I advanced, perplexed me, occupied as I was by the emotions which the occurrences of the day had produced. Night was far advanced, when I came to the half-way resting-place, and seated myself beside the foun-tain. The stars shone at intervals, as the clouds passed from over them; the dark pines rose before me, and every here and there a broken tree lay on the ground (it was a scene of wonderful solemnity, and stirred strange thoughts within me.) I wept bitterly; and clasping my hands in agony, I exclaimed, "Oh! stars and clouds, and winds, ye are all about to mock me: if ye really pity me, crush sensation and memory; let me become as nought; but if not, depart, depart, and leave me in darkness."

These were wild and miserable thoughts; but I cannot describe to you how the eternal twinkling of the stars weighed upon me, and how I listened to every blast of wind, as if it were a dull, ugly siroc° on its way to consume me.

Morning dawned before I arrived at the village of Chamounix; I took no rest, but returned immediately to Geneva. Even in my own heart I could give no expression to my sensations—they weighed on me with a mountain's weight, and their excess destroyed my agony beneath them. Thus I returned home, and entering the house, pre-sented myself to the family. My haggard and wild appearance awoke intense alarm; but I answered no question, scarcely did I speak. I felt as if I were placed under a ban—as if I had no right to claim their sympa-thies—as if never more might I enjoy companionship with them. Yet even thus I loved them to adoration; and to save them, I resolved to dedicate myself to my most abhorred task. The prospect of such an occupation made every other circumstance of existence pass before me like a dream; and that thought only had to me the reality of life.

---

*siroc:* Sirocco, a blistering wind that blows into Europe from Northern Africa.

# CHAPTER XVIII

Day after day, week after week, passed away on my return to Geneva; and I could not collect the courage to recommence my work, I feared the vengeance of the disappointed fiend, yet I was unable to overcome my repugnance to the task which was enjoined me. I found that I could not compose a female without again devoting several months to profound study and laborious disquisition. I had heard of some discoveries having been made by an English philosopher, the knowledge of which was material to my success, and I sometimes thought of obtaining my father's consent to visit England for this purpose; but I clung to every pretence of delay, and shrunk from taking the first step in an undertaking whose immediate necessity began to appear less absolute to me. A change indeed had taken place in me: my health, which had hitherto declined, was now much restored; and my spirits, when unchecked by the memory of my unhappy promise, rose proportionably. My father saw this change with pleasure, and he turned his thoughts towards the best method of eradicating the remains of my melancholy, which every now and then would return by fits, and with a devouring blackness overcast the approaching sunshine. At these moments I took refuge in the most perfect solitude. I passed whole days on the lake alone in a little boat, watching the clouds, and listening to the rippling of the waves, silent and listless. But the fresh air and bright sun seldom failed to restore me to some degree of composure; and, on my return, I met the salutations of my friends with a readier smile and a more cheerful heart.

It was after my return from one of these rambles, that my father, calling me aside, thus addressed me:—

"I am happy to remark, my dear son, that you have resumed your former pleasures, and seem to be returning to yourself. And yet you are still unhappy, and still avoid our society. For some time I was lost in conjecture as to the cause of this; but yesterday an idea struck me, and if it is well founded, I conjure you to avow it. Reserve on such a point would be not only useless, but draw down treble misery on us all."

I trembled violently at his exordium, and my father continued—

"I confess, my son, that I have always looked forward to your marriage with our dear Elizabeth as the tie of our domestic comfort, and the stay of my declining years. You were attached to each other from your earliest infancy; you studied together, and appeared, in dispositions and tastes, entirely suited to one another. But so blind is the experience of man, that what I conceived to be the best assistants to my plan, may have entirely destroyed it. You, perhaps, regard her as your sister, without any wish that she might become your wife. Nay, you may have met with another whom you may love; and, considering yourself as bound in honour to Elizabeth, this struggle may occasion the poignant misery which you appear to feel."

"My dear father, re-assure yourself. I love my cousin tenderly and sincerely. I never saw any woman who excited, as Elizabeth does, my warmest admiration and affection. My future hopes and prospects are entirely bound up in the expectation of our union."

"The expression of your sentiments on this subject, my dear Victor, gives me more pleasure than I have for some time experienced. If you feel thus, we shall assuredly be happy, however present events may cast a gloom over us. But it is this gloom which appears to have taken so strong a hold of your mind, that I wish to dissipate. Tell me, therefore, whether you object to an immediate solemnisation of the marriage. We have been unfortunate, and recent events have drawn us from that everyday tranquillity befitting my years and infirmities. You are younger; yet I do not suppose, possessed as you are of a competent fortune, that an early marriage would at all interfere with any future plans of honour and utility that you may have formed. Do not suppose, however, that I wish to dictate happiness to you, or that a delay on your part would cause me any serious uneasiness. Interpret my words with candour, and answer me, I conjure you, with confidence and sincerity."

I listened to my father in silence, and remained for some time incapable of offering any reply. I revolved rapidly in my mind a multitude of thoughts, and endeavoured to arrive at some conclusion. Alas! to me the idea of an immediate union with my Elizabeth was one of horror and dismay. I was bound by a solemn promise, which I had not yet fulfilled, and dared not break; or, if I did, what manifold miseries might not impend over me and my devoted family! Could I enter into a festival with this deadly weight yet hanging round my neck, and bowing me to the ground? I must perform my engagement, and let the monster depart with his mate, before I allowed myself to enjoy the delight of an union from which I expected peace.

I remembered also the necessity imposed upon me of either journeying to England, or entering into a long correspondence with those philosophers of that country, whose knowledge and discoveries were of indispensable use to me in my present undertaking. The latter method of obtaining the desired intelligence was dilatory and unsatisfactory: besides, I had an insurmountable aversion to the idea of engaging myself in my loathsome task in my father's house, while in habits of familiar intercourse with those I loved. I knew that a thousand fearful accidents might occur, the slightest of which would disclose a tale to thrill all connected with me with horror. I was aware also that I should often lose all self-command, all capacity of hiding the harrowing sensations that would possess me during the progress of my unearthly occupation. I must absent myself from all I loved while thus employed. Once commenced, it would quickly be achieved, and I might be restored to my family in peace and happiness. My promise fulfilled, the monster would depart for ever. Or (so my fond fancy imaged) some accident might meanwhile occur to destroy him, and put an end to my slavery for ever.

These feelings dictated my answer to my father. I expressed a wish to visit England; but, concealing the true reasons of this request, I clothed my desires under a guise which excited no suspicion, while I urged my desire with an earnestness that easily induced my father to comply. After so long a period of an absorbing melancholy, that resembled madness in its intensity and effects, he was glad to find that I was capable of taking pleasure in the idea of such a journey, and he hoped that change of scene and varied amusement would, before my return, have restored me entirely to myself.

The duration of my absence was left to my own choice; a few months, or at most a year, was the period contemplated. One paternal kind precaution he had taken to ensure my having a companion. Without previously communicating with me, he had, in concert with Elizabeth, arranged that Clerval should join me at Strasburgh. This interfered with the solitude I coveted for the prosecution of my task; yet at the commencement of my journey the presence of my friend could in no way be an impediment, and truly I rejoiced that thus I should be saved many hours of lonely, maddening reflection. Nay, Henry might stand between me and the intrusion of my foe. If I were alone, would he not at times force his abhorred presence on me, to remind me of my task, or to contemplate its progress?

To England, therefore, I was bound, and it was understood that my union with Elizabeth should take place immediately on my return. My father's age rendered him extremely averse to delay. For myself, there was one reward I promised myself from my detested toils — one consolation for my unparalleled sufferings; it was the prospect of that day when, enfranchised from my miserable slavery, I might claim Elizabeth, and forget the past in my union with her.

I now made arrangements for my journey; but one feeling haunted me, which filled me with fear and agitation. During my absence I should

leave my friends unconscious of the existence of their enemy, and
unprotected from his attacks, exasperated as he might be by my departure.) But he had promised to follow me wherever I might go; and
would he not accompany me to England? This imagination was dreadful in itself, but soothing, inasmuch as it supposed the safety of my
friends. I was agonised with the idea of the possibility that the reverse
of this might happen. But through the whole period during which I was
the slave of my creature, I allowed myself to be governed by the impulses
of the moment; and my present sensations strongly intimated that the
fiend would follow me, and exempt my family from the danger of his
machinations.

It was in the latter end of September that I again quitted my native
country. My journey had been my own suggestion, and Elizabeth,
therefore, acquiesced: but she was filled with disquiet at the idea of my
suffering, away from her, the inroads of misery and grief. It had been
her care which provided me a companion in Clerval—and yet a man is
blind to a thousand minute circumstances, which call forth a woman's
sedulous attention. She longed to bid me hasten my return,—a thousand conflicting emotions rendered her mute, as she bade me a tearful
silent farewell.

I threw myself into the carriage that was to convey me away, (hardly
knowing whither I was going, and careless of what was passing around.)
I remembered only, and it was with a bitter anguish that I reflected on
it, to order that my chemical instruments should be packed to go with
me. Filled with dreary imaginations, I passed through many beautiful
and majestic scenes; but my eyes were fixed and unobserving. I could
only think of the bourne of my travels,° and the work which was to
occupy me whilst they endured.

After some days spent in listless indolence, during which I traversed
many leagues, I arrived at Strasburgh, where I waited two days for
Clerval. He came. Alas, how great was the contrast between us! He was
alive to every new scene; joyful when he saw the beauties of the setting
sun, and more happy when he beheld it rise, and recommence a new
day. He pointed out to me the shifting colours of the landscape, and
the appearances of the sky. "This is what it is to live," he cried, "now
I enjoy existence! But you, my dear Frankenstein, wherefore are
you desponding and sorrowful?" In truth, I was occupied by gloomy
thoughts, and neither saw the descent of the evening star, nor the

---

*the bourne of my travels:* End or goal.

golden sunrise reflected in the Rhine. —And you, my friend, would be
far more amused with the journal of Clerval, who observed the scenery
with an eye of feeling and delight, than in listening to my reflections. I,
a miserable wretch, haunted by a curse that shut up every avenue to
enjoyment. )

We had agreed to descend the Rhine in a boat from Strasburgh to
Rotterdam, whence we might take shipping for London. During this
voyage, we passed many willowy islands, and saw several beautiful
towns. We stayed a day at Manheim, and, on the fifth from our departure from Strasburgh, arrived at Mayence. The course of the Rhine
below Mayence becomes much more picturesque. The river descends
rapidly, and winds between hills, not high, but steep, and of beautiful
forms. We saw many ruined castles standing on the edges of precipices,
surrounded by black woods, high and inaccessible. This part of the
Rhine, indeed, presents a singularly variegated landscape. In one spot
you view rugged hills, ruined castles overlooking tremendous precipices, with the dark Rhine rushing beneath; and, on the sudden turn of
a promontory, flourishing vineyards, with green sloping banks, and a
meandering river, and populous towns occupy the scene.

We travelled at the time of the vintage, and heard the song of the
labourers, as we glided down the stream. Even I, depressed in mind,
and my spirits continually agitated by gloomy feelings, even I was
pleased. I lay at the bottom of the boat, and, as I gazed on the cloudless
blue sky, I seemed to drink in a tranquillity to which I had long been a
stranger. And if these were my sensations, who can describe those of
Henry? He felt as if he had been transported to Fairy-land, and enjoyed
a happiness seldom tasted by man. "I have seen," he said, "the most
beautiful scenes of my own country; I have visited the lakes of Lucerne
and Uri, where the snowy mountains descend almost perpendicularly
to the water, casting black and impenetrable shades, which would cause
a gloomy and mournful appearance, were it not for the most verdant
islands that relieve the eye by their gay appearance; I have seen this lake
agitated by a tempest, when the wind tore up whirlwinds of water, and
gave you an idea of what the water-spout must be on the great ocean,
and the waves dash with fury the base of the mountain, where the priest
and his mistress° were overwhelmed by an avalanche, and where their
dying voices are still said to be heard amid the pauses of the nightly
wind; I have seen the mountains of La Valais, and the Pays de Vaud: but

*the priest and his mistress:* Reference to local tale from Rhine-North Westphalia region
of Germany.

this country, Victor, pleases me more than all those wonders. The mountains of Switzerland are more majestic and strange; but there is a charm in the banks of this divine river, that I never before saw equalled. Look at that castle which overhangs yon precipice; and that also on the island, almost concealed amongst the foliage of those lovely trees; and now that group of labourers coming from among their vines; and that village half hid in the recess of the mountain. Oh, surely, the spirit that inhabits and guards this place has a soul more in harmony with man, than those who pile the glacier, or retire to the inaccessible peaks of the mountains of our own country."

Clerval! beloved friend! even now it delights me to record your words, and to dwell on the praise of which you are so eminently deserving. He was a being formed in the "very poetry of nature." His wild and enthusiastic imagination was chastened by the sensibility of his heart. His soul overflowed with ardent affections, and his friendship was of that devoted and wondrous nature that the worldly-minded teach us to look for only in the imagination. But even human sympathies were not sufficient to satisfy his eager mind. The scenery of external nature, which others regard only with admiration, he loved with ardour:—

      ————The sounding cataract
   Haunted him like a passion: the tall rock,
   The mountain, and the deep and gloomy wood,
   Their colours and their forms, were then to him
   An appetite; a feeling, and a love,
   That had no need of a remoter charm,
   By thought supplied, or any interest
   Unborrow'd from the eye.°

And where does he now exist? Is this gentle and lovely being lost for ever? Has this mind, so replete with ideas, imaginations fanciful and magnificent, which formed a world, whose existence depended on the life of its creator;—has this mind perished? Does it now only exist in my memory? No, it is not thus; your form so divinely wrought, and beaming with beauty, has decayed, but your spirit still visits and consoles your unhappy friend.

Pardon this gush of sorrow; these ineffectual words are but a slight tribute to the unexampled worth of Henry, but they soothe my heart,

---

*The sounding . . . from the eye:* Adapted from lines 76–83 of William Wordsworth's poem "Lines composed a few miles above Tintern Abbey" (1798).

overflowing with the anguish which his remembrance creates. I will
proceed with my tale.

Beyond Cologne we descended to the plains of Holland; and we
resolved to post the remainder of our way; for the wind was contrary,
and the stream of the river was too gentle to aid us.

Our journey here lost the interest arising from beautiful scenery;
but we arrived in a few days at Rotterdam, whence we proceeded by sea
to England. It was on a clear morning, in the latter days of December,
that I first saw the white cliffs of Britain. The banks of the Thames presented a new scene; they were flat, but fertile, and almost every town
was marked by the remembrance of some story. We saw Tilbury Fort,
and remembered the Spanish armada; Gravesend, Woolwich, and Green-
wich, places which I had heard of even in my country.

At length we saw the numerous steeples of London, St. Paul's towering above all, and the Tower famed in English history.

## CHAPTER XIX

London was our present point of rest; we determined to remain
several months in this wonderful and celebrated city. Clerval desired the
intercourse of the men of genius and talent who flourished at this time;
but this was with me a secondary object; I was principally occupied with
the means of obtaining the information necessary for the completion of
my promise, and quickly availed myself of the letters of introduction
that I had brought with me, addressed to the most distinguished natural philosophers.

If this journey had taken place during my days of study and happiness, it would have afforded me inexpressible pleasure. But a blight had
come over my existence, and I only visited these people for the sake of
the information they might give me on the subject in which my interest
was so terribly profound. Company was irksome to me; when alone, I
could fill my mind with the sights of heaven and earth; the voice of
Henry soothed me, and I could thus cheat myself into a transitory
peace. But busy, uninteresting, joyous faces brought back despair to
my heart. I saw an insurmountable barrier placed between me and my
fellow-men; this barrier was sealed with the blood of William and Justine; and to reflect on the events connected with those names filled my
soul with anguish.

But in Clerval I saw the image of my former self; he was inquisitive,
and anxious to gain experience and instruction. The difference of

manners which he observed was to him an inexhaustible source of instruction and amusement. He was also pursuing an object he had long had in view. His design was to visit India, in the belief that he had in his knowledge of its various languages, and in the views he had taken of its society, the means of materially assisting the progress of European *Slavery* colonisation and trade. In Britain only could he further the execution of his plan. He was for ever busy; and the only check to his enjoyments was my sorrowful and dejected mind. I tried to conceal this as much as possible, that I might not debar him from the pleasures natural to one, who was entering on a new scene of life, undisturbed by any care or bitter recollection. I often refused to accompany him, alleging another engagement, that I might remain alone. I now also began to collect the materials necessary for my new creation, and this was to me like the torture of single drops of water continually falling on the head. Every thought that was devoted to it was an extreme anguish, and every word that I spoke in allusion to it caused my lips to quiver, and my heart to palpitate.

After passing some months in London, we received a letter from a person in Scotland, who had formerly been our visitor at Geneva. He mentioned the beauties of his native country, and asked us if those were not sufficient allurements to induce us to prolong our journey as far north as Perth, where he resided. Clerval eagerly desired to accept this invitation; and I, although I abhorred society, wished to view again mountains and streams, and all the wondrous works with which Nature adorns her chosen dwelling-places.

We had arrived in England at the beginning of October, and it was now February. We accordingly determined to commence our journey towards the north at the expiration of another month. In this expedition we did not intend to follow the great road to Edinburgh, but to visit Windsor, Oxford, Matlock, and the Cumberland lakes, resolving to arrive at the completion of this tour about the end of July. I packed up my chemical instruments, and the materials I had collected, resolving to finish my labours in some obscure nook in the northern highlands of Scotland.

We quitted London on the 27th of March, and remained a few days at Windsor, rambling in its beautiful forest. This was a new scene to us mountaineers; the majestic oaks, the quantity of game, and the herds of stately deer, were all novelties to us.

From thence we proceeded to Oxford. As we entered this city, our minds were filled with the remembrance of the events that had been transacted there more than a century and a half before. It was here that

Charles I. had collected his forces. (This city had remained faithful to him, after the whole nation had forsaken his cause to join the standard of parliament and liberty.)The memory of that unfortunate king, and his companions, the amiable Falkland, the insolent Goring, his queen, and son, gave a peculiar interest to every part of the city, which they might be supposed to have inhabited. (The spirit of elder days found a dwelling here, and we delighted to trace its footsteps.)If these feelings had not found an imaginary gratification, the appearance of the city had yet in itself sufficient beauty to obtain our admiration. The colleges are ancient and picturesque; the streets are almost magnificent; and the lovely Isis, which flows beside it through meadows of exquisite verdure, is spread forth into a placid expanse of waters, which reflects its majestic assemblage of towers, and spires, and domes, embosomed among aged trees.

I enjoyed this scene; and yet my enjoyment was embittered both by the memory of the past, and the anticipation of the future. I was formed for peaceful happiness. During my youthful days discontent never visited my mind; and if I was ever overcome by *ennui*, the sight of what is beautiful in nature, or the study of what is excellent and sublime in the productions of man, could always interest my heart, and communicate elasticity to my spirits. But I am a blasted tree; the bolt has entered my soul; and I felt then that I should survive to exhibit, what I shall soon cease to be—a miserable spectacle of wrecked humanity, pitiable to others, and intolerable to myself.)

We passed a considerable period at Oxford, rambling among its environs, and endeavouring to identify every spot which might relate to the most animating epoch of English history. Our little voyages of discovery were often prolonged by the successive objects that presented themselves. We visited the tomb of the illustrious Hampden, and the field on which that patriot fell. (For a moment my soul was elevated from its debasing and miserable fears, to contemplate the divine ideas of liberty and self-sacrifice, of which these sights were the monuments and the remembrancers.) For an instant I dared to shake off my chains, and look around me with a free and lofty spirit; but the iron had eaten into my flesh, and I sank again, trembling and hopeless, into my miserable self.

We left Oxford with regret, and proceeded to Matlock, which was our next place of rest. The country in the neighbourhood of this village resembled, to a greater degree, the scenery of Switzerland; but every thing is on a lower scale, and the green hills want the crown of distant white Alps, which always attend on the piny mountains of my native country. We visited the wondrous cave, and the little cabinets of natural history, where the curiosities are disposed in the same manner as in the collections at Servox and Chamounix. The latter name made me tremble, when pronounced by Henry; and I hastened to quit Matlock, with which that terrible scene was thus associated.

From Derby, still journeying northward, we passed two months in Cumberland and Westmorland. I could now almost fancy myself among the Swiss mountains. The little patches of snow which yet lingered on the northern sides of the mountains, the lakes, and the dashing of the rocky streams, were all familiar and dear sights to me. Here also we made some acquaintances, who almost contrived to cheat me into happiness. The delight of Clerval was proportionably greater than mine; his mind expanded in the company of men of talent, and he found in his own nature greater capacities and resources than he could have imagined himself to have possessed while he associated with his inferiors. "I could pass my life here," said he to me; "and among these mountains I should scarcely regret Switzerland and the Rhine."

But he found that a traveller's life is one that includes much pain amidst its enjoyments. His feelings are for ever on the stretch; and when he begins to sink into repose, he finds himself obliged to quit that on which he rests in pleasure for something new, which again engages his attention, and which also he forsakes for other novelties.

We had scarcely visited the various lakes of Cumberland and Westmorland, and conceived an affection for some of the inhabitants, when the period of our appointment with our Scotch friend approached, and we left them to travel on. For my own part I was not sorry. I had now neglected my promise for some time, and I feared the effects of the daemon's disappointment. He might remain in Switzerland, and wreak his vengeance on my relatives. This idea pursued me, and tormented me at every moment from which I might otherwise have snatched repose and peace. I waited for my letters with feverish impatience: if they were delayed, I was miserable, and overcome by a thousand fears; and when they arrived, and I saw the superscription of Elizabeth or my father, I hardly dared to read and ascertain my fate. Sometimes I thought that the fiend followed me, and might expedite my remissness by murdering my companion. When these thoughts possessed me, I would not quit Henry for a moment, but followed him as his shadow, to protect him from the fancied rage of his destroyer. I felt as if I had committed some great crime, the consciousness of which haunted me. I was guiltless, but I had indeed drawn down a horrible curse upon my head, as mortal as that of crime.

I visited Edinburgh with languid eyes and mind; and yet that city might have interested the most unfortunate being. Clerval did not like it so well as Oxford: for the antiquity of the latter city was more pleasing to him. But the beauty and regularity of the new town of Edinburgh, its romantic castle and its environs, the most delightful in the world, Arthur's Seat, St. Bernard's Well, and the Pentland Hills, compensated him for the change, and filled him with cheerfulness and admiration. But I was impatient to arrive at the termination of my journey.

We left Edinburgh in a week, passing through Coupar, St. Andrew's, and along the banks of the Tay, to Perth, where our friend expected us. But I was in no mood to laugh and talk with strangers, or enter into their feelings or plans with the good humour expected from a guest; and accordingly I told Clerval that I wished to make the tour of Scotland alone. "Do you," said I, "enjoy yourself, and let this be our rendezvous. I may be absent a month or two; but do not interfere with my motions, I entreat you: leave me to peace and solitude for a short time; and when I return, I hope it will be with a lighter heart, more congenial to your own temper."

Henry wished to dissuade me; but, seeing me bent on this plan, ceased to remonstrate. He entreated me to write often. "I had rather be with you," he said, "in your solitary rambles, than with these Scotch people, whom I do not know: hasten then, my friend, to return, that I may again feel myself somewhat at home, which I cannot do in your absence."

Having parted from my friend, I determined to visit some remote spot of Scotland, and finish my work in solitude. I did not doubt but that the monster followed me, and would discover himself to me when I should have finished, that he might receive his companion.

With this resolution I traversed the northern highlands, and fixed on one of the remotest of the Orkneys as the scene of my labours. It was a place fitted for such a work, being hardly more than a rock, whose high sides were continually beaten upon by the waves. The soil was barren, scarcely affording pasture for a few miserable cows, and oatmeal for its inhabitants, which consisted of five persons, whose gaunt and scraggy limbs gave tokens of their miserable fare. Vegetables and bread, when they indulged in such luxuries, and even fresh water, was to be procured from the main land, which was about five miles distant.

On the whole island there were but three miserable huts, and one of these was vacant when I arrived. This I hired. It contained but two rooms, and these exhibited all the squalidness of the most miserable penury. The thatch had fallen in, the walls were unplastered, and the door was off its hinges. I ordered it to be repaired, bought some furniture, and took possession; an incident which would, doubtless, have occasioned some surprise, had not all the senses of the cottagers been benumbed by want and squalid poverty. As it was, I lived ungazed at and unmolested, hardly thanked for the pittance of food and clothes which I gave; so much does suffering blunt even the coarsest sensations of men.

*Dick*

In this retreat I devoted the morning to labour; but in the evening, when the weather permitted, I walked on the stony beach of the sea, to listen to the waves as they roared and dashed at my feet. It was a monotonous yet ever-changing scene. I thought of Switzerland; it was far different from this desolate and appalling landscape. Its hills are covered with vines, and its cottages are scattered thickly in the plains. Its fair lakes reflect a blue and gentle sky; and, when troubled by the winds, their tumult is but as the play of a lively infant, when compared to the roarings of the giant ocean.

In this manner I distributed my occupations when I first arrived; but, as I proceeded in my labour, it became every day more horrible and irksome to me. Sometimes I could not prevail on myself to enter my laboratory for several days; and at other times I toiled day and night in order to complete my work. It was, indeed, a filthy process in which I was engaged. During my first experiment, a kind of enthusiastic frenzy had blinded me to the horror of my employment; my mind was intently fixed on the consummation of my labour, and my eyes were shut to the horror of my proceedings. But now I went to it in cold blood, and my heart often sickened at the work of my hands.

*1st Experiment*

*2nd*

Thus situated, employed in the most detestable occupation, immersed in a solitude where nothing could for an instant call my attention from the actual scene in which I was engaged, my spirits became unequal; I grew restless and nervous. Every moment I feared to meet my persecutor. Sometimes I sat with my eyes fixed on the ground, fearing to raise them, lest they should encounter the object which I so much dreaded to behold. I feared to wander from the sight of my fellow-creatures, lest when alone he should come to claim his companion.

In the mean time I worked on, and my labour was already considerably advanced. I looked towards its completion with a tremulous and eager hope, which I dared not trust myself to question, but which was intermixed with obscure forebodings of evil, that made my heart sicken in my bosom.

## CHAPTER XX

I sat one evening in my laboratory; the sun had set, and the moon was just rising from the sea; I had not sufficient light for my employment, and I remained idle, in a pause of consideration of whether I should leave my labour for the night, or hasten its conclusion by an unremitting attention to it. As I sat, a train of reflection occurred to me, which led me to consider the effects of what I was now doing. Three years before I was engaged in the same manner, and had created a fiend whose unparalleled barbarity had desolated my heart, and filled it for ever with the bitterest remorse. I was now about to form another being, of whose dispositions I was alike ignorant; she might become ten thousand times more malignant than her mate, and delight, for its own sake, in murder and wretchedness. He had sworn to quit the neighbourhood of man, and hide himself in deserts; but she had not; and she, who in all probability was to become a thinking and reasoning animal, might refuse to comply with a compact made before her creation. They might even hate each other; the creature who already lived loathed his own deformity, and might he not conceive a greater abhorrence for it when it came before his eyes in the female form? She also might turn with disgust from him to the superior beauty of man; she might quit him, and he be again alone, exasperated by the fresh provocation of being deserted by one of his own species. *what species?*

Even if they were to leave Europe, and inhabit the deserts of the new world, yet one of the first results of those sympathies for which the daemon thirsted would be children, and a race of devils would be propagated upon the earth, who might make the very existence of the species of man a condition precarious and full of terror. Had I a right, for my own benefit, to inflict this curse upon everlasting generations? I had before been moved by the sophisms of the being I had created; I had been struck senseless by his fiendish threats: but now, for the first time, the wickedness of my promise burst upon me; I shuddered to think that future ages might curse me as their pest, whose selfishness had not hesitated to buy its own peace at the price, perhaps, of the existence of the whole human race.

I trembled, and my heart failed within me; when, on looking up, I saw, by the light of the moon, the daemon at the casement. A ghastly grin wrinkled his lips as he gazed on me, where I sat fulfilling the task which he had allotted to me. Yes, he had followed me in my travels; he had loitered in forests, hid himself in caves, or taken refuge in wide and desert heaths; and he now came to mark my progress, and claim the fulfillment of my promise.

As I looked on him, his countenance expressed the utmost extent of malice and treachery, I thought with a sensation of madness on my promise of creating another like to him, and trembling with passion, tore to pieces the thing on which I was engaged. The wretch saw me destroy the creature on whose future existence he depended for happiness, and, with a howl of devilish despair and revenge, withdrew.

I left the room, and, locking the door, made a solemn vow in my own heart never to resume my labours; and then, with trembling steps, I sought my own apartment. I was alone; none were near me to dissipate the gloom, and relieve me from the sickening oppression of the most terrible reveries.

Several hours passed, and I remained near my window gazing on the sea; it was almost motionless, for the winds were hushed, and all nature reposed under the eye of the quiet moon. A few fishing vessels alone specked the water, and now and then the gentle breeze wafted the sound of voices, as the fishermen called to one another. I felt the silence, although I was hardly conscious of its extreme profundity, until my ear was suddenly arrested by the paddling of oars near the shore, and a person landed close to my house.

In a few minutes after, I heard the creaking of my door, as if some one endeavoured to open it softly. I trembled from head to foot; I felt a presentiment of who it was, and wished to rouse one of the peasants who dwelt in a cottage not far from mine; but I was overcome by the sensation of helplessness, so often felt in frightful dreams, when you in vain endeavour to fly from an impending danger, and was rooted to the spot.

Presently I heard the sound of footsteps along the passage; the door opened, and the wretch whom I dreaded appeared. Shutting the door, he approached me, and said, in a smothered voice—

"You have destroyed the work which you began; what is it that you intend? Do you dare to break your promise? I have endured toil and misery: I left Switzerland with you; I crept along the shores of the Rhine, among its willow islands, and over the summits of its hills. I have dwelt many months in the heaths of England, and among the deserts of Scotland. I have endured incalculable fatigue, and cold, and hunger; do you dare destroy my hopes?"

"Begone! I do break my promise; never will I create another like yourself, equal in deformity and wickedness."

*monster calls F a slave*

"Slave, I have reasoned with you, but you have proved yourself unworthy of my condescension. Remember that I have power; you believe yourself miserable, but I can make you so wretched that the light of day will be hateful to you. You are my creator, but I am your master;—obey!"

"The hour of my irresolution is past, and the period of your power is arrived. Your threats cannot move me to do an act of wickedness; but they confirm me in a determination of not creating you a companion in vice. Shall I, in cool blood, set loose upon the earth a daemon, whose delight is in death and wretchedness? Begone! I am firm, and your words will only exasperate my rage."

The monster saw my determination in my face, and gnashed his teeth in the impotence of anger. "Shall each man," cried he, "find a wife for his bosom, and each beast have his mate, and I be alone? I had feelings of affection, and they were requited by detestation and scorn. Man! you may hate; but beware! your hours will pass in dread and misery, and soon the bolt will fall which must ravish from you your happiness for ever. Are you to be happy, while I grovel in the intensity of my wretchedness? You can blast my other passions; but revenge remains— revenge, henceforth dearer than light or food! I may die; but first you, my tyrant and tormentor, shall curse the sun that gazes on your misery. Beware; for I am fearless, and therefore powerful. I will watch with the wiliness of a snake, that I may sting with its venom. Man, you shall repent of the injuries you inflict."

*SATAN*

"Devil, cease; and do not poison the air with these sounds of malice. I have declared my resolution to you, and I am no coward to bend beneath words. Leave me; I am inexorable."

"It is well. I go; but remember, I shall be with you on your wedding-night."

I started forward, and exclaimed, "Villain! before you sign my death-warrant, be sure that you are yourself safe."

I would have seized him; but he eluded me, and quitted the house with precipitation. In a few moments I saw him in his boat, which shot across the waters with an arrowy swiftness, and was soon lost amidst the waves.

All was again silent; but his words rung in my ears. I burned with rage to pursue the murderer of my peace, and precipitate him into the ocean. I walked up and down my room hastily and perturbed, while my imagination conjured up a thousand images to torment and sting me. Why had I not followed him, and closed with him in mortal strife? But I had suffered him to depart, and he had directed his course towards

the main land. I shuddered to think who might be the next victim sacrificed to his insatiate revenge. And then I thought again of his
words—"*I will be with you on your wedding-night.*" That then was the
period fixed for the fulfilment of my destiny. In that hour I should die,
and at once satisfy and extinguish his malice. The prospect did not
move me to fear; yet when I thought of my beloved Elizabeth,—of her
tears and endless sorrow, when she should find her lover so barbarously
snatched from her,—tears, the first I had shed for many months,
streamed from my eyes, and I resolved not to fall before my enemy
without a bitter struggle.

The night passed away, and the sun rose from the ocean; my feelings became calmer, if it may be called calmness, when the violence of
rage sinks into the depths of despair. I left the house, the horrid scene
of the last night's contention, and walked on the beach of the sea,
which I almost regarded as an insuperable barrier between me and my
fellow-creatures; nay, a wish that such should prove the fact stole across
me. I desired that I might pass my life on that barren rock, wearily, it is
true, but uninterrupted by any sudden shock of misery. If I returned, it
was to be sacrificed, or to see those whom I most loved die under the
grasp of a daemon whom I had myself created.

I walked about the isle like a restless spectre, separated from all it
loved, and miserable in the separation. When it became noon, and the
sun rose higher, I lay down on the grass, and was overpowered by a
deep sleep. I had been awake the whole of the preceding night, my
nerves were agitated, and my eyes inflamed by watching and misery.
The sleep into which I now sunk refreshed me; and when I awoke, I
again felt as if I belonged to a race of human beings like myself, and I
began to reflect upon what had passed with greater composure; yet still
the words of the fiend rung in my ears like a death-knell, they appeared
like a dream, yet distinct and oppressive as a reality.

The sun had far descended, and I still sat on the shore, satisfying my
appetite, which had become ravenous, with an oaten cake, when I saw
a fishing-boat land close to me, and one of the men brought me a
packet; it contained letters from Geneva, and one from Clerval, entreating me to join him. He said that he was wearing away his time fruitlessly
where he was; that letters from the friends he had formed in London
desired his return to complete the negotiation they had entered into for
his Indian enterprise. He could not any longer delay his departure; but
as his journey to London might be followed, even sooner than he now
conjectured, by his longer voyage, he entreated me to bestow as much
of my society on him as I could spare. He besought me, therefore, to

leave my solitary isle, and to meet him at Perth, that we might proceed southwards together. This letter in a degree recalled me to life, and I determined to quit my island at the expiration of two days.

Yet, before I departed, there was a task to perform, on which I shuddered to reflect: I must pack up my chemical instruments; and for that purpose I must enter the room which had been the scene of my odious work, and I must handle those utensils, the sight of which was sickening to me. The next morning, at daybreak, I summoned sufficient courage, and unlocked the door of my laboratory. The remains of the half-finished créature, whom I had destroyed, lay scattered on the floor, and I almost felt as if I had mangled the living flesh of a human being. I paused to collect myself, and then entered the chamber. With trembling hand I conveyed the instruments out of the room; but I reflected that I ought not to leave the relics of my work to excite the horror and suspicion of the peasants; and I accordingly put them into a basket, with a great quantity of stones, and, laying them up, determined to throw them into the sea that very night; and in the mean time I sat upon the beach, employed in cleaning and arranging my chemical apparatus.

Nothing could be more complete than the alteration that had taken place in my feelings since the night of the appearance of the daemon. I had before regarded my promise with a gloomy despair, as a thing that, with whatever consequences, must be fulfilled; but I now felt as if a film had been taken from before my eyes, and that I, for the first time, saw clearly. The idea of renewing my labours did not for one instant occur to me; the threat I had heard weighed on my thoughts, but I did not reflect that a voluntary act of mine could avert it. I had resolved in my own mind, that to create another like the fiend I had first made would be an act of the basest and most atrocious selfishness; and I banished from my mind every thought that could lead to a different conclusion.

Between two and three in the morning the moon rose; and I then, putting my basket aboard a little skiff, sailed out about four miles from the shore. The scene was perfectly solitary: a few boats were returning towards land, but I sailed away from them. I felt as if I was about the commission of a dreadful crime, and avoided with shuddering anxiety any encounter with my fellow-creatures. At one time the moon, which had before been clear, was suddenly overspread by a thick cloud, and I took advantage of the moment of darkness, and cast my basket into the sea: I listened to the gurgling sound as it sunk, and then sailed away from the spot. The sky became clouded; but the air was pure, although chilled by the north-east breeze that was then rising. But it refreshed me, and filled me with such agreeable sensations, that I resolved to prolong my stay on the water; and, fixing the rudder in a direct position, stretched myself at the bottom of the boat. Clouds hid the moon, every thing was obscure, and I heard only the sound of the boat, as its keel cut through the waves; the murmur lulled me, and in a short time I slept soundly.

I do not know how long I remained in this situation, but when I awoke I found that the sun had already mounted considerably. The wind was high, and the waves continually threatened the safety of my little skiff. I found that the wind was north-east, and must have driven me far from the coast from which I had embarked. I endeavoured to change my course, but quickly found that, if I again made the attempt, the boat would be instantly filled with water. Thus situated, my only resource was to drive before the wind. I confess that I felt a few sensations of terror. I had no compass with me, and was so slenderly acquainted with the geography of this part of the world, that the sun was of little benefit to me. I might be driven into the wide Atlantic, and feel all the tortures of starvation, or be swallowed up in the immeasurable waters that roared and buffeted around me. I had already been out many hours, and felt the torment of a burning thirst, a prelude to my other sufferings. I looked on the heavens, which were covered by clouds that flew the wind, only to be replaced by others: I looked upon the sea, it was to be my grave. "Fiend," I exclaimed, "your task is already fulfilled!" I thought of Elizabeth, of my father, and of Clerval; all left behind, on whom the monster might satisfy his sanguinary and merciless passions. This idea plunged me into a reverie, so despairing and frightful, that even now, when the scene is on the point of closing before me for ever, I shudder to reflect on it.

Some hours passed thus; but by degrees, as the sun declined towards the horizon, the wind died away into a gentle breeze, and the sea became free from breakers. But these gave place to a heavy swell: I felt sick, and hardly able to hold the rudder, when suddenly I saw a line of high land towards the south.

Almost spent, as I was, by fatigue, and the dreadful suspense I endured for several hours, this sudden certainty of life rushed like a flood of warm joy to my heart, and tears gushed from my eyes.

How mutable are our feelings, and how strange is that clinging love we have of life even in the excess of misery! I constructed another sail with a part of my dress, and eagerly steered my course towards the land. It had a wild and rocky appearance; but, as I approached nearer, I easily perceived the traces of cultivation. I saw vessels near the shore, and found myself suddenly transported back to the neighbourhood of civilised man. I carefully traced the windings of the land, and hailed a steeple which I at length saw issuing from behind a small promontory. As I was in a state of extreme debility, I resolved to sail directly towards the town, as a place where I could most easily procure nourishment. Fortunately, I had money with me. As I turned the promontory, I perceived a small, neat town and a good harbour, which I entered, my heart bounding with joy at my unexpected escape.

As I was occupied in fixing the boat and arranging the sails, several people crowded towards the spot. They seemed much surprised at my appearance; but, instead of offering me any assistance, whispered together with gestures that at any other time might have produced in me a slight sensation of alarm. As it was, I merely remarked that they spoke English; and I therefore addressed them in that language: "My good friends," said I, "will you be so kind as to tell me the name of this town, and inform me where I am?"

"You will know that soon enough," replied a man with a hoarse voice. "May be you are come to a place that will not prove much to your taste; but you will not be consulted as to your quarters, I promise you."

I was exceedingly surprised on receiving so rude an answer from a stranger; and I was also disconcerted on perceiving the frowning and angry countenances of his companions. "Why do you answer me so roughly?" I replied; "surely it is not the custom of Englishmen to receive strangers so inhospitably."

"I do not know," said the man, "what the custom of the English may be; but it is the custom of the Irish to hate villains."

While this strange dialogue continued, I perceived the crowd rapidly increase. Their faces expressed a mixture of curiosity and anger, which annoyed, and in some degree alarmed me. I enquired the way to the inn; but no one replied. I then moved forward, and a murmuring sound arose from the crowd as they followed and surrounded me; when an ill-looking man approached, tapped me on the shoulder, and said, "Come, sir, you must follow me to Mr. Kirwin's, to give an account of yourself."

"Who is Mr. Kirwin? Why am I to give an account of myself? Is not this a free country?"

"Ay, sir, free enough for honest folks. Mr. Kirwin is a magistrate; and you are to give an account of the death of a gentleman who was found murdered here last night."

This answer startled me; but I presently recovered myself. I was innocent; that could easily be proved: accordingly I followed my conductor in silence, and was led to one of the best houses in the town. I was ready to sink from fatigue and hunger; but, being surrounded by a crowd, I thought it politic to rouse all my strength, that no physical debility might be construed into apprehension or conscious guilt. Little did I then expect the calamity that was in a few moments to overwhelm me, and extinguish in horror and despair all fear of ignominy or death.

I must pause here; for it requires all my fortitude to recall the memory of the frightful events which I am about to relate, in proper detail, to my recollection.

## CHAPTER XXI

I was soon introduced into the presence of the magistrate, an old benevolent man, with calm and mild manners. He looked upon me, however, with some degree of severity: and then, turning towards my conductors, he asked who appeared as witnesses on this occasion.

About half a dozen men came forward; and, one being selected by the magistrate, he deposed, that he had been out fishing the night before with his son and brother-in-law, Daniel Nugent, when, about ten o'clock, they observed a strong northerly blast rising, and they accordingly put in for port. It was a very dark night, as the moon had not yet risen; they did not land at the harbour, but, as they had been accustomed, at a creek about two miles below. He walked on first, carrying a part of the fishing tackle, and his companions followed him at some distance. As he was proceeding along the sands, he struck his foot against something, and fell at his length on the ground. His companions came up to assist him; and, by the light of their lantern, they found that he had fallen on the body of a man, who was to all appearance dead. Their first supposition was, that it was the corpse of some person who had been drowned, and was thrown on shore by the waves; but, on examination, they found that the clothes were not wet, and even that the body was not then cold. They instantly carried it to the cottage of an old woman near the spot, and endeavoured, but in vain, to restore it to life. It appeared to be a handsome young man, about five and twenty years of age. He had apparently been strangled; for there was no sign of any violence, except the black mark of fingers on his neck.

The first part of this deposition did not in the least interest me; but when the mark of the fingers was mentioned, I remembered the murder of my brother, and felt myself extremely agitated; my limbs trembled, and a mist came over my eyes, which obliged me to lean on a chair for support. The magistrate observed me with a keen eye, and of course drew an unfavourable augury from my manner.

The son confirmed his father's account: but when Daniel Nugent was called, he swore positively that, just before the fall of his companion, he saw a boat, with a single man in it, at a short distance from the shore; and, as far as he could judge by the light of a few stars, it was the same boat in which I had just landed.

A woman deposed, that she lived near the beach, and was standing at the door of her cottage, waiting for the return of the fishermen, about an hour before she heard of the discovery of the body, when she saw a boat, with only one man in it, push off from that part of the shore where the corpse was afterwards found.

Another woman confirmed the account of the fishermen having brought the body into her house; it was not cold. They put it into a bed, and rubbed it; and Daniel went to the town for an apothecary, but life was quite gone.

Several other men were examined concerning my landing; and they agreed, that, with the strong north wind that had arisen during the night, it was very probable that I had beaten about for many hours, and had been obliged to return nearly to the same spot from which I had departed. Besides, they observed that it appeared that I had brought the body from another place, and it was likely, that as I did not appear to know the shore, I might have put into the harbour ignorant of the distance of the town of * * * from the place where I had deposited the corpse.

Mr. Kirwin, on hearing this evidence, desired that I should be taken into the room where the body lay for interment, that it might be observed what effect the sight of it would produce upon me. This idea was probably suggested by the extreme agitation I had exhibited when the mode of the murder had been described. I was accordingly conducted, by the magistrate and several other persons, to the inn. I could not help being struck by the strange coincidences that had taken place during this eventful night; but, knowing that I had been conversing with several persons in the island I had inhabited about the time that the body had been found, I was perfectly tranquil as to the consequences of the affair.

I entered the room where the corpse lay, and was led up to the coffin. How can I describe my sensations on beholding it? I feel yet parched with horror, nor can I reflect on that terrible moment without shuddering and agony. The examination, the presence of the magistrate and witnesses, passed like a dream from my memory, when I saw the lifeless form of Henry Clerval stretched before me. I gasped for breath; and, throwing myself on the body, I exclaimed, "Have my murderous machinations deprived you also, my dearest Henry, of life? Two I have already destroyed; other victims await their destiny: but you, Clerval, my friend, my benefactor—"

The human frame could no longer support the agonies that I endured, and I was carried out of the room in strong convulsions.

A fever succeeded to this. I lay for two months on the point of death: my ravings, as I afterwards heard, were frightful; I called myself the murderer of William, of Justine, and of Clerval. Sometimes I entreated my attendants to assist me in the destruction of the fiend by whom I was tormented; and at others, I felt the fingers of the monster already grasping my neck, and screamed aloud with agony and terror. Fortunately, as I spoke my native language, Mr. Kirwin alone understood me; but my gestures and bitter cries were sufficient to affright the other witnesses.

Why did I not die? More miserable than man ever was before, why did I not sink into forgetfulness and rest? Death snatches away many blooming children, the only hopes of their doting parents: how many brides and youthful lovers have been one day in the bloom of health and hope, and the next a prey for worms and the decay of the tomb! Of what materials was I made, that I could thus resist so many shocks, which, like the turning of the wheel, continually renewed the torture?

But I was doomed to live; and, in two months, found myself as awaking from a dream, in a prison, stretched on a wretched bed, surrounded by gaolers, turnkeys, bolts, and all the miserable apparatus of a dungeon. It was morning, I remember, when I thus awoke to understanding: I had forgotten the particulars of what had happened, and only felt as if some great misfortune had suddenly overwhelmed me; but when I looked around, and saw the barred windows, and the squalidness of the room in which I was, all flashed across my memory, and I groaned bitterly.

This sound disturbed an old woman who was sleeping in a chair beside me. She was a hired nurse, the wife of one of the turnkeys, and her countenance expressed all those bad qualities which often characterise that class. The lines of her face were hard and rude, like that of persons accustomed to see without sympathising in sights of misery. Her tone expressed her entire indifference; she addressed me in English, and the voice struck me as one that I had heard during my sufferings:—

"Are you better now, sir?" said she.

*English Spoken in Prison*

I replied in the same language, with a feeble voice, "I believe I am; but if it be all true, if indeed I did not dream, I am sorry that I am still alive to feel this misery and horror."

*He is screwed*

"For that matter," replied the old woman, "if you mean about the gentleman you murdered, I believe that it were better for you if you were dead, for I fancy it will go hard with you! However, that's none of my business; I am sent to nurse you, and get you well; I do my duty with a safe conscience; it were well if every body did the same."

*taste of his own medicine*

*living in a dream*

I turned with loathing from the woman who could utter so unfeeling a speech to a person just saved, on the very edge of death; but I felt languid, and unable to reflect on all that had passed. The whole series of my life appeared to me as a dream; I sometimes doubted if indeed it were all true, for it never presented itself to my mind with the force of reality.

*like the monster*

As the images that floated before me became more distinct, I grew feverish; a darkness pressed around me: no one was near me who soothed me with the gentle voice of love; no dear hand supported me. The physician came and prescribed medicines, and the old woman prepared them for me; but utter carelessness was visible in the first, and the expression of brutality was strongly marked in the visage of the second. Who could be interested in the fate of a murderer, but the hangman who would gain his fee?

These were my first reflections; but I soon learned that Mr. Kirwin had shown me extreme kindness. He had caused the best room in the prison to be prepared for me (wretched indeed was the best); and it was he who had provided a physician and a nurse. It is true, he seldom came to see me; for, although he ardently desired to relieve the sufferings of every human creature, he did not wish to be present at the agonies and miserable ravings of a murderer. He came, therefore, sometimes, to see that I was not neglected; but his visits were short, and with long intervals.

One day, while I was gradually recovering, I was seated in a chair, my eyes half open, and my cheeks livid like those in death. I was overcome by gloom and misery, and often reflected I had better seek death than desire to remain in a world which to me was replete with wretchedness. At one time I considered whether I should not declare myself guilty, and suffer the penalty of the law, less innocent than poor Justine had been. Such were my thoughts, when the door of my apartment was opened, and Mr. Kirwin entered. His countenance expressed sympathy and compassion; he drew a chair close to mine, and addressed me in French—

*what is the significance of the languages?     french = kindness?*

"I fear that this place is very shocking to you; can I do any thing to make you more comfortable?"

"I thank you; but all that you mention is nothing to me: on the whole earth there is no comfort which I am capable of receiving."

"I know that the sympathy of a stranger can be but of little relief to one borne down as you are by so strange a misfortune. But you will, I hope, soon quit this melancholy abode; for, doubtless, evidence can easily be brought to free you from the criminal charge."

"That is my least concern: I am, by a course of strange events, become the most miserable of mortals. Persecuted and tortured as I am and have been, can death be any evil to me?"

"Nothing indeed could be more unfortunate and agonising than the strange chances that have lately occurred. You were thrown, by some surprising accident, on this shore, renowned for its hospitality; seized immediately, and charged with murder. The first sight that was presented to your eyes was the body of your friend, murdered in so unaccountable a manner, and placed, as it were, by some fiend across your path."

As Mr. Kirwin said this, notwithstanding the agitation I endured on this retrospect of my sufferings, I also felt considerable surprise at the knowledge he seemed to possess concerning me. I suppose some astonishment was exhibited in my countenance; for Mr. Kirwin hastened to say—

"Immediately upon your being taken ill, all the papers that were on your person were brought to me, and I examined them that I might discover some trace by which I could send to your relations an account of your misfortune and illness. I found several letters, and, among others, one which I discovered from its commencement to be from your father. I instantly wrote to Geneva: nearly two months have elapsed since the departure of my letter.—But you are ill; even now you tremble: you are unfit for agitation of any kind."

"This suspense is a thousand times worse than the most horrible event: tell me what new scene of death has been acted, and whose murder I am now to lament?"

"Your family is perfectly well," said Mr. Kirwin, with gentleness; "and some one, a friend, is come to visit you."

I know not by what chain of thought the idea presented itself, but it instantly darted into my mind that the murderer had come to mock at my misery, and taunt me with the death of Clerval, as a new incitement for me to comply with his hellish desires. I put my hand before my eyes, and cried out in agony—

"Oh! take him away! I cannot see him; for God's sake, do not let him enter!"

Mr. Kirwin regarded me with a troubled countenance. He could not help regarding my exclamation as a presumption of my guilt, and said, in rather a severe tone —

"I should have thought, young man, that the presence of your father would have been welcome, instead of inspiring such violent repugnance."

"My father!" cried I, while every feature and every muscle was relaxed from anguish to pleasure: "is my father indeed come? How kind, how very kind! But where is he, why does he not hasten to me?"

My change of manner surprised and pleased the magistrate; perhaps he thought that my former exclamation was a momentary return of delirium, and now he instantly resumed his former benevolence. He rose, and quitted the room with my nurse, and in a moment my father entered it.

Nothing, at this moment, could have given me greater pleasure than the arrival of my father. I stretched out my hand to him, and cried —

[handwritten margin note: Not even Elizabeth?]

"Are you then safe — and Elizabeth — and Ernest?"

My father calmed me with assurances of their welfare, and endeavoured, by dwelling on these subjects so interesting to my heart, to raise my desponding spirits; but he soon felt that a prison cannot be the abode of cheerfulness. "What a place is this that you inhabit, my son!" said he, looking mournfully at the barred windows, and wretched appearance of the room. "You travelled to seek happiness, but a fatality seems to pursue you. And poor Clerval —"

The name of my unfortunate and murdered friend was an agitation too great to be endured in my weak state; I shed tears.

"Alas! yes, my father," replied I; "some destiny of the most horrible kind hangs over me, and I must live to fulfil it, or surely I should have died on the coffin of Henry." [handwritten margin note: Wanted to die w/ Henry?]

We were not allowed to converse for any length of time, for the precarious state of my health rendered every precaution necessary that could ensure tranquillity. Mr. Kirwin came in, and insisted that my strength should not be exhausted by too much exertion. But the appearance of my father was to me like that of my good angel, and I gradually recovered my health.

As my sickness quitted me, I was absorbed by a gloomy and black melancholy, that nothing could dissipate. The image of Clerval was for ever before me, ghastly and murdered. More than once the agitation into which these reflections threw me made my friends dread a dangerous relapse. Alas! why did they preserve so miserable and detested a life? It was surely that I might fulfil my destiny, which is now drawing to a close. Soon, oh! very soon, will death extinguish these throbbings, and relieve me from the mighty weight of anguish that bears me to the dust; and, in executing the award of justice, I shall also sink to rest. Then the appearance of death was distant, although the wish was ever present to my thoughts; and I often sat for hours motionless and speechless, wishing for some mighty revolution that might bury me and my destroyer in its ruins.

The season of the assizes approached. I had already been three months in prison; and although I was still weak, and in continual danger of a relapse, I was obliged to travel nearly a hundred miles to the county-town, where the court was held. Mr. Kirwin charged himself with every care of collecting witnesses, and arranging my defence. I was spared the disgrace of appearing publicly as a criminal, as the case was not brought before the court that decides on life and death. The grand jury rejected the bill, on its being proved that I was on the Orkney Islands at the hour the body of my friend was found; and a fortnight after my removal I was liberated from prison.

My father was enraptured on finding me freed from the vexations of a criminal charge, that I was again allowed to breathe the fresh atmosphere, and permitted to return to my native country. I did not participate in these feelings; for to me the walls of a dungeon or a palace were alike hateful. The cup of life was poisoned for ever; and although the sun shone upon me, as upon the happy and gay of heart, I saw around me nothing but a dense and frightful darkness, penetrated by no light but the glimmer of two eyes that glared upon me. Sometimes they were the expressive eyes of Henry, languishing in death, the dark orbs nearly covered by the lids, and the long black lashes that fringed them; sometimes it was the watery, clouded eyes of the monster, as I first saw them in my chamber at Ingolstadt.

My father tried to awaken in me the feelings of affection. He talked of Geneva, which I should soon visit—of Elizabeth and Ernest; but these words only drew deep groans from me. Sometimes, indeed, I felt a wish for happiness; and thought, with melancholy delight, of my beloved cousin; or longed, with a devouring *maladie du pays,*° to see once more the blue lake and rapid Rhone, that had been so dear to me in early childhood: but my general state of feeling was a torpor, in which a prison was as welcome a residence as the divinest scene in

*maladie du pays:* Homesickness (Fr.).

nature; and these fits were seldom interrupted but by paroxysms of anguish and despair. At these moments I often endeavoured to put an end to the existence I loathed; and it required unceasing attendance and vigilance to restrain me from committing some dreadful act of violence.

Yet one duty remained to me, the recollection of which finally triumphed over my selfish despair. It was necessary that I should return without delay to Geneva, there to watch over the lives of those I so fondly loved; and to lie in wait for the murderer, that if any chance led me to the place of his concealment, or if he dared again to blast me by his presence, I might, with unfailing aim, put an end to the existence of the monstrous image which I had endued with the mockery of a soul still more monstrous. My father still desired to delay our departure, fearful that I could not sustain the fatigues of a journey: for I was a shattered wreck,—the shadow of a human being. My strength was gone. I was a mere skeleton; and fever night and day preyed upon my wasted frame.

Still, as I urged our leaving Ireland with such inquietude and impatience, my father thought it best to yield. We took our passage on board a vessel bound for Havre-de-Grace, and sailed with a fair wind from the Irish shores. It was midnight. I lay on the deck, looking at the stars, and listening to the dashing of the waves. I hailed the darkness that shut Ireland from my sight; and my pulse beat with a feverish joy when I reflected that I should soon see Geneva. The past appeared to me in the light of a frightful dream; yet the vessel in which I was, the wind that blew me from the detested shore of Ireland, and the sea which surrounded me, told me too forcibly that I was deceived by no vision, and that Clerval, my friend and dearest companion, had fallen a victim to me and the monster of my creation. I repassed, in my memory, my whole life; my quiet happiness while residing with my family in Geneva, the death of my mother, and my departure for Ingolstadt. I remembered, shuddering, the mad enthusiasm that hurried me on to the creation of my hideous enemy, and I called to mind the night in which he first lived. I was unable to pursue the train of thought; a thousand feelings pressed upon me, and I wept bitterly.

Ever since my recovery from the fever, I had been in the custom of taking every night a small quantity of laudanum; for it was by means of this drug only that I was enabled to gain the rest necessary for the preservation of life. Oppressed by the recollection of my various misfortunes, I now swallowed double my usual quantity, and soon slept profoundly. But sleep did not afford me respite from thought and mis-

*Sleep scares him*

ery; my dreams presented a thousand objects that scared me. Towards
morning I was possessed by a kind of night-mare; I felt the fiend's grasp *night mare*
in my neck, and could not free myself from it; groans and cries rung in
my ears. My father, who was watching over me, perceiving my restlessness, awoke me; the dashing waves were around: the cloudy sky above;
the fiend was not here: a sense of security, a feeling that a truce was
established between the present hour and the irresistible, disastrous
future, imparted to me a kind of calm forgetfulness, of which the human
mind is by its structure peculiarly susceptible. *can forget for now.*

# CHAPTER XXII

The voyage came to an end. We landed, and proceeded to Paris. I
soon found that I had overtaxed my strength, and that I must repose
before I could continue my journey. My father's care and attentions
were indefatigable; but he did not know the origin of my sufferings,
and sought erroneous methods to remedy the incurable ill. He wished *like the monster*
me to seek amusement in society. I abhorred the face of man. Oh, not
abhorred! they were my brethren, my fellow-beings, and I felt attracted
even to the most repulsive among them, as to creatures of an angelic
nature and celestial mechanism. But I felt that I had no right to share
their intercourse. I had unchained an enemy among them, whose joy it *monster doesn't enjoy it though.*
was to shed their blood, and to revel in their groans. How they would,
each and all, abhor me, and hunt me from the world, did they know my
unhallowed acts, and the crimes which had their source in me!

My father yielded at length to my desire to avoid society, and strove
by various arguments to banish my despair. Sometimes he thought that
I felt deeply the degradation of being obliged to answer a charge of
murder, and he endeavoured to prove to me the futility of pride.

"Alas! my father," said I, "how little do you know me. Human *no pride*
beings, their feelings and passions, would indeed be degraded if such a
wretch as I felt pride. Justine, poor unhappy Justine, was as innocent as *rlt?*
I, and she suffered the same charge; she died for it; and I am the cause
of this—I murdered her. William, Justine, and Henry—they all died
by my hands."

My father had often, during my imprisonment, heard me make the
same assertion; when I thus accused myself, he sometimes seemed to
desire an explanation, and at others he appeared to consider it as the
offspring of delirium, and that, during my illness, some idea of this kind
had presented itself to my imagination, the remembrance of which I

preserved in my convalescence. I avoided explanation, and maintained a continual silence concerning the wretch I had created. I had a persuasion that I should be supposed mad; and this in itself would for ever have chained my tongue. But, besides, I could not bring myself to disclose a secret which would fill my hearer with consternation, and make fear and unnatural horror the inmates of his breast. I checked, therefore, my impatient thirst for sympathy, and was silent when I would have given the world to have confided the fatal secret. Yet still words like those I have recorded, would burst uncontrollably from me. I could offer no explanation of them; but their truth in part relieved the burden of my mysterious woe.

Upon this occasion my father said, with an expression of unbounded wonder, "My dearest Victor, what infatuation is this? My dear son, I entreat you never to make such an assertion again."

"I am not mad," I cried energetically; "the sun and the heavens, who have viewed my operations, can bear witness of my truth. I am the assassin of those most innocent victims; they died by my machinations. A thousand times would I have shed my own blood, drop by drop, to have saved their lives; but I could not, my father, indeed I could not sacrifice the whole human race."

The conclusion of this speech convinced my father that my ideas were deranged, and he instantly changed the subject of our conversation, and endeavoured to alter the course of my thoughts. He wished as much as possible to obliterate the memory of the scenes that had taken place in Ireland, and never alluded to them, or suffered me to speak of my misfortunes.

As time passed away I became more calm: misery had her dwelling in my heart, but I no longer talked in the same incoherent manner of my own crimes; sufficient for me was the consciousness of them. By the utmost self-violence, I curbed the imperious voice of wretchedness, which sometimes desired to declare itself to the whole world; and my manners were calmer and more composed than they had ever been since my journey to the sea of ice.

A few days before we left Paris on our way to Switzerland, I received the following letter from Elizabeth:—

"My dear Friend,

"It gave me the greatest pleasure to receive a letter from my uncle dated at Paris; you are no longer at a formidable distance, and I may hope to see you in less than a fortnight. My poor cousin, how much you must have suffered! I expect to see you looking even more ill than when you quitted Geneva. This winter has been passed most miserably, tortured as I have been by anxious suspense; yet I hope to see peace in your countenance, and to find that your heart is not totally void of comfort and tranquillity.

"Yet I fear that the same feelings now exist that made you so miserable a year ago, even perhaps augmented by time. I would not disturb you at this period, when so many misfortunes weigh upon you; but a conversation that I had with my uncle previous to his departure renders some explanation necessary before we meet.

"Explanation! you may possibly say; what can Elizabeth have to explain? If you really say this, my questions are answered, and all my doubts satisfied. But you are distant from me, and it is possible that you may dread, and yet be pleased with this explanation; and, in a probability of this being the case, I dare not any longer postpone writing what, during your absence, I have often wished to express to you, but have never had the courage to begin.

"You well know, Victor, that our union had been the favourite plan of your parents ever since our infancy. We were told this when young, and taught to look forward to it as an event that would certainly take place. We were affectionate playfellows during childhood, and, I believe, dear and valued friends to one another as we grew older. But as brother and sister often entertain a lively affection towards each other, without desiring a more intimate union, may not such also be our case? Tell me, dearest Victor. Answer me, I conjure you, by our mutual happiness, with simple truth—Do you not love another?

"You have travelled; you have spent several years of your life at Ingolstadt; and I confess to you, my friend, that when I saw you last autumn so unhappy, flying to solitude, from the society of every creature, I could not help supposing that you might regret our connection, and believe yourself bound in honour to fulfil the wishes of your parents, although they opposed themselves to your inclinations. But this is false reasoning. I confess to you, my friend, that I love you, and that in my airy dreams of futurity you have been my constant friend and companion. But it is your happiness I desire as well as my own, when I declare to you, that our marriage would render me eternally miserable, unless it were the dictate of your own free choice. Even now I weep to think, that, borne down as you are by the cruellest misfortunes, you may stifle, by the word _honour_, all hope of that love and happiness which would alone restore you to yourself. I, who have so disinterested an affection for you, may increase your miseries tenfold, by being an obstacle to your wishes. Ah! Victor, be assured that your cousin and playmate has too sincere a love for you not to be made miserable by this supposition. Be happy, my friend; and if you obey me in this one request, remain satisfied that nothing on earth will have the power to interrupt my tranquillity.

"Do not let this letter disturb you; do not answer tomorrow, or the next day, or even until you come, if it will give you pain. My uncle will send me news of your health; and if I see but one smile on your lips when we meet, occasioned by this or any other exertion of mine, I shall need no other happiness.

"ELIZABETH LAVENZA.

"Geneva, May 18th, 17—."

This letter revived in my memory what I had before forgotten, the threat of the fiend — "*I will be with you on your wedding-night!*" Such was my sentence, and on that night would the daemon employ every art to destroy me, and tear me from the glimpse of happiness which promised partly to console my sufferings. On that night he had determined to consummate his crimes by my death. Well, be it so; a deadly struggle would then assuredly take place, in which if he were victorious I should be at peace, and his power over me be at an end. If he were vanquished, I should be a free man. Alas! what freedom? such as the peasant enjoys when his family have been massacred before his eyes, his cottage burnt, his lands laid waste, and he is turned adrift, homeless, penniless, and alone, but free. Such would be my liberty, except that in my Elizabeth I possessed a treasure; alas! balanced by those horrors of remorse and guilt, which would pursue me until death.

Sweet and beloved Elizabeth! I read and re-read her letter, and some softened feelings stole into my heart, and dared to whisper paradisiacal dreams of love and joy; but the apple was already eaten, and the angel's arm bared to drive me from all hope. Yet I would die to make her happy. If the monster executed his threat, death was inevitable; yet, again, I considered whether my marriage would hasten my fate. My destruction might indeed arrive a few months sooner; but if my torturer should suspect that I postponed it, influenced by his menaces, he would surely find other, and perhaps more dreadful means of revenge. He had vowed *to be with me on my wedding-night*, yet he did not consider that threat as binding him to peace in the mean time; for, as if to show me that he was not yet satiated with blood, he had murdered Clerval immediately after the enunciation of his threats. I resolved, therefore, that if my immediate union with my cousin would conduce either to hers or my father's happiness, my adversary's designs against my life should not retard it a single hour.

In this state of mind I wrote to Elizabeth. My letter was calm and affectionate. "I fear, my beloved girl," I said, "little happiness remains for us on earth; yet all that I may one day enjoy is centred in you. Chase away your idle fears; to you alone do I consecrate my life, and my endeavours for contentment. I have one secret, Elizabeth, a dreadful one; when revealed to you, it will chill your frame with horror, and then, far from being surprised at my misery, you will only wonder that I survive what I have endured. I will confide this tale of misery and terror to you the day after our marriage shall take place; for, my sweet cousin, there must be perfect confidence between us. But until then, I conjure you, do not mention or allude to it. This I most earnestly entreat, and I know you will comply."

In about a week after the arrival of Elizabeth's letter, we returned to Geneva. The sweet girl welcomed me with warm affection; yet tears were in her eyes, as she beheld my emaciated frame and feverish cheeks. I saw a change in her also. She was thinner, and had lost much of that heavenly vivacity that had before charmed me; but her gentleness, and soft looks of compassion, made her a more fit companion for one blasted and miserable as I was.

The tranquillity which I now enjoyed did not endure. Memory brought madness with it; and when I thought of what had passed, a real insanity possessed me; sometimes I was furious, and burnt with rage, sometimes low and despondent. I neither spoke, nor looked at any one, but sat motionless, bewildered by the multitude of miseries that overcame me. *Partner is the only one who helps him*

Elizabeth alone had the power to draw me from these fits; her gentle voice would soothe me when transported by passion, and inspire me with human feelings when sunk in torpor. She wept with me, and for me. When reason returned, she would remonstrate, and endeavour to inspire me with resignation. Ah! it is well for the unfortunate to be resigned, but for the guilty there is no peace. The agonies of remorse poison the luxury there is otherwise sometimes found in indulging the excess of grief.

Soon after my arrival, my father spoke of my immediate marriage with Elizabeth. I remained silent.

"Have you, then, some other attachment?"

"None on earth. I love Elizabeth, and look forward to our union with delight. Let the day therefore be fixed; and on it I will consecrate myself, in life or death, to the happiness of my cousin."

"My dear Victor, do not speak thus. Heavy misfortunes have befallen us; but let us only cling closer to what remains, and transfer our

love for those whom we have lost, to those who yet live. Our circle will
be small, but bound close by the ties of affection and mutual misfortune.(And when time shall have softened your despair, new and dear
objects of care will be born to replace those of whom we have been so
cruelly deprived.") *new life*

Such were the lessons of my father. But to me the remembrance of
the threat returned: nor can you wonder, that, omnipotent as the fiend
had yet been in his deeds of blood,(I should almost regard him as invincible) and that when he had pronounced the words, "I shall be with
you on your wedding-night," I should regard the threatened fate as
unavoidable. But death was no evil to me, if the loss of Elizabeth were
balanced with it; and I therefore, with a contented and even cheerful
countenance, agreed with my father, that if my cousin would consent,
the ceremony should take place in ten days, and thus put, as I imagined,
the seal to my fate.

*invincible*

Great God! if for one instant I had thought what might be the hellish intention of my fiendish adversary, I would rather have banished
myself for ever from my native country, and wandered a friendless out-
cast over the earth, than have consented to this miserable marriage.
But, as if possessed of magic powers, the monster had blinded me to his
real intentions; and when I thought that I had prepared only my own
death, I hastened that of a far dearer victim.

As the period fixed for our marriage drew nearer, whether from
cowardice or a prophetic feeling, I felt my heart sink within me. But I
concealed my feelings by an appearance of hilarity, that brought smiles
and joy to the countenance of my father, but hardly deceived the ever-
watchful and nicer eye of Elizabeth. She looked forward to our union
with placid contentment, not unmingled with a little fear, which past
misfortunes had impressed, that what now appeared certain and tangible
happiness, might soon dissipate into an <u>airy dream</u>, and leave no trace
but deep and everlasting regret. *dream*

Preparations were made for the event; congratulatory visits were
received; and all wore a smiling appearance. I shut up, as well as I could,
in my own heart the anxiety that preyed there, and entered with seeming earnestness into the plans of my father, although they might only
serve as the decorations of my tragedy. Through my father's exertions,
a part of the inheritance of Elizabeth had been restored to her by the
Austrian government. A small possession on the shores of Como° 
belonged to her. It was agreed that, immediately after our union, we

***Como:*** A large lake in Italy.

should proceed to Villa Lavenza, and spend our first days of happiness beside the beautiful lake near which it stood.

In the mean time I took every precaution to defend my person, in case the fiend should openly attack me. I carried pistols and a dagger constantly about me, and was ever on the watch to prevent artifice; and by these means gained a greater degree of tranquillity. Indeed, as the period approached, the threat appeared more as a delusion, not to be regarded as worthy to disturb my peace, while the happiness I hoped for in my marriage wore a greater appearance of certainty, as the day fixed for its solemnisation drew nearer, and I heard it continually spoken of as an occurrence which no accident could possibly prevent.

Elizabeth seemed happy; my tranquil demeanour contributed greatly to calm her mind. But on the day that was to fulfil my wishes and my destiny, she was melancholy, and a presentiment of evil pervaded her; and perhaps also she thought of the dreadful secret which I had promised to reveal to her on the following day. My father was in the mean time overjoyed, and, in the bustle of preparation, only recognised in the melancholy of his niece the diffidence of a bride.

After the ceremony was performed, a large party assembled at my father's; but it was agreed that Elizabeth and I should commence our journey by water, sleeping that night at Evian, and continuing our voyage on the following day. The day was fair, the wind favourable, all smiled on our nuptial embarkation.

Those were the last moments of my life during which I enjoyed the feeling of happiness. We passed rapidly along: the sun was hot, but we were sheltered from its rays by a kind of canopy, while we enjoyed the beauty of the scene, sometimes on one side of the lake, where we saw Mont Salêve, the pleasant banks of Montalègre, and at a distance, surmounting all, the beautiful Mont Blanc, and the assemblage of snowy mountains that in vain endeavour to emulate her; sometimes coasting the opposite banks, we saw the mighty Jura opposing its dark side to the ambition that would quit its native country, and an almost insurmountable barrier to the invader who should wish to enslave it.

I took the hand of Elizabeth: "You are sorrowful, my love. Ah! if you knew what I have suffered, and what I may yet endure, you would endeavour to let me taste the quiet and freedom from despair, that this one day at least permits me to enjoy."

"Be happy, my dear Victor," replied Elizabeth; "there is, I hope, nothing to distress you; and be assured that if a lively joy is not painted in my face, my heart is contented. Something whispers to me not to depend too much on the prospect that is opened before us; but I will not listen to such a sinister voice. Observe how fast we move along, and how the clouds, which sometimes obscure and sometimes rise above the dome of Mont Blanc, render this scene of beauty still more interesting. Look also at the innumerable fish that are swimming in the clear waters, where we can distinguish every pebble that lies at the bottom. What a divine day! how happy and serene all nature appears! *nature*

Thus Elizabeth endeavoured to divert her thoughts and mine from all reflection upon melancholy subjects. But her temper was fluctuating; joy for a few instants shone in her eyes, but it continually gave place to distraction and reverie.

The sun sunk lower in the heavens; we passed the river Drance, and observed its path through the chasms of the higher, and the glens of the lower hills. The Alps here come closer to the lake, and we approached the amphitheatre of mountains which forms its eastern boundary. The spire of Evian shone under the woods that surrounded it, and the range of mountain above mountain by which it was overhung.

The wind, which had hitherto carried us along with amazing rapidity, sunk at sunset to a light breeze; the soft air just ruffled the water, and caused a pleasant motion among the trees as we approached the shore, from which it wafted the most delightful scent of flowers and hay. The sun sunk beneath the horizon as we landed; and as I touched the shore, I felt those cares and fears revive, which soon were to clasp me, and cling to me for ever. *land brings cares*

## CHAPTER XXIII

It was eight o'clock when we landed; we walked for a short time on the shore, enjoying the transitory light, and then retired to the inn, and contemplated the lovely scene of waters, woods, and mountains, obscured in darkness, yet still displaying their black outlines.

The wind, which had fallen in the south, now rose with great violence in the west. The moon had reached her summit in the heavens, and was beginning to descend; the clouds swept across it swifter than the flight of the vulture, and dimmed her rays, while the lake reflected the scene of the busy heavens, rendered still busier by the restless waves that were beginning to rise. Suddenly a heavy storm of rain descended.

*night scary* I had been calm during the day; but so soon as night obscured the shapes of objects, a thousand fears arose in my mind. I was anxious and watchful, while my right hand grasped a pistol which was hidden in my bosom; every sound terrified me; but I resolved that I would sell my life dearly, and not shrink from the conflict until my own life, or that of my adversary, was extinguished.

Elizabeth observed my agitation for some time in timid and fearful silence; but there was something in my glance which communicated terror to her, and trembling she asked, "What is it that agitates you, my dear Victor? What is it you fear?"

"Oh! peace, peace, my love," replied I; "this night, and all will be safe: but this night is dreadful, very dreadful."

I passed an hour in this state of mind, when suddenly I reflected how fearful the combat which I momentarily expected would be to my wife, and I earnestly entreated her to retire, resolving not to join her until I had obtained some knowledge as to the situation of my enemy.

She left me, and I continued some time walking up and down the passages of the house, and inspecting every corner that might afford a retreat to my adversary. But I discovered no trace of him, and was beginning to conjecture that some fortunate chance had intervened to prevent the execution of his menaces; when suddenly I heard a shrill and dreadful scream. It came from the room into which Elizabeth had retired. As I heard it, the whole truth rushed into my mind, my arms dropped, the motion of every muscle and fibre was suspended; I could feel the blood trickling in my veins, and tingling in the extremities of my limbs. This state lasted but for an instant; the scream was repeated, and I rushed into the room.

Great God! why did I not then expire! Why am I here to relate the destruction of the best hope, and the purest creature of earth? She was there, lifeless and inanimate, thrown across the bed, her head hanging down, and her pale and distorted features half covered by her hair. Every where I turn I see the same figure—her bloodless arms and relaxed form flung by the murderer on its bridal bier. Could I behold this, and live? Alas! life is obstinate, and clings closest where it is most hated. For a moment only did I lose recollection; I fell senseless on the ground.

When I recovered, I found myself surrounded by the people of the inn; their countenances expressed a breathless terror: but the horror of others appeared only as a mockery, a shadow of the feelings that oppressed me. I escaped from them to the room where lay the body of Elizabeth, my love, my wife, so lately living, so dear, so worthy. She had been moved from the posture in which I had first beheld her; and now, as she lay, her head upon her arm, and a handkerchief thrown across her face and neck, I might have supposed her asleep. I rushed towards her, and embraced her with ardour; but the deadly languor and coldness of the limbs told me, that what I now held in my arms had ceased to be the Elizabeth whom I had loved and cherished. The murderous mark of the fiend's grasp was on her neck, and the breath had ceased to issue from her lips.

While I still hung over her in the agony of despair, I happened to look up. The windows of the room had before been darkened, and I felt a kind of panic on seeing the pale yellow light of the moon illuminate the chamber. The shutters had been thrown back; and, with a sensation of horror not to be described, I saw at the open window a figure the most hideous and abhorred. A grin was on the face of the monster; he seemed to jeer, as with his fiendish finger he pointed towards the corpse of my wife. I rushed towards the window, and drawing a pistol from my bosom, fired; but he eluded me, leaped from his station, and, running with the swiftness of lightning, plunged into the lake.

The report of the pistol brought a crowd into the room. I pointed to the spot where he had disappeared, and we followed the track with boats; nets were cast, but in vain. After passing several hours, we returned hopeless, most of my companions believing it to have been a form conjured up by my fancy. After having landed, they proceeded to search the country, parties going in different directions among the woods and vines.

I attempted to accompany them, and proceeded a short distance from the house; but my head whirled round, my steps were like those of a drunken man, I fell at last in a state of utter exhaustion; a film covered my eyes, and my skin was parched with the heat of fever. In this state I was carried back, and placed on a bed, hardly conscious of what had happened; my eyes wandered around the room, as if to seek something that I had lost.

After an interval, I arose, and, as if by instinct, crawled into the room where the corpse of my beloved lay. There were women weeping around—I hung over it, and joined my sad tears to theirs—all this time no distinct idea presented itself to my mind; but my thoughts rambled to various subjects, reflecting confusedly on my misfortunes, and their cause. I was bewildered in a cloud of wonder and horror. The death of William, the execution of Justine, the murder of Clerval, and lastly of my wife; even at that moment I knew not that my only remaining friends were safe from the malignity of the fiend; my father even now might be writhing under his grasp, and Ernest might be dead at his feet. This idea made me shudder, and recalled me to action. I started up, and resolved to return to Geneva with all possible speed.

There were no horses to be procured, and I must return by the lake; but the wind was unfavourable, and the rain fell in torrents. However, it was hardly morning, and I might reasonably hope to arrive by night. I hired men to row, and took an oar myself; for I had always experienced relief from mental torment in bodily exercise. But the overflowing misery I now felt, and the excess of agitation that I endured, rendered me incapable of any exertion. I threw down the oar; and leaning my head upon my hands, gave way to every gloomy idea that arose. If I looked up, I saw the scenes which were familiar to me in my happier time, and which I had contemplated but the day before in the company of her who was now but a shadow and a recollection. Tears streamed from my eyes. The rain had ceased for a moment, and I saw the fish play in the waters as they had done a few hours before; they had then been observed by Elizabeth. Nothing is so painful to the human mind as a great and sudden change. The sun might shine, or the clouds might lower: but nothing could appear to me as it had done the day before. A fiend had snatched from me every hope of future happiness: no creature had ever been so miserable as I was; so frightful an event is single in the history of man.

But why should I dwell upon the incidents that followed this last overwhelming event? Mine has been a tale of horrors; I have reached their *acme*, and what I must now relate can but be tedious to you. Know that, one by one, my friends were snatched away; I was left desolate. My own strength is exhausted; and I must tell, in a few words, what remains of my hideous narration.

I arrived at Geneva. My father and Ernest yet lived; but the former sunk under the tidings that I bore. I see him now, excellent and venerable old man! his eyes wandered in vacancy, for they had lost their charm and their delight—his Elizabeth, his more than daughter, whom he doted on with all that affection which a man feels, who in the decline of life, having few affections, clings more earnestly to those that remain. Cursed, cursed be the fiend that brought misery on his grey hairs, and doomed him to waste in wretchedness! He could not live under the horrors that were accumulated around him; the springs of existence suddenly gave way: he was unable to rise from his bed, and in a few days he died in my arms.

What then became of me? I know not; I lost sensation, and chains and darkness were the only objects that pressed upon me. Sometimes, indeed, I dreamt that I wandered in flowery meadows and pleasant vales with the friends of my youth; but I awoke, and found myself in a

dungeon. Melancholy followed, but by degrees I gained a clear conception of my miseries and situation, and was then released from my prison.
For they had called me mad; and during many months, as I understood,
a solitary cell had been my habitation.

*like the monster*

Liberty, however, had been an useless gift to me, had I not, as I
awakened to reason, at the same time awakened to revenge. As the
memory of past misfortunes pressed upon me, I began to reflect on
their cause—the monster whom I had created, the miserable daemon
whom I had sent abroad into the world for my destruction. I was possessed by a maddening rage when I thought of him, and desired and
ardently prayed that I might have him within my grasp to wreak a great
and signal revenge on his cursed head.

Nor did my hate long confine itself to useless wishes; I began to
reflect on the best means of securing him; and for this purpose, about a
month after my release, I repaired to a criminal judge in the town, and
told him that I had an accusation to make; that I knew the destroyer of
my family; and that I required him to exert his whole authority for the
apprehension of the murderer.

The magistrate listened to me with attention and kindness:—"Be
assured, sir," said he, "no pains or exertions on my part shall be spared
to discover the villain."

"I thank you," replied I; "listen, therefore, to the deposition that I
have to make. It is indeed a tale so strange, that I should fear you would
not credit it, were there not something in truth which, however wonderful, forces conviction. The story is too connected to be mistaken for
a dream, and I have no motive for falsehood." My manner, as I thus
addressed him, was impressive, but calm; I had formed in my own heart
a resolution to pursue my destroyer to death; and this purpose quieted
my agony, and for an interval reconciled me to life. I now related my
history, briefly, but with firmness and precision, marking the dates with
accuracy, and never deviating into invective or exclamation.

The magistrate appeared at first perfectly incredulous, but as I continued he became more attentive and interested; I saw him sometimes
shudder with horror, at others a lively surprise, unmingled with disbe-
lief, was painted on his countenance.

When I had concluded my narration, I said, "This is the being
whom I accuse, and for whose seizure and punishment I call upon you
to exert your whole power. It is your duty as a magistrate, and I believe
and hope that your feelings as a man will not revolt from the execution
of those functions on this occasion."

This address caused a considerable change in the physiognomy of my own auditor. He had heard my story with that half kind of belief that is given to a tale of spirits and supernatural events; but when he was called upon to act officially in consequence, the whole tide of his incredulity returned. He, however, answered mildly, "I would willingly afford you every aid in your pursuit; but the creature of whom you speak appears to have powers which would put all my exertions to defiance. Who can follow an animal which can traverse the sea of ice, and inhabit caves and dens where no man would venture to intrude? Besides, some months have elapsed since the commission of his crimes, and no one can conjecture to what place he has wandered, or what region he may now inhabit."

"I do not doubt that he hovers near the spot which I inhabit; and if he has indeed taken refuge in the Alps, he may be hunted like the chamois, and destroyed as a beast of prey. But I perceive your thoughts: you do not credit my narrative, and do not intend to pursue my enemy with the punishment which is his desert."

As I spoke, rage sparkled in my eyes; the magistrate was intimidated: — "You are mistaken," said he, "I will exert myself; and if it is in my power to seize the monster, be assured that he shall suffer punishment proportionate to his crimes. But I fear, from what you have yourself described to be his properties, that this will prove impracticable; and thus, while every proper measure is pursued, you should make up your mind to disappointment."

"That cannot be; but all that I can say will be of little avail. My revenge is of no moment to you; yet, while I allow it to be a vice, I confess that it is the devouring and only passion of my soul. My rage is unspeakable, when I reflect that the murderer, whom I have turned loose upon society, still exists. You refuse my just demand: I have but one resource; and I devote myself, either in my life or death, to his destruction."

I trembled with excess of agitation as I said this; there was a frenzy in my manner, and something, I doubt not, of that haughty fierceness which the martyrs of old are said to have possessed. But to a Genevan magistrate, whose mind was occupied by far other ideas than those of devotion and heroism, this elevation of mind had much the appearance of madness. He endeavoured to soothe me as a nurse does a child, and reverted to my tale as the effects of delirium.

"Man," I cried, "how ignorant art thou in thy pride of wisdom! Cease; you know not what it is you say."

I broke from the house angry and disturbed, and retired to meditate on some other mode of action.

## CHAPTER XXIV

My present situation was one in which all voluntary thought was
swallowed up and lost. I was hurried away by fury; revenge alone endowed
me with strength and composure; it moulded my feelings, and allowed
me to be calculating and calm, at periods when otherwise delirium or
death would have been my portion.

My first resolution was to quit Geneva for ever; my country, which,
when I was happy and beloved, was dear to me, now, in my adversity,
became hateful. I provided myself with a sum of money, together with
a few jewels which had belonged to my mother, and departed.

And now my wanderings began, which are to cease but with life. I
have traversed a vast portion of the earth, and have endured all the
hardships which travellers, in deserts and barbarous countries, are wont
to meet. How I have lived I hardly know; many times have I stretched
my failing limbs upon the sandy plain, and prayed for death. But
revenge kept me alive; I dared not die, and leave my adversary in being.

When I quitted Geneva, my first labour was to gain some clue by
which I might trace the steps of my fiendish enemy. But my plan was
unsettled; and I wandered many hours round the confines of the town,
uncertain what path I should pursue. As night approached, I found
myself at the entrance of the cemetery where William, Elizabeth, and
my father reposed. I entered it, and approached the tomb which marked
their graves. Every thing was silent, except the leaves of the trees, which
were gently agitated by the wind; the night was nearly dark; and the
scene would have been solemn and affecting even to an uninterested
observer. The spirits of the departed seemed to flit around, and to cast
a shadow, which was felt but not seen, around the head of the mourner.

The deep grief which this scene had at first excited quickly gave way
to rage and despair. They were dead, and I lived; their murderer also
lived, and to destroy him I must drag out my weary existence. I knelt
on the grass, and kissed the earth, and with quivering lips exclaimed,
"By the sacred earth on which I kneel, by the shades that wander near
me, by the deep and eternal grief that I feel, I swear; and by thee, O
Night, and the spirits that preside over thee, to pursue the daemon, who
caused this misery, until he or I shall perish in mortal conflict. For this
purpose I will preserve my life: to execute this dear revenge, will I again

behold the sun, and tread the green herbage of earth, which otherwise should vanish from my eyes for ever. And I call on you, spirits of the dead; and on you, wandering ministers of vengeance, to aid and conduct me in my work. Let the cursed and hellish monster drink deep of agony; let him feel the despair that now torments me." *spirits*

I had begun my adjuration with solemnity, and an awe which almost assured me that the shades of my murdered friends heard and approved my devotion; but the furies possessed me as I concluded, and rage choked my utterance.

I was answered through the stillness of night by a loud and fiendish laugh. It rung on my ears long and heavily; the mountains re-echoed it, and I felt as if all hell surrounded me with mockery and laughter. Surely in that moment I should have been possessed by frenzy, and have destroyed my miserable existence, but that my vow was heard, and that I was reserved for vengeance. The laughter died away; when a well-known and abhorred voice, apparently close to my ear, addressed me in an audible whisper — "I am satisfied: miserable wretch! you have determined to live, and I am satisfied." *Monsters existence serves to torture victor*

I darted towards the spot from which the sound proceeded; but the devil eluded my grasp. Suddenly the broad disk of the moon arose, and shone full upon his ghastly and distorted shape, as he fled with more than mortal speed.

I pursued him; and for many months this has been my task. Guided by a slight clue, I followed the windings of the Rhone, but vainly. The blue Mediterranean appeared; and, by a strange chance, I saw the fiend enter by night, and hide himself in a vessel bound for the Black Sea. I took my passage in the same ship; but he escaped, I know not how.

Amidst the wilds of Tartary and Russia, although he still evaded me, I have ever followed in his track. Sometimes the peasants, scared by this horrid apparition, informed me of his path; sometimes he himself, who feared that if I lost all trace of him, I should despair and die, left some mark to guide me. The snows descended on my head, and I saw the print of his huge step on the white plain. To you first entering on life, to whom care is new, and agony unknown, how can you understand what I have felt, and still feel? Cold, want, and fatigue, were the least pains which I was destined to endure; I was cursed by some devil, and carried about with me my eternal hell; yet still a spirit of good followed and directed my steps; and, when I most murmured, would suddenly extricate me from seemingly insurmountable difficulties. Sometimes, when nature, overcome by hunger, sunk under the exhaustion, a repast was prepared for me in the desert, that restored and inspired me. The fare was, indeed, coarse, such as the peasants of the country ate; but I will not doubt that it was set there by the spirits that I had invoked to aid me. Often, when all was dry, the heavens cloudless, and I was parched by thirst, a slight cloud would bedim the sky, shed the few drops that revived me, and vanish.

I followed, when I could, the courses of the rivers; but the daemon generally avoided these, as it was here that the population of the country chiefly collected. In other places human beings were seldom seen; and I generally subsisted on the wild animals that crossed my path. I had money with me, and gained the friendship of the villagers by distributing it; or I brought with me some food that I had killed, which, after taking a small part, I always presented to those who had provided me with fire and utensils for cooking.

My life, as it passed thus, was indeed hateful to me, and it was during sleep alone that I could taste joy. O blessed sleep! often, when most miserable, I sank to repose, and my dreams lulled me even to rapture. The spirits that guarded me had provided these moments, or rather hours, of happiness, that I might retain strength to fulfill my pilgrimage. Deprived of this respite, I should have sunk under my hardships. During the day I was sustained and inspirited by the hope of night: for in sleep I saw my friends, my wife, and my beloved country; again I saw the benevolent countenance of my father, heard the silver tones of my Elizabeth's voice, and beheld Clerval enjoying health and youth. Often, when wearied by a toilsome march, I persuaded myself that I was dreaming until night should come, and that I should then enjoy reality in the arms of my dearest friends. What agonising fondness did I feel for them! how did I cling to their dear forms, as sometimes they haunted even my waking hours, and persuade myself that they still lived! At such moments vengeance, that burned within me, died in my heart, and I pursued my path towards the destruction of the daemon, more as a task enjoined by heaven, as the mechanical impulse of some power of which I was unconscious, than as the ardent desire of my soul.

What his feelings were whom I pursued I cannot know. Sometimes, indeed, he left marks in writing on the barks of the trees, or cut in stone, that guided me, and instigated my fury. "My reign is not yet over," (these words were legible in one of these inscriptions;) "you live, and my power is complete. Follow me; I seek the everlasting ices of the north, where you will feel the misery of cold and frost, to which I am impassive. You will find near this place, if you follow not too tardily, a dead hare; eat, and be refreshed. Come on, my enemy; we have yet to wrestle for our lives; but many hard and miserable hours must you endure until that period shall arrive."

Scoffing devil! Again do I vow vengeance; again do I devote thee, miserable fiend, to torture and death. Never will I give up my search, until he or I perish; and then with what ecstasy shall I join my Elizabeth, and my departed friends, who even now prepare for me the reward of my tedious toil and horrible pilgrimage!

As I still pursued my journey to the northward, the snows thickened, and the cold increased in a degree almost too severe to support. The peasants were shut up in their hovels, and only a few of the most hardy ventured forth to seize the animals whom starvation had forced from their hiding-places to seek for prey. The rivers were covered with ice, and no fish could be procured; and thus I was cut off from my chief article of maintenance.

The triumph of my enemy increased with the difficulty of my labours. One inscription that he left was in these words:—"Prepare! your toils only begin: wrap yourself in furs, and provide food; for we shall soon enter upon a journey where your sufferings will satisfy my everlasting hatred."

My courage and perseverance were invigorated by these scoffing words; I resolved not to fail in my purpose; and, calling on Heaven to support me, I continued with unabated fervour to traverse immense deserts, until the ocean appeared at a distance, and formed the utmost boundary of the horizon. Oh! how unlike it was to the blue seas of the south! Covered with ice, it was only to be distinguished from land by its superior wildness and ruggedness. The Greeks wept for joy when they beheld the Mediterranean from the hills of Asia, and hailed with rapture the boundary of their toils. I did not weep; but I knelt down, and, with a full heart, thanked my guiding spirit for conducting me in safety to the place where I hoped, notwithstanding my adversary's gibe, to meet and grapple with him.

Some weeks before this period I had procured a sledge and dogs, and thus traversed the snows with inconceivable speed. I know not whether the fiend possessed the same advantages; but I found that, as before I had daily lost ground in the pursuit, I now gained on him: so much so, that when I first saw the ocean, he was but one day's journey in advance, and I hoped to intercept him before he should reach the beach. With new courage, therefore, I pressed on, and in two days arrived at a wretched hamlet on the sea-shore. I enquired of the inhabitants concerning the fiend, and gained accurate information. A gigantic monster, they said, had arrived the night before, armed with a gun and many pistols; putting to flight the inhabitants of a solitary cottage, through fear of his terrific appearance. He had carried off their store of winter food, and, placing it in a sledge, to draw which he had seized on a numerous drove of trained dogs, he had harnessed them, and the same night, to the joy of the horror-struck villagers, had pursued his journey across the sea in a direction that led to no land; and they conjectured that he must speedily be destroyed by the breaking of the ice, or frozen by the eternal frosts.

On hearing this information, I suffered a temporary access of despair. He had escaped me; and I must commence a destructive and almost endless journey across the mountainous ices of the ocean,—amidst cold that few of the inhabitants could long endure, and which I, the native of a genial and sunny climate, could not hope to survive. Yet at the idea that the fiend should live and be triumphant, my rage and vengeance returned, and, like a mighty tide, overwhelmed every other feeling. After a slight repose, during which the spirits of the dead hovered round, and instigated me to toil and revenge, I prepared for my journey.

I exchanged my land-sledge for one fashioned for the inequalities of the Frozen Ocean; and purchasing a plentiful stock of provisions, I departed from land.

I cannot guess how many days have passed since then; but I have endured misery, which nothing but the eternal sentiment of a just retribution burning within my heart could have enabled me to support. Immense and rugged mountains of ice often barred up my passage, and I often heard the thunder of the ground sea, which threatened my destruction. But again the frost came, and made the paths of the sea secure.

By the quantity of provision which I had consumed, I should guess that I had passed three weeks in this journey; and the continual protraction of hope, returning back upon the heart, often wrung bitter drops of despondency and grief from my eyes. Despair had indeed almost secured her prey, and I should soon have sunk beneath this misery. Once, after the poor animals that conveyed me had with incredible toil gained the summit of a sloping ice-mountain, and one, sinking under his fatigue, died, I viewed the expanse before me with anguish, when suddenly my eye caught a dark speck upon the dusky plain. I strained my sight to discover what it could be, and uttered a wild cry of ecstasy when I distinguished a sledge, and the distorted proportions of a well-known form within. Oh! with what a burning gush did hope revisit my heart! warm tears filled my eyes, which I hastily wiped away, that they might not intercept the view I had of the daemon; but still my sight was dimmed by the burning drops, until, giving way to the emotions that oppressed me, I weep aloud. ~~Criesulvensves daemon~~

But this was not the time for delay: I disencumbered the dogs of their dead companion, gave them a plentiful portion of food; and, after an hour's rest, which was absolutely necessary, and yet which was bitterly irksome to me, I continued my route. The sledge was still visible; nor did I again lose sight of it, except at the moments when for a short time some ice-rock concealed it with its intervening crags. I indeed perceptibly gained on it; and when, after nearly two days' journey, I beheld my enemy at no more than a mile distant, my heart bounded within me.

But now, when I appeared almost within grasp of my foe, my hopes were suddenly extinguished, and I lost all traces of him more utterly than I had ever done before. A ground sea was heard; the thunder of its progress, as the waters rolled and swelled beneath me, became every moment more ominous and terrific. I pressed on, but in vain. The wind arose; the sea roared; and, as with the mighty shock of an earthquake, it split, and cracked with a tremendous and overwhelming sound. The work was soon finished: in a few minutes a tumultuous sea rolled between me and my enemy, and I was left drifting on a scattered piece of ice, that was continually lessening, and thus preparing for me a hideous death.

In this manner many appalling hours passed; several of my dogs died; and I myself was about to sink under the accumulation of distress, when I saw your vessel riding at anchor, and holding forth to me hopes of succour and life. I had no conception that vessels ever came so far north, and was astounded at the sight. I quickly destroyed part of my sledge to construct oars; and by these means was enabled, with infinite fatigue, to move my ice-raft in the direction of your ship. I had determined, if you were going southward, still to trust myself to the mercy of the seas rather than abandon my purpose. I hoped to induce you to grant me a boat with which I could pursue my enemy. But your direction was northward. You took me on board when my vigour was exhausted, and I should soon have sunk under my multiplied hardships into a death which I still dread — for my task is unfulfilled.

Oh! when will my guiding spirit, in conducting me to the daemon, allow me the rest I so much desire; or must I die, and he yet live? If I do, swear to me, Walton, that he shall not escape; that you will seek him, and satisfy my vengeance in his death. And do I dare to ask of you to undertake my pilgrimage, to endure the hardships that I have

undergone? No; I am not so selfish. Yet, when I am dead, if he should
appear; if the ministers of vengeance should conduct him to you, swear
that he shall not live—swear that he shall not triumph over my accumulated woes, and survive to add to the list of his dark crimes. He is
eloquent and persuasive; and once his words had even power over my
heart; but trust him not. His soul is as hellish as his form, full of treachery and fiendlike malice. Hear him not; call on the manes° of William,
Justine, Clerval, Elizabeth, my father, and of the wretched Victor, and
thrust your sword into his heart. I will hover near, and direct the steel
aright.

Walton, in continuation.

August 26th, 17—.

You have read this strange and terrific story, Margaret; and do you
not feel your blood congeal with horror, like that which even now
curdles mine? Sometimes, seized with sudden agony, he could not continue his tale; at others, his voice broken, yet piercing, uttered with
difficulty the words so replete with anguish. His fine and lovely eyes
were now lighted up with indignation, now subdued to downcast sorrow, and quenched in infinite wretchedness. Sometimes he commanded
his countenance and tones, and related the most horrible incidents with
a tranquil voice, suppressing every mark of agitation; then, like a volcano bursting forth, his face would suddenly change to an expression of
the wildest rage, as he shrieked out imprecations on his persecutor.

His tale is connected, and told with an appearance of the simplest
truth, yet I own to you that the letters of Felix and Safie, which he
showed me, and the apparition of the monster seen from our ship,
brought to me a greater conviction of the truth of his narrative than his
asseverations, however earnest and connected. Such a monster has then
really existence! I cannot doubt it; yet I am lost in surprise and admiration. Sometimes I endeavoured to gain from Frankenstein the particulars of his creature's formation: but on this point he was impenetrable.

"Are you mad, my friend?" said he; "or whither does your senseless
curiosity lead you? Would you also create for yourself and the world a
daemoniacal enemy? Peace, peace! learn my miseries, and do not seek
to increase your own."

Frankenstein discovered that I made notes concerning his history:
he asked to see them, and then himself corrected and augmented them

---

***manes:*** Spirits of the dead; shades (Latin).

*unreliable narrator*

in many places; but principally in giving the life and spirit to the conver
sations he held with his enemy. "Since you have preserved my narration," said he, "I would not that a mutilated one should go down to
posterity."

Thus has a week passed away, while I have listened to the strangest
tale that ever imagination formed. My thoughts, and every feeling of
my soul, have been drunk up by the interest for my guest, which this
tale, and his own elevated and gentle manners, have created. I wish to
soothe him; yet can I counsel one so infinitely miserable, so destitute of
every hope of consolation, to live? Oh, no! the only joy that he can now
know will be when he composes his shattered spirit to peace and death.
Yet he enjoys one comfort, the offspring of solitude and delirium: he
believes, when in dreams he holds converse with his friends, and derives     *dreams*
from that communion consolation for his miseries, or excitements to
his vengeance, that they are not the creations of his fancy, but the beings
themselves who visit him from the regions of a remote world. This faith
gives a solemnity to his reveries that render them to me almost as
imposing and interesting as truth.

Our conversations are not always confined to his own history and
misfortunes. On every point of general literature he displays unbounded
knowledge, and a quick and piercing apprehension. His eloquence is
forcible and touching; nor can I hear him, when he relates a pathetic
incident, or endeavours to move the passions of pity or love, without
tears. What a glorious creature must he have been in the days of his
prosperity, when he is thus noble and godlike in ruin! He seems to feel
his own worth, and the greatness of his fall.

"When younger," said he, "I believed myself destined for some
great enterprise. My feelings are profound; but I possessed a coolness
of judgment that fitted me for illustrious achievements. This sentiment
of the worth of my nature supported me, when others would have been
oppressed; for I deemed it criminal to throw away in useless grief those
talents that might be useful to my fellow-creatures. When I reflected on
the work I had completed, no less a one than the creation of a sensitive
and rational animal, I could not rank myself with the herd of common
projectors. But this thought, which supported me in the commencement of my career, now serves only to plunge me lower in the dust. All
my speculations and hopes are as nothing; and, like the archangel who
aspired to omnipotence, I am chained in an eternal hell. My imagination was vivid, yet my powers of analysis and application were intense;
by the union of these qualities I conceived the idea, and executed the
creation of a man. Even now I cannot recollect, without passion, my

*Calls monster a man*

reveries while the work was incomplete. I trod heaven in my thoughts, now exulting in my powers, now burning with the idea of their effects. From my infancy I was imbued with high hopes and a lofty ambition; but how am I sunk! Oh! my friend, if you had known me as I once was, you would not recognise me in this state of degradation. Despondency rarely visited my heart; a high destiny seemed to bear me on, until I fell, never, never again to rise." *Paradise Lost*

Must I then lose this admirable being? I have longed for a friend; I have sought one who would sympathise with and love me. Behold, on these desert seas I have found such a one; but, I fear, I have gained him only to know his value, and lose him. I would reconcile him to life, but he repulses the idea.

"I thank you, Walton," he said, "for your kind intentions towards so miserable a wretch; but when you speak of new ties, and fresh affections, think you that any can replace those who are gone? Can any man be to me as Clerval was; or any woman another Elizabeth? Even where the affections are not strongly moved by any superior excellence, the companions of our childhood always possess a certain power over our minds, which hardly any later friend can obtain. They know our infantine dispositions, which, however they may be afterwards modified, are never eradicated; and they can judge of our actions with more certain conclusions as to the integrity of our motives. A sister or a brother can never, unless indeed such symptoms have been shown early, suspect the other of fraud or false dealing, when another friend, however strongly he may be attached, may, in spite of himself, be contemplated with suspicion. But I enjoyed friends, dear not only through habit and association, but from their own merits; and wherever I am, the soothing voice of my Elizabeth, and the conversation of Clerval, will be ever whispered in my ear. They are dead; and but one feeling in such a solitude can persuade me to preserve my life. If I were engaged in any high undertaking or design, fraught with extensive utility to my fellow-creatures, then could I live to fulfil it. But such is not my destiny; I must pursue and destroy the being to whom I gave existence; then my lot on earth will be fulfilled, and I may die."

My beloved Sister,                                    September 2d.
I write to you, encompassed by peril, and ignorant whether I am ever doomed to see again dear England, and the dearer friends that inhabit it. I am surrounded by mountains of ice, which admit of no escape, and threaten every moment to crush my vessel. The brave fellows, whom I have persuaded to be my companions, look towards me

for aid; but I have none to bestow. There is something terribly appalling in our situation, yet my courage and hopes do not desert me. Yet it is terrible to reflect that the lives of all these men are endangered through me. If we are lost, my mad schemes are the cause. *overreach*

And what, Margaret, will be the state of your mind? You will not hear of my destruction, and you will anxiously await my return. Years will pass, and you will have visitings of despair, and yet be tortured by hope. Oh! my beloved sister, the sickening failing of your heart-felt expectations is, in prospect, more terrible to me than my own death. But you have a husband, and lovely children; you may be happy: Heaven bless you, and make you so!

My unfortunate guest regards me with the tenderest compassion. He endeavours to fill me with hope; and talks as if life were a possession which he valued. He reminds me how often the same accidents have happened to other navigators, who have attempted this sea, and, in spite of myself, he fills me with cheerful auguries. Even the sailors feel the power of his eloquence: when he speaks, they no longer despair; he rouses their energies, and, while they hear his voice, they believe these vast mountains of ice are mole-hills, which will vanish before the resolutions of man. These feelings are transitory; each day of expectation delayed fills them with fear, and I almost dread a mutiny caused by this despair.

September 5th.

A scene has just passed of such uncommon interest, that although it is highly probable that these papers may never reach you, yet I cannot forbear recording it.

We are still surrounded by mountains of ice, still in imminent danger of being crushed in their conflict. The cold is excessive, and many of my unfortunate comrades have already found a grave amidst this scene of desolation. Frankenstein has daily declined in health: a feverish fire still glimmers in his eyes; but he is exhausted, and, when suddenly roused to any exertion, he speedily sinks again into apparent lifelessness.

I mentioned in my last letter the fears I entertained of a mutiny. This morning, as I sat watching the wan countenance of my friend—his eyes half closed, and his limbs hanging listlessly,—I was roused by half a dozen of the sailors, who demanded admission into the cabin. They entered, and their leader addressed me. He told me that he and his companions had been chosen by the other sailors to come in deputation to me, to make me a requisition, which, in justice, I could not refuse. We were immured in ice, and should probably never escape; but they feared that if, as was possible, the ice should dissipate, and a free passage be opened, I should be rash enough to continue my voyage, and lead them into fresh dangers, after they might happily have surmounted this. They insisted, therefore, that I should engage with a solemn promise, that if the vessel should be freed I would instantly direct my course southward.

This speech troubled me. I had not despaired; nor had I yet conceived the idea of returning, if set free. Yet could I, in justice, or even in possibility, refuse this demand? I hesitated before I answered; when Frankenstein, who had at first been silent, and, indeed, appeared hardly to have force enough to attend, now roused himself; his eyes sparkled, and his cheeks flushed with momentary vigour. Turning towards the men, he said— *Frankenstein tells them to overreach*

"What do you mean? What do you demand of your captain? Are you then so easily turned from your design? Did you not call this a glorious expedition? And wherefore was it glorious? Not because the way was smooth and placid as a southern sea, but because it was full of dangers and terror; because, at every new incident, your fortitude was to be called forth, and your courage exhibited; because danger and death surrounded it, and these you were to brave and overcome. For this was it a glorious, for this was it an honourable undertaking. You were hereafter to be hailed as the benefactors of your species; your names adored, as belonging to brave men who encountered death for honour, and the benefit of mankind. And now, behold, with the first imagination of danger, or, if you will, the first mighty and terrific trial of your courage, you shrink away, and are content to be handed down as men who had not strength enough to endure cold and peril; and so, poor souls, they were chilly, and returned to their warm firesides. Why, that requires not this preparation; ye need not have come thus far, and dragged your captain to the shame of a defeat, merely to prove yourselves cowards. Oh! be men, or be more than men. Be steady to your purposes, and firm as a rock. This ice is not made of such stuff as your hearts may be; it is mutable, and cannot withstand you, if you say that it shall not. Do not return to your families with the stigma of disgrace marked on your brows. Return as heroes who have fought and conquered, and who know not what it is to turn their backs on the foe."

He spoke this with a voice so modulated to the different feelings expressed in his speech, with an eye so full of lofty design and heroism, that can you wonder that these men were moved? They looked at one another, and were unable to reply. I spoke; I told them to retire, and consider of what had been said: that I would not lead them farther north, if they strenuously desired the contrary; but that I hoped that, with reflection, their courage would return.

They retired, and I turned towards my friend; but he was sunk in languor, and almost deprived of life.

How all this will terminate, I know not; but I had rather die than return shamefully,—my purpose unfulfilled. Yet I fear such will be my fate; the men, unsupported by ideas of glory and honour, can never willingly continue to endure their present hardships.

September 7th.

The die is cast; I have consented to return, if we are not destroyed. Thus are my hopes blasted by cowardice and indecision; I come back ignorant and disappointed. It requires more philosophy than I possess, to bear this injustice with patience. *Turned around, sad*

*Frank dead*                                    September 12th.

It is past; I am returning to England. I have lost my hopes of utility and glory;—I have lost my friend. But I will endeavour to detail these bitter circumstances to you, my dear sister; and, while I am wafted towards England, and towards you, I will not despond.

September 9th, the ice began to move, and roarings like thunder were heard at a distance, as the islands split and cracked in every direction. We were in the most imminent peril; but, as we could only remain passive, my chief attention was occupied by my unfortunate guest, whose illness increased in such a degree, that he was entirely confined to his bed. The ice cracked behind us, and was driven with force towards the north; a breeze sprung from the west, and on the 11th the passage towards the south became perfectly free. When the sailors saw this, and that their return to their native country was apparently assured, a shout of tumultuous joy broke from them, loud and long-continued. Frankenstein, who was dozing, awoke, and asked the cause of the tumult. "They shout," I said, "because they will soon return to England."

"Do you then really return?"

"Alas! yes; I cannot withstand their demands. I cannot lead them unwillingly to danger, and I must return."

"Do so, if you will; but I will not. You may give up your purpose, but mine is assigned to me by Heaven, and I dare not. I am weak; but surely the spirits who assist my vengeance will endow me with sufficient strength." Saying this, he endeavoured to spring from the bed, but the exertion was too great for him; he fell back, and fainted.

It was long before he was restored; and I often thought that life was entirely extinct. At length he opened his eyes; he breathed with difficulty, and was unable to speak. The surgeon gave him a composing draught, and ordered us to leave him undisturbed. In the mean time he told me, that my friend had certainly not many hours to live.

His sentence was pronounced; and I could only grieve, and be patient. I sat by his bed, watching him; his eyes were closed, and I thought he slept; but presently he called to me in a feeble voice, and, bidding me come near, said—"Alas! the strength I relied on is gone; I feel that I shall soon die, and he, my enemy and persecutor, may still be in being. Think not, Walton, that in the last moments of my existence I feel that burning hatred, and ardent desire of revenge, I once expressed; but I feel myself justified in desiring the death of my adversary. During these last days I have been occupied in examining my past conduct; nor do I find it blameable. In a fit of enthusiastic madness I created a rational creature, and was bound towards him, to assure, as far as was in my power, his happiness and well-being. This was my duty; but there was another still paramount to that. My duties towards the beings of my own species had greater claims to my attention, because they included a greater proportion of happiness or misery. Urged by this view, I refused, and I did right in refusing, to create a companion for the first creature. He showed unparalleled malignity and selfishness, in evil: he destroyed my friends; he devoted to destruction beings who possessed exquisite sensations, happiness, and wisdom; nor do I know where this thirst for vengeance may end. Miserable himself, that he may render no other wretched, he ought to die. The task of his destruction was mine, but I have failed. When actuated by selfishness and vicious motives, I asked you to undertake my unfinished work; and I renew this request now, when I am only induced by reason and virtue.

"Yet I cannot ask you to renounce your country and friends, to fulfil this task; and now, that you are returning to England, you will have little chance of meeting with him. But the consideration of these points, and the well balancing of what you may esteem your duties, I leave to you; my judgment and ideas are already disturbed by the near approach of death. I dare not ask you to do what I think right, for I may still be misled by passion.

"That he should live to be an instrument of mischief disturbs me; in other respects, this hour, when I momentarily expect my release, is the only happy one which I have enjoyed for several years. The forms of the beloved dead flit before me, and I hasten to their arms. Farewell, Walton! Seek happiness in tranquillity, and avoid ambition, even if it be

only the apparently innocent one of distinguishing yourself in science
and discoveries. Yet why do I say this? I have myself been blasted in
these hopes, yet another may succeed."

His voice became fainter as he spoke; and at length, exhausted by
his effort, he sunk into silence. About half an hour afterwards he
attempted again to speak, but was unable; he pressed my hand feebly,
and his eyes closed for ever, while the irradiation of a gentle smile passed
away from his lips.

Margaret, what comment can I make on the untimely extinction of
this glorious spirit? What can I say, that will enable you to understand
the depth of my sorrow? All that I should express would be inadequate
and feeble. My tears flow; my mind is overshadowed by a cloud of disappointment. But I journey towards England, and I may there find
consolation.

I am interrupted. What do these sounds portend? It is midnight;
the breeze blows fairly, and the watch on deck scarcely stir. Again; there
is a sound as of a human voice, but hoarser; it comes from the cabin
where the remains of Frankenstein still lie. I must arise, and examine.
Good night, my sister.

Great God! what a scene has just taken place! I am yet dizzy with
the remembrance of it. I hardly know whether I shall have the power to
detail it; yet the tale which I have recorded would be incomplete without this final and wonderful catastrophe.

I entered the cabin, where lay the remains of my ill-fated and admirable friend. Over him hung a form which I cannot find words to
describe; gigantic in stature, yet uncouth and distorted in its proportions. As he hung over the coffin, his face was concealed by long locks
of ragged hair; but one vast hand was extended, in colour and apparent
texture like that of a mummy. When he heard the sound of my approach,
he ceased to utter exclamations of grief and horror, and sprung towards
the window. Never did I behold a vision so horrible as his face, of such
loathsome yet appalling hideousness. I shut my eyes involuntarily, and
endeavoured to recollect what were my duties with regard to this
destroyer. I called on him to stay.

He paused, looking on me with wonder; and, again turning towards
the lifeless form of his creator, he seemed to forget my presence, and
every feature and gesture seemed instigated by the wildest rage of some
uncontrollable passion.

"That is also my victim!" he exclaimed: "in his murder my crimes
are consummated; the miserable series of my being is wound to its close!
Oh, Frankenstein! generous and self-devoted being! what does it avail

that I now ask thee to pardon me? I, who irretrievably destroyed thee by destroying all thou lovedst. Alas! he is cold, he cannot answer me."

His voice seemed suffocated; and my first impulses, which had suggested to me the duty of obeying the dying request of my friend, in destroying his enemy, were now suspended by a mixture of curiosity and compassion. I approached this tremendous being; I dared not again raise my eyes to his face, there was something so scaring and unearthly in his ugliness. I attempted to speak, but the words died away on my lips. The monster continued to utter wild and incoherent self-reproaches. At length I gathered resolution to address him in a pause of the tempest of his passion: "Your repentance," I said, "is now superfluous. If you had listened to the voice of conscience, and heeded the stings of remorse, before you had urged your diabolical vengeance to this extremity, Frankenstein would yet have lived."

"And do you dream?" said the daemon; "do you think that I was then dead to agony and remorse?—He," he continued, pointing to the corpse, "he suffered not in the consummation of the deed—oh! not the ten-thousandth portion of the anguish that was mine during the lingering detail of its execution. A frightful selfishness hurried me on, while my heart was poisoned with remorse. Think you that the groans of Clerval were music to my ears? My heart was fashioned to be susceptible of love and sympathy; and, when wrenched by misery to vice and hatred, it did not endure the violence of the change, without torture such as you cannot even imagine.

"After the murder of Clerval, I returned to Switzerland, heartbroken and overcome. I pitied Frankenstein; my pity amounted to horror: I abhorred myself. But when I discovered that he, the author at once of my existence and of its unspeakable torments, dared to hope for happiness; that while he accumulated wretchedness and despair upon me, he sought his own enjoyment in feelings and passions from the indulgence of which I was for ever barred, then impotent envy and bitter indignation filled me with an insatiable thirst for vengeance. I recollected my threat, and resolved that it should be accomplished. I knew that I was preparing for myself a deadly torture; but I was the slave, not the master, of an impulse, which I detested, yet could not disobey. Yet when she died!—nay, then I was not miserable. I had cast off all feeling, subdued all anguish, to riot in the excess of my despair. Evil thenceforth became my good. Urged thus far, I had no choice but to adapt my nature to an element which I had willingly chosen. The completion of my demoniacal design became an insatiable passion. And now it is ended; there is my last victim!"

I was first touched by the expressions of his misery; yet, when I called to mind what Frankenstein had said of his powers of eloquence and persuasion, and when I again cast my eyes on the lifeless form of my friend, indignation was rekindled within me. "Wretch!" I said, "it is well that you come here to whine over the desolation that you have made. You throw a torch into a pile of buildings; and, when they are consumed, you sit among the ruins, and lament the fall. Hypocritical fiend! if he whom you mourn still lived, still would he be the object, again would he become the prey, of your accursed vengeance. It is not pity that you feel; you lament only because the victim of your malignity is withdrawn from your power."

"Oh, it is not thus—not thus," interrupted the being; "yet such must be the impression conveyed to you by what appears to be the purport of my actions. Yet I seek not a fellow-feeling in my misery. No sympathy may I ever find. When I first sought it, it was the love of virtue, the feelings of happiness and affection with which my whole being overflowed, that I wished to be participated. But now, that virtue has become to me a shadow, and that happiness and affection are turned into bitter and loathing despair, in what should I seek for sympathy? I am content to suffer alone, while my sufferings shall endure: when I die, I am well satisfied that abhorrence and opprobrium should load my memory. Once my fancy was soothed with dreams of virtue, of fame, and of enjoyment. Once I falsely hoped to meet with beings, who, pardoning my outward form, would love me for the excellent qualities which I was capable of unfolding. I was nourished with high thoughts of honour and devotion. But now crime has degraded me beneath the meanest animal. No guilt, no mischief, no malignity, no misery, can be found comparable to mine. When I run over the frightful catalogue of my sins, I cannot believe that I am the same creature whose thoughts were once filled with sublime and transcendent visions of the beauty and the majesty of goodness. But it is even so; the fallen angel becomes a malignant devil. Yet even that enemy of God and man had friends and associates in his desolation; I am alone.

"You, who call Frankenstein your friend, seem to have a knowledge of my crimes and his misfortunes. But, in the detail which he gave you of them, he could not sum up the hours and months of misery which I endured, wasting in impotent passions. For while I destroyed his hopes, I did not satisfy my own desires. They were for ever ardent and craving; still I desired love and fellowship, and I was still spurned. Was there no injustice in this? Am I to be thought the only criminal, when all human kind sinned against me? Why do you not hate Felix, who drove his friend from his door with contumely? Why do you not execrate the rustic who sought to destroy the saviour of his child? Nay, these are virtuous and immaculate beings! I, the miserable and the abandoned, am an abortion, to be spurned at, and kicked, and trampled on. Even now my blood boils at the recollection of this injustice.

"But it is true that I am a wretch. I have murdered the lovely and the helpless; I have strangled the innocent as they slept, and grasped to death his throat who never injured me or any other living thing. I have devoted my creator, the select specimen of all that is worthy of love and admiration among men, to misery; I have pursued him even to that irremediable ruin. There he lies, white and cold in death. You hate me; but your abhorrence cannot equal that with which I regard myself. I look on the hands which executed the deed; I think on the heart in which the imagination of it was conceived, and long for the moment when these hands will meet my eyes, when that imagination will haunt my thoughts no more.

"Fear not that I shall be the instrument of future mischief. My work is nearly complete. Neither yours nor any man's death is needed to consummate the series of my being, and accomplish that which must be done; but it requires my own. Do not think that I shall be slow to perform this sacrifice. I shall quit your vessel on the ice-raft which brought me thither, and shall seek the most northern extremity of the globe; I shall collect my funeral pile, and consume to ashes this miserable frame, that its remains may afford no light to any curious and unhallowed wretch, who would create such another as I have been. I shall die. I shall no longer feel the agonies which now consume me, or be the prey of feelings unsatisfied, yet unquenched. He is dead who called me into being; and when I shall be no more, the very remembrance of us both will speedily vanish. I shall no longer see the sun or stars, or feel the winds play on my cheeks. Light, feeling, and sense will pass away; and in this condition must I find my happiness. Some years ago, when the images which this world affords first opened upon me, when I felt the cheering warmth of summer, and heard the rustling of the leaves and the warbling of the birds, and these were all to me, I should have wept to die; now it is my only consolation. Polluted by crimes, and torn by the bitterest remorse, where can I find rest but in death?

"Farewell! I leave you, and in you the last of human kind whom these eyes will ever behold. Farewell, Frankenstein! If thou wert yet alive, and yet cherished a desire of revenge against me, it would be better satiated in my life than in my destruction. But it was not so; thou didst seek my extinction, that I might not cause greater wretchedness;

and if yet, in some mode unknown to me, thou hadst not ceased to think and feel, thou wouldst not desire against me a vengeance greater than that which I feel. Blasted as thou wert, my agony was still superior to thine; for the bitter sting of remorse will not cease to rankle in my wounds until death shall close them for ever.

"But soon," he cried, with sad and solemn enthusiasm, "I shall die, and what I now feel be no longer felt. Soon these burning miseries will be extinct. I shall ascend my funeral pile triumphantly, and exult in the agony of the torturing flames. The light of that conflagration will fade away; my ashes will be swept into the sea by the winds. My spirit will sleep in peace; or if it thinks, it will not surely think thus. Farewell."

He sprung from the cabin window, as he said this, upon the ice-raft which lay close to the vessel. He was soon borne away by the waves, and lost in darkness and distance.

THE END

# PART TWO

# *Frankenstein* in Cultural Context

# Cultural Documents
# and Illustrations

## EDITOR'S NOTE

Several factors make it difficult to choose a representative sample of
contextual documents for Mary Shelley's *Frankenstein*. The first is the
intertextuality of the novel, its frequent overt and covert allusions to
and engagements with many other texts. In addition is the intertextuality of the reader, the fact that few of us come to the novel without some
prior experience of popular or cinematic versions of *Frankenstein*. And
finally there is the issue of volume, the glutton's plateful of contextual
documents from which to choose. Hence the documents included here
are necessarily a small sample, selected to highlight a problematic of the
novel that has been of continuing interest to readers over *Frankenstein*'s almost two-hundred-year history: the making of a monster.

Irish artist Richard Rothwell, who enjoyed great—albeit brief—popularity in England during the late 1820s and early 1830s, painted this portrait of Mary Shelley, c. 1840. A testament to Rothwell's fame and Shelley's standing as a literary figure, the painting was exhibited at the Royal Academy of London in 1840, nine years after the 1831 edition of *Frankenstein*, when Mary Shelley was 43.

National Portrait Gallery, London, UK / Photo © Tarker / Bridgeman Images.

JOHN MILTON

## *From* Paradise Lost
## A Poem in Twelve Books (1673)

*In 1673 English poet and political writer John Milton published the second, twelve-book edition of* Paradise Lost, *his great epic of humankind's first sin and expulsion from Eden. Milton's influence on* Frankenstein *is evidenced by the fact that* Paradise Lost *is both the source of the novel's epigraph and one of the three books that provides the Monster's education. From reading* Paradise Lost, *the Monster learns his rights as a created being. During their first interview, for instance, the Monster tells Franken-stein, "Remember, that I am thy creature; I ought to be thy Adam; but I am rather the fallen angel, whom thou drivest from joy for no misdeed. Every where I see bliss, from which I alone am irrevocably excluded."*

*Several editions of* Paradise Lost *were published during the eighteenth century, and it is not known which edition Mary Shelley read or consulted for her novel. The excerpts included here are taken from the 1794 edition published by brothers Henry and John Richter, because of its possible connec-tion with Mary's father William Godwin. The Richter edition was published during the year of the Treason Trials, a government prosecution against political radicals and radical organizations. The Trials connect Godwin, who wrote a pamphlet challenging the prosecution's definition of treason, with Henry Richter, who was indicted for treason under this prosecution and published his* Paradise Lost *while under indictment.*

*The first passage presented below comes from Book IV of* Paradise Lost. *The speaker is Satan, "the fallen angel" the Monster refers to; after bat-tling many doubts, Satan reaffirms his desire to subvert God by doing evil and destroying God's new creation, humankind. The second passages, from Book X, show Adam bewailing his fallen condition and questioning his relationship to God.*

```
      . . . horror and doubt distract
20    His¹ troubled thoughts, and from the bottom stir
      The Hell within him; for within him Hell
      He brings, and round about him, nor from Hell
      One step no more than from himself can fly
      By change of place: now conscience wakes despair
25    That slumber'd, wakes the bitter memory
      Of what he was, what is, and what must be
```

¹ *his:* Satan's.

Worse; of worse deeds worse sufferings must ensue.
Sometimes towards Eden, which now in his view
Lay pleasant, his griev'd look he fixes sad;
Sometimes towards Heav'n and the full-blazing sun,
30  Which now sat high in his meridian towre:[2]
Then much revolving, thus in sighs began.
O thou that with surpassing glory crown'd,
Look'st from thy sole dominion like the God
Of this new world; at whose sight all the stars
35  Hide their diminish'd heads; to thee I call,
But with no friendly voice, and add thy name,
O Sun, to tell thee how I hate thy beams,
That bring to my remembrance from what state
I fell, how glorious once above thy sphere;
40  Till Pride and worse Ambition threw me down
Warring in Heaven against Heaven's matchless King:
Ah wherefore! He deserv'd no such return
From me, whom he created what I was
In that bright eminence, and with his good
45  Upbraided none; nor was his service hard.
What could be less than to afford him praise,
The easiest recompence, and pay him thanks,
How due! yet all his good prov'd ill in me,
And wrought but malice; lifted up so high
50  I sdein'd[3] subjection, and thought one step higher
Would set me highest, and in a moment quit[4]
The debt immense of endless gratitude,
So burthensome, still paying, still to owe;
Forgetful what from him I still receiv'd,
55  And understood not that a grateful mind
By owing owes not, but still pays, at once
Indebted and discharg'd; what burden then?
O had his powerful destiny ordain'd
Me some inferior Angel, I had stood
60  Then happy; no unbounded hope had rais'd
Ambition. Yet why not? some other power
As great might have aspir'd, and me though mean[5]
Drawn to his part; but other Powers as great
Fell not, but stand unshaken, from within
65  Or from without, to all temptations arm'd.

[2]*his meridian tower:* That is, the sun is in the meridian.
[3]*sdein'd:* Disdained.
[4]*quit:* Pay off.
[5]*mean:* Inferior in status.

Hadst thou the same free will and power to stand?
Thou hadst: whom hast thou then or what to accuse,
But Heav'ns free Love dealt equally to all?
Be then his love accurs'd, since love or hate,
70   To me alike, it deals eternal woe.
Nay curs'd be thou; since against his thy will
Chose freely what it now so justly rues.
Me miserable! which way shall I fly
Infinite wrath, and infinite despair?
75   Which way I fly is Hell; myself am Hell;
And in the lowest deep a lower deep
Still threatening to devour me opens wide,
To which the Hell I suffer seems a Heav'n.
O then at last relent: is there no place
80   Left for repentance, none for pardon left?
None left but by submission; and that word
Disdain forbids me, and my dread of shame
Among the Spirits beneath, whom I seduc'd
With other promises and other vaunts
85   Than to submit, boasting I could subdue
The omnipotent. Ay me! they little know
How dearly I abide that boast so vain,
Under what torments inwardly I groan:
While they adore me on the throne of Hell,
90   With diadem and scepter high advanc'd
The lower still I fall, only supreme
In misery; such joy ambition finds.
But say I could repent and could obtain
By act of grace my former state; how soon
95   Would highth⁶ recal high thoughts, how soon unsay
What feign'd submission swore: ease would recant
Vows made in pain, as violent and void.
For never can true reconcilement grow
Where wounds of deadly hate have pierc'd so deep:
100  Which would but lead me to a worse relapse,
And heavier fall: so should I purchase dear
Short intermission bought with double smart.
This knows my punisher; therefore as far
From granting he, as I from begging peace:
105  All hope excluded thus, behold in stead
Of us out-cast, exil'd, his new delight,
Mankind created, and for him this world.

---

⁶*highth:* Height or elevation.

So farewel hope, and with hope farewel fear,
Farewel remorse: all good to me is lost;
110    Evil be thou my good; by thee at least
Divided empire with Heav'ns King I hold
By thee, and more than half perhaps will reign;
As Man ere long, and this new World shall know.

                                  [Book IV, lines 18–113]

. . . . . . . . . . . . . . . . . . . . . . . . . . . . . . . . . . .

720    O miserable of happy! is this the end
Of this new glorious World, and me so late
The glory of that glory, who now become
Accurs'd of blessed, hide me from the face
Of God, whom to behold was then my highth
725    Of happiness! yet well, if here would end
The misery; I deserv'd it, and would bear
My own deservings; but this will not serve;
All that I eat or drink, or shall beget,
Is propagated curse. O voice once heard
730    Delightfully, Increase and multiply,
Now death to hear! for what can I increase
Or multiply, but curses on my head?
Who of all ages to succeed, but feeling
The evil on him brought by me, will curse
735    My Head? Ill fare our ancestor impure,
For this we may thank Adam; but his thanks
Shall be the execration; so besides
Mine own[7] that bide upon me, all from me
Shall with a fierce reflux on me redound,
740    On me as on their natural center light
Heavy, though in their place. O fleeting joys
Of Paradise, dear bought with lasting woes!
Did I request thee, Maker, from my clay
To mould me man, did I solicit thee
745    From darkness to promote me, or here place
In this delicious garden? as my will
Concur'd not to my being, it were but right
And equal to reduce me to my dust,
Desirous to resign, and render back
750    All I receiv'd, unable to perform
Thy terms too hard, by which I was to hold
The good I sought not. To the loss of that,

---

[7] *mine own:* My own curses.

Sufficient penalty, why hast thou added
The sense of endless woes?

[Book X, lines 720–54]

. . . . . . . . . . . . . . . . . . . . . . . . . . . . . . . . . . . . . .

. . . Ah, why should all mankind
For one man's fault thus guiltless be condemn'd,
If guiltless? But from me what can proceed,
825    But all corrupt, both mind and will deprav'd,
Not to do only, but to will the same
With me? how can they then acquitted stand
In sight of God? Him after all Disputes
Forc't I absolve.[8] All my evasions vain
830    And reasonings, though through mazes lead me still
But to my own conviction: first and last
On me, me only, as the source and spring
Of all corruption, all the blame lights due;
So might the wrath. Fond wish! couldst thou support
835    That burden heavier than the Earth to bear
Than all the World much heavier, though divided
With that bad woman?[9] Thus what thou desirest,
And what thou fearest, alike destroys all hope
Of refuge, and concludes thee miserable
840    Beyond all past example and future,
To Satan only like both crime and doom.
O Conscience, into what abyss of fears
And horrors hast thou driv'n me; out of which
I find no way, from deep to deeper plung'd!

[Book X, lines 822–44]

### WILLIAM GODWIN

## *From* Things as They Are; or, the Adventures of Caleb Williams (1794)

*William Godwin, father of Mary Shelley and the person to whom she dedicates* Frankenstein, *was an English political philosopher and novelist. Observing the rapid decline in influence that Godwin experienced during*

---

[8] *Forc't I absolve:* That is, Adam realizes he must absolve God of responsibility for his own condition.
[9] *that bad woman:* That is, Eve.

*his lifetime, William Hazlitt writes in* The Spirit of the Age; Or, Contemporary Portraits (1825),

> *Mr. Godwin's person is not known, he is not pointed out in the street, his conversation is not courted, his opinions are not asked, he is at the head of no cabal, belongs to no party in the State, he has no train of admirers, no one thinks it worth his while even to traduce and vilify him, he has scarcely friend or foe, the world make a point (as Goldsmith used to say) of taking no more notice of him than if such an individual had never existed; he is to all ordinary intents and purposes dead and buried; but the author of* Political Justice *and of* Caleb Williams *can never die.*

*These observations have proven to be prescient as Godwin continues to survive through the two major works Hazlitt names.* Caleb Williams, *a work embodying Godwin's political ideals, follows the story of its eponymous hero as he struggles to expose a murder by his employer, Ferdinando Falkland. Similar to Victor, Caleb creates a monster by being curious about forbidden knowledge and refusing to heed warnings of potential danger: Falkland eventually admits his murderous deed to Caleb, but then pursues him for the rest of the novel. In the following passage, taken from Chapter VI of Book II, Caleb explains his state of mind.*

[M]y steps, by some mysterious fatality, were directed to the private apartment at the end of the library. Here, as I looked round, my eye was suddenly caught by the trunk mentioned in the first pages of my narrative.

My mind was already raised to its utmost pitch. In a window-seat of the room lay a number of chisels and other carpenter's tools. I know not what infatuation instantaneously seized me. The idea was too powerful to be resisted. I forgot the business upon which I came, the employment of the servants, and the urgency of general danger. I should have done the same if the flames that seemed to extend as they proceeded, and already surmounted the house, had reached this very apartment. I snatched a tool suitable for the purpose, threw myself upon the ground, and applied with eagerness to a magazine which inclosed all for which my heart panted. After two or three efforts, in which the energy of uncontrollable passion was added to my bodily strength, the fastenings gave way, the trunk opened, and all that I sought was at once within my reach.

I was in the act of lifting up the lid, when Mr. Falkland entered, wild, breathless, distracted in his looks! He had been brought home from a considerable distance by the sight of the flames. At the moment of his appearance the lid dropped down from my hand. He no sooner saw me than his eyes emitted sparks of rage. He ran with eagerness to a brace of loaded pistols which hung in the room, and, seizing one, presented it to my head. I saw his design, and sprang to avoid it; but, with the same rapidity with which he had formed his resolution, he changed it, and instantly went to the window, and flung the pistol into the court below. He bade me begone with his usual irresistible energy; and, overcome as I was already by the horror of the detection, I eagerly complied. . . . .

The reader can with difficulty form a conception of the state to which I was now reduced. My act was in some sort an act of insanity; but how undescribable are the feelings with which I looked back upon it! It was an instantaneous impulse, a short-lived and passing alienation of mind; but what must Mr. Falkland think of that alienation? To any man a person who had once shown himself capable of so wild a flight of the mind, must appear dangerous: how must he appear to a man under Mr. Falkland's circumstances? I had just had a pistol held to my head, by a man resolved to put a period to my existence. That indeed was past; but what was it that fate had yet in reserve for me! The insatiable vengeance of a Falkland, of a man whose hands were, to my apprehension, red with blood, and his thoughts familiar with cruelty and murder. How great were the resources of his mind, resources henceforth to be confederated for my destruction! This was the termination of an ungoverned curiosity, an impulse that I had represented to myself as so innocent or so venial.

In the high tide of boiling passion I had overlooked all consequences. . . . No thought of future security had reached my mind. I had acted upon no plan. I had conceived no means of concealing my deed, after it had once been effected. But it was over now. One short minute had effected a reverse in my situation, the suddenness of which the history of man, perhaps is unable to surpass. . . .

I had now every thing to fear. And yet what was my fault? It proceeded from none of those errors which are justly held up to the aversion of mankind; my object had been neither wealth, nor the means of indulgence, nor the usurpation of power. No spark of malignity had harboured in my soul. I had always reverenced the sublime mind of Mr. Falkland; I reverenced it still. My offence had merely been a mistaken thirst of knowledge. Such however it was, as to admit neither of forgiveness nor remission. This epoch was the crisis of my fate, dividing what may be called the offensive part from the defensive, which has been the sole business of my remaining years. Alas! my offence was short, not aggravated by any sinister intention: but the reprisals I was to suffer are long, and can terminate only with my life!

In the state in which I found myself, when the recollection of what I had done flowed back upon my mind, I was incapable of any resolution. All was chaos and uncertainty within me. My thoughts were too full of horror to be susceptible of activity. I felt deserted of my intellectual powers, palsied in mind, and compelled to sit in speechless expectation of the misery to which I was destined. To my own conception I was like a man, who, though blasted with lightning, and deprived for ever of the power of motion, should yet retain the consciousness of his situation. Death-dealing despair was the only idea of which I was sensible.

## MARY WOLLSTONECRAFT

### *From* Maria: or, the Wrongs of Woman (1798)

*Mary Wollstonecraft, like her husband William Godwin, followed up her political tracts with a novel that depicted her philosophical views. Unlike Godwin, however, Wollstonecraft neither finished nor saw the book to print. Wollstonecraft, who is best remembered for* A Vindication of the Rights of Woman *(1792) — a critical response to Edmund Burke's conservative* Reflections on the Revolution in France *(1790) — died on September 10, 1797, leaving behind an unfinished manuscript that Godwin published the following year.* Maria: or, the Wrongs of Woman *follows the story of its eponymous heroine as she struggles to survive in an insane asylum to which her libertine husband has forcibly committed her, and works through the painful memories of her childhood and disastrous marriage. In the following passage from chapter 5, Jemima, a lower-class attendant in the asylum who befriends Maria, tells the story of her mother's death and her own subsequent tribulations. The suffering that Jemima endures due to a lack of maternal care is particularly pertinent to* Frankenstein, *for the absence of this care, in fact of a mother, has often been seen as crucial in the creature's becoming a monster.*

"My father," said Jemima, "seduced my mother, a pretty girl, with whom he lived fellow-servant; and she no sooner perceived the natural, the dreaded consequence, than the terrible conviction flashed on her — that she was ruined. Honesty, and a regard for her reputation, had been the only principles inculcated by her mother; and they had been so forcibly impressed, that she feared shame, more than the poverty to which it would lead. Her incessant importunities to prevail upon my father to screen her from reproach by marrying her, as he had promised in the fervour of seduction, estranged him from her so completely, that her very person became distasteful to him; and he began to hate, as well as despise me, before I was born.

"My mother, grieved to the soul by his neglect, and unkind treatment, actually resolved to famish herself; and injured her health by the attempt; though she had not sufficient resolution to adhere to her project, or renounce it entirely. Death came not at her call; yet sorrow, and the methods she adopted to conceal her condition, still doing the work of a house-maid, had such an effect on her constitution, that she died in the wretched garret, where her virtuous mistress had forced her to take refuge in the very pangs of labour, though my father, after a slight reproof, was allowed to remain in his place—allowed by the mother of six children, who, scarcely permitting a footstep to be heard, during her month's indulgence, felt no sympathy for the poor wretch, denied every comfort required by her situation.

"The day my mother died, the ninth after my birth, I was consigned to the care of the cheapest nurse my father could find; who suckled her own child at the same time, and lodged as many more as she could, in two cellar-like apartments.

"Poverty, and the habit of seeing children die off her hands, had so hardened her heart, that the office of a mother did not awaken the tenderness of a woman; nor were the feminine caresses which seem a part of the rearing of a child, ever bestowed on me. The chicken has a wing to shelter under; but I had no bosom to nestle in, no kindred warmth to foster me. Left in dirt, to cry with cold and hunger till I was weary, and sleep without ever being prepared by exercise, or lulled by kindness to rest; could I be expected to become any thing but a weak and rickety babe? Still, in spite of neglect, I continued to exist, to learn to curse existence, [her countenance grew ferocious as she spoke,] and the treatment that rendered me miserable, seemed to sharpen my wits. Confined then in a damp hovel, to rock the cradle of the succeeding tribe, I looked like a little old woman, or a hag shrivelling into nothing. The furrows of reflection and care contracted the youthful cheek, and gave a sort of supernatural wildness to the ever watchful eye. During this period, my father had married another fellow-servant, who loved him less, and knew better how to manage his passion, than my mother. She likewise proving with child, they agreed to keep a shop: my step-mother, if, being an illegitimate offspring, I may venture thus to characterize her, having obtained a sum of a rich relation, for that purpose.

"Soon after her lying-in, she prevailed on my father to take me home, to save the expence of maintaining me, and of hiring a girl to assist her in the care of the child. I was young, it was true, but appeared a knowing little thing, and might be made handy. Accordingly I was brought to her house; but not to a home—for a home I never knew. Of this child, a daughter, she was extravagantly fond; and it was a part of my employment, to assist to spoil her, by humouring all her whims, and bearing all her caprices. Feeling her own consequence, before she could speak, she had learned the art of tormenting me, and if I ever dared to resist, I received blows, laid on with no compunctious hand, or was sent to bed dinnerless, as well as supperless. I said that it was a part of my daily labour to attend this child, with the servility of a slave; still it was but a part. I was sent out in all seasons, and from place to place, to carry burdens far above my strength, without being allowed to draw near the fire, or ever being cheered by encouragement or kindness. No wonder then, treated like a creature of another species, that I began to envy, and at length to hate, the darling of the house. Yet, I perfectly remember, that it was the caresses, and kind expressions of my step-mother, which first excited my jealous discontent. Once, I cannot forget it, when she was calling in vain her wayward child to kiss her, I ran to her, saying, 'I will kiss you, ma'am!' and how did my heart, which was in my mouth, sink, what was my debasement of soul, when pushed away with—'I do not want you, pert thing!' Another day, when a new gown had excited the highest good humour, and she uttered the appropriate *dear*, addressed unexpectedly to me, I thought I could never do enough to please her; I was all alacrity, and rose proportionably in my own estimation.

"As her daughter grew up, she was pampered with cakes and fruit, while I was, literally speaking, fed with the refuse of the table, with her leavings. A liquorish tooth is, I believe, common to children, and I used to steal any thing sweet, that I could catch up with a chance of concealment. When detected, she was not content to chastize me herself at the moment, but, on my father's return in the evening (he was a shopman), the principal discourse was to recount my faults, and attribute them to the wicked disposition which I had brought into the world with me, inherited from my mother. He did not fail to leave the marks of his resentment on my body, and then solaced himself by playing with my sister.—I could have murdered her at those moments. To save myself from these unmerciful corrections, I resorted to falsehood, and the untruths which I sturdily maintained, were brought in judgment against me, to support my tyrant's inhuman charge of my natural propensity to vice. Seeing me treated with contempt, and always being fed and dressed better, my sister conceived a contemptuous opinion of me, that proved an obstacle to all affection; and my father, hearing continually of my faults, began to consider me as a curse entailed on him for his sins: he was therefore easily prevailed on to bind me apprentice to one of my step-mother's friends, who kept a slop-shop in Wapping. I was represented (as it was said) in my true colours; but she 'warranted,' snapping her fingers, 'that she should break my spirit or heart.'

"My mother replied, with a whine, 'that if any body could make me better, it was such a clever woman as herself; though, for her own part, she had tried in vain; but good-nature was her fault.'

"I shudder with horror, when I recollect the treatment I had now to endure. Not only under the lash of my task-mistress, but the drudge of the maid, apprentices and children, I never had a taste of human kindness to soften the rigour of perpetual labour. I had been introduced as an object of abhorrence into the family; as a creature of whom my step-mother, though she had been kind enough to let me live in the house with her own child, could make nothing. I was described as a wretch, whose nose must be kept to the grinding stone—and it was held there with an iron grasp. It seemed indeed the privilege of their superior nature to kick me about, like the dog or cat. If I were attentive, I was called fawning, if refractory, an obstinate mule, and like a mule I received their censure on my loaded back. Often has my mistress, for some instance of forgetfulness, thrown me from one side of the kitchen to the other, knocked my head against the wall, spit in my face, with various refinements on barbarity that I forbear to enumerate, though they were all acted over again by the servant, with additional insults, to which the appellation of *bastard,* was commonly added, with taunts or sneers. But I will not attempt to give you an adequate idea of my situation, lest you, who probably have never been drenched with the dregs of human misery, should think I exaggerate.

"I stole now, from absolute necessity,—bread; yet whatever else was taken, which I had it not in my power to take, was ascribed to me. I was the filching cat, the ravenous dog, the dumb brute, who must bear all; for if I endeavoured to exculpate myself, I was silenced, without any enquiries being made, with 'Hold your tongue, you never tell truth.' Even the very air I breathed was tainted with scorn; for I was sent to the neighbouring shops with Glutton, Liar, or Thief, written on my forehead. This was, at first, the most bitter punishment; but sullen pride, or a kind of stupid desperation, made me, at length, almost regardless of the contempt, which had wrung from me so many solitary tears at the only moments when I was allowed to rest.

"Thus was I the mark of cruelty till my sixteenth year; and then I have only to point out a change of misery; for a period I never knew. Allow me first to make one observation. Now I look back, I cannot help attributing the greater part of my misery, to the misfortune of having been thrown into the world without the grand support of life—a mother's affection. I had no one to love me; or to make me respected, to enable me to acquire respect. I was an egg dropped on the sand; a pauper by nature, hunted from family to family, who belonged to nobody—and nobody cared for me. I was despised from my birth, and denied the chance of obtaining a footing for myself in society. Yes; I had not even the chance of being considered as a fellow-creature—yet all the people with whom I lived, brutalized as they were by the low cunning of trade, and the despicable shifts of poverty, were not without bowels,[1] though they never yearned for me. I was, in fact, born a slave, and chained by infamy to slavery during the whole of existence, without having any companions to alleviate it by sympathy, or teach me how to rise above it by their example."

## PARACELSUS
# Writings on creation (1531–1538)

*If Wollstonecraft's novel* Maria *helps elucidate the critical role a mother plays in the development and well-being of a child, Paracelsus's discourse on creation explains the philosophical necessity for a woman in the creation of another being. Paracelsus was a physician, alchemist, and philosopher recognized as the founder of modern toxicology. Born Philippus Aureolus Theophrastus Bombastus von Hohenheim, he named himself Paracelsus, meaning "next to Celsus," a first-century Roman encyclopaedist known for his medical text* De Medicina. *Paracelsus believed that the well-being of an individual depended upon the harmony of humankind with nature. In the following passage, Paracelsus explains the crucial importance of the mother figure in the creation and sustaining of humankind. According to*

[1] *bowels:* Archaic term for seat of the emotions; compare heart.

From *Paracelsus: Selected Writings.* (Bollingen, No. 28) Ed. Jolande Jacobi, translated by Norbert Guterman. Copyright © 1951 by Bollingen Foundation. Renewed by Princeton University Press in 1979. Reprinted by permission of Princeton University Press.

*Paracelsus, God meant woman to be not only a participant in creation but the most important component. Creating life without both man and woman, as Victor does, would be an abomination in Paracelsus's estimation, since he believes that "God wills to make man out of two, and not out of one; he wills man composed of two and not of one alone" (p. 209 in this volume). Although Victor has read Paracelsus, he seems to have missed this crucial point. Viewed in this light, Victor might have doomed the creature from its very "birth" by creating it on his own, thereby distorting the natural harmony and order of creation.*

God wills man as man, and woman as woman, and He wills that both should be of the human kind.

God created man directly from the matrix. He took him from the matrix and made a man of him. . . . And then He gave him a matrix of his own—woman. . . . To the end that henceforth there may be two of them, and yet only one; two kinds of flesh, and yet only one, not two. This means that neither of them is perfect alone, that only both together are the whole man. . . . Thus the son is created from the *limbus*—the father—but he is shaped, built, and endowed with his complexions in the matrix . . . just as the first man was created in the macrocosm, the Great World.

There are three different kinds of matrix: the first is the water on which the spirit of God was borne, and this was the maternal womb in which heaven and earth were created. Then heaven and earth each in turn became a matrix, in which Adam, the first man, was formed by the hand of God. Then woman was created out of man; she became the maternal womb of all men, and will remain so to the end of the world. Now, what did that first matrix contain within itself? Being the kingdom of God, it encompassed the spirit of God. The world encloses the eternal, by which it is at the same time surrounded. Woman is enclosed in her skin as in a house, and everything that is within it forms, as it were, a single womb. Even though the female body was taken from the male, it cannot be compared to it. It is true that in shape it is similar to the male body, for woman too is formed as a human being, and like man she carries God's image in her. But in everything else, in its essence, properties, nature, and peculiarities, it is completely different from the male body. Man suffers as man, woman suffers as woman; but both suffer as creatures beloved by God.

Just as heaven and earth close to form a shell, so the maternal body is a closed vessel. . . . An empty matrix in which no child is contained is like heaven and earth before they contained anything living. Since man is a child of the cosmos, and is himself the microcosm, he must be begotten, each time anew, by his mother. And just as he was created of the four elements of the world even in the beginning, so he will be created in the future again and again. For the Creator created the world once, and then He rested. Thus He also made heaven and earth and formed them into a matrix, in which man is conceived, born, and nourished as though in an outer mother, when he no longer rests in his own mother. Thus life in the world is like life in the matrix. The child in the maternal body lives in the inner firmament, and outside the mother's body it lives in the outer firmament. For the matrix is the Little World and has in it all the kinds of heaven and earth.

Woman is like the earth and all the elements, and in this sense she must be considered a matrix; she is the tree which grows from the earth, and the child is like the fruit that is born of the tree. Just as a tree stands in the earth and belongs not only to the earth but also to the air and the water and the fire, so all the four elements are in woman—for the Great Field, the lower and the upper sphere of the world, consists of these—and in the middle of it stands the tree; woman is the image of the tree. Just as the earth, its fruits, and the elements are created for the sake of the tree and in order to sustain it, so the members of woman, all her qualities, and her whole nature exist for the sake of her matrix, her womb.

God willed that the seed of man should not be sown in the body of the elements—not in the earth—but in woman; that his image should be conceived in her and born through her and not from the field of the world. And yet woman in her own way is also a field of the earth and not at all different from it. She replaces it, so to speak, she is the field and the garden mould in which the child is sown and planted, then growing up to be a man.

He who contemplates woman should see in her the maternal womb of man; she is man's world, from which he is born. But no one can see from what force man actually is born. For just as God once created man in His likeness, so He still creates him today.

How can one be an enemy of woman—whatever she may be? The world is peopled with her fruits, and that is why God lets her live so long, however loathsome she may be.

A woman is like a tree bearing fruit. And man is like the fruit that the tree bears. . . . The tree must be well nourished until it has everything by which to give that for the sake of which it exists. But consider how much injury the tree can bear, and how much less the pears! By that much woman is also superior to man. Man is to her what the pear is to the tree. The pear falls, but the tree remains standing. The tree continues to care for the other fruit in order itself to survive; therefore it must also receive much, suffer much, bear up with much, for the sake of its fruits, in order that they may thrive well and happily.

Woman's season of blossoming occurs when she conceives. At this hour she is in bloom, and the blossoming is followed by the fruit, that is to say, the child. . . . When a tree blossoms, it is always because of the fruit that desires to ripen in it, and the tree in which no fruit lies hidden does not blossom. . . . If a virgin is ever to blossom, she must bear fruit. . . . For this is the nature of woman, that she is transformed as soon as she conceives; and then all things in her are like a summer, there is no snow, no frost, and no winter, but only pleasure and delight.

Just as a house is a work and is visible, and its master is also a work and is visible, so the master is a work of God, and the house a work of the master. In the same way it must be understood that we have the works visible before our eyes, and when we discover the master of the work, he is also visible to us. In things eternal, faith makes all the works visible; in things corporeal, but not visible, the light of nature makes all things visible. . . . Do not judge a thing that can become visible by its present invisibility. A child that is being conceived is already a man, although it is not yet visible. . . . It already resembles the visible man.

When the seed is received in the womb, nature combines the seed of the man and the seed of the woman. Of the two seeds the better and stronger will form the other according to its nature. . . . The seed from the man's brain and that from the woman's brain make together only one brain; but the child's brain is formed according to the one which is the stronger of the two, and it becomes like this seed, but never completely like it. For the second seed breaks the force of the first, and this always results in a change of nature. And the more different the two seeds are in their innate complexions, the more the change will be manifest.

When the seeds of all members come together in the matrix, this matrix combines the seed of the head with the seed of the brain, etc., in its own way . . . putting each in its proper place, and thus each single member is placed where it belongs, just as a carpenter builds a house from pieces of wood. Then every seed lies as it is supposed to lie in the mother, which is also called a microcosm. Only life is not there, nor is the soul. . . . But the seed of a single man does not yet make a complete man. God wills to make man out of two, and not out of one; he wills man composed of two and not of one alone. For if man were born of the seed of one individual, he would not change in nature. His child would be just as he is, in the manner of a walnut tree, which is reborn of itself alone, and therefore is entirely like the one from which it is born. In all trees, the same always comes from the same; similarly all walnut trees bear the same nuts, without any difference. The same is true of man. If he had been born only of one individual, he would be like his father, and this father would be his father and his mother in one. Then there would be only people of one kind, and each would look like the other, and all would have the same nature. But the mixing of the seeds of man and woman results in so much change that no individual can be like the other. . . . Each individual's seed breaks the unity of the other, and that is why no man is like another.

At first the herb grows from the root, then a flower grows from the herb, and in the end the seed grows from the flower; the seed is the vital sap, the *quinta essentia* of the herb. For nothing grows without a seed, nothing is born without a seed, nothing multiplies without a seed, and in all fruits of the earth the seed is the most precious, the most noble part, which should be most valued and prized.

A good tree brings good fruits. If the mother is healthy like healthy earth, and if her body is fertile, then the tree too is good and bears good fruit. But for the children there is another matter of importance: a good fruit can be born only of a good seed. . . . A tree of the earth bears fruit again and again, without always requiring a new seed; the tree of woman only when a new seed is planted in it, namely, by man. Therefore much depends upon the seed; if it is worthless, the tree cannot improve it. What is true of the tree is also true of the seed; both must be fit. And if both are good, together they produce something good: the fruit.

A bad seed produces a bad tree, which brings bad fruit. Only the evil seed is not the man himself, nor is the good seed; for the good seed is God, and the evil seed is the devil, and man is only the field. If a good seed falls into a man, it grows from him, since this man is its field, his heart is its tree, and his works are its fruits. Cannot a field that bears weeds be weeded and cleansed of this bad fruit, so that another, good seed can be planted in it? . . . Or cannot a good field be sown with bad seeds? Indeed it can! Every field is ordered by its seed, and no seed by its field. For the seed is the master of the field. Every man is like a field, neither entirely good nor entirely bad, but of an uncertain kind. . . . If a good seed falls into the field, and the soil receives it, it grows to be good. If a bad seed falls into the field and is received, it grows to be bad. Therefore it is not the soil of the field that decides the matter; it is neither good nor bad. It is like a body of water, coloured by the colours that fall on the water.

## The Execution of William Burke (1829)
## [Broadside]

*Although he reads Paracelsus, Victor certainly does not adhere to the scientist's advice on creation, opting instead to make by himself the creature from human and animal parts:*

> *I collected bones from charnel-houses; and disturbed, with profane fingers, the tremendous secrets of the human frame. . . . The dissecting room and the slaughter-house furnished many of my materials[.]*
> *(p. 58 in this volume)*

*Victor's admission of stealing parts from a "charnel-house" (a repository for bones or corpses) might surprise modern readers, but it probably would not have elicited a raised eyebrow from Shelley's contemporaries. While Victor states that he gets most of the necessary human material from "the dissecting room," the truth is that during the early nineteenth century medical schools had a very difficult time supplying the number of human bodies needed for professional and classroom dissection. One of the major causes of the shortage of bodies was existing English law which permitted dissection only of those who had been condemned to death or dissection by the courts. As a result, a black market for dead bodies arose as "body snatchers" or "Resurrectionists" exhumed dead bodies and sold them to medical professionals in need of corpses. Because body snatching became so pervasive, families sometimes kept watch over the graves of the recently deceased for several days, and some wealthy families even placed iron bars over coffins to prevent theft.*

*The Burke and Hare murders, which occurred over a period of 10 months in 1828, helped excite public outrage against the illicit use of dead bodies. Irish immigrants William Burke and William Hare killed sixteen people and sold the cadavers to Doctor Robert Knox, who used them for his anatomy lectures. The combined actions of Burke and Hare, and the imitators who followed, known as "Burkers," helped forward the passage of the Anatomy Act of 1832, which broadened the scope of bodies permitted for dissection, thereby obviating the need for illegally obtained corpses. The following document reproduces a broadside featuring William Burke's confession as well as describing his death. Burke's dead body was legally available for dissection; ironically it remains on display at the Anatomy Museum of the*

*Edinburgh Medical School. Broadsides were large posters intended to announce events or proclamations; they were often sold at public executions as a kind of souvenir. This "Execution" broadside, probably produced to capitalize on the Burke and Hare scandal, was available for sale at Burke's hanging.*

## EXECUTION.

A Full and Particular account of the Execution of W. BURKE, who was hanged at Edinburgh on Wednesday the 28th January, 1829; also, an account of his conduct and behaviour since his condemnation, and on the Scaffold.

Early on Wednesday morning, the Town of Edinburgh was filled with an immense croud of spectators, from all places of the surrounding country, to witness the execution of a Monster, whose crime stands unparalleled in the annals of Scotland : viz.—for cruelly murdering Margery M'Conegal, and afterwards selling her body to the Doctors in October last.

Whilst this unhappy man was under sentence, he made the following Confession—that he had been engaged in this murderous traffic from Christmas, 1827, until the murder of the woman Docherty, or M'Conegal, in October last; during which period, he had butchered Sixteen of his fellow-creatures, and that he had no accomplice but Hare,—that they perpetrated these fearful atrocities by suffocation. When they succeeded in making their victims drunk, the one held the mouth and nostrils, whilst the other went upon the body, and in this manner was the woman Docherty killed; they then sold her body to Doctor——in his rooms, and received payment at his house—and that they were never Resurrectionests; all the bodies they sold being murdered, except one, who died a natural death in Hare's house.

At an early hour on Tuesday, he was taken in a coach from the jail on the Calton-hill to the Lock-up, a prison immediately adjacent to the place of execution. He spent the day in silence, reading, and devotion, and on Tuesday night he slept soundly for several hours. About seven o'clock, the two Catholic clergymen arrived, and were admitted into the cell, and they were soon after followed by the Rev. Mr Marshall: The religious ceremonies being performed, he talked firmly, declared that death had no terrors, and expressed a hope of pardon and happiness. During the night, Burke stated that he was happy, that he had at last been arrested in his career of crime, and brought to justice. Though he had been a great offender, yet he rested on the atonement of the Saviour for salvation. When the irons were knocked off, he exclaimed, "Thank God these are off, and all will be off shortly." Shortly after eight o'clock, the procession set out for the place of execution. Bailies Crichton and Small, with a party of town officers, first ascended the scaffold, and they were followed by Burke, supported by the two Catholic Clergymen. He was dressed in decent black clothes, and was perfectly firm and composed. The moment he appeared, the crowd set up an appalling shout, which continued for several minutes. The murderer and the Catholic clergymen then knelt down and spent a few minutes in devotion, and the religious exercises were concluded by a prayer from the Rev. Mr Marshall. As soon as the executioner proceeded to do his duty, the cries of "Burke him, Burke him, give him no rope," and many others of a similar complexion, were vociferated in voices loud with indignation. Burke, in the mean time, stood perfectly unmoved, and gazed around till the cap was drawn over his face, and shut the world for ever from his view.

The executioner having completed his preparations and placed the signal in Burke's hand, the magistrates, ministers, and attendants left the scaffold. The crowd again set up another long and loud cheer, which was followed by cries for "Hare, Hare!" "Where is Hare?" "Hang Hare!" and so on. Burke lifted his hands and ejaculated a prayer of a few sentences — then dropt the napkin, and momently the drop fell. The struggle was neither long nor apparently severe; but at every convulsive motion, a loud huzza arose from the multitude, which was several times repeated even after the last agonies of humanity were past. During the time of the wretched man's suspension, not a single indication of pity was observable among the vast crowd — on the contrary, every countenance wore the lively aspect of a gala day, while puns and jokes on the occasion were freely bandied about, and produced bursts of laughter and merriment, which were not confined to the juvenile spectators alone — "*Burke* Hare too!" "Wash blood from the land!" "One cheer more" and similar exclamations, were repeated in different directions, until the culprit was cut down, about nine o'clock, when one general and tremendous huzza closed the awful exhibition — and the multitude immediately thereafter began to disperse.

Burke's body is to be dissected, and his Skeleton to be preserved, in order that posterity may keep in remembrance his atrocious crimes.

PRICE ONE PENNY

# EXECUTION.

## A Full and Particular account of the Execution of W. BURKE, who was hanged at Edinburgh on Wednesday the 28th January, 1829; also, an account of his conduct and behaviour since his condemnation, and on the Scaffold.

Early on Wednesday morning, the Town of Edinburgh was filled with an immense croud of spectators, from all places of the surrounding country, to witness the execution of a Monster, whose crime stands unparalleled in the annals of Scotland: viz.—for cruelly murdering Margery M'Conegal, and afterwards selling her body to the Doctors in October last.

Whilst this unhappy man was under sentence, he made the following Confession:—that he had been engaged in this murderous traffic from Christmas, 1827, until the murder of the woman Docherty, or M'Conegal, in October last; during which period, he had butchered Sixteen of his fellow-creatures, and that he had no accomplice but Hare,—that they perpetrated these fearful atrocities by suffocation. When they succeeded in making their victims drunk, the one held the mouth and nostrils, whilst the other went upon the body, and in this manner was the woman Docherty killed; they then sold her body to Doctor ——— in his rooms, and received payment at his house—and that they were never Resurrectionests; all the bodies they sold being murdered, except one, who died a natural death in Hare's house.

At an early hour on Tuesday, he was taken in a coach from the jail on the Calton-hill to the Lock-up, a prison immediately adjacent to the place of execution. He spent the day in silence, reading, and devotion, and on Tuesday night he slept soundly for several hours. About seven o'clock, the two Catholic clergymen arrived, and were admitted into the cell, and they were soon after followed by the Rev. Mr Marshall; The religious ceremonies being performed, he talked firmly, declared that death had no terrors, and expressed a hope of pardon and happiness. During the night, Burke stated that he was happy, that he had at last been arrested in his career of crime, and brought to justice. Though he had been a great offender, yet he rested on the atonement of the Saviour for salvation. When the irons were knocked off, he exclaimed, "Thank God these are off, and all will be off shortly." Shortly after eight o'clock, the procession set out for the place of execution. Bailies Crichton and Small, with a party of town officers, first ascended the scaffold, and they were followed by Burke, supported by the two Catholic Clergymen. He was dressed in decent black clothes, and was perfectly firm and composed. The moment he appeared, the crowd set up an appalling shout, which continued for several minutes. The murderer and the Catholic clergymen then knelt down and spent a few minutes in devotion, and the religious exercises were concluded by a prayer from the Rev. Mr Marshall. As soon as the executioner proceeded to do his duty, the cries of "Burke him, Burke him, give him no rope," and many others of a similar complexion, were vociferated in voices loud with indignation. Burke, in the mean time, stood perfectly unmoved, and gazed around till the cap was drawn over his face, and shut the world for ever from his view.

The executioner having completed his preparations and placed the signal in Burke's hand, the magistrates, ministers, and attendants left the scaffold. The crowd again set up another long and loud cheer, which was followed by cries for "Hare, Hare!" "Where is Hare?" "Hang Hare!" and so on. Burke lifted his hands and ejaculated a prayer of a few sentences—then dropt the napkin, and momently the drop fell. The struggle was neither long nor apparently severe; but at every convulsive motion, a loud huzza arose from the multitude, which was several times repeated even after the last agonies of humanity were past. During the time of the wretched man's suspension, not a single indication of pity was observable among the vast crowd—on the contrary, every countenance wore the lively aspect of a gala day, while puns and jokes on the occasion were freely bandied about, and produced bursts of laughter and merriment, which were not confined to the juvenile spectators alone—"Burke Hare too!" "Wash blood from the land!" "One cheer more!" and similar exclamations, were repeated in different directions, until the culprit was cut down, about nine o'clock, when one general and tremendous huzza closed the awful exhibition—and the multitude immediately thereafter began to disperse.

Burke's body is to be dissected, and his Skeleton to be preserved, in order that posterity may keep in remembrance his atrocious crimes.

### PRICE ONE PENNY.

Facsimile of the Execution of William Burke broadside. National Library of Scotland.

HUMPHRY DAVY

# A Discourse, Introductory to a Course of Lectures on Chemistry (1802)

*Victor learns from lectures at the University of Ingolstadt much of the science he uses to make his creature. The last stage of Victor's education is his introduction to modern chemistry as presented by M. Waldman, whose lecture closely conforms to sections of Sir Humphry Davy's Discourse. Davy, who dabbled in poetry as a youth and was a friend of poets Samuel Taylor Coleridge and Robert Southey, remains best known for discovering alkali and alkaline earth metals. Davy's Discourse, printed here in its entirety, suggests the ways in which a (mis)education in the absolute power of science over nature might not only produce a creature predisposed to become a monster but also make a monster of the scientist Victor Frankenstein.*

Chemistry is that part of Natural Philosophy which relates to those intimate actions of bodies upon each other, by which their appearances are altered, and their individuality destroyed.

This science has for its objects all the substances found upon our globe. It relates not only to the minute alterations in the external world, which are daily coming under the cognizance of our senses, and which, in consequence, are incapable of affecting the imagination; but likewise to the great changes, and convulsions in nature, which, occurring but seldom, excite our curiosity, or awaken our astonishment.

The phaenomena of combustion, of the solution of different substances in water, of the agencies of fire; the production of rain, hail, and snow, and the conversion of dead matter into living matter by vegetable organs, all belong to chemistry: and, in their various and apparently capricious appearances, can be accurately explained only by an acquaintance with the fundamental and general chemical principles.

Chemistry, considered as a systematic arrangement of facts, is of later origin than most of the other sciences; yet certain of its processes and operations have been always more or less connected with them; and, lately, by furnishing new instruments and powers of investigation, it has greatly contributed to increase their perfection, and to extend their applications.

Mechanical Philosophy, regarded as the science of the motions of the masses of matter, in its theories and practices, is, to a certain extent, dependent upon chemical laws. How, in fact, can the mechanic calculate with accuracy upon the powers of solids, fluids, or gases, in communicating motion to each other, unless he is previously acquainted with their particular chemical affinities, or propensities to remain disunited, or to combine? It is to chemistry that he is indebted for the knowledge of the nature and properties of the substances he employs; and he is obliged to that science for the artificial production of the most powerful and most useful of his agents.

Natural History and chemistry are attached to each other by very intimate ties. For, whilst the first of these sciences treats of the general external properties of bodies, the last unfolds their internal constitution and ascertains their intimate nature. Natural history examines the beings and substances of the external world, chiefly in their permanent and unchanging forms: whereas chemistry, by studying them in the laws of their alterations, developes and explains their active powers, and the particular exertions of those powers.

It is only in consequence of chemical discoveries that that part of natural history which relates to mineral substances has assumed the form of a science. Mineralogy, at a period not very distant from the present, consisted merely of a collection of terms badly arranged according to certain vague external properties of substances. It is now founded upon a beautiful and methodical classification; and that chiefly in consequence of the comparison of the intimate composition of the bodies it represents, with their obvious forms and appearances. The mind of the mineralogist is no longer perplexed by endeavours to discover the loose and varying analogies between the colours, the shapes, and the weights of different substances. By means of the new method of analysis, he is furnished with instruments of investigation immediately applicable, and capable of producing uniform and accurate results.

Even Botany and Zoology as branches of natural history, though independent of chemistry as to their primary classifications, yet are related to it, so far as they treat of the constitution and functions of vegetables and animals. How dependent, in fact, upon chemical processes are the nourishment and growth of organized beings: their various alterations of form, their constant production of new substances, and finally their death and decomposition, in which nature seems to take unto herself those elements and constituent principles which, for a while, she had lent to a superior agent as the organs and instruments of the spirit of life!

And in pursuing this view of the subject, Medicine and Physiology, those sciences which connect the preservation of the health of the human being with the abstruse philosophy of organized nature, will be found to have derived from chemistry most of their practical applications, and many of the analogies which have contributed to give to their scattered

facts order and systematic arrangement. The art of preparing those substances, which operate powerfully upon animal bodies, and which, according to their different modes of exhibition, are either efficient remedies, or
active poisons, is purely chemical. Indeed the want of an acquaintance
with scientific principles in the processes of pharmacy has often been productive of dangerous consequences; and the study of the simple and
unvarying agencies of dead matter ought surely to precede investigations
concerning the mysterious and complicated powers of life. Knowing very
little of the laws of his own existence, man has nevertheless derived some
useful information from researches concerning the nature of respiration;
and the composition and properties of animal organs even in their dead
state. And if the connection of chemistry with physiology has given rise
to some visionary and seductive theories; yet even this circumstance has
been useful to the public mind in exciting it by doubt, and in leading it
to new investigations. A reproach, to a certain degree just, has been
thrown upon those doctrines known by the name of the chemical physiology; for in the applications of them, speculative philosophers have been
guided rather by the analogies of words than of facts. Instead of slowly
endeavouring to lift up the veil concealing the wonderful phaenomena of
living nature; full of ardent imaginations, they have vainly and presump-
tuously attempted to tear it asunder.

Though Astronomy, in its sublime views and its mathematical principles, is far removed from chemistry, yet to this science it is indebted
for many of its instruments of experiment. The progress of the astronomer has been in some measure commensurate with that of the chemical
artist, who, indeed, by his perfection of the materials used for the astro-
nomical apparatus, has afforded to the investigating philosopher the
means of tracing the revolutions of the planets, and of penetrating into
space, so as to discover the forms and appearances of the distant parts
of the universe.

It would be unnecessary to pursue this subject to a greater extent.
Fortunately for man, all the different parts of the human mind are possessed of certain harmonious relations; and it is even difficult to draw
the line of distinction between the sciences; for, as they have for their
objects only dead and living nature, and as they consist of expressions
of facts more or less analogous, they must all be possessed of certain ties
of connection, and of certain dependencies on each other. The man of
true genius, who studies science in consequence of its application, pointing out to himself a definite end, will make use of all the instruments
of investigation which are necessary for his purposes: and in the search
of discovery, he will rather pursue the plans of his own mind than be

limited by the artificial divisions of language. Following extensive views, he will combine together mechanical, chemical, and physiological knowledge, whenever this combination may be essential: in consequence, his facts will be connected together by simple and obvious analogies; and, in studying one class of phaenomena more particularly, he will not neglect its relations to other classes.

But chemistry is not valuable simply in its connections with the sciences, some of which are speculative and remote from our habitual passions and desires; it applies to most of the processes and operations of common life; to those processes on which we depend for the gratification of our wants; and which, in consequence of their perfection and extension by means of scientific principles, have become the sources of the most refined enjoyments and delicate pleasures of civilized society.

Agriculture, to which we owe our means of subsistence, is an art intimately connected with chemical science. For, though the common soil of the earth will produce vegetable food, yet it can only be made to produce it in the greatest quantity, and of the best quality, in consequence of the adoption of methods of cultivation dependent upon scientific principles. The knowledge of the composition of soils, of the food of vegetables, of the modes in which their products must be treated, so as to become fit for the nourishment of animals, is essential to the cultivation of land; and his exertions are profitable and useful to society, in proportion as he is more of a chemical philosopher. Since, indeed, this truth has been understood, and since the importance of agriculture has been generally felt, the character of the agriculturist has become more dignified and more refined. No longer a mere machine of labour, he has learned to think and to reason. He is aware of his usefulness to his fellow men; and he is become at once the friend of nature and the friend of society.

The Working of Metals is a branch of technical chemistry; and it would be a sublime, though a difficult task to ascertain the effects of this art upon the progress of the human mind. It has afforded to man the powers of defence against savage animals: it has enabled him to cultivate the ground, to build houses, cities, and ships, and to model much of the surface of the earth after his own imaginations of beauty. It has furnished instruments connected not only with his sublime enjoyments, but likewise with his crimes and his miseries; it has enabled him to oppress and destroy, to conquer and protect.

The arts of Bleaching and Dyeing, which the habits and fashions of society have made important, are purely chemical. To destroy and produce colours, to define the causes of the changes they undergo, and to exhibit the modes in which they may be rendered durable, demand an intimate acquaintance with chemistry. The artist, who merely labours with his hands, is obliged to theory for his discovery of the most useful of his practices: and permanent and brilliant ornamental colours, which rival the most beautiful tints of nature, are artificially composed from their elements by means of human inventions.

Tanning, and the Preparation of Leather, are chemical processes, which, though extremely simple, are of great importance to society. The modes of impregnating skin with the tanning principle of the vegetable kingdom, so as to render it strong, and insoluble in water, and the methods of preparing it for this impregnation, have been reduced to scientific principles. And if the improvements resulting from new investigations have not been uniformly adopted by manufacturers, it appears to be owing rather to the difficulty occurring in inducing workmen to form new habits, to a want of certain explanations of the minutiae of the operations, and, perhaps in some measure, to the common prejudice against novelties, than to any defect in the general theory of the art, as laid down by chemical philosophers, and demonstrated by their experiments.

But, amongst the chemical arts, few perhaps are more important than those of Porcelain and Glass making. To them we owe many of those elegant vessels and utensils which have contributed to the health and delicacy of civilized nations. They have furnished instruments of experiments for most of the sciences; and, consequently, have become the remote causes of some of the discoveries made in those sciences. Without instruments of glass, the gases could never have been discovered, or their combinations ascertained; the minute forms and appearances of natural objects could not have been investigated; and, lastly, the sublime researches of the moderns concerning heat and light would have been wholly lost to us.

This subject might be much enlarged upon; for it is difficult to examine any of our common operations or labours without finding them more or less connected with chemistry. By means of this science man has employed almost all the substances in nature either for the satisfaction of his wants, or the gratification of his luxuries. Not contented with what is found upon the surface of the earth, he has penetrated into her bosom, and has even searched the bottom of the ocean, for the purpose of allaying the restlessness of his desires, or of extending and increasing his power. He is to a certain extent ruler of all the elements that surround him; and he is capable of using not only common matter according to his will and inclinations, but likewise of subjecting to his purposes the ethereal principles of heat and light. By his inventions they are elicited from the atmosphere; and under his control they become, according to circumstances, instruments of comfort and enjoyment, or of terror and destruction.

To be able indeed to form an accurate estimate of the effects of chemical philosophy, and the arts and sciences connected with it, upon the human mind, we ought to examine the history of society, to trace the progress of improvement, or more immediately to compare the uncultivated savage with the being of science and civilization.

Man, in what is called a state of nature, is a creature of almost pure sensation. Called into activity only by positive wants, his life is passed either in satisfying the cravings of the common appetites, or in apathy, or in slumber. Living only in moments, he calculates but little on futurity. He has no vivid feelings of hope, or thoughts of permanent and powerful action. And, unable to discover causes, he is either harassed by superstitious dreams, or quietly and passively submissive to the mercy of nature and the elements. How different is man informed through the beneficence of the Deity, by science, and the arts! Knowing his wants, and being able to provide for them, he is capable of anticipating future enjoyments, and of connecting hope with an infinite variety of ideas. He is in some measure independent of chance or accident for his pleasures. Science has given to him an acquaintance with the different relations of the parts of the external world; and more than that, it has bestowed upon him powers which may be almost called creative; which have enabled him to modify and change the beings surrounding him, and by his experiments to interrogate nature with power, not simply as a scholar, passive and seeking only to understand her operations, but rather as a master, active with his own instruments.

But, though improved and instructed by the sciences, we must not rest contented with what has been done; it is necessary that we should likewise do. Our enjoyment of the fruits of the labours of former times should be rather an enjoyment of activity than of indolence; and, instead of passively admiring, we ought to admire with that feeling which leads to emulation.

Science has done much for man, but it is capable of doing still more; its sources of improvement are not yet exhausted; the benefits that it has conferred ought to excite our hopes of its capability of conferring new benefits; and, in considering the progressiveness of our nature, we may reasonably look forward to a state of greater cultivation and happiness than that we at present enjoy.

As a branch of sublime philosophy, chemistry is far from being perfect. It consists of a number of collections of facts, connected together by different relations; but as yet it is not furnished with a precise and beautiful theory. Though we can perceive, develope, and even produce, by means of our instruments of experiment, an almost infinite variety of minute phaenomena, yet we are incapable of determining the general laws by which they are governed; and, in attempting to define them, we are lost in obscure, though sublime imaginations concerning unknown agencies. That they may be discovered, however, there is every reason to believe. And who would not be ambitious of becoming acquainted with the most profound secrets of nature; of ascertaining her hidden operations; and of exhibiting to men that system of knowledge which relates so intimately to their own physical and moral constitution?

The future is composed merely of images of the past, connected in new arrangements by analogy, and modified by the circumstances and feelings of the moment; our hopes are founded upon our experience; and in reasoning concerning what may be accomplished, we ought not only to consider the immense field of research yet unexplored, but likewise to examine the latest operations of the human mind, and to ascertain the degree of its strength and activity.

At the beginning of the seventeenth century, very little was known concerning the philosophy of the intimate actions of bodies on each other: and before this time vague ideas, superstitious notions, and inaccurate practices, were the only effects of the first efforts of the mind to establish the foundations of chemistry. Men either were astonished and deluded by their first inventions, so as to become visionaries, and to institute researches after imaginary things, or they employed them as instruments for astonishing and deluding others, influenced by their dearest passions and interests, by ambition, or the love of money. Hence arose the dreams of Alchemy concerning the philosopher's stone and the elixir of life. Hence for a long while the other metals were destroyed, or rendered useless, by experiments designed to transmute them into gold; and for a long while the means of obtaining earthly immortality were sought for amidst the unhealthy vapours of the laboratory. These views of things have passed away, and a new science has gradually arisen. The dim and uncertain twilight of discovery, which gave to objects false or indefinite appearances, has been succeeded by the steady light of truth, which has shown the external world in its distinct forms, and in its true relations to human powers. The composition of the atmosphere, and the properties of the gases, have been ascertained; the phaenomena of electricity have been developed; the lightnings have been taken from the clouds; and, lastly, a new influence has been discovered, which has enabled man to produce from combinations of dead matter effects which were formerly occasioned only by animal organs.

The human mind has been lately active and powerful; but there is very little reason for believing that the period of its greatest strength is passed; or even that it has attained its adult state. We find in all its exertions not only the health and vigour, but likewise the awkwardness of youth. It has gained new powers and faculties; but it is as yet incapable of using them with readiness and efficacy. Its desires are beyond its abilities; its different parts and organs are not firmly knit together, and they seldom act in perfect unity.

Unless any great physical changes should take place upon the globe, the permanency of the arts and sciences is rendered certain, in consequence of the diffusion of knowledge by means of the invention of printing: and those words which are the immutable instruments of thought, are become the constant and widely-diffused nourishment of the mind, the preservers of its health and energy. Individuals, in consequence of interested motives or false views, may check for a time the progress of knowledge; moral causes may produce a momentary slumber of the public spirit; the adoption of wild and dangerous theories, by ambitious or deluded men, may throw a temporary opprobrium on literature: but the influence of true philosophy will never be despised; the germs of improvement are sown in minds even where they are not perceived; and sooner or later the spring-time of their growth must arrive.

In reasoning concerning the future hopes of the human species, we may look forward with confidence to a state of society in which the different orders and classes of men will contribute more effectually to the support of each other than they have hitherto done. This state indeed seems to be approaching fast; for, in consequence of the multiplication of the means of instruction, the man of science and the manufacturer are daily becoming more nearly assimilated to each other. The artist, who formerly affected to despise scientific principles, because he was incapable of perceiving the advantages of them, is now so far enlightened, as to favour the adoption of new processes in his art, whenever they are evidently connected with a diminution of labour. And the increase of projectors, even to too great an extent, demonstrates the enthusiasm of the public mind in its search after improvement. The arts and sciences also are in a high degree cultivated, and patronized by the rich and privileged orders. The guardians of civilization and of refinement, the most powerful and respected part of society, are daily growing more attentive to the realities of life; and, giving up many of their unnecessary enjoyments, in consequence of the desire to be useful, are becoming the friends and protectors of the labouring part of the community. The unequal division of property and of labour, the difference of rank and condition amongst mankind, are the sources of power in civilized life, its moving causes, and even its very soul: and, in considering and hoping that the human species is capable of becoming more enlightened and more happy, we can only expect that the great whole of society should be ultimately connected together by means of knowledge and the useful arts; that they should act as the children of one great parent, with one determinate end, so that no power may be rendered useless, no exertions thrown away. In this view we do not look to distant ages, or amuse ourselves with brilliant, though delusive dreams, concerning the infinite improveability of man, the annihilation of labour, disease, and even death. But we reason by analogy from simple facts. We consider only a state of human progression arising out of its present condition. We look for a time that we may reasonably expect, for a bright day of which we already behold the dawn.

So far our considerations have been general; so far we have examined chemistry, chiefly with regard to its great agency upon the improvement of society, as connected with the increasing perfection of the different branches of natural philosophy and the arts. At present it remains for us only to investigate the effects of the study of this science upon particular minds, and to ascertain its powers of increasing that happiness which arises out of the private feelings and interests of individuals.

The quantity of pleasure which we are capable of experiencing in life, appears to be in a great measure connected with the number of independent sources of enjoyment in our possession. And, though one great object of desire, connected with great exertions, must more or less employ the most powerful faculties of the soul; yet a certain variety of trains of feeling, and of ideas, is essential to its health and permanent activity. In considering the relations of the pursuit of chemistry to this part of our nature, we cannot but perceive, that the contemplation of the various phaenomena in the external world is eminently fitted for giving a permanent and placid enjoyment to the mind. For the relations of these phaenomena are perpetually changing; and, consequently, they are uniformly obliging us to alter our modes of thinking. Also the theories that represent them are only approximations to truth; and they do not fetter the mind by giving to it implicit confidence, but are rather the instruments that it employs for the purpose of gaining new ideas.

A certain portion of physical knowledge is essential to our existence; and all efficient exertion is founded upon an accurate and minute acquaintance with the properties of the different objects surrounding us. The germ of power indeed is native; but it can only be nourished by the forms of the external world. The food of the imagination is supplied by the senses, and all ideas existing in the human mind are representations of parts of nature accurately delineated by memory, or tinged with the glow of passion, and formed into new combinations by fancy. In this view researches concerning the phaenomena of corpuscular action may be said to be almost natural to the mind, and to arise out of its instinctive feelings. The objects that are nearest to man are the first to occupy his attention: from considering their agencies on each other he becomes capable of predicting effects; in modifying these effects he gains activity; and science becomes the parent of the strength and independence of his faculties.

The appearances of the greater number of natural objects are originally delightful to us, and they become still more so when the laws by which they are governed are known, and when they are associated with ideas of order and utility. The study of nature, therefore, in her various operations must be always more or less connected with the love of the beautiful and sublime: and, in consequence of the extent and indefiniteness of the views it presents to us, it is eminently calculated to gratify and keep alive the more powerful passions and ambitions of the soul; which, delighting in the anticipation of enjoyment, is never satisfied with knowledge; and which is, as it were, nourished by futurity, and rendered strong by hope.

In common society, to men collected in great cities, who are wearied by the constant recurrence of similar artificial pursuits and objects, and who are in need of sources of permanent attachment, the cultivation of chemistry, and the physical sciences, may be eminently beneficial. For in all their applications they exhibit an almost infinite variety of effects connected with a simplicity of design. They demonstrate that every being is intended for some definite end or purpose. They attach feelings of importance even to inanimate objects: and they furnish to the mind means of obtaining enjoyment unconnected with the labour or misery of others.

To the man of business, or of mechanical employment, the pursuit of experimental research may afford a simple pleasure, unconnected with the gratification of unnecessary wants, and leading to such an expansion of the faculties of the mind as must give to it dignity and power. To the refined and fashionable classes of society it may become a source of consolation and of happiness, in those moments of solitude when the common habits and passions of the world are considered with indifference. It may destroy diseases of the imagination, owing to too deep a sensibility; and it may attach the affections to objects, permanent, important, and intimately related to the interests of the human species. Even to persons of powerful minds, who are connected with society by literary, political, or moral relations, an acquaintance with the science that represents the operations of nature cannot be wholly useless. It must strengthen their habits of minute discrimination; and, by obliging them to use a language representing simple facts, may tend to destroy the influence of terms connected only with feeling. The man who has been accustomed to study natural objects philosophically, to be perpetually guarding against the delusions of the fancy, will not readily be induced to multiply words so as to forget things. From observing in the relations of inanimate things fitness and utility, he will reason with deeper reverence concerning beings possessing life; and, perceiving in all the phaenomena of the universe the designs of a perfect intelligence, he will be averse to the turbulence and passion of hasty innovations, and will uniformly appear as the friend of tranquillity and order.

## LUIGI GALVANI

### De viribus electricitatis in motu musculari commentarius

*When experiments in galvanism, the science dealing with the action of conductors of electricity, were limited to using electricity to produce twitching in the body parts of frogs and other animals, as in the 1791 print of Luigi Galvani's experiments, they seem relatively benign. And although Galvani did not animate a corpse, he is credited with discovering bioelectricity.*

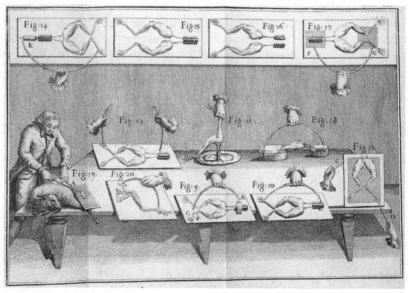

*De viribus electricitatis in motu musculari commentarious* (Commentary on the effect of electricity on muscular motion).
Courtesy of the National Library of Medicine.

## HENRY R. ROBINSON

# "A Galvinized Corpse" (1836)

Henry R. Robinson's 1836 American political cartoon, "A Galva-nized Corpse," indicates that when scientists extend their range from frogs to humans they might be perceived as the devil's disciples. In the cartoon, the devil on the right tells his worried companion: "can't you see that it's all for our gain that he should be galvanized into activity again?"

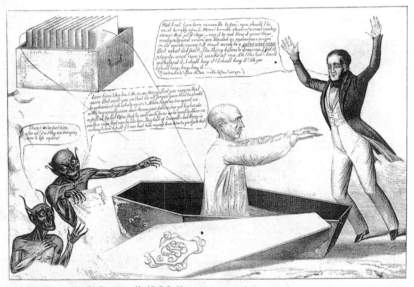

"A Galvanized Corpse" (1836). Library of Congress.

JAMES WHALE

## Frankenstein's Laboratory (1931)

*Victor's use of "instruments of life" to "infuse a spark of being" (p. 59 in this volume) into his creature gestures toward contemporary experiments in galvanism. It is James Whale's* Frankenstein *(1931), however, that emphasizes the technology of life-creation. The still from the film shows some of the additions to Mary Shelley's text, most notably Victor's lab-coat, the fully equipped laboratory, and the hunchbacked assistant Igor, that have become part of the popular conception of Victor as mad scientist.*

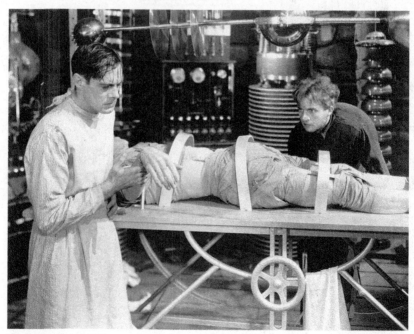

Frankenstein's laboratory in James Whale's *Frankenstein* (1931).
© Universal Pictures/Photofest.

## ERASMUS DARWIN

### *From* The Temple of Nature; or, The Origin of Society—A poem, with philosophical notes (1803)

*While theories of galvanism certainly influenced Mary Shelley's writing, so too did the theories of "spontaneous vitality" espoused by scientists such as Erasmus Darwin.* Grandfather of the famous Charles Darwin—author of The Origin of Species *(1859)* and The Descent of Man *(1871)—Erasmus was himself an evolutionist philosopher and scientist. In the "Additional Notes" section of his posthumously published* The Temple of Nature, *Darwin explains his ideas about both the evolution of species in "a perpetual state of improvement" and spontaneous vitality. Shelley learned about Darwin's theory of spontaneous vitality from her husband and Lord Byron:*

> *Many and long were the conversations between Lord Byron and Shelley, to which I was a devout but nearly silent listener. During one of these, various philosophical doctrines were discussed, and among others the nature of the principle of life, and whether there was any probability of its ever being discovered and communicated. They talked of the experiments of Dr. Darwin, (I speak not of what the Doctor really did, or said that he did, but, as more to my purpose, of what was then spoken of as having been done by him,) who preserved a piece of vermicelli in a glass case, till by some extraordinary means it began to move with voluntary motion. (p. 23 in this volume)*

> *The passage from Darwin presented below does not indicate that he witnessed "a piece of vermicelli" begin "to move with voluntary motion," but as Shelley states, for her the truth of the experiments did not matter so much as "what was then spoken of as having been done by him." Victor takes as a given the idea that life can spontaneously occur; for him, creating life is a matter of unlocking "the spark" that excites inanimate material into life.*

### SPONTANEOUS VITALITY OF MICROSCOPIC ANIMALS.

Hence without parent by spontaneous birth
Rise the first specks of animated earth.

—CANTO. I. I. 247

*Preliminary observations.*

II. Concerning the spontaneous production of the smallest microscopic animals it should be first observed, that the power of reproduction distinguishes organic being, whether vegetable or animal, from inanimate nature. The circulation of fluids in vessels may exist in hydraulic machines, but the power of reproduction belongs alone to life. This reproduction of plants and of animals is of two kinds, which may be termed solitary and sexual. The former of these, as in the reproduction of the buds of trees, and of the bulbs of tulips, and of the polypus, and aphis, appears to be the first or most simple mode of generation, as many of these organic beings afterwards acquire sexual organs, as the flowers of seedling trees, and of seedling tulips, and the autumnal progeny of the aphis. See Phytologia.[1]

Secondly, it should be observed, that by reproduction organic beings are gradually enlarged and improved; which may perhaps more rapidly and uniformly occur in the simplest modes of animated being; but occasionally also in the more complicated and perfect kinds. Thus the buds of a seedling tree, or the bulbs of seedling tulips, become larger and stronger in the second year than the first, and thus improve till they acquire flowers or sexes; and the aphis, I believe, increases in bulk to the eighth or ninth generation, and then produces a sexual progeny. Hence the existence of spontaneous vitality is only to be expected to be found in the simplest modes of animation, as the complex ones have been formed by many successive reproductions.

*Experimental facts.*

III. By the experiments of Buffon, Reaumur, Ellis, Ingenhouz,[2] and others, microscopic animals are produced in three or four days, according to the warmth of the season, in the infusions of all vegetable or animal matter. One or more of these gentlemen put some boiling veal broth into a phial previously heated in the fire, and sealing it up hermetically or with melted wax, observed it to be replete with animalcules in three or four days. . . .

---

[1] The reference is to Erasmus Darwin's 1800 book *Phytologia; or, The Philosophy of agriculture and gardening. With the theory of draining morasses and with an improved construction of the drill plough.*

[2] Georges-Louis Leclerc, Comte de Buffon (1707–1788), French naturalist now best known for his theories of evolution; he wrote a 36-volume treatise on *Natural History, general and particular.* Réne-Antoine Ferchault de Réaumur (1683–1757), French scientist of manifold interests in botany and natural history, including artificial incubation. John Ellis (c. 1710–1776), British naturalist interested in zoophytes who specialized in the study of corals. Jan Ingenhousz (1730–1799), Dutch physiologist who studied the gases emitted by plants.

Not only microscopic animals appear to be produced by a spontaneous vital process, and then quickly improve by solitary generation like the buds of trees, or like the polypus and aphis, but there is one vegetable body, which appears to be produced by a spontaneous vital process, and is believed to be propagated and enlarged in so short a time by solitary generation as to become visible to the naked eye; I mean the green matter first attended to by Dr. Priestley,[3] and called by him conferva fontinalis. The proofs, that this material is a vegetable, are from its giving up so much oxygen, when exposed to the sunshine, as it grows in water, and from its green colour.

Dr. Ingenhouz asserts, that by filling a bottle with well-water, and inverting it immediately into a basin of well-water, this green vegetable is formed in great quantity; and he believes, that the water itself, or some substance contained in the water, is converted into this kind of vegetation, which then quickly propagates itself.

M. Girtanner[4] asserts, that this green vegetable matter is not produced by water and heat alone, but requires the sun's light for this purpose, as he observed by many experiments, and thinks it arises from decomposing water deprived of a part of its oxygen, and laughs at Dr. Priestley for believing that the seeds of this conferva, and the parents of microscopic animals, exist universally in the atmosphere, and penetrate the sides of glass jars; Philos. Magazine for May 1800.[5]

Besides this green vegetable matter of Dr. Priestley, there is another vegetable, the minute beginnings of the growth of which Mr. Ellis observed by his microscope near the surface of all putrefying vegetable or animal matter, which is the mucor or mouldiness; the vegetation of which was amazingly quick so as to be almost seen, and soon became so large as to be visible to the naked eye. It is difficult to conceive how the seeds of this mucor can float so universally in the atmosphere as to fix itself on all putrid matter in all places.

*Theory of Spontaneous Vitality.*

IV. In animal nutrition the organic matter of the bodies of dead animals, or vegetables, is taken into the stomach, and there suffers decompositions and new combinations by a chemical process. Some parts of it are however absorbed by the lacteals as fast as they are produced by this

---

[3] Joseph Priestley (1733–1804), political radical, controversial Dissenting clergyman, and well-regarded naturalist best known for his experiments with electricity and gases.

[4] Christoph Girtanner (1760–?), German physician and writer on medical subjects.

[5] Abbreviation for *Philosophical Magazine*, a scientific journal.

process of digestion; in which circumstance this process differs from common chemical operations.

In vegetable nutrition the organic matter of dead animals, or vegetables, undergoes chemical decompositions and new combinations on or beneath the surface of the earth; and parts of it, as they are produced, are perpetually absorbed by the roots of the plants in contact with it; in which this also differs from common chemical processes. Hence the particles which are produced from dead organic matter by chemical decompositions or new consequent combinations, are found proper for the purposes of the nutrition of living vegetable and animal bodies, whether these decompositions and new combinations are performed in the stomach or beneath the soil. . . .

It may be here added, that the production and properties of some kinds of inanimate matter, are almost as difficult to comprehend as those of the simplest degrees of animation. Thus the elastic gum, or caoutchouc, and some fossile bitumens, when drawn out to a great length, contract themselves by their elasticity, like an animal fibre by stimulus. The laws of action of these, and all other elastic bodies, are not yet understood; as the laws of the attraction of cohesion, to produce these effects, must be very different from those of general attraction, since the farther the particles of elastic bodies are drawn from each other till they separate, the stronger they seem to attract; and the nearer they are pressed together, the more they seem to repel; as in bending a spring, or in extending a piece of elastic gum; which is the reverse to what occurs in the attractions of disunited bodies; and much wants further investigation. So the spontaneous production of alcohol or of vinegar, by the vinous and acetous fermentations, as well as the production of a mucus by putrefaction which will contract when extended, seems almost as difficult to understand as the spontaneous production of a fibre from decomposing animal or vegetable substances, which will contract when stimulated, and thus constitutes the primordium of life.

Some of the microscopic animals are said to remain dead for many days or weeks, when the fluid in which they existed is dried up, and quickly to recover life and motion by the fresh addition of water and warmth. Thus the chaos redivivum of Linnaeus[6] dwells in vinegar and in bookbinders paste: it revives by water after having been dried for years,

---

[6]Carl Linnaeus (1707–1778), Swedish botanist best known for his system of taxonomy (biological classification).

and is both oviparous and viviparous; Syst. Nat.[7] Thus the vorticella[8] or wheel animal, which is found in rain water that has stood some days in leaden gutters, or in hollows of lead on the taps of houses, or in the slime or sediment left by such water, though it discovers no sign of life except when in the water, yet it is capable of continuing alive for many months though kept in a dry state. In this state it is of a globulous shape, exceeds not the bigness of a grain of sand, and no signs of life appear; but being put into water, in the space of half an hour a languid motion begins, the globule turns itself about, lengthens itself by slow degrees, assumes the form of a lively maggot, and most commonly in a few minutes afterwards puts out its wheels, swimming vigorously through the water as if in search of food; or else, fixing itself by the tail, works the wheels in such a manner as to bring its food to its mouth; English Encyclopedia, Art. Animalcule.[9] Thus some shell-snails in the cabinets of the curious have been kept in a dry state for ten years or longer, and have revived on being moistened with warmish water; Philos. Transact.[10] So eggs and seeds after many months torpor, are revived by warmth and moisture; hence it may be concluded, that even the organic particles of dead animals may, when exposed to a due degree of warmth and moisture, regain some degree of vitality, since this is done by more complicate animal organs in the instances above mentioned.

The hydra of Linnaeus, which dwells in the rivers of Europe under aquatic plants, has been observed by the curious of the present time, to revive after it has been dried, to be restored after being mutilated, to multiply by being divided, to be propagated from small portions, to live after being inverted; all which would be best explained by the doctrine of spontaneous reproduction from organic particles not yet completely decomposed.

To this should be added, that these microscopic animals are found in all solutions of vegetable or animal matter in water; as black pepper steeped in water, hay suffered to become putrid in water, and the water of dunghills, afford animalcules in astonishing numbers. See Mr. Ellis's

[7] Abbreviation for *Systema Naturae*, the work by Carl Linnaeus that presented his system of taxonomy; first edition 1735, twelfth and much expanded edition 1766–68.

[8] It is possible that what Mary Shelley heard as "vermicelli," a kind of pasta (p. 23 in this volume), was in fact the word "vorticella"; it is also possible that Byron and Shelley themselves misunderstood the "vorticella" experiment.

[9] The *English Encyclopedia*, a 10-volume text published in London in 1802; "Art. Animalcule," abbreviation for "article on animalcule."

[10] Abbreviation for *Philosophical Transactions of the Royal Society of London for improving natural knowledge*, the first peer-reviewed science journal.

curious account of Animalcules produced from an infusion of Potatoes and Hempseed; Philos. Transact. Vol. LIX. from all which it would appear, that organic particles of dead vegetables and animals during their usual chemical changes into putridity or acidity, do not lose all their organization or vitality, but retain so much of it as to unite with the parts of living animals in the process of nutrition, or unite and produce new complicate animals by secretion as in generation, or produce very simple microscopic animals or microscopic vegetables, by their new combinations in warmth and moisture.

And finally, that these microscopic organic bodies are multiplied and enlarged by solitary reproduction without sexual intercourse till they acquire greater perfection or new properties. Lewenhoek[11] observed in rain-water which had stood a few days, the smallest scarcely visible microscopic animalcules, and in a few more days he observed others eight times as large; English Encyclop. Art. Animalcule.

*Conclusion.*

There is therefore no absurdity in believing that the most simple animals and vegetables may be produced by the congress of the parts of decomposing organic matter, without what can properly be termed generation, as the genus did not previously exist; which accounts for the endless varieties, as well as for the immense numbers of microscopic animals.

The green vegetable matter of Dr. Priestley, which is universally produced in stagnant water, and the mucor, or mouldiness, which is seen on the surface of all putrid vegetable and animal matter, have probably no parents, but a spontaneous origin from the congress of the decomposing organic particles, and afterwards propagate themselves. Some other fungi, as those growing in close wine-vaults, or others which arise from decaying trees, or rotten timber, may perhaps be owing to a similar spontaneous production, and not previously exist as perfect organic beings in the juices of the wood, as some have supposed. In the same manner it would seem, that the common esculent mushroom is produced from horse dung at any time and in any place, as is the common practice of many gardiners; Kennedy on Gardening.[12]

---

[11] Antonie van Leeuwenhoek (1632–1723), Dutch tradesman and lensmaker; using his own handcrafted microscope, he was the first to observe single-celled organisms, which he termed "animalcules."

[12] John Kennedy, *A Treatise upon Planting, Gardening, and the Management of the Hothouse,* c. 1777.

*Appendix.*
The knowledge of microscopic animals is still in its infancy: those already known are arranged by Mr. Muller[13] into [. . .] classes; but it is probable, that many more classes, as well as innumerable individuals, may be discovered by improvements of the microscope, as Mr. Herschell[14] has discovered so many thousand stars, which were before invisible, by improvements of the telescope.

## SAMUEL TAYLOR COLERIDGE

### *From* The Rime of the Ancyent Marinere, In Seven Parts (1798)

*Although scientists during the Romantic period neither created spontaneous life nor resurrected a cadaver, poets such as Samuel Taylor Coleridge brought to life such spectacular imaginings through poetry. Coleridge's* The Rime of the Ancyent Marinere *details the story of a sailor who kills an innocent albatross. Similar to Victor, the mariner suffers because he commits an act against nature; in addition, the actions of both men have a ripple effect on the communities to which they belong, and lead to the deaths of innocent people. The nested narratives of* Frankenstein *might well be a nod to the as-told-to narrative structure of Coleridge's poem. One could go further: just as the Ancyent Marinere must wear the albatross around his neck as a symbol of his transgression against nature, Victor's creature leaves a blackened fingerprint on the necks of each of his strangling victims, a fingerprint that hauntingly reminds Victor of his mistakes. Shelley, who throughout her life held Coleridge and his poem in high regard, references and quotes* The Rime *several times in her novel. The first four parts of the poem, detailing the killing of the albatross and its immediate consequences, are presented here, from the original 1798 version.*

---

[13]Otto Friedrich Müller (1730–1784), Danish naturalist and taxonomist.
[14]William Herschel (1738–1822), British astronomer and composer known for his discoveries of planets, moons, and stars.

## ARGUMENT.

How a Ship having passed the Line was driven by Storms to the cold Country towards the South Pole; and how from thence she made her course to the Tropical Latitude of the Great Pacific Ocean; and of the strange things that befell; and in what manner the Ancyent Marinere came back to his own Country.

## I.

It is an ancyent Marinere,
    And he stoppeth one of three:
"By thy long grey beard and thy glittering eye
    "Now wherefore stoppest me?

"The Bridegroom's doors arc open'd wide,      5
    "And I am next of kin;
"The Guests are met, the Feast is set,—
    "May'st hear the merry din.

But still he holds the wedding-guest—
    There was a Ship, quoth he—     10
"Nay, if thou'st got a laughsome tale,
    "Marinere! come with me."

He holds him with his skinny hand,
    Quoth he, there was a Ship—
"Now get thee hence, thou grey-beard Loon!     15
    "Or my Staff shall make thee skip.

He holds him with his glittering eye—
    The wedding guest stood still
And listens like a three year's child;
    The Marinere hath his will.     20

The wedding-guest sate on a stone,
    He cannot chuse but hear:
And thus spake on that ancyent man,
    The bright-eyed Marinere.

The Ship was cheer'd, the Harbour clear'd— 25
  Merrily did we drop
Below the Kirk,[1] below the Hill,
  Below the Light-house top.

The Sun came up upon the left,
  Out of the Sea came he: 30
And he shone bright, and on the right
  Went down into the Sea.[2]

Higher and higher every day,
  Till over the mast at noon—[3]
The wedding-guest here beat his breast, 35
  For he heard the loud bassoon.

The Bride hath pac'd into the Hall,
  Red as a rose is she;
Nodding their heads before her goes
  The merry Minstrelsy. 40

The wedding-guest he beat his breast,
  Yet he cannot chuse but hear:
And thus spake on that ancyent Man,
  The bright-eyed Marinere.

Listen, Stranger! Storm and Wind, 45
  A Wind and Tempest strong!
For days and weeks it play'd us freaks—
  Like Chaff we drove along.

Listen, Stranger! Mist and Snow,
  And it grew wond'rous cauld: 50
And Ice mast-high came floating by
  As green as Emerauld.

---

[1] *Kirk:* Church
[2] The ship heads south.
[3] They arrive at the equator.

And thro' the drifts the snowy clifts[4]
Did send a dismal sheen;
Ne shapes of men ne beasts we ken[5]—                    55
The Ice was all between.

The Ice was here, the Ice was there,
The Ice was all around:
It crack'd and growl'd, and roar'd and howl'd—
Like noises of a swound.[6]                              60

At length did cross an Albatross,
Thorough[7] the Fog it came;
And an[8] it were a Christian Soul,
We hail'd it in God's name.

The Marineres gave it biscuit-worms,                     65
And round and round it flew:
The Ice did split with a Thunder-fit;[9]
The Helmsman steer'd us thro'.

And a good south wind sprung up behind,[10]
The Albatross did follow;                                70
And every day for food or play
Came to the Marinere's hollo!

In mist or cloud on mast or shroud[11]
It perch'd for vespers nine,[12]
Whiles all the night thro' fog smoke-white,              75
Glimmer'd the white moon-shine.

"God save thee, ancyent Marinere!
    "From the fiends that plague thee thus—

---

[4] *clifts:* Ciffs.
[5] *ken:* Discern.
[6] *swound:* Swoon.
[7] *Thorough:* Through.
[8] *an:* As if.
[9] *Thunder-fit:* Clap of thunder.
[10] The ship sails north.
[11] *shroud:* Heavy rope to fasten the mast.
[12] *vespers nine:* Nine evenings.

"Why look'st thou so?"—with my cross bow
    I shot the Albatross.                  80


## II.

The Sun came up upon the right,[13]
    Out of the Sea came he;
And broad as a weft[14] upon the left
    Went down into the Sea.

And the good south wind still blew behind,      85
    But no sweet Bird did follow
Ne any day for food or play
    Came to the Marinere's hollo!

And I had done an hellish thing
    And it would work 'em woe:          90
For all averr'd, I had kill'd the Bird
    That made the Breeze to blow.

Ne dim ne red, like God's own head,
    The glorious Sun uprist:
Then all averr'd, I had kill'd the Bird      95
    That brought the fog and mist.
'Twas right, said they, such birds to slay
    That bring the fog and mist.

The breezes blew, the white foam flew,
    The furrow follow'd free:         100
We were the first that ever burst
    Into that silent Sea.

Down dropt the breeze, the Sails dropt down,
    'Twas sad as sad could be
And we did speak only to break      105
    The silence of the Sea.

---

[13] The ship sails north after passing Cape Horn.
[14] *weft:* Crosswise threads on a loom.

All in a hot and copper sky
    The bloody sun at noon,
Right up above the mast did stand,[15]
    No bigger than the moon.                               110

Day after day, day after day,
    We stuck, ne breath ne motion,
As idle as a painted Ship
    Upon a painted Ocean.

Water, water, every where                                  115
    And all the boards did shrink;
Water, water, every where,
    Ne any drop to drink.

The very deeps did rot: O Christ!
    That ever this should be!                              120
Yea, slimy things did crawl with legs
    Upon the slimy Sea.

About, about, in reel and rout
    The Death-fires[16] danc'd at night;
The water, like a witch's oils,                            125
    Burnt green and blue and white.

And some in dreams assured were
    Of the Spirit that plagued us so:[17]
Nine fathom deep he had follow'd us
    From the Land of Mist and Snow.                        130

And every tongue thro' utter drouth
    Was wither'd at the root;
We could not speak no more than if
    We had been choked with soot.

---

[15] The ship is at the equator in the Pacific Ocean.

[16] *Death-fires*: St. Elmo's fire, an atmospheric glow on a ship's mast or rigging, seen as an evil omen.

[17] One of the spirits of the middle air.

Ah wel-a-day! what evil looks                                    135
  Had I from old and young;
Instead of the Cross the Albatross
  About my neck was hung.


**III.**

I saw a something in the Sky
  No bigger than my fist;                                        140
At first it seem'd a little speck
  And then it seem'd a mist:
It mov'd and mov'd, and took at last
  A certain shape, I wist.[18]

A speck, a mist, a shape, I wist!                                145
  And still it ner'd and ner'd;
And, an[19] it dodg'd a water-sprite,
  It plung'd and tack'd and veer'd.

With throat unslack'd, with black lips bak'd
  Ne could we laugh, ne wail:                                    150
Then while thro' drouth all dumb they stood
I bit my arm and suck'd the blood
  And cry'd, A sail! a sail!

With throat unslack'd, with black lips bak'd
  Agape they hear'd me call:                                     155
Gramercy![20] they for joy did grin
And all at once their breath drew in
  As[21] they were drinking all.

She doth not tack from side to side—
  Hither to work us weal                                         160
Withouten wind, withouten tide
  She steddies with upright keel.


---

[18] *wist:* Knew.
[19] *an:* As if.
[20] *Gramercy:* Great thanks.
[21] *As:* As if.

The western wave was all a flame,
    The day was well nigh done!
Almost upon the western wave                165
    Rested the broad bright Sun;
When that strange shape drove suddenly
    Betwixt us and the Sun.

And strait the Sun was fleck'd with bars
    (Heaven's mother send us grace)        170
As if thro' a dungeon grate he peer'd
    With broad and burning face.

Alas! (thought I, and my heart beat loud)
    How fast she neres and neres!
Are those *her* Sails that glance in the Sun    175
    Like restless gossameres?[22]

Are those *her* naked ribs, which fleck'd
    The sun that did behind them peer?
And are those two all, all the crew,
    That woman and her fleshless Pheere?[23]    180

    Are those her ribs, which fleck'd the Sun,
        Like the bars of a dungeon grate?
    And are these two all, all the crew
        That woman and her Mate?

This Ship, it was a plankless Thing,[24]    185
    A rare Anatomy!
A plankless Spectre — and it mov'd
    Like a Being of the Sea!
The Woman and a fleshless Man
    Therein sate merrily.    190

*His* bones were black with many a crack,
    All black and bare, I ween;[25]

---

[22] *gossameres:* Airborne cobwebs.
[23] *Pheere:* Companion.
[24] Lines 185–90 were first published in 1912, although Coleridge had wanted them added in 1800.
[25] *ween:* Think.

Jet-black and bare, save wherewith rust
Of mouldy damps and charnel crust
   They're patch'd with purple and green. 195

*Her* lips are red, *her* looks are free,[26]
   *Her* locks are yellow as gold:
Her skin is as white as leprosy,
And she is far liker Death than he;
   Her flesh makes the still air cold. 200

The naked Hulk alongside came
   And the Twain were playing dice;
"The Game is done! I've won, I've won!"
   Quoth she, and whistled thrice.

A gust of wind sterte up behind 205
   And whistled thro' his bones;
Thro' the holes of his eyes and the hole of his mouth
   Half-whistles and half-groans.

With never a whisper in the Sea
   Oft darts the Spectre-ship; 210
While clombe above the Eastern bar [27]
The horned Moon,[28] with one bright Star
   Almost atween the tips.

One after one by the horned Moon
   (Listen, O Stranger! to me) 215
Each turn'd his face with a ghastly pang
   And curs'd me with his ee.[29]

Four times fifty living men,
   With never a sigh or groan,
With heavy thump, a lifeless lump 220
   They dropp'd down one by one.

[26] *free:* Brazen, libidinous.
[27] *bar:* Horizon.
[28] *horned Moon:* It is a common superstition among sailors that something evil is about to happen whenever a star dogs the moon [Coleridge's note].
[29] *ee:* Eye.

Their souls did from their bodies fly,—
   They fled to bliss or woe;
And every soul it pass'd me by,
   Like the whiz of my Cross-bow.   225


**IV.**

"I fear thee, ancient Marinere!
   "I fear thy skinny hand;
"And thou art long and lank and brown
   "As is the ribb'd Sea-sand.

"I fear thee and thy glittering eye   230
   "And thy skinny hand so Brown—
Fear not, fear not, thou wedding guest!
   This body dropt not down.

Alone, alone, all all alone
   Alone on the wide wide Sea;   235
And Christ would take no pity on
   My soul in agony.

The many men so beautiful,
   And they all dead did lie!
And a million million slimy things   240
   Liv'd on—and so did I.

I look'd upon the rotting Sea,
   And drew my eyes away;
I look'd upon the eldritch[30] deck,
   And there the dead men lay.   245

I look'd to Heaven, and try'd to pray;
   But or[31] ever a prayer had gusht,
A wicked whisper came and made
   My heart as dry as dust.

[30] *eldritch:* eerie.
[31] *or:* Before.

I clos'd my lids and kept them close,                    250
  Till the balls like pulses beat;
For the sky and the sea, and the sea and the sky
Lay like a load on my weary eye,
  And the dead were at my feet.

The cold sweat melted from their limbs,              255
  Ne rot, ne reck did they;
The look with which they look'd on me,
  Had never pass'd away.

An orphan's curse would drag to Hell
  A spirit from on high:                                        260
But O! more horrible than that
  Is the curse in a dead man's eye!
Seven days, seven nights I saw that curse,
  And yet I could not die.

The moving Moon went up the sky                     265
  And no where did abide:
Softly she was going up
  And a star or two beside—

Her beams bemock'd the sultry main
  Like morning frosts yspread;[32]                      270
But where the ship's huge shadow lay,
The charmed water burnt alway
  A still and awful red.

Beyond the shadow of the ship
  I watch'd the water-snakes:                             275
They mov'd in tracks of shining white;
And when they rear'd, the elfish light
  Fell off in hoary flakes.

Within the shadow of the ship
  I watch'd their rich attire:                                280
Blue, glossy green, and velvet black

[32] *yspread:* Overspread.

They coil'd and swam; and every track
  Was a flash of golden fire.

O happy living things! no tongue
  Their beauty might declare:            285
A spring of love gusht from my heart,
  And I bless'd them unaware!
Sure my kind saint took pity on me,
  And I bless'd them unaware.

The self-same moment I could pray;       290
  And from my neck so free[33]
The Albatross fell off, and sank
  Like lead into the sea.

## JOHANN WOLFGANG VON GOETHE

## *From* The Sorrows of Young Werther (1774)

*If Coleridge's* The Rime of the Ancyent Marinere *imagines a grim, gothic world outside the self created by humankind's transgressions, Johann Wolfgang von Goethe's* The Sorrows of Young Werther *imagines a gothic psyche within the self created by personal tribulation. At the forefront of the* German Sturm und Drang *(Storm and Stress) movement in the mid- to-late-eighteenth century, Goethe first published his tale of a love-tormented hero in 1774. The success of the book helped establish a phenomenon known as* Werther-Fieber *(Werther-Fever), which saw men throughout Europe dress like Werther; reportedly, some further emulated their hero by committing suicide.* Sorrows *is one of the three books that the creature reads when acquiring language. Werther and the creature have in common experiences of suffering caused by unrequited love. In the section of Goethe's novel presented here, Werther explains the ways in which "that which makes a man happy . . . become[s] the source of his misery."*

---

[33]Free of the Albatross.

August 18th

Must it ever be thus,—that the source of our happiness must also be the fountain of our misery? The full and ardent sentiment which animated my heart with the love of nature, overwhelming me with a torrent of delight, and which brought all paradise before me, has now become an insupportable torment, a demon which perpetually pursues and harasses me. When in bygone days I gazed from these rocks upon yonder mountains across the river, and upon the green, flowery valley before me, and saw all nature budding and bursting around; the hills clothed from foot to peak with tall, thick forest trees; the valleys in all their varied windings, shaded with the loveliest woods; and the soft river gliding along amongst the lisping reeds, mirroring the beautiful clouds which the soft evening breeze wafted across the sky,—when I heard the groves about me melodious with the music of birds, and saw the million swarms of insects dancing in the last golden beams of the sun, whose setting rays awoke the humming beetles from their grassy beds, whilst the subdued tumult around directed my attention to the ground, and I there observed the arid rock compelled to yield nutriment to the dry moss, whilst the heath flourished upon the barren sands below me, all this displayed to me the inner warmth which animates all nature, and filled and glowed within my heart. I felt myself exalted by this overflowing fulness to the perception of the Godhead, and the glorious forms of an infinite universe became visible to my soul! Stupendous mountains encompassed me, abysses yawned at my feet, and cataracts fell headlong down before me; impetuous rivers rolled through the plain, and rocks and mountains resounded from afar. In the depths of the earth I saw innumerable powers in motion, and multiplying to infinity; whilst upon its surface, and beneath the heavens, there teemed ten thousand varieties of living creatures. Everything around is alive with an infinite number of forms; while mankind fly for security to their petty houses, from the shelter of which they rule in their imaginations over the wide-extended universe. Poor fool! in whose petty estimation all things are little. From the inaccessible mountains, across the desert which no mortal foot has trod, far as the confines of the unknown ocean, breathes the spirit of the eternal Creator; and every atom to which he has given existence finds favour in his sight. Ah, how often at that time has the flight of a bird, soaring above my head, inspired me with the desire of being transported to the shores of the immeasurable waters, there to quaff the pleasures of life from the foaming goblet of the Infinite, and to partake, if but for a moment even, with the confined powers of my soul, the beatitude of that Creator who accomplishes all things in himself, and through himself!

My dear friend, the bare recollection of those hours still consoles me. Even this effort to recall those ineffable sensations, and give them utterance, exalts my soul above itself, and makes me doubly feel the intensity of my present anguish.

It is as if a curtain had been drawn from before my eyes, and, instead of prospects of eternal life, the abyss of an ever open grave yawned before me. Can we say of anything that it exists when all passes away, when time, with the speed of a storm, carries all things onward, — and our transitory existence, hurried along by the torrent, is either swallowed up by the waves or dashed against the rocks? There is not a moment but preys upon you, — and upon all around you, not a moment in which you do not yourself become a destroyer. The most innocent walk deprives of life thousands of poor insects: one step destroys the fabric of the industrious ant, and converts a little world into chaos. No: it is not the great and rare calamities of the world, the floods which sweep away whole villages, the earthquakes which swallow up our towns, that affect me. My heart is wasted by the thought of that destructive power which lies concealed in every part of universal nature. Nature has formed nothing that does not consume itself, and every object near it: so that, surrounded by earth and air, and all the active powers, I wander on my way with aching heart; and the universe is to me a fearful monster, for ever devouring its own offspring.

*Translated by R. D. Boylan*

## FRANKENSTEIN AND POLITICAL CARTOONS

*From the mid-nineteenth century to the present day, many cartoonists have reused, reimagined, and manipulated Shelley's creature for their own ideological ends.*

Perhaps best known for illustrating Lewis Carroll's *Alice's Adventures in Wonderland,* John Tenniel used the image of Frankenstein's monster for political ends more than once while writing for the satirical British magazine *Punch.* In his 1866 political cartoon "The Brummagem Frankenstein," Tenniel represents the newly enfranchised working class as a massive threatening monster. *Brummagem* was a slang term for the city of Birmingham, considered a center of radical working-class politics. Hulton Archive/Getty Images.

In 1882, Tenniel returned to Mary Shelley's figure with "The Irish Fran-kenstein," a political cartoon that figures the Irish Fenian movement—revolutionaries dedicated to the overthrow of British rule in Ireland—as a gigantic, animalistic, knife-wielding monster. Hulton Archive/Getty Images.

Clifford K. Berryman, "Are WE Frankensteins?" (1940). Commenting on the political events that led to World War II, Pulitzer Prize–winning cartoonist Clifford K. Berryman imagined Adolf Hitler's rise in Frankensteinian terms, with Benito Mussolin (the prime minister of Italy from 1922 to 1943) and Joseph Stalin (leader of the Soviet Union from the late 1920s to 1953) together cast in Victor's role.

Library of Congress.

Steve Greenberg, "Frankenfish" (2009). GMOs (genetically modified organisms) or "Franken food"—food either genetically modified in a lab or grown using hormones, steroids, and other scientific modifications—has been a major source of inspiration for contemporary political cartoons. Steve Greenberg's 2002 cartoon imagines a scientist employed by the Genetically Altered Salmon Research corporation as a cross between Victor Frankenstein of the 1931 movie *Frankenstein* and his assistant Igor, and the monstrous fish as his now edible creature. Steve Greenberg, Ventura County Star (Calif.) 2002.

### FRANKENSTEIN ON THE BIG SCREEN

*Since its introduction to film with Thomas Edison's Kinetogram, Frankenstein has enjoyed lasting relevance as a motion picture. As times have changed, however, so have the portrayals of Shelley's main characters—none more so than the creature.*

The EDISON
# KINETOGRAM

VOL. 2                   MARCH 15, 1910                   No. 4

SCENE FROM
**FRANKENSTEIN**
FILM No. 6604

When played by Charles Ogle in Edison's *Frankenstein*, The Edison Kinetogram (1910), the creature looks more like a beast than a human. Courtesy of Billy Rose Theatre Collection, New York Public Library.

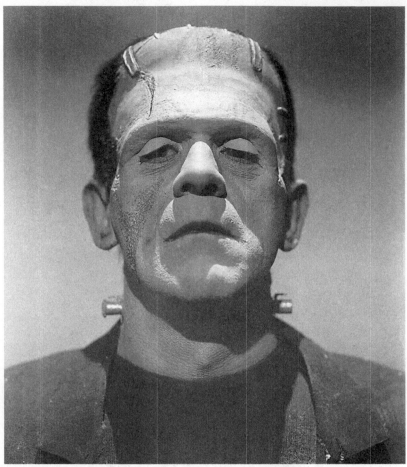

In perhaps the most famous portrayal of the creature, Boris Karloff in
James Whale's 1931 *Frankenstein* appears part man and part machine, with
two bolts protruding from his neck—an accoutrement that remains popular in contemporary portrayals of the creature.
© Universal/Photofest.

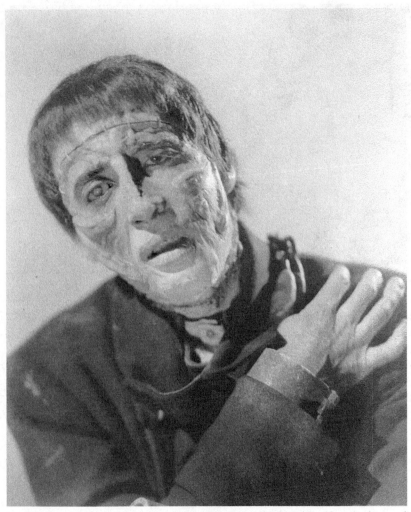

In Terence Fisher's *The Curse of Frankenstein* (1957), the three-eyed creature played by Christopher Lee is even more grotesque than the creature played by Karloff, and is especially terrifying in color film.
© Warner Bros. Pictures/Photofest.

Offering both a new take on the story and a new look for the creature, the Stuart Beattie film *I, Frankenstein* (2014) trades the hideous for the handsome. Based on the graphic novel of the same name by Kevin Grevioux, *I, Frankenstein* follows the creature (Aaron Eckhart), later named Adam, as he battles numerous demons, led by Naberius (Bill Nighy), that seek to destroy him and all of humanity. Although reluctant at first, Adam eventually agrees to protect humans by hunting demons.

Ben King/© Lionsgate/Courtesy Everett Collection.

Even the creature's ostensible bride-to-be has undergone dramatic changes in costume and makeup over the years. One of the first and still most popular portrayals of the creature's bride, Elsa Lancaster in James Whale's 1935 *The Bride of Frankenstein* has shock-wave hair and pale skin but a very human visage. By contrast, Helena Bonham Carter's bride in *Mary Shelley's Frankenstein* (1994), directed by Kenneth Branagh, is deformed with monstrous stitches crisscrossing her face, neck, ravaged scalp, and mutilated eye.

© Universal/Photofest.

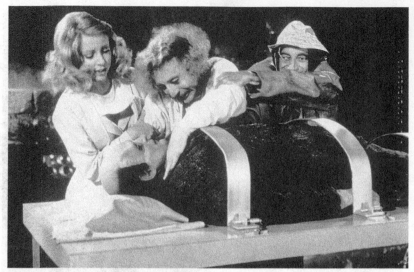

Of course, not all filmic adaptations of *Frankenstein* have been grim or even serious in nature. Mel Brooks and Gene Wilder famously parodied Shelley's novel and earned an Academy Award nomination (adapted screenplay) in the process. Their satirical 1974 *Young Frankenstein* follows Dr. Frederick Frankenstein (Gene Wilder) as he tries to escape the legacy left by his mad-scientist grandfather, Victor.
TM & Copyright © 20th Century Fox Film Corp./Everett Collection.

*Opposite page:* Although Hollywood is responsible for the majority of *Frankenstein* films produced for theatres, several foreign films also offer versions of Shelley's novel. In 1971, Mel Welles directed *Lady Franken-stein* (or *La Figlia di Frankenstein*), an Italian horror film written by Edward di Lorenzo. The film follows Tania Frankenstein as she attempts to learn from her father, Baron Frankenstein, the skills needed to reanimate a corpse. When the creature Tania creates kills the Baron, she manipulates his assistant into killing an attractive young man so that she can perform a brain transplant. In a new twist to *Frankenstein* adaptations, the movie is, as the promotional poster shows, highly sexual in nature.

Everett Collection.

Even American artist Andy Warhol coproduced a foreign film version of *Frankenstein*. Directed by Paul Morrissey and titled *Andy Warhol's Flesh for Frankenstein*, it is a 1973 Italian-French horror film that follows the Serbian Baron von Frankenstein as he tries unsuccessfully to create a perfect Serbian race. Like *Lady Frankenstein*, Warhol's movie is highly sexual in nature.

Everett Collection.

## FRANKENSTEIN TOYS, VIDEO GAMES, AND CHILDREN'S BOOKS

In 2010, Mattel launched a line of monster-inspired toys, supported by short cartoons retailing their teen adventures, called Monster High. The line includes dolls fashioned from famous science fiction and monster movie characters, including zombies, vampires, Dracula, and Frankenstein's creature. Combining fashion with a Frankenstein motif, Mattel claims that this "Create-A-Monster" toy package allows girls to "Take monster design to a whole new level." The "Frankie Stein" doll pictured here ("I was brought to unlife as a teenager, so I'm still a bit scary-naïve about the ways of the monster world") is promoted as "the daughter of Frankenstein," thereby perpetuating the pop culture confusion about the creature (the monster, presumably the father of Frankie) and his creator (Victor Frankenstein).

In 2009, Storm City Games released *The Island of Dr. Frankenstein*, an adventure game for Nintendo Wii. Players control a young mechanic, "Frankie," as he "chat[s] with numerous classical monsters who live there, collect[s] clues to solve a big mystery, and tr[ies] to fix all the broken machines on the island."

Elements of Shelley's novel have even found their way into children's books. In 2013, R.L. Stine published *Frankenstein's Dog* in his *Goosebumps Most Wanted* series with Scholastic Press, a company best known for marketing educational materials to young readers. In the story, Kat has to visit her uncle Vic Frankenstein, who is described on the book's back cover as "a quiet, gentle man, a scientist interested in building robots with artificial intelligence." The cover of the book shows Uncle Vic's dog Poochie, whose stitched-together visage recalls that of Frankenstein's original creature.

# PART THREE

# *Frankenstein*: A Case Study in Contemporary Criticism

# A Critical History of *Frankenstein*

In 1992 I began the Critical History for the first edition of this book by noting the increase in academic criticism of *Frankenstein* after 1970 or so. Updating that Critical History for the second edition (2000), I found an even more striking increase: of the more than four hundred entries under "Mary Shelley Frankenstein" listed in the online MLA Bibliography, over half were published after 1990. Interest shows no sign of abating; for the years between 2001 and 2014, the same search terms again yielded more than four hundred entries. Not surprisingly, however, the foci of criticism have shifted. Prior to 1970, most critics discussed Mary Shelley rather than her novel; nonbiographical criticism did focus on the novel, but as a subset of a more significant category such as Romanticism, as a minor incident in some major and predominantly masculine literary tradition. After 1970 critical attention interrogated both *Frankenstein*'s fit in established literary traditions and the status of those traditions themselves, with feminist critics in particular asking why women writers had been excluded from the Romantic canon. But feminist criticism itself tended to exclude considerations of class and race in the novel, and one of the most interesting developments of 1990s *Frankenstein* criticism was a new attention to those issues. Another shift in critical focus, which like the first began around 1970 and took a slightly different turn after 1990, has to do with whether the novel had attained high-culture status. As the post-1970 critique of the Romantic canon paralleled a more general tendency in literary studies to analyze how and why literature canons are constructed, so the new attention to *Frankenstein* as a fit subject for academic criticism paralleled a reevaluation of popular culture as similarly available to scholarly analysis. From this perspective, what is striking about 1990s *Frankenstein* criticism is an increased attention from practitioners not only of haute critique, especially deconstruction, but also of cultural studies; in other words, the novel remained a fit in both high and low culture. The trend toward cultural studies of *Frankenstein*, especially its science, has continued since 2000, and there has also been a turn toward newer critical theories. In what follows I trace in more detail these and other shifts in the critical history of *Frankenstein*. I track these shifts chronologically, centering first on post-1970 criticism, then on work of the 1990s, and finally on developments since 2000. I also attempt to prepare for the critical methodologies exemplified in Part Three of this book by showing how the *Frankenstein* criticism using those methodologies developed from earlier criticism.

Mary Shelley's first critic was her husband Percy. Although his essay "On *Frankenstein*" wasn't published until 1832 (ten years after his death), it was written in 1817 and apparently intended to counter potentially hostile reviews of the novel. This review raises two issues that persist in later criticism. The first is a question: Who is responsible for the monster's monstrosity? For Percy, the novel's "direct moral" (264) is that human intolerance created the monster: "divide . . . a social being from society, and you impose upon him the irresistible obligations [of] malevolence and selfishness"; more simply, "[t]reat a person ill, and he will become wicked." But Percy also suggests that no one can finally be held responsible. The creature's crimes are not "the offspring of an unaccountable propensity to evil," so they are not his fault, but neither are they the fault of Victor Frankenstein: rather they are "the children, as it were, of necessity and human nature." As early as 1824, however, one commentator insisted that Victor "ought to have reflected on the means of giving happiness to the being of his creation" rather than abusing the creature for "crimes to which his [own] negligence gave rise" ("The Anniversary" 199), and many later critics continued to find Victor responsible for the creature's misdeeds.

Criticism has also pursued the second issue raised in Percy's review, the ways that sensational fiction might (mis)educate its readers. After praising *Frankenstein* as "a source of powerful and profound emotion" (263), Percy distinguishes between feeling and rational responses to that emotion. The reader interested in "anything beside[s] a new love-story" will respond to the "elementary feelings" that are the novel's subject; only the reader "accustomed to reason deeply" on the "origin and tendency" of such feelings, however, can "sympathize, to the full extent," with the events they produce. This last readership, fit audience though few, capable of reasoned and therefore full sympathy, should be educated by reading the novel and thus become capable of grasping its "direct moral." But nineteenth-century commentators were divided about *Frankenstein*'s moral effect. Many early reviewers, less sanguine than Percy, felt the emotions stirred by the novel would feed sensation rather than education. In 1818 John Croker concluded that the novel would please only readers with "deplorably vitiated" tastes (385), since it "fatigues the feelings without interesting the understanding" and "inculcates no lesson of conduct, manners, or morality." Another early reviewer, writing in *Edinburgh Magazine*, feared the novel would appeal to an already "desperately inflamed . . . appetite . . . for every sort of wonder"; most troubling was "the expression 'Creator,' applied to a mere human being" (253), for "wild and irregular theories" of this sort may shock "some of our highest and most reverential feelings."

Concerns about *Frankenstein*'s moral effects persisted among nineteenth-century critics, but M. A. Goldberg's 1959 article was perhaps the first modern interpretation to recover this sense of *Frankenstein*'s moral purpose. In her view, *Frankenstein*'s "moral context" was the eighteenth-century aesthetic that taking "pleasure in terror" has "ethical and social implications" (28–29), and so the terror *Frankenstein* inspires was meant to instill its moral lesson. During the 1990s there was a new critical attention to the "ethical and social implications" of teaching such lessons, in other words of pedagogy itself. Maureen McLane read the novel as "a parable of pedagogic failure" (959), the failure of "the promise of the humanities . . . as a route to humanization." Alan Richardson argued that *Frankenstein* shows how an education "predicated on inequality" (157) is "a form of tyranny," while Anne McWhir used the novel to suggest that a teacher "recogniz[e] her own role as oppressor—manipulating texts for authoritarian ends—as well as her own sympathy" with the oppressed (86–87). Although critical attention to pedagogy lessens after 2000, in 2006 Eric Sonstroem reported on the classroom use of FrankenMOO, an electronic textual space, and in 2010 Melissa Bissonette proposed using *Frankenstein* in "a pedagogy of alienation" (108) that would challenge students toward both sympathy with and judgment of the monster.

Another problematic indicated by nineteenth-century commentators and revived by M. A. Goldberg is *Frankenstein*'s cultural status. By relocating the novel in its social context, Goldberg reconciled its popular elements with its high moral seriousness, thereby closing a gap between low-culture and high-culture status. *Frankenstein* has since received the academic imprimatur with an MLA Approaches to Teaching volume in 1990, Mary Lowe-Evans's Twayne book in 1993, and five essays in *The Cambridge Companion to Mary Shelley* of 2003 (edited by Esther Shor). But the question of *Frankenstein*'s status has remained vexed, in part because of the novel's prodigious popularity. It has been reprinted in dozens of English-language editions and translated into Japanese, Arabic, Urdu, Malayam, and most European languages; the 1942 Armed Services and overseas editions were clearly aimed at a popular audience, as were the 1945 comic book and the many "simplified" versions designed for children. *Frankenstein*'s presence in other forms of popular culture was manifested in the 1990s in such artefacts as the Topps Comics official adaptation of *Kenneth Branagh's Mary Shelley's Frankenstein*, the Wishbone Classics *Frankenstein* as retold by Michael Burgan, an Absolut Shelley vodka ad, and in 2013 Derek Marks's graphic novel *An Illustrated Biography of Mary Shelley*. The story's appeal is further evidenced in the number of nineteenth-century melodramas and twentieth-century horror movies based (however loosely) on the novel, and there is a long history of critical attention to *Frankenstein* movies—Donald Glut in 1973, Radu Florescu in 1975, Albert LaValley and William Nestrick in 1979, Patrick McLeod in 1980. This attention continued in the 1990s, with Steven Forry's comprehensive study of *Frankenstein* adaptations (including texts of six plays) and with articles on mad scientist movies in general (Christopher Toumey), on *Frankenstein* movies in particular (Robert Chamberlain, A. C. Goodson, James Heffernan), on cinematic and other visualizations of the monster (Jane Davidson), and on filmic and other variants of the text (myself, William St Clair). Interest in *Frankenstein* films continued in scholarship after 2000. Kay Picart wrote about "Visualizing the Monstrous in *Frankenstein* Films," while Scott Juengel discussed filmic fetishizations of the face. Mark Poindexter focused on the series of Universal films featuring the creature, Bouriana Zakharieva on Kenneth Branagh's version. In the 2000s, scholarship on popular mediations of the novel included a boomlet in drawing connections between *Frankenstein* and Shelley Jackson's hypertext *Patchwork Girl*; many analyses, such as those by Teresa Dobson and Rebecca Luce-Kapler, Laura Schackelford, and Christopher Keep, used the new critical method of media studies, indicating another aspect of the continuing popularity of *Frankenstein*. The "*Frankenstein* in Cultural Context" section of this book provides many more examples of the creature's continuing presence in popular culture.

In the first collection of academic criticism on *Frankenstein*, published in 1979, editors George Levine and U. C. Knoepflmacher evinced some unease at applying "the 'high seriousness' of the Arnoldian literary critic" (xii) to *Frankenstein*. Their tone is half-joking, but it does indicate the difficulties of attempting both to account for *Frankenstein*'s "persistent hold" on the popular imagination and to "rescue" it for high culture from the abyss of low culture. One early branch of "rescue" criticism established a high-culture pedigree for Mary Shelley's novel by taking her philosophical and political ideas seriously. In 1965 Burton Pollin demonstrated *Frankenstein*'s "respectable philosophical intent" (108) by analyzing the monster's education in terms of Locke's *Essay Concerning Human Understanding* and Condillac's *Treatise on the Sensations*. Criticism after 1970 increasingly compared Mary's political ideas with those of her father William Godwin, and this work by Lee Sterrenburg (1979) and Katherine Powers (1980) continued after 1990. Gregory Maertz, for instance, saw *Frankenstein* as appropriating and rewriting Godwin's novel *St. Leon*, while Marilyn May suggested a more anxious intertextual relation between Mary's work and her father's. Since 2000, attention to Mary's philosophical ideas has concentrated less on the influence of earlier texts and more on a discourse shared with her contemporaries. Ana Acosta, for example, analyzed the function of Volney's *Ruins* (1791) in Mary's text. In a more new historicist strain, Clara Tuite read the novel in terms of the "monster of 'overpopulation'" (142) predicated in T. R. Malthus's *Essay on the Principle of Population*, Robert Anderson read it in light of Robert Owen's theories of social reproduction, and Christopher Rovee read it in relation to the contemporary discourse on the aesthetics of the Elgin Marbles.

After 1970, some scholars based claims for *Frankenstein*'s high-culture status on its literary rather than its philosophical lineage. Taking their cue from the novel's subtitle, critics such as William Hildebrand read Victor as a Promethean overreacher, while in 1973 L. J. Swingle situated Mary Shelley in the Romantic literary tradition of concern with the problem of knowledge. Such readings located *Frankenstein* in a masculine literary tradition reaching from Aeschylus's *Prometheus Bound* to Percy Shelley's *Prometheus Unbound*, a strategy that often amounted to hooking a popular novel by a woman to a train of literary classics by men. In 1979 Peter Dale Scott emphasized Mary's departures from Percy's influence, and after 2000 several comparisons of *Frankenstein* with other Romantic texts stressed the ambiguities of such intertextuality: Beth Lau's "Romantic Ambivalence in *Frankenstein* and *The Rime of the Ancient Mariner*," Astrida Tantillo's "*Werther, Frankenstein*, and Girardian Mediated Desire," and Leslie and Walter Minot's "*Frankenstein* and *Christabel*: Intertextuality, Biography, and Gothic Ambiguity." As early as 1967, P. D. Fleck had contended that Mary's novel critiqued the idealism of much Romantic literature, and that revisionist trend has continued. After 1970 critics such as John Reed, James O'Rourke ("Nothing"), and Elsie B. Michie argued for Mary's "resistance to Romanticism" (Michie 32). In the 1990s a plethora of studies linked Mary with women Romantic writers (Stephen Behrendt) and also stressed her departures from masculine Romantic ideas about creativity (Mary Favret, *Romantic*, and Jerome Bump), incest (Leila May), linguistic development (Christian Bok), and autobiography (Richard Lansdown). The critical interest in *Frankenstein*'s uneasy status as a Romantic text continued in post-2000 scholarship. Elizabeth Dolan connected Mary to women Romantics in her *Seeing Suffering in Women's Literature of the Romantic Era*, while other scholars expanded the scope of Romanticism to include such figures as Baudelaire (Jürgen Klein), such activities as mountaineering (Jane Nardin), and such concepts as nationalism (Deidre Lynch) and race (Peter Kitson).

Also in the 1990s, the Mary Shelley once seen as a hanger-on of Romanticism was reevaluated as a precursor of literary figures from Ivan Turgenev (Richard Freeborn) to Doris Lessing (Norma Rowen, "*Frankenstein* Revisited") and Phyllis Gotlieb (Dominick Grace). As early as 1973, Mary's novel was touted by Brian Aldiss as a precursor of science fiction; in 1990 Reuben Ellis claimed *Frankenstein* for the sub-genre known as speculative fiction, and in 2002 George Slusser compared the novel with other works of speculative fiction. In 1981 Judith Spector gave such claims a feminist twist by calling Mary the mother of science fiction, and in 1991 Jenny Newman connected Mary to modern feminist science fiction writers. And it seems fitting that science fiction, itself located somewhere between escapist trash and serious social commentary, should find a forerunner in *Frankenstein*. Recent critics have linked the novel with other genres, most persuasively Emma Raub in "*Frankenstein* and the Mute Figure of Melodrama." Where some of the novel's earliest critics denigrated *Frankenstein*'s horror elements, some of the latest critics have read the novel to re-evaluate the popular genre of the Gothic. Connections have been made between *Frankenstein* and Gothic authors (Ashley Lancaster) and Gothic film (Jules Law). Sue Chaplin included a discussion of *Frankenstein* in her book *The Gothic and the Rule of Law, 1764–1820*. More generally, Jonathan Crimmins used *Frankenstein* to explore his concept of Gothic's two vectors, Theodora Goss her concept of the Gothic technological imaginary, and Jerrold Hogle ("*Frankenstein*") the concept of the neo-Gothic.

Alongside these claims for *Frankenstein*'s relation to popular genres, however, were continued arguments for the novel's high-culture status. Many post-1970s critics found in *Frankenstein* no simple tale of schlock horror but a complex narrative technique and a sophisticated understanding of the problems of interpretation. For Gay Clifford, *Frankenstein*'s technique of first-person narration demonstrates the three narrators' solipsism; for Richard Dunn, the novel's three-narrative form "structurally dramatizes the failure of human community" (408); for Beth Newman, *Frankenstein*'s frame structure and embedded stories show the inadequacy of conventional modes of interpretation. In the 1990s many claims for the novel's literary sophistication were made in high-theory modes. Thomas Dutoit read the creature through Michel Foucault's theorization of the body as spectacle, while Ellen Goldner worked insightfully with Foucault's theories of discipline as well as spectacle. Readings also exfoliated from deconstruction's interest in *différance*/deferral (Jerrold Hogle, "Otherness"), supplements (Bok) and traces (Bernard Duyfhuizen), figuration (Steven Vine, "Filthy"), and monstrosity (Peter Brooks, "What"). Critics after 2000 returned to many of these theoretical models. Anna Clark saw in the creature an example of the narrative theory of "protagonism" (245), and Criscillia Benford and Gregory O'Dea also used narratology to examine *Frankenstein*. Deconstructors continued to produce readings of the novel: Jessie Givner addressed "the monster of representation" (287), Luis Rosa adapted Derrida's concept of the wound of reading to *Frankenstein*, and Peter Melville read the creature's various encounters through the lens of Derrida's writings on hospitality. More recent critical methodologies have also proved amenable to *Frankenstein*; Andrew Burkett, for instance, exhaustively analyzes the turn to *Frankenstein* in Romantic digital humanities initiatives (for one such, see *The Godwin-Shelley Archive*). Witness too the convincing readings in new economic criticism (Charles Lewis), animal studies (Stephanie Rowe), disability studies (Essaka Joshua, Mark Mossman), and posthumanism (Sarah Fuller).

*Frankenstein* has consistently attracted the attention of psychoanalytic critics. Psychoanalytic readings during the 1970s were concerned with the novel's characters, its author, and its structure. Morton Kaplan

saw in Victor a son's classic oedipal desire to displace the father and
marry the mother, and in the monster a return of Victor's repressed
desire for and hatred of the mother. U. C. Knoepflmacher called the
novel "a fantasy designed to relieve [Mary's] deep personal anxieties"
about her relation to her parents (92). J. M. Hill interpreted it as Mary's
attempt to detach herself by "authorial otherness" from her obsessive
desire for a mother's love (339–40); in contrast, Marc Rubenstein saw
Mary as searching for an origin in her mother. Some readings applied
Freudian concepts to the novel's structure. Daniel Cottom read the
narrative's careful organizing structure as a Freudian displacement of
repressed disorder; for Joseph Kestner, the novel's tale-within-a-tale
structure demonstrated a kind of narcissism. In the 1990s Freudian readings moved away from character, author, and narrative structure to
more theoretical concerns. Steven Vine's "Hellish Sport" analyzed the
novel in terms of Freud's joke theory, while essays by Christine Berthin
and Ruth Parkin-Gounelas revisited standard definitions of the Freudian uncanny. Departing from Freud, post-2000 psychoanalytic critics
turne to the concept of trauma (Diane Hoeveler, and James O'Rourke,
*Sex*), Slavoj Žižek's theorization of the ugly (Denise Gigante, James C.
Hatch), and Julia Kristeva's theory of abjection (Panagiota Petkow).

Judith Pike's elegant reading in 1995 of the creature as fetishized
corpse drew on Freudian but also on Lacanian concepts, and in the
1990s Lacanian readings became a growth industry. Peter Brooks's
1979 Lacanian reading was very influential in the 1990s, especially his
use of the concept of "language as relation" ("'Godlike'" 208) to
analyze the novel's failures of communication. John Lamb took off
from Brooks in his analysis of the monster's "fall into language" (311),
and both Jerrold Hogle ("Otherness") and Gerhard Joseph referenced
Brooks as they discussed *Frankenstein* in terms of the Lacanian idea of
the unconscious as structured like a language. Articles by Diana Negra
and Rhonda Kercsmar read Victor in terms of a problematic suggested
by Lacanian theory, the split or fragmented subjectivity resulting from
a failure to fully enter the Symbolic order. Lacanian theories of desire
featured in post-2000 essays by Haidee Kotze and Ying-chiao Lin,
Lacanian ideology critique in Patricia Comitini's 2006 essay.

As in psychoanalytic criticism, *Frankenstein* remains a hardy perennial
in feminist criticism. This sizable and still growing body of readings has
provided instructive re-visions of many earlier sites of criticism: Mary
Shelley's relations with her parents and her husband; evaluations both of
*Frankenstein* as a literary text and of its thematics; the utility of other

critical methodologies when turned to a woman's text; most generally, all the ramifications of the fact that the novel was written by a woman. *Frankenstein* was first published anonymously, and most early reviewers assumed it was written by a man; in 1818, for instance, Walter Scott attributed it to Percy Shelley (614). Some seventy years later Richard Garnett postulated that *Frankenstein* was far superior to anything Mary Shelley wrote after her husband's death because "her brain, magnetized by his companionship, was capable of an effort never to be repeated" (v). Florence Marshall, a contemporary of Garnett, reversed these magnetic poles by claiming that Percy Shelley's achievements were due "in great measure" (1: 2) to his wife's "sustaining and refining influence" (2: 325); however, she also admitted that Mary's "free growth" as a writer was "checked" by her marriage. Written at a time when women's domestic roles and marriage itself were being reevaluated, these comments prefigure some of the concerns of feminist criticism during other periods of reevaluation.

Feminist critics of the 1970s and 1980s revised many earlier judgments of *Frankenstein*'s author, and these readings were in turn revised in the 1990s and again after 2000. Earlier critics had postulated that Percy Shelley's revisions of and additions to the novel made him a "minor collaborator" (Rieger xviii), "though always in keeping with Mary's conception" (Murray 67). Against this view, in 1988 Anne Mellor assembled a body of evidence from the early manuscript versions to argue that Percy often seriously misrepresented Mary's intentions. Although not specifically feminist, in 1996 Charles Robinson's introduction to his edition of the several *Frankenstein* manuscripts corrected all three of these judgments. Other feminist critics gave new attention to Mary's relations with her mother, Mary Wollstonecraft: in 1976 Janet Todd traced the parallels between Mary's fiction and her mother's, and in the 1990s essays by Rhonda Batchelor and Elisabeth Bronfen analyzed the effects of Wollstonecraft's fiction and politics on her daughter.

Post-1970s feminist attention to constructing a history of women's literature began to rewrite earlier views of *Frankenstein* as a literary text. Feminists placed and replaced *Frankenstein* in several literary histories. Against critics such as Ronald Paulson, who located the novel in a masculine tradition of the Gothic, Ellen Moers in 1979 called it a female Gothic and Marcia Tillotson in 1983 explored the implications of that new alignment. In 1999 Debra Best linked *Frankenstein* to the genre of the domestic novel. Source studies have changed direction too. Where Stuart Curran saw the echoes of *Paradise Lost* in *Frankenstein* as relatively straightforward, in 1979 Sandra Gilbert and Susan Gubar argued that the novel dramatizes "the blind rejection of women by misogynistic/Miltonic patriarchy" (243), and in 1991 Stephanie Kiceluk problematized that argument by pointing to Mary's "assimilation" of Milton's misogyny (112–13). Another change in views of *Frankenstein* emerged from the French feminist concept of *l'écriture féminine*. Some critics now saw the novel's narrative structure as feminine and feminist: for Devon Hodges, *Frankenstein* critiques a masculine narrative pattern of sequence and closure intended to master the text; for James Carson, the three male narrators are a woman's commentary on "the male expropriation of the voice of the conventionally passive female" (435); for Mary Poovey, the novel's three narratives are a network of relations that allow the author to efface but also to express her unladylike wish for literary fame. One element of Poovey's work was especially influential: her analysis of the 1831 revisions was picked up by Henriette Power in 1988, and again by 1990s feminist readings that saw in Mary's 1831 introduction her desire to be "acknowledged as the novel's ultimate author" (Leader 186). Several 1990s critics continued the new emphasis on the subversiveness of *Frankenstein*'s narrative structure. James Davis discerned three women's stories that "ironically mirror" (308) the three men's stories in which they are embedded; Susan Winnett saw the novel's narrative pattern as a critique of "ending and sense making" (510); Joyce Zonana used Safie's absent letters to argue that *Frankenstein* is "an articulated frame surrounding a speaking silence" (180) and as such resists "the act of appropriation which is reading." Several of *Frankenstein*'s thematics were reevaluated by feminist critics in the 1970s and again in the 1990s (Ellen Rose). By the 2000s, many strands of feminist criticism had played out, but a few persisted. An early focus was the issue of procreation. In 1979 Ellen Moers used Mary's experience of her mother (who died giving birth to her) to read *Frankenstein* as "a horror story of maternity" (85) that is "most feminine" (85) when it expresses a mother's "revulsion against newborn life" (81), and in 1982 essays by both Mary Jacobus and Barbara Johnson saw in the novel "the unresolvable contradictions inherent in being female" (Johnson 9). In 1972 Robert Kiely argued that Victor's presumption was not his Promethean usurpation of divine creativity but rather his "attempt to usurp the power of woman" in procreation (165); in 1995 David del Principe made a similar point about Victor's "patrilineal erasure of the womb" (13), and in 2006 Galia Benziman analyzed the fantasy of male birth in *Frankenstein*. By the 1990s, the centrality of procreation to *Frankenstein* had been "virtually established" (Richard Sanderson 49); one nexus of interest pursued by A. James Wohlpart (1998), Cynthia Pon (2000), and Harriet Hustis (2003) was the relation between procreation and responsible creativity. Another recurring thematic in feminist criticism is the novel's representation of domesticity as necessary yet somehow "inadequate" to its tasks (Goodwin 93). In 1979 Kate Ellis argued that the three narrators' tales dramatize the deficiencies of the bourgeois family; twenty years later, Jacqueline Labbe addressed the problematic of the wifely ideal in *Frankenstein*. In 1993 Vanessa Dickerson pointed to the number of women characters in the novel who "nurture and love unto death" (85), and Siobhan Craig (1994) and Nancy Fredricks (1996) noted such characters' difficulties in achieving subjectivity. In a 2000 essay, Margit Stange broadened the scope of such analyses by postulating that Victor's destruction of the female creature "dramatizes the violent and punishing recruitment of woman into the liberal republic" (310).

Finally, feminist criticism has added to earlier critical methodologies and opened a way for new ones. I have already cited the additions to source studies and to narratology; the work just noted on the problematic of women's subjectivity enriches the feminist/Lacanian analyses done in the 1980s by Margaret Homans, Rosemary Jackson, and Elissa Marder; and it is at least arguable that gender studies of *Frankenstein* built on the concerns of feminist criticism. William Veeder's 1986 book turned feminist analyses of the concept of androgyny to *Frankenstein*'s constructions of gender; in 1993 Bette London applied French feminist theories of specularity to the spectacle of masculinity in *Frankenstein*, and Colleen Hobbs explored Victor's masculine hysteria. Building on the theoretical work of Judith Butler, in the 1990s Veronica Hollinger wrote about performing gender in the novel and Susan Stryker addressed performing transgender rage in *Frankenstein*. Gender studies of *Frankenstein* continued in the 2000s with Russell Kilbourn's analysis of the novel's visual codings of masculinity and Polly Gould's analysis of its narratives of gender difference.

Another new body of work in *Frankenstein* criticism has emerged from queer theory. Essays by Frann Michel, Eric Daffron, and James McGavran analyzed the novel in terms of Eve Kosofsky Sedgwick's work on homosociality and homosexual panic. Michael Laplace-Sinatra discussed the homoerotic elements of Mary Shelley's novel that were closed down by Kenneth Branagh's film, while both George Haggerty and Mair Rigby read the novel as an example of the queer Gothic.

Marxist readings of *Frankenstein* were relatively thin on the ground in the 1990s and the 2000s, but they often provided instructive revisions of other criticism. As early as 1967, Stephen Crafts used Herbert Marcuse's Marxist theory to draw a parallel between the oppressed and victimized monster and both the "technologically oppressed" of industrial capitalism and a Third World victimized by the First World (98). In 1983 Paul O'Flinn argued that both the novel and the movie versions function as "straightforward allegory" (199) of the class struggle, and in 2005 Jonathan Jones used the novel to trace the ideologies of socialization inherent in contemporary theories of language acquisition. Where early psychoanalytical criticism saw the monster as Victor's doppelgänger, the Marxist concept of alienation offered an economic rather than psychological explanation of this split. Being alienated from their own labor and its products results in what Marx called "misshapen" workers, and in 1983 Franco Moretti argued that the monster represents this deformed proletariat; in 1988 Michie saw both the monster and the novel as "objective products which alienate the artist/worker" (32). Other psychoanalytic approaches were shifted by Marxist analysis from a personal to a political register. Rather than seeing *Frankenstein*'s family relations as Freudian incest fantasies, in 1983 Anca Vlasopolos interpreted Victor's tendency toward incest as a form of class selection and exclusion; in 1991 Sarah Goodwin reworked another Freudian theory by reading the monster as a figure for a "political uncanny" (104). Marxist criticism also broadened feminist analyses of gender relations in the novel: both Vlasopolos and Cottom analyzed the class-specific traits that qualify only certain women for elevation into the Frankenstein family. In 1983 Burton Hatlen saw in the novel a "revolutionary" (42) critique of class as well as gender hierarchies, and in 1992 Lamb revised earlier source studies with his claim that *Frankenstein* exposes "the illusory nature of bourgeois individualism" as set out in *Paradise Lost* (306).

The greatest growth in post-1990 criticism of the novel occurred in cultural studies, and that trend continued in the 2000s. Cultural studies of *Frankenstein* in the 1980s included John Rieder's article on the cultural work of science fiction, Chris Baldick's book on discursive forms of the Frankenstein monster in nineteenth-century culture, and Gayatri Spivak's reading of the novel as a text of "English cultural identity" (254). In 1993 Marie-Hélène Huet connected the novel's monstrous birth to alchemical and Renaissance writing on generation and monstrosity, and in 1996 Jonathan Glance placed Victor's dreams in the context of eighteenth- and nineteenth-century dream theory. Several 1990s articles followed Spivak in reformulating questions of cultural difference in *Frankenstein*: Margo Perkins and Adam Komisaruk focused on class difference, for example. Following Tim Marshall's *Murdering to Dissect* (1995), in 2006 Silvia Granata discussed the novel in terms of contemporary anatomy literature. Other areas of cultural studies of *Frankenstein* after 2000 included the creation of artificial life (Jürgen Barkhoff, Ricarda Vidal) and of automatons (Julia Douthwaite and Daniel Richter), polar exploration (Adriana Craciun, Laurie Garrison), resurrection (Nicola Trott, Carolyn Williams, Sharon Ruston), the law (Jonathan Grossman), popular religion (Jasper Cragwall), education (John Bugg, Frances Ferguson), and radical politics (James Brown, Colene Bentley, Patrick Vincent). Finally, three magisterial cultural studies of *Frankenstein* appeared in the 2000s: Susan Hitchcock's *Franken-stein: A Cultural History*, Elizabeth Young's *Black* Frankenstein: *The Making of an American Metaphor*, and Susan Wolfson and Ronald Levao's *Mary Wollstonecraft Shelley: The Annotated* Frankenstein.

The bull market in cultural studies of *Frankenstein* is analyses of its science. Stephen Bann called *Frankenstein* "a congeries of scientific and philosophical problems" (1), and cultural studies of these problems have followed a revisionist course that mirrors changes in cultural views of science itself. In 1818 an anonymous reviewer in *Gentleman's Maga-zine* chastised "the pride of Science" with which Victor "presumes to take upon himself" the construction of a human being (334), and Wal-ter Scott too disapproved of Victor's "rash researches" (617) in "physi-ological discovery" (618). Many later scholars took the novel's science less seriously, considering it inaccurate pseudoscience. In 1976, how-ever, John Dussinger clarified the importance of alchemical science to Victor's endeavors, in 1984 Samuel Vasbinder defended Mary's knowl-edge of early-nineteenth-century science, and in 1987 Sergio Perosa located *Frankenstein* in the context of a late-eighteenth-century hope that science and imagination might work together. Later critics came to see in the novel a critique of scientific claims to absolute knowledge and benevolent power. In line with a post-1960s reaction against war-related science and a post-1970s attention to bioethics, 1980s critics such as Theodore Ziolkowski and Ray Hammond emphasized the novel's representation of scientific irresponsibility and the consequences thereof. Mellor read the novel as a feminist critique of masculine science, and Laura Kranzler argued that Victor's creation of life and modern science's sperm banks and artificial wombs show a similar "masculine desire to claim female (re)productivity for themselves" (45). 1990s readings of the novel's science followed some of these paths and branched out to others. Like Vasbinder, several critics placed *Frankenstein* in a scien-tific context, linking Victor's science to Rosicrucianism (Marie Roberts), to experimental biology (Jon Turney), to radical (Marilyn Butler) and

Romantic (Marina Benjamin) science, and to the debate in Romantic science over vitalism and materialism (Maurice Hindle, Martin Willis). Other 1990s critics saw *Frankenstein*'s scientific context as one of transition or tension: a transition from occult philosophy to modern science (David Ketterer), or from "alchemical notions" (Vernon 271) to "the scientific principles of Chemistry and Physics"; or a tension between natural magic and Enlightenment rationality (Crosbie Smith), or between alchemical and modern techniques of creation (Rowen, "Making"), or between secluded and social scientific work (Alan Rauch). Some critics pointed to the failures of Victor's science. The hope for unity between science and imagination that Perosa noted was shown by Michael Manson and Robert Stewart to have failed, while Carmine Sarracino examined that failure in light of a Vedic critique of Western dualistic science. The articles by Mary Favret followed up on earlier feminist critiques of masculinist science, as did Ludmilla Jordanova's analysis of the gendering of science, and Kiceluk's essay continued Kranzler's critique of contemporary technology. That critique went in a new direction with Jay Clayton, who connected Victor's monster with analyses of the modern cyborg, and Mark Hansen, who read *Frankenstein* as an example of "machinic textuality" (603).

Some scientific questions examined in earlier criticism returned after 2000, such as bioethics (Shane Denson), while other critics moved on to such areas as botany (Carlos Seligo) and voltaic electricity (Richard Sha). An area of particular interest for post-2000 *Frankenstein* critics was medical science. Alan Bewell's groundbreaking analysis of the language of obstetrics in *Frankenstein* (1988) was followed after 2000 by attention to the medical gaze in the novel (Emma Liggins) and by critics locating *Frankenstein* in a series of nineteenth-century novels about medicine (Janis Caldwell, Sylvia Pamboukian). Perhaps the best indication of this recent turn to science studies is the 2008 collection of essays edited by Christa Knellwolf and Jane Goodall: Frankenstein's Science, the first book devoted entirely to that subject.

Another subset of cultural studies which has proved hospitable to *Frankenstein* is ecocriticism. While the importance of nature in Romanticism has long been acknowledged, in 2006 Bill Phillips claimed that *Frankenstein* demonstrated the importance of the environment as well. More specifically, Paul Outka explored the novel's juxtapositions between natural and unnatural environments and Helena Feder focused on the significance of the novel's mountains and bodies of water. Taking a slightly different direction, Katey Castellano traced the critical progression from feminist to ecofeminist readings of *Frankenstein*.

I close this critical history with postcolonial criticism, one of the newer methodologies to take on *Frankenstein* in the 1990s. Joseph Lew saw in the novel a critique of the contemporary discourse of Orientalism, Jeffrey Cass "the spectre of a colonialist paradigm" (39). D. S. Neff connected the novel with contemporary perceptions of Hindus ("Hostages") and with the construction of high-caste Hindus in Joseph Lawrence's 1811 book *The Empire of the Nairs* ("'Paradise'"). H. L. Malchow provided a wide-ranging discussion of how *Frankenstein* and the melodrama based on it both drew on contemporary ideas of race. Post-2000 postcolonial approaches to the novel have been equally various. Karen Piper claimed that *Frankenstein* is linked less with Orientalism than with "the 'problem' of indigeneity and European 'discovery'" (64). Where Paul Stock focused on the "fractious interactions between Europeans and non-Europeans" in *Frankenstein* (337), John Ball found in the assembling and abandonment of the creature "a specifically West Indian imperial connection" (35).

Each of the essays in this collection follows from the critical history I have been sketching. David Collings's piece reflects changes in psychoanalytic criticism of *Frankenstein* by exploring the relation between Lacanian theory and ideology critique. Warren Montag's Marxist essay first locates *Frankenstein* in history and then shows how history operates as a force within the text. My essay in feminist criticism focuses on problematics of domesticity in conjunction with the related set of problematics posed by a gendered science. Grant F. Scott's queer reading uses Lynd Ward's woodblock illustrations to a 1934 edition of *Frankenstein* to explore elements of homoeroticism and homosexual panic in the novel. Allan Lloyd Smith's postcolonial approach analyzes how contemporary attitudes toward race and slavery function in representations of the creature. Siobhan Carroll's essay in ecocriticism foregrounds the context of contemporary debates about polar ice and climate change. As these essays' various methodologies all converge on *Frankenstein*, they testify to the endurance of critical interest in Mary Shelley and her novel.

## WORKS CITED

Acosta, Ana M. *Reading Genesis in the Long Eighteenth Century: From Milton to Mary Shelley*. Aldershot, UK: Ashgate, 2006. Print.

Aldiss, Brian. *Billion Year Spree: A History of Science Fiction*. New York: Doubleday, 1973. Print.

Anderson, Robert. " 'Misery Made Me a Fiend': Social Reproduction in Mary Shelley's *Frankenstein* and Robert Owen's Early Writings." *Nineteenth-Century Contexts* 24.4 (2002): 417–38. Print.

"The Anniversary." *Knight's Quarterly Magazine* 3 (Aug.–Nov. 1824): 195–99. Print.

Baldick, Chris. *In Frankenstein's Shadow: Myth, Monstrosity, and Nineteenth-Century Writing.* Oxford: Clarendon, 1987. Print.

Ball, John Clement. "Imperial Monstrosities: *Frankenstein*, the West Indies, and V. S. Naipaul." *Ariel* 32.3 (2001): 31–58. Print.

Bann, Stephen. Introduction. Frankenstein, *Creation* 1–15.

———, ed. Frankenstein, *Creation and Monstrosity.* London: Reaktion, 1994. Print.

Barkhoff, Jürgen. "Perfecting Nature—Surpassing God: The Dream of Creating Artificial Humans around 1800." *Science, Technology and the German Cultural Imagination.* Eds. C. Emden and D Midgley. Berlin: Peter Lang, 2005. 39–55. Print.

Batchelor, Rhonda. "The Rise and Fall of the Eighteenth Century's Authentic Feminine Voice." *Eighteenth-Century Fiction* 6.4 (July 1994): 347–68. Print.

Behrendt, Stephen. "Mary Shelley, *Frankenstein*, and the Woman Writer's Fate." Feldman and Kelley 69–87.

Benford, Criscillia. " 'Listen to my tale': Multilevel Structure, Narrative Sense Making, and the Inassimilable in Mary Shelley's *Frankenstein*." *Narrative* 18.3 (2010): 324–46. Print.

Benjamin, Marina. "Elbow Room: Women Writers on Science, 1790–1840." *Science and Sensibility: Gender and Scientific Enquiry 1780–1945.* Ed. Benjamin. Oxford: Basil Blackwell, 1991. 27–59. Print.

Bentley, Colene. "Family, Humanity, Polity: Theorizing the Basis and Boundaries of Political Community in *Frankenstein*." *Criticism* 47.3 (2005): 325–51. Print.

Benziman, Galia. "Challenging the Biological: The Fantasy of Male Birth as a Nineteenth-Century Narrative of Ethical Failure." *Women's Studies* 35.4 (2006): 375–95. Print.

Berthin, Christine. "Family Secrets and a Shameful Disease: 'Aberrations of Mourning' in *Frankenstein*." *Q/W/E/R/T/Y* 3 (1993): 53–60. Print.

Best, Debra E. "The Monster in the Family: A Reconsideration of *Frankenstein*'s Domestic Relationships." *Women's Writing* 6.3 (1999): 365–84. Print.

Bewell, Alan. "An Issue of Monstrous Desire: *Frankenstein* and Obstetrics." *Yale Journal of Criticism* 2.1 (Fall 1988): 105–28. Print.

Bissonette, Melissa Bloom. "Teaching the Monster: *Frankenstein* and Critical Thinking." *College Literature* 37.3 (2010): 106–20. Web. 11 November 2014.

Bok, Christian. "The Monstrosity of Representation: *Frankenstein* and Rousseau." *English Studies in Canada* 18.4 (Dec. 1992): 415–32. Print.

Bronfen, Elisabeth. "Rewriting the Family: Mary Shelley's *Frankenstein* in Its Biographical/Textual Context." Bann, Frankenstein, *Creation* 16–38.

Brooks, Peter. " 'Godlike Science/Unhallowed Arts': Language, Nature, and Monstrosity." Levine and Knoepflmacher, *Endurance* 205–20.

———. "What Is a Monster? (According to *Frankenstein*)." *Body Work: Objects of Desire in Modern Narrative*. Cambridge: Harvard UP, 1993. 199–220. Print.

Brown, James. "Through the Looking Glass: Victor Frankenstein and Robert Owen." *Extrapolation* 43.2 (2002): 263–76. Web. 11 November 2014.

Bugg, John. " 'Master of Their Language': Education and Exile in Mary Shelley's *Frankenstein*." *Huntington Library Quarterly* 68.4 (2005): 655–66. Print.

Bump, Jerome. "Mary Shelley's Subversion of Male Myths of Creativity in *Frankenstein*." *The Ethics of Popular Culture from Frankenstein to Cyberculture*. Kilgore, TX: 2d Dimension, 1995. 18–42. Print.

Burkett, Andrew. "Mediating Monstrosity: Media, Information, and Mary Shelley's *Frankenstein*." *Studies in Romanticism* 51.3 (2012): 579–605. Print.

Butler, Marilyn. Introduction. *Frankenstein or the Modern Prometheus: The 1818 Text*. By Mary Shelley. Oxford: Oxford UP, 1993. ix–lvii. Print.

Caldwell, Janis McLarren. *Literature and Medicine in Nineteenth-Century Britain: From Mary Shelley to George Eliot*. Cambridge: Cambridge UP, 2004. Print.

Carson, James B. "Bringing the Author Forward: *Frankenstein* through Mary Shelley's Letters." *Criticism* 30.4 (Fall 1988): 431–53. Print.

Cass, Jeffrey. "The Contestatory Gothic in Mary Shelley's *Frankenstein* and J. W. Polidori's *Ernestus Berchtold*: The Spectre of a Colonialist Paradigm." *JAISA* 1.2 (Spr. 1996): 33–41. Print.

Castellano, Katey. "Feminism to Ecofeminism: The Legacy of Gilbert and Gubar's Readings of Mary Shelley's *Frankenstein* and *The Last*

*Man."* *Gilbert and Gubar's* The Madwoman in the Attic *After Thirty Years.* Ed. Annette R. Federico. Columbia: U of Missouri P, 2009. 76–93. Print.

Chamberlain, Robert. "The Cultural Context of *Frankenstein* in Films: Oppression or Carnival?" Proc. of the Conf. on Film and American Culture. Williamsburg: Roy R. Charles Center, College of William and Mary, 1994. 7–14. Print.

Chaplin, Sue. *The Gothic and the Rule of Law, 1764–1820.* Houndmills, UK: Palgrave, 2007. Print.

Clark, Anna E. *"Frankenstein*: or, the Modern Protagonist." *ELH* 81.1 (Spr. 2014): 248–66. Print.

Clayton, Jay. "Concealed Circuits: *Frankenstein's* Monster, the Medusa, and the Cyborg." *Raritan* 15.4 (Spr. 1996): 53–69. Print.

Clifford, Gay. "Caleb Williams and *Frankenstein*: First-Person Narratives and 'Things as They Are'." *Genre* 10 (Win. 1977): 601–17. Print.

Comitini, Patricia. "The Limits of Discourse and the Ideology of Form in Mary Shelley's *Frankenstein.*" *Keats-Shelley Journal* 55 (2006): 179–98. Print.

Cottom, Daniel. *"Frankenstein* and the Monster of Representation." *Sub-Stance* 28 (1980): 60–71. Print.

Craciun, Adriana. "Writing the Disaster: Franklin and *Frankenstein.*" *Nineteenth Century Literature* 65.4 (2011): 433–80. Print.

Crafts, Stephen. *"Frankenstein*: Camp Curiosity or Premonition?" *Catalyst* 3 (Sum. 1967): 96–103. Print.

Cragwall, Jasper. *Lake Methodism: Polite Literature and Popular Religion in England, 1780–1830.* Athens: Ohio UP, 2013. Print.

Craig, Siobhan. "Monstrous Dialogues: Erotic Discourse and the Dialogic Constitution of the Subject in *Frankenstein.*" *A Dialogue of Voices: Feminist Literary Theory and Bakhtin.* Ed. Karen Hohne and Helen Wussow. Minneapolis: U of Minnesota P, 1994. 83–96. Print.

Crimmins, Jonathan. "Mediation's Sleight of Hand: The Two Vectors of the Gothic in Mary Shelley's *Frankenstein.*" *Studies in Romanticism* 52.4 (2013): 561–83. Print.

[Croker, John.] Rev. of *Frankenstein; or, The Modern Prometheus. Quarterly Review* 18 (Jan. 1818): 379–85. Print.

Curran, Stuart. "The Siege of Hateful Contraries: Shelley, Mary Shelley, Byron, and *Paradise Lost.*" *Milton and the Line of Vision.* Ed. Joseph Wittreich, Jr. Madison: U of Wisconsin P, 1975. 209–30. Print.

Daffron, Eric. "Male Bonding: Sympathy and Shelley's *Frankenstein*." *Nineteenth-Century Contexts* 21.3 (1999): 415–35. Print.

Davidson, Jane P. "Golem — Frankenstein — Golem of Your Own." *Journal of the Fantastic in the Arts* 7.2–3 (1996): 228–43. Print.

Davis, James P. "*Frankenstein* and the Subversion of the Masculine Voice." *Women's Studies* 21.3 (1992): 307–22. Print.

del Principe, David. "Misbegotten, Unbegotten, Forgotten: Vampires and Monsters in the Works of Ugo Tarchetti, Mary Shelley, Bram Stoker, and the Gothic Tradition." *Forum Italicum* 29.1 (Spr. 1995): 3–25. Print.

Denson, Shane. "*Frankenstein*, Bioethics, and Technological Ireversibility." *Studies in Irreversibility: Texts and Contexts*. Ed. Benjamin Schreier. Cambridge: Cambridge Scholars, 2007. 134–66. Print.

Dickerson, Vanessa D. "The Ghost of a Self: Female Identity in Mary Shelley's *Frankenstein*." *Journal of Popular Culture* 27.3 (Win. 1993): 79–91. Print.

Dobson, Teresa, and Rebecca Luce-Kapler. "Stitching Texts: Gender and Geography in *Frankenstein* and *Patchwork Girl*." *Changing English* 12.2 (2005): 265–77. Print.

Dolan, Elizabeth A. *Seeing Suffering in Women's Litereature of the Romantic Era*. Aldershot, UK: Ashgate, 2008. Print.

Douthwaite, Julia V., and Daniel Richter. "The *Frankenstein* of the French Revolution: Nogaret's Automaton Tale of 1790." *European Romantic Review* 20.3 (2009): 381–411. Print.

Dunn, Richard J. "Narrative Distance in *Frankenstein*." *Studies in the Novel* 6.4 (Win. 1974): 408–17. Print.

Dussinger, John A. "Kinship and Guilt in Mary Shelley's *Frankenstein*." *Studies in the Novel* 8.1 (Spr. 1976): 38–55. Print.

Dutoit, Thomas. "Re-specting the Face as the Moral (of ) Fiction in Mary Shelley's *Frankenstein*." *Modern Language Notes* 109.5 (Dec. 1994): 847–71. Print.

Duyfhuizen, Bernard. "Periphrastic Naming in Mary Shelley's *Frankenstein*." *Studies in the Novel* 27.4 (Win. 1995): 477–92. Print.

Ellis, Kate. "Monsters in the Garden: Mary Shelley and the Bourgeois Family." Levine and Knoepflmacher, *Endurance* 123–42.

Ellis, Reuben J. "Mary Shelley Reading Ludvig Holberg: A Subterranean Fantasy at the Outer Edge of *Frankenstein*." *Extrapolation* 31.4 (Win. 1990): 317–25. Print.

Favret, Mary A. *Romantic Correspondence: Women, Politics, and the Fiction of Letters*. Cambridge: Cambridge UP, 1993. Print.

————. "A Woman Writes the Fiction of Science: The Body in *Fran-kenstein*." *Genders* 14 (Fall 1992): 50–65. Print.

Feder, Helena. "'A Blot upon the Earth': Nature's 'Negative' and the Production of Monstrosity in *Frankenstein*." *Journal of Ecocriticism* 2.1 (2010): 55–66. Print.

Feldman, Paula R., and Theresa M. Kelley, eds. *Romantic Women Writers: Voices and Countervoices*. Hanover: UP of New England, 1995. Print.

Ferguson, Frances. "Generationalizing: Romantic Social Forms and the Case of Mary Shelley's *Frankenstein*." *Partial Answers* 8.1 (2010): 97–118. Print.

Fleck, P. D. "Mary Shelley's Notes to Shelley's Poems and *Frankenstein*." *Studies in Romanticism* 6 (1967): 226–54. Print.

Florescu, Radu. *In Search of Frankenstein*. Boston: New York Graphic Society, 1975. Print.

Forry, Steven Earl. *Hideous Progenies: Dramatizations of Frankenstein from Mary Shelley to the Present*. Philadelphia: U of Pennsylvania P, 1990. Print.

[Rev. of] *Frankenstein; or, The Modern Prometheus*. *Edinburgh Magazine and Literary Miscellany* 2 (?Mar. 1818): 249–53. Facsim. rpt. in Reiman Vol. 7. 819–23. Print.

[Rev. of] *Frankenstein; or, The Modern Prometheus*. *Gentleman's Magazine* ns 88 (Apr. 1818): 334–35. Print.

Fredricks, Nancy. "On the Sublime and the Beautiful in Shelley's *Frankenstein*." *Essays in Literature* 23.2 (Fall 1996): 178–89. Print.

Freeborn, Richard. "*Frankenstein* and Bazarov." *New Zealand Slavonic Journal* (1994): 33–44. Print.

Fuller, Sarah Canfield. "Reading the Cyborg in Mary Shelley's *Frankenstein*." *Journal of the Fantastic in the Arts* 14.2 [53] (2003): 217–27. Print.

Garnett, Richard. Introduction. *Tales and Stories by Mary Wollstonecraft Shelley*. London: William Paterson, 1891. i–xi. Print.

Garrison, Laurie. "Imperial Vision in the Arctic: Fleeting Looks and Pleasurable Distractions in Barker's Panorama and Shelley's *Frankenstein*." *Romanticism and Victorianism on the Net* 52 (2008): n. pag. Web. 10 November 2014.

Gigante, Denise. "Facing the Ugly: The Case of *Frankenstein*." *ELH* 67.2 (2000): 565–87. Print.

Gilbert, Sandra, and Susan Gubar. *The Madwoman in the Attic: The Woman Writer and the Nineteenth-Century Literary Imagination*. New Haven: Yale UP, 1979. Print.

Givner, Jessie. "The Revolutionary Turn: Mary Shelley's *Franken-stein.*" *Gothic Studies* 2.3 (2000): 274–91. Print.

Glance, Jonathan C. "'Beyond the Usual Bounds of Reverie?': Another Look at the Dreams in *Frankenstein.*" *Journal of the Fantastic in the Arts* 7.4 (1996): 30–47. Print.

Glut, Donald F. *The Frankenstein Legend: A Tribute to Mary Shelley and Boris Karloff.* Metuchen, NJ: Scarecrow, 1973. Print.

Goldberg, M. A. "Moral and Myth in Mrs. Shelley's *Frankenstein.*" *Keats-Shelley Journal* 8.1 (Win. 1959): 27–38. Print.

Goldner, Ellen J. "Monstrous Body, Tortured Soul: *Frankenstein* at the Juncture between Discourses." *Genealogy and Literature.* Ed. Lee Quinby. Minneapolis: U of Minnesota P, 1995. 28–47. Print.

Goodson, A. C. "*Frankenstein* in the Age of Prozac." *Literature and Medicine* 15.1 (Spr. 1996): 16–32. Print.

Goodwin, Sarah Webster. "Domesticity and Uncanny Kitsch in 'The Rime of the Ancient Mariner' and *Frankenstein.*" *Tulsa Studies in Women's Literature* 10.1 (Spr. 1991): 93–108. Print.

Goss, Theodora. "From Superhuman to Posthuman: The Gothic Technological Imaginary in Mary Shelley's *Frankenstein* and Octavia Butler's *Xenogenesis.*" *MFS* 53.3 (2007): 434–59. Print.

Gould, Polly. "Sexual Polarities: Shelley's *Frankenstein* and Polar Exploration as a Search for Origins beyond 'Women.'" *Nordlit* 23 (2008): 103–18.

Grace, Dominick. "*Frankenstein*, Motherhood, and Phyllis Gotlieb's *O Master Caliban!*" *Extrapolation* 46.1 (2005): 90–102. Web. 10 November 2014.

Granata, Silvia. "Anatomists and Public Opinion: Literary Representations of a Troubled Relationship." *Il Confronto Letterario* 23.45 [1] (2006): 97–115. Print.

Grossman, Jonathan H. *The Art of Alibi: English Law Courts and the Novel.* Baltimore, MD: Johns Hopkins UP, 2002. Print.

Haggerty, George E. "'Dung, Guts and Blood': Sodomy, Abjection and Gothic Fiction in the Early Nineteenth Century." *Gothic Studies* 18.2 (2006): 35–51. Print.

Hammond, Ray. *The Modern Frankenstein: Fiction Becomes Fact.* Poole, UK: Blandford, 1986. Print.

Hansen, Mark. "'Not thus, after all, would life be given': Technesis, Technology and the Parody of Romantic Poetics in *Frankenstein.*" *Studies in Romanticism* 36.4 (Win. 1997): 575–609. Print.

Hatch, James C. "Disruptive Affects: Shame, Disgust, and Sympathy in *Frankenstein.*" *European Romantic Review* 19.1 (2008): 33–49. Print.

Hatlen, Burton. "Milton, Mary Shelley, and Patriarchy." *Bucknell Review* 28.2 (1983): 19–47. Print.

Heffernan, James A. W. "Looking for the Monster: *Frankenstein* and Film." *Critical Inquiry* 24.1 (Aut. 1997): 133–58. Print.

Hildebrand, William H. "On Three Prometheuses: Shelley's Two and Mary's One." *Serif* 11.2 (1974): 3–11. Print.

Hill, J. M. "*Frankenstein* and the Physiognomy of Desire." *American Imago* 32.4 (1975): 335–58. Print.

Hindle, Maurice. "Vital Matters: Mary Shelley's *Frankenstein* and Romantic Science." *Critical Survey* 2.1 (1990): 29–35. Print.

Hitchcock, Susan Tyler. *Frankenstein: A Cultural History.* New York: Norton, 2007.

Hobbs, Colleen. "Reading the Symptoms: An Exploration of Repression and Hysteria in Mary Shelley's *Frankenstein.*" *Studies in the Novel* 25.2 (Sum. 1993): 152–69. Print.

Hodges, Devon. "*Frankenstein* and the Feminine Subversion of the Novel." *Tulsa Studies in Women's Literature* 2.2 (Fall 1983): 155–64. Print.

Hoeveler, Diane Long. "Fantasy, Trauma, and Gothic Daughters: *Frankenstein* as Therapy." *Prism(s)* 8 (2000): 7–28. Print.

Hogle, Jerrold E. "*Frankenstein* as Neo-gothic: From the Ghost of the Counterfeit to the Monster of Abjection." *Romanticism, History and the Possibilities of Genre: Re-forming Literature 1789–1837.* Ed. Tilottama Rajan and Julia M. Wright. Cambridge: Cambridge UP, 1998. 176–210. Print.

———. "Otherness in *Frankenstein*: The Confinement/Autonomy of Fabrication." *New Casebooks*: Frankenstein. By Mary Shelley. Ed. Fred Botting. New York: St. Martin's, 1995. 206–34. Print.

Hollinger, Veronica. "Putting on the Feminine: Gender and Negativity in *Frankenstein* and *The Handmaid's Tale.*" *Negation, Critical Theory, and Postmodern Textuality.* Ed. Daniel Fischlin. Boston: Kluwer, 1994. 203–24. Print.

Homans, Margaret. *Bearing the Word: Language and Female Experience in Nineteenth-Century Women's Writing.* Chicago: U of Chicago P, 1986. Print.

Huet, Marie-Hélène. *Monstrous Imagination.* Cambridge: Harvard UP, 1993. Print.

Hustis, Harriet. "Responsible Creativity and the 'Modernity' of Mary Shelley's *Frankenstein.*" *SEL* 43.4 (2003): 845–58. Print.

Jackson, Rosemary. "Narcissism and Beyond: A Psychoanalytic Reading of *Frankenstein* and Fantasies of the Double." *Aspects of*

*Fantasy: Selected Essays from the Second International Conference on the Fantastic in Literature and Film.* Ed. William Coyle. Westport, CT: Greenwood, 1986. 45–53. Print.

Jacobus, Mary. "Is There a Woman in This Text?" *New Literary History* 14.1 (Aut. 1982): 117–41. Print.

Johnson, Barbara. "My Monster/My Self." *Diacritics* 12.2 (Sum. 1982): 2–10. Print.

Jones, Jonathan. "Hidden Voices: Language and Ideology in Philosophy of Language of the Eighteeenth Century and Mary Shelley's *Frankenstein.*" *Textual Practice* 19.3 (2005): 265–87. Print.

Jordanova, Ludmilla. "Melancholy Reflection: Constructing an Identity for Unveilers of Nature." Bann, Frankenstein, *Creation* 60–76.

Joseph, Gerhard. "Virginal Sex, Vaginal Text: The 'Folds' of *Frankenstein.*" *Virginal Sexuality and Textuality in Victorian Literature.* Ed. Lloyd Davis. Albany: State U of New York P, 1993. 25–32. Print.

Joshua, Essaka. "'Blind Vacancy': Sighted Culture and Voyeuristic Historiography in Mary Shelley's *Frankenstein.*" *European Romantic Review* 22.1 (2011): 49–69. Print.

Juengel, Scott J. "Face, Figure, Physiognomics: Mary Shelley's *Frankenstein* and the Moving Image." *Novel* 33.3 (2000): 353–76. Print.

Kaplan, Morton. "Fantasy of Paternity and the Doppelgänger: Mary Shelley's *Frankenstein.*" *The Unspoken Motive: A Guide to Psychoanalytic Literary Criticism.* Ed. Kaplan and Robert Kloss. New York: Free Press, 1973. 119–45. Print.

Keep, Christopher. "Growing Intimate with Monsters: Shelley Jackson's *Patchwork Girl* and the Gothic Nature of Hypertext." *Romanticism on the Net* 41–42 (2006): n. pag. Web. 9 November 2014.

Kercsmar, Rhonda Ray. "Displaced Apocalypse and Eschatological Anxiety in *Frankenstein.*" *South Atlantic Quarterly* 95.3 (Sum. 1995): 729–51. Print

Kestner, Joseph. "Narcissism and Beyond: A Psychoanalytic Reading of *Frankenstein* and Fantasies of the Double." *Aspects of Fantasy: Selected Essays from the Second International Conference on the Fantastic in Literature and Film.* Ed. William Coyle. Westport: Greenwood, 1986. 45–53. Print.

Ketterer, David. "*Frankenstein*'s 'Conversion' from Natural Magic to Modern Science—and a Shifted (and Converted) Last Draft Insert." *Science Fiction Studies* 24.1 (Mar. 1997): 57–78. Print.

Kiceluk, Stephanie. "Made in His Image: Frankenstein's Daughters." *Michigan Quarterly Review* 30.1 (Win. 1991): 110–26. Print.

Kiely, Robert. *The Romantic Novel in England.* Cambridge: Harvard UP, 1972. Print.

Kilbourn, Russell J.A. "American Frankenstein: Modernity's Monstrous Progeny." *Mosaic* 38.3 (2005): 167–84. Web. 9 November 2014.

Kitson, Peter. *Romantic Literature, Race, and Colonial Encounter.* New York: Palgrave Macmillan, 2007. Print.

Klein, Jürgen. "Aesthetics of Coldness: The Romantic Scene and a Glimpse at Baudelaire." *1650–1850* 9 (2003): 79–105. Print.

Knellwolf, Christa, and Jane Goodall, eds. *Frankenstein's Science: Experimentation and Discovery in Romantic Culture, 1780–1830.* Aldershot, UK: Ashgate, 2008. Print.

Knoepflmacher, U. C. "Thoughts on the Aggression of Daughters." Levine and Knoepflmacher, *Endurance* 88–119.

Komisaruk, Adam. "'So Guided by a Silken Cord': *Frankenstein*'s Family Values." *Studies in Romanticism* 38.3 (1999): 409–41. Print.

Kotze, Haidee. "Desire, Gender, Power, Language: A Psychoanalytic Reading of Mary Shelley's *Frankenstein*." *Literator* 21.1 (2000): 53–67. Print.

Kranzler, Laura. "*Frankenstein* and the Technological Future." *Foundation* 44 (Win. 1988–89): 42–49. Print.

Labbe, Jacqueline M. "A Monstrous Fiction: *Frankenstein* and the Wifely Ideal." *Women's Writing* 6.3 (1999): 345–63. Print.

Lamb, John B. "Mary Shelley's *Frankenstein* and Milton's Monstrous Myth." *Nineteenth-Century Fiction* 47.3 (Dec. 1992): 303–19. Print.

Lancaster, Ashley Craig. "From Frankenstein's Monster to Lester Ballard: The Evolving Gothic Monster." *Midwest Quarterly* 49.2 (2008): 132–48. Print.

Lansdown, Richard. "Beginning Life: Mary Shelley's Introduction to *Frankenstein*." *The Critical Review* 35 (1995): 81–94. Print.

Laplace-Sinatra, Michael. "Science, Gender, and Otherness in Shelley's *Frankenstein* and Kenneth Branagh's Film Adaptation." *European Romantic Review* 9.2 (1998): 253–70. Print.

Lau, Beth. "Romantic Ambivalence in *Frankenstein* and *The Rime of the Ancient Mariner*." *Fellow Romantics: Male and Female British Writers, 1790–1835.* Ed. Lau. Farnham, UK: Ashgate, 2009. 71–97. Print.

LaValley, Albert J. "The Stage and Film Children of *Frankenstein*: A Survey." Levine and Knoepflmacher, *Endurance* 243–89.

Law, Jules. "Being There: Gothic Violence and Virtuality in *Franken-stein, Dracula*, and *Strange Days*." *ELH* 73.4 (2006): 975–96. Print.

Leader, Zachary. *Revision and Romantic Authorship*. Oxford: Claren-don, 1996. Print.

Levine, George, and U. C. Knoepflmacher. Preface. *Endurance* xi–xvi.

———, eds. *The Endurance* of Frankenstein: *Essays on Mary Shelley's Novel*. Berkeley: U of California P, 1979. Print.

Lew, Joseph W. "The Deceptive Other: Mary Shelley's Critique of Orientalism in *Frankenstein*." *Studies in Romanticism* 30.2 (Sum. 1991): 255–83. Print.

Lewis, Charles R. *A Coincidence of Wants: The Novel and Classical Economics*. New York: Garland, 2000. Print.

Liggins, Emma. "The Medical Gaze and the Female Corpse: Looking at Bodies in Mary Shelley's *Frankenstein*." *Studies in the Novel* 32.2 (2000): 129–46. Print.

Lin, Ying-chiao. "The Dialect of Law and Desire in Mary Shelley's *Frankenstein*: A Lacanian Reading." *NTU Studies in Language and Literature* 14 (2005): 21–54. Print.

London, Bette. "Mary Shelley, *Frankenstein*, and the Spectacle of Masculinity." *PMLA* 108.2 (Mar. 1993): 253–67. Print.

Lowe-Evans, Mary. Frankenstein: *Mary Shelley's Wedding Guest*. New York: Twayne, 1993. Print.

Lynch, Deidre Shauna. "The (Dis)Locations of Romantic National-ism: Shelley, Staël, and the Home-Schooling of Monsters." *The Literary Channel: The Inter-National Invention of the Novel*. Ed. Margaret Cohen and Carolyn Dever. Princeton: Princeton UP, 2002. 194–224. Print.

Maertz, Gregory. "Family Resemblances: Intertextual Dialogue between Father and Daughter Novelists in Godwin's *St. Leon* and Shelley's *Frankenstein*." *University of Mississippi Studies in English* ns 11–12 (1993–1995): 303–20. Print.

Malchow, H. L. *Gothic Images of Race in Nineteenth-Century Britain*. Stanford: Stanford UP, 1996. Print.

Manson, Michael, and Robert Scott Stewart. "Heroes and Hideous-ness: *Frankenstein* and Failed Unity." *SubStance* 71/72 (1993): 228–42. Print.

Marder, Elissa. "The Mother Tongue in *Phèdre* and *Frankenstein*." *Yale French Studies* 76 (1989): 59–77. Print.

Marks, Derek. *An Illustrated Biography of Mary Shelley*. Web. 15 June 2014. <http://exhibitions.nypl.org/biblion/outsiders/shelleys -ghost/illustrated-biography-mary-shelley>

Marshall, Florence. *The Life and Letters of Mary Wollstonecraft Shelley.* 2 vols. London: Bentley, 1889. Print.

Marshall, Tim. *Murdering to Dissect: Grave-Robbing, Frankenstein and the Anatomy Literature.* Manchester: Manchester UP, 1995. Print.

Martin, Philip W., and Robin Jarvis, eds. *Reviewing Romanticism.* New York: St. Martin's, 1992. Print.

May, Leila Silvana. "Sibling Rivalry in Mary Shelley's *Frankenstein.*" *SEL 1500–1900* 35.4 (Aut. 1995): 669–85. Print.

May, Marilyn. "Publish and Perish: William Godwin, Mary Shelley, and the Public Appetite for Scandal." *Papers on Language and Literature* 26.4 (Fall 1990): 489–512. Print.

McGavran, James Holt. " 'Insurmountable Barriers to Our Union': Homosocial Male Bonding, Homosexual Panic, and Death on the Ice in *Frankenstein.*" *European Romantic Review* 11.1 (2000): 46–67. Print.

McLane, Maureen Noelle. "Literate Species: Populations, 'Humanities,' and *Frankenstein.*" *ELH* 63.4 (Win. 1996): 959–88. Print.

McLeod, Patrick G. "Frankenstein: Unbound and Otherwise." *Extrapolation* 21.2 (Sum. 1980): 158–66. Print.

McWhir, Anne. "Teaching the Monster to Read: Mary Shelley, Education and *Frankenstein.*" *The Educational Legacy of Romanticism.* Ed. John Willinsky. Waterloo, ON: Wilfrid Laurier UP, 1990. 73–92. Print.

Mellor, Anne K. *Mary Shelley: Her Life, Her Fiction, Her Monsters.* New York: Routledge, 1988. Print.

Melville, Peter. "Monstrous Ingratitude: Hospitality in Mary Shelley's *Frankenstein.*" *European Romantic Review* 19.2 (2008): 179–85. Print.

Michel, Frann. "Lesbian Panic and Mary Shelley's *Frankenstein.*" *GLQ* 2.3 (1995): 237–52. Print.

Michie, Elsie B. "Production Replaces Creation: Market Forces and *Frankenstein* as Critique of Romanticism." *Nineteenth-Century Contexts* 12.1 (1988): 27–33. Print.

Minot, Leslie Ann, and Walter S. Minot. "*Frankenstein* and *Christabel*: Intertextuality, Biography, and Gothic Ambiguity." *European Romantic Review* 15.1 (2004): 23–49. Print.

Moers, Ellen. "Female Gothic." Levine and Knoepflmacher, *Endurance* 77–87.

Moretti, Franco. *Signs Taken for Wonders: Essays in the Sociology of Literary Forms.* Trans. Susan Fischer, David Forgacs, and David Miller. London: Verso, 1983. Print.

Mossman, Mark. "Acts of Becoming: Autobiography, *Frankenstein*, and the Postmodern Body." *Postmodern Culture* 11.3 (2001). Web. 10 September 2014.

Murray, E. B. "Shelley's Contribution to Mary's *Frankenstein*." *Keats-Shelley Memorial Bulletin* 29 (1978): 50–68. Print.

Nardin, Jane. "A Meeting on the Mer de Glace: *Frankenstein* and the History of Alpine Mountaineering." *Women's Writing* 6.3 (1999): 441–49. Print.

Neff, D. S. "The 'Paradise of the Mothersons': *Frankenstein* and *The Empire of the Nairs*." *Journal of English and Germanic Philology* 95.2 (Apr. 1996): 204–22. Print.

———. "Hostages to Empire: The Anglo-Indian Problem in *Frankenstein*, *The Curse of Kehama*, and *The Missionary*." *European Romantic Review* 8.4 (Fall 1997): 386–408. Print.

Negra, Diana. "Coveting the Feminine: Victor Frankenstein, Norman Bates, and Buffalo Bill." *Literature Film Quarterly* 24.2 (1996): 193–200. Print.

Nestrick, William. "Coming to Life: *Frankenstein* and the Nature of Film Narrative." Levine and Knoepflmacher, *Endurance* 290–315.

Newman, Beth. "Narratives of Seduction and the Seductions of Narrative: The Frame Structure of *Frankenstein*." *ELH* 53.1 (Spr. 1986): 141–63. Print.

Newman, Jenny. "Mary and the Monster: Mary Shelley's *Frankenstein* and Maureen Duffy's *Gor Saga*." *Where No Man Has Gone Before: Women and Science Fiction*. Ed. Lucie Armitt. London: Routledge, 1991. 85–96. Print.

O'Dea, Gregory. "Framing the Frame: Embedded Narratives, Enabling Texs, and *Frankenstein*." *Romanticism on the Net* 31 (2003). Web. 15 June 2014.

O'Flinn, Paul. "Production and Reproduction: The Case of *Frankenstein*." *Literature and History* 9.2 (Aut. 1983): 194–213. Print.

O'Rourke, James. " 'Nothing More Unnatural': Mary Shelley's Revision of Rousseau." *ELH* 56.3 (Fall 1989): 543–69. Print.

———. *Sex, Lies, and Autobiography: The Ethics of Confession*. Charlottesville: U of Virginia P, 2006. Print.

Outka, Paul. "Posthuman/Postnatural: Ecocriticism and the Sublime in Mary Shelley's *Frankenstein*." *Environmental Criticism for the Twenty-First Century*. Ed. Stephanie LeMenager, Teresa Shewry, and Ken Hiltner. New York: Routledge, 2012. 31–48. Print.

Pamboukian, Sylvia A. *Doctoring the Novel: Medicine and Quackery from Shelley to Doyle*. Athens: Ohio UP, 2012. Print.

Parkin-Gounelas, Ruth. "Learning What we have Forgotten: Repetition as Remembrance in Early Nineteenth-Century Gothic." *European Romantic Review* 6.2 (Win. 1996): 213–26. Print.

Paulson, Ronald. "Gothic Fiction and the French Revolution." *ELH* 48.3 (Fall 1981): 532–54. Print.

Perkins, Margo V. "The Nature of Otherness: Class and Difference in Mary Shelley's *Frankenstein.*" *Studies in the Humanities* 19.1 (June 1992): 27–42. Print.

Perosa, Sergio. "Franklin to Frankenstein: A Note on Lightning and Novels." *Science and Imagination in XVIIIth-Century British Culture.* Ed. Sergio Rossi. Milan: Unicopli, 1987. 321–28 Print.

Petkow, Panagiota. "Getting Dirty with the Body: Abjection in Mary Shelley's *Frankenstein.*" *Gramma* 11 (2003): 31–38. Print.

Phillips, Bill. "*Frankenstein* and Mary Shelley's 'wet ungenial summer'." *Atlantis* 28.2 (2006): 59–68. Print.

Picart, Caroline Joan ("Kay") S. "Visualizing the Monstrous in *Frankenstein* Films." *Pacific Coast Philology* 35.1 (2000): 17–34. Print.

Pike, Judith. "Resurrection of the Fetish in *Gradiva, Frankenstein,* and *Wuthering Heights.*" Feldman and Kelley 150–68.

Piper, Karen. "Inuit Diasporas: *Frankenstein* and the Inuit in England." *Romanticism* 13.1 (2007): 63–75. Print.

Poindexter, Mark. "The Diverse Discourses of *Frankenstein* and Its Retellings." *Journal of Evolutionary Psychology* 22.11-2 (2001): 2–23. Print.

Pollin, Burton R. "Philosophical and Literary Sources of *Frankenstein.*" *Comparative Literature* 17.2 (Spr. 1965): 97–108. Print.

Pon, Cynthia. " 'Passage' in Mary Shelley's *Frankenstein*: Toward a Feminist Figure of Humanity?" *Modern Language Studies* 30.2 (2000): 33–50. Print.

Poovey, Mary. *The Proper Lady and the Woman Writer: Ideology as Style in the Works of Mary Wollstonecraft, Mary Shelley, and Jane Austen.* Chicago: U of Chicago P, 1984. Print.

Power, Henriette Lazardis. "The Text as Trap: The Problem of Difference in Mary Shelley's *Frankenstein.*" *Nineteenth-Century Contexts* 12.1 (1988): 85–103. Print.

Powers, Katherine Richardson. *The Influence of William Godwin on the Novels of Mary Shelley.* New York: Arno, 1980. Print.

Raub, Emma. "*Frankenstein* and the Mute Figure of Melodrama." *Modern Drama* 55.4 (2012): 437–58. Print.

Rauch, Alan. "The Monstrous Body of Knowledge in Mary Shelley's *Frankenstein.*" *Studies in Romanticism* 34.2 (Sum. 1995): 227–53. Print.

Reed, John R. "Will and Fate in *Frankenstein*." *Bulletin of Research in the Humanities* 83 (1980): 319–38. Print.

Reiman, Donald H., ed. *The Romantics Reviewed: Contemporary Reviews of British Romantic Writers.* 8 vols. New York: Garland, 1972. Print.

Richardson, Alan. "From *Emile* to *Frankenstein*: The Education of Monsters." *European Romantic Review* 1.2 (Win. 1991): 147–62. Print.

Rieder, John. "Embracing the Alien: Science Fiction in Mass Culture." *Science Fiction Studies* 9.1 (Mar. 1982): 26–37. Print.

Rieger, James. Introduction. *Frankenstein; or, The Modern Prometheus (The 1818 Text).* By Mary Shelley. Ed. Rieger. 1974. Chicago: U of Chicago P, 1982. xi–xxxvii. Print.

Rigby, Mair. " 'Do you share my madness?': *Frankenstein*'s Queer Gothic." *Queering the Gothic.* Ed. William Hughes and Andrew Smith. Manchester: Manchester UP, 2009. 36–54. Print.

Roberts, Marie. "Mary Shelley: Immortality, Gender and the Rosy Cross." Martin and Jarvis 60–68. Print.

Robinson, Charles E., ed. *The* Frankenstein *Notebooks: A Facsimile Edition of Mary Shelley's Novel, 1816–1817* (2 parts). Vol. IX of *The Manuscripts of the Younger Romantics.* Ed. Donald H. Reiman et al. 9 vols. New York: Garland, 1996. Print.

Rosa, Luis Othoniel. "Wound-Readers: Derrida and *Frankenstein*'s Monster." *Canadian Review of Comparative Literature/Revue canadienne de littérature comparée* 38.4 (2011): 463–81. Print.

Rose, Ellen Cronan. "Custody Battles: Reproducing Knowledge about *Frankenstein*." *New Literary History* 26.4 (Aut. 1995): 809–32. Print.

Rovee, Christopher. "Monsters, Marbles, and Miniatures: Mary Shelley's Reform Aesthetic." *Studies in the Novel* 36.2 (2004): 147–69. Print.

Rowe, Stephanie. " 'Listen to me': *Frankenstein* as an Appeal to Mercy and Justice, on Behalf of the Persecuted Animals." *Humans and Other Animals in Eighteenth-Century British Culture: Representation, Hybridity, Ethics.* Ed. Frank Palmeri. Burlington, VT: Ashgate, 2006. 137–52. Print.

Rowen, Norma. "*Frankenstein* Revisited: Doris Lessing's *The Fifth Child*." *Journal of the Fantastic in the Arts* 2.3 (1990): 41–49. Print.

———. "The Making of Frankenstein's Monster: Post-Golem, Pre-Robot." *State of the Fantastic. Selected Essays from the Eleventh International Conference on the Fantastic in the Arts, 1990.* Ed. Nicholas Ruddick. Westport: Greenwood, 1992. 169–77. Print.

Rubenstein, Marc A. "'My Accursed Origin': The Search for the Mother in *Frankenstein.*" *Studies in Romanticism* 15 (Spr. 1976): 165–94. Print.

Ruston, Sharon. "Resurrecting *Frankenstein.*" *Keats-Shelley Review* 19 (2005): 97–116. Print.

St. Clair, William. "The Impact of *Frankenstein.*" *Mary Shelley in Her Times.* Ed. Betty T. Bennett and Stuart Curran. Baltimore: Johns Hopkins UP, 2000. 38–63. Print.

Sanderson, Richard K. "Glutting the Maw of Death: Suicide and Procreation in *Frankenstein.*" *South Central Review* 9.2 (Sum. 1992): 49–64. Print.

Sarracino, Carmine. "Natural Law and the Monster." *Connecticut Review* 15.1 (1993): 23–32. Print.

Schackelford, Laura. "Subject to Change: The Monstrosity of Media in Shelley Jackson's *Patchwork Girl*; or, a Modern Monster and Other Posthumanist Critiques of the Instrumental." *Camera Obscura* 21.63 [3] (2006): 61–100. Print.

Scott, Peter Dale. "Vital Artifice: Mary, Percy, and the Psychopolitical Integrity of *Frankenstein.*" Levine and Knoepflmacher, *Endurance* 172–202.

[Scott, Walter.] "Remarks on *Frankenstein, or the Modern Prometheus; a novel.*" *Blackwood's Edinburgh Magazine* 2 (Mar. 1818): 613–20. Facsim. rpt. in Reiman Vol. 7, 73–80. Print.

Seligo, Carlos. "The Monsters of Botany and Mary Shelley's *Frankenstein.*" *Science Fiction, Critical Frontiers.* Ed. Karen Sayer and John Moore. Basingstoke: Palgrave Macmillan, 2000. 69–84. Print.

Sha, Richard C. "Volta's Battery, Animal Electricity, and *Frankenstein.*" *European Romantic Review* 23.1 (Feb. 2012): 21–41. Print.

Shelley, Percy Bysshe. "On *Frankenstein.*" 1832. *The Complete Works of Percy Bysshe Shelley.* Ed. Roger Ingpen and Walter E. Peck. 10 vols. New York: Gordian, 1965. 6: 263–65. Print.

*Shelley-Godwin Archive, The.* www.shelleygodwinarchive.org/contents /frankenstein. Web. 15 June 2014.

Shor, Esther, ed. *The Cambridge Companion to Mary Shelley.* Cambridge: Cambridge UP, 2003. Print.

Slusser, George. "The *Frankenstein* Barrier." *Fiction 2000: Cyberpunk and the Future of Narrative.* Ed. Slusser and Tom Shippey. Athens: U of Georgia P, 1992. 46–71. Print.

———. "Future Liberty: Benjamin Constant in the Light of Speculative Fiction." *Historical Reflections/Réflexions Historiques* 28.3 (2002): 493–512. Print.

Smith, Crosbie. "*Frankenstein* and Natural Magic." Bann, Franken-stein, *Creation* 39–59.

Smith, Johanna M. " 'Hideous Progenies': Texts of *Frankenstein*." *Texts and Textuality: Textual Instability, Theory, Interpretation, and Pedagogy.* Ed. Philip Cohen. New York: Garland, 1997. 121–40. Print.

Sonstroem, Eric. "Do You Really Want a Revolution? CyberTheory Meets Real-Life Pedagogical Practice in FrankenMOO and the Conventional Literature Classroom." *College Literature* 33.3 (2006): 148–70. Print.

Spector, Judith A. "Science Fiction and the Sex War: A Womb of One's Own." *Literature and Psychology* 31.1 (1981): 21–32. Print.

Spivak, Gayatri Chakravorty. "Three Women's Texts and a Critique of Imperialism." *Critical Inquiry* 12.1 (1985): 243–61. Print.

Stange, Margit. " 'You must create a female': Republican Order and its Natural Base in *Frankenstein*." *Women's Studies* 29.3 (2000): 309–31. Print.

Sterrenburg, Lee. "Mary Shelley's Monster: Politics and Psyche in *Frankenstein*." Levine and Knoepflmacher, *Endurance* 143–71.

Stock, Paul. "The Shelleys and the Idea of 'Europe'." *European Romantic Review* 19.4 (2008): 335–50. Print.

Stryker, Susan. "My Words to Victor Frankenstein above the Village of Chamounix: Performing Transgender Rage." *GLQ* 1 (1994): 237–54. Print.

Swingle, L. J. "Frankenstein's Monster and its Romantic Relatives: Problems of Knowledge in English Romanticism." *Texas Studies in Literature and Language* 15.1 (Spr. 1973): 51–65. Print.

Tantillo, Astrida Orle. "*Werther, Frankenstein,* and Girardian Mediated Desire." *Studia Neophilologica* 80.2 (2008): 177–87. Print.

Tillotson, Marcia. " 'A Forced Solitude': Mary Shelley and the Creation of Frankenstein's Monster." *The Female Gothic.* Ed. Juliann E. Fleenor. Montreal: Eden, 1983. 167–75. Print.

Todd, Janet. "Frankenstein's Daughter: Mary Shelley and Mary Wollstonecraft." *Women and Literature* 4.2 (Fall 1976): 18–27. Print.

Toumey, Christopher P. "The Moral Character of Mad Scientists: A Cultural Critique of Science." *Science, Technology, and Human Values* 17.4 (Aut. 1992): 411–37. Print.

Trott, Nicola. "Loves of the Triangle: William, Mary, and Percy Bysshe." *Wordsworth Circle* 31.1 (2000): 2–13. Print.

Tuite, Clara. "Frankenstein's Monster and Malthus's 'Jaundiced Eye': Population, Body Politics, and the Monstrous Sublime." *Eighteenth-Century Life* 22.1 (1998): 141–55. Print.

Turney, Jon. *Frankenstein's Footprints: Science, Genetics, and Popular Culture.* New Haven: Yale UP, 1998. Print.

Vasbinder, Samuel Holmes. *Scientific Attitudes in Mary Shelley's Frankenstein.* Ann Arbor: UMI, 1984. Print.

Veeder, William. *Mary Shelley and Frankenstein: The Fate of Androgyny.* Chicago: U of Chicago P, 1986. Print.

Vernon, Peter. "*Frankenstein*: Science and Electricity." *Études Anglaises* 50.3 (July–Sep. 1997): 270–83. Print.

Vidal, Ricarda. "Man's Creation of Man: From the Cruel Nature of de Sade and Mary Shelley to F. T. Marinetti's Mechanical Son." *Prism(s)* 13 (2005): 27–46. Print.

Vincent, Patrick. " 'This Wretched Mockery of Justice': Mary Shelley's *Frankenstein* and Geneva." *European Romantic Review* 18.5 (2007): 645–61. Print.

Vine, Steven. "Filthy Types: *Frankenstein*, Figuration, Femininity." *Critical Survey* 8.3 (1996): 246–58. Print.

———. "Hellish Sport: Irony in *Frankenstein*." *Q/W/E/R/T/Y* 3 (1993): 105–14. Print.

Vlasopolos, Anca. "*Frankenstein*'s Hidden Skeleton: The Psycho-Politics of Oppression." *Science Fiction Studies* 10.2 (July 1983): 125–36. Print.

Williams, Carolyn. " 'Inhumanly Brought Back to Life and Misery': Mary Wollstonecraft, *Frankenstein*, and the Royal Humane Society." *Women's Writing* 8.2 (2001): 213–34. Print.

Willis, Martin. "*Frankenstein* and the Soul." *Essays in Criticism* 45.1 (Jan. 1995): 24–35. Print.

Winnett, Susan. "Coming Unstrung: Women, Men, Narrative, and Principles of Pleasure." *PMLA* 105.3 (May 1990): 505–18. Print.

Wohlpart, A. James. "A Tradition of Male Poetics: Mary Shelley's *Frankenstein* as an Allegory of Art." *Midwest Quarterly* 39.3 (1998): 265–79. Print.

Wolfson, Susan J., and Ronald L. Levao, eds. *Mary Wollstonecraft Shelley: The Annotated* Frankenstein. Cambridge MA: Harvard-Belknap, 2012. Print.

Young, Elizabeth. *Black* Frankenstein: *The Making of an American Metaphor.* New York: New York UP, 2008. Print.

Zakharieva, Bouriana. "*Frankenstein* of the Nineties: The Composite Body." *Canadian Review of Comparative Literature/Revue canadienne de littérature comparée* 23.3 (Sep. 1996): 739–52. Print.

Ziolkowski, Theodore. "Science, *Frankenstein*, and Myth." *Sewanee Review* 89.1 (Win. 1981): 34–56. Print.

Zonana, Joyce. " 'They Will Prove the Truth of My Tale': Safie's Letters as the Feminist Core of Mary Shelley's *Frankenstein*." *Journal of Narrative Technique* 21.2 (Spr. 1991): 170–84. Print.

# Psychoanalytic Criticism
## and *Frankenstein*

## WHAT IS PSYCHOANALYTIC CRITICISM?

It seems natural to think about novels in terms of dreams. Like dreams, literary works are fictions, inventions of the mind that, although based on reality, are by definition not literally true. Like a literary work, a dream may have some truth to tell, but, like a literary work, it may need to be interpreted before that truth can be grasped. We can live vicariously through romantic fictions, much as we can through daydreams. Terrifying novels and nightmares affect us in much the same way, plunging us into an atmosphere that continues to cling, even after the last chapter has been read—or the alarm clock has sounded.

The notion that dreams allow such psychic explorations, of course, like the analogy between literary works and dreams, owes a great deal to the thinking of Sigmund Freud, the famous Austrian psychoanalyst who in 1900 published a seminal essay, *The Interpretation of Dreams*. But is the reader who feels that Emily Brontë's *Wuthering Heights* is dreamlike—who feels that Mary Shelley's *Frankenstein* is nightmarish—necessarily a Freudian literary critic? To some extent the answer has to be yes. We are all Freudians, really, whether or not we have read a single work by Freud. At one time or another, most of us have referred to ego, libido, complexes, unconscious desires, and sexual repression. The premises of Freud's thought have changed the way the Western world thinks about itself. Psychoanalytic criticism has influenced the teachers our teachers studied with, the works of scholarship and criticism they read, and the critical and creative writers *we* read as well. What Freud did was develop a language that described, a model that explained, a theory that encompassed human psychology. Many of the elements of psychology he sought to describe and explain are present in the literary works of various ages and cultures, from Sophocles' *Oedipus Rex* to Shakespeare's *Hamlet* to works being written in our own day. When the great novel of the twenty-first century is written, many of these same elements of psychology will probably inform its discourse as well. If, by understanding human psychology according to Freud, we can appreciate literature on a new level, then we should acquaint ourselves with his insights.

Freud's theories are either directly or indirectly concerned with the nature of the unconscious mind. Freud didn't invent the notion of the unconscious; others before him had suggested that even the supposedly "sane" human mind was conscious and rational only at times, and even then at possibly only one level. But Freud went further, suggesting that the powers motivating men and women are *mainly* and *normally* unconscious.

Freud, then, powerfully developed an old idea: that the human mind is essentially dual in nature. He called the predominantly passional, irrational, unknown, and unconscious part of the psyche the *id*, or "it." The *ego*, or "I," was his term for the predominantly rational, logical, orderly, conscious part. Another aspect of the psyche, which he called the *superego*, is really a projection of the ego. The superego almost seems to be outside of the self, making moral judgments, telling us to make sacrifices for good causes even though self-sacrifice may not be quite logical or rational. And, in a sense, the superego *is* "outside," since much of what it tells us to do or think we have learned from our parents, our schools, or our religious institutions.

What the ego and superego tell us *not* to do or think is repressed, forced into the unconscious mind. One of Freud's most important contributions to the study of the psyche, the theory of repression, goes something like this: much of what lies in the unconscious mind has been put there by consciousness, which acts as a censor, driving underground unconscious or conscious thoughts or instincts that it deems unacceptable. Censored materials often involve infantile sexual desires, Freud postulated. Repressed to an unconscious state, they emerge only in disguised forms: in dreams, in language (so-called Freudian slips), in

creative activity that may produce art (including literature), and in neurotic behavior.

According to Freud, all of us have repressed wishes and fears; we all
have dreams in which repressed feelings and memories emerge disguised, and thus we are all potential candidates for dream analysis. One
of the unconscious desires most commonly repressed is the childhood
wish to displace the parent of our own sex and take his or her place
in the affections of the parent of the opposite sex. This desire really
involves a number of different but related wishes and fears. (A boy—
and it should be remarked in passing that Freud here concerns himself
mainly with the male—may fear that his father will castrate him, and he
may wish that his mother would return to nursing him.) Freud referred
to the whole complex of feelings by the word *oedipal*, naming the complex after the Greek tragic hero Oedipus, who unwittingly killed his
father and married his mother.

Why are oedipal wishes and fears repressed by the conscious side
of the mind? And what happens to them after they have been censored?
As Roy P. Basler puts it in *Sex, Symbolism, and Psychology in Literature*
(1975), "from the beginning of recorded history such wishes have been
restrained by the most powerful religious and social taboos, and as a
result have come to be regarded as 'unnatural,'" even though "Freud
found that such wishes are more or less characteristic of normal human
development":

> In dreams, particularly, Freud found ample evidence that such
> wishes persisted. . . . Hence he conceived that natural urges, when
> identified as "wrong," may be repressed but not obliterated. . . .
> In the unconscious, these urges take on symbolic garb, regarded
> as nonsense by the waking mind that does not recognize their
> significance. (14)

Freud's belief in the significance of dreams, of course, was no more
original than his belief that there is an unconscious side to the psyche.
Again, it was the extent to which he developed a theory of how dreams
work—and the extent to which that theory helped him, by analogy, to
understand far more than just dreams—that made him unusual, important, and influential beyond the perimeters of medical schools and psy-
chiatrists' offices.

The psychoanalytic approach to literature not only rests on the theories of Freud; it may even be said to have *begun* with Freud, who was
interested in writers, especially those who relied heavily on symbols.

Such writers regularly cloak or mystify ideas in figures that make sense only when interpreted, much as the unconscious mind of a neurotic disguises secret thoughts in dream stories or bizarre actions that need to be interpreted by an analyst. Freud's interest in literary artists led him to make some unfortunate generalizations about creativity; for example, in the twenty-third lecture in *Introductory Lectures on Psycho-Analysis* (1922), he defined the artist as "one urged on by instinctive needs that are too clamorous" (314). But it also led him to write creative literary criticism of his own, including an influential essay on "The Relation of a Poet to Daydreaming" (1908) and "The Uncanny" (1919), a provocative psychoanalytic reading of E. T. A. Hoffman's supernatural tale "The Sandman."

Freud's application of psychoanalytic theory to literature quickly caught on. In 1909, only a year after Freud had published "The Relation of a Poet to Daydreaming," the psychoanalyst Otto Rank published *The Myth of the Birth of the Hero.* In that work, Rank subscribes to the notion that the artist turns a powerful, secret wish into a literary fantasy, and he uses Freud's notion about the "oedipal" complex to explain why the popular stories of so many heroes in literature are so similar. A year after Rank had published his psychoanalytic account of heroic texts, Ernest Jones, Freud's student and eventual biographer, turned his attention to a tragic text: Shakespeare's *Hamlet.* In an essay first published in the *American Journal of Psychology,* Jones, like Rank, makes use of the oedipal concept: he suggests that Hamlet is a victim of strong feelings toward his mother, the queen.

Between 1909 and 1949, numerous other critics decided that psychological and psychoanalytic theory could assist in the understanding of literature. I. A. Richards, Kenneth Burke, and Edmund Wilson were among the most influential to become interested in the new approach. Not all of the early critics were committed to the approach; neither were all of them Freudians. Some followed Alfred Adler, who believed that writers wrote out of inferiority complexes, and others applied the ideas of Carl Gustav Jung, who had broken with Freud over Freud's emphasis on sex and who had developed a theory of the *collective* unconscious. According to Jungian theory, a great work of literature is not a disguised expression of its author's personal, repressed wishes; rather, it is a manifestation of desires once held by the whole human race but now repressed because of the advent of civilization.

It is important to point out that among those who relied on Freud's models were a number of critics who were poets and novelists as well. Conrad Aiken wrote a Freudian study of American literature, and poets such as Robert Graves and W. H. Auden applied Freudian insights when writing critical prose. William Faulkner, Henry James, James Joyce, D. H. Lawrence, Marcel Proust, and Toni Morrison are only a few of the novelists who have either written criticism influenced by Freud or who have written novels that conceive of character, conflict, and creative writing itself in Freudian terms. The poet H. D. (Hilda Doolittle) was actually a patient of Freud's and provided an account of her analysis in her book *Tribute to Freud*. By giving Freudian theory credibility among students of literature that only they could bestow, such writers helped to endow earlier psychoanalytic criticism with a largely Freudian orientation that has begun to be challenged only in the last few decades.

The willingness, even eagerness, of writers to use Freudian models in producing literature and criticism of their own consummated a relationship that, to Freud and other pioneering psychoanalytic theorists, had seemed fated from the beginning; after all, therapy involves the close analysis of language. René Wellek and Austin Warren included "psychological" criticism as one of the five "extrinsic" approaches to literature described in their influential book *Theory of Literature* (1942). Psychological criticism, they suggest, typically attempts to do at least one of the following: provide a psychological study of an individual writer; explore the nature of the creative process; generalize about "types and laws present within works of literature"; or theorize about the psychological "effects of literature upon its readers" (81). Entire books on psychoanalytic criticism began to appear, such as Frederick J. Hoffman's *Freudianism and the Literary Mind* (1945).

Probably because of Freud's characterization of the creative mind as "clamorous" if not ill, psychoanalytic criticism written before 1950 tended to psychoanalyze the individual author. Poems were read as fantasies that allowed authors to indulge repressed wishes, to protect themselves from deep-seated anxieties, or both. A perfect example of author analysis would be Marie Bonaparte's 1933 study of Edgar Allan Poe. Bonaparte found Poe to be so fixated on his mother that his repressed longing emerges in his stories in images such as the white spot on a black cat's breast, said to represent mother's milk.

A later generation of psychoanalytic critics often paused to analyze the characters in novels and plays before proceeding to their authors. But not for long, since characters, both evil and good, tended to be seen by these critics as the author's potential selves, or projections of various repressed aspects of his or her psyche. For instance, in *A Psychoanalytic Study of the Double in Literature* (1970), Robert Rogers begins with the view that human beings are double or multiple in nature. Using this assumption, along with the psychoanalytic concept of "dissociation" (best known by its result, the dual or multiple personality), Rogers concludes that writers reveal instinctual or repressed selves in their books, often without realizing that they have done so.

In the view of critics attempting to arrive at more psychological insights into an author than biographical materials can provide, a work of literature is a fantasy or a dream—or at least so analogous to daydream or dream that Freudian analysis can help explain the nature of the mind that produced it. The author's purpose in writing is to gratify secretly some forbidden wish, in particular an infantile wish or desire that has been repressed into the unconscious mind. To discover what the wish is, the psychoanalytic critic employs many of the terms and procedures developed by Freud to analyze dreams.

The literal surface of a work is sometimes spoken of as its "manifest content" and treated as a "manifest dream" or "dream story" would be treated by a Freudian analyst. Just as the analyst tries to figure out the "dream thought" behind the dream story—that is, the latent or hidden content of the manifest dream—so the psychoanalytic literary critic tries to expose the latent, underlying content of a work. Freud used the words *condensation* and *displacement* to explain two of the mental processes whereby the mind disguises its wishes and fears in dream stories. In condensation, several thoughts or persons may be condensed into a single manifestation or image in a dream story; in displacement, an anxiety, a wish, or a person may be displaced onto the image of another, with which or whom it is loosely connected through a string of associations that only an analyst can untangle. Psychoanalytic critics treat metaphors as if they were dream condensations; they treat metonyms—figures of speech based on extremely loose, arbitrary associations—as if they were dream displacements. Thus figurative literary language in general is treated as something that evolves as the writer's conscious mind resists what the unconscious tells it to picture or describe. A symbol is, in Daniel Weiss's words, "a meaningful concealment of truth as the truth promises to emerge as some frightening or forbidden idea" (20).

In a 1970 article entitled "The 'Unconscious' of Literature," Norman Holland, a literary critic trained in psychoanalysis, succinctly sums up the attitudes held by critics who would psychoanalyze authors, but without quite saying that it is the *author* that is being analyzed by the psychoanalytic critic. "When one looks at a poem psychoanalytically," he writes, "one considers it as though it were a dream or as though some ideal patient [were speaking] from the couch in iambic pentameter." One "looks for the general level or levels of fantasy associated with the language. By level I mean the familiar stages of childhood development—oral [when desires for nourishment and infantile sexual desires overlap], anal [when infants receive their primary pleasure from defecation], urethral [when urinary functions are the locus of sexual pleasure], phallic [when the penis or, in girls, some penis substitute is of primary interest], oedipal." Holland continues by analyzing not Robert Frost but Frost's poem "Mending Wall" as a specifically oral fantasy that is not unique to its author. "Mending Wall" is "about breaking down the wall which marks the separated or individuated self so as to return to a state of closeness to some Other"—including and perhaps essentially the nursing mother (" 'Unconscious' " 136, 139).

While not denying the idea that the unconscious plays a role in creativity, psychoanalytic critics such as Holland began to focus more on the ways in which authors create works that appeal to *our* repressed wishes and fantasies. Consequently, they shifted their focus away from the psyche of the author and toward the psychology of the reader and the text. Holland's theories, which have concerned themselves more with the reader than with the text, have helped to establish another school of critical theory: reader-response criticism. Elizabeth Wright explains Holland's brand of modern psychoanalytic criticism in this way: "What draws us as readers to a text is the secret expression of what we desire to hear, much as we protest we do not. The disguise must be good enough to fool the censor into thinking that the text is respectable, but bad enough to allow the unconscious to glimpse the unrespectable" (117).

Holland is one of dozens of critics who have revised Freud significantly in the process of revitalizing psychoanalytic criticism. Another such critic is R. D. Laing, whose controversial and often poetical writings about personality, repression, masks, and the double or "schizoid" self have (re)blurred the boundary between creative writing and psychoanalytic discourse. Yet another is D. W. Winnicott, an "object relations" theorist who has had a significant impact on literary criticism. Critics influenced by Winnicott and his school have questioned the tendency to see reader/text as an either/or construct; instead, they have seen reader and text (or audience and play) in terms of a *relationship* taking place in what Winnicott calls a "transitional" or "potential" space—space in which binary terms such as *real* and *illusory, objective* and *subjective,* have little or no meaning.

Psychoanalytic theorists influenced by Winnicott see the transitional or potential reader/text (or audience/play) space as being *like* the space entered into by psychoanalyst and patient. More important, they also see it as being similar to the space between mother and infant: a space characterized by trust in which categorizing terms such as *knowing* and *feeling* mix and merge and have little meaning apart from one another.

Whereas Freud saw the mother-son relationship in terms of the son and his repressed oedipal complex (and saw the analyst-patient relationship in terms of the patient and the repressed "truth" that the analyst could scientifically extract), object-relations analysts see both relationships as *dyadic*—that is, as being dynamic in both directions. Consequently, they don't depersonalize analysis or their analyses. It is hardly surprising, therefore, that contemporary literary critics who apply object-relations theory to the texts they discuss don't depersonalize critics or categorize their interpretations as "truthful," at least not in any objective or scientific sense. In the view of such critics, interpretations are made of language—itself a transitional object—and are themselves the mediating terms or transitional objects of a relationship.

Like critics of the Winnicottian school, the French structuralist theorist Jacques Lacan focused on language and language-related issues. He treated the unconscious *as* a language and, consequently, viewed the dream not as Freud did (that is, as a form and symptom of repression) but rather as a form of discourse. Thus we may study dreams psychoanalytically to learn about literature, even as we may study literature to learn more about the unconscious. In Lacan's seminar on Poe's "The Purloined Letter," a pattern of repetition like that used by psychoanalysts in their analyses is used to arrive at a reading of the story. According to Wright, "the new psychoanalytic structural approach to literature" employs "analogies from psychoanalysis . . . to explain the workings of the text as distinct from the workings of a particular author's, character's, or even reader's mind" (125).

Lacan, however, did far more than extend Freud's theory of dreams, literature, and the interpretation of both. More significantly, he took Freud's whole theory of psyche and gender and added to it a crucial third term—that of language. In the process, he both used and significantly developed Freud's ideas about the oedipal stage and complex.

Lacan pointed out that the pre-oedipal stage, in which the child at first does not even recognize its independence from its mother, is also a pre*verbal* stage, one in which the child communicates without the medium of language, or—if we insist on calling the child's communications a language—in a language that can only be called *literal*. ("Coos," certainly, cannot be said to be figurative or symbolic.) Then, while still in the pre-oedipal stage, the child enters the *mirror* stage.

During the mirror period, the child comes to view itself and its mother, later other people as well, *as* independent selves. This is the stage in which the child is first able to fear the aggressions of another, to desire what is recognizably beyond the self (initially the mother), and, finally, to want to compete with another for the same desired object. This is also the stage at which the child first becomes able to feel sympathy with another being who is being hurt by a third, to cry when another cries. All of these developments, of course, involve projecting beyond the self and, by extension, constructing one's own self (or "ego" or "I") as others view one—that is, as *another*. Such constructions, according to Lacan, are just that: constructs, products, artifacts—fictions of coherence that in fact hide what Lacan called the "absence" or "lack" of being.

The mirror stage, which Lacan also referred to as the *imaginary* stage, is fairly quickly succeeded by the oedipal stage. As in Freud, this stage begins when the child, having come to view itself as self and the father and mother as separate selves, perceives gender and gender differences between its parents and between itself and one of its parents. For boys, gender awareness involves another, more powerful recognition, for the recognition of the father's phallus as the mark of his difference from the mother involves, at the same time, the recognition that his older and more powerful father is also his rival. That, in turn, leads to the understanding that what once seemed wholly his and even indistinguishable from himself is in fact someone else's: something properly desired only at a distance and in the form of socially acceptable *substitutes*.

The fact that the oedipal stage roughly coincides with the entry of the child into language is extremely important for Lacan. For the linguistic order is essentially a figurative or "Symbolic" order (Lacan sometimes refers to it as the *grand Autre*, or "big Other"); words are not the things they stand for but are, rather, stand-ins or substitutes for those things. Hence boys, who in the most critical period of their development have had to submit to what Lacan called the "Law of the Father"—a law that prohibits direct desire for and communicative intimacy with what has been the boy's whole world—enter more easily into the realm of language and the Symbolic order than do girls, who have never really had to renounce that which once seemed continuous with the self: the mother. The gap that has been opened up for boys, which includes the gap between signs and what they substitute—the gap marked by the phallus and encoded with the boy's sense of his maleness—has not opened up for girls, or has not opened up in the same way, to the same degree.

For Lacan, the father need not be present to trigger the oedipal stage; nor does his phallus have to be seen to catalyze the boy's (easier) transition into the Symbolic order. Rather, Lacan argued, a child's recognition of its gender is intricately tied up with a growing recognition of the system of names and naming, part of the larger system of substitutions we call language. A child has little doubt about who its mother is, but who is its father, and how would one know? The father's claim rests on the mother's *word* that he is in fact the father; the father's relationship to the child is thus established through language and a system of marriage and kinship—names—that in turn is basic to rules of everything from property to law. The name of the father (*nom du père,* which in French sounds like *non du père*) involves, in a sense, nothing of the father—nothing, that is, except his word or name.

Lacan's development of Freud has had several important results. First, his sexist-seeming association of maleness with the Symbolic order, together with his claim that women cannot therefore enter easily into the order, has prompted feminists not to reject his theory out of hand but, rather, to look more closely at the relation between language and gender, language and women's inequality. Some feminists have gone so far as to suggest that the social and political relationships between male and female will not be fundamentally altered until language itself has been radically changed. (That change might begin dialectically, with the development of some kind of "feminine language" grounded in the presymbolic, literal-to-imaginary communication between mother and child.)

Second, Lacan's theory has proved of interest to deconstructors and other poststructuralists, in part because it holds that the ego (which in Freud's view is as necessary as it is natural) is a product or construct. The ego-artifact, produced during the mirror stage, *seems* at once unified, consistent, and organized around a determinate center. But this unified self, or ego, is a fiction produced via the exclusion (Freud would say repression) of certain discontinuous elements and the yoking together of others as if they were continuous. In *The Four Fundamental Concepts of Psychoanalysis,* Lacan uses the term *objet petit a*—*petit a* being a shortened form of *petit autre,* meaning "small other"—to refer to that "from which subject, in order to constitute itself, has separated" (103). The fiction of the unified self ultimately takes its toll. The *objet petit a* becomes at once "the eternally lacking object" and "the cause of desire" that is akin to restlessness, anxiety. In the meantime, the self that feels the "lack" remains a collection of fragments fictively yoked together. It is the job of the Lacanian psychoanalyst to "deconstruct," as it were, the ego, to show its continuities to be contradictions as well.

\* \* \*

In the essay that follows, David Collings sees *Frankenstein* as a novel consisting of two realms: one proper and public and dominated by language and law (that of Alphonse Frankenstein and the De Lacey family), the other private—even secret—and incommunicable (that of Victor Frankenstein and his monster). These two worlds correspond, in Collings's view, to Lacan's Symbolic and Imaginary orders. In the first world, trials are held and language reigns supreme; the second exists outside society and language, containing only Victor and his double.

Collings, using Lacan's concepts, suggests that Victor's passage from the Imaginary into the Symbolic realms has been incomplete. He points out that we learn near the beginning of the novel that Victor's studies have included "neither the structure of languages, nor the code of governments, nor the politics of various states" (p. 44 in this volume)—all of which, as Collings points out, are associated with what Lacan calls the Symbolic order.

If Victor had fully and entirely emerged from the Imaginary order and entered the Symbolic, Collings goes on to say, he would have resolved what both Freud and Lacan would call his oedipal conflict by marrying a substitute for his mother. Instead, Victor rejects Elizabeth (whose nature and story nearly double that of his mother) and chooses to look into "the physical secrets of the world"—nature in "her hiding places" (p. 44, 52). Thus, in Collings's words, Victor continues "spurning the social realm in favor of the bodily mother, whom he attempts to recover by creating the monster" (p. 325). Pointing out that the death of Victor's mother and the later creation of the monster are closely intertwined within the text, Collings goes on to show the numerous ways in which the monster represents not a mother substitute but the body of the mother lost on entrance into the Symbolic order.

Of course, Victor *has* partially emerged from the pre-oedipal mirror stage and entered into some of the terms of the patriarchal or Symbolic order. If he hadn't, he couldn't speak to teachers or function at a university. As a result of the fact that he has partially emerged into the Symbolic order, his attempt to recreate the body of the lost mother is botched—as botched as his passage out of the Imaginary order has been rough and incomplete. His creation ends up resembling his own mirror image more than it does his maternal object.

But what a terrifying mental image it is! Lacan maintained that the infant is "jubilant" upon seeing its own reflected image as such. This is because the image is, in Collings's words, a "pleasingly coherent" picture from which "the child constructs the fiction of a unified ego," thereby "warding off the possibility" that the self—and even the body—"may be an assortment of disjointed and unrelated parts." Victor's monstrous mirror image, instead of "warding off" that prospect, explicitly represents "the body as a random assemblage" and "reveal[s] . . . that the unified self is a fiction" (p. 328).

Collings further explains the horror Victor feels upon looking onto the creature, and into its eyes, by citing Mladen Dolar's development of Lacanian theory. Dolar argues that, at the mirror stage, we necessarily see ourselves from the outside, as others see us, in the process losing " 'that uniqueness that one could enjoy in one's self-being' ": what Lacan referred to as "the object *a*," that which we will from then on desire but never regain (p. 329). When Victor sees the monster, according to Collings, he "does not encounter himself as another person" but, rather, "that element of the self" that human beings irretrievably lose when they first recognize themselves in a mirror (p. 329). In the moment he regains that object of desire, Victor also "lose[s] the lack that makes him human."

Thus, according to Collings's Lacanian reading, "When the monster awakes, he embodies both the maternal Thing and the object *a*, both the lost maternal body and the missing element of Victor himself. He is doubly impossible, representing two taboos at once" (p. 330), and in creating him Shelley envisioned a form of desire unidentified by either Freud or Lacan. For beyond the longing for coherent being, beyond the desire to defy the taboo against oedipal incest, she has revealed "the wish to recover what one was before one became human: to become a monster" (p. 331).

Shelley, Collings argues, subsequently attempts to "humanize" the position of the monster, to suggest that no monstrousness is innate but is, rather, only grotesque in the eyes of some society and its ideology. She carries out her critique of cultural norms regarding the desirable and the undesirable—the good, the bad, and the ugly—by allowing that which is "doubly impossible, . . . two taboos at once," to speak and express its *own* desire: specifically, to enter society, have a bride and a family, and, in short, enter the Symbolic order!

It is at this point that Collings's essay begins fully to justify its title, for what follows is a discussion that enlarges its focus on individual development through the Imaginary, mirror, oedipal, and Symbolic stages to include certain collective social fantasies alluded to in the essay's first paragraph. According to these fantasies, which are the products of ideology, there is "someone," i.e., some minority group, who gets some kind of pleasure—*jouissance*—from monstrous behavior of a type "civilized" people don't desire. What people subject to the ideology may not be able to see — but what the psychoanalytic approach to texts and their culture exposes — is the horribly fictive nature of these myths of difference. It also suggests something even more basic, namely, that just as the Victor Frankensteins of the world may want to be monsters, those unfairly tagged as monsters only want to be people.

                                                              Ross C Murfin

## PSYCHOANALYTIC CRITICISM: A SELECTED BIBLIOGRAPHY

### Psychoanalytic and Psychological Criticism: General Texts

Barry, Peter. *Beginning Theory: An Introduction to Literary and Cultural Theory*. 3rd ed. Manchester: Manchester UP, 2009. Print. See ch. 5, "Psychoanalytic Criticism."

Berger, Arthur Asa. *Media Analysis Techniques*. 5th ed. Thousand Oaks: Sage, 2014. Print. See ch. 3, "Psychoanalytic Criticism."

Brown, Kathleen L. *Teaching Literary Theory Using Film Adaptations*. Jefferson: McFarland, 2009. Print. See ch. 1, "Psychoanalytic Criticism."

Dobie, Ann B. *Theory into Practice: An Introduction to Literature*. 4th ed. Boston: Wadsworth, 2015. Print. See ch. 4, "Psychological Criticism."

Eagleton, Terry. *Literary Theory: An Introduction*. Anniv. ed. Minneapolis: U of Minnesota P, 2008. Print. See ch. 5, "Psychoanalysis."

Ellmann, Maud, ed. *Psychoanalytic Literary Criticism*. 1994. New York: Routledge, 2013. Print.

Fry, Paul H. *Theory of Literature*. New Haven: Yale UP, 2012. Print. See the section "Author (Reader) and Psyche."

Holland, Norman N. *Holland's Guide to Psychoanalytic Psychology and Literature-and-Psychology*. New York: Oxford UP, 1990. Print.

——. "The 'Unconscious' of Literature: The Psychoanalytic Approach." *Contemporary Criticism*. Ed. Malcolm Bradbury and David Palmer. London: Arnold, 1970. 130–53. Print.

Lapsley, Rob. "Psychoanalytic Criticism." *The Routledge Companion to Critical and Cultural Theory*. Ed. Paul Wake and Simon Malpas. 2nd ed. New York: Routledge, 2013. 73–86. Print.

Rabaté, Jean-Michel. *The Cambridge Introduction to Literature and Psychoanalysis.* New York: Cambridge UP, 2014. Print.

Sugg, Richard, ed. *Jungian Literary Criticism.* Evanston: Northwestern UP, 1992. Print.

Vice, Sue, ed. *Psychoanalytic Criticism: A Reader.* Cambridge: Blackwell, 1996. Print.

Vine, Steve, ed. *Literature in Psychoanalysis: A Reader.* New York: Palgrave Macmillan, 2005. Print.

Wellek, René, and Austin Warren. *Theory of Literature.* 1949. Rev. ed. New York: Mariner, 1984. Print. See ch. 7, "Literature and Psychology."

Wright, Elizabeth. "Modern Psychoanalytic Criticism." *Modern Literary Theory: A Comparative Introduction.* Ed. Ann Jefferson and David Robey. 2nd ed. London: Batsford, 1986. 113–33. Print.

———. *Psychoanalytic Criticism: A Reappraisal.* 2nd ed. New York: Routledge, 1998. Print.

———. *Psychoanalytic Criticism: Theory in Practice.* 1984. New York: Routledge, 2002. Print.

### Freud and Lacan

Althusser, Louis. *Writings on Psychoanalysis: Freud and Lacan.* Ed. Olivier Corpet and François Matheron. Trans. Jeffrey Mehlman. New York: Columbia UP, 1996. Print.

Berg, Henk de. *Freud's Theory and Its Use in Literary and Cultural Studies: An Introduction.* Rochester: Camden, 2004. Print.

Bowie, Malcolm. *Lacan.* Cambridge: Harvard UP, 1991. Print.

Boxer, Sarah. *In the Floyd Archives.* New York: Pantheon, 2001. Print.

Evans, Dylan. *An Introductory Dictionary of Lacanian Psychoanalysis.* London: Routledge, 1996. Print.

Feldstein, Richard, Bruce Fink, and Maire Jaanus, eds. *Reading Seminar XI: Lacan's Four Fundamental Concepts of Psychoanalysis.* Albany: State U of New York P, 1995. Print.

Fink, Bruce. *The Lacanian Subject: Between Language and Jouissance.* Princeton: Princeton UP, 1995. Print.

Frankland, Graham. *Freud's Literary Culture.* Cambridge: Cambridge UP, 2000. Print.

Freud, Sigmund. *The Freud Reader.* Ed. Peter Gay. New York: Norton, 1989. Print.

———. *Introductory Lectures on Psycho-Analysis.* 1915–17. Trans. Joan Riviere. London: Allen, 1922. Print.

————. *The Penguin Freud Reader*. Ed. Adam Phillips. London: Penguin, 2006. Print.

————. *Standard Edition of the Complete Psychological Works of Sigmund Freud*. Trans. and gen. ed. James Strachey. 24 vols. 1953–74. New York: Vintage, 2001. Print. See esp. *The Interpretation of Dreams* (1900), vol. 4, part 1; "The Relation of the Poet to Daydreaming" (1908), in vol. 9; and "The Uncanny," in vol. 17.

H. D. *Tribute to Freud*. 1956. 2nd ed. New York: New Directions, 2012. Print.

Hill, Philip. *Lacan for Beginners*. 1997. Danbury: For Beginners, 2009. Print.

Hoffman, Frederick J. *Freudianism and the Literary Mind*. 1945. New York: Grove, 1959. Print.

Homer, Sean. *Jacques Lacan*. New York: Routledge, 2005. Print.

Lacan. Jacques. "Desire and the Interpretation of Desire in Hamlet." Felman 11–52.

————. *Écrits: The First Complete Edition in English*. Trans. Bruce Fink. New York: Norton, 2006. Print. Includes Lacan's "Seminar on 'The Purloined Letter.'" 6–48.

————. *Écrits: A Selection*. 1966. Trans. Alan Sheridan. New York: Routledge, 2001. Print.

————. *The Seminar of Jacques Lacan, Book I: Freud's Papers on Technique, 1953–1954*. Ed. Jacques-Alain Miller. Trans. John Forrester. New York: Norton, 1988. Print.

————. *The Seminar of Jacques Lacan, Book II: The Ego in Freud's Theory and in the Technique of Psychoanalysis, 1954–1955*. Ed. Jacques-Alain Miller. Trans. Sylvana Tomaselli. New York: Norton, 1988. Print.

————. *The Seminar of Jacques Lacan, Book VII: The Ethics of Psychoanalysis, 1959–1960*. Ed. Jacques-Alain Miller. Trans. Dennis Porter. New York: Norton, 1992. Print. Includes Lacan's seminar on Sophocles' Antigone. 243–87.

————. *The Seminar of Jacques Lacan, Book XI: The Four Fundamental Concepts of Psychoanalysis, 1964*. Ed. Jacques-Alain Miller. Trans. Alan Sheridan. New York: Norton, 1998. Print.

————. *The Seminar of Jacques Lacan, Book XX, Encore: On Feminine Sexuality, The Limits of Love and Knowledge, 1972–1973*. Ed. Jacques-Alain Miller. Trans. Bruce Fink. New York: Norton, 1998. Print.

Leader, Darian, and Judy Groves. *Introducing Lacan: A Graphic Guide*. 1995. Cambridge: Icon, 2005. Print.

Lee, Jonathan Scott. *Jacques Lacan.* Boston: Twayne, 1990. Print.

MacCannell, Juliet Flower. *Figuring Lacan: Criticism and the Cultural Unconscious.* 1986. New York: Routledge, 2014. Print.

Meisel, Perry. *The Literary Freud.* New York: Routledge, 2007. Print.

O'Neill, John, ed. *Freud and the Passions.* University Park: Penn State UP, 1996. Print.

Ragland, Ellie. *Essays on the Pleasures of Death: From Freud to Lacan.* New York: Routledge, 1995. Print.

Roudinesco, Elisabeth. *Jacques Lacan.* Trans. Barbara Bray. New York: Columbia UP, 1997. Print.

Schneiderman, Stuart. *Jacques Lacan: The Death of an Intellectual Hero.* Cambridge: Harvard UP, 1983. Print.

Thurschwell, Pamela. *Sigmund Freud.* 2nd ed. New York: Routledge, 2009. Print.

Weber, Samuel. *The Legend of Freud.* 1982. Expanded ed. Stanford: Stanford UP, 2000. Print.

Žižek, Slavoj. *How to Read Lacan.* 2006. London: Granta, 2011. Print.

———. *Looking Awry: An Introduction to Jacques Lacan through Popular Culture.* Cambridge: MIT P, 1991. Print.

## Other Influential Psychoanalytic and Psychological Theorists

Bloom, Harold. *The Anxiety of Influence: A Theory of Poetry.* 1973. 2nd ed. New York: Oxford UP, 1997. Print.

Jung, C. G. *The Collected Works of C. G. Jung.* Ed. and trans. Gerhard Adler and R. F. C. Hull. 20 vols. Princeton: Princeton UP, 1960–90. Print. See esp. vol. 9, part 1, *The Archetypes and the Collective Unconscious* (1969). Vols. 1–19 available online.

Klein, Melanie. *The Selected Melanie Klein.* Ed. Juliet Mitchell. New York: Free Press, 1987. Print.

Kristeva, Julia. *The Kristeva Reader.* Ed. Toril Moi. 1986. New York: Blackwell, 1996. Print.

———. *Revolution in Poetic Language.* 1974. Trans. Margaret Waller. New York: Columbia UP, 1984. Print.

Winnicott, Donald W. *Playing and Reality.* 1971. New York: Routledge, 2005. Print.

Wood, Kelsey. *Žižek: A Reader's Guide.* Malden: Wiley, 2012. Print.

Žižek, Slavoj. *The Metastases of Enjoyment: Six Essays on Woman and Causality.* New York: Verso, 1994. Print.

————. *The Sublime Object of Ideology.* 1989. 2nd ed. New York: Verso, 2009. Print.

## Intersections with Feminist, Gender, and Queer Approaches

Barr, Marleen S., and Richard Feldstein, eds. *Discontented Discourses: Feminism/Textual Intervention/Psychoanalysis.* Urbana: U of Illinois P, 1989. Print.

Baruch, Elaine Hoffman. *Women, Love, and Power: Literary and Psychoanalytic Perspectives.* New York: New York UP, 1991. Print.

Bowlby, Rachel. *Still Crazy After All These Years: Women, Writing, & Psychoanalysis.* 1992. New York: Routledge, 2010. Print.

Bruhm, Steven. *Reflecting Narcissus: A Queer Aesthetic.* Minneapolis: U of Minnesota P, 2000. Print.

Butler, Judith. *Bodies That Matter: On the Discursive Limits of "Sex."* 1993. New York: Routledge, 2011. Print.

————. *Gender Trouble: Feminism and the Subversion of Identity.* 1990. New York: Routledge, 2010. Print.

Carlin, Claire L. *Women Reading Corneille: Feminist Psychocriticisms of Le Cid.* New York: Peter Lang, 2000. Print.

Chodorow, Nancy. *The Reproduction of Mothering: Psychoanalysis and the Sociology of Gender.* 1978. Berkeley: U of California P, 1999. Print.

de Lauretis, Teresa. *The Practice of Love: Lesbian Sexuality and Perverse Desire.* Bloomington: Indiana UP, 1994. Print.

Elliott, Patricia. *From Mastery to Analysis: Theories of Gender in Psychoanalytic Feminism.* Ithaca: Cornell UP, 1991. Print.

Fleeger, Jennifer. *Mismatched Women: The Siren's Song Through the Machine.* New York: Oxford UP, 2014. Print.

Gallop, Jane. *Thinking Through the Body.* New York: Columbia UP, 1988. Print.

Garner, Shirley Nelson, Claire Kahane, and Madelon Sprengnether, eds. *The (M)other Tongue: Essays in Feminist Psychoanalytic Interpretation.* Ithaca: Cornell UP, 1985. Print.

Greven, David. *The Fragility of Manhood: Hawthorne, Freud, and the Politics of Gender.* Columbus: Ohio State UP, 2012. Print.

Grosz, Elizabeth. *Jacques Lacan: A Feminist Introduction.* New York: Routledge, 1990. Print.

Irigaray, Luce. *This Sex Which Is Not One*. 1977. Trans. Catherine Porter. Ithaca: Cornell UP, 1985. Print.

———. *Speculum of the Other Woman*. 1974. Trans. Gillian C. Gill. Ithaca: Cornell UP, 1985. Print.

Jacobus, Mary. *Reading Woman: Essays in Feminist Criticism*. New York: Columbia UP, 1986. Print. See esp. "Is There a Woman in This Text?" (1971).

Johnson, Barbara. *The Feminist Difference: Literature, Psychoanalysis, Race, and Gender*. Cambridge: Harvard UP, 1998. Print. See esp. the section "Literary Differences: Psychoanalysis, Race, and Gender."

Long, Margherita. *This Perversion Called Love: Reading Tanizaki, Feminist Theory, and Freud*. Stanford: Stanford UP, 2009. Print.

MacCannell, Juliet Flower. *The Regime of the Brother: After the Patriarchy*. New York: Routledge, 1991. Print.

Mitchell, Juliet. *Psychoanalysis and Feminism: A Radical Reassessment of Freudian Psychoanalysis*. 1974. New York: Basic Books, 2000. Print.

Mitchell, Juliet, and Jacqueline Rose. eds. Introduction I and Introduction II. *Feminine Sexuality: Jacques Lacan and the école freudienne*. By Lacan. Trans. J. Rose. New York: Norton, 1982. 1–57. Print.

Pitcher, John A. *Chaucer's Feminine Subjects: Figures of Desire in* The Canterbury Tales. New York: Palgrave Macmillan, 2012. Print.

Rohy, Valerie. *Lost Causes: Narrative, Etiology, and Queer Theory*. Oxford: Oxford UP, 2015. Print.

Rose, Jacqueline. *Sexuality in the Field of Vision*. 1986. New York: Verso, 2006. Print.

Samuels, Robert. *Hitchcock's Bi-Textuality: Lacan, Feminisms, and Queer Theory*. Albany: State of U of New York P, 1998. Print.

———. *Writing Prejudices: The Psychoanalysis and Pedagogy of Discrimination from Shakespeare to Toni Morrison*. Albany: State U of New York P, 2001. Print.

Schanoes, Veronica L. *Fairy Tales, Myth, and Psychoanalytic Theory: Feminism and Retelling the Tale*. Burlington, VT: Ashgate, 2014. Print.

Segal, Naomi. *The Unintended Reader: Feminism and* Manon Lescaut. 1986. Cambridge: Cambridge UP, 2010. Print. See Part III, "Theory," for a feminist critique of Freud and Lacan.

Stockton, Will. *Playing Dirty: Sexuality and Waste in Early Modern Comedy*. Minneapolis: U of Minnesota P, 2011. Print.

Weed, Elizabeth. "Feminist Psychoanalytic Literary Criticism." *The Cambridge Companion to Feminist Literary Theory*. Ed. Ellen Rooney. Cambridge: Cambridge UP, 2006. 261–82. Print.

## Intersections with Other Critical Perspectives

Apollon, Willy, and Richard Feldstein, eds. *Lacan, Politics, Aesthetics*. Albany: State U of New York P, 1996. Print. Intersection with cultural studies.

———. *The Freudian Body: Psychoanalysis and Art*. New York: Columbia UP, 1986. Print. Intersection with deconstruction.

Bracher, Mark. *Lacan, Discourse, and Social Change: A Psychoanalytic Cultural Criticism*. Ithaca: Cornell UP, 1993. Print.

Campbell, Jan. *Arguing with the Phallus: Feminist, Queer, and Postcolonial Theory—A Psychoanalytic Contribution*. New York: Zed, 2000. Print.

Fradenburg, L. O. Aranye. *Sacrifice Your Love: Psychoanalysis, Historicism, Chaucer*. Minneapolis: U of Minnesota P, 2002. Print.

Gana, Nouri. *Signifying Loss: Toward a Poetics of Narrative Mourning*. Lewisburg, PA: Bucknell UP, 2011. Print. Intersection with deconstruction and postcolonial theory.

Kille, D. Andrew. *Psychological Biblical Criticism*. Minneapolis: Fortress, 2001. Print.

Kofman, Sarah. *The Childhood of Art: An Interpretation of Freud's Aesthetics*. 1970. Trans. Winifred Woodhull. New York: Columbia UP, 1988. Print. Intersection with deconstruction.

Lundberg, Christian. *Lacan in Public: Psychoanalysis and the Science of Rhetoric*. Tuscaloosa: U of Alabama P, 2012. Print.

Macdonald, Molly. *Hegel and Psychoanalysis: A New Interpretation of Phenomenology of Spirit*. New York: Routledge, 2013. Print.

Marcus, Laura, and Ankhi Mukherjee, eds. *A Concise Companion to Psychoanalysis, Literature, and Culture*. Malden: Wiley, 2014. Print. Impact of psychoanalytic theory on literature, cultural theory, feminist and gender studies, translation studies, and film.

Plasa, Carl, ed. *Toni Morrison: Beloved*. New York: Columbia UP, 1998. Print. See Ch. 5, "'It's Not Over Just Because It Stops': Post-colonialism, Psychoanalysis, History."

Rollins, Wayne G. *Soul and Psyche: The Bible in Psychological Perspective*. Minneapolis: Fortress, 1999. Print.

Van Boheemen-Saaf, Christine. *Joyce, Derrida, Lacan, and the Trauma of History: Reading, Narrative, and Postcolonialism*. Cambridge: Cambridge UP, 1999. Print.

## Further Reading on Psychoanalytic
## and Psychological Criticism

Armstrong, Philip. *Shakespeare in Psychoanalysis.* New York: Routledge, 2001. Print.

Berman, Emanuel, ed. *Essential Papers on Literature and Psychoanalysis.* New York: New York UP, 1993. Print.

Brill, Susan B. "Critical Descriptions, or Moving Beyond Freud: A Wittgensteinian-Based Psychological Criticism." *Wittgenstein and Critical Theory: Beyond Postmodern Criticism and Toward Descriptive Investigations.* Athens: Ohio UP, 1995. 33–52. Print.

Britton, Ronald. *Belief and Imagination: Explorations in Psychoanalysis.* London & New York: Routledge, 1998. Print.

Brophy, Kevin. *Creativity: Psychoanalysis, Surrealism and Creative Writing.* Carlton South: Melbourne UP, 1998. Print.

Easthope, Anthony. *The Unconscious.* New York: Routledge, 1999. Print.

Ginsburg, Nancy, and Roy Ginsburg, eds. *Psychoanalysis and Culture at the Millennium.* New Haven: Yale UP, 1999. Print.

Gunn, Daniel. *Psychoanalysis and Fiction: An Exploration of Literary and Psychoanalytic Borders.* Cambridge: Cambridge UP, 1988. Print.

Jackson, Leonard. *Literature, Psychoanalysis and the New Sciences of Mind.* 2000. New York: Routledge, 2014. Print.

Jacobus, Mary. *The Poetics of Psychoanalysis: In the Wake of Klein.* New York: Oxford UP, 2005. Print.

Lechte, John, ed. *Writing and Psychoanalysis: A Reader.* New York: Arnold, 1996. Print.

Lesser, Simon O. *Fiction and the Unconscious.* Boston: Beacon, 1957. Print. On ego psychology.

Phillips, Adam. *Promises, Promises: Essays on Literature and Psychoanalysis.* London: Faber, 2000. Print.

———. *Side Effects.* New York: Hamish Hamilton, 2006. Print.

Rimmon-Kenan, Shlomith, ed. *Discourse in Psychoanalysis and Literature.* 1987. New York: Routledge, 2014. Print.

Rogers, Robert A. *A Psychoanalytic Study of the Double in Literature.* Detroit: Wayne State UP, 1970. Print.

Roland, Alan. *Dreams and Drama: Psychoanalytic Criticism, Creativity and the Artist.* Middletown: Wesleyan UP, 2003. Print.

Rothenberg, Molly Anne, Dennis A. Foster, and Slavoj Žižek, eds. *Perversion and the Social Relation.* Durham: Duke UP, 2003. Print.

Rudnytsky, Peter L., ed. *Transitional Objects and Potential Spaces: Literary Uses of D. W. Winnicott.* New York: Columbia UP, 1993. Print.

Sodré, Ignês. *Imaginary Existences: A Psychoanalytic Exploration of Phantasy, Fiction, Dreams and Daydreams.* New York: Routledge, 2014. Print.

Tate, Claudia. *Psychoanalysis and Black Novels: Desire and the Protocols of Race.* New York: Oxford UP, 1998. Print.

Weiss, Daniel. *The Critic Agonistes: Psychology, Myth, and the Art of Fiction.* Seattle: U of Washington P, 1985. Print.

Wright, Elizabeth. *Speaking Desires Can Be Dangerous: The Poetics of the Unconscious.* Malden: Polity, 1999. Print.

Yoshida, Hiromi. *Joyce and Jung: The "Four Stages of Eroticism" in* A Portrait of the Artist As a Young Man. New York: Lang, 2006. Print.

### Psychoanalytic and Psychological Readings

Basler, Roy P. *Sex, Symbolism, and Psychology in Literature.* 1948. New York: Octagon, 1975. Print.

Berman, Jeffrey. *Narcissism and the Novel.* New York: New York UP, 1990. Print.

Bersani, Leo. *Baudelaire and Freud.* Berkeley: U of California P, 1977. Print.

Bettelheim, Bruno. *The Uses of Enchantment: The Meaning and Importance of Fairy Tales.* 1976. New York: Vintage, 2010. Print.

Bodkin, Maud. *Archetypal Patterns in Poetry: Psychological Studies of Imagination.* London: Oxford UP, 1934. Print.

Bonaparte, Marie. *The Life and Works of Edgar Allan Poe: A Psycho-Analytic Interpretation.* 1933. Trans. John Rodker. London: Imago, 1949. Print.

Cameron, Ed. *The Psychopathology of the Gothic Romance: Perversion, Neuroses and Psychoses in Early Works of the Genre.* Jefferson: McFarland, 2010. Print.

Crews, Frederick C. *The Sins of the Fathers: Hawthorne's Psychological Themes.* 1966. Berkeley: U of California P, 1989. Print.

Dervin, Daniel. *A "Strange Sapience": The Creative Imagination of D. H. Lawrence.* Amherst: U of Massachusetts P, 1984. Print.

Francis, Samuel. *The Psychological Fictions of J. G. Ballard.* New York: Continuum, 2011. Print.

Hertz, Neil. *The End of the Line: Essays on Psychoanalysis and the Sublime.* 1985. Rev. ed. Aurora: Davies Group, 2009.

Jacobus, Mary. *First Things: The Maternal Imaginary in Literature, Art, and Psychoanalysis.* New York: Routledge, 1995. Print.

Jones, Ernest. *Hamlet and Oedipus.* 1949. New York: Norton, 1976. Print.

———. "The Oedipus-Complex as an Explanation of Hamlet's Mystery: A Study in Motive." *American Journal of Psychology* 21.1 (1910): 72–113. Print.

McDayter, Ghislaine, ed. *Untrodden Regions of the Mind: Romanticism and Psychoanalysis.* Lewisburg, PA: Bucknell UP, 2002. Print.

Mills, Alice. *Stuckness in the Fiction of Mervyn Peake.* New York: Rodopi, 2005. Print.

Rank, Otto. *The Myth of the Birth of the Hero: A Psychological Interpretation of Mythology.* 1909. 2nd ed. Trans. Gregory C. Richter and E. James Lieberman. Baltimore: Johns Hopkins UP, 2004. Print.

Reinhard, Kenneth, and Julia Reinhard Lupton. *After Oedipus: Shakespeare in Psychoanalysis.* 1993. 2nd ed. Aurora, CO: Davies Group, 2009. Print.

Rickels, Laurence A. *Aberrations of Mourning.* 1988. Minneapolis: U of Minnesota P, 2011. Print.

Rollin, Lucy, and Mark I. West. *Psychoanalytic Responses to Children's Literature.* 1999. Jefferson: McFarland, 2008. Print.

Rollins, Wayne G., and D. Andrew Kille, eds. *Psychological Insight into the Bible: Texts and Readings.* Grand Rapids: Eerdsmans, 2007. Print.

Ross, Ciaran. *Beckett's Art of Absence: Rethinking the Void.* New York: Palgrave Macmillan, 2011. Print.

Sartre, Jean-Paul. *Mallarmé: or, the Poet of Nothingness.* 1953. Trans. Ernest Sturm. University Park: Penn State UP, 1991. Print.

Schapiro, Barbara A. *The Romantic Mother: Narcissistic Patterns in Romantic Poetry.* Baltimore: Johns Hopkins UP, 1983. Print.

Schwenger, Peter. *Fantasm and Fiction: On Textual Envisioning.* Stanford: Stanford UP, 1999. Print.

Storey, Robert F. *Pierrots on the Stage of Desire: Nineteenth-Century French Literary Artists and the Comic Pantomime.* 1985. Princeton: Princeton UP, 2014. Print.

Trigo, Benigno, ed. *Kristeva's Fiction.* Albany: State U of New York P, 2013. Print.

Waldman, Suzanne M. *The Demon and the Damozel: Dynamics of Desire in the Works of Christina Rossetti and Dante Gabriel Rossetti.* Athens: Ohio UP, 2008. Print.

Wallingford, Katharine. *Robert Lowell's Language of the Self.* 1988. Chapel Hill: U of North Carolina P, 2012. Print.

Webster, Brenda. *Yeats: A Psychoanalytic Study.* 1973. Bloomington, IN: iUniverse.com, 2000. Print.

Woodman, Ross. *Sanity, Madness, Transformation: The Psyche in Romanticism.* Toronto: U of Toronto P, 2009. Print.

## Lacanian Psychoanalytic Studies of Literature

Azari, Ehsan. *Lacan and the Destiny of Literature: Desire, Jouissance and the Sinthome in Shakespeare, Donne, Joyce and Ashbery.* London: Continuum, 2008. Print.

Davis, Robert Con, ed. *The Fictional Father: Lacanian Readings of the Text.* Amherst: U of Massachusetts P, 1981. Print.

———. *Lacan and Narration: The Psychoanalytic Difference in Narrative Theory.* Baltimore: Johns Hopkins UP, 1983. Print.

Felman, Shoshana, ed. *Literature and Psychoanalysis: The Question of Reading: Otherwise.* Baltimore: Johns Hopkins UP, 1982. Print.

Homans, Margaret. *Bearing the Word: Language and Female Experience in Nineteenth-Century Women's Writing.* Chicago: U of Chicago P, 1986. Print.

Mellard, James M. *Using Lacan, Reading Fiction.* Urbana: U of Illinois P, 1991. Print.

———. *Beyond Lacan.* Albany: State U of New York P, 2006. Print.

Muller, John P., and William J. Richardson, eds. *The Purloined Poe: Lacan, Derrida, and Psychoanalytic Reading.* Baltimore: Johns Hopkins UP, 1988. Print.

Rabaté, Jean-Michel. *Jacques Lacan: Psychoanalysis and the Subject of Literature.* New York: Palgrave, 2001. Print.

Rapaport, Herman. *Between the Sign and the Gaze.* Ithaca: Cornell UP, 1994. Print.

Salecl, Renata, and Slavoj Žižek, eds. *Gaze and Voice as Love Objects.* Durham: Duke UP, 1996. Print.

## Psychoanalytic Readings of *Frankenstein*

Benziman, Galia. "Challenging the Biological: The Fantasy of Male Birth as a Nineteenth-Century Narrative of Ethical Failure." *Women's Studies* 35.4 (2006): 375–95. Print.

Comitini, Patricia. "The Limits of Discourse and the Ideology of Form in Mary Shelley's *Frankenstein*." *Keats-Shelley Journal* 55 (2006): 179–98. Print.

Copjec, Joan. "Vampires, Breast-Feeding, and Anxiety." Copjec 117–39.

Dolar, Mladen. " 'I Shall Be with You on Your Wedding-Night': Lacan and the Uncanny." *October* 58 (1991): 5–23. Print.

Kercsmar, Rhonda Ray. "Displaced Apocalypse and Eschatological Anxiety in *Frankenstein*." *South Atlantic Quarterly* 95 (1996): 729–51. Print.

Knoepflmacher, U. C. "Thoughts on the Aggression of Daughters." *The Endurance of* Frankenstein: *Essays on Mary Shelley's Novel*. Ed. George Levine and Knoepflmacher. Berkeley: U of California P, 1979. 88–119. Print.

London, Bette. "Mary Shelley, *Frankenstein*, and the Spectacle of Masculinity." *PMLA* 108 (1993): 253–67. Print.

Petkow, Panagiota. "Getting Dirty with the Body: Abjection in Mary Shelley's *Frankenstein*." *Gramma* 11 (2003): 31–38. Print.

Pike, Judith. "Resurrection of the Fetish in *Gradiva, Frankenstein,* and *Wuthering Heights*." *Romantic Women Writers: Voices and Countervoices*. Ed. Paula R. Feldman and Theresa M. Kelley. Hanover: UP of New England, 1995. 150–68. Print.

Rieder, John. " 'A Filthy Type': The Motif of the Fecal Child in *Frankenstein*." *Gothic Studies* 3.1 (2001): 24–31. Print.

# A PSYCHOANALYTIC PERSPECTIVE

### DAVID COLLINGS

## The Monster and the Maternal Thing: Mary Shelley's Critique of Ideology

It might seem odd to argue that Mary Shelley's *Frankenstein*, apparently about something as outlandish as the creation of a monster and all that follows, might ultimately expose the way ideology operates in modern societies. It might seem even more strange to make this argument using the resources of psychoanalytic theory. Yet this is one of the great virtues of such theory in the wake of Jacques Lacan: it can at once decipher the significance of the uncanny and clarify the relation between the construction of desire and of modern society, primarily because it conceives of society as the product of a collective fantasy, as a psychoanalytic construct in its own right. Lacan and Shelley both suggest that society orients itself toward the fantasy of an impossible fulfillment which, if ever realized, would be the source of great dread — and that such a fantasy supports ideology by allowing us to blame the divided condition of the psyche or of society on others. Conflating utopias and monsters, Shelley anticipates Lacanian theory, urging us to recognize the limits of the emancipatory dream, accept the conflicts of modern society, and thereby undo the very logic that enables prejudice and exclusion.

The world of *Frankenstein* is deeply divided. On the one hand, there is a social order rooted in kinship, marriage, and legality, related to what Lacan calls the Symbolic order, exemplified by the dutiful father and judge Alphonse Frankenstein, the families of the Frankensteins and the De Laceys, the possibility of Victor's marriage with Elizabeth, the responsible science of M. Krempe, and the operation of law in the trial of Justine and the imprisonment of Victor. On the other hand, there is the domain of rivalry between Victor and his creature, resembling Lacan's Imaginary order, exemplified by the curious solitude of each, the fact that neither can belong to a family, their endless fascination with each other, and their utter incapacity to communicate their situation to anyone else (except of course Robert Walton, the novel's narrator). Victor's obsession with his double compels him to resist or attack his father, friend, and potential wife whenever they threaten that self. His solitude is so profound that his obsession with and fear of the monster would amount to madness were it not that another person, Walton, encounters the monster in the novel's final pages.

The early pages of Victor's story emphasize the distinctively oedipal quality of his solitude. As a young scholar, Victor studies "neither the structure of languages, nor the code of governments, nor the politics of various states," all subjects associated with the Symbolic order, but rather "the physical secrets of the world" (p. 44 in this volume). Moreover, within the physical sciences, he pursues the outmoded and semimagical arts of Agrippa, Paracelsus, and Albertus Magnus in defiance of his father's prohibition, as if replaying the oedipus complex in his intellectual pursuits. A similar oedipal drama is performed after Victor arrives at the university. The ugly, forbidding M. Krempe scoffs at the alchemists (p. 51), but Waldman indirectly praises them and describes modern chemistry in sexually resonant terms: the modern masters "penetrate into the recesses of nature, and show how she works in her hiding places" (p. 52).

While Victor's oedipal yearnings are familiar, they do not lead him toward the normative resolution, in which the son relinquishes his mother and desires a person who resembles her. Margaret Homans argues that in effect the son gives up the physical mother and desires a figurative representation of her, a substitute for her in the realm of language or social relations. She proposes that Victor's development is typical because he attempts to re-create his mother in his scientific, intellectual project and thus in the realm of language (9–10, 101–2, 107). But the novel presents Elizabeth, not the monster, as the ideal figure for the mother; her personality and biography almost duplicate Caroline Frankenstein's, as if she is in fact the perfect person to complete the oedipal drama. Victor resists the seemingly inevitable marriage to Elizabeth, leaves home, and chooses another, forbidden erotic object: the mystery of how nature works in "her" hiding places—the mystery of the feminine body. That is, he chooses to take exactly the opposite of the typical path, spurning the social realm in favor of the bodily mother, whom he attempts to recover by creating the monster.

This relation between the mother and monster is made clear in the episodes surrounding Victor's going to the university. The break from the family represents Victor's entrance into the public world and his separation from his mother. Thus her death immediately before his leaving is highly appropriate; it represents Victor's separation from her and the loss consequent on accepting his place in the Symbolic order. Despite himself, Victor must leave her behind, tell himself not to grieve over his loss (p. 49), and go on to begin a career. Yet, as we have seen, once he gets to the university he refuses to participate in authorized scientific activities and falls prey to his longing for forbidden knowledge. He identifies with his mother, recovering her body in his own as he attempts to become pregnant himself, to labor in childbirth, and to watch the child awaken, gesture, and attempt to speak (see pp. 55–59). He also attempts to re-create her by reassembling her dead body, as it were, from "bones from charnel-houses" (p. 58), animating it, and looking up at it (as would a child at its mother) as he lies in bed (p. 60).

In the midst of these depictions of the monster's infantile and maternal attributes comes Victor's dream:

> I thought I saw Elizabeth, in the bloom of health, walking in the streets of Ingolstadt. Delighted and surprised, I embraced her; but as I imprinted the first kiss on her lips, they became livid with the hue of death; her features appeared to change, and I thought that I held the corpse of my dead mother in my arms; a shroud

enveloped her form, and I saw the graveworms crawling in the folds of the flannel. (p. 60)

In a reversal of the normative shift, here the potential lover (Elizabeth) transforms back into the dead mother she is supposed to replace. For Victor, feminine sexuality can never be separated from the mother he has lost; as soon as he imagines touching Elizabeth, the figurative substitute for her turns back into her physical form, and then—impossibly—into the all-too-literal and present form of the monster itself, whom Victor, immediately after this passage, sees upon awakening from his dream. In effect, all women are for him the dead mother, the all-too-physical person he left when he went to the university. Furthermore, because he entered the university on the condition that he leave behind the dead mother, she necessarily appears as a monstrously physical intruder in the world of masculine learning. It would be impossible for Elizabeth to walk in Ingolstadt without seeming to be a visitor from the dead, nor could the product of Victor's rapturous discovery of "the cause of generation and life" (p. 56) arise without being recognized as a walking corpse. Clearly, the turn from erotic ideal to grotesque body horrifies Victor, and in this respect he is a responsible citizen of the Symbolic realm, longing for Elizabeth rather than the mother. Yet this horror is so strong, and this dream so necessary, because of his unspeakable desire for the secret of the dead mother's body, for that element of her that has no substitute.

What Lacan would call the Imaginary nature of his relation to the monster is further reinforced in the visual imagery of the passage: when Victor awakens, he sees, "by the dim and yellow light of the moon, as it forced its way through the window shutters," the monster, who fixes on Victor "his eyes, if eyes they may be called" (p. 60). A peculiar and intense sight dominates in this passage: a haunting light cast on a ghastly figure, framed by the window, who gazes back with inhuman eyes. This seems to be the return of a deeply repressed mirror stage in which the monster is Victor's own reflection. As if to emphasize the prelinguistic nature of this moment, Shelley goes on to write: "His jaws opened, and he muttered some inarticulate sounds, while a grin wrinkled his cheeks" (p. 60). The mirrorlike quality of Victor's encounter with the monster is clearer elsewhere in the novel where the nearly hallucinatory image recurs: at the destruction of the female monster ("I trembled, and my heart failed within me; when, on looking up, I saw, by the light of the moon, the dæmon at the casement" [p. 144]) and, most clearly, at the death of Elizabeth (p. 167). In all these passages, the window represents the mirror, a framed surface on which always appears the face of the demonic double.

All this is complicated by Shelley's account of the conception of the novel:

> When I placed my head on my pillow, I did not sleep, nor could I be said to think. My imagination, unbidden, possessed and guided me, gifting the successive images that arose in my mind with a vividness far beyond the usual bounds of reverie. I saw—with shut eyes, but acute mental vision,—I saw the pale student of unhallowed arts kneeling beside the thing he had put together. . . . I opened [my eyes] in terror. . . . I wished to exchange the ghastly image of my fancy for the realities around. I see them still; the very room, the dark *parquet*, the closed shutters, with the moonlight struggling through, and the sense I had that the glassy lake and white high Alps were beyond. (Introduction p. 24)

Shelley's emphasis on the haunting "vividness" of this "acute mental vision" locates it outside of ordinary, waking sight—in the Imaginary realm. Her reference to "the realities around" leads her to further mental images, "sense[d]" through the closed shutters, of the lake and Alps, or perhaps of the Alps reflected in the lake, another kind of mirror, and the intense seeing of the original vision (emphasized through the repetition of the words "I saw") is repeated late in the passage ("I see them still").

For both Shelley and her character Victor Frankenstein, creation takes place neither in the Symbolic moment of uttering words (as in the Biblical Genesis) nor even of writing them but in the moment of an astonishing visual literalization when what they "see" comes to life. Anne Mellor has quite justifiably discussed Victor's creation of the monster as a masculine attempt to circumvent the maternal, to usurp and destroy the life-giving power of feminine sexuality (220–32). But the strong parallels of the two creation scenes suggest instead that Victor circumvents normative sexuality with a sexuality of the Imaginary in which the child can re-create the dead mother in a prelinguistic, visual mode.

It is important that this visual imagery is most intense in moments both of creating (the novel, the monster) and of killing (the female monster, Elizabeth): by tying together these apparently opposite motifs, this imagery points to the way the novel operates according to the logic of the Imaginary, rather than the more familiar and normative Symbolic order. The female monster and Elizabeth represent not simply feminine sexuality but its function within the world of the Symbolic, that is, of kinship and filiation: Elizabeth as a married sexual partner and the female monster as a potential partner in creating a new society in South America—a new "chain of existence" (p. 130) that, as Peter Brooks points out, would be a new "systematic network of relation" akin to the Symbolic order (593). If we apply this reading to Mary Shelley as author, it suggests that literary creation is for her a form of matricide, of killing the kind of mother that is subordinated to a father or husband. Perhaps it is even a way to kill herself as such a mother. Barbara Johnson argues this point, emphasizing the subtle link between the italics in the passages on the creating of the book and the killing of Elizabeth (Johnson 8–9). In both cases, the italics culminate in a moment of a creation or murder rendered with a familiar kind of imagistic intensity. On some level, the novel hints that creation through hallucinatory power, through the literal realization of a mental image, threatens to destroy sexual reproduction itself.

But if the category of the Imaginary goes far to explaining these unusually constructed scenes, it cannot by itself explain what is so terrifying in the monster. After all, one can see one's face in a mirror without going into shock. While the monster clearly occupies a place in the Imaginary realm, he does so in an unusual way, one that Lacanian theory also helps explain. Lacan argues that the infant is "jubilant" on seeing the reflected image precisely because that image, so pleasingly coherent, gives the child the illusion that the body itself is also coherent. From this image the child constructs the fiction of a unified ego, warding off the possibility that one is not in fact one, that the body may be an assortment of disjointed and unrelated parts. To some extent, then, the child identifies with the mirror-image to defend against the possibility of a fragmented body-image (*Ecrits* 1–5). When Victor sees the monster in the mirrorlike scenes throughout the novel, in effect he sees what the mirror-image is supposed to hide from him: the image of the body as a random assemblage. These scenes travesty the normative mirror-scene, undermine the ego, and reveal what neither Victor nor we wish to know: that the unified self is a fiction. Only now is it clear that by attempting to reconstruct the maternal body excluded by the Symbolic order, Victor produced a body that threatens the Imaginary order as well. What precedes language must in some way also precede the ego itself.

But this analysis still does not fully explain Victor's response to the creature. One would expect Victor to be familiar with the idea of the assembled body, since he gathered the parts of dead bodies himself. In fact, when he contemplates the creature just before it comes to life, he approves of his work and finds it beautiful. But once the creature opens its eyes, he cannot bear the sight. In this haunting version of the mirror-scene, everything works as if Victor looks in the mirror *and sees the image begin to have a life of its own*, moving in ways that do not reflect his gestures, and (worst of all) looking back with its own "dull yellow" eyes, "if eyes they may be called" (p. 60).

Simply imagining such a scene happening to us can give us the creeps as well. But why? Mladen Dolar explains that when one seizes upon the fiction of a unified self in the mirror-stage by identifying with something outside the self, one loses "that uniqueness that one could enjoy in one's self-being," the element that Lacan calls the object *a*. To become a subject, one must lose an element of the subject forever: this loss enables one to care about the world of objects, to make demands on the world, and to desire (Dolar 13; cf. Lacan, *Ecrits* 5–6). Instead of merely existing as a unique being, for example, the child begins to pay attention to the mirror and to replicate the activities of other children (Lacan, *Ecrits* 18–19). Lacan argues that this loss structures desire, which will always seek what it is lacking: the object *a*. And this loss also marks the moment of the foreclosure of the Real, that notoriously difficult Lacanian category, that largely mythical condition without lack or representation that accordingly appears as a hole or gap from the perspective of the Symbolic or Imaginary orders (see Žižek, *Sublime* 170). Thus ordinarily when we look in the mirror, the image reflects us but itself lacks the extra element that would make it a person, too. Oddly, then, we can only recognize ourselves in an image that in fact fails to depict us: we become human when something essential is subtracted from us. What shocks Victor is simply that the image comes to life, as if this essential thing has been added back. "The double," writes Dolar, "is the same as me plus the object *a*, that invisible part of being added to my image" (13). Victor does not encounter himself as another person: that would be startling enough, to be sure, but not as strange as actually seeing as an image that element of the self that one loses when one recognizes one's reflection in the mirror. Suddenly he sees what it would be like to be an image and be complete, too: to appear in the world *and lack nothing*.

We might think that Victor would be ecstatic at gaining such access to wholeness. But in such a moment he would lose the lack that makes him human, the form of desire that gives him subjectivity, the invisible thing that made the visible world significant to him. As Dolar writes, he has now gained "something too much" by losing "the loss that made it possible to deal with a coherent reality" (13). In short, he has encountered the Lacanian Real in such a way that his sense of ordinary reality is in danger of disappearing entirely.

Shelley makes this uncanny moment possible when she takes advantage of the conventions of supernatural fiction and allows the impossible to take place. By imagining such a counterfactual scenario, she indirectly reveals much about the nature of desire. Dolar argues that to some extent Victor represents the Enlightenment project insofar as he seeks to confer an unprecedented blessing on humanity. But the realization of his project is far worse than what it sought to correct (17–18). There is something frustrating about imagining a utopia and not watching it come to pass, but it is even worse if the seemingly impossible ideal is actually realized. The advent of a genuine utopia would in fact destroy the need for political activity or the desire for a different future. It would obliterate the lack that drives historical change. Similarly, when Victor succeeds in realizing his wish to revive what he has lost, he need no longer sustain a separate image, name, or identity. The encounter with the Real at least potentially shatters him as a human subject. The novel thus suggests that the Symbolic, the Imaginary, and the sense of ordinary reality itself depend on the primordial loss of the maternal body; to revive it is to threaten the order of the world.

If, as I have argued, the monster is the resurrected maternal body, how can he also capture the lost part of the self? What is the relation between the two readings I have given of the creation scene so far? Lacan argues that the primordial lost object is the mother; she is the Thing whose absence structures desire and the unconscious, just as the prohibition of incest with her anchors all further elaborations of the law (*Ethics* 67–68). But to capture the significance of Shelley's monster, one must add a twist or two to Lacan's analysis. When the monster awakes, he embodies both the maternal Thing and the object $a$, both the lost maternal body and the missing element of Victor himself. He is doubly impossible, representing two taboos at once. On some level, Shelley's point does not seem so difficult: after all, it makes sense that in the mirror-stage, when one loses access to the prior, disorganized but undivided bodily mode, one simultaneously loses the earliest version of the maternal body as well. But the creation scene implicitly suggests that the element we seek in desire—the object $a$—is to be found in a body so formless that it has no gender and does not even constitute a person. By writing a novel not only about the double (all in all, a rather familiar topic in the Gothic) but about something that travesties the coherent body image as well, Shelley uncovers an element of desire Lacan never quite theorized: the longing to rejoin and/or to be something that a person who has been through the mirror stage can imagine only as a monster. Behind the fascination with the double, behind the longing to violate the incest taboo, lies the wish to recover what one was before one became human: to become a monster.

One reason that this reading seems a little implausible is that the novel suggests it only on occasion—for example, through Victor's dream—but usually emphasizes other aspects of the creature. The fact that the monster is a "man" and, later in the novel, can confront Victor "man" to man, seeking a female mate and demanding a form of justice, places the creature on a somewhat more familiar footing, even if still uncanny. Perhaps the idea that the creature is his masculine double helps Victor ward off the even more frightening wish that he be the dead mother. The ultimate forbidden object, it seems, is the maternal Thing.

The novel's depiction of Victor's project is already provocative enough. But even more radically, it allows the supposed impossible object to speak and to desire. With this simple step, Mary Shelley places limits upon Victor's entire way of relating to his creature, suggesting that the creature, existing with a human consciousness of its own, is someone other than a projection of Victor's psyche. In effect, she tries to humanize the position of the impossible object, to imagine what it would be like for a monster to sustain personhood when everybody around him treats him as an utterly alien being. In this way, she shows that the monster "is not 'in itself' monstrous, [for] there is no inherent monstrousness," only whatever fails to fit into "the facile categorizing of the social and cultural order" (Musselwhite 59). If we follow Shelley and try to look at the world through the creature's eyes, human desire—whether that of Victor or of the novel's other characters—appears to be steeped in illusions. In this way Shelley carries out a wholesale critique of the structure of desire and challenges her readers to recognize its ideological dimension.

The creature's bizarre form of embodiment is clear in his own mirror-scene. Having "admired the perfect forms of [his] cottagers," he looks into a pool and is terrified, "unable to believe that it was indeed I who was reflected in the mirror" (p. 104). In a gesture that should remind us of Victor's response to him, he cannot identify the image with himself, for evidently he sees there a form of bodily incoherence not compatible with the "I," the ego he wants to protect. Strangely enough, the creature's image is alien even to him—as if his very body literalizes a principle threatening to every possible form of subjectivity. This scene establishes that those who respond to his appearance with hostility are not deranged; the creature himself finds his appearance unbearable.

Of course, the monster does not accept his status, for he longs to enter the social world, belong to a family, converse, and have a sexual partner. He wishes, in short, to enter the Symbolic order. If Victor creates the monster in order to revolt against the Symbolic, the monster protests against being excluded from it. He understands his condition well: early in their conversation high in the Alps when Victor cries out, " 'Begone! relieve me from the sight of your detested form,' " the monster replies by placing his hands over Victor's eyes (p. 94), mocking his fixation on the sight of his form (Brooks 592). In the narrative that follows, the monster attempts to replace his appearance with his words (Brooks 593), just as he attempts to cut across the dual relation between Victor and himself with his demands for a female partner who could offer him a social and sexual relation.

Despite his best efforts, however, the creature remains caught on the margins of the Symbolic. The story the monster tells Victor, primarily about his acquisition of language from the De Lacey family, dramatizes this marginal position. Crouching there in the lean-to next to the family's cottage, he can listen to everything that people say but cannot participate in their conversations. He can learn the words, but he cannot share in the social exchange of words and must remain an invisible presence unknown to the family. It is no surprise that the monster learns along with Safie, as if he, too, is both foreign and a woman. Critics have remarked that he is thus placed in the position of the woman who, like Eve or Mary Shelley, eavesdrops on the conversations of men (see, for example, Gilbert and Gubar 238). As a result, his condition is similar to that of woman in Lacanian theory. As Jacqueline Rose puts it, "woman is excluded *by* the nature of words" but not "*from* the nature of words" (49), on the one hand being given a sexual and gender identity through language and on the other being excluded from language as it is based in the father's name. Oddly enough, the creature becomes defined by language without receiving the name-of-the-father, in effect dramatizing the condition of women in most Western cultures, whose names come from men and who thus remain in one sense nameless.

Shelley dramatizes these problematic qualities of language when she renders the elder De Lacey blind. This father seems to have forgotten about the Imaginary and to live entirely within the world of words. Hardly moving from his place in the cottage, he only speaks, listens to someone read, and teaches people words: like Safie and the monster, he too is a consummate listener, but because he is already the master of the language and need not see the objects to which words refer. In effect, he represents the blindness of language, its apparent indifference to the body and to sight. This old man has almost ceased to be an actual father and become a parodic version of the name-of-the-father, the father as nothing but names.

Although the father's blindness might indicate that he is so alienated from the visual world he need no longer see it, the monster interprets that blindness differently. Perhaps the old man, unable to see the monster, will accept him simply because he speaks. Blindness to the Imaginary may allow some tolerance for a body that travesties it. But in the crucial moment of the monster's attempt to be accepted, Felix rushes in and violently ejects the monster from the cottage, and in the following days the entire family flees the scene. The monster's failure demonstrates that language is not indifferent but hostile to the monstrous body, as if Victor's cry to the monster ("Begone!") merely made explicit the exclusionary principle that allows people to exchange words with each other in the first place.

So Safie and the monster are ultimately quite different. She is accepted into the cottage, after all, while he must remain outside. She has the name "Safie," while he has none. She can speak the language to others, while the creature discovers that he cannot do so safely. She has a story to tell that depicts the wrongs of woman, as if to echo one of the feminist fictions written by Mary Shelley's mother, Mary Wollstonecraft. But the monster is denied even this form of protest; only an unspeakable secret can explain him. If Safie represents woman as she is accepted into language and the family, the monster embodies woman as she is excluded from the world of images and words. He is even more foreign than she, representing what will always remain nameless and threatening in her.

The monster's condition is made clear again when he describes his experience as a reader. Recognizing that he is "similar, yet at the same time strangely unlike to the beings concerning whom" he reads in Goethe, Plutarch, or Milton (p. 115), he finds himself in an oblique relation to language. If we regard books as language preserved in print, then we can understand why the monster cannot find anyone like himself in them. Books exclude the bodies of the dead and preserve only their words, whereas the monster is pieced together solely out of fragments of corpses. The monster embodies precisely what books cannot preserve.

The stories that books tell also have a way of replacing the body with words. Milton's *Paradise Lost*, the myth of origins that the monster reads, attributes origins not to physical nature but to the disembodied Word of God at the creation. Milton's God is somewhat like a divine version of the Lacanian father, who lacks any direct physical link with the child and thus establishes his paternal authority through words, claiming that the child belongs to him. Indeed, that God goes even further, dispensing with nature or any other physical force and creating the world out of his own Word, as if no mother of the world were necessary. Milton, following Biblical tradition, substitutes the father's words for the mother's body as origin so radically that the latter almost disappears. The story that the monster finds in Victor's papers is very different: it tells of a bodily, maternal origin, as if the monster were produced out of the mother's body without her ever entering into sexual relations, as if she could create life without the participation of a father and without reference to the order of filiation or gender. Here we find the opposite of Milton's myth of paternal origin: a celibate, solitary, and material creation. Thus the monster finds his origins in a kind of anti-Symbolic story, indeed an anti-story, which confusedly tells how bodies come from bodies without the need for a sexual relation, how "birth" takes place without the need for parents, in effect how the monster has no familial position worthy of the name. With such an anti-story in his pocket, the monster must remain nameless, for a name comes with a story that tells how one originates in social and sexual relations, in kinship, and thus in language.

If, as I have argued, the creature's image is intolerable to him, if no person is willing to respond to him sympathetically, and if he is utterly caught within an alien order of being, how does he manage to sustain any kind of relation to the world? He does so only by demanding that he be given access to ordinary human experience, asking Victor to make him a partner with whom he could enter into social and sexual relations. It turns out that the creature is like the rest of us: he lacks what he wants. Of course, his situation is unique, for what he wants is an approximation of the relations we usually take for granted. Yet that he is divided from his object suggests that he is no monster but simply a desiring subject; he is not the maternal Thing at all, for his bodily incoherence gives him access to no special mode of being but only blocks his access to satisfaction. It appears that no person, not even one who supposedly represents the object of desire, ever truly has access to a mythical condition of fulfillment. If Victor wants to be a monster, the monster just wants to be another person. In a deeply ironic gesture, Shelley suggests (as does Lacan) that the category of the Real is ultimately empty, even if it persists as a dimension of our experience; that the maternal Thing does not exist, even if its prohibition continues to anchor the structure of law; and that we never possessed the lost object in the first place, even if we continue to seek it (cf. Lacan, *Ethics* 118). As Žižek puts it, the paradox is that "this Thing is retroactively produced by the very process of symbolization, i.e., that it emerges in the very gesture of its loss" (*Tarrying* 37).

Because of this impasse, the creature establishes his relation to the world almost entirely by threatening Victor in more and more aggressive ways, eventually killing nearly every member of Victor's circle— most tellingly, the virtuous Elizabeth on her wedding night. The creature takes these actions as his only recourse in the long negotiation with Victor over his demand for a spouse. The fact that the monster limits his aggression to those whom Victor loves, all of whom happen to be exemplary in their sexual purity, allows many readers to construct almost allegorical readings of the book. For example, critics have argued that the monster represents the sexuality of Victor himself, which, in his hysterical condition, he wishes to repudiate (Hobbs), the sexuality that this sentimental family—and Shelley herself—represses (Hall), or the "fatal materiality of all life" and the stain of "impure birth" that, according to Shelley, "a civilized order" and especially this family "must keep at bay" (Youngquist 348–49). Such readings in effect suggest that the monster is a figure for what Lacan calls *jouissance,* a form of enjoyment so extravagant that society sustains the moral law out of recoil against it (*Ethics* 179–90).

Of course, Shelley provides many details that support such readings. But one must proceed with caution here. To read the monster as if he is the sexuality of Victor or of his family is to forget that in this novel he is also a person separate from them in character and motivation. By his own account in his final speech to Walton, these murders are anything but pleasurable. He is thus a figure of monstrous enjoyment only in the eyes of others, just as he is the maternal Thing not to himself but others. To them, the fact that his appearance threatens their sense of selfhood must mean his form of satisfaction is equally inhuman. If he is physically intolerable, he must be ethically intolerable as well. It is no surprise, then, to realize that for Lacan the illusory nature of these projections is the same: he argues that nobody actually experiences *jouissance* per se, for it is as impossible to gain access to it as to the Real or to the maternal Thing (*Ethics* 203). It is a mythic experience, one we imagine that someone *else* (usually of another class, race, gender, or sexual orientation) might experience but that civilized people avoid (or, in another version, a bliss of which they have been deprived). It seems likely that Shelley makes these readings plausible precisely so that she can discredit the myth of *jouissance* in the same way that she undoes the myth of the maternal Thing: her goal, it seems, is to destroy the belief—whether Victor's or ours—that some form of bodily, sexual, or emotional plenitude exists elsewhere, even while she shows that this myth underlies the very logic of desire.

As the creature destroys more and more of the people in Victor's circle and isolates his creator further, the two of them gradually move into the mode of direct rivalry. Because each sees the other as blocking his desire, each becomes ever more obsessed with wounding the other. The complexity of their relation now takes on the simplicity of the Imaginary: the monster is fated to define himself in relation to Victor, and vice versa, each becoming the other's double, the mirror-self that haunts his every step. In the eyes of the law, they are indistinguishable: witnesses in Ireland mistake the dark figure in the boat for Victor (p. 152), and later when Victor tries to gain the law's help in tracking down the monster, the judge assumes he is mad (p. 171). Caught in this relation to the double, each sees the other as his rival self, attacking the other and getting revenge in an endless spiral of violence, each revealing in this way what Lacan identifies as the aggressive, paranoid structure of the ego. Rivalry becomes a directly destructive force, reducing everything to the opposition between the Imaginary pair—an opposition that is never resolved by the intervention of a Symbolic law but that expires at last only with their deaths.

As if to emphasize the impasses of the Imaginary, Shelley allows this Imaginary mode to expand beyond Victor and the monster and threaten to organize the structure of her entire novel, whose series of identifications and projections ultimately includes the reader. The creature's anti-Symbolic tale becomes one in which one narrator identifies with another, who introduces yet a third, in a regress of tale within tale, mirror within mirror. I have no space to repeat here what critics have already discussed: the many resemblances between the narrators Mary Shelley and Margaret Saville (the woman who receives Walton's letters and whose initials are also M. S.), Mary Shelley and Walton, Walton and Victor, Victor and the monster, the monster and Safie, and Safie and Mary Shelley (see, among others, Brooks 603 and Rubenstein 168–72). Nor can I review the ways in which characters in the novel are orphaned and motherless (Gilbert and Gubar 227–28), with the result that they tend to create an identity through finding doubles of themselves in other orphans. I can only point to the psychoanalytic coherence of this duplication of narratives, which, like the monster's tale to Victor in the heart of the novel, follow from and return to Victor's horrified gaze into the monster's face. We read all the stories in the novel as if a hand is over our eyes, too, and at any moment it will be lifted and the novel will transform from something read into something seen—perhaps someone seen in the mirror.

But Shelley does not entirely abandon her novel to this logic. Instead of having Walton sign the last letter and thereby complete the Chinese-box structure of her work, she leaves the crucial final message from the monster unsigned, hinting that in some way it breaks out of the logic of the Imaginary. The monster gets the last word. Here he explains what I discussed above: that he did not take satisfaction in his crimes, that he is not ethically monstrous. By dispelling the illusion of his enjoyment and emphasizing his own ordinary desire for fellowship, he provides an alternative to Victor's project. Implicitly, in this final speech Shelley answers a question that Victor's narrative poses. If we are to renounce the illusion of the maternal Thing and of *jouissance*, what remains to us as subjects? Are we to renounce desire itself and live without hope? The monster's wish for ordinary life, complete with its attendant frustrations and conflicts, suggests that for Shelley, as for Lacan, the best path is to affirm the deadlock of ordinary desire rather than seeking to escape it through any kind of utopian condition (cf. *Ethics* 291–301). Insofar as desire is always oriented toward a lost object, it is best to affirm the wish for that as well—even if in the knowledge that it is forever lost.

How does such an answer bear upon the many political questions that this novel raises? As I have argued, the creature is (like) a woman; others have shown how he is also a racially marked person, a revolutionary or member of a radical mob, a member of the working class, and a sexual deviant. He can represent so many possibilities only because in his monstrosity "he can stand for everything that our culture has to repress" (Dolar 19). The monster is not any *one* of these things, nor can culture exorcise him by addressing any one political problem. Rather, the creature reveals the general structure of ideological projection per se, the abstract category by virtue of which ideology can operate. Thus "psychoanalysis differs from other interpretations by its insistence on the formal level of the uncanny rather than on its content" (Dolar 20). Zizek argues, in a discussion of totalitarianism and anti-Semitism, that ideology operates by imagining that some social force—whether Jews, women, workers, blacks, gays—blocks social unity. "Society is not prevented from achieving its full identity because of Jews" or any other group but "by its own antagonistic nature, by its own immanent blockage, and it 'projects' this internal negativity into the figure of the 'Jew'"—or, Shelley might add, of the monster (*Sublime* 127). Shelley, neither an Enlightenment radical in the mode of Victor nor a sentimental conservative in the mode of the Frankenstein family, advocates a self-consciously disillusioned form of ideology critique in which one accepts and affirms the deadlock of social and sexual relations. Long before Lacan, she formulated an ethics for those of us who live after the Enlightenment and the French Revolution, one that relinquishes the dream of emancipation and sustains instead a postutopian form of political hope.

## WORKS CITED

Brooks, Peter. "Godlike Science/Unhallowed Arts: Language and Monstrosity in *Frankenstein.*" *New Literary History* 9 (1978): 591–605. Print.

Dolar, Mladen. "'I Shall Be with You on Your Wedding-Night': Lacan and the Uncanny." *October* 58 (1991): 5–23. Print.

Gilbert, Sandra M., and Susan Gubar. *The Madwoman in the Attic: The Woman Writer and the Nineteenth-Century Literary Imagination*. New Haven: Yale UP, 1979. Print.

Hall, Jean. "*Frankenstein:* The Horrifying Otherness of Family." *Essays in Literature* 17 (1990): 179–89. Print.

Hobbs, Colleen. "Reading the Symptoms: An Exploration of Repression and Hysteria in Mary Shelley's *Frankenstein.*" *Studies in the Novel* 25 (1993): 252–69. Print.

Homans, Margaret. *Bearing the Word: Language and Female Experience in Nineteenth-Century Women's Writing*. Chicago: U of Chicago P, 1986. Print.

Johnson, Barbara. "My Monster/My Self." *Diacritics* 12 (1982): 2–10. Print.

Lacan, Jacques. *Ecrits: A Selection*. Trans. Alan Sheridan. New York: Norton, 1977. Print.

———. *The Seminar of Jacques Lacan, Book VII. The Ethics of Psychoanalysis: 1959–1960*. Ed. Jacques-Alain Miller. Trans. Dennis Porter. New York: Norton, 1992. Print.

Mellor, Anne K. "Possessing Nature: The Female in *Frankenstein.*" *Romanticism and Feminism*. Ed. Mellor. Bloomington: Indiana UP, 1988. 220–32. Print.

Musselwhite, David E. *Partings Welded Together: Politics and Desire in the Nineteenth-Century English Novel*. New York: Methuen, 1987. Print.

Rose, Jacqueline. Introduction II. *Feminine Sexuality: Lacan and the école freudienne.* Ed. Juliet Mitchell and Rose. New York: Norton, 1982. 27–57. Print.

Rubenstein, Marc. "'My Accursed Origin': The Search for the Mother in *Frankenstein.*" *Studies in Romanticism* 15 (1976): 165–94. Print.

Youngquist, Paul. "*Frankenstein:* The Mother, the Daughter, and the Monster." *Philological Quarterly* 70 (1991): 339–59. Print.

Žižek, Slavoj. *The Sublime Object of Ideology.* New York: Verso, 1989. Print.

———. *Tarrying With the Negative: Kant, Hegel, and the Critique of Ideology.* Durham: Duke UP, 1993. Print.

# Feminist Criticism
## and *Frankenstein*

### WHAT IS FEMINIST CRITICISM?

Feminist criticism comes in many forms, and feminist critics have a variety of goals. Some have been interested in rediscovering the works of women writers overlooked by a masculine-dominated culture. Others have revisited books by male authors and reviewed them from a woman's point of view to understand how they both reflect and shape the attitudes that have held women back. A number of contemporary feminists have turned to topics as various as women in postcolonial societies, women's autobiographical writings, lesbians and literature, womanliness as masquerade, and the role of film and other popular media in the construction of the feminine gender.

Until a few years ago, however, feminist thought tended to be classified not according to topic but, rather, according to country of origin. This practice reflected the fact that, during the 1970s and early 1980s, French, American, and British feminists wrote from somewhat different perspectives.

French feminists tended to focus their attention on language, analyzing the ways in which meaning is produced. They concluded that language as we commonly think of it is a decidedly male realm. Drawing on the ideas of the psychoanalytic philosopher Jacques Lacan, they reminded us that language is a realm of public discourse. A child enters the linguistic realm just as it comes to grasp its separateness from its mother, just about the time that boys identify with their father, the family representative of culture. The language learned reflects a binary logic that opposes such terms as active/passive, masculine/feminine, sun/moon, father/mother, head/heart, son/daughter, intelligent/sensitive, brother/sister, form/matter, phallus/vagina, reason/emotion. Because this logic tends to group with masculinity such qualities as light, thought, and activity, French feminists said that the structure of language is phallocentric: it privileges the phallus and, more generally, masculinity by associating them with things and values more appreciated by the (masculine-dominated) culture. Moreover, French feminists suggested, "masculine desire dominates speech and posits woman as an idealized fantasy-fulfillment for the incurable emotional lack caused by separation from the mother" (Jones, "Inscribing" 83).

French feminists associated language with separation from the mother. Its distinctions, they argued, represent the world from the male point of view. Language systematically forces women to choose: either they can imagine and represent themselves as men imagine and represent them (in which case they may speak, but will speak as men) or they can choose "silence," becoming in the process "the invisible and unheard sex" (Jones, "Inscribing" 83).

But some influential French feminists maintained that language only seems to give women such a narrow range of choices. There is another possibility, namely, that women can develop a feminine language. In various ways, early French feminists such as Annie Leclerc, Xavière Gauthier, and Marguerite Duras suggested that there is something that may be called *l'écriture féminine*: women's writing. More recently, Julia Kristeva has said that feminine language is *semiotic*, not *symbolic*. Rather than rigidly opposing and ranking elements of reality, rather than symbolizing one thing but not another in terms of a third, feminine language is rhythmic and unifying. If from the male perspective it seems fluid to the point of being chaotic, that is a fault of the male perspective.

According to Kristeva, feminine language is derived from the pre-oedipal period of fusion between mother and child. Associated with the maternal, feminine language is not only a threat to culture, which is patriarchal, but also a medium through which women may be creative in new ways. But Kristeva paired her central, liberating claim—that truly feminist innovation in all fields requires an understanding of the relation between maternity and feminine creation—with a warning. A feminist language that refuses to participate in "masculine" discourse, that places its future entirely in a feminine, semiotic discourse, risks being politically marginalized by men. That is to say, it risks being relegated to the outskirts (pun intended) of what is considered socially and politically significant. Kristeva, who associated feminine writing with the female body, was joined in her views by other leading French feminists. Hélène Cixous, for instance, also posited an essential connection between the woman's body, whose sexual pleasure has been repressed and denied expression, and women's writing. "Write your self. Your body must be heard," Cixous urged; once they learn to write their bodies, women will not only realize their sexuality but enter history and move toward a future based on a "feminine" economy of giving rather than the "masculine" economy of hoarding (Cixous, "Laugh" 880). For Luce Irigaray, women's sexual pleasure (*jouissance*) cannot be expressed by the dominant, ordered, "logical," masculine language. Irigaray explored the connection between women's sexuality and women's language through the following analogy: as women's *jouissance* is more multiple than men's unitary, phallic pleasure ("woman has sex organs just about everywhere"), so "feminine" language is more diffusive than its "masculine" counterpart. ("That is undoubtedly the reason . . . her language . . . goes off in all directions and . . . he is unable to discern the coherence," Irigaray writes [*This Sex* 101–03].) Cixous's and Irigaray's emphasis on feminine writing as an expression of the female body drew criticism from other French feminists. Many argued that an emphasis on the body either reduces "the feminine" to a biological essence or elevates it in a way that shifts the valuation of masculine and feminine but retains the binary categories. For Christine Fauré, Irigaray's celebration of women's difference failed to address the issue of masculine dominance, and Catherine Clément, a Marxist-feminist, warned that *poetic* descriptions of what constitutes the feminine will not challenge that dominance in the realm of production. The boys will still make the toys, and decide who gets to use them. In her effort to redefine women as political rather than as sexual beings, Monique Wittig called for the abolition of the sexual categories that Cixous and Irigaray retained and revalued as they celebrated women's writing.

American feminist critics of the 1970s and early 1980s shared with French critics both an interest in and a cautious distrust of the concept of feminine writing. Annette Kolodny, for instance, worried that the "richness and variety of women's writing" will be missed if we see in it only its "feminine mode" or "style" ("Some Notes" 78). And yet Kolodny herself proceeded, in the same essay, to point out that women have had their own style, which includes reflexive constructions (e.g. "she found herself crying") and particular, recurring themes (clothing and self-fashioning are mentioned by Kolodny; other American feminists have focused on madness, disease, and the demonic).

Interested as they became in the "French" subject of feminine style, American feminist critics began by analyzing literary texts rather than philosophizing abstractly about language. Many reviewed the great works by male writers, embarking on a revisionist rereading of literary tradition. These critics examined the portrayals of women characters, exposing the patriarchal ideology implicit in such works and showing how clearly this tradition of systematic masculine dominance is inscribed in our literary tradition. Kate Millett, Carolyn Heilbrun, and Judith Fetterley, among many others, created this model for American feminist criticism, a model that Elaine Showalter came to call "the feminist critique" of "male-constructed literary history" ("Poetics" 128).

Meanwhile another group of critics including Sandra Gilbert, Susan Gubar, Patricia Meyer Spacks, and Showalter herself created a somewhat different model. Whereas feminists writing "feminist critique" analyzed works by men, practitioners of what Showalter used to refer to as "gynocriticism" studied the writings of those women who, against all odds, produced what she calls "a literature of their own." In *The Female Imagination* (1975), Spacks examined the female literary tradition to find out how great women writers across the ages have felt, perceived themselves, and imagined reality. Gilbert and Gubar, in *The Madwoman in the Attic* (1979), concerned themselves with well-known women writers of the nineteenth century, but they too found that general concerns, images, and themes recur, because the authors that they wrote about lived "in a culture whose fundamental definitions of literary authority" were "both overtly and covertly patriarchal" (45–46).

If one of the purposes of gynocriticism was to (re)study well-known women authors, another was to rediscover women's history and culture, particularly women's communities that nurtured female creativity. Still another related purpose was to discover neglected or forgotten women writers and thus to forge an alternative literary tradition, a canon that better represents the female perspective by better representing the literary works that have been written by women. Showalter, in *A Literature of Their Own* (1977), admirably began to fulfill this purpose, providing a remarkably comprehensive overview of women's writing through three of its phases. She defined these as the Feminine, Feminist, and Female phases, phases during which women first imitated a masculine tradition (1840–80), then protested against its standards and values (1880–1920), and finally advocated their own autonomous, female perspective (1920 to the present).

With the recovery of a body of women's texts, attention returned to a question raised in 1978 by Lillian Robinson: Shouldn't feminist criticism need to formulate a theory of its own practice? Won't reliance on theoretical assumptions, categories, and strategies developed by men and associated with nonfeminist schools of thought prevent feminism from being accepted as equivalent to these other critical discourses? Not all American feminists came to believe that a special or unifying theory of feminist practice was urgently needed; Showalter's historical approach to women's culture allowed a feminist critic to use theories based on non-feminist disciplines. Kolodny advocated a playful pluralism that encompasses a variety of critical schools and methods. But Jane Marcus and others responded that if feminists adopt too wide a range of approaches, they may relax the tensions between feminists and the educational establishment necessary for political activism.

The question of whether feminism weakens or fortifies itself by emphasizing its separateness—and by developing unity through separateness—was one of several areas of debate within American feminism during the 1970s and early 1980s. Another area of disagreement touched on earlier, between feminists who stress universal feminine attributes (the feminine imagination, feminine writing) and those who focus on the political conditions experienced by certain groups of women at certain times in history, paralleled a larger distinction between American feminist critics and their British counterparts.

While it gradually became customary to refer to an Anglo-American tradition of feminist criticism, British feminists tended to distinguish themselves from what they saw as an American overemphasis on texts linking women across boundaries and decades and an underemphasis on popular art and culture. They regarded their own critical practice as more political than that of North American feminists, whom they sometimes faulted for being uninterested in historical detail. They joined such American critics as Myra Jehlen in suggesting that a continuing preoccupation with women writers may bring about the dangerous result of placing women's texts outside the history that conditions them.

British feminists felt that the American opposition to male stereotypes that denigrate women often leads to counterstereotypes of feminine virtue that ignore real differences of race, class, and culture among women. In addition, they argued that American celebrations of individual heroines falsely suggest that powerful individuals may be immune to repressive conditions and may even imply that any individual can go through life unconditioned by the culture and ideology in which she or he lives.

Similarly, the American endeavor to recover women's history—for example, by emphasizing that women developed their own strategies to gain power within their sphere—was seen by British feminists as an endeavor that mystifies male oppression, disguising it as something that has created for women a special world of opportunities. More important from the British standpoint, the universalizing and essentializing tendencies in both American practice and French theory disguise women's oppression by highlighting sexual difference, suggesting that a dominant system is impervious to political change. By contrast, British feminist theory emphasized an engagement with historical process in order to promote social change.

By now the French, American, and British approaches have so thoroughly critiqued, influenced, and assimilated one another that the work of most Western practitioners is no longer easily identifiable along national boundary lines. Instead, it tends to be characterized according to whether the category of woman is the major focus in the exploration of gender and gender oppression or, alternatively, whether the interest in sexual difference encompasses an interest in other differences that also define identity. The latter paradigm encompasses the work of feminists of color, Third World (preferably called postcolonial) feminists, and lesbian feminists, many of whom have asked whether the universal category of woman constructed by certain French and North American predecessors is appropriate to describe women in minority groups or non-Western cultures.

These feminists stress that, while all women are female, they are something else as well (such as African American, lesbian, Muslim, Pakistani). This "something else" is precisely what makes them, their problems, and their goals different from those of other women. As Amrit Wilson has pointed out, Asian women living in Britain are expected by their families and communities to preserve Asian cultural traditions; thus, the expression of personal identity through clothing involves a much more serious infraction of cultural rules than it does for a Western woman. Gloria Anzaldúa has spoken personally and eloquently about the experience of many women on the margins of Eurocentric North American culture. "I am a border woman," she writes in *Borderlands/ La Frontera: The New Mestiza* (1987). "I grew up between two cultures, the Mexican (with a heavy Indian influence) and the Anglo. . . . Living on the borders and in margins, keeping intact one's shifting and multiple identity and integrity is like trying to swim in a new element, an 'alien' element" (i).

Instead of being divisive and isolating, this evolution of feminism into feminisms has fostered a more inclusive, global perspective. The era of recovering women's texts—especially texts by white Western women—has been succeeded by a new era in which the goal is to recover entire cultures of women. Two important figures of this new era are Trinh T. Minh-ha and Gayatri Spivak. Spivak, in works such as *In Other Worlds: Essays in Cultural Politics* (1987) and *Outside in the Teaching Machine* (1993), has shown how political independence (generally looked upon by metropolitan Westerners as a simple and beneficial historical and political reversal) has complex implications for "subaltern" or subproletarian women.

The understanding of woman not as a single, deterministic category but rather as the nexus of diverse experiences has led some white, Western, majority feminists like Jane Tompkins and Nancy K. Miller to advocate and practice personal or autobiographical criticism. Once reluctant to inject themselves into their analyses for fear of being labeled idiosyncratic, impressionistic, and subjective by men, some feminists are now openly skeptical of the claims to reason, logic, and objectivity that have been made in the past by male critics. With the advent of more personal feminist critical styles has come a powerful new interest in women's autobiographical writings.

Shari Benstock, who has written personal criticism in her book *Textualizing the Feminine* (1991), was one of the first feminists to argue that traditional autobiography is a gendered, "masculinist" genre. Its established conventions, feminists have recently pointed out, call for a life-plot that turns on action, triumph through conflict, intellectual self-discovery, and often public renown. The body, reproduction, children, and intimate interpersonal relationships are generally well in the background and often absent. Arguing that the lived experiences of women and men differ—women's lives, for instance, are often characterized by interruption and deferral—Leigh Gilmore has developed a theory of women's self-representation in her book *Autobiographics: A Feminist Theory of Self-Representation* (1994).

Autobiographics and personal criticism are only two of a number of recent developments in contemporary feminist criticism. Others alluded to in the first paragraph of this introduction—lesbian studies, performance or "masquerade" theory, and studies of the role played by film and various other "technologies" in shaping gender today—are so prominent in contemporary gender criticism that they are discussed in a separate introduction (see "What Are Gender Criticism and Queer Theory?" pp. 381–400 in this volume). Although that introduction will outline several of the differences between the feminist and gender approaches, the fact of this overlap should remind us that categories obscure similarities even as they help us make distinctions. Feminist criticism is, after all, a form of gender criticism, and gender criticism as we have come to know it could never have developed without feminist criticism.

Johanna M. Smith begins the essay that follows by discussing the nineteenth-century doctrine of "separate spheres" (p. 360), which worked to keep middle-class women at home maintaining a household, raising children, and creating a reenergizing refuge from the workplace for their husbands. So many women characters in *Frankenstein* embrace the domestic life that the novel might seem to advocate the doctrine of separate spheres, but in fact, as Smith points out, it ultimately critiques both " 'the feminine sphere of domesticity' " and its counterpart, " 'the masculine sphere of discovery' " (p. 362).

Smith grounds the terms of that critique in Mary Shelley's dual identity as an author (indeed, as the daughter of authors) and as the wife of a famous writer, Percy Shelley. Smith provides numerous examples both of the tension between those two roles—for instance, Mary's decision to write but to publish anonymously—and of the "negotiations" required of a woman writer (p. 362). (As an example of the attempt to negotiate or resolve the tensions between her gender-coded roles and the public and private spheres, Smith cites Mary's willingness to let Percy edit *Frankenstein*, thereby allowing the novel to become a collaborative effort, however slightly so.)

Turning her attention from author to text, Smith finds the same sorts of tensions and negotiations in *Frankenstein*. She finds them in Victor's father, Alphonse, whose gentle rule at home makes him something of a "feminine patriarch" (p. 364), and in Henry Clerval "a model of internalized complementarity, of conjoined masculine and feminine traits" (p. 365). Most important, she finds them in Victor's "conflicted" attitude (p. 366) toward what he describes as the "secluded and domestic" life he experienced as a child, the "cooped up" (p. 366) state deemed natural for children as well as for women by the doctrine of separate spheres.

Although some men and women are able successfully to negotiate, respectively, their way into the realm of public adventure and achievement on one hand, or peace with themselves as they remain confined in its gender-coded alternative on the other, Victor Frankenstein is not among them. In addition to doing the bad work of using science to create a monster, he becomes, in turn, the epitome of the "bad father," demanding rather than deserving gratitude and abandoning rather than supporting his "'child'" (p. 367). Smith suggests that the failure of his "domestic instruction" to "produce a better Victor" (p. 365) may be read as an implicit if incomplete critique of the doctrine of separate spheres.

When Smith turns her attention to science, we might expect to read that science is a masculine undertaking in the public arena of discovery. Instead Smith distinguishes between kinds of science, using Thomas Kuhn's concept of paradigm shifts and Michel Foucault's concept of a genealogy of subjugated knowledges to suggest that the transition from alchemy (Victor's father calls it "sad trash" [p. 45]) and the work of the "electricians" to modern chemistry as understood by Erasmus Darwin and Humphry Davy is a scientific paradigm shift (p. 371). Thus, alchemy and the science of the electricians are subjugated knowledges that have, as it were, been domesticated and feminized in the sense that they have been declared off-limits in the public life of masculine knowledges.

Victor's transition from alchemy to modern science is "incomplete" (p. 372), Smith argues, and because he (not unlike his author, who was similarly torn between spheres deemed irreconcilable by many) has not yet left the old paradigm behind, he retires with his modern knowledge of chemistry to what he calls the "solitary chamber" of alchemy to create a monster whose subsequent rebellion may be seen as analogous to Mary Shelley's incipient but incomplete rebellion against and transition from the doctrine of separate spheres. Thus, according to Smith, a "feminist adaptation of Kuhn's and Foucault's ideas can show" that, "as the monster enacts the insurrection of subjugated sciences he also enacts Victor's rebellion against domesticity" (p. 373).

Smith's essay exemplifies feminist criticism in a number of ways. Her analysis of Mary Shelley as a novelist and wife advances the historic interest of French and American feminists in women's writing and writers. Her emphasis on the role played by culturally pervasive ideologies in shaping the experiences of women and women writers (according to their social class) and the content and structure of literary texts advances the historical interest of British feminism and of cultural feminist criticism. Smith's essay exemplifies contemporary feminist thought insofar as it overlaps with gender criticism, whose practitioners tend to be less interested in "essential" differences between women and men than in the gender-coded differences that society constructs and imposes (through such mechanisms as the nineteenth-century doctrine of separate spheres). Equally contemporary—and equally relevant to gender theory—is the emphasis Smith places on science, a form of knowledge that has played no small role in defining and perpetuating gender differences but whose paradigms, as Smith suggests, can be adapted to serve the ends of feminist analysis, feminist critique.

Ross C Murfin

# FEMINIST CRITICISM:
## A SELECTED BIBLIOGRAPHY

### Feminist Theory: Classic Texts, General Approaches, Collections

Abel, Elizabeth, and Emily K. Abel, eds. *The Signs Reader: Women, Gender, and Scholarship.* Chicago: U of Chicago P, 1983. Print.

Alaimo, Stacy, and Susan J. Hekman, eds. *Material Feminisms.* Bloomington: Indiana UP, 2008. Print.

Barrett, Michèle, and Anne Phillips. *Destabilizing Theory: Contemporary Feminist Debates.* Stanford: Stanford UP, 1992. Print.

Benstock, Shari, ed. *Feminist Issues in Literary Scholarship.* Bloomington: Indiana UP, 1987. Print.

de Beauvoir, Simone. *The Second Sex.* 1949. Trans. and ed. H. M. Parshley. New York: Vintage, 1974. Print.

de Lauretis, Teresa, ed. *Feminist Studies/Critical Studies.* Bloomington: Indiana UP, 1986. Print.

Eagleton, Mary, ed. *Feminist Literary Theory: A Reader.* 2nd ed. Oxford: Blackwell, 1996. Print.

Fetterley, Judith. *The Resisting Reader: A Feminist Approach to American Fiction.* Bloomington: Indiana UP, 1978. Print.

Fuss, Diana. *Essentially Speaking: Feminism, Nature and Difference.* New York: Routledge, 1989. Print.

Gallop, Jane. *Around 1981: Academic Feminist Critical Theory.* New York: Routledge, 1992. Print.

Gilbert, Sandra M., and Susan Gubar, eds. *Feminist Literary Theory and Critism: A Norton Reader.* New York: Norton, 2007. Print.

Greer, Germaine. *The Female Eunuch.* New York: McGraw, 1971. Print.

hooks, bell. *Feminist Theory: From Margin to Center.* Boston: South End, 1984. Print.

Keohane, Nannerl O., Michelle Z. Rosaldo, and Barbara C. Gelpi, eds. *Feminist Theory: A Critique of Ideology.* Chicago: U of Chicago P, 1982. Print.

Kolodny, Annette. "Dancing Through the Minefield: Some Observations on the Theory, Practice, and Politics of a Feminist Literary Criticism." Rpt. in Showalter, *New Feminist Criticism* 144–67. Print.

———. "Some Notes on Defining a 'Feminist Literary Criticism.'" *Critical Inquiry* 2 (1975): 75–92. Print.

Lovell, Terry, ed. *British Feminist Thought: A Reader.* Oxford: Basil Blackwell, 1990. Print.

Malson, Micheline, et al., eds. *Feminist Theory in Practice and Process.* Chicago: U of Chicago P, 1986. Print.

Meese, Elizabeth. *Crossing the Double-Cross: The Practice of Feminist Criticism.* Chapel Hill: U of North Carolina P, 1986. Print.

Miller, Nancy K., ed. *The Poetics of Gender.* New York: Columbia UP, 1986. Print.

Millett, Kate. *Sexual Politics.* Garden City: Doubleday, 1970. Print.

Nicholson, Linda, ed. *The Second Wave: A Reader in Feminist Theory.* New York: Routledge, 1997. Print.

Rich, Adrienne. *On Lies, Secrets, and Silence: Selected Prose, 1966–1979.* New York: Norton, 1979. Print.

Showalter, Elaine, ed. *The New Feminist Criticism: Essays on Women, Literature, and Theory.* New York: Pantheon, 1985. Print.

———. "Toward a Feminist Poetics." *New Feminist Criticism* 125–43.

———. "Women's Time, Women's Space: Writing the History of Feminist Criticism." *Tulsa Studies in Women's Literature* 3 (1984): 29–43. Print. Rpt. in Benstock, *Feminist Issues in Literary Scholarship* 30–44.

*Signs@40: Feminist Scholarship through Four Decades.* Spec. issue of *Signs* 40 (2014). Ed. Andrew Mazzaschi. Web. 14 November 2014. <http://signsat40.signsjournal.org.>

Stimpson, Catherine R. "Feminist Criticism." *Redrawing the Boundaries: The Transformation of English and American Literary Studies.* Ed. Stephen Greenblatt and Giles Gunn. New York: MLA, 1992. 251–70. Print.

———. *Where the Meanings Are: Feminism and Cultural Spaces.* New York: Methuen, 1988. Print.

Warhol-Down, Robyn R., and Diane Price Herndl, eds. *Feminisms: An Anthology of Literary Criticism and Theory.* Rev. ed. New Brunswick: Rutgers UP, 2007. Print.

Weed, Elizabeth, ed. *Coming to Terms: Feminism, Theory, Politics.* New York: Routledge, 1989. Print.

Woolf, Virginia. *A Room of One's Own.* New York: Harcourt, 1929. Print.

## French Feminist Theory

Cixous, Hélène. *"Coming to Writing" and Other Essays.* Ed. Deborah Jenson. Trans. Sarah Cornell. Cambridge: Harvard UP, 1991. Print.

———. "The Laugh of the Medusa." Trans. Keith Cohen and Paula Cohen. *Signs* 1 (1976): 875–94. Print.

———. *The Newly Born Woman.* Trans. Betsy Wing. Minneapolis: U of Minnesota P, 1986. Print.

*Feminist Readings: French Texts/American Contexts.* Spec. issue of *Yale French Studies* 62 (1981). Ed. Colette Gaudin. Print.

*Feminist Theory.* Spec. issue of *Signs* 7.1 (1981). Print.

Irigaray, Luce. *An Ethics of Sexual Difference.* Trans. Carolyn Burke and Gillian C. Gill. Ithaca: Cornell UP, 1993. Print.

———. *This Sex Which Is Not One.* Trans. Catherine Porter. Ithaca: Cornell UP, 1985. Print.

Jardine, Alice A. *Gynesis: Configurations of Woman and Modernity.* Ithaca: Cornell UP, 1985. Print.

Jones, Ann Rosalind. "Inscribing Femininity: French Theories of the Feminine." *Making a Difference: Feminist Literary Criticism.* Ed. Gayle Green and Coppélia Kahn. London: Methuen, 1985. 80–112. Print.

———. "Writing the Body: Toward an Understanding of *L'Écriture féminine.*" Showalter, *New Feminist Criticism* 361–77.

Kristeva, Julia. *Desire in Language: A Semiotic Approach to Literature and Art.* Ed. Leon S. Roudiez. Trans. Thomas Gora, Alice Jardine, and Leon S. Roudiez. New York: Columbia UP, 1980. Print.

Marks, Elaine, and Isabelle de Courtivron, eds. *New French Feminisms: An Anthology.* Amherst: U of Massachusetts P, 1980. Print.

Moi, Toril, ed. *French Feminist Thought: A Reader.* Oxford: Basil Blackwell, 1987. Print.

Spivak, Gayatri Chakravorty. "French Feminism in an International Frame." *Yale French Studies* 62 (1981): 154–84. Print.

Stanton, Domna C. "Language and Revolution: The Franco-American Dis-Connection." *The Future of Difference.* Ed. Hester Eisenstein and Alice Jardine. Boston: G. K. Hall, 1980. 73–87. Print.

Wittig, Monique. *Les Guérillères.* 1969. Trans. David Le Vay. New York: Avon, 1973. Print.

## Women's Writing and Creativity

Abel, Elizabeth, ed. *Writing and Sexual Difference.* Chicago: U of Chicago P, 1982. Print.

Abel, Elizabeth, Marianne Hirsch, and Elizabeth Langland, eds. *The Voyage In: Fictions of Female Development.* Hanover: UP of New England, 1983. Print.

Auerbach, Nina. *Communities of Women: An Idea in Fiction.* Cambridge: Harvard UP, 1978. Print.

Benstock, Shari. "Reading the Signs of Women's Writing." *Tulsa Studies in Women's Literature* 4 (1985): 5–15. Print.

Diehl, Joanne Feit. "Come Slowly Eden: An Exploration of Women Writers and Their Muse." *Signs* 3 (1978): 572–87. Print.

DuPlessis, Rachel Blau. *The Pink Guitar: Writing as Feminist Practice.* New York: Routledge, 1990. Print.

Finke, Laurie. *Feminist Theory, Women's Writing.* Ithaca: Cornell UP, 1992. Print.

Gilbert, Sandra M., and Susan Gubar. *The Madwoman in the Attic: The Woman Writer and the Nineteenth-Century Literary Imagination.* New Haven: Yale UP, 1979. Print.

Homans, Margaret. *Bearing the Word: Language and Female Experience in Nineteenth-Century Women's Writing.* Chicago: U of Chicago P, 1986. Print.

Jacobus, Mary, ed. *Women Writing and Writing about Women.* New York: Barnes, 1979. Print.

Miller, Nancy K., ed. *The Poetics of Gender.* New York: Columbia UP, 1986. Print.

———. *Subject to Change: Reading Feminist Writing.* New York: Columbia UP, 1988. Print.

Montefiore, Janet. "Feminine Identity and the Poetic Tradition." *Feminist Review* 13 (1983): 69–94. Print.

Newton, Judith Lowder. *Women, Power and Subversion: Social Strategies in British Fiction, 1778–1860.* Athens: U of Georgia P, 1981. Print.

Poovey, Mary. *The Proper Lady and the Woman Writer: Ideology as Style in the Works of Mary Wollstonecraft, Mary Shelley, and Jane Austen.* Chicago: U of Chicago P, 1984. Print.

Showalter, Elaine. *Daughters of Decadence: Women Writers of the Fin-de-Siècle.* New Brunswick: Rutgers UP, 1993. Print.

———. *A Literature of Their Own: British Women Novelists from Brontë to Lessing.* Princeton: Princeton UP, 1977. Print.

———. "Women Who Write Are Women." *New York Times Book Review* I (December 16, 1984): 31–33. Print.

### Women's History/Women's Studies

Bridenthal, Renate, et al., ed. *Becoming Visible: Women in European History.* Rev. ed. Boston: Houghton Mifflin, 1998. Print.

Donovan, Josephine. "Feminism and Aesthetics." *Critical Inquiry* 3 (1977): 605–8. Print.

Farnham, Christie, ed. *The Impact of Feminist Research in the Academy.* Bloomington: Indiana UP, 1987. Print.

Kelly, Joan. *Women, History & Theory: The Essays of Joan Kelly.* Chicago: U of Chicago P, 1984. Print.

McConnell-Ginet, Sally, et al., eds. *Woman and Language in Literature and Society.* New York: Praeger, 1980. Print.

Mitchell, Juliet, and Ann Oakley, eds. *The Rights and Wrongs of Women.* London: Penguin, 1976. Print.

Riley, Denise. *"Am I That Name?": Feminism and the Category of Women in History.* Minneapolis: U of Minnesota P, 1988. Print.

Rowbotham, Sheila. *Woman's Consciousness, Man's World.* Harmondsworth, UK: Penguin, 1973. Print.

Spacks, Patricia Meyer. *The Female Imagination.* New York: Knopf, 1975. Print.

### Feminisms and Sexualities

Fausto-Sterling, Anne. *Sexing the Body: Gender, Politics and the Construction of Sexuality.* New York: Basic, 2000. Print.

Snitow, Ann, Christine Stansell, and Sharon Thompson, eds. *Powers of Desire: The Politics of Sexuality.* New York: Monthly Review, 1983. Print.

Stryker, Susan, ed. *The Transgender Studies Reader.* London: Routledge, 2006. Print.

Vance, Carole S., ed. *Pleasure and Danger: Exploring Female Sexuality.* Boston: Routledge, 1984. Print.

## Feminism, Race, Class, and Nationality

Anzaldúa, Gloria. *BorderlandsLa Frontera: The New Mestiza.* San Francisco: Spinsters/Aunt Lute, 1987. Print.

Christian, Barbara. *Black Feminist Criticism: Perspectives on Black Women Writers.* New York: Pergamon, 1985. Print.

Collins, Patricia Hill. *Black Feminist Thought: Knowledge, Consciousness, and the Politics of Empowerment.* Boston: Hyman, 1990. Print.

hooks, bell. *Ain't I a Woman? Black Women and Feminism.* Boston: South End, 1981. Print.

———. *Black Looks: Race and Representation.* Boston: South End, 1992. Print.

Mitchell, Juliet. *Woman's Estate.* New York: Pantheon, 1971. Print.

Moraga, Cherrie, and Gloria Anzaldúa, eds. *This Bridge Called My Back: Writings by Radical Women of Color.* New York: Kitchen Table, 1981. Print.

Newton, Judith, and Deborah Rosenfelt, eds. *Feminist Criticism and Social Change: Sex, Class, and Race in Literature and Culture.* New York: Methuen, 1985. Print.

Newton, Judith Lowder, Mary P. Ryan, and Judith R. Walkowitz, eds. *Sex and Class in Women's History.* London: Routledge, 1983. Print.

Pryse, Marjorie, and Hortense Spillers, eds. *Conjuring: Black Women, Fiction, and Literary Tradition.* Bloomington: Indiana UP, 1985. Print.

Robinson, Lillian S. *Sex, Class, and Culture.* 1978. New York: Methuen, 1986. Print.

Smith, Barbara. *The Truth That Never Hurts: Writing on Race, Gender, and Freedom.* New Brunswick: Rutgers UP, 1998. Print. See esp. "Toward a Black Feminist Criticism."

## Women's Self-Representation and Personal Criticism

Benstock, Shari, ed. *The Private Self: Theory and Practice of Women's Autobiographical Writings.* Chapel Hill: U of North Carolina P, 1988. Print.

Brodski, Bella, and Celeste Schenck, eds. *Life/Lines: Theorizing Women's Autobiography.* Ithaca: Cornell UP, 1988. Print.

Gilmore, Leigh. *Autobiographics: A Feminist Theory of Self-Representation.* Ithaca: Cornell UP, 1994. Print.

Miller, Nancy K. *Getting Personal: Feminist Occasions and Other Autobiographical Acts.* New York: Routledge, 1991. Print.

### Intersections between Feminist and Film Theory

Carson, Diane, Janice R. Welsch, and Linda Dittmar, eds. *Multiple Voices in Feminist Film Criticism.* Minneapolis: U of Minnesota P, 1994. Print.

de Lauretis, Teresa. *Alice Doesn't: Feminism, Semiotics, Cinema.* Bloomington: Indiana UP, 1986. Print.

———. *The Cinematic Apparatus.* London: Macmillan, 1980. Print.

Doane, Mary Ann, Patricia Mellencamp, and Linda Williams, eds. *Re-vision: Essays in Feminist Film Criticism.* Frederick, MD: University Publications of America, 1984. Print.

Erens, Patricia, ed. *Issues in Feminist Film Criticism.* Bloomington: Indiana UP, 1990. Print.

McHugh, Kathleen, and Vivian Sobchack, eds. *Beyond the Gaze: Recent Approaches to Film Feminisms.* Spec. issue of *Signs* 30.1 (Aut. 2004). Print.

Modleski, Tania. *Feminism without Women: Culture and Criticism in a "Postfeminist" Age.* New York: Routledge, 1991. Print.

Mulvey, Laura. *Visual and Other Pleasures.* Bloomington: Indiana UP, 1989. Print.

Penley, Constance, ed. *Feminism and Film Theory.* New York: Routledge, 1988. Print.

### Intersections between Feminism and Queer Theory

Case, Sue-Ellen. *Feminist and Queer Performance: Critical Strategies.* Basingstoke, UK: Palgrave Macmillan, 2009. Print.

Giffney, Noreen. "Denormatizing Queer Theory: More Than (Simply) Lesbian and Gay Studies." *Feminist Theory* 5.1 (2004): 73–78. Print.

Green, Adam I. "Gay but Not Queer: Toward a Post-Queer Study of Sexuality." *Theory and Society* 31 (2002): 521–45. Print.

Harris, Laura Alexandra. "Queer Black Feminism: The Pleasure Principle." *Feminist Review* 54 (Aut. 1996): 3–30. Print.

Lovaas, Karen E., et al., eds. *LGBT Studies and Queer Theory: New Conflicts, Collaborations, and Contested Terrain.* New York: Routledge. 2007. Print.

Piontek, Thomas. *Queering Gay and Lesbian Studies.* Urbana: U of Illinois P, 2006. Print.

Richardson, Diane, et al., eds. *Intersections between Feminist and Queer Theory*. Houndmills: Palgrave Macmillan, 2006. Print.

Weed, Elizabeth, and Naomi Schor, eds. *Feminism Meets Queer Theory*. Indianapolis: Indiana UP, 1997. Print.

## Intersections between Feminism and Postcolonial Theory and Criticism

Anzaldúa, Gloria. *Borderlands/La Frontera: The New Mestiza*. San Francisco: Spinsters/Aunt Lute, 1987. Print.

Azim, Firdous. *The Colonial Rise of the Novel*. London: Routledge, 1993. Print.

Emberley, Julia. *Thresholds of Difference: Feminist Critique, Native Women's Writings, Postcolonial Theory*. Toronto: U of Toronto P, 1993. Print.

Ghosh, Bishnupriya, and Brinda Bose, eds. *Interventions: Feminist Dialogues on Third World Women's Literature and Film*. New York: Garland, 1997. Print.

Jayawardena, Kumari. *Feminism and Nationalism in the Third World*. New Delhi: Kali for Women, 1986. Print.

Kwok, Pui-lan. *Postcolonial Imagination and Feminist Theology*. Louisville, KY: Westminster John Knox, 2005. Print.

Lewis, Reina, and Sara Mills, eds. *Feminist Postcolonial Theory: A Reader*. Edinburgh: Edinburgh UP, 2003. Print.

McClintock, Anne, Aamir Mufti, and Ella Shohat, eds. *Dangerous Liaisons: Gender, Nation, and Postcolonial Perspectives*. Minneapolis: U of Minnesota P, 1997. Print.

Mills, Sara. *Gender and Colonial Space*. Manchester and New York: Manchester UP, 2005. Print.

Mohanty, Chandra Talpade, et al., eds. *Third World Women and the Politics of Feminism*. Bloomington: Indiana UP, 1991. Print.

Schipper, Mineke, ed. *Unheard Words: Women and Literature in Africa, the Arab World, Asia, the Caribbean, and Latin America*. London: Allison, 1985. Print.

Sharpe, Jenny. *Allegories of Empire: The Figure of the Woman in the Colonial Text*. Minneapolis. U of Minnesota P, 1993. Print.

Spivak, Gayatri Chakravorty. *In Other Worlds: Essays in Cultural Politics*. New York: Methuen, 1987. Print.

———. *Outside in the Teaching Machine*. New York: Routledge, 1993. Print.

Wilson, Amrit. *Finding a Voice: Asian Women in Britain*. 1979. London: Virago, 1980. Print.

Yeğenoğlu, Meyda. *Colonial Fantasies: Towards a Feminist Reading of Orientalism*. Cambridge UP, 1998 Print.

## Intersections between Feminism and Other Critical Approaches

Armstrong, Nancy, ed. *Literature as Women's History I*. Spec. issue of *Genre* 19–20 (1986–1987). Print.

Barrett, Michèle. *Women's Oppression Today: Problems in Marxist Feminist Analysis*. London: Verso, 1980. Print.

Belsey, Catherine, and Jane Moore, eds. *The Feminist Reader: Essays in Gender and the Politics of Literary Criticism*. New York: Basil Blackwell, 1989. Print.

Benjamin, Jessica. *The Bonds of Love: Psychoanalysis, Feminism, and the Problem of Domination*. New York: Pantheon, 1988. Print.

Benstock, Shari. *Textualizing the Feminine: On the Limits of Genre*. Norman: U of Oklahoma P, 1991. Print.

Butler, Judith, and Joan W. Scott, eds. *Feminists Theorize the Political*. New York: Routledge, 1992. Print.

Delphy, Christine. *Close to Home: A Materialist Analysis of Women's Oppression*. Trans. and ed. Diana Leonard. Amherst: U of Massachusetts P, 1984. Print.

Deutscher, Penelope. *Yielding Gender: Feminism, Deconstruction, and the History of Philosophy*. London: Routledge, 1997. Print.

Dimock, Wai-chee. "Feminism, New Historicism, and the Reader." *American Literature* 63 (1991): 601–22. Print.

Elam, Diane. *Feminism and Deconstruction*. London: Routledge, 1994. Print.

Felman, Shoshana. "Women and Madness: The Critical Fallacy." *Diacritics* 5 (1975): 2–10.

———, ed. *Literature and Psychoanalysis: The Questions of Reading: Otherwise*. Baltimore: Johns Hopkins UP, 1982. Print.

*Feminism and Deconstruction*. Spec. issue of *Feminist Studies* 14 (1988). Print.

Flynn, Elizabeth A., and Patrocinio P. Schweickart, eds. *Gender and Reading: Essays on Readers, Texts and Contexts*. Baltimore: Johns Hopkins UP, 1986. Print.

Gaard, Greta, and Patrick D. Murphy, eds. *Ecofeminist Literary Criticism: Theory, Interpretation, Pedagogy.* Urbana: U of Illinois P, 1998. Print.

Gallop, Jane. *The Daughter's Seduction: Feminism and Psychoanalysis.* Ithaca: Cornell UP, 1982. Print.

Gamer, Shirley Nelson. *The (M)other Tongue: Essays in Feminist Psychoanalytic Interpretation.* Ithaca: Cornell UP, 1985. Print.

Gilligan, Carol. *In a Different Voice: Psychological Theory and Women's Development.* Cambridge: Harvard UP, 1982. Print.

Hartsock, Nancy C. M. *Money, Sex, and Power: Toward a Feminist Historical Materialism.* Boston: Northeastern UP, 1985. Print.

Higonnet, Margaret, and Joan Templeton, eds. *Reconfigured Spheres: Feminist Explorations of Literary Space.* Amherst: U of Massachusetts P, 1994. Print.

Hohne, Karen, and Helen Wussow, eds. *A Dialogue of Voices: Feminist Literary Theory and Bakhtin.* Minneapolis: U of Minnesota P, 1994. Print.

Holland, Nancy J., ed. *Feminist Interpretations of Jacques Derrida.* University Park: Pennsylvania State UP, 1997. Print.

Kaplan, Cora. *Sea Changes: Essays on Culture and Feminism.* London: Verso, 1986. Print.

Landry, Donna, and Gerald Maclean. *Materialist Feminisms.* Cambridge: Blackwell, 1993. Print.

Meese, Elizabeth, and Alice Parker, eds. *The Difference Within: Feminism and Critical Theory.* Philadelphia: John Benjamins, 1989.

Newton, Judith Lowder. *Starting Over: Feminism and the Politics of Cultural Critique.* Ann Arbor: U of Michigan P, 1994. Print.

Nicholson, Linda J., ed. *Feminism/Postmodernism.* New York: Routledge, 1990. Print.

Riviere, Joan. "Womanliness as Masquerade." *The International Journal of Psycho-Analysis* 10 (1929): 303–13. Rpt. in *Formations of Fantasy.* Ed. Victor Burgin, James Donald, and Cora Kaplan. New York: Methuen, 1986. 35–44. Print.

Mitchell, Juliet, and Jacqueline Rose, eds. Introduction I and Introduction II. *Feminine Sexuality: Jacques Lacan and the école freudienne.* By Lacan. Trans. J. Rose. New York: Norton, 1982. 1–57. Print.

Sargent, Lydia, ed. *Women and Revolution: A Discussion of the Unhappy Marriage of Marxism and Feminism.* Montreal: Black Rose, 1981. Print.

Weedon, Chris. *Feminist Practice and Poststructuralist Theory.* New York: Basil Blackwell, 1987. Print.

## Feminist Readings

Armour, Ellen T. *Deconstruction, Feminist Theology, and the Problem of Difference: Subverting the Race/Gender Divide.* Chicago: U of Chicago P, 1999. Print.

Deutscher, Penelope. *Yielding Gender: Feminism, Deconstruction, and the History of Philosophy.* London: Routledge, 1997. Print.

Flynn, Elizabeth A., and Patrocinio P. Schweickart, eds. *Gender and Reading: Essays on Readers, Texts, and Contexts.* Baltimore: Johns Hopkins UP, 1986. Print.

Gaard, Greta, and Patrick D. Murphy, eds. *Ecofeminist Literary Criticism: Theory, Interpretation, Pedagogy.* Urbana: U of Illinois P, 1998. Print.

Holland, Nancy J., ed. *Feminist Interpretations of Jacques Derrida.* University Park: Pennsylvania State UP, 1997. Print.

Orr, Elaine Neil. *Subject to Negotiation: Reading Feminist Criticism and American Women's Fictions.* Charlottesville: UP of Virginia, 1997. Print.

Straus, Barrie Ruth, ed. *Skirting the Texts: Feminisms' Re-reading of Medieval and Renaissance Texts: A Special Issue on Feminism, Theory, and Medieval and Renaissance Texts.* Spec. issue of *Exemplaria* 4.1 (Spring 1992). Print.

## Feminist Criticism of *Frankenstein*

Carson, James B. "Bringing the Author Forward: *Frankenstein* through Mary Shelley's Letters." *Criticism* 30.4 (Fall 1988): 431–53. Print.

Castellano, Katey. "Feminism to Ecofeminism: The Legacy of Gilbert and Gubar's Readings of Mary Shelley's *Frankenstein* and *The Last Man*." *Gilbert and Gubar's* The Madwoman in the Attic *After Thirty Years*. Ed. Annette R. Federico Columbia: U of Missouri P, 2009. 76–93. Print.

Gilbert, Sandra M., and Susan Gubar. *The Madwoman in the Attic: The Woman Writer and the Nineteenth-Century Literary Imagination.* New Haven: Yale UP, 1979. Print.

Homans, Margaret. *Bearing the Word: Language and Female Experience in Nineteenth-Century Woman's Writing.* Chicago: U of Chicago P, 1986. Print.

Kranzler, Laura. "Frankenstein and the Technological Future." *Foundation* 44 (Win. 1988–89): 42–49. Print.

Labbe, Jacqueline M. "A Monstrous Fiction: *Frankenstien* and the Wifely Ideal." *Women's Writing* 6.3 (1999): 345–63. Print.

Pon, Cynthia. "'Passage' in Mary Shelley's *Frankenstein:* Toward a Feminist Figure of Humanity?" *Modern Language Studies* 30.2 (2000): 33–50. Print.

Spivak, Gayatri Chakravorty. "Three Women's Texts and a Critique of Imperialism." *Critical Inquiry* 12.1 (1985): 243–61. Print.

Stange, Margit. "'You must create a female': Republican Order and its Natural Base in *Frankenstien.*" *Women's Studies* 29.3 (2000): 309–31. Print.

## A FEMINIST PERSPECTIVE

### JOHANNA M. SMITH

### "Cooped Up" with "Sad Trash": Domesticity and the Sciences in *Frankenstein*

It is important to note that *Frankenstein* was published anonymously, that its woman author kept her identity hidden. Similarly, no women in the novel speak directly: everything we hear from and about them is filtered through the three male narrators. In addition, these women seldom venture far from home, while the narrators and most of the novel's other men engage in quests and various public occupations. These facts exemplify the nineteenth century's emerging concept of separate spheres, a concept that itself exemplifies a middle-class ideology of domesticity. That is, as the man's public sphere of commerce and activity was kept distinct from the woman's private sphere of home and passivity, and as certain traits (such as aggression) were coded as "naturally" masculine while the complementary traits (such as nurturance) were coded as "naturally" feminine, the woman's sphere and attributes were delimited to the domestic. I begin by discussing the workings of this ideology where one might expect to find them, in the life of the woman writer Mary Shelley and in the domestic relations of her novel *Frankenstein*. I then go on to show how the binaries that structure the ideology of separate spheres also structure the contemporary science that *Frankenstein* critiques.

   First, some caveats. Recently some feminist scholars have argued
that the focus on separate spheres which has long characterized feminist
criticism has outlived its usefulness. Certainly it is true that upper-class
women were less restricted by this ideology than middle-class women,
and working-class women continued to do paid work outside the home;
indeed, the domestic sphere of upper- and middle-class ladies was maintained by the labor of working-class women, especially that of their servants. It is also true that some middle-class women were able to turn
an ideology of domesticity to limited account in the public sphere: by a
sort of extended domesticity which validated their reforming work in
such public institutions as workhouses and prisons, and by writing novels that "participate[d] in national issues . . . otherwise conducted by
men" (Kelly 200). By and large, however, middle-class women were
expected to maintain a home for their menfolk. And that home was to
be not only, as one of domesticity's stoutest ideologues put it, "a relief
from the severer duties of life," but also a protection from the taint of
those duties (Sarah Ellis 12); a man could thus "pursue the necessary
avocation of the day" but also "keep as it were a separate soul for his
family, his social duty, and his God" (Sarah Ellis 20). Hence it seems to
me still useful to explore the problems that such ideological expectations posed for some women.
   We might infer from *Frankenstein*'s women that Mary Shelley
accepted and even approved the concept of separate and gendered
spheres; Elizabeth in particular is a veritable catalog of ideologically
sound feminine qualities. Yet it is also true that Elizabeth and the domestic sphere she represents fail signally in their *raison d'être*, which is to
prepare young men like Victor Frankenstein to resist the temptations of
the public sphere. The novel shows that the private virtues inculcated in
the home by the domestic affections cannot arm men against the public
sphere unless they emulate these feminine and domestic qualities. And
while Victor often reiterates his "warmest admiration" (p. 133 in this
volume) for Elizabeth's qualities, he perceives them not as his model but
as a "reward" and "consolation" for his trials (p. 134). Similarly, while
he may wax eloquent on the domestic "lesson of patience, of charity,
and of self-control" taught him as a child (p. 41), his quest for scientific
glory demonstrates that none of this lesson took. These contradictions
may suggest that domestic affection can instill its lessons only if it is
"hardy enough to survive in the world outside the home" (Kate Ellis
140), but *Frankenstein* also dramatizes how difficult is that achievement. From this point of view, *Frankenstein* may be said to critique a
bifurcated social order "that separates 'outer' and 'inner,' the masculine

sphere of discovery and the feminine sphere of domesticity" (Kate Ellis 124). How could the home be both a nursery of public virtue and a shelter from the public sphere? Indeed, what would be the use of the "separate soul" touted by Sarah Ellis if its qualities were never activated in/for the public sphere? Although an ideology of domesticity attempts to paper over such contradictions, they are glaringly represented in the Victor Frankenstein who "procrastinate[s] all that related to my feelings of affection" (p. 58) for home and family in order to pursue masculine scientific labors in the public sphere.

Similar contradictions appear in Mary Shelley's negotiations between public and private in her career as a woman writer. In her 1831 introduction to *Frankenstein*, she recalls that her private, domestic role — "the cares of a family" (p. 21) — long kept her from fulfilling her desire for the public fame her parents had won through writing. Even when she went public with *Frankenstein* in 1818, she remained to some extent private by publishing it anonymously. Some of this desire for privacy may have been due to Mary's various family relations. She was certainly aware of the contumely directed at her mother's unconventional life and at both her parents for their radical writing, and her husband Percy and their friend Lord Byron had been similarly vilified for their lives and work. After her elopement Mary had come in for her own share of public comment on her private life, such as the rumors, which she knew of, that her father had sold her to Percy (*Letters* 1:4). Furthermore, "as the daughter of two literary celebrities" (May 493) Mary at birth "immediately entered the speculative economy of the marketplace"; publishing anonymously, then, may have reduced the pressure of expectations on "a name so heavily intertextualized" (Duyfhuizen 477). In conjunction with these personal reasons for desiring privacy, however, may well have been cultural pressures, gendered expectations about women's writing.

The negotiations necessary for a woman to write her way into the public sphere are hinted in the history of a letter Mary wrote to Percy on 30 September 1817. On this date *Frankenstein* was with the publisher, halfway between a private and a public state; Percy, not Mary, was in London editing the proofs. In her letter Mary animadverted at length on the politics of a pamphlet by the radical William Cobbett, and Percy apparently showed these private comments on public affairs to their mutual friend Leigh Hunt, editor of the weekly *Examiner*. Without informing Mary, Hunt then made these comments public by quoting them in an editorial. Although he did not name Mary, he did make a point of her gender, describing her as "a lady of what is called a masculine understanding, that is to say, of great natural abilities not obstructed by a bad education" (qtd. in *Letters* 1:54, fn.2). Mary's letter reads somewhat breathlessly—like much of the manuscript *Frankenstein*, for instance, it is punctuated only by dashes—and she felt it "cut a very foolish figure" in print (1:53). Had she known Hunt would make her remarks public, she told Percy, she would have written with "more print-worthy dignity"; instead, the letter was "so femininely [sic] expressed that all men of letters will on reading it acquit me of having a masculine understanding."

What this incident illuminates is the separate spheres of writing and of literacy. That is, Hunt genders "great natural abilities" as masculine, and such abilities would be showcased in the "print-worthy dignity" of a masculine Latinate prose—the product of a public-school and university education, available at this time only to men, which taught writing on the model of Latin prose. Natural abilities "obstructed" by the "bad" education most women could expect to receive, in contrast, are feminized—obscured, weakened. Letters in particular were often characterized as "femininely expressed," that is, ill-spelt and rambling prattle, and like the private letter, the public genre of the epistolary novel was "long associated with women's writing" (Behrendt 71). For Mary Shelley to name herself as *Frankenstein*'s author, then, might be to endanger her status as honorary man, to risk having her "masculine understanding" impugned as "femininely expressed." Small wonder that a woman writer, especially a woman writer as visible in the specular and speculative economy of the marketplace as Mary Shelley (May 493), might attempt to evade a harsh judgment from "men of letters" by publishing anonymously. Even her apparently straightforward claiming of the novel in her 1831 introduction shows these "tensions between the public Mary Shelley and the private one" (Poovey 118), as several feminist critics have pointed out. Stephen Behrendt calls the introduction Mary's "explicit" and public claim to authorship (84); in contrast, Vanessa Dickerson finds in it further evidence of authorial "passivity" (80); Veronica Hollinger argues that Mary was indeed "careful to represent herself" as an "acceptable . . . version of the woman author," but that this very masquerade, like the "equally conventional portraits" of the novel's women characters, hints that such versions of womanliness are only masquerade, merely an "exemplary performance created in response to male desire" (212–14). And since we know that Percy Shelley laid a heavy editorial hand on the first versions of his wife's manuscript, one might call the novel itself such a performance. It remains important, however, to insist on the tensions of performing gender. In other words, Mary Shelley's willingness to accept her husband's editorial revisions is analogous to *Frankenstein*'s oppressively feminine women: all are efforts to negotiate between public and private, between masculine understanding and feminine expression, between domestic ideology and domestic practice. I turn now to the novel, to show how domestic relationships in *Frankenstein* embody this complex and uneasy set of negotiations.

At first blush, the Frankenstein home seems a model of gender relations under domestic ideology. Not only are Alphonse and Caroline joined in "bonds of devoted affection" (p. 40), they are model parents, "possessed by the very spirit of kindness and indulgence" (p. 44) toward their children. Furthermore, they parent together: they are joint "agents and creators" of Victor's childhood joys; he derives as much pleasure from his father's "smile of benevolent pleasure" as from his mother's "tender caresses"; both parents teach Victor moral lessons of "self-control," gently guiding him with "a silken cord" (p. 41). This shared parenting suggests that fathers have important functions in the feminine domestic sphere; indeed, I would argue that, as a Good Father, Alphonse is feminized. His nurturant qualities were commonly coded as feminine, and it is significant that before his marriage he "relinquished all his public functions" (p. 41) as syndic, and withdrew from the man's sphere of government into the woman's sphere of home. And although he played the traditional masculine role of protector by rescuing Caroline from want, after their marriage this role is domesticated when he "shelter[s] her, as a fair exotic is sheltered by the gardener, from every rougher wind" (p. 41). In these ways Alphonse becomes a sort of feminine patriarch, and his gentle rule by "silken cord" is the reverse of paternal tyranny.

Also ideologically sound is the harmony among the household's children, for it arises from traits that are gendered as opposite yet complementary. This emphasis on gender harmony is particularly apparent in several of Mary's revisions. In her rough draft, for instance, an electrical storm produced "a very different effect" on each child: Victor wanted "to analyze its causes," his friend Henry Clerval "said that the fairies and giants were at war," and Elizabeth "attempted a picture of it" (Robinson 36). Although such differences are retained in the 1831 *Frankenstein*, the focus shifts to Victor and Elizabeth, and to how "diversity and contrast . . . drew us nearer together" (p. 43). For example, Elizabeth "contemplate[s] with a serious and satisfied spirit" the appearance of things while Victor "delight[s] in investigating their causes," but no "disunion or dispute" ensues (p. 43). Throughout the novel, such gendered differences—here, between feminine passivity and masculine activity—are represented as complementary. Thus, although young Victor and Henry actively prepare for public futures while Elizabeth simply exists "like a shrine-dedicated lamp in our peaceful home" (p. 45), what might seem an opposition between the separate gendered spheres is rewritten as complementary difference. And although Elizabeth is little more than "the living spirit of love to soften and attract," as such she performs specifically feminine functions for her men. Her "sympathy," smile, "sweet glance," etc., are "ever there to bless and animate" the boys; she teaches Henry "the real loveliness of beneficence"; crucially, her very presence "subdue[s]" Victor to "a semblance of her own gentleness" (p. 45).

If Elizabeth's femininity is a complement to the boys' masculinity, Henry is a model of internalized complementarity, of conjoined masculine and feminine traits. When Victor is ill at Ingolstadt, Henry takes the role of "kind and attentive nurse" (p. 63) that Elizabeth wished for herself (p. 65). Although Henry aspires to be numbered among the "adventurous benefactors of our species," this masculine "passion for adventurous exploit" is tempered when Elizabeth directs his "soaring ambition" toward "doing good" (p. 45). Unlike Victor's "mad enthusiasm" (p. 158), in short, Henry's "wild and enthusiastic imagination was chastened by the sensibility of his heart" (p. 137). Clearly, Victor's "eager desire" to learn "the *physical* secrets of the world" should have been balanced by Henry's preoccupation with "the *moral* relations of things" (p. 44, emphases added).

Why, then, does this enclave of domestic virtues not produce a better Victor? Why does he not profit from the "lesson of patience, of charity, of self-control" taught by his model parents and embodied in Elizabeth and Henry? Why does he not remain within the boundaries marked off by the "silken cord" of domestic instruction and affection? To ask these questions, of course, is to buy into a "great myth of the Enlightenment" (Rowen 46), the myth of human capacity to be perfected by education and nurture. This myth of perfectibility is central to the politics of Mary Shelley's parents, and while she was skeptical of such optimism her work throughout is deeply engaged with the problematic of education. Hence it is worth asking why Victor's domestic education was so signal a failure, and I approach the question via Victor's complicated relations to feminine domesticity and masculine science.

## COOPED UP

Despite Victor's insistence on his perfect childhood, his reaction to this "remarkably secluded and domestic" home life (p. 50) is in fact conflicted. On the one hand, he is "reluctant" to leave home for university, because there he will have to be "[his] own protector"; on the other hand, he has often felt "cooped up" at home and has "longed to enter the world" (p. 50). This admission jars, especially when one compares it with Victor's earlier statement that "gratitude" to his parents "assisted the developement of filial love" (p. 44). I want to argue, however, that it is this very gratitude that makes him feel "cooped up." Gratitude, no matter how heartfelt, implies obligation to the benefactor, which in turn implies that the benefactor is one up until the debt of gratitude is discharged. It also implies the need to keep track of one's obligations, and most of the relations in the novel are permeated by this bookkeeping mentality. Grateful for Henry's nursing, Victor asks "How shall I ever repay you?" (p. 64); Felix De Lacey sees Safie as the "treasure" that will "fully reward his toil and hazard" in rescuing her father (p. 111); even the creature fumes when "the reward of [his] benevolence" in saving the drowning girl turns out to be "ingratitude" (p. 125). This emotional quid pro quo is most evident, however, in the novel's domestic relations. In this sense the Frankenstein family is "a paradigm of the social contract based on economic terms" (Dussinger 52), for kinship and domestic affection are "secondary to the indebtedness incurred by promises exchanged for gifts." That is, in this family what seems freely given in fact requires something in exchange, so that the relation between parents and children is one of "unpayable debt."

Rather than Victor's picture of "bonds of devoted affection" and a "silken cord" of guidance, then, what emerges is a pattern of constricting domestic relations. Among the Frankensteins, a gift requires gratitude and so produces a sense of obligation, a debt that can be discharged only by endless repetitions of this pattern. Consider Victor's description of the parent-child relation.

> I was . . . their child, the innocent and helpless creature *bestowed* on them by Heaven, whom to bring up to good, and whose future lot it was in their hands to direct to happiness or misery, according as they fulfilled their *duties* towards me. With this deep consciousness of what they *owed* towards the being to which they had *given* life, . . . while . . . I received a lesson of patience, of charity, and of self-control, I was so guided by a silken cord, that all seemed but one train of enjoyment to me. (p. 41, emphases added)

Alphonse and Caroline pay off their debt of gratitude to "Heaven" by fulfilling the duties they owe their child. Victor in turn owes gratitude for the life they have given him and for their care, and this obligation forms the cord that, no matter how silken, confines him within the family. Hence he repeats this pattern when he contemplates creating a new species. The members of his species "would *owe* their being to me," he gloats, and thus "No father could *claim* the *gratitude* of his child so completely as I should deserve theirs" (p. 57, emphases added). The distinction Victor makes here, between really deserving gratitude and merely claiming it, is important because it indicates the difference between a good father and a bad one. A good father, like Alphonse, fulfills his duties to his child and thus deserves its gratitude; a bad father, like Victor, does not fulfill his duties and in fact abandons his "child," so he may claim gratitude but does not in fact deserve it. Furthermore, bad father Victor produces a bad son, not the embodied filial gratitude he had hoped for but rather "my own spirit . . . forced to destroy all that was dear to me" (p. 75). It might seem that the creature's rampage against Victor's dear ones is the opposite of good son Victor's gratitude toward his loving family and its feminized patriarch. But if the creature is Victor's "own spirit"—the bad son lurking within the good son— and if bad sons are produced by bad fathers, then is Alphonse somehow a bad father? To ask this question is again to teeter on the brink of the Enlightenment myth of nurture, to suggest that parents make or create their children and are therefore responsible for the child who turns out badly. *Frankenstein*, I think, does show the importance of parental nurture, but it does not thereby absolve the child of agency in, and responsibility for, what we might call self-creation or self-nurture. But even if Alphonse is not a bad father, questions remain about a domestic ideology in which the novel is so invested but which so spectacularly fails.

Is there in fact something destructive about the good domesticity Mary Shelley seems to advocate? Thomas Dutoit claims that "the real monster" in this novel is "the domestic scene and its discourse on virtue, happiness, and affection"—specifically, its "fiction of the domestic union of happiness and virtue" (867)—and many feminist critics agree. Sarah Goodwin points out that "violence is at the heart of every home in the novel" and that the monster "gives expression" to this "repressed violence in the home" (100, 101). Hollinger argues that the novel's violence results partly from "the repression required to internalize the masquerade" of femininity, and that the creature "destroys precisely those realms of the domestic most closely associated with conventional femininity" (210, 212). This last point is made obvious in the creature's victims: young William living at home under Elizabeth's care, the servant Justine whose devotion to her mistress and resignation to her fate embody class as well as gender-specific domestic subordination, Henry the paradigm of masculine and feminine traits in harmony, Elizabeth the domestic icon, Alphonse the feminized patriarch. In this sense, as Victor's murderous "spirit" the monster reveals the dark side of the Frankenstein family's oppressive domesticity.

Even before the monster's outbreak, however, we can see this dark side in the relations of Caroline Beaufort, Elizabeth Lavenza, and Justine Moritz to the Frankensteins. In the first place, it is class selection that determines which women are tapped to enter the upper-class Frankenstein family. Although plunged into straw-plaiting poverty by her father's business failure, Caroline's lineage and beauty mark her as still deserving the "rank and magnificence" (p. 39) he once enjoyed; by marrying her, then, Alphonse is restoring the status quo, rescuing Caroline from a working-class milieu and returning her to her proper place. Furthermore, as Anca Vlasopolos points out, such "aristocratic protectionism . . . encourages, in fact engineers, incest" (126) by closing the family off from otherness or difference. This pattern is especially overt in the adoption of Elizabeth. Because Elizabeth is a nobleman's daughter, visibly "of a different stock" from her rude guardians (p. 42), Caroline rescues her from the lower orders; under the "powerful protection" (p. 43) of the Frankenstein family, Elizabeth rapidly becomes Victor's "more than sister" (p. 43). Difference is further excluded as Elizabeth takes on all the family's feminine roles: Victor's quasi-sister and destined to be his wife, after Caroline's death Elizabeth takes her "place" as his mother (p. 49). Although Justine is brought less fully into the family, she is perhaps the most Frankensteinized: when Caroline rescues her from her mother, Justine so "imitate[s] her phraseology and manners" (p. 66) as to become her clone. The Frankenstein family's incestuous pattern of reproducing itself by excluding difference could hardly be clearer.

This insistent replication of the domestic icon also shows how completely and destructively the pattern of indebtedness permeates the Frankenstein definition of femininity. That is, although the Frankenstein family opens to receive these three, they then become subject to its gratitude/obligation debt economy and its pattern of repetitions. We first see Caroline as a daughter, discharging her obligations to her father, and it is the tableau of her paying her last respects that first captivates Alphonse. After he becomes her "protecting spirit," she almost literally owes all she has to this marriage, and the benevolence with which he "shelter[s]" and "surround[s]" her further enjoins gratitude (p. 41). As Caroline tries to discharge her obligations by "act[ing] in her turn the guardian angel to the afflicted" (p. 41)—that is, by becoming a Frankenstein—her benevolence takes the usual form of the "gift" that induces obligation and requires gratitude. When she gives Justine an education, for instance, "This benefit was fully repaid," for Justine becomes "the most grateful little creature in the world" (p. 66). Eventually, however, when she acts the guardian angel by nursing Elizabeth, Caroline discharges her debt with her own life. Elizabeth, indebted to Caroline for rescue from peasant life, then discharges this debt by taking Caroline's place as the Frankenstein ideal of femininity. Victor's dream, that his kiss kills Elizabeth and turns her into his dead mother, is proleptic of the price she will pay. Justine is perhaps the most pathetic victim of this pattern of replicated femininity. Exhausted by her Caroline-like maternal care in searching for William, she falls asleep; her likeness to the miniature of Caroline reminds the monster of all women's indifference to him, and in a rage he plants the miniature on her; it becomes circumstantial evidence of the crime for which Justine is convicted, "blackest ingratitude" (p. 81) toward her benefactors. Like Caroline and Elizabeth, Justine pays her obligations to the Frankensteins with her life, and furthermore dies all but convinced that she is in fact a "monster" (p. 83) of ingratitude. The domestic enclave of affective relations turns out to be not an alternative to but a mirror of the public sphere of economic relations.

My final example of this pattern is the female monster whom Victor creates and destroys in a kind of parody of Frankensteinian benevolence. The monster's desire for a mate "as hideous as myself" (p. 129) is an "ironic repetition" (Vine 253) of Victor's desire for Elizabeth, "the material form of his ideal self-representation"; and because Victor destroys the monsterette, the monster retaliates by destroying Elizabeth. Of course, Victor assumed that he rather than Elizabeth would be the monster's target, and in one sense he is correct: Elizabeth dies not because she is Elizabeth but because she is the object of Victor's desire. In other words, just as women are interchangeable within the domestic circle, here Elizabeth and the monsterette are simply counters in the struggle between Victor and the monster. Like Elizabeth's, the monsterette's creation and destruction dramatize how women function not in their own right but rather as signs of and conduits for men's relations with other men.[1]

[1] For analyses of other works that enact this traffic in women, see Sedgwick.

Before leaving this thematic of domesticity, it is worth discussing the monsterette and Safie as examples of the otherness that the Frankenstein family circle works so hard to exclude. I have been stressing the interchangeability of Elizabeth and the monsterette, but there is one difference between them, at least in Victor's mind: while Elizabeth is firmly located in the family circle of replication and controlled desire, a monsterette "might refuse to comply with a compact made before her creation" (p. 144), might desire where she shouldn't, might in short become "an independent site of production" (Vine 256). This unpredictability connects her with another outsider: the Arabian Safie, whose "independence of spirit" (p. 111) leads her to defy her father's "tyrannical mandate" (p. 113) and travel across Europe to rejoin Felix. And like the monsterette's, albeit less drastically, Safie's independence is neutralized; the challenge she might otherwise represent to a domestic ideology is in effect "absorbed" by various cultural norms (Vlasopolos 132). For one thing, her desire to marry Felix is acceptable in class terms, for she finds "enchanting" the prospect of "tak[ing] a rank in society" (p. 112); it is also acceptable in the terms of a "European 'Orientalist' construction of the East" (Zonana 173), for she chooses Felix in part to avoid "returning to Asia, and being immured within the walls of a haram" (pp. 111–12). In addition, unlike Henry or Walton, Safie seeks adventure not for its own sake or to benefit humankind but to get a man. It is thus apt that she joins the De Lacey family, for while their interactive domestic style stands in stark contrast to the rigid gift/debt structure of the Frankensteins, it is nonetheless a conventionally middle-class separate-spheres arrangement: Felix is "employed out of doors" (p. 101), for instance, while his sister Agatha's work consists of "arranging the cottage" (p. 99). Finally, just as Victor's family takes in only a select few women, so the De Lacey family circle opens only to admit the beautiful Safie. That Felix, like Victor, excludes the ugly monster indicates again how strictly men control the domestic sphere.


## SAD TRASH

This section covers the kinds of scientific knowledge the novel explores: the alchemical sciences of Albertus Magnus, Paracelsus, and Cornelius Agrippa that Victor's father dismisses as "sad trash" (p. 45); the experiments of the "electricians," late-eighteenth-century scientists testing the powers and uses of electricity; and the modern chemistry, modeled on the work of Erasmus Darwin and Humphry Davy, that Victor embraces. The masculinism of Victor's science has been exhaustively argued by Anne Mellor, and I have made this argument myself. But one could also make the case, as Crosbie Smith does, that *Frankenstein* is less anti-science than "structured by powerful tensions" (39) among *kinds* of science: "the textual lore of Paracelsianism" (Schaffer 93), the spectacular demonstrations of the "electricians," and the achievements of modern chemistry. Hence Mary Shelley's novel is not "a simple moralistic tale of masculinist, scientific overreaching" (Jordanova 60); rather it is an exploration of "different modes of knowledge" (74), of "practices that manipulated nature," of "the desire for mastery."[2] Hence too, we can see that Victor's attempt to leave behind a domestic life is also an effort to leave behind the sad trash of alchemy, and that his attempt to move into a public life is also an effort at mastery over masculine scientific knowledges. Developing these parallels will reveal that, just as the ideology of domesticity relegates certain qualities to the devalued feminine sphere, so modern science relegates other kinds of science to the realm of "sad trash." To trace Victor's move from alchemy to chemistry is thus to trace the tensions and conflicts of contemporary gendered science.

I approach these tensions and conflicts with the help of two theoretical models: Thomas Kuhn's concept of paradigm shifts in scientific knowledge and Michel Foucault's concept of a genealogy of subjugated knowledges. Kuhn defines a paradigm as a "model from which spring particular coherent traditions of scientific research" (11); texts such as Antoine Lavoisier's *Chemistry* provide successful paradigms because they "define the legitimate problems and methods of a research field" (Kuhn 10). A successful paradigm in turn affects "the structure of the group that practices the field" (18), since there is now a "more rigid definition of the field" itself (19). Those practitioners who reject the new paradigm are "read out of the profession" and their form of science is marginalized; in contrast, researchers who share the paradigm also share "the same rules and standards for scientific practice" (11), and that consensus enables "normal science," or "the genesis and continuation of a particular research tradition." But any paradigm has a limited utility; hence the second element of Kuhn's thesis, the paradigm shift. An

---

[2] See "A Critical History of *Frankenstein*" (pp. 267–99) for other forms of science operating in the novel.

anomaly of some sort emerges that cannot be accommodated by the current dominant paradigm; an increased "professional awareness" (67) of that anomaly then induces "a state of growing crisis"; the crisis, however, "loosens the rules of normal puzzle-solving in ways that ultimately permit a new paradigm to emerge" (80). Once this paradigm shift has occurred, it "necessitates a redefinition" (103) of the pertinent science that constitutes a "scientific revolution" (90). That is, "[t]he transition from a paradigm in crisis to a new one" (84) involves "a reconstruction of the field from new fundamentals," as a result of which the "old problems" may be relegated to another science or to the category of the "unscientific." Despite the metaphor of revolution, however, Kuhn here suggests a transition between rather than a struggle of knowledges, and to foreground this element of struggle I turn to my second theoretical model, Foucault's genealogy of subjugated knowledges. A genealogy in Foucault's sense is not so much a history as a tactic or a strategy: genealogies function to oppose "the effects of the centralising powers which are linked to the institution and function of an organized scientific discourse" (Foucault 83). In this sense a genealogy is "an insurrection of subjugated knowledges" (81), "a return of knowledge[s]" which had been "disqualified" as "popular," or as "inadequate to their task," or as "beneath the required level of cognition or scientificity."

What is the relevance of all this for *Frankenstein*? Kuhn's example of preparadigm science is the researches of "electricians" in the first half of the eighteenth century; his example of paradigm science is the modern, post-Lavoisier chemistry which emerged from that research and which so entrances Victor. Thus Victor's move from alchemy to chemistry via the electricians is a paradigm shift in miniature. But as natural philosophy was systematized into the study of the laws of nature, searches into "hidden and ultimate causes" (Smith 41) rather than laws were increasingly "assigned to an ancient metaphysics" such as natural magic or alchemy. As Victor continues to "investigat[e the] causes" of things (42), then, his paradigm shift is incomplete. Furthermore, alchemy and the researches of the electricians become what Kuhn would call superseded paradigms but also what Foucault would call subjugated knowledges. And a feminist adaptation of Kuhn's and Foucault's ideas can show how, as the monster enacts the insurrection of subjugated sciences, he also enacts Victor's rebellion against domesticity. To see why this is so, we need to begin with Victor's first "preceptors" (45), Paracelsus and Cornelius Agrippa, for if they were alchemists they were also physicians and thus scientists.

Paracelsus was "a magician, psychologist, astrologer, diviner, pharmacist, philosopher, metaphysician, teacher, reformer, and alchemist" but "first and foremost" a physician (Poncé). He anticipated antisepsis and germ theory, developed mineral medicines to supersede the prevailing Galenic organic remedies, invented chemical urinalysis and chemical therapy, and suggested the biochemical theory of digestion. And he developed all this chemical medicine from his "revolutionized . . . alchemical thought" (Poncé); indeed, Paracelsus called alchemy one of the four "fundamental part[s], or pillars, of true medicine" (2: 148). It follows that "the stars . . . complete and perfect the work of the physician," and it also follows that "[i]f you wish to attain the ends you anticipate you must have heaven kindly and benignant to you" (2: 149, 151). Victor appears not to have read that far, but he may well have derived from Paracelsus his sense of the alchemist's power over a feminine nature. As Paracelsus puts it,

[although] Nature is so keen and subtle in her operations. . . ,
[s]he brings nothing to the light that is at once perfect in itself,
but leaves it to be perfected by man. This method of perfection
is called Alchemy. . . . [Its] methods of treatment have rivaled
Nature, and have . . . mastered her properties. (2: 149)

Including Nature's property of life: "certain medicines" (2: 108) protect the body "altogether from diseases," and there are "means of attaining long life" and of "driving away . . . death" (2: 110). Furthermore, through his "art and industry" (1: 121) the alchemist can bring to life a homunculus, i.e., a man originating in the sperm (2: 334) and then "begotten without the female body and the natural womb" (1: 124). Small wonder that Victor believes he can achieve the power to "banish disease from the human frame" (p. 47), to "render man invulnerable to any but a violent death," even to generate life.

Such powers are also important thematics in Cornelius Agrippa, early-sixteenth-century Cabalist, alchemist, physician, and experimenter in breeding life from putrefying matter (Rowen 169). The volume (p. 46) of Agrippa that Victor happens upon may have been the *Occult Philosophy*, for this book on the alchemical operations of what Agrippa calls "natural magic" offers several theories which would interest Victor: that "the Passions of the Mind can work out of themselves upon another[']s Body" (Agrippa 145) when "inflamed with a strong imagination"; that "the reviving of the dead" (58) may be accomplished by "perfect men" (127) exercising "the powers of their soul"; and that such powers must be exercised in secret.[3] Agrippa warns that "[e]very Magical experiment fleeth the publike, seeks to be hid, is strengthened by silence, but is destroyed by publication" (349), so "it behoveth a Magicall operator, . . . to manifest to none, neither his work nor place, nor time." But he also characterizes natural magic as the revealing of secrets: what seem the natural magician's " 'incredible miracles'" (qtd. in Henry 589) are often the work of nature, for natural magic simply " 'make[s] known the hidden and secret powers of nature.'"

I am deliberately stressing the contradictory thematic of secrecy here, because it is this ambiguous paradigm of powers and secrets with which Victor begins his scientific education. Before turning to that education, however, I stress again that Victor's first preceptors, the alchemists, cannot simply be dismissed as nonscientists. The operations of natural magic were " 'derived from nature and in harmony with it'" (Agrippa, qtd. in Henry 589), and natural magicians were " 'careful explorers of nature[,] only directing what nature has formerly prepared'"; for this reason, natural magic was considered a "branch of science" (Kieckhefer 9). Thus the pertinent distinction is not between false science (alchemy or natural magic) and true science (chemistry) but between a discredited form of science and a newly dominant scientific paradigm.

From childhood Victor has been as attracted as any alchemist to the secrets of nature. The world was "a secret which I desired to divine," and repeatedly he tells us of his obsessive curiosity about "the hidden laws of nature" (p. 43), his "eager desire" to learn "the secrets of heaven and earth" (p. 44), his "fervent longing to penetrate the secrets of nature" (p. 46). At first Victor finds in the alchemists "men who had penetrated deeper and knew more" (p. 46), who promise a full revelation of nature's powers and secrets. But then, to use Kuhn's terms, an anomaly occurs that cannot be explained by Victor's current dominant paradigm, viz., the great oak being "utterly destroyed" during a thunderstorm. A "man of great research in natural philosophy" explains this phenomenon in terms of "electricity and galvanism," and while this explanation satisfies Victor it also "overthrow[s]" the theories of his alchemists (p. 47). What ensues is, again in Kuhn's terms, crisis: "It

---

[3]Albertus Magnus, another of Victor's alchemist mentors, is thought to have written a *Book of Secrets*, and his book *On Alchemy* warns against revealing its secrets (Kieckhefer 142, 140). He was also interested in "artificial creation" (Rowen 169); he is variously supposed to have constructed a brass housekeeper and a talking head (his pupil Thomas Aquinas is said to have destroyed the latter because of its distracting chat [Kieckhefer 142]).

seemed to me as if nothing would or could ever be known," says Victor; "[a]ll that had so long engaged my attention suddenly grew despicable." His paradigm shift then begins, as he turns from the "would-be science" of the alchemists to the "secure" science of mathematics, and it continues with his studies in natural philosophy at the University of Ingolstadt.

But Ingolstadt is an anomalous choice for a shift from alchemy to modern science. On the one hand, it was known for its preeminence in the modern experimental sciences: as early as 1675 its scientific apparatus made it a "tourist attraction," and in 1780 an Ingolstadt professor was recognized for his translation of a work on electricity (Heilbron 103, 143). On the other hand, Ingolstadt was also known as the home of the Illuminati, a secret society of freethinkers who operated by "direct communication with the holy spirit" (Vernon 274) rather than by "verifiable and repeatable" scientific experimentation. Victor's experience there is similarly anomalous: when he hears M. Waldman deliver a "panegyric upon modern chemistry" he converts to that science, but he simultaneously reverts to the visions of "boundless grandeur" he earlier associated with the alchemists (p. 51). Waldman's panegyric is a virtual checklist of the achievements of modern chemists (Smith 49): "They ascend into the heavens" alludes to the scientific investigations conducted by balloonists; "they have discovered how the blood circulates, and the nature of the air we breathe" is a reference to Harvey and Lavoisier respectively; and "they can . . . mimic the earthquake" recalls the experiments of Priestley and others in producing with electricity the effects of earthquakes (p. 52). But when Victor, having heard all these wonders of modern chemistry, vows to "explore unknown powers, and unfold to the world the deepest mysteries of creation" (p. 53), his emphasis on "powers" recalls Paracelsus, and his emphasis on revealing "deepest mysteries" recalls Agrippa's view that natural magic reveals nature's "hidden and secret powers." In other words, the distinction between the alchemy phase and the chemistry phase of Victor's education is "blurred" (Ketterer 61); the paradigm shift between the two is incomplete. As Victor's education proceeds, again chemistry—his studies in the scientific community of Ingolstadt and his improvements of chemical instruments—leads back to alchemy: he retreats to a "solitary chamber" (p. 58) as recommended by Agrippa. While his act of solitary creation might be seen as the apotheosis of masculine science dispensing with female reproduction, it might also be seen as the achievement of the alchemists' dream: discovering first "the cause of generation and life" (p. 56) and then the power of "bestowing animation

upon lifeless matter."[4] And certainly chemistry and alchemy join when
Victor animates the creature: using the scientific "instruments of life"
(p. 59), he fulfills Paracelsus's promise of "driving away death." Despite
Victor's conversion to modern chemistry, then, "significant traces of . . .
the alchemist and natural magician remain" (Ketterer 64).

We might say that Victor is still in crisis, and I would suggest that
his crisis is a microcosm of the position of chemistry itself at the turn of
the nineteenth century. Of course, the paradigm shift from alchemy to
chemistry occurring at this time was sometimes smooth. When Waldman locates the "foundations" (p. 53) of modern science in alchemy,
for example, he is following one accepted line of thought; as late as
1834 the historian of science William Whewell still considered alchemy
"the mother of Chemistry" (OED def.1 of alchemy). Leading modern
chemist Humphry Davy was called " 'the Father and Founder of philo-
sophic alchemy'" (qtd. in Lawrence 222), and Waldman's panegyric on
modern chemistry often echoes the chemical/alchemical Davy (compare Waldman's speech with Davy pp. 215–25). In a successful paradigm shift such as this, there is an "appropriation" (Henry 587) of the
older paradigm's "most naturalistic and rational aspects" into the newer
one. But there is also a concurrent dismissal of less useful elements to,
in Foucault's terms, subjugated knowledge — the popular, the inadequate, the insufficiently "scientific."[5]

The late-eighteenth- and early-nineteenth-century crisis of chemistry arose as elements of it were being thus disqualified. These were the
elements tainted with the science of the electricians, and physiologists
working in "medical electricity" were particularly suspect. Such men
signified " 'a new medical Prometheanism, the belief that mechanical
means could fix the malfunctioning body'" or even reanimate it (qtd.
in Marshall 5). But because the boundary between life and death was
still "widely held" to be "fluid" and "reversible," such medical Prometheuses might be seen not as healers but as "tormentors of the dead"
(Jordanova 66–67). Victor's studies in anatomy and physiology (p. 55),
not to mention his "instruments of life" (p. 59), thus link him to these
discredited elements of chemistry. Furthermore, Mary's Introduction

---

[4]McWhir makes the intriguing argument that "Nature is parthenogenic, a female
principle whose laws govern man's being" (77), and hence that Victor is "simply a man
who understands and employs a principle of nature."

[5]Or magical — one electrician complained that his lower-class audience was " 'so
barbarously ignorant, that they have taken me for a Magician'" (qtd. in Heilbron 164).

refers to the electrician Luigi Galvani, and his records of his electrical tests on frog parts are particularly pertinent to *Frankenstein*. Galvani's interest in discovering "concealed properties" (23) recalls Victor's interest in discovering nature's secrets, and statements such as "my heart burned with desire" (40) recall the "ardour" (p. 60) with which Victor approaches his studies. Galvani's experiments themselves seem to foreshadow Victor's, and the one in which, using the "customary [electrical] devices" (96), Galvani created movement in an amputated human arm and leg seems a prototype of Victor's "dabbl[ing] among the unhallowed damps of the grave" (p. 57).[6]

If Victor is Promethean in these ways, it's a short step to maintain that Shelley intends to critique "the aspiration of modern masculinist scientists to be technically creative divinities" (Hindle 23). As I have been suggesting, however, it is possible to read the novel rather as an exploration of the tensions called into being by such aspirations, specifically the tensions in the paradigm shift from alchemy to chemistry. One final tension particularly pertinent to *Frankenstein* is the fact that early-nineteenth-century science operated in a separate-spheres structure. On the one hand, some experimental science took place in universities and other institutions; as Davy points out, however, men and women of all classes might conduct experiments on their own (pp. 224–25). Crucially, many men who studied science worked "in a domestic rather than an institutional setting" (Jordanova 63), and many had the help of female relatives; Galvani's wife often helped him with his electrical tests, and drawings of the electricians' workspaces show that women featured in their experiments.

The resultant tension for the scientist is very like the tension already explored in my "Cooped Up" section. The scientist who is "collaborating with female relatives" (Jordanova 64) yet trying to forge a "masculine professional identit[y]" is analogous to a Victor trying to negotiate between the feminized domestic sphere and the masculine sphere of science. Victor's "workshop of filthy creation" (p. 58) is thus resonant in a number of ways that draw together the elements of my analysis. The workshop itself—not a domestic space but not quite an institutional setting—indicates Victor's difficulties in escaping the domestic sphere so as to create a masculine professional identity. The solitude of the workshop indicates Victor's return to an alchemical paradigm, but the product of the workshop is the return of that paradigm from its status

---

[6]On such connections, Marshall's book is invaluable.

as subjugated knowledge or "sad trash." And if "filthy creation" in the workshop suggests the "attempt to exclude or repress the maternal" (Pike 155) that is characteristic of a separate-spheres culture, the monster also suggests the destructiveness consequent on such "cooping up." Finally, as evidence of the crisis of early-nineteenth-century chemistry, Victor's creation is also evidence of the gendering of the sciences, and thus it dramatizes how the separation of the spheres and the dualities of the sciences are equally Mary Shelley's subject in *Frankenstein*.

## WORKS CITED

Agrippa, Cornelius. *Three Books of Occult Philosophy*. 1531. London: Chthonios, 1987. Print.

Bann, Stephen, ed. Frankenstein, *Creation and Monstrosity*. London: Reaktion, 1994. Print.

Behrendt, Stephen. "Mary Shelley, *Frankenstein*, and the Woman Writer's Fate." Feldman and Kelley 69–87.

Cunningham, Andrew, and Rosemary Jardine, eds. *Romanticism and the Sciences*. Cambridge: Cambridge UP, 1990. Print.

Dickerson, Vanessa D. "The Ghost of a Self: Female Identity in Mary Shelley's *Frankenstein*." *Journal of Popular Culture* 27.3 (Win. 1993): 79–91. Print.

Dussinger, John A. "Kinship and Guilt in Mary Shelley's *Frankenstein*." *Studies in the Novel* 8.1 (Spr. 1976): 38–55. Print.

Dutoit, Thomas. "Re-specting the Face as the Moral (of ) Fiction in Mary Shelley's *Frankenstein*." *Modern Language Notes* 109.5 (Dec. 1994): 847–71. Print.

Duyfhuizen, Bernard. "Periphrastic Naming in Mary Shelley's *Frankenstein*." *Studies in the Novel* 27.4 (Win. 1995): 477–92. Print.

Ellis, Kate. "Monsters in the Garden: Mary Shelley and the Bourgeois Family." *The Endurance of* Frankenstein: *Essays on Mary Shelley's Novel*. Ed. George Levine and U. C. Knoepflmacher. Berkeley: U of California P, 1979. 123–42. Print.

Ellis, Sarah Stickney. *The Women of England: Their Social Duties and Domestic Habits*. 1838. Victorian Women Writers Project. Web. www.dlib.indiana.edu/collections/vwwp. 17 September 2015.

Feldman, Paula R., and Theresa M. Kelley, eds. *Romantic Women Writers: Voices and Countervoices*. Hanover, NH: UP of New England, 1995. Print.

Foucault, Michel. "Two Lectures." *Power/Knowledge. Selected Interviews and Other Writings 1972–1977.* Ed. Colin Gordon. Trans. Gordon et al. London: Harvester, 1980. 78–108. Print.

Galvani, Luigi. *Commentary on the Effect of Electricity on Muscular Motion.* 1791. Trans. Robert Montraville Green. Cambridge, MA: Elizabeth Licht, 1953. Print.

Goodwin, Sarah Webster. "Domesticity and Uncanny Kitsch in 'The Rime of the Ancient Mariner' and *Frankenstein.*" *Tulsa Studies in Women's Literature* 10.1 (Spr. 1991): 93–108. Print.

Heilbron, J. L. *Electricity in the 17th and 18th Centuries.* Berkeley: U of California P, 1979. Print.

Henry, John. "Magic and Science in the Sixteenth and Seventeenth Centuries." *Companion to the History of Modern Science.* Ed. R. C. Olby et al. London: Routledge, 1996. 583–96. Print.

Hindle, Maurice. Introduction. *Frankenstein.* By Mary Shelley. Ed. Hindle. New York: Penguin, 2007. Print.

Hollinger, Veronica. "Putting on the Feminine: Gender and Negativity in *Frankenstein* and *The Handmaid's Tale.*" *Negation, Critical Theory, and Postmodern Textuality.* Ed. Daniel Fischlin. Boston: Kluwer, 1994. 203–24. Print.

Jordanova, Ludmilla. "Melancholy Reflection: Constructing an Identity for Unveilers of Nature." Bann, Frankenstein, *Creation* 60–76.

Kelly, Gary. "Romantic Fiction." *The Cambridge Companion to British Romanticism.* Ed. Stuart Curran. Cambridge: Cambridge UP, 1993. 196–215. Print.

Ketterer, David. "*Frankenstein*'s 'Conversion' from Natural Magic to Modern Science—and a Shifted (and Converted) Last Draft Insert." *Science Fiction Studies* 24.1 (Mar. 1997): 57–78. Print.

Kieckhefer, Richard. *Magic in the Middle Ages.* Cambridge: Cambridge UP, 1989. Print.

Kuhn, Thomas S. *The Structure of Scientific Revolutions.* 2nd ed. Chicago: U of Chicago P, 1970. Print.

Lawrence, Christopher. "The power and the glory: Humphry Davy and Romanticism." Cunningham and Jardine 213–27.

Marshall, Tim. *Murdering to Dissect: Grave-Robbing,* Frankenstein *and the Anatomy Literature.* Manchester: Manchester UP, 1995. Print.

May, Marilyn. "Publish and Perish: William Godwin, Mary Shelley, and the Public Appetite for Scandal." *Papers on Language and Literature* 26.4 (Fall 1990): 489–512. Print.

McWhir, Anne. "Teaching the Monster to Read: Mary Shelley, Education and *Frankenstein.*" *The Educational Legacy of*

*Romanticism.* Ed. John Willinsky. Waterloo, Canada: Wilfrid Laurier UP, 1990. 73–92. Print.

Mellor, Anne K. *Mary Shelley: Her Life, Her Fiction, Her Monsters.* New York: Routledge, 1988. Print.

Paracelsus. *The Hermetic and Alchemical Writings of Aureolus Philippus Theophrastus Bombast, of Hohenheim, called Paracelsus the Great.* 1896. 2 vols. Ed. Arthur Edward Waite. Berkeley: Shambhala, 1976. Print.

Pike, Judith. "Resurrection of the Fetish in *Gradiva, Frankenstein,* and *Wuthering Heights.*" Feldman and Kelley 150–68.

Poncé, Charles. Foreword. Paracelsus, *Hermetical and Alchemical Writings.* N. Pag. Print.

Poovey, Mary. *The Proper Lady and the Woman Writer: Ideology as Style in the Works of Mary Wollstonecraft, Mary Shelley, and Jane Austen.* Chicago: U of Chicago P, 1984. Print.

Robinson, Charles E., ed. *The* Frankenstein *Notebooks: A Facsimile Edition of Mary Shelley's Novel, 1816–1817* (2 parts). Vol. IX of *The Manuscripts of the Younger Romantics.* Ed. Donald H. Reiman et al. 9 vols. New York: Garland, 1996. Print.

Rowen, Norma. "*Frankenstein* Revisited: Doris Lessing's *The Fifth Child.*" *Journal of the Fantastic in the Acts* 2.3 (1990): 41–49. Print.

Schaffer, Simon. "Genius in Romantic Natural Philosophy." Cunningham and Jardine 82–98.

Sedgwick, Eve Kosofsky. *Between Men: English Literature and Male Homosocial Desire.* New York: Columbia UP, 1985. Print.

Shelley, Mary. *The Letters of Mary Wollstonecraft Shelley.* Ed. Betty T. Bennett. 3 vols. Baltimore: Johns Hopkins UP, 1980–88. Print.

Smith, Crosbie. "*Frankenstein* and Natural Magic." Bann, Frankenstein, *Creation* 39–59.

Vernon, Peter. "*Frankenstein:* Science and Electricity." *Études Anglaises* 50.3 (July–Sep. 1997): 270–83. Print.

Vine, Steven. "Filthy Types: *Frankenstein,* Figuration, Femininity." *Critical Survey* 8.3 (1996): 246–58. Print.

Vlasopolos, Anca. "*Frankenstein*'s Hidden Skeleton: The Psycho-Politics of Oppression." *Science Fiction Studies* 10.2 (July 1983): 125–36. Print.

Zonana, Joyce. "'They Will Prove the Truth of My Tale': Safie's Letters as the Feminist Core of Mary Shelley's *Frankenstein.*" *Journal of Narrative Technique* 21.2 (Spr. 1991): 170–84. Print.

# Gender Criticism, Queer Theory, and *Frankenstein*

## WHAT ARE GENDER CRITICISM AND QUEER THEORY?

Among the most exciting and influential developments in the field of literary studies, gender criticism and queer theory participate in a broad philosophical discourse that extends far beyond literature, far beyond the arts in general. The critical *practices* of those who explore the representation of women and men in works by male or female, lesbian or gay writers inevitably grow out of and contribute to a larger and more generally applicable *theoretical* discussion of how gender and sexuality are constantly shaped by and shaping institutional structures and attitudes, artifacts and behaviors.

Feminist criticism was accorded academic legitimacy in American universities "around 1981," Jane Gallop claims in her book *Around 1981: Academic Feminist Literary Theory* (1992). With Gallop's title and approximation in mind, Naomi Schor has since estimated that "around 1985, feminism began to give way to what has come to be called gender studies" (275). Some would argue that feminist criticism became academically legitimate well before 1981. Others would take issue with the notion that feminist criticism and women's studies have been giving way to gender criticism and gender studies, and with the either/or distinction that such a claim implies. Taken together, however, Gallop and

Schor provide us with a useful fact—that of feminist criticism's historical precedence—and a chronological focus on the early to mid-1980s, a period during which the feminist approach was unquestionably influential and during which new interests emerged, not all of which were woman centered.

Feminist and gender criticism are not polar opposites but, rather, exist along a continuum of attitudes toward sex and sexism, sexuality and gender, language and the literary canon. There are, however, a few distinctions to be made between those critics whose writings are inevitably identified as being toward one end of the continuum or the other.

One distinction is based on focus: as the word implies, *feminists* have concentrated their efforts on the study of women and women's issues. Gender criticism, by contrast, has not been woman centered. It has tended to view the male and female sexes—and the masculine and feminine genders—in terms of a complicated continuum, much as we are viewing feminist and gender criticism. Critics like Diane K. Lewis have raised the possibility that black women may be more like white men in terms of familial and economic roles, like black men in terms of their relationships with whites, and like white women in terms of their relationships with men. Lesbian gender critics have asked whether lesbian women are really more like straight women than they are like gay (or for that matter straight) men. That we refer to gay and lesbian studies as gender studies has led some to suggest that gender studies is a misnomer; after all, homosexuality is not a gender. This objection may easily be answered once we realize that one purpose of gender criticism is to criticize gender as we commonly conceive of it, to expose its insufficiency and inadequacy as a category.

Another distinction between feminist and gender criticism is based on the terms *gender* and *sex*. As de Lauretis suggests in *Technologies of Gender* (1987), feminists of the 1970s tended to equate gender with sex, gender difference with sexual difference. But that equation doesn't help us explain "the differences among women, . . . the differences *within women*." After positing that "we need a notion of gender that is not so bound up with sexual difference," de Lauretis provides just such a notion by arguing that "gender is not a property of bodies or something originally existent in human beings"; rather, it is "the product of various social technologies, such as cinema" (2). Gender is, in other words, a construct, an effect of language, culture, and its institutions. It is gender, not sex, that causes a weak old man to open a door for an athletic young woman. And it is gender, not sex, that may cause one young woman to expect old men to behave in this way, another to view this kind of behavior as chauvinistic and insulting, and still another to have mixed feelings (hence de Lauretis's phrase "differences *within women*") about "gentlemanly gallantry."

Still another related distinction between feminist and gender criticism is based on the essentialist views of many feminist critics and the constructionist views of many gender critics (both those who would call themselves feminists and those who would not). Stated simply and perhaps too reductively, the term *essentialist* refers to the view that women are essentially different from men. *Constructionist*, by contrast, refers to the view that most of those differences are characteristics not of the male and female sex (nature) but, rather, of the masculine and feminine genders (nurture). Because of its essentialist tendencies, "radical feminism," according to the influential gender critic Eve Kosofsky Sedgwick, "tends to deny that the meaning of gender or sexuality has ever significantly changed; and more damagingly, it can make future change appear impossible" (*Between Men* 13).

Most obviously essentialist would be those feminists who emphasize the female body, its difference, and the manifold implications of that difference. The equation made by some avant-garde French feminists between the female body and the *maternal* body has proved especially troubling to some gender critics, who worry that it may paradoxically play into the hands of extreme conservatives and fundamentalists seeking to reestablish patriarchal family values. In her book *The Reproduction of Mothering* (1978), Nancy Chodorow, a sociologist of gender, admits that what we call "mothering"—not having or nursing babies but mothering more broadly conceived—is commonly associated not just with the feminine gender but also with the female sex, often considered nurturing by nature. But she critically interrogates the common assumption that it is in women's nature or biological destiny to "mother" in this broader sense, arguing that the separation of home and workplace brought about by the development of capitalism and the ensuing industrial revolution made mothering *appear* to be essentially a woman's job in modern Western society.

If sex turns out to be gender where mothering is concerned, what differences *are* grounded in sex—that is, nature? *Are* there *essential* differences between men and women—other than those that are purely anatomical and anatomically determined (for example, a man can exclusively take on the job of feeding an infant milk, but he may not do so from his own breast)? A growing number of gender critics would answer the question in the negative. Sometimes referred to as "extreme constructionists" and "postfeminists," these critics have adopted the viewpoint of philosopher Judith Butler, who in her book *Gender Trouble* (1990) predicts that "sex, by definition, will be shown to have been gender all along" (8). As Naomi Schor explains their position, "there is nothing outside or before culture, no nature that is not always and already enculturated" (278).

Whereas a number of feminists celebrate women's difference, postfeminist gender critics would agree with Chodorow's statement that men have an "investment in difference that women do not have" (Eisenstein and Jardine 14). They see difference as a symptom of oppression, not a cause for celebration, and would abolish it by dismantling gender categories and, ultimately, destroying gender itself. Since gender categories and distinctions are embedded in and perpetuated through language, gender critics like Monique Wittig have called for the wholesale transformation of language into a nonsexist, and nonheterosexist, medium.

Language has proved the site of important debates between feminist and gender critics, essentialists and constructionists. Gender critics have taken issue with those French feminists who have spoken of a feminine language and writing and who have grounded differences in language and writing in the female body.[1] For much the same reason, they have disagreed with those French-influenced Anglo-American critics who, like Toril Moi and Nancy K. Miller, have posited an essential relationship between sexuality and textuality. (In an essentialist sense, such critics have suggested that when women write, they tend to break the rules of plausibility and verisimilitude that men have created to evaluate fiction.) Gender critics like Peggy Kamuf posit a relationship only between *gender* and textuality, between what most men and women *become* after they are born and the way in which they write. They are therefore less interested in the author's sexual "signature"—in whether the author was a woman writing—than in whether the author was (to borrow from Kamuf) "Writing like a Woman."

Feminists like Miller have suggested that no man could write the "female anger, desire, and selfhood" that Emily Brontë, for instance, inscribed in her poetry and in *Wuthering Heights* (72). In the view of gender critics, it is and has been possible for a man to write like a woman,

---

[1] Because feminist/gender studies, not unlike sex/gender, should be thought of as existing along a continuum of attitudes and not in terms of simple opposition, attempts to highlight the difference between feminist and gender criticism are inevitably prone to reductive overgeneralization and occasional distortion. Here, for instance, French feminism is made out to be more monolithic than it actually is. Hélène Cixous has said that a few men (such as Jean Genet) have produced "feminine writing," although she suggests that these are exceptional men who have acknowledged their own bisexuality.

a woman to write like a man. Shari Benstock, a noted feminist critic whose investigations into psychoanalytic and poststructuralist theory have led her increasingly to adopt the gender approach, poses the following question to herself in *Textualizing the Feminine* (1991): "Isn't it precisely 'the feminine' in Joyce's writings and Derrida's that carries me along?" (45). In an essay entitled "Unsexing Language: Pronominal Protest in Emily Dickinson's 'Lay this Laurel,'" Anna Shannon Elfenbein has argued that "like Walt Whitman, Emily Dickinson crossed the gender barrier in some remarkable poems," such as "We learned to like the Fire / By playing Glaciers—when a Boy—" (Elfenbein 215).

It is also possible, in the view of most gender critics, for women to read as men, men as women. The view that women can, and indeed have been forced to, read as men has been fairly noncontroversial. Everyone agrees that the literary canon is largely "androcentric" and that writings by men have tended to "immasculate" women, forcing them to see the world from a masculine viewpoint. But the question of whether men can read as women has proved to be yet another issue dividing feminist and gender critics. Some feminists suggest that men and women have some essentially different reading strategies and outcomes, while gender critics maintain that such differences arise entirely out of social training and cultural norms. One interesting result of recent attention to gender and reading is Elizabeth A. Flynn's argument that women in fact make the best interpreters of imaginative literature. Based on a study of how male and female students read works of fiction, she concludes that women come up with more imaginative, open-ended readings of stories. Quite possibly the imputed hedging and tentativeness of women's speech, often seen by men as disadvantages, are transformed into useful interpretive strategies—receptivity combined with critical assessment of the text—in the act of reading (Flynn and Schweickart 286).

In singling out a catalyst of the gender approach, many historians of criticism have pointed to Michel Foucault. In his *History of Sexuality* (1976, tr. 1978), Foucault distinguished sexuality (that is, sexual behavior or practice) from sex, calling the former a "technology of sex." De Lauretis, who has deliberately developed her theory of gender "along the lines of . . . Foucault's theory of sexuality," explains his use of "technology" this way: "Sexuality, commonly thought to be a natural as well as a private matter, is in fact completely constructed in culture according to the political aims of the society's dominant class" (*Technologies* 2, 12).

Influenced by Foucault, some gay and lesbian gender critics associated with the development of queer theory have argued that the heterosexual/homosexual distinction is as much a cultural construct as is the masculine/feminine dichotomy. Arguing that sexuality is a continuum, not a fixed and static set of binary oppositions, a number of gay and lesbian critics have critiqued heterosexuality as a norm, arguing that it has been an enforced corollary and consequence of what Gayle Rubin has referred to as the sex/gender system. (Those subscribing to this system assume that persons of the male sex should be masculine, that masculine men are attracted to women, and therefore that it is natural for masculine men to be attracted to women and unnatural for them to be attracted to men.) Lesbian gender critics have also taken issue with their feminist counterparts on the grounds that they proceed from fundamentally heterosexual and even heterosexist assumptions. Particularly offensive to lesbians like the poet-critic Adrienne Rich have been those feminists who, following Doris Lessing, have implied that to make the lesbian choice is to make a statement, to act out feminist hostility against men. Rich has called heterosexuality "a beachhead of male dominance" that, "like motherhood, needs to be recognized and studied as a political institution" ("Compulsory Heterosexuality" 143, 145).

If there is such a thing as reading like a woman and such a thing as reading like a man, how then do lesbians read? Are there gay and lesbian ways of reading? Many would say that there are. Rich, by reading Emily Dickinson's poetry as a lesbian—by not assuming that "heterosexual romance is the key to a woman's life and work"—has introduced us to a poet somewhat different from the one heterosexual critics have made familiar (*Lies* 158). As for gay reading, Wayne Koestenbaum has defined "the (male twentieth-century first world) gay reader" as one who "reads resistantly for inscriptions of his condition, for texts that will confirm a social and private identity founded on a desire for other men. . . . Reading becomes a hunt for histories that deliberately foreknow or unwittingly trace a desire felt not by author but by reader, who is most acute when searching for signs of himself" (Boone and Cadden 176–77).

Lesbian critics have produced a number of compelling reinterpretations, or inscriptions, of works by authors as diverse as Emily Dickinson, Virginia Woolf, and Toni Morrison. As a result of these provocative readings, significant disagreements have arisen between straight and lesbian critics and among lesbian critics as well. Perhaps the most famous and interesting example of this kind of interpretive controversy involves the claim by Adrienne Rich and Barbara Smith that Morrison's novel *Sula* can be read as a lesbian text—and author Toni Morrison's counterclaim that it cannot.

Gay male critics have produced a body of readings no less revisionist and controversial, focusing on writers as staidly classic as Henry James and Wallace Stevens. In Melville's *Billy Budd* and *Moby-Dick*, Robert K. Martin suggests, a triangle of homosexual desire exists. In the latter novel, the hero must choose between a captain who represents "the imposition of the male on the female" and a "Dark Stranger" (Queequeg) who "offers the possibility of an alternate sexuality, one that is less dependent upon performance and conquest" (5).

Masculinity as a complex construct producing and reproducing a constellation of behaviors and goals, many of them destructive (like performance and conquest) and most of them injurious to women, has become the object of an unprecedented number of gender studies. A 1983 issue of *Feminist Review* contained an essay entitled "Anti-Porn: Soft Issue, Hard World," in which B. Ruby Rich suggested that the "legions of feminist men" who examine and deplore the effects of pornography on women might better "undertake the analysis that can tell us why men like porn (not, piously, why this or that exceptional man does *not*)" (67). The advent of gender criticism makes precisely that kind of analysis possible. Stephen H. Clark, who alludes to Rich's challenge, reads T. S. Eliot "as a man." Responding to "Eliot's implicit appeal to a specifically masculine audience—" 'You! hypocrite lecteur!—mon semblable,—mon *frère!*' "—Clark concludes that poems like "Sweeney Among the Nightingales" and "Gerontion," rather than offering what they are usually said to offer—"a social critique into which a misogynistic language accidentally seeps"—instead articulate a masculine "psychology of sexual fear and desired retaliation" (Clark 173).

Some gender critics focusing on masculinity have analyzed "the anthropology of boyhood," a phrase coined by Mark Seltzer in an article in which he comparatively reads, among other things, Stephen Crane's *The Red Badge of Courage*, Jack London's *White Fang*, and the first *Boy Scouts of America* handbook (Boone and Cadden 150). Others have examined the fear men have that artistry is unmasculine, a guilty worry that surfaces perhaps most obviously in "The Custom-House," Hawthorne's lengthy preface to *The Scarlet Letter*. Still others have studied the representation in literature of subtly erotic disciple-patron relationships, relationships like the ones between Nick Carraway and Jay Gatsby, Charlie Marlow and Lord Jim, Doctor Watson and Sherlock Holmes, and any number of characters in Henry James's stories. Not all of these studies have focused on literary texts. Because the movies have played a primary role in gender construction during our lifetimes, gender critics have analyzed the dynamics of masculinity (vis-à-vis femininity and androgyny) in films from *Rebel Without a Cause* to *Tootsie* to last year's Academy Award nominees. One of the "social technologies" most influential in (re)constructing gender, film is one of the media in which today's sexual politics is most evident.

The term *queer*—long used pejoratively to refer to homosexuals, especially male homosexuals—has been reclaimed and embraced by queer theorists, who apply it to both sexual relations and critical practice. With reference to sexual relations, *queer* encompasses any practice or behavior that a person engages in without reproductive aims and without regard for social or economic considerations. As a critical term, *queer* refers to writings that question generally accepted associations and identities involving sex, gender, and sexuality. As queer theorist Annamarie Jagose wrote in her book *Queer Theory* (1996), "queer is less an identity than a critique of identity" (65). Moreover, queer theorists seek to keep the term *queer* flexible and resist the tendency to turn it into a "pride word" simply meaning homosexual. Seeking to avoid the normalization of *queer*, David Halperin asserted in *Saint Foucault: Towards a Gay Hagiography* (1995) that "Queer is by definition *whatever* is at odds with the normal, the legitimate, the dominant. *There is nothing in particular to which it necessarily refers*"(62).

Queer theory is an outgrowth of gender criticism and, more specifically, of gay and lesbian criticism. In fact, the term *queer theory* is generally credited to gender theorist Teresa de Lauretis, who in 1991 edited a special issue of the journal *differences* entitled *Queer Theory: Lesbian and Gay Sexualities*. Queer theory diverges from gender criticism, however, in its emphasis on sexuality and in its broader insistence that the multifaceted and fluid character of identity negates efforts to categorize people on the basis of any one characteristic. It also diverges from gay and lesbian criticism in that its approach is more theoretically oriented than text-centered and insofar as some gay and lesbian critics advance an essentialist view of sexuality as biologically based. Moreover, unlike practitioners of gay and lesbian criticism, who tend to assume that sexual identity defines textual representations, queer theorists argue that representations define the contours of sexual identity. Like most gender, gay, and lesbian critics, however, queer theorists draw on the work of Foucault as well as Rich, Sedgwick, and Judith Butler.

In his *History of Sexuality*, Foucault suggested that the Western conception of homosexuality was largely an invention of the nineteenth century—as was heterosexuality, its "normal" opposite. (Before that time, people spoke of "acts of sodomy" but not of homosexual *persons*.) By historicizing sexuality, Foucault made it possible to argue that all the categories and assumptions that operate when we think about sex, sexual difference, gender, and sexuality are the products of cultural discourses and thus social, rather than natural, artifacts.

Rich extended Foucault's theories in an essay entitled "Compulsory Heterosexuality and Lesbian Existence" (1980), in which she claimed that "heterosexuality [is] a beachhead of male dominance", that, "like motherhood, needs to be recognized and studied as a political institution." Subsequently, Butler argued in *Gender Trouble: Feminism and the Subversion of Identity* (1990) that sexual difference is also culturally produced and thus indistinguishable from gender. Sedgwick, in her book *Between Men: English Literature and Male Homosocial Desire* (1985), adapted feminist criticism to analyze relationships between men, between male characters in literary works, and, most importantly, between gender and sexuality. She later specifically critiqued the gender category "sexual orientation" in *Epistemology of the Closet* (1990), stating that "it is a rather amazing fact that, of the very many dimensions along which the genital activity of one person can be differentiated from another . . . , precisely one, the gender of object choice, emerged . . . and has remained . . . *the* dimension denoted by the now ubiquitous category of 'sexual orientation'" (8).

Building on these insights, queer theorists have questioned the "solidarity" and "pride" aspects of homosexual liberation movements. They argue, among other things, that lesbians and gays should not be grouped together given that their separate histories are defined by gender differences. For example, lesbians, as women, have been more affected than gay men by pay discrimination issues. Moreover, queer theorists have taken the position that liberation movements that are specifically gay or specifically lesbian ultimately encourage the development of new sets of gender-based norms that divide more than they unite.

Queer theorists are wary of identity politics, believing that identity is flexible and that categorization on the basis of a single shared characteristic is inappropriate. They question, for example, whether African American lesbians really have more in common with white, upper-middle-class lesbians than they do with heterosexual African American women. Queer theorists have also argued that identity politics tends to reinforce a web of heterosexual and heterosexist "norms." As such, some have even questioned whether it is wise to view "coming out" as the assumption of a "transformative identity."

Queer theorists, who favor coalition politics over what they view as exclusionary identity politics, seek to destabilize popular conceptions of normality and sexuality and to undermine the heterosexual/homosexual opposition. To this end, they focus attention on those who do not easily fit into the socially constructed categories of gender and sexuality (such as bisexuals, transvestites, transgendered persons, and transsexuals) and explore from a nonjudgmental perspective behaviors and practices that are often considered deviant (such as fetishes, autoeroticism, and sadomasochism). They ultimately aim to show that representations—whether in novels, movies, ads, or other media—are culturally dependent and fallible, not some sort of received or objective truth. By "queering the text"—by revealing within cultural representations the signs of what Rich called "compulsory heterosexuality" and by showing that meaning is the relative product of prevailing discourses—queer theorists seek to show that the truly "queer" thing is how quick we are to label, categorize, and judge.

The tenets of queer theory are reflected in numerous works of literary and cultural criticism. Early examples include Thomas Yingling's *Hart Crane and the Homosexual Text* (1990), Jonathan Goldberg's *Sodometries* (1992), and Michael Moon's *Disseminating Whitman* (1993). Other critics whose analyses are informed by queer theory include Lauren Berlant, Richard Bozorth, Joseph Bristow, Christopher Craft, Lisa Duggan, Elizabeth Freeman, Christopher Lane, Jeff Nunokawa, and Michael Warner. Berlant and Freeman's "Queer Nationality," which appeared in Berlant's collection *The Queen of America Goes to Washington City: Essays on Sex and Censorship* (1997), discussed the ways in which a national network of gay and lesbian affinity groups has sought to use everything from local rituals to mass-culture spectacles to alter America's self-perception as a heterosexual nation. Bozorth's book *Auden's Games of Knowledge: Poetry and the Meanings of Homosexuality* (2001) argued that Auden's poetry addresses and reflects the psychological and political meanings of same-sex desire. Some queer theorists have even suggested that the approach lends itself to the "queering" of other socially constructed categories. As Mimi Nguyen wrote in her essay "Why Queer Theory?" (1999): "It's impossible . . . to imagine that 'queer' only skews gender and sexuality, and not race or class or nation, as if we might line up our social categories like cans in a cupboard" (n.p.).

In the essay that follows, Grant F. Scott focuses on the wood block illustrations of *Frankenstein* done by Lynd Ward for a deluxe edition of the novel published in 1934 by Harrison Smith and Robert Haas. Although Ward may have been trying to take advantage of James Whale's 1931 film adaptation of the novel, Scott sees his illustrations as being more "Gothic in atmosphere and psychology" (p. 401 in this volume). He cites as a "vital context for understanding Ward's designs" (p. 401) an early nineteenth-century stage version of the novel by Richard Brinsley Peake. Peake had "deprive[d] the monster of speech, relying on pantomime," focusing the eyes of the audience on the body of the actor (p. 391). It was the success of these early theatrical adaptations that kept interest in the novel alive—as well as interest in "the creature's powerfully muscular body" (p. 404). Ward's illustrations, Scott argues, with their focus on the masculine body, "offer a sustained queer reading of Mary Shelley's novel, one that balances a psychological with a political dimension" (p. 407).

Whereas the first of Ward's illustrations might have represented the threshold of creation, it instead "fast-forwards to Victor's bed chamber some time after Victor has fled the laboratory and endured a few hours of restless sleep" (p. 408). The creature "towers over his supine creator," but "[w]hereas Shelley's text describes the creature in infantile terms, . . . Ward's design focuses on the creature's mature and emphatically masculine body" (p. 410). Scott argues that Ward's erotically charged image of the creature "revises the dream Victor has before this encounter, which involves him kissing Elizabeth who then turns into his mother's corpse" (p. 410). It "converts a necrophilic oedipal fantasy into a nightmare of what Eve Sedgwick describes as 'homosexual panic,' the revelation of an unspeakable same-sex desire" (p. 410). In making his argument, Scott also credits the work of earlier queer theorists, who had argued that it was Victor's growing awareness of his latent homosexual attraction to his monster that caused his psyche to become unstable and riven by contradictions.

Returning to Ward's first engraving, Scott points out that whereas it reveals even the hair on the creature's massive body, it shows his head to be small, thereby again stressing the creature's physicality. A pair of "oversized hands," which are said to echo the illustration by Theodor von Hoist found on the title page of the 1831 edition, and "in a broader sense the creation scene of Michelangelo's Sistine fresco and the sculpture of David, acts as a coded reference to homosexuality. . . . In the pivotal bed-chamber scene, more importantly, the creature looms over Frankenstein like a grotesque David with his enormous hands and aggressively sharp nails, suggesting the dangers of erotic transgression" (p. 412).

Ward's subsequent depiction of the face-off between Victor and the monster on a glacier in the Alps is said by Scott to depict the "open defiance and provocative sexuality of the creature . . . even more dramatically" (p. 414). Once again, it is the creature's body, scantily clad and seen from behind, as if by readers viewing it in the text, that "dominates the compositional space" (p. 416). Making a move more typical of critical race theory than queer theory, Scott argues that the creature's simian, bestial appearance in the engraving conforms to the nineteenth-century image of the racial as well as sexual Other. It is the image of the animalistic black man that was part of "the nineteenth-century discourse of slavery" (p. 417). And Scott sounds as much like a Marxist as a race- or sexuality-oriented critic when he goes on to analyze the clothes worn by Ward's two figures. He argues that they turn one figure into an industrial laborer or deck hand and the other, Victor, into something like a "foreman or factory owner" (p. 419). This "othering" of the creature's class complements rather than contradicts the othering of his race and sexuality, since the transgressions of racial, class, and sexual boundaries were deeply interinvolved in the white Western psyche and could easily serve as tropes for one another.

In a subsequent treatment of Ward's rendering of the scene in which Shelley's monster is horrified to see his own reflection in a pool, Scott notes how sharply it differs from Shelley's verbal depiction. Whereas the latter emphasizes the monster's horrified recognition of his own ugliness, the former offers a "portrait of the racial other that visually gestures to Gaugin's paintings of native Tahitians" and "Shakespeare's Caliban before Prospero arrived on the island and transformed him into 'a savage and deformed slave'" (p. 421). In the edition's ensuing pages, Ward depicts the creature under attack, first by the mob that hurls all sorts of projectiles his way, then by Felix, who in Shelley's words "dashed me to the ground, and struck me violently with a stick" (p. 425). In the first of these illustrations, Scott maintains, the creature is subject "to the kind of public humiliation and ostracism experienced by homosexuals in late eighteenth- and early nineteenth-century Britain" (p. 422). Scott argues that the second image sexualizes the episode, turning the stick into a spiked phallic object threatening to penetrate the creature from behind. It makes a disturbing connection—one that Ward makes not only in subsequent renderings but also in his illustrations of other works—"between homoeroticism and sadistic acts of violence" (p. 428). In what Scott calls "the most shocking of all the images, the creature radically tests the viewer's sympathy for him by exacting his own terrible revenge on Victor's youngest brother William" (p. 428). Ward's illustration, in Scott's words, "utterly transforms the almost accidental nature of the assault as it is described in Mary

Shelley's own text"; here, "the creature pulverizes the boy like a rag doll, obliterating his victim's face" (p. 428). Not only is the image a violent one, not only does it turn the killing into a sexual crime via the "phallic extension" of the creature's "left leg" (p. 429), but it also—given the victim's age—shades suggestively into the terrifying territory in which male homosexuals are suspected of being pedophiles.

In the final pages of his essay, Scott discusses the association Mary Shelley's novel makes between sexuality and crime, its "queer use of the word 'consummation,'" and Ward's decision to represent various scenes of incarceration (pp. 433–36). Justine, imprisoned for a crime that Victor's creature committed, is said by Scott to be "the scapegoat on which Victor projects his monstrous shame" (p. 433). Ward's image of the jailed Turk represents, in Scott's view, the creature's "monstrous foreignness" (p. 433) at any number of levels—including one on which the wicked, unnatural, and bestial-looking Turk signifies the subhuman monstrosity of the sodomite.

The essay concludes with an analysis of Ward's final illustration, which presents the murdered Elizabeth in "a highly eroticized portrait that drapes a languorous figure across the bed, her form falling provocatively toward the viewer." In this final design, "pictorial energies" are expended "for the careful erotic deployment of Elizabeth's body, as Ward re-inscribes for the viewer an apparently heteronormative view of Victor's sexuality. As Victor himself does in the text, Ward uses heterosexuality as a defense against the temptation of the protagonist's powerful homosexual attraction to his creation" (p. 440). This very interesting turn in Scott's argument seems to suggest that Ward, having used his illustrations to explore the theme of homosexual desire in *Frankenstein*, chose to close out his series safely, with a heterosexually erotic image that rescues Victor, perhaps the reader and himself, from undesirable suspicion.

Though it is sensitive to issues of race and class in Shelley's novel, Scott's essay best exemplifies the kind of critical reading associated with queer theory. It points out instances, some latent but others quite blatant, of same-sex desire, finds instances of the "homosexual panic" (p. 441) often felt when male-male desire presents itself, and it makes deft use of other critics, such as Sedgwick, who have uncovered the homosocial and homoerotic themes and motifs in literary works. Finally, the essay takes queer theory to a metalevel, performing a queer reading of a set of illustrations that, in turn, perform a queer reading of a novel not usually viewed in homoerotic terms.

# GENDER CRITICISM AND QUEER THEORY: A SELECTED BIBLIOGRAPHY

## Gender Criticism and Theory: General Texts, Studies

Benstock, Shari. *Textualizing the Feminine: Essays on the Limits of Genre*. Norman: U of Oklahoma P, 1991. Print.

Berg, Temma F., et al., eds. *Engendering the Word: Feminist Essays in Psychosexual Poetics*. Urbana: U of Illinois P, 1989. Print.

Boone, Joseph A., and Michael Cadden, eds. *Engendering Men: The Question of Male Feminist Criticism*. New York: Routledge, 1990. Print. See especially the essays by Wayne Koestenbaum and Mark Seltzer.

Butler, Judith. *Gender Trouble: Feminism and the Subversion of Identity*. New York: Routledge, 1990. Print. For a new introduction by the author, see the 1999 edition.

Chodorow, Nancy. *The Reproduction of Mothering: Psychoanalysis and the Sociology of Gender*. Updated ed. Berkeley: U of California P, 1999. Print.

Clark, Stephen H. "Testing the Razor: T. S. Eliot's *Poems* 1920." Berg et al. 167–89.

Eisenstein, Hester, and Alice Jardine, eds. *The Future of Difference*. Boston: G. K. Hall, 1980. Print.

Elfenbein, Anna Shannon. "Unsexing Language: Pronomial Protest in Emily Dickinson's 'Unlay this Laurel'." Berg et al. 208–23.

Flood, Michael. *The Men's Bibliography: A Comprehensive Bibliography of Writing on Men, Masculinities, Gender, and Sexualities*. 19th ed. Canberra: 2008. *The Men's Bibliography*. Web. 21 January 2010.

Foucault, Michel. *The History of Sexuality*. Trans. Robert Hurley. Vol. 1. New York: Pantheon, 1978. Print.

Garber, Marjorie. *Vested Interests: Cross-Dressing and Cultural Anxiety*. New York: Routledge, 1992. Print.

Goodman, Lizbeth. *Literature and Gender*. London: Routledge, 1996. Print.

Halberstam, Judith. *Female Masculinity*. Durham: Duke UP, 1998. Print.

Halperin, David. *Saint Foucault: Towards a Gay Hagiography*. Oxford: Oxford UP, 1997. Print.

hooks, bell. *We Real Cool: Black Men and Masculinity*. London: Routledge, 2004. Print.

Kamuf, Peggy. "Writing Like a Woman." *Women and Language in Literature and Society.* New York: Praeger, 1980. 284–99. Print.

Miller, Nancy K. *Subject to Change: Reading Feminist Writing.* New York: Columbia UP, 1988. Print.

Rich, B. Ruby. "Anti-Porn: Soft Issue, Hard Word." *Feminist Review* 13 (Spr. 1983): 56–67.

Rubin, Gayle. "The Traffic in Women: Notes on the 'Political Economy' of Sex." *Toward an Anthropology of Women.* Ed. Rayna R. Reiter. New York: Monthly Review, 1975. 157–210. Print.

Schor, Naomi. "Feminist and Gender Studies." *Introduction to Scholarship in Modern Languages and Literatures.* Ed. Joseph Gibaldi. New York: MLA, 1992. 262–87. Print.

Sedgwick, Eve Kosofsky. *Between Men: English Literature and Male Homosocial Desire.* New York: Columbia UP, 1985. Print.

———. "Gender Criticism." *Redrawing the Boundaries: The Transformation of English and American Literary Studies.* Eds. Stephen Greenblatt and Giles Gunn. New York: MLA, 1992. 271–302. Print.

## Gay and Lesbian Criticism/Sexualities Criticism

Abelove, Henry, Michèle Aina Barale, and David Halperin, eds. *The Lesbian and Gay Reader.* New York: Routledge, 1993. Print. Contains Gayle Rubin's essay "Thinking Sex: Notes for a Radical Theory of the Politics of Sexuality."

de Lauretis, Teresa. *Technologies of Gender: Essays on Theory, Film, and Fiction.* Bloomington: Indiana UP, 1987. Print.

Dollimore, Jonathan. *Sexual Dissidence: Augustine to Wilde, Freud to Foucault.* Oxford: Clarendon, 1991. Print.

Edelman, Lee. *Homographesis: Essays in Gay Literary and Cultural Theory.* New York: Routledge, 1994. Print.

Floyd, Kevin. *The Reification of Desire: Toward a Queer Marxism.* Minneapolis: U of Minnesota P, 2009. Print.

Haggerty, George E., and Bonnie Zimmerman, eds. *Professions of Desire: Lesbian and Gay Studies in Literature.* New York: MLA, 1995. Print.

Hall, Donald E. *Reading Sexualities: Hermeneutic Theory and the Future of Queer Studies.* London: Routledge, 2009. Print.

Halperin, David M. *One Hundred Years of Homosexuality and Other Essays on Greek Love.* New York: Routledge, 1990. Print.

Kollar, Veronika. *Lesbian Discourses: Images of a Community.* New York: Routledge, 2008. Print.

Munt, Sally, ed. *New Lesbian Criticism: Literary and Cultural Readings*. New York: Harvester Wheatsheaf, 1992. Print.

Raitt, Suzanne. *Volcanos and Pearl Divers: Essays in Lesbian Feminist Studies*. London: Onlywomen, 1995. Print.

Rich, Adrienne. "Compulsory Heterosexuality and Lesbian Existence." *Signs* 5 (Sum. 1980): 631–60. Print.

Stimpson, Catharine R. "Zero Degree Deviancy: The Lesbian Novel in English." *Critical Inquiry* 8 (1981): 363-79. Print.

Wittig, Monique. *The Straight Mind and Other Essays*. Boston: Beacon, 1992. Print. See especially "One Is Not Born a Woman" and "The Mark of Gender."

## Queer Theory

Beemyn, Brett, and Mickey Eliason, eds. *Queer Studies: A Lesbian, Gay, Bisexual, and Transgender Anthology*. New York: New York UP, 1996. Print.

Butler, Judith. *Bodies That Matter: On the Discursive Limits of "Sex."* New York: Routledge, 1993. Print.

Corber, Robert, ed. *Queer Studies: An Interdisciplinary Reader*. Malden, MA: Blackwell, 2003. Print.

de Lauretis, Teresa, ed. *Queer Theory: Lesbian and Gay Sexualities*. Spec. issue of *differences* 3.2 (1991). Print.

Duberman, Martin, ed. *Queer Representations: Reading Lives, Reading Cultures*. New York: New York UP, 1997. Print.

Halberstam, Judith. *In a Queer Time and Place: Transgender Bodies, Subcultural Lives*. New York: New York UP, 2005. Print.

Jagose, Annamarie. *Queer Theory: An Introduction*. New York: New York UP, 1997. Print.

Nguyen, Mimi. "Why Queer Theory?" 1999. Web. www.theory.org .uk/ctr-que4.htm. 19 September 2015.

Sedgwick, Eve Kosofsky. *Epistemology of the Closet*. Berkeley: U of California P, 1990. Print.

———. *Tendencies*. Durham: Duke UP, 1993. Print.

Sinfield, Alan. *Cultural Politics—Queer Reading*. 2nd ed. London: Routledge, 2005. Print.

Sullivan, Nikki. *A Critical Introduction to Queer Theory*. Edinburgh: Edinburgh UP, 2003. Print.

Valocchi, Stephen, and Robert J. Corber, eds. *Queer Studies: An Interdisciplinary Reader*. Malden, MA: Blackwell, 2003. Print.

## Intersections of Feminist and Gender Studies

Case, Sue-Ellen. *Feminist and Queer Performance: Critical Strategies.* Basingstoke: Palgrave Macmillan, 2009. Print.

Giffney, Noreen. "Denormatizing Queer Theory: More Than (Simply) Lesbian and Gay Studies." *Feminist Theory* 5.1 (2004): 73–78. Print.

Green, Adam I. "Gay but Not Queer: Toward a Post-Queer Study of Sexuality." *Theory and Society* 31 (2002): 521–45. Print.

Harris, Laura Alexandra. "Queer Black Feminism: The Pleasure Principle." *Feminist Review* 54 (Aut. 1996): 3–30. Print.

Lovaas, Karen E., et al., eds. *LGBT Studies and Queer Theory: New Conflicts, Collaborations, and Contested Terrain.* New York: Routledge, 2007. Print.

Piontek, Thomas. *Queering Gay and Lesbian Studies.* Urbana: U of Illinois P, 2006. Print.

Richardson, Diane, et al., eds. *Intersections Between Feminist and Queer Theory.* Houndmills: Palgrave Macmillan, 2006. Print.

Weed, Elizabeth, and Naomi Schor, eds. *Feminism Meets Queer Theory.* Indianapolis: Indiana UP, 1997. Print.

Wilchins, Riki. *Queer Theory, Gender Theory: An Instant Primer.* Los Angeles: Alyson, 2004. Print.

## Intersections with Film Theory

Aaron, Michele, ed. *New Queer Cinema.* New Brunswick: Rutgers UP, 2004. Print. See especially B. Ruby Rich's essay "New Queer Cinema."

Carson, Diane, Janice R. Welsch, and Linda Dittmar, eds. *Multiple Voices in Feminist Film Criticism.* Minneapolis: U of Minnesota P, 1994. Print.

de Lauretis, Teresa. *Alice Doesn't: Feminism, Semiotics, Cinema.* Bloomington: Indiana UP, 1986. Print.

Dyer, Richard. *Now You See It: Studies in Lesbian and Gay Film.* 2nd ed. London: Routledge, 2003. Print.

Griffiths, Robin. *Queer Cinema in Europe.* Bristol: Intellect, 2008. Print.

Modleski, Tania. *Feminism without Women: Culture and Criticism in a "Postfeminist" Age.* New York: "Routledge, 1991. Print.

Mulvey, Laura. *Visual and Other Pleasures.* 2nd ed. Houndmills: Palgrave Macmillan, 2009. Print.

Penley, Constance. *Feminism and Film Theory*. New York: Routledge, 1988. Print.

William, David Foster. *Queer Issues in Contemporary Latin American Cinema*. Austin: U of Texas P, 2003. Print.

### Intersections with Postcolonial Theory and Criticism

Desai, Jigna. *Beyond Bollywood: The Cultural Politics of South Asian Diasporic Film*. New York: Routledge, 2004. Print.

Hawley, John C, ed. *Postcolonial and Queer Theories: Intersections and Essays*. Westport: Greenwood, 2001. Print.

Mills, Sara. *Gender and Colonial Space*. Manchester: Manchester UP, 2005. Print.

Spivak, Gayatri Chakravorty. *In Other Worlds: Essays in Cultural Politics*. New York: Methuen, 1987. Print.

——. *Outside in the Teaching Machine*. New York: Routledge, 1993. Print.

### Gender Readings

Berlant, Lauren. *The Female Complaint: On the Unfinished Business of Sentimentality in American Culture*. Durham: Duke UP, 2008. Print.

Brown, Anne E., and Marjanne E. Goozé, eds. *International Women's Writing: New Landscapes of Identity*. Westport: Greenwood, 1995. Print.

Bruder, Helen P., ed. *Women Reading William Blake*. New York: Palgrave Macmiiian, 2007. Print.

Claridge, Laura, and Elizabeth Langland, eds. *Out of Bounds: Male Writing and Gender(ed) Criticism*. Amherst: U of Massachusetts P, 1980. Print.

Michie, Elsie. *Outside the Pale: Cultural Exclusion, Gender Difference, and the Victorian Writer*. Ithaca: Cornell UP, 1993. Print.

### Gay, Lesbian, and Queer Readings

Breen, Margaret Sönser. *Narratives of Queer Desire: Deserts of the Heart*. Basingstoke: Palgrave Macmillan, 2009. Print.

Bristow, Joseph, ed. *Sexual Sameness: Textual Differences in Lesbian and Gay Writing*. New York: Routledge, 1992. Print.

Craft, Christopher. *Another Kind of Love: Male Homosexual Desire in English Discourse, 1850–1920.* Berkeley: U of California P, 1994. Print.

Creech, James. *Closet Writing/Gay Reading: The Case of Melville's Pierre.* Chicago: U of Chicago P, 1993. Print.

Flannery, Denis. *On Sibling Love, Queer Attachment and American Writing.* Aldershot: Ashgate, 2007. Print.

Galvin, Mary E. *Queer Poetics: Five Modernist Women Writers.* Westport: Greenwood, 1999. Print.

Hoffman, Warren. *The Passing Game: Queering Jewish American Culture.* Syracuse: Syracuse UP, 2009. Print.

Lilly, Mark, ed. *Lesbian and Gay Writing: An Anthology of Critical Essays.* Philadelphia: Temple UP, 1990. Print.

Martin, Robert K. *Hero, Captain, and Stranger: Male Friendship, Social Critique, and Literary Form in the Sea Novels of Herman Melville.* Chapel Hill: U of North Carolina P, 1986. Print.

Packard, Chris. *Queer Cowboys and Other Erotic Male Friendships in Nineteenth-Century American Literature.* New York: Palgrave Macmillan, 2005. Print.

Puar, Jasbir. *Terrorist Assemblages: Homonationalism in Queer Times.* Durham, NC: Duke UP, 2008. Print.

Rich, Adrienne. *On Lies, Secrets, and Silence: Selected Prose, 1966–1979.* New York: Norton, 1979. Print.

Samuels, Robert. *Hitchcock's Bi-Textuality: Lacan, Feminisms, and Queer Theory.* Albany: State U of New York P, 1998.

Sedgwick, Eve Kosofsky, ed. "Queerer Than Fiction." Spec. issue of *Studies in the Novel* 28.3 (Fall 1996). Print.

Traub, Valerie. *Desire and Anxiety: Circulations of Sexuality in Shakespearean Drama.* London: Routledge, 1992. Print.

### Gender and Queer Readings of *Frankenstein*

Fuller, Sarah Canfield. "Reading the Cyborg in Mary Shelley's *Frankenstein.*" *Journal of the Fantastic in the Arts* 14.2 [53] (2003): 217–27. Print.

Gould, Polly. "Sexual Polarities: Shelley's *Frankenstein* and Polar Exploration as a Search for Origins Beyond 'Woman'." *Nordlit* 23 (2008): 103–18. Print.

Haggerty, George E. "'Dung, Guts and Blood': Sodomy, Abjection and Gothic Fiction in the Early Nineteenth Century." *Gothic Studies* 18.2 (2006): 35–51. Print.

Kilbourn, Russell J. A. "American Frankenstein: Modernity's Monstrous Progeny." *Mosaic* 38.3 (2005): 167–84. Web. www .umanitoba.ca/mosaic. 14 June 2014.

Komisaruk, Adam. "'So Guided by a Silken Cord': *Frankenstein*'s Family Values." *Studies in Romanticism* 38.3 (1999): 409–41. Print.

Laplace-Sinatra, Michael. "Science, Gender, and Otherness in Shelley's *Frankenstein* and Kenneth Branagh's Film Adaptation." *European Romantic Review* 9.2 (1998): 253–70. Print.

Michel, Frann. "Lesbian Panic and Mary Shelley's *Frankenstein*." *GLQ* 2.3 (1995): 237–52. Print.

## A GENDER/QUEER PERSPECTIVE

### GRANT F. SCOTT

### Victor's Secret: Queer Gothic in Lynd Ward's Illustrations to *Frankenstein* (1934)

Over the years book illustrators have found Mary Shelley's *Frankenstein* a rich canvas for visual exploration. Graphic artists such as Carl Lagerquist (1922), Nino Carbe (1932), Everett Henry (1934), Berni Wrightson (1983), and Barry Moser (1984) created evocative adaptations of the book's dramatic scenes that offer perceptive interpretations of plot and character. The most widely reproduced series, however, belongs to Lynd Ward, who executed his woodblock designs for a deluxe edition of the novel published in 1934 by Harrison Smith and Robert Haas. Issuing its handsomely printed and boxed volume during the height of the holiday season, the firm no doubt wished to capitalize on Ward's earlier success with his four wordless, "graphic" novels, *Gods' Man* (1929), *Madman's Drum* (1930), *Wild Pilgrimage* (1932), and *Prelude to a Million Years* (1933). They also sought to take advantage of the recent popularity of James Whale's film adaptation of *Frankenstein* (1931), which had done well enough at the box office to merit a sequel.[1]

---

[1] In spite of being published in the same month as the stock market crash, *Gods' Man* sold 20,000 copies in its first three years. Whale's first adaptation was followed by *Bride of Frankenstein* in 1935.

That the slipcase illustration bears a striking resemblance to black-and-white screen titles of the period is further evidence that the publishers sought to woo a larger audience eager to read the novel after seeing the film.[2]

Ironically, though, Ward's detailed images depart from the film aesthetic that influenced the work of his fellow illustrators and return us to an earlier nineteenth-century tradition of adaptation, not least in their use of the medium of woodblock engraving. Although indebted to German expressionism and characteristic of high modernism in their splintered and fractured style, Ward's illustrations are fundamentally Gothic in atmosphere and psychology (figure 1). The aggressive passages of woodblock gouging as well as the macabre and sinister facial expressions of the human figures subvert realism and replace a conventional mimetic or cinematic style with a darkly surreal mental landscape reminiscent of the Gothic imaginary. The extreme contrasts of black and white, tilting picture planes, shifting points of view, abrupt foreshortenings, and dramatic rays of light only confirm our sense that Ward is exploring a psychological space more in keeping with the Gothic terrain of Mary Shelley's novel.

In this sense, a vital context for understanding Ward's designs is the early nineteenth-century stage history of *Frankenstein*. The first adaptation of Mary Shelley's novel, Richard Brinsley Peake's *Presumption; or, The Fate of Frankenstein* (English Opera House, 1823), was an enormous popular success and within three years spawned at least fifteen other English and French dramatizations of the book.[3] Jean Toussant Merle and Antoine Nicolas Béraud's *Le Monstre et le magicien* (Théâtre de la Porte Saint-Martin, Paris, 1826) was almost as popular as Peake's melodrama, and inspired a translation by John Kerr, *The Monster and Magician; or, The Fate of Frankenstein* (Royal West London Theatre, 1826), along with Henry M. Milner's *The Man and the Monster; or, The Fate of Frankenstein* (Royal Coburg Theatre, 1826). Each of these plays took its cue from Peake (not Mary Shelley) in emphasizing stage spectacle and special effects, domestic melodrama, comedy, and music.

That creative stagecraft and riveting spectacle were the primary means of captivating large audiences is clear from a Covent Garden

---

[2]For a good online image of the cover plus digital reproductions of all the woodcut designs, see http://paganpressbooks.com/jpl/LYNDWARD.HTM
[3]Steven Earl Forry, *Hideous Progenies: Dramatizations of "Frankenstein" from Mary Shelley to the Present* (Philadelphia: University of Pennsylvania Press, 1990), 34.

Figure 1. From *Frankenstein, or The Modern Prometheus* by Mary Woll-stonecraft Shelley with engravings on wood by Lynd Ward (New York: Harrison Smith and Robert Haas, 1934), opposite p. 26. Lynd Ward's illustrations in this edition, henceforth referenced in captions as "Ward's *Frankenstein*," exhibit German expressionist, high modernist, and gothic influences.

By permission of Robin Ward Savage and Nanda Weedon Ward. Reproduced with the permission of Rare Books and Manuscripts, Special Collections Library, the Pennsylvania State University Libraries.

playbill of July 9, 1824, which announced that "among the many striking effects of this Piece, the following will be displayed: Mysterious and
terrific appearance of the Demon from the Laboratory of Frankenstein.
DESTRUCTION of a COTTAGE by FIRE. And the FALL of an
AVALANCHE."[4] All four of the 1820 productions mentioned above
cut Robert Walton's frame narrative, reorganize Mary Shelley's novel
around the creation scene, and base the action on dramatic confrontations between the creature and the plays' various characters. Unlike the
novel, which culminates with the eloquent soliloquies of Frankenstein
and his creature, these plays end with both characters grappling each
other and perishing in spectacular natural catastrophes. H.M. Milner's
script, in fact, contains not a single word of dialogue in the final two
scenes but instead gives detailed instructions about how to stage the
final pursuit. It even provides a diagram showing the actors' positions
around the rim of the volcano. In *Presumption,* moreover, Peake's directions often emphasize the creature's visual stationing: "in attitude before
Frankenstein," "on an eminence of the bush, or a projecting rock,"
"climbing the outside of the Portico . . . with burning brand." The final
prompt instructs the surviving characters to "form a picture as the curtain falls,"[5] leaving the audience with a tableau that anticipates Lynd
Ward's spatial arrangement of his own figures.

Undoubtedly the most important departure from the original novel
and the most influential alteration for later adaptations was Peake's
decision to deprive the monster of speech, a move that focused the
audience's attention on gesture and pantomime, and on the physical
presence of the role's first actor, T.P. Cooke. As Jeffrey Cox states in
discussing the emergence of pantomime in the period, Peake's revision
highlighted "the new dramatic power of moments of muteness."[6] It
meant, too, of course, that the audience's eyes were fixed on the body
of the actor and the repertoire of striking attitudes he could perform. It
was no accident that T.P. Cooke, a former sailor who by one estimate
played the role 365 times over his career,[7] was physically imposing and
wore a close-fitting cotton tunic that accentuated his athletic physique.

[4]Quoted in Elizabeth Nitchie, *Mary Shelley: Author of "Frankenstein."* (New Brunswick,
NJ: Rutgers University Press, 1953), 233.
[5]Jeffrey N. Cox, ed., *Seven Gothic Dramas 1789–1825* (Athens: Ohio University
Press, 1992), 399, 403, 413, 425. See also H.M. Milner's play, which, after an earlier
scene of combat, states: "a general picture is formed, on which the Drop falls" (cited in
Forry, *Hideous Progenies,* 198).
[6]Jeffrey N. Cox, "Re-viewing Romantic Drama," *Literature Compass* 1 (2004): 18.
[7]Forry, *Hideous Progenies,* 11.

H.M. Milner's play also called for the monster to wear "close vest and leggings . . . heightened with blue, as if to show the muscles, &c".[8] Many contemporary reviews applauded Cooke's ability to strike effective poses and to express the monster's character through his body movements and countenance.[9]

The popular success of these theatre pieces led to a resurgence of interest in Mary Shelley's novel and prompted its immediate republication in 1823 and a subsequent revised volume in 1831, which became the standard and first illustrated edition.[10] Capitalizing on the visual power of the recent stage productions, the firm of Colburn and Bentley commissioned two engravings by Theodor von Holst as the book's frontispiece and title page (figures 2 and 3). What is striking about these images is the way they not only reflect the pantomimic qualities of the theatrical performances with their exaggerated gestures and telegraphed emotion, but recall the hybrid nature of these plays, their confluence of Gothic horror and domestic melodrama. While the frontispiece offers us a veritable storehouse of Gothic stage props all jumbled together in the cramped space of Victor's castle/laboratory, the title page presents a sentimental tableau: a teary Frankenstein bidding farewell to Elizabeth in a feminized green space of plants and flowers. The crucifix that she wears combined with the background church serve to counter the blasphemous birth represented in the frontispiece and reinforce the conventional morality offered by the stage versions. More important, particularly for the later realizations of Lynd Ward, is Holst's attention in the frontispiece to the creature's powerfully muscular body and the fact that he portrays him neither as hideous nor as deformed—as the *monster* we expect—but as remarkably human. Like the illustrations that accompanied published editions of Peake's *Presumption* and its offshoots, the creature appears largely indistinguishable from the other human characters.[11]

The gender ambivalence of Holst's figure, who appears to have the body of a man and the head of a woman, suggests another crucial

[8]Ibid., 190.

[9]Douglas William Hoehn, "The First Season of *Presumption!: Or, The Fate of Frankenstein.*" *Theatre Studies* 26–27(1979): 83.

[10]For the influence of stage versions on the printing and copyright history of the novel, see William St. Clair, "The Impact of *Frankenstein*," in *Mary Shelley in Her Times,* eds. Betty T. Bennett and Stuart Curran (Baltimore and London: Johns Hopkins University Press, 2000), 38–63.

[11]See the three illustrations of T.P. Cooke reproduced in Forry, *Hideous Progenies,* 18–20.

Figure 2. Theodor von Holst's frontispiece to Colburn and Bentley's 1831 edition of *Frankenstein, or, the Modern Prometheus.*
© The British Library/The Image Works.

Figure 3. Theodor von Holst's title page to Colburn and Bentley's 1831 edition of *Frankenstein, or, the Modern Prometheus.*
Private Collection/Bridgeman Images.

Gothic influence on Ward's engravings and may explain why they have never been afforded serious consideration as works of critical interpretation; I mean their often frank and (for the time-period) disturbing homoerotic content. Ward's illustrations constitute the earliest attempt in the medium to offer a sustained queer reading of Mary Shelley's novel, one that balances a psychological with a political dimension.[12] These designs in fact anticipate like-minded critical investigations of *Frankenstein* by about sixty-five years.[13] While Ward's interpretation lays the foundation for such later theoretical readings, it also mediates the novel's homoeroticism through the illustrator's own socialist politics of the early 1930s and his concerns about race. Ward's critique of capitalism, depression-era labor conditions in America, and the increasing division between classes and races is apparent in his earlier graphic novel, *Wild Pilgrimage* (1932), which subtly informs his visual narrative in the engravings for *Frankenstein*.[14]

[12]As Elizabeth Young has recently shown in her insightful study, the Edison studio *Frankenstein* (1910) directed by J. Searle Dawley and James Whale's *Bride of Frankenstein* (1935) are the two earliest cinematic adaptations to offer salient homoerotic interpretations of Mary Shelley's novel. Since there is no evidence that he knew the Edison *Frankenstein* (1910), Ward's illustrations are historically important for offering the first known visual interpretation of this aspect of the novel. See *Black Frankenstein: The Making of an American Metaphor* (New York and London: New York University Press, 2008).

[13]It is not until the mid-1980s that scholars such as Eve K. Sedgwick and l.ouis Crompton begin theorizing the idea of homosexuality in Gothic and Romanic literature generally, and not until fifteen years after their pioneering studies that *Frankenstein* itself starts gaining momentum among critics as a work that insightfully exploits the complexities of male same-sex desire. See Eve K. Sedgwick, *Between Men: English Literature and Male Homosocial Desire* (New York: Columbia University Press, 1985) and Louis Crompton, *Byron and Greek Love: Homophobia in 19th-Century England* (Berkeley: University of California Press, 1985). Arguably the most astute and entertaining homoerotic reading of the novel is still *The Rocky Horror Picture Show* (1975), which gleefully and unabashedly portrays a transsexual Frankenstein whose sole purpose in creating the creature is to provide himself with a "new playmate" who will attend to his master's sexual pleasure. That *Rocky Horror* was critically ahead of its time is demonstrated by an article published in the same year as the film. In "*Frankenstein* and the Physiognomy of Desire," J. M. Hill specifically rejects homosexuality as a viable lens through which to understand Victor's relationships with other male characters: "He never either desires or identifies with a male peer" and rather than the ideal lover, "Walton and Clerval become versions of the desired mother (for Frankenstein" (*American Imago* 32 [1975]: 347, 357). For another early homoerotic reading of the creation scene, see Liz Lochhead's play, *Blood and Ice* (Edinburgh: Salamander Press, 1982), 21.

[14]In the 1930s Ward was committed to a number of progressive organizations such as the American League against War and Fascism and the American Artists' Congress, and became directly involved in their campaigns. No doubt he drew his inspiration from his father, the Methodist minister Harry F. Ward, who was a radical social activist and with Roger Baldwin one of the founders of the American Civil Liberties Union. Ward kept in close correspondence with his father and also helped disseminate his ideas at this time by illustrating his work *In Place of Profit: Social Incentives in the Soviet Union* (1933). See

## I

Lynd Ward's direct presentation of the creature's sexuality becomes apparent in the first full-page engraving of him (figure 4). Chapter Five of the novel begins with a vignette that shows Victor Frankenstein brooding in his secret laboratory high above the town. Surrounded by chemical instruments that emit braids of smoke, he seems to pause on the threshold of creation, deliberating over whether to take the next decisive step. In the book, of course, he does, but Ward chooses not to show the dramatic infusion of "a spark of being" or provide any representation of Victor's famous description of the creature. Instead he fast-forwards to Victor's bed chamber some time after Victor has fled the laboratory and endured a few hours of restless sleep. Ward illustrates the following passage from Shelley's novel:

> I beheld the wretch—the miserable monster whom I had created. He held up the curtain of the bed; and his eyes, if eyes they may be called, were fixed on me. His jaws opened, and he muttered some inarticulate sounds, while a grin wrinkled his cheeks. He might have spoken, but I did not hear; one hand was stretched out, seemingly to detain me, but I escaped, and rushed down stairs.[15]

In this second encounter, which inverts the hierarchy of the initial animation scene where the creature "lay at [Victor's] feet" (p. 59), he now towers over his supine creator. Whereas Shelley's text describes the creature in infantile terms, as an innocent smiling baby who mumbles and reaches out to his parent, Ward's design focuses on the creature's mature and emphatically masculine body. The creature's overture to Victor is most eloquently expressed in the rich darkness and mystery that surrounds the genital area and the illuminated curve of the penis.[16]

---

Perry Willett, *The Silent Shout: Frans Masereel, Lynd Ward, and the Novel in Woodcuts* (Bloomington: Indiana University Libraries, 1997), 38–39, and Ophelia Gilbert, "Lynd Ward," in *American Writers for Children, 1900–1960,* ed. John Cech, *Dictionary of Literary Biography,* vol. 22 (Detroit: Gale Research, 1983), 331.

[15]Mary Wollstonecraft Shelley, *Frankenstein or The Modern Prometheus,* with engravings on wood by Lynd Ward (New York: Harrison Smith and Robert Haas, 1934), 54–55. References in footnotes 26, 27, and 40 are also to this edition, which was reprinted in facsimile by Dover Publications (2009). All other references to the novel are taken from the Bedford text, pp. 19–189.

[16]Ward's homoerotic interpretation of this scene from the novel is made even more explicit if we consider the first version of the woodcut rejected by the publisher. It shows considerably larger genitals and a more well-defined penis. See Lynd Ward, *Storyteller without Words: The Wood Engravings of Lynd Ward* (New York: Harry N. Abrams, 1974), 288.

Figure 4. The first full-page engraving of the creature from Ward's *Frankenstein*, opposite p. 54.

The text of the 1831 novel figures the creature as Victor's infant son, his Adam; Ward's image, by contrast, intuitively responds to the subtext, the creature's role as male companion and lover. This role is much more apparent in an early draft of Mary Shelley's chapter, where in place of "the accomplishment of his toils" (1831), she had written that Victor beholds "my man compleated."[17]

The exhibition of the creature's powerfully erotic body along with the homoerotic charge of the scene revises the dream Victor has before this encounter, which involves him kissing Elizabeth who then turns into his mother's corpse with "grave-worms crawling in the folds of the flannel" (p. 60). In this illustration, Ward converts a necrophilic oedipal fantasy into a nightmare of what Eve Sedgwick describes as "homosexual panic," the revelation of an unspeakable same-sex desire.[18] "From Victor's paranoid perspective," as Mair Rigby insightfully argues, "he cannot help but read the Monster's desire as a sexual threat and its gaze, together with the physical reach through the curtains towards his body, figures his bedchamber as a potentially 'sodomitical' space."[19] Most recent queer readings situate the novel within the genre of "paranoid Gothic" and see Victor's highly unstable and conflicted emotional state as the consequence of his latent homosexual attraction to the creature. They trace the permutations of Victor's divided consciousness and his painful oscillation between homoerotic longing for the creature and homophobic loathing at the buried emotions it raises in him. As Eric Daffron states, the novel sets up an uneasy continuum between nonsexual, homosocial bonds between Victor and his friends Waldman, Walton, and Clerval, and the central homo-erotic bond with his creation that is deviant and dangerous.[20] In this understanding, as explored further by James Holt McGavran, "the masculine fear of being dominated by another man combines with powerful but unconscious homophobic feelings of panic and loathing, driving Victor simultaneously to reject his monster/lover/himself and yet to bond with him negatively

---

[17]Charles Robinson, ed., *Frankenstein or The Modern Prometheus: The Original Two-Volume Novel of 1816–1817 from the Bodleian Library Manuscripts* (Oxford: Bodleian Library, 2008), 276.

[18]Sedgwick, *Between Men*, 89.

[19]"'Do you share my madness?': *Frankenstein's* Queer Gothic," in *Queering the Gothic*, eds. William Hughes and Andrew Smith (Manchester: Manchester University Press, 2009), 44.

[20]"Male Bonding: Sympathy and Shelley's *Frankenstein*," *Nineteenth-Century Contexts* 21 (1999): 415–35.

so as to assure their mutual destruction."[21] This negative bond is symbolized earlier in Ward's depiction of the "old and beautiful oak" that is struck by lightning and becomes "a blasted stump" (p. 47). The implication of Victor's thrilling revulsion over the prospect of physical intimacy with his creature and the threat of violence that this union implies is what lends Ward's design its disturbing power. Victor's sexual ambivalence is most clearly reflected in the contrasting features of Ward's engraving. The eroticism of the creature's body (the intimate, and for woodblock engraving, highly unusual detail of body *hair*), its contoured muscular chest and the dark assertion of his sex, are set against an abnormally small head, hooded eyes, and grim mouth. Together with the large, claw-like hands, the asymmetry of the abdominal cavity, and the snaky folds of the curtain, which imply an ancient biblical sin, these more sinister features signify what is deviant and "monstrous" about the creature and his proposition. Reinforcing the centrality of this encounter for Ward's reading of the novel is the motif of oversized hands, which in echoing Holst's frontispiece, and in a broader sense the creation scene of Michelangelo's Sistine fresco and the sculpture of David, acts as a coded reference to homosexuality. A number of the illustrations in the edition represent hands not only as fragmentary body parts floating in isolation on the page but as disjoined from the hands of other human figures. When they do meet, as in a later tailpiece (figure 5), Victor's left hand struggles to prevent the proportionately larger hand of the creature from seizing him. This vignette revises "The Creation of Adam" on the Sistine ceiling by reiterating the touching into life as a murderous contest rather than a tender beckoning. In the pivotal bed-chamber scene, more importantly, the creature looms over Frankenstein like a grotesque David with his enormous hands and aggressively sharp nails suggesting the dangers of erotic transgression.

---

[21] "'Insurmountable Barriers to Our Union': Homosocial Male Bonding, Homosexual Panic, and Death on the Ice in *Frankenstein*," *European Romantic Review* 11 (Winter 2000): 46–47. For additional readings in this vein, see also Siobhan Craig, "Monstrous Dialogues: Erotic Discourse and the Dialogic Constitution of the Subject in *Frankenstein*," in *A Dialogue of Voices: Feminist Literary Theory and Bakhtin*, ed. Karen Hohne and Helen Wussow (Minneapolis: University of Minnesota Press, 1994), 83–96; George Haggerty, *Queer Gothic* (Urbana: Illinois University Press, 2006); and Christopher Nagle, *Sexuality and the Culture of Sensibility in the British Romantic Era* (Basingstoke: Palgrave Macmillan, 2007), 132–36.

Figure 5. A tailpiece from Ward's *Frankenstein* showing the creature's oversized hands, p. 211.
By permission of Robin Ward Savage and Nanda Weedon Ward. Reproduced with the permission of Rare Books and Manuscripts, Special Collections Library, the Pennsylvania State University Libraries.

In its unabashed rendering of the creature's desire, Ward's engraving culminates an evolution of complex visual responses to what George Haggerty has called the novel's primal scene.[22] The title page of Peake's *Frankenstein* in Dicks' Standard Plays (1823) takes liberty with the "gestures of conciliation"[23] as indicated by the stage directions, transforming them into a tentative erotic query (figure 6). Holst's frontispiece (1831), as we have seen, hints at the creature's dismay at discovering its own bisexual or androgynous nature, and the later illustration by Carl Lagerquist (1922), the most daring of these earlier designs, depicts a naked, muscular creature striding toward a recumbent Frankenstein, whose legs are splayed and face aghast. Lagerquist's creature balances a terrifying visage and aggressive movement with sexual modesty as he grabs the bed curtain to cover his genitals (figure 7).[24] It is only Ward who completely undresses the creature, stations him much closer to the picture plane and collapses Victor's character with the viewer's, thereby augmenting the psychosexual threat. The ragged edges of the print

[22] Haggerty, *Queer Gothic*, 53.

[23] Cox, *Seven Gothic Dramas*, 399.

[24] Mary Wollstonecraft Shelley, *Frankenstein or The Modern Prometheus* (Boston and New York: Cornhill Publishing, 1922), opposite p. 44.

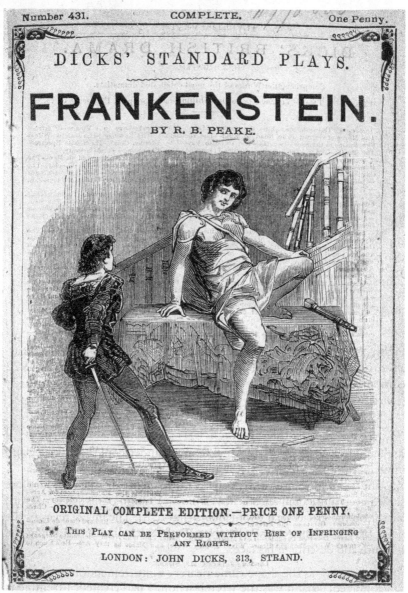

Figure 6. Title page from Richard Brinsley Peake's 1823 play *Franken-stein. A Romantic Drama, in Three Acts.*

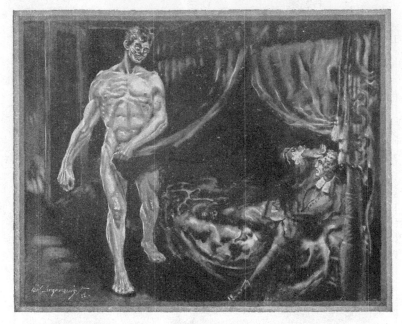

I BEHELD THE WRETCH, THE MISERABLE MONSTER WHOM I HAD CREATED

Figure 7. Carl Lagerquist's representation of the creature's initial appearance to a cowering Victor, opposite p. 44 in Cornhill Publishing's 1922 edition of *Frankenstein*.
Courtesy of Grant F. Scott.

itself and its lack of verbal or visual framing underscore the intimacy and immediacy of the creature's demand.

The open defiance and provocative sexuality of the creature are staged even more dramatically in Ward's illustration of his stand-off with Victor on the glacier near Mont Blanc (figure 8). The image reverses the point of view of the text, which gives Victor's account of beholding the creature and describing his face:

> I perceived, as the shape came nearer (sight tremendous and abhorred!) that it was the wretch whom I had created. I trembled with rage and horror, resolving to wait his approach, and then close with him in mortal combat. He approached; his countenance bespoke bitter anguish, combined with disdain and malignity, while its unearthly ugliness rendered it almost too horrible for human eyes. (p. 92)

Figure 8. The creature confronts Victor on the glacier near Mont Blanc, from Ward's *Frankenstein*, opposite p. 106.
By permission of Robin Ward Savage and Nanda Weedon Ward. Reproduced with the permission of Rare Books and Manuscripts, Special Collections Library, the Pennsylvania State University Libraries.

As opposed to the early nineteenth-century stage adaptations of *Frankenstein*, Ward stations us *behind* the creature and refuses to represent the "unearthly ugliness" of the creature's countenance, aligning viewers with the creature's perceptive field rather than Victor's. Instead of his face or his voice, Ward chooses to accentuate the creature's powerful and expressive body. The creature's dark form dominates the compositional space and dwarfs that of his creator, who raises his arms in a pantomime of fury. If in the text Victor "overwhelm[s] him with words" (p. 92), in the design the creature's menacing image effectively mutes his creator's flurry of epithets.

More important than inequality of scale is the defiant stance the creature assumes, throwing his arms back and thrusting forward his chest and pelvis. The scene recalls the first dramatic encounter between Victor and his creature in *Presumption* in which "The Demon advances forward, breaks through the balustrade or railing of [the] gallery . . . jumps on the table beneath, and from thence leaps on the stage, stands in attitude before Frankenstein, who had started up in terror; they gaze for a moment at each other."[25] The scene also replays the initial encounter in Frankenstein's bedroom, but reverses the positions of the figures and magnifies the creature's attitude and confidence of statement. Significantly, Ward has arranged the figures and the tilting picture plane so that Victor is level with the creature's groin, not his face as indicated by Mary Shelley's text. What is "too horrible for human eyes" turns out here to be the direct manifestation of the creature's erotic desire. We witness a homoerotic rather than an existential challenge as Victor is enraged less by the hideousness of his appearance or heinousness of his crimes than by his sexual presumption.

While Victor calls the creature a "Devil," "daemon," and "fiend" in this episode of the novel (p. 92), Ward represents him here in simian terms suggesting a more atavistic and racial than Christian reading of his threat.[26] The engraving thus depicts the clash between Victor and his creature in terms that resonate with the nineteenth-century discourse of slavery and the race politics of America in the 1930s. The arc

---

[25]Cox, *Seven Gothic Dramas*, 399.
[26]It is worth noting that an early vignette also represents the faces of the three magistrates presiding over Justine's trial as simian (83), and a later one shows members of the Irish mob who assail Victor as bearing animal-like features (199). Their legal judgment, as Ward seems to suggest, originates from the same place as the creature's nature.

of knotted vertebrae protruding from his neck, the long swept-back arms, enlarged hands, and pointed nails all evidence a bestial, apelike nature and imply that the creature conforms to stereotypes of black men as animalistic.[27] Attired in the standard suit of the nineteenth-century aristocrat and representing the natural philosopher as gentleman, Victor faces his primitive double and tries to resist the imminent reversion to an animal, sexual, and racial Other that he represents. Put in a slightly different way, the rebellious, insouciant Caliban confronts his master Prospero, demanding his attention and the recognition of his claim. In this respect, and in the context of homosexuality, the most menacing threat here is miscegenation, a potentially explosive union between Victor as the white master and the creature as his dark, half-naked male servant.

In his choice of clothing for the two figures, further, Ward alludes to an evident class conflict between the antagonists, thus politicizing the homoerotic tension in a way that modern queer theory typically ignores. We see the capitalist-owner and the worker, or, more suggestively, a denizen of the naval-yard, a dockhand displaying his bare upper torso and outfitted in skin-tight sailor breeches. In a number of woodcut designs from his earlier graphic novel, *Wild Pilgrimage* (1932), Ward focuses on men at work and shows them laboring in the factory, the forge, and on the farm.[28] Many of the images in *Wild Pilgrimage* in fact decry the effects of industrial labor, extol the virtues of rural work, and exemplify Ward's commitment to social activism. A repeated image in the series shows the working-class protagonist standing up against figures of authority such as the foreman or factory owner, scenes that clearly anticipate the over-the-shoulder point of view of the creature's confrontation with Victor (figure 9). Several scenes also illustrate what

[27]The vignette that precedes Chapter 16 (151) reinforces these allusions by showing the creature's elongated limbs and chimpanzee-like acrobatics as he balances between the branches of crooked trees. For a full treatment of the racial discourse in *Frankenstein*, see Allan Lloyd Smith, "'This Thing of Darkness': Racial Discourse in Mary Shelley's *Frankenstein*," *Gothic Studies* 6 (Nov. 2004): 208–22; rpt. in this volume p. 547–67.

[28]As Ward writes in his introduction to the novel, the protagonist, like the creature, "is not a beautiful person. . . . It seemed to me that an individual who was less than well favored by nature in terms of physical appearance would experience a more dramatic contrast between what is happening in outer reality and the thoughts, urges, and desires that compose the inner world." See Art Spiegelman, ed., *Lynd Ward: Gods' Man, Madman's Drum, Wild Pilgrimage* (New York: Library of America, 2010), 795.

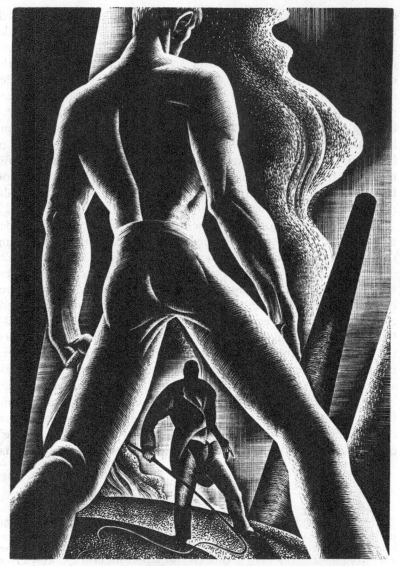

Figure 9. Illustration with over-the-shoulder perspective from Lynd Ward's *Wild Pilgrimage* (1932), 88 pages into unpaginated book.

By permission of Robin Ward Savage and Nanda Weedon Ward. Reproduced with the permission of Rare Books and Manuscripts, Special Collections Library, the Pennsylvania State University Libraries.

Art Spiegelman calls "odd sexual subcurrents,"[29] connecting agricultural labor with male companionship and homoerotic desire, and class conflict with acts of violent assault and phallic aggression. In *Wild Pilgrimage,* the factory owner is not only dwarfed by the worker but is several times viewed from between his towering legs, a point of view that eroticizes the encounter and also entangles it with issues of power and domination. Along with several of the other *Frankenstein* illustrations, figure 8 struggles to balance compassion for the economic oppression of the working class with a strange electric pull toward the sexual dynamism implicit in the dialectic between capitalist owner and proletarian worker.

## II

If the creature embodies and enacts Victor's homosexual dream-fantasy in these two illustrations, he pays a steep price for his transgression in the ensuing pages and bears the burden of Victor's own guilt. The creature's abiding response to his "crime" seems to be humiliation and shame as Ward repeatedly depicts him covering or shielding his face from the viewer and other characters.[30] In fact, we never directly see the creature's face again; either he turns his back to us, covers his head with his arms or hands, looks down or to the side (his ragged locks of hair shielding his face), or is foreshortened so that his head is obscured and his body dominates the picture space. In the smaller chapter headings and tailpieces, he is also represented synecdochally as a body part, in most cases a hand or arm.

The only time he reveals his face occurs when he is alone and sees himself "in a transparent pool" (figure 10), an image that, like the figure in Holst's frontispiece design and the various portraits of T.P. Cooke accompanying printed editions of Richard Peake's play, succeeds in humanizing the creature. In this respect, Ward follows the

---

[29]Ibid., xvi.
[30]The haunting sequence of eight lightly colored woodcut portraits that Barry Moser designed to accompany the creature's narrative in a later edition of *Frankenstein* (1984) differ most obviously from Ward's designs in that they represent the creature's face emerging toward us, out of an amniotic sea of darkness. See Mary Shelley, *Frankenstein; or, The Modern Prometheus: The 1818 Text in Three Volumes,* illus. Barry Moser, afterword by Joyce Carol Oates (Berkeley: University of California Press, 1984), 103–47.

Figure 10. The creature sees himself in a transparent pool, from Ward's *Frankenstein*, opposite p. 124.

many scenes in *Presumption* that represent him as curious and reflective, scenes that show "his sensitiveness of light and air," his admiration and wonder at the prospect of fire, and his developing aesthetic sensibility as he delights in the sound of Felix's flute and "gently places" a bouquet of flowers in a basket.[31] As the creature himself relates in Shelley's novel:

> At first I started back, unable to believe that it was indeed I who was reflected in the mirror; and when I became fully convinced that I was in reality the monster I am, I was filled with the bitterest sensations of despondence and mortification. Alas! I did not yet entirely know the fatal effects of this miserable deformity. (p. 104)

Ward's reflected image of the creature shows no signs of deformity and is markedly different from this account and the grisly face we see in the first picture of him. The appearance in the reflection is symmetrical, free of scarring or stitching, and evidences no patchwork ugliness, "dun white sockets" or "shriveled complexion" (p. 60). On the contrary, the eyes are large, round, and open, the nostrils wide, the lips lightly traced but uniform and straight. Ward offers a portrait of the racial other that visually gestures to Gauguin's paintings of native Tahitians and to Shakespeare's Caliban before Prospero arrived on the island and transformed him into "a savage and deformed slave." In his inverted reflection, moreover, we see the creature free from the social or moral stigma of other human beings, the church, or his tormentor, Victor, redeemed here as the kind of "natural" self who spontaneously rescues Agatha from the stream in *Presumption*. Emerging from the undergrowth at the lake's edge, his locks of hair drooping like lank weeds, the creature is associated with the earth and the world of Nature. The water serves to purify his face of deformity and like the inverted perspective helps the viewer see him anew. Rather than the ravaged outer mask Victor constructs and describes, this image invites us to bear witness to the vital innocence of the creature's soul. In this respect the portrait is testament to Ward's romanticized view of indigenous peoples and subjects of racial difference. The creature is made over from grotesque avatar of a lower order to idealized noble savage.

The idyll represented in this engraving is all too brief, however, as it is framed by scenes where the creature is shown suffering the consequences of Victor's punitive moral fury. The first full-page illustration

---

[31] Cox, *Seven Gothic Dramas*, 403, 407.

of this kind witnesses him under attack by a mob of enraged villagers who hurl a variety of projectiles at him (figure 11), a scene that recalls "The Martyrdom of St. Stephen" in Doré's *Bible Gallery*, which Ward would have known, and also the dramatic conclusions of the plays by Richard Peake and H.M. Milner where gypsies and armed peasants pursue the creature to his demise. Instead of retaliating, the creature weakly shields his upper body and seems to endure rather than sensibly flee his persecutors who treat him to the kind of public humiliation and ostracism experienced by homosexuals in late eighteenth and early nineteenth-century Britain. Many alleged sodomites were exposed in the "pillory" and subjected to the execrations of a crowd pelting them with refuse, rotten fish, dead animals, and other objects.[32] Consistent with the way that religious convictions continued to prevail over reformist thought in the England of Mary Shelley's day, Ward represents the punishment as coming from the direction of the church, itself framed in the triangle formed by the creature's thighs and groin. Again, it is not his hideous appearance but rather his homosexuality that provokes the attack, his mortal sin against Mosaic Law and God's authority.

This image, moreover, vividly recalls the fate of runaway slaves in the antebellum South, alluding to their pursuit, capture, and eventual hanging, and to the prevalence of the Ku Klux Klan and lynching mobs contemporaneous with Ward's illustrations. For the audience in the 1930s it may have evoked the Scottsboro trial (1931), in which an all-white jury sentenced to death nine black youths for allegedly raping two white women in Alabama. Despite widespread protests, the number of lynchings of black men actually rose in the first half of the decade, and a national anti-lynching bill was defeated in [C]ongress the year after Ward's edition was published. That Ward was consciously aware of this climate is more apparent in *Wild Pilgrimage*, where the hero directly witnesses the lynching of a black man and then experiences a haunting nightmare that features images of multiple lynchings, including a dangling noose intended for him (figure 12). The *Frankenstein* engraving of the creature's persecution also brings to mind the final sequence in James Whale's film where an angry mob of townspeople carrying torches and leading dogs chase the creature to an abandoned

[32] See Crompton, *Byron and Greek Love*, 14, 21–22, 31–32, 163–66, and Michael Sibalis, "Male Homosexuality in the Age of Enlightenment and Revolution, 1680–1850," in *Gay Life and Culture: A World History*, ed. Robert Aldrich (London: Thames & Hudson, 2006), 113.

Figure 11. The creature attacked by a mob of enraged villagers, from Ward's *Frankenstein*, opposite p. 114.

By permission of Robin Ward Savage and Nanda Weedon Ward. Reproduced with the permission of Rare Books and Manuscripts, Special Collections Library, the Pennsylvania State University Libraries.

Figure 12. Illustration of a nightmare about lynching from Lynd Ward's *Wild Pilgrimage* (1932), 43 pages into the unpaginated book.

windmill and then set it alight. As Elizabeth Young has persuasively shown, this episode resonates with contemporary accounts of lynchings.[33]

The next image of punishment is far more brutal and more violently realized than the equivalent scene in the stage productions of the 1820s where the creature is typically fired upon, wounded, and then retaliates by setting fire to the cottage. Here the creature is shown writhing on the ground, his body radically foreshortened and hence much smaller and more vulnerable than in earlier engravings (figure 13). Ward pictures the agonizing aftermath of the scene where Felix, Agatha, and Sadie suddenly return to their cottage and witness the creature kneeling before old man De Lacey and begging for his protection. As the creature relates:

> Who can describe their horror and consternation on behold-
> ing me? Agatha fainted; and Safie, unable to attend to her
> friend, rushed out of the cottage. Felix darted forward, and
> with supernatural force tore me from his father, to whose knees
> I clung: in a transport of fury, he dashed me to the ground and
> struck me violently with a stick. (p. 121)

In Ward's image, which exceeds and embellishes the text, Felix is wrapped less in a "transport of fury" than he is shown methodically enacting a sadistic punishment, a form of brutal justice that is exaggerated by the pointed spike affixed to the top of the weapon (hardly a "stick"). Ward sexualizes the scene from the novel, inverting the power dynamic between Victor and the creature in their earlier confrontation on the ice. The creature's prone position on the ground, combined with the phallic cord of wood raised aloft by Felix and the fact that both characters are shown with their legs spread apart, persuade us that what we see, like Agatha and Safie who shield their eyes in the background, is a violent rape. The spiked weapon aimed at the creature's exposed buttocks suggests an act of violent penetration and visually echoes the razor-sharp knife Victor holds in a later portrait that shows him in his foul bone shop assembling the female creature (figure 14). Later, Felix's crude weapon evolves into the image of a rapier (p. 178), which is shown enacting the pledge Victor elicits from his surrogate Walton, whom he had ordered to "thrust" his sword into the creature's "heart"

[33]Young, *Black Frankenstein*, 177.

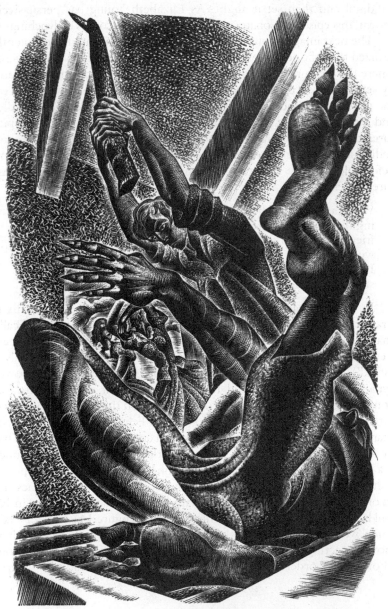

Figure 13. The creature attacked in the cottage by the old man's son, from Ward's *Frankenstein*, opposite p. 150.
By permission of Robin Ward Savage and Nanda Weedon Ward. Reproduced with the permission of Rare Books and Manuscripts, Special Collections Library, the Pennsylvania State University Libraries.

Figure 14. Victor assembling the female creature in his workshop, from Ward's *Frankenstein*, opposite p. 186.
By permission of Robin Ward Savage and Nanda Weedon Ward. Reproduced with the permission of Rare Books and Manuscripts, Special Collections Library, the Pennsylvania State University Libraries.

(p. 178). On the very next page, moreover, the weapon metamorphoses yet again into a jutting iceberg from which the creature recoils (figure 15). Toward the end, as Ward intuits, Victor's sex is increasingly projected as a punitive weapon even within the natural landscape, and it is this murderous symbol of eroticism that ultimately emerges as the book's source of real monstrosity.

Interestingly, sequences in both *Wild Pilgrimage* (1932) and *Prelude to a Million Tears* (1933) anticipate the disturbing connection that Ward makes here between homoeroticism and sadistic acts of violence. In the former novel, as we have seen, an early series of images retails a lynching; in both books there are sequences that show the brutal suppression of a peaceful assembly of workers by authorities wielding billy clubs; and in *Prelude* one woodcut features a patriotic demonstration in which a soldier seizes the protagonist by the back of the neck and forces him to look at an American flag, a scene reminiscent of fellatio (figure 16). In both novels Ward sexualizes the violence by foregrounding the phallic weapons of the authority figures and accentuating their tight clothing and prominent, muscular buttocks (figure 17).

Similar to the representations in these earlier graphic novels, the depictions of persecution in *Frankenstein* show Victor's spirit of revenge, a spirit that parries the creature's homoerotic desire with his own brutal form of anal-sadistic justice.[34] A scant ten pages later, however, Ward dramatically counters the creature's victimization in the edition's last full-page illustration of him. In the most shocking of all the images, the creature radically tests the viewer's sympathy for him by exacting his own terrible revenge on Victor's youngest brother William, a small child (figure 18). No earlier illustrated edition of the novel chooses to represent this or the creature's other crimes, and the murders in *Presumption* and *The Man and the Monster* occur offstage. In fact, H.M. Milner contrives the escape of his child by having his mother Emmeline distract the creature with music from her flute. Ward's picture of this murder, by contrast, far exceeds all the stage adaptations in savagery and utterly transforms the almost accidental nature of the assault as it is described in Mary Shelley's own text ("I grasped his throat to silence him, and in a moment he lay dead at my feet" [p. 126]). In the engraving, the creature pulverizes the boy like a rag doll, obliterating his victim's face in

---

[34] In legal cases involving sodomy in nineteenth-century America, as Jonathan Katz argues, the descriptions of anal intercourse almost always included the word "assault," even if the act was consensual and did not involve force or coercion. See *Love Stories: Sex between Men before Homosexuality* (Chicago: University of Chicago Press, 2001), 70–71.

Figure 15. The creature recoils from an iceberg, from Ward's *Franken-stein*, p. 242.
By permission of Robin Ward Savage and Nanda Weedon Ward. Reproduced with the permission of Rare Books and Manuscripts, Special Collections Library, the Pennsylvania State University Libraries.

the process. The murder appears premeditated but also furtive, concealed as it is from the background village (with its two church spires) by a rocky barrier and protective rushes. As in the previous woodcut, Ward implies a sexual crime by darkening the tone of the print, sinking the action beneath the surface of the ground, obscuring both figures' faces, and representing the creature's arousal in the phallic extension of his left leg. This is dark retribution indeed, shading into pedophilia, and seems to more than compensate for his own earlier rape and beating at the hands of Felix.[35]

In realizing these episodes of escalating vengeance and violence, Ward senses the queer use of the word "consummation" in the text and

[35] There are clear parallels here with the protagonist of *Wild Pilgrimage,* who begins to erode our sympathy when he sexually assaults the wife of a farmer who has hired him as a day laborer. A later eruption of violence in a dream sequence where he decapitates a factory owner and brandishes his own head is similarly problematic and implies a connection between homoeroticism and the protagonist's own murderous longings. We might also detect parallels here between the image of William's murder and the creature's drowning of the little girl in Whale's *Frankenstein,* an accident that is later presumed by the girl's father, the townsfolk and original film audiences to be a homicide. (The sequence of shots that reveals the accidental nature of the incident was not added to the film until many years later.)

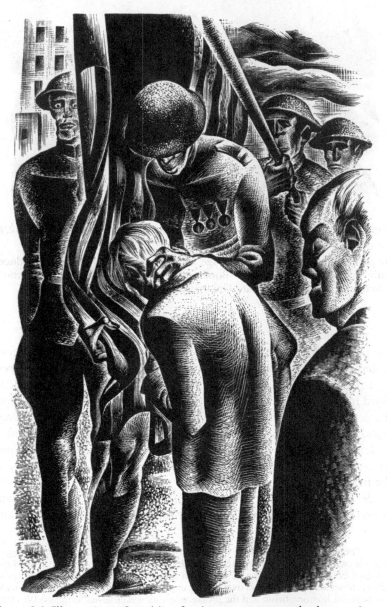

Figure 16. Illustration of a soldier forcing a protestor to look at an American flag from Lynd Ward's *Prelude to a Million Years* (1933), 21 pages into the unpaginated book.

By permission of Robin Ward Savage and Nanda Weedon Ward. Reproduced with the permission of Rare Books and Manuscripts, Special Collections Library, the Pennsylvania State University Libraries.

Figure 17. Illustration of brutal, sexualized authority figures from Lynd Ward's *Wild Pilgrimage* (1932), 93 pages into the unpaginated work.
By permission of Robin Ward Savage and Nanda Weedon Ward. Reproduced with the permission of Rare Books and Manuscripts, Special Collections Library, the Pennsylvania State University Libraries.

the connection Mary Shelley draws between it and the ideas of sexuality and crime. The illustration of William anticipates the creature's own climactic act of psychological aggression against his master: "That is also my victim!", exclaims the creature to Walton near the conclusion, "in his murder my crimes are consummated" (p. 185). Moments later, the creature points at Victor's corpse and states: "he suffered not in

Figure 18. The creature murdering Victor's younger brother William, from Ward's *Frankenstein*, opposite p. 160.

the consummation of the deed." In place of the (heterosexual) non-consummation of Victor's wedding night the novel substitutes the creature's posthumous consummation with his creator, a strange union that represents the climax of their love in a double crime — patricide and the legal and theological "crime against nature" that Jonathan Katz reminds us of in his study of homosexuality, a felony of father love and love between men.[36]

That the creature is triply condemned for his deviance — by angry peasants, by the De Lacey family, *and* by the criminal justice system — becomes starkly apparent in two prominent engravings of incarceration wherein the prisoners serve as surrogates for his transgressive desires.[37] These full-page illustrations show Justine, the Frankenstein family's servant, and the Turkish merchant whom Felix rescues from a jail cell in Paris as jailed fugitives who mirror the creature's plight (figures 19 and 20). Like the creature, Justine covers her face in shame and despair after being forced to confess the killing of William ("I almost began to think that I was the monster that he said I was," she says [p. 83]). The shape and position of her enlarged hands parallel those of the creature, the rushes she kneels upon foreshadow those found in the scene where the creature murders William, and both the chains and the mounting stairs seen through the prison bars evoke the architecture of the watchtower in James Whale's *Frankenstein* (1931), where the creature is imprisoned and tortured by the lab assistant Fritz. Even the water jug in the foreground anticipates the culinary objects that will be hurled at the creature in the later scene. If she serves as the imprisoned symbol of the creature's unlawful desires, Justine can also be seen as the scapegoat on which Victor projects his own monstrous shame and despair as well as his fears of being feminized by his creature's affection.

In contrast with Justine, Ward offers a xenophobic representation of the Turk as a symbol of the creature's monstrous foreignness. Unrepentant and staring at us with beady, diabolical eyes, the Turk is a far more malevolent inmate than the Frankenstein family's gentle servant. His skeletal hands and elongated fingers again parallel those of the creature, but they are much more prominent than Justine's and much more

---

[36] Katz, *Love Stories*, 6.
[37] The headpiece of Chapter 11, situated between these two full-page illustrations, portrays the creature as an escaped convict, crawling on his hands and knees through a barren landscape and turning his face away from us to observe the moon, which looks like an eye of surveillance. If we are attending to the racial discourse in Ward's illustrations, the figure also resembles a runaway slave.

Figure 19. The servant Justine jailed for the murder of William, from Ward's *Frankenstein*, opposite p. 90.

By permission of Robin Ward Savage and Nanda Weedon Ward. Reproduced with the permission of Rare Books and Manuscripts, Special Collections Library, the Pennsylvania State University Libraries.

Figure 20. The jailed Turkish merchant, from Ward's *Frankenstein*, opposite p. 136.

expressive of deviancy and machination. He looks nothing like "the unfortunate Mahometan" described in Mary Shelley's text, who awaits "in despair the execution of the barbarous sentence" (p. 111), but is curled up like a giant spider, reminding us of the "vile insect" Victor calls the creature on the Alpine glacier (p. 92). On the dark, glowering image of the Turk, then, Ward projects Victor's view of the creature as consumed with aberrant desire, as not only wicked, unnatural, and foreign but subhuman, a view, as Louis Crompton has shown, that is consonant with legal and journalistic discourse in nineteenth-century England which frequently referred to sodomites as brutish and bestial and often represented the scourge of homosexuality as emanating from abroad.[38]

## III

Having dwelt at such length on the psycho-sexual, class, and racial battle between Victor and his creature, it is surprising that Ward does not lend these issues and his two main characters prominence of place in the final wood engravings. Given the illustrations of confrontation earlier in the sequence and the violent clash that signals the denouement in the major stage adaptations of the 1820s, we anticipate vivid evocations of the breathless pursuit across the arctic tundra or perhaps a stirring image of Victor's "wild cry of ecstasy" and "burning gush" of hope as he spies the creature in the near distance (p. 176). But scenes such as these are nowhere to be found, a striking omission, particularly in the light of the images of passionate confrontation seen in his earlier woodcut novel, *Prelude to a Million Years* (1933), and the final sequence of *Wild Pilgrimage,* where in addition to episodes of police brutality, Ward shows the hero brutally stabbing and beheading a factory owner and strangling a policeman (figure 21).[39]

[38] Crompton, *Byron and Greek Love*, 52–56.

[39] In more indirect and purely aesthetic terms, Ward's remarks about the process of engraving are also germane here and to my earlier remarks about hand imagery: "Working with a woodblock takes on the aspects of a struggle between antagonists. The wood is reluctant, the artist determined, and it is reasonable to suggest that that battle of wills brings about a result quite different from those media in which the band of the artist moves brush or pencil or crayon freely over the working surface. . . . The result is an emotional involvement between man and material that, enduring over the years, somehow takes on the character of an addiction, or a love affair, or something similarly irrational" ("The Way of Wood Engraving," Spiegelman, *Lynd Ward*, 775).

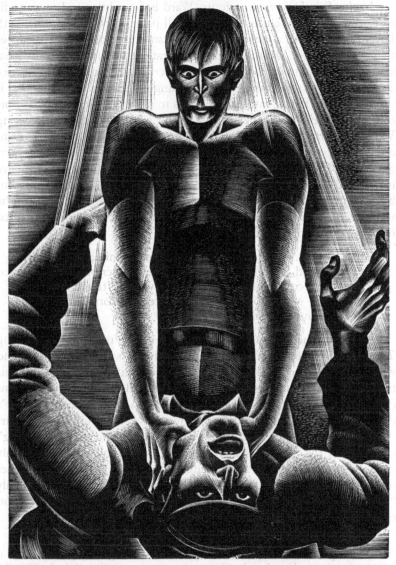

Figure 21. Illustration of a policeman being strangled by the hero of Lynd Ward's *Wild Pilgrimage* (1932), 92 pages into the unpaginated book.

By permission of Robin Ward Savage and Nanda Weedon Ward. Reproduced with the permission of Rare Books and Manuscripts, Special Collections Library, the Pennsylvania State University Libraries.

In the *Frankenstein* woodcuts, Ward is far subtler and more indirect, offering two curiously static full-page portraits of Elizabeth
Lavenza along with a handful of smaller and more anticlimactic scenes
that portray Victor and the creature separately and diminish their visual
status. After the murder of William, the creature assumes the status of
a ghost in Ward's narrative, overwhelming his victims off camera, as it
were, and then fading into the shadows to taunt Victor.[40] The first portrait of Elizabeth shows her calmly sitting by a large window awaiting
Victor's return from abroad. The scene may recall the domestic tranquility represented by Holst in his title page engraving and by Lagerquist in his later illustration of Victor entreating his new bride to retire
to her bed chamber, but the window grids evoke a jail cell and thus
bring to mind the earlier incarcerations of Justine and the Turk. In the
second, more compelling woodcut, Ward depicts Victor's horrified
response on seeing his dead bride:

> Great God! . . . She was there, lifeless and inanimate, thrown
> across the bed, her head hanging down, and her pale and distorted
> features half covered by her hair. Everywhere I turn I see the
> same figure—her bloodless arms and relaxed form flung by the
> murderer on its bridal bier. (p. 167)

Following the lead of his predecessor Henry Fuseli, whose painting
*The Nightmare* (1781) influenced Mary Shelley's own description and
which his image so frankly adapts, Ward sexualizes the scene but this
time in a way that appears far more conventional than his earlier designs
(figure 22).[41] He erases all evidence of violence from Mary Shelley's
description—the figure's "distorted features," evidence of the "murderous mark of the fiend's grasp . . . on her neck," and the body "flung"
callously on the bed by the creature (p. 167)—in favor of a highly
eroticized portrait that drapes a languorous figure across the bed, her
form falling provocatively towards the viewer. Her body is certainly
"relaxed," as Mary Shelley writes, but in a state of post-coital abandon
rather than mutilated death.

---

[40]Although he seldom appears directly in the remaining designs, his presence is
nonetheless palpable. If we look carefully at the engraving of Clerval's body (200), for
example, it is possible to detect a giant fist in the form of background clouds, and opposite the seated portrait of Elizabeth (216), the outline of his face in the curtains.
[41]Ward may also have had in mind one of the original posters for Whale's *Frankenstein* (1931), which shows, beneath the famous image of Boris Karloff's haunting face
and the film's title, Elizabeth sprawled out on the edge of the bed as in Fuseli. Probably
because the producers did not want to risk losing their audience, this poster overtly het-
erosexualizes the scene and the creature's threat, portraying him as a stalker and rapist.

Figure 22. Elizabeth after being murdered by the creature, from Ward's *Frankenstein*, opposite p. 226.

As a bedroom scene, this final full-page illustration echoes the initial encounter between Victor and the creature but now substitutes Elizabeth as the object of Victor's gaze. In place of homosexual Ward promises a conventionally heterosexual intercourse that features a dead bride as the erotic object, bringing to mind Victor's original dream of Elizabeth metamorphosing into the corpse of his mother. The image prefigures subsequent lines from the text where, recovering from his shock, Victor "rushe[s] towards her, and embrace[s] her with ardour" (p. 167). In compensating for the earlier scene of homosexual terror, this one hyperbolizes a standard voyeuristic male fantasy. Ward ignores the events that transpire immediately after this moment in the novel, which involve the protagonist's violent emotional clash with the creature, events that climax in the discharge of Victor's pistol. All pictorial energies are reserved instead for the careful erotic deployment of Elizabeth's body, as Ward re-inscribes for the viewer an apparently heteronormative view of Victor's sexuality. As Victor himself does in the text, Ward uses heterosexuality as a defense against the temptation of the protagonist's powerful homosexual attraction to his creation. "In using women as objects of [their own] power," Eric Daffron has argued, the protagonists "deflect some of the homoerotic tension in the novel."[42] The sexual objectification and idealization of Elizabeth—who only remotely resembles the rather sexless figure in the two illustrations of her earlier in the edition—serves to offset and partially neutralize the male characters' expression of same-sex desire.

And yet there is another way of reading the wedding-night scene that reinforces rather than vitiates the homoerotic interpretation that Ward has explored. Several details from the image suggest that Victor and the creature share the body of Elizabeth and that she functions as a conduit for the homoerotic bond between them. Because her form is eroticized rather than depicted more realistically as bearing the physical marks of strangulation, it is implied that the creature has sexually assaulted her, a conclusion affirmed by parallels with Fuseli's painting that shows a horse's head aimed at the female figure's pudendum and a monstrous incubus perched atop her stomach.

Ward's departure from the novel in vacating the creature's image from the background window ("I saw at the open window a figure the most hideous and abhorred" [p. 168]) allows him to open up an implied viewing space in front of the picture for Victor and the creature to occupy together, both able now to gaze on Elizabeth's voluptuous form. Her body, then, like Justine's earlier, becomes the site of contest between the two male protagonists, who vent the murderous frustration of their homoerotic stand-off through her.

## IV

As I have argued, Ward's woodcut engravings extend the visual tradition of Gothic theater as it was realized in early nineteenth-century stage adaptations of *Frankenstein* by playwrights such as Richard Brinsley Peake and H.M. Milner. The designs incorporate the muteness of the creature and the individual actor's ability to express character through pantomimic gesture and vivid pictorial attitudes. Ward is also sensitive to the images of the creature that accompanied various published editions of the plays, images which complicate his monstrosity by normalizing and humanizing his figure and also by juxtaposing the Gothic horror of his threat with the relief of domestic melodrama. In addition, as we have seen, the engravings build on important book illustrations of the creature by Theodor von Holst and Carl Lagerquist. These artists begin to explore his gender identity and awakening sexuality, but Ward offers a far more revealing and subversive portrait of the creature's deviance, his challenge to Victor's patriarchal codes of masculine power. Of all these visual representations, Ward's most fully realize the homoerotic tensions in Mary Shelley's novel, recognizing the psychic terror implied in the creature's warning to Victor about being with him on his wedding night.

If Ward's illustrations are prescient in exploring repressed desire, homosexual panic, and homophobia in Shelley's novel, they also historicize homosexuality in ways that later modern critics of the Gothic tend to overlook. The engravings pay close attention to the problem of labor as well as to class and race upheaval in depression-era America. Ward's visual representations offer no simple liberal message about the status of the oppressed or about the relationship between homoeroticism and these various forms of social rebellion, but pose questions that complicate our response to Mary Shelley's original novel. Building on his portrait of the working-class protagonist in *Wild Pilgrimage,* the illustrations vex our relationship to the creature who at once acts as the sympathetic protagonist of the story, gay lover, oppressed laborer, victimized racial other, and, in the most ambivalent design in the book, violent felon.

Figure 23. Final tailpiece from Ward's *Frankenstein*, showing the creature's arm engulfed in flames, p. 259.
By permission of Robin Ward Savage and Nanda Weedon Ward. Reproduced with the permission of Rare Books and Manuscripts, Special Collections Library, the Pennsylvania State University Libraries.

At the same time, Ward attempts to recuperate, even commemorate the creature's example at the very end of the book. The final tailpiece shows his arm engulfed by flames and serves as an effective reminder of his earlier persecution and suffering (figure 23). This image also forges a visual link with the working-class hero of *Wild Pilgrimage*, whose arm we see wrapped in flames in one of that novel's final images, and the sculptor-hero of *Prelude to a Million Years*, who embraces his artwork as the world bursts into fire around him. In representing the creature's own promised action—"I shall ascend my funeral pile triumphantly," as he states at the end of Shelley's novel, "and exult in the agony of the torturing flames" (p. 189)—Ward diverges from the endings imagined by playwrights such as Milner, Peake, and Kerr, who show the creature succumbing to the larger forces of nature, and places the creature's fate in his own hands. In this way he ennobles, even martyrs the creature whose form is not obscured by the elements, as it is in the conclusions of the earlier plays, but made visible in a spectacular Promethean blaze.

## Acknowledgment

Special thanks to Amze Emmons, Garrett Gallinot, Melanie Henry, and Alex Nagorski for their illuminating commentary on Lynd Ward's engravings, and to an anonymous reader for helpful advice on an earlier draft.

## WORKS CITED

Cox, Jeffrey N. "Re-viewing Romantic Drama." *Literature Compass* 1.1 (2003/2004): n.p. Web. 6 June 2014.

———, ed. *Seven Gothic Dramas 1789–1825*. Athens: Ohio UP, 1992. Print.

Craig, Siobhan. "Monstrous Dialogue: Erotic Discourse and the Dialogic Construction of the Subject in *Frankenstein*." *A Dialogue of Voices: Feminist Literary Theory and Bakhtin*. Ed. Karen Hohne and Helen Wussow. Minneapolis: U of Minnesota P, 1994. 83–96. Print.

Crompton, Louis. *Byron and Greek Love: Homophobia in Nineteenth-Century England*. Berkeley: U of California P, 1985. Print.

Daffron, Eric. "Male Bonding: Sympathy and Shelley's *Frankenstein*." *Nineteenth-Century Contexts* 21 (1999): 415–35. Print.

Forry, Stephen Earl. *Hideous progenies: Dramatizations of* Frankenstein *from Mary Shelley to the Present.* Philadelphia: U of
Pennsylvania P, 1990. Print.

Gilbert, Ophelia. "Lynd Ward." *American Writers for Children,
1900–1960.* Ed. John Cech. *Dictionary of Literary Biography,*
vol. 22. Detroit: Gale, 1983. 326–33. Print.

Haggerty, George E. *Queer Gothic.* Urbana: Illinois UP, 2006. Print.

Hill, J. M. "*Frankenstein* and the Physiognomy of Desire." *American
Imago* 32 (1975): 335–58. Print.

Hoehn, Douglas William. "The First Season of *Presumption! or,
The Fate of Frankenstein.*" *Theatre Studies* 26–27 (1979/1981):
79–88. Print.

Katz, Jonathan. *Love Stories: Sex between Men before Homosexuality.*
Chicago: U of Chicago P, 2001. Print.

Lockhead, Liz. *Blood and Ice.* Edinburgh: Salamander, 1982. Print.

McGavran, James Holt. "'Insurmountable Barriers to Our Union':
Homosocial Male Bonding, Homosexual Panic, and Death on the
Ice in *Frankenstein.*" *European Romantic Review* 11 (Win. 2000):
46–67. Print.

Nagle, Christopher. *Sexuality and the Culture of Sensibility in the
British Romantic Era.* Basingstoke: Palgrave Macmillan, 2007.
Print.

Nitchie, Elizabeth. *Mary Shelley: Author of* Frankenstein. New Brunswick: Rutgers UP, 1953. Print.

Peake, Richard Brinsley. *Frankenstein. A Romantic Drama in Three
Acts.* London: John Dicks, c. 1823. Dicks' Standard Plays,
no. 431. Print.

Rigby, Mair. "'Do You Share My Madness?': *Frankenstein*'s Queer
Gothic." *Queering the Gothic.* Ed. William Hughes and Andrew
Smith. Manchester: Manchester UP, 2009. 36–54. Print.

Robinson, Charles, ed. *Frankenstein or the Modern Prometheus: The
Original Two-Volume Novel of 1816–1817 from the Bodleian
Library Manuscripts.* Oxford: Bodleian, 2008. Print.

Sedgwick, Eve Kosofsky. *Between Men: English Literature and Male
Homosocial Desire.* New York: Columbia UP, 1985. Print.

Shelley, Mary Wollstonecraft. *Frankenstein, or, the Modern Prometheus.*
London: Colburn and Bentley, 1831. Print.

———. *Frankenstein or the Modern Prometheus.* Boston: Cornhill,
1922. Print.

———. *Frankenstein: or, the Modern Prometheus. The 1818 Text in
Three Volumes.* Illustrated by Barry Moser. Berkeley: U of California P, 1984. Print.

————. *Frankenstein or the Modern Prometheus.* Engravings by Lynn Ward. New York: Harrison Smith and Robert Haas, 1934. Print.

Sibalis, Michael. "Male Homosexuality in the Age of Enlightenment and Revolution 1680-1850." *Gay Life and Culture: A World History.* Ed. Robert Aldrich. London: Thames & Hudson, 2006. 103–24. Print.

Smith, Allan Lloyd. "'This Thing of Darkness': Racial Discourse in Mary Shelley's *Frankenstein.*" *Gothic Studies* 6 (Nov. 2004): 208-22. Print. Rpt. in this volume pp. 547–67.

Spiegelman, Art. "The Way of Wood Engraving." *Lynd Ward: Gods' Man, Madman's Drum, Wild Pilgrimage.* Ed. Spiegelman. New York: Library of America, 2010. 765–75. Print.

St. Clair, William. "The Impact of *Frankenstein.*" *Mary Shelley in her Times.* Ed. Betty T. Bennett and Stuart Curran. Baltimore: Johns Hopkins UP, 2000. 38–63. Print.

Ward, Lynd. *Prelude to a Million Years.* New York: Harrison Smith and Robert Haas, 1933. Print.

————. *Storyteller without Words: The Wood Engravings of Lynd Ward.* New York: Abrams, 1974. Print.

————. *Wild Pilgrimage.* New York: Harrison Smith and Robert Haas, 1932. Print.

Willett, Perry. *The Silent Shout: Franz Masereel, Lynn Ward, and the Novel in Woodcuts.* Bloomington: Indiana U Libraries, 1997. Print.

Young, Elizabeth. *Black Frankenstein: The Making of an American Metaphor.* New York: New York UP, 2008. Print.

# Marxist Criticism and *Frankenstein*

## WHAT IS MARXIST CRITICISM?

To the question "What is Marxist criticism?" it may be tempting to respond with another question: "What does it matter?" In light of the rapid and largely unanticipated demise of Soviet-style communism in the former USSR and throughout Eastern Europe, it is understandable to suppose that Marxist literary analysis would disappear too, quickly becoming an anachronism in a world enamored with full-market capitalism.

In fact, however, there is no reason why Marxist criticism should weaken, let alone disappear. It is, after all, a phenomenon distinct from Soviet and Eastern European communism, having had its beginnings nearly eighty years before the Bolshevik revolution and having thrived since the 1940s, mainly in the West—not as a form of communist propaganda but rather as a form of critique, a discourse for interrogating *all* societies and their texts in terms of certain specific issues. Those issues—including race, class, and the attitudes shared within a given culture—are as much with us as ever, not only in contemporary Russia but also in the United States.

The argument could even be made that Marxist criticism has been strengthened by the collapse of Soviet-style communism. There was a time, after all, when few self-respecting Anglo-American journals would use Marxist terms or models, however illuminating, to analyze Western issues or problems. It smacked of sleeping with the enemy. With the collapse of the Kremlin, however, old taboos began to give way. Even the staid *Wall Street Journal* now seems comfortable using phrases like "worker alienation" to discuss the problems plaguing the American business world.

The assumption that Marxist criticism will die on the vine of a moribund political system rests in part on another mistaken assumption, namely, that Marxist literary analysis is practiced only by people who would like to see society transformed into a Marxist-communist state, one created through land reform, the redistribution of wealth, a tightly and centrally managed economy, the abolition of institutionalized religion, and so on. In fact, it has never been necessary to be a communist political revolutionary to be classified as a Marxist literary critic. (Many of the critics discussed in this introduction actually *fled* communist societies to live in the West.) Nor is it necessary to like only those literary works with a radical social vision or to dislike books that represent or even reinforce a middle-class, capitalist worldview. It is necessary, however, to adopt what most students of literature would consider a radical definition of the purpose and function of literary criticism.

More traditional forms of criticism, according to the Marxist critic Pierre Macherey, "set . . . out to deliver the text from its own silences by coaxing it into giving up its true, latent, or hidden meaning." Inevitably, however, non-Marxist criticism "intrude[s] its own discourse between the reader and the text" (qtd. in Bennett 107). Marxist critics, by contrast, do not attempt to discover hidden meanings in texts. Or if they do, they do so only after seeing the text, first and foremost, as a material product to be understood in broadly historical terms. That is to say, a literary work is first viewed as a product *of* work (and hence of the realm of production and consumption we call economics). Second, it may be looked upon as a work that *does* identifiable work of its own. At one level, that work is usually to enforce and reinforce the prevailing ideology, that is, the network of conventions, values, and opinions to which the majority of people uncritically subscribe.

This does not mean that Marxist critics merely describe the obvious. Quite the contrary: the relationship that the Marxist critic Terry Eagleton outlines in *Criticism and Ideology* (1978) among the soaring cost of books in the nineteenth century, the growth of lending libraries, the practice of publishing "three-decker" novels (so that three borrowers could be reading the same book at the same time), and the changing *content* of those novels is highly complex in its own way. But the complexity Eagleton finds is not that of the deeply buried meaning of the text. Rather, it is that of the complex web of social and economic relationships that were prerequisite to the work's production. Marxist criticism does not seek to be, in Eagleton's words, "a passage from text to reader." Indeed, "its task is to show the text as it cannot know itself, to manifest those conditions of its making (inscribed in its very letter) about which it is necessarily silent" (43).

As everyone knows, Marxism began with Karl Marx, the nineteenth-century German philosopher best known for writing *Das Kapital*, the seminal work of the communist movement. What everyone doesn't know is that Marx was also the first Marxist literary critic (much as Sigmund Freud, who psychoanalyzed E. T. A. Hoffmann's supernatural tale "The Sandman," was the first Freudian literary critic). During the 1830s Marx wrote critical essays on writers such as Goethe and Shakespeare (whose tragic vision of Elizabethan disintegration he praised).

The fact that Marxist literary criticism began with Marx himself is hardly surprising, given Marx's education and early interests. Trained in the classics at the University of Bonn, Marx wrote literary imitations, his own poetry, a failed novel, and a fragment of a tragic drama (*Oulanem*) before turning to contemplative and political philosophy. Even after he met Friedrich Engels in 1843 and began collaborating on works such as *The German Ideology* and *The Communist Manifesto*, Marx maintained a keen interest in literary writers and their works. He and Engels argued about the poetry of Heinrich Heine, admired Hermann Freiligrath (a poet critical of the German aristocracy), and faulted the playwright Ferdinand Lassalle for writing about a reactionary knight in the Peasants' War rather than about more progressive aspects of German history.

As these examples suggest, Marx and Engels would not—indeed, could not—think of aesthetic matters as being distinct and independent from such things as politics, economics, and history. Not surprisingly, they viewed the alienation of the worker in industrialized, capitalist societies as having grave consequences for the arts. How can people mechanically stamping out things that bear no mark of their producer's individuality (people thereby "reified," turned into things themselves) be expected to recognize, produce, or even consume things of beauty? And if there is no one to consume something, there will soon be no one to produce it, especially in an age in which production (even of something like literature) has come to mean *mass* (and therefore profitable) production.

In *The German Ideology* (1846), Marx and Engels expressed their sense of the relationship between the arts, politics, and basic economic reality in terms of a general social theory. Economics, they argued, provides the "base" or "infrastructure" of society, but from that base emerges a "superstructure" consisting of law, politics, philosophy, religion, and art.

Marx later admitted that the relationship between base and superstructure may be indirect and fluid: every change in economics may not be reflected by an immediate change in ethics or literature. In *The Eighteenth Brumaire of Louis Bonaparte* (1852), he came up with the word *homology* to describe the sometimes unbalanced, often delayed, and almost always loose correspondence between base and superstructure. And later in that same decade, while working on an introduction to his *Political Economy*, Marx further relaxed the base–superstructure relationship. Writing on the excellence of ancient Greek art (versus the primitive nature of ancient Greek economics), he conceded that a gap sometimes opens up between base and superstructure—between economic forms and those produced by the creative mind.

Nonetheless, *at* base the old formula was maintained. Economics remained basic and the connection between economics and superstructural elements of society was reaffirmed. Central to Marxism and Marxist literary criticism was and is the following "materialist" insight: consciousness, without which such things as art cannot be produced, is not the source of social forms and economic conditions. It is, rather, their most important product.

Marx and Engels, drawing upon the philosopher G. W. F. Hegel's theories about the dialectical synthesis of ideas out of theses and antitheses, believed that a revolutionary class war (pitting the capitalist class against a proletarian, antithetical class) would lead eventually to the synthesis of a new social and economic order. Placing their faith not in the idealist Hegelian dialectic but, rather, in what they called "dialectical materialism," they looked for a secular and material salvation of humanity—one in, not beyond, history—via revolution and not via divine intervention. And they believed that the communist society eventually established would be one capable of producing new forms of consciousness and belief and therefore, ultimately, great art.

The revolution anticipated by Marx and Engels did not occur in their century, let alone lifetime. When it finally did take place, it didn't happen in places where Marx and Engels had thought it might be successful: the United States, Great Britain, and Germany. It happened, rather, in 1917 Russia, a country long ruled by despotic czars but also enlightened by the works of powerful novelists and playwrights, including Chekhov, Pushkin, Tolstoy, and Dostoyevsky.

Perhaps because of its significant literary tradition, Russia produced revolutionaries like V.I. Nikolai Lenin, who shared not only Marx's interest in literature but also his belief in literature's ultimate importance. But it was not without some hesitation that Lenin endorsed the significance of texts written during the reign of the czars. Well before 1917 he had questioned what the relationship should be between a society undergoing a revolution and the great old literature of its bourgeois past.

Lenin attempted to answer that question in a series of essays on Tolstoy that he wrote between 1908 and 1911. Tolstoy—the author of *War and Peace* and *Anna Karenina*—was an important nineteenth-century Russian writer whose views did not accord with all of those of young Marxist revolutionaries. Continuing interest in a writer like Tolstoy may be justified, Lenin reasoned, given the primitive and unenlightened economic order of the society that produced him. Since superstructure usually lags behind base (and is therefore usually *more* primitive), the attitudes of a Tolstoy were relatively progressive when viewed in light of the monarchical and precapitalist society out of which they arose.

Moreover, Lenin also reasoned, the writings of the great Russian realists would *have* to suffice, at least in the short run. Lenin looked forward, in essays like "Party Organization and Party Literature," to the day in which new artistic forms would be produced by progressive writers with revolutionary political views and agendas. But he also knew that a great proletarian literature was unlikely to evolve until a thoroughly literate proletariat had been produced by the educational system.

Lenin was hardly the only revolutionary leader involved in setting up the new Soviet state who took a strong interest in literary matters. In 1924 Leon Trotsky published a book called *Literature and Revolution*, which is still acknowledged as a classic of Marxist literary criticism.

Trotsky worried about the direction in which Marxist aesthetic theory seemed to be going. He responded skeptically to groups like Proletkult, which opposed tolerance toward pre- and nonrevolutionary writers, and which called for the establishment of a new, proletarian culture. Trotsky warned of the danger of cultural sterility and risked unpopularity by pointing out that there is no necessary connection between the quality of a literary work and the quality of its author's politics.

In 1927 Trotsky lost a power struggle with Josef Stalin, a man who believed, among other things, that writers should be "engineers" of "human souls." After Trotsky's expulsion from the Soviet Union, views held by groups like Proletkult and the Left Front of Art (LEF), and by theorists such as Nikolai Bukharin and A. A. Zhdanov, became more prevalent. Speaking at the First Congress of the Union of Soviet Writers in 1934, the Soviet author Maxim Gorky called for writing that would "make labor the principal hero of our books." It was at the same writers' congress that "socialist realism," an art form glorifying workers and the revolutionary State, was made Communist party policy and the official literary form of the USSR.

Of those critics active in the USSR after the expulsion of Trotsky and the unfortunate triumph of Stalin, two critics stand out. One, Mikhail Bakhtin, was a Russian, later a Soviet, critic who spent much of his life in a kind of internal exile. Many of his essays were written in the 1930s and not published in the West or translated until the late 1960s. His work comes out of an engagement with the Marxist intellectual tradition as well as out of an indirect, even hidden, resistance to the Soviet government. It has been important to Marxist critics writing in the West because his theories provide a means to decode submerged social critique, especially in early modern texts. He viewed language—especially literary texts—in terms of discourses and dialogues. Within a novel written in a society in flux, for instance, the narrative may include an official, legitimate discourse, plus another infiltrated by challenging comments and even retorts. In a 1929 book on Dostoyevsky and a 1940 study titled *Rabelais and His World*, Bakhtin examined what he calls "polyphonic" novels, each characterized by a multiplicity of voices or discourses. In Dostoyevsky the independent status of a given character is marked by the difference of his or her language from that of the narrator. (The narrator's voice, too, can in fact be a dialogue.) In works by Rabelais, Bakhtin finds that the (profane) language of the carnival and of other popular festivals plays against and parodies the more official discourses, that is, of the king, church, or even socially powerful intellectuals. Bakhtin influenced modern cultural criticism by showing, in a sense, that the conflict between "high" and "low" culture takes place not only between classic and popular texts but also between the "dialogic" voices that exist within many books—whether "high" or "low."

The other subtle Marxist critic who managed to survive Stalin's dictatorship and his repressive policies was Georg Lukács. A Hungarian who had begun his career as an "idealist" critic, Lukács had converted to Marxism in 1919; renounced his earlier, Hegelian work shortly thereafter; visited Moscow in 1930–31; and finally emigrated to the USSR in 1933, just one year before the First Congress of the Union of Soviet Writers met. Lukács was far less narrow in his views than the most strident Stalinist Soviet critics of the 1930s and 1940s. He disliked much socialist realism and appreciated prerevolutionary, realistic novels that broadly reflected cultural "totalities"—and were populated with characters representing human "types" of the author's place and time. (Lukács was particularly fond of the historical canvasses painted by the early-nineteenth-century novelist Sir Walter Scott.) But like his more rigid and censorious contemporaries, he drew the line at accepting non-revolutionary, modernist works like James Joyce's *Ulysses*. He condemned movements like Expressionism and Symbolism, preferring works with "content" over more decadent, experimental works characterized mainly by "form."

With Lukács its most liberal and tolerant critic from the early 1930s until well into the 1960s, the Soviet literary scene degenerated to the point that the works of great writers like Franz Kafka were no longer read, either because they were viewed as decadent, formal experiments or because they "engineered souls" in "nonprogressive" directions. Officially sanctioned works were generally ones in which artistry lagged far behind the politics (no matter how bad the politics were).

Fortunately for the Marxist critical movement, politically radical critics *outside* the Soviet Union were free of its narrow, constricting policies and, consequently, able fruitfully to develop the thinking of Marx, Engels, and Trotsky. It was these non-Soviet Marxists who kept Marxist critical theory alive and useful in discussing all *kinds* of literature, written across the entire historical spectrum.

Perhaps because Lukács was the best of the Soviet communists writing Marxist criticism in the 1930s and 1940s, non-Soviet Marxists tended to develop their ideas by publicly opposing those of Lukács. German dramatist and critic Bertolt Brecht countered Lukács by arguing that art ought to be viewed as a field of production, not as a container of "content." Brecht also criticized Lukács for his attempt to enshrine realism at the expense not only of other "isms" but also of poetry and drama, both of which had been largely ignored by Lukács.

Even more outspoken was Brecht's critical champion Walter Benjamin, a German Marxist who, in the 1930s, attacked those conventional and traditional literary forms conveying a stultifying "aura" of culture. Benjamin praised Dadaism and, more important, new forms of art ushered in by the age of mechanical reproduction. Those forms—including radio and film—offered hope, he felt, for liberation from capitalist culture, for they were too new to be part of its stultifyingly ritualistic traditions.

But of all the anti-Lukácsians outside the USSR who made a contribution to the development of Marxist literary criticism, the most important was probably Théodor Adorno. Leader since the early 1950s of the

Frankfurt school of Marxist criticism, Adorno attacked Lukács for his dogmatic rejection of nonrealist modern literature and for his belief in the primacy of content over form. Art does not equal science, Adorno insisted. He went on to argue for art's autonomy from empirical forms of knowledge and to suggest that the interior monologues of modernist works (by Beckett and Proust) reflect the fact of modern alienation in a way that Marxist criticism ought to find compelling.

In addition to turning against Lukács and his overly constrictive canon, Marxists outside the Soviet Union were able to take advantage of insights generated by non-Marxist critical theories being developed in post–World War II Europe. One of the movements that came to be of interest to non-Soviet Marxists was structuralism, a scientific approach to the study of humankind whose proponents believed that all elements of culture, including literature, could be understood as parts of a system of signs. Using modern linguistics as a model, structuralists like Claude Lévi-Strauss broke the myths of various cultures into "mythemes" in an attempt to show that there are structural correspondences or homologies between the mythical elements produced by various human communities across time.

Of the European structuralist Marxists, one of the most influential was Lucien Goldmann, a Rumanian critic living in Paris. Goldmann combined structuralist principles with Marx's base-superstructure model in order to show how economics determines the mental structures of social groups, which are reflected in literary texts. Goldmann rejected the idea of individual human genius, choosing to see works, instead, as the "collective" products of "trans-individual" mental structures. In early studies, such as *The Hidden God* (1955), he related seventeenth-century French texts (such as Racine's *Phèdre*) to the ideology of Jansenism. In later works, he applied Marx's base-superstructure model even more strictly, describing a relationship between economic conditions and texts unmediated by an intervening, collective consciousness.

In spite of his rigidity and perhaps because of his affinities with structuralism, Goldmann came to be seen in the 1960s as the proponent of a kind of watered-down, "humanist" Marxism. He was certainly viewed that way by the French Marxist Louis Althusser, a disciple not of Lévi-Strauss and structuralism but rather of the psychoanalytic theorist Jacques Lacan and of the Italian communist Antonio Gramsci, famous for his writings about ideology and "hegemony." (Gramsci used the latter word to refer to the pervasive, weblike system of assumptions and values that shapes the way things look, what they mean, and therefore what reality *is* for the majority of people within a culture.)

Like Gramsci, Althusser viewed literary works primarily in terms of their relationship to ideology, the function of which, he argued, is to (re)produce the existing relations of production in a given society. Dave Laing, in *The Marxist Theory of Art* (1978), has attempted to explain this particular insight of Althusser's by saying that ideologies, through the "ensemble of habits, moralities, and opinions" that can be found in any literary text, "ensure that the work-force (and those responsible for re-producing them in the family, school, etc.) are maintained in their position of subordination to the dominant class" (91). This is not to say that Althusser thought of the masses as a brainless multitude following only the dictates of the prevailing ideology: Althusser followed Gramsci in suggesting that even working-class people have some freedom to struggle against ideology and to change history. Nor is it to say that Althusser saw ideology as being a coherent, consistent force. In fact, he saw it as being riven with contradictions that works of literature sometimes expose and even widen. Thus Althusser followed Marx and Gramsci in believing that although literature must be seen in *relation* to ideology, it—like all social forms—has some degree of autonomy.

Althusser's followers included Pierre Macherey, who in *A Theory of Literary Production* (1966) developed Althusser's concept of the relationship between literature and ideology. A realistic novelist, he argued, attempts to produce a unified, coherent text, but instead ends up producing a work containing lapses, omissions, gaps. This happens because within ideology there are subjects that cannot be covered, things that cannot be said, contradictory views that aren't recognized as contradictory. (The critic's challenge, in this case, is to supply what the text cannot say, thereby making sense of gaps and contradictions.)

But there is another reason why gaps open up and contradictions become evident in texts. Works don't just reflect ideology (which Goldmann had referred to as "myth" and which Macherey refers to as a system of "illusory social beliefs"); they are also "fictions," works of art, *products* of ideology that have what Goldmann would call a "worldview" to offer. What kind of product, Macherey implicitly asks, is identical to the thing that produced it? It is hardly surprising, then, that Balzac's fiction shows French peasants in two different lights, only one of which is critical and judgmental, only one of which is baldly ideological. Writing approvingly on Macherey and Macherey's mentor Althusser in *Marxism and Literary Criticism* (1976), Terry Eagleton says: "It is by giving ideology a determinate form, fixing it within certain fictional limits, that art is able to distance itself from [ideology], thus revealing . . . [its] limits" (19).

\* \* \*

A follower of Althusser, Macherey is sometimes referred to as a "post-Althusserian Marxist." Eagleton, too, is often described that way, as is his American contemporary Fredric Jameson. Jameson and Eagleton, as well as being post-Althusserians, are also among the few Anglo-American critics who have closely followed and significantly developed Marxist thought.

Before them, Marxist interpretation in English was limited to the work of a handful of critics: Christopher Caudwell, Christopher Hill, Arnold Kettle, E. P. Thompson, and Raymond Williams. Of these, Williams was perhaps least Marxist in orientation: he felt that Marxist critics, ironically, tended too much to isolate economics from culture; that they overlooked the individualism of people, opting instead to see them as "masses"; and that even more ironically, they had become an elitist group. But if the least Marxist of the British Marxists, Williams was also by far the most influential. Preferring to talk about "culture" instead of ideology, Williams argued in works such as *Culture and Society 1780–1950* (1958) that culture is "lived experience" and, as such, an interconnected set of social properties, each and all grounded in and influencing history.

Terry Eagleton's *Criticism and Ideology* (1978) is in many ways a response to the work of Williams. Responding to Williams's statement in *Culture and Society*, that "there are in fact no masses; there are only ways of seeing people as masses" (289), Eagleton writes: "That men and women really are now unique individuals was Williams's (unexceptionable) insistence; but it was a proposition bought at the expense of perceiving the fact that they must mass and fight to achieve their full individual humanity. One has only to adapt Williams's statement to 'There are in fact no classes; there are only ways of seeing people as classes' to expose its theoretical paucity" (*Criticism* 29)

Eagleton goes on, in *Criticism and Ideology*, to propose an elaborate theory about how history—in the form of "general," "authorial," and "aesthetic" ideology—enters texts, which in turn may revivify, open up, or critique those same ideologies, thereby setting in motion a process that may alter history. He shows how texts by Jane Austen, Matthew Arnold, Charles Dickens, George Eliot, Joseph Conrad, and T. S. Eliot deal with and transmute conflicts at the heart of the general and authorial ideologies behind them: conflicts between morality and individualism, individualism and social organicism and utilitarianism.

As all this emphasis on ideology and conflict suggests, a modern British Marxist like Eagleton, even while acknowledging the work of a

British Marxist predecessor like Williams, is more nearly developing the ideas of continental Marxists like Althusser and Macherey. That holds, as well, for modern American Marxists like Fredric Jameson. For although he makes occasional, sympathetic references to the works of Williams, Thompson, and Hill, Jameson makes far more *use* of Lukács, Adorno, and Althusser as well as non-Marxist structuralist, psychoanalytic, and poststructuralist critics.

In the first of several influential works, *Marxism and Form* (1971), Jameson takes up the question of form and content, arguing that the former is "but the working out" of the latter "in the realm of superstructure" (329). (In making such a statement Jameson opposes not only the tenets of Russian Formalists, for whom content had merely been the fleshing out of form, but also those of so-called vulgar Marxists, who tended to define form as mere ornamentation or window dressing.) In his later work *The Political Unconscious* (1981), Jameson uses what in *Marxism and Form* he had called "dialectical criticism" to synthesize out of structuralism and poststructuralism, Freud and Lacan, Althusser and Adorno, a set of complex arguments that can only be summarized reductively.

The fractured state of societies and the isolated condition of individuals, he argues, may be seen as indications that there originally existed an unfallen state of something that may be called "primitive communism." History—which records the subsequent divisions and alienations—limits awareness of its own contradictions and of that lost, Better State, via ideologies and their manifestation in texts whose strategies essentially contain and repress desire, especially revolutionary desire, into the collective unconscious. (In Conrad's *Lord Jim*, Jameson shows, the knowledge that governing classes don't *deserve* their power is contained and repressed by an ending that metaphysically blames Nature for the tragedy and that melodramatically blames wicked Gentleman Brown.)

As demonstrated by Jameson in analyses like the one mentioned above, textual strategies of containment and concealment may be discovered by the critic, but only by the critic practicing dialectical criticism, that is to say, a criticism aware, among other things, of its *own* status as ideology. All thought, Jameson concludes, is ideological; only through ideological thought that knows itself as such can ideologies be seen through and eventually transcended.

In the Marxist interpretation of *Frankenstein* that follows, Warren Montag begins his interpretive encounter with Mary Shelley's novel by arguing that a literary work creates the illusion of autonomy while depending, in fact, on history for meaning. (He thus steers a course between Althusser, for whom literary works are at least semiautonomous, and critics like Eagleton, for whom they are not.) Montag proceeds, then, by attempting to "[ascertain] the character of the second decade of the nineteenth century, and more generally the period of English (and to a certain extent European) history between the French Revolution of 1789 and the period of relative social stability that set in with the passage of the Reform Bill in 1832 in England" (p. 469 in this volume).

Using the text to establish that the novel is set in the 1790s, the period of the French Revolution, Montag shows how the novel at once reveals and masks that fact, telling us that Victor Frankenstein is planning to create his monster one hundred and fifty years *after* the *English* Revolution (of 1642). The passage referring to that earlier revolt against monarchy turns out to be surprisingly conservative in its implications — *oddly* conservative, in fact, given Mary Shelley's supposed radicalism. Montag explains that conservatism by remounting E. P. Thompson's argument that the French Revolution had produced a kind of monster in Europe, a mood of amorality and anarchy that had infected England and come to raise fears, even among some radicals, that England itself was on the brink of chaos.

After all, the formation of the working class *as* a class had led to revolutionary working-class political movements such as the Luddite movement, which in turn had led to violent mass demonstrations and machine-smashing incidents. These movements and incidents had shown English working people to be militant and combative toward the middle class as well as toward the aristocracy. Mary Shelley had seen this as well as anyone, and the sight could only have made her fearful, if also excited. "Shelley's work," according to Montag, "is incontestably interwoven in this history: it bears witness to the birth of that monster, simultaneously the object of pity and fear, the industrial working class" (p. 472).

We come to realize as we follow Montag's argument further, however, that to read *Frankenstein* as a work in which monster equals proletariat is to read as a somewhat simplistic Marxist critic. So Montag proceeds to another level of the text, as well as to other levels of Marxist critical discourse that we may associate with Macherey, Eagleton, and Jameson. To find the history in the text — rather than seeing the text as a simpleminded allegory of history — Montag goes back to it in search of "the contradictions, discrepancies, and inconsistencies that the work displays but does not address or attempt to resolve" (p. 474). In doing so, he begins practicing a form of Marxism that combines Macherey's conviction that the profoundest historical meaning of a work lies in what the work *cannot* say, what ideology of the day will not *let* it say, with a neo-Hegelian interest in form. For the telling contradictions Montag finds in *Frankenstein*, the discrepancies that hide what it cannot say as often involve disruptions of aesthetic unity as they do contradictory ideas or "contents."

What *Frankenstein* leaves out—what is conspicuously and significantly absent—is not that in creating a working class, England has created a monster. That, rather, is what the work virtually says outright. It is, rather, that science, or more precisely the technology that the Age of Reason has made possible (and that the Enlightenment would tell us will assure human progress), can in fact be alienating and dehumanizing, could in fact cause society to grow, if anything, weaker and turn human beings into a lower form of life. In making that absence in the text present, Marxist criticism surely makes *Frankenstein* present in the temporal as well as in the spatial sense—that is, as a work able to speak provocatively of and to the historical epoch in which it is now being read.

Ross C Murfin

## MARXIST CRITICISM:
## A SELECTED BIBLIOGRAPHY

### Marxist Criticism: General Texts

Baxendall, Lee, comp. *Marxism and Aesthetics: A Selective Annotated Bibliography*. New York: Humanities, 1968. Print.

Bennett, Tony, *Formalism and Marxism*. London: Methuen, 1979. Print.

Bullock, Chris, and David R. Peck, comps. *Guide to Marxist Literary Criticism*. Bloomington: Indiana UP, 1980. Print. Bibliography of Marxist writings.

Craig, David, ed. *Marxists on Literature: An Anthology*. Baltimore: Penguin, 1975. Print.

Demetz, Peter. *Marx, Engels, and the Poets: Origins of Marxist Literary Criticism*. 1959. Rev. and enl. by author and trans. Jeffrey L. Sammons. Chicago: U of Chicago P, 1967. Print.

Dobie, Ann B. *Theory into Practice: An Introduction to Literary Criticism*. 3d ed. Boston: Wadsworth, 2009. Print. See ch. 5, "Marxist Criticism."

Eagleton, Terry. *Criticism and Ideology: A Study in Marxist Literary Theory*. 1976. Rpt. London: Verso, 2006. Print.

———. *Marxism and Literary Criticism*. London: Methuen, 1976. Rpt. with new preface by author. New York: Routledge, 2002. Print.

————, and Drew Milne, eds. *Marxist Literary Theory: A Reader.* Cambridge: Blackwell, 1996. Print.

Forgacs, David. "Marxist Literary Theories." *Modern Literary Theory: A Comparative Introduction.* Eds. Ann Jefferson and David Robey. Totowa, NJ: Barnes & Noble, 1986. Print.

Frow, John. *Marxism and Literary History.* Cambridge: Harvard UP, 1986. Print.

Goldstein, Philip. *The Politics of Literary Theory: An Introduction to Marxist Criticism.* Tallahassee: Florida State UP, 1990. Print.

Groden, Michael, and Martin Kreiswirth, eds. *The Johns Hopkins Guide to Literary Theory and Criticism.* 2d ed. Baltimore: Johns Hopkins UP, 2005. Print. See "Marxist Theory and Criticism."

Haslett, Moyra. *Marxist Literary and Cultural Theories.* New York: St. Martin's, 2000. Print.

Hyman, Stanley Edgar. "The Marxist Criticism of Literature." *The Antioch Review* 7.4 (Win. 1947): 541–68. Print.

Jackson, Leonard. *The Dematerialisation of Karl Marx: Literature and Marxist Theory.* New York: Longman, 1994. Print.

Laing, Dave. *The Marxist Theory of Art: An Introductory Survey.* Boulder: Westview, 1978. Print.

LeRoy, Gaylord C., and Ursula Beitz, eds. *Preserve and Create: Essays in Marxist Literary Criticism.* New York: Humanities, 1973. Print.

*Marxism and Literature Revisited.* Spec. issue of *Mediations* 24.2 (Spr. 2009). Print.

Marxists Internet Archive, http://www.marxists.org. Web. 28 June 2013. See especially "Literary Criticism."

*Mediations: Journal of the Marxist Literary Group.* Marxist Literary Group (at U of Illinois at Chicago). Print. http://mediations journal.org/about. Web. 25 June 2013.

Mulhern, Francis, ed. *Contemporary Marxist Literary Criticism.* New York: Longman, 1992. Print.

Paananen, Victor N. *British Marxist Criticism.* New York: Garland, 2000. Print. Introductions and annotated bibliographies for eight critics.

Selden, Raman, Peter Widdowson, and Peter Brooker. *A Reader's Guide to Contemporary Literary Theory.* 5th ed. New York: Pearson, 2005. Print. See ch. 5, "Marxist Theories."

Slaughter, Cliff. *Marxism, Ideology, and Literature.* Atlantic Highlands, NJ: Humanities, 1980. Print.

Tyson, Lois. *Critical Theory Today: A User-Friendly Guide.* 3d. ed. New York: Routledge, 2014. Print. See ch. 3, "Marxist Criticism."

## Marx, Engels, Lenin, and Trotsky

Engels, Friedrich. *The Condition of the Working Class in England.* 1845. Ed. David McLellan. New York: Oxford UP, 1993. Print.

Lenin, Vladimir I. *Articles on Tolstoy.* Moscow: Foreign Languages Publishing, 1951. Print.

———. *On Literature and Art.* Moscow: Progress, 1967. Print. See especially "Party Organization and Party Literature" (1905).

Marx, Karl. *Das Kapital (Capital).* Vol. 1. 1867. Trans. Ben Fowkes. New York: Vintage, 1976. Print.

———. *A Contribution to the Critique of Political Economy.* 1859. Ed. Maurice Dobb. Trans. S. W. Ryazanskaya. New York: International, 1970. Print.

———. *The Eighteenth Brumaire of Louis Bonaparte.* 1852. Trans. Daniel De Leon. 1897. New York: Mondial, 2005. Print.

———. *Selected Writings.* Ed. David McLellan. 1977. 2d ed. Oxford: Oxford UP, 2000. Print.

———, and Friedrich Engels. *The Communist Manifesto.* 1848. Trans Samuel Moore. 1888. Ed. David McLellan. New York: Oxford UP, 1992. Print. Includes authors' prefaces written after 1848.

———. *The German Ideology.* Print. 1932. Ed. C. J. Arthur. New York: International, 1970. Part 1, with selections from Parts 2 and 3 and supplementary texts.

Trotsky, Leon. *Literature and Revolution.* 1924. Ed. William Keach. Trans. Rose Strunsky. Chicago: Haymarket, 2005. Print.

## Influential Marxist Literary Studies

Bakhtin, Mikhail. *The Dialogic Imagination: Four Essays.* 1975. Ed. Michael Holquist. Trans. Caryl Emerson and Holquist. Austin: U of Texas P, 1981. Print.

———. *Problems of Dostoevsky's Poetics.* 1929. Trans. R. W. Rotsel. Ann Arbor: Ardis, 1973. Print.

———. *Rabelais and His World.* 1965. Trans. Hélène Iswolsky. Bloomington: Indiana UP, 1984. Print.

Benjamin, Walter. *Illuminations.* 1955. Ed. Hannah Arendt. Trans. Harry Zohn. New York: Harcourt, 1968. Print. See especially "The Work of Art in the Age of Mechanical Reproduction" (1936).

Brecht, Bertolt. *Brecht on Theatre: The Development of an Aesthetic.* Ed. John Willett. New York: Hill and Wang, 1964. Print.

Caudwell, Christopher. *Illusion and Reality: A Study of the Sources of Poetry.* London: Macmillan, 1937. Print.

——. *Studies in a Dying Culture.* London: John Lane, Bodley Head, 1938. Print.

Eagleton, Terry. *Criticism and Ideology: A Study in Marxist Literary Theory.* London: NLB, 1976. New ed. with new intro. by author. New York: Verso, 2006. Print.

Goldmann, Lucien. *The Hidden God: A Study of Tragic Vision in the Pensées of Pascal and the Tragedies of Racine.* 1955. Trans. Philip Thody. New York: Humanities, 1964. Print.

——. *Towards a Sociology of the Novel.* 1963. Trans. Alan Sheridan. London: Tavistock, 1975. Print.

Jameson, Fredric. *Marxism and Form: Twentieth-Century Dialectical Theories of Literature.* Princeton: Princeton UP, 1971. Print.

——. *The Political Unconscious: Narrative as a Socially Symbolic Act.* Ithaca: Cornell UP, 1981. Print.

Kettle, Arnold. *An Introduction to the English Novel.* 1951–53. London: Routledge, 2015. Print.

——. *Literature and Liberation: Selected Essays.* Eds. Graham Martin and W. R. Owens. New York: Manchester UP, 1988. Print.

Lukács, Georg. *Essays on Realism.* 1931–40. Ed. Rodney Livingstone. Trans. David Fernbach. Cambridge: MIT, 1980. Print.

——. *The Historical Novel.* 1937. Trans. Hannah Mitchell and Stanley Mitchell. London: Merlin, 1962. Rpt. Lincoln: U of Nebraska P, 1983. Print.

——. *Studies in European Realism: A Sociological Survey of the Writings of Balzac, Stendhal, Zola, Tolstoy, Gorki and Others.* 1948. Trans. Edith Bone. London: Hillway, 1950. Print.

——. *The Theory of the Novel: A Historico-Philosophical Essay on the Forms of Great Epic Literature.* 1920. Trans. Anna Bostock. London: Merlin, 1971. Print.

Macherey, Pierre. *A Theory of Literary Production.* 1966. Trans. Geoffrey Wall. New York: Routledge, 2006. Print.

——, and Étienne Balibar. "On Literature as an Ideological Form." 1978. *Contemporary Marxist Literary Criticism.* Ed. Francis Mulhern. New York: Longman, 1992. 34–54. Print.

Williams, Raymond. *Culture and Society: 1780–1950.* 1958. New York: Columbia UP, 1983. Print.

——. *Marxism and Literature.* Oxford: Oxford UP, 1977. Print.

## Other Influential Marxist Studies

Adorno, Theodor. *Prisms*. 1967. Trans. Samuel Weber and Shierry Weber. Cambridge: MIT, 1981. Print.

Althusser, Louis. *For Marx*. 1965. Trans. Ben Brewster. New York: Pantheon, 1969. Print.

———. *Lenin and Philosophy and Other Essays*. Trans. Ben Brewster. London: Verso, 1971. Print. See especially "Ideology and Ideological State Apparatuses (Notes Toward an Investigation)" (1969), and "A Letter on Art" (1966).

———, and Étienne Balibar. *Reading* Capital. 1968. Trans. Ben Brewster. London: New Left, 1970. Print.

Benjamin, Walter. *The Arcades Project*. Ed. Rolf Tiedemann. 1972. Trans. Howard Eiland and Kevin McLaughlin. Cambridge: Belknap P, 1999. Print.

Gramsci, Antonio. *Selections from the Prison Notebooks*. Eds. and trans. Quintin Hoare and Geoffrey Nowell Smith. London: Lawrence & Wishart, 1971. Print.

Jameson, Fredric. *Postmodernism, or, The Cultural Logic of Late Capitalism*. Durham: Duke UP, 1991. Print.

Marcuse, Herbert. *One-Dimensional Man: Studies in the Ideology of Advanced Industrial Society*. 1964. Boston: Beacon, 1991. Print.

Thompson, E. P. *The Making of the English Working Class*. London: Victor Gollancz, 1963. Print.

———. *William Morris: Romantic to Revolutionary*. London: Lawrence & Wishart, 1955. Print.

Williams, Raymond. *The Long Revolution*. New York: Columbia UP, 1961. Print.

Wilson, Edmund. *To the Finland Station: A Study in the Writing and Acting of History*. New York: Harcourt, 1940. Print.

## Further Reading on Marxist Criticism

Anderson, Perry. *The Origins of Postmodernity*. New York: Verso, 1998. Print.

Baraka, Amiri. *Daggers and Javelins: Essays*. New York: Morrow, 1984. Print.

Bennett, Tony. *Outside Literature*. New York: Routledge, 1990. Print.

Benton, Ted. *The Rise and Fall of Structural Marxism: Louis Althusser and His Influence*. New York: St. Martin's, 1984. Print.

Bisztray, George. *Marxist Models of Literary Realism*. New York: Columbia UP, 1974. Print.

Burnham, Clint. *The Jamesonian Unconscious: The Aesthetics of Marxist Theory.* Durham: Duke UP, 1995. Print.

Day, Gary. *Class.* New York: Routledge, 2001. Print.

*Décalages: An Althusser Studies Journal.* Los Angeles: Occidental College. Semi-annual journal, available at http://scholar.oxy.edu /decalages. Web. 25 June 2013.

Dimock, Wai Chee, and Michael T. Gilmore, eds. *Rethinking Class: Literary Studies and Social Formations.* New York: Columbia UP, 1994. Print.

Dowling, William C. *Jameson, Althusser, Marx: An Introduction to The Political Unconscious.* Ithaca: Cornell UP, 1984. Print.

Donahue, Brian. "Marxism, Postmodernism, Žižek." *Postmodern Culture* 12.2 (2002): 57 paragraphs. Web. 8 August 2015.

Eagleton, Terry. "Marxism and the Future of Criticism." *Writing the Future.* Ed. David Wood. New York: Routledge, 1990. 177–80. Print.

———. *Walter Benjamin: or, Towards a Revolutionary Criticism.* London: Verso, 1981. Print.

Elliott, Gregory, ed. *Althusser: A Critical Reader.* Cambridge: Blackwell, 1994. Print.

Gugelberger, Georg, ed. *Marxism in African Literature.* Trenton: African World, 1985. Print.

Hawthorn, Jeremy. *Identity and Relationship: Contribution to Marxist Theory of Literary Criticism.* London: Lawrence & Wishart, 1973. Print.

Higgins, John. *Raymond Williams: Literature, Marxism and Cultural Materialism.* New York: Routledge, 1999. Print.

———, ed. *The Raymond Williams Reader.* Malden, MA: Wiley, 2001. Print.

Homer, Sean. *Fredric Jameson: Marxism, Hermeneutics, Postmodernism.* New York: Routledge, 1998. Print.

Ives, Peter, and Rocco Lacorte, eds. *Gramsci, Language, and Translation.* Lanham: Lexington, 2010. Print.

Jameson, Fredric. *The Ideologies of Theory: Essays, 1971–1986.* 2 vols. 1988. Updated ed. New York: Verso, 2009. Print.

———. *The Jameson Reader.* Michael Hardt and Kathi Weeks, eds. Malden, MA: Wiley, 2000. Print.

Johnson, Pauline. *Marxist Aesthetics: The Foundations within Everyday Life for an Emancipated Consciousness.* 1984. Abingdon: Routledge, 2012. Print.

Kadarkay, Arad, ed. *The Lukács Reader.* Cambridge, MA: Blackwell, 1995. Print.

Lavelle, John F. *Blue Collar, Theoretically: A Post-Marxist Approach to Working Class Literature.* Jefferson: McFarland, 2012. Print.

LeRoy, Gaylord, and Ursula Beitz. "The Marxist Approach to Modernism." *Journal of Modern Literature* 3.5 (July 1974): 1158–74. Print.

Lesjak, Carolyn. "Reading Dialectically." *Criticism* 55.2 (2013): 233–77. Print.

Levine, Ira A. *Left-Wing Dramatic Theory in the American Theater.* Ann Arbor: U of Michigan Research P, 1985. Print.

Marcuse, Herbert. *The Aesthetic Dimension: Toward a Critique of Marxist Aesthetics.* 1977. Trans. and rev. Herbert Marcuse and Erica Sherover. Boston: Beacon, 1978. Print.

Markels, Julian. "Toward a Marxian Reentry to the Novel." *Narrative* 4.3 (Oct. 1996): 197–217. Print.

Mehring, Franz. *The Lessing Legend.* 1892. Abridged. Trans. A. S. Grogan. New York: Critics, 1938. Print.

Murphy, James F. *The Proletarian Moment: The Controversy over Leftism in Literature.* Urbana: U of Illinois P, 1991. Print.

Nelson, Cary, and Lawrence Grossberg, eds. *Marxism and the Interpretation of Culture.* Urbana: U of Illinois P, 1988. Print. See especially Section VI, "The Politics of Theory and Interpretation."

Nordquist, Joan, comp. *Fredric Jameson: A Bibliography.* Santa Cruz, CA: Reference & Research, 2001. Print.

Plekhanov, G. V. *Art and Social Life.* 1912. Ed. Andrew Rothstein. London: Lawrence & Wishart, 1953. Print.

Rabinovitch, Rachel. *How to Become a Poet Today: Notes on the Poetic-Industrial Complex.* N.p.: Pascal Editions, 2013. Kindle file.

Regan, Stephen, ed. *The Eagleton Reader.* Malden, MA: Wiley, 1998. Print. See especially Part I, "Literary Criticism," and Part III, "Marxism and Critical Theory."

San Juan, Jr., E. *From the Masses, to the Masses: Third-World Literature and Revolution.* Minneapolis: Mep, 1994. Print.

Sumner, Charles. "The Turn Away from Marxism, or Why We Read the Way We Read Now." *diacritics* 40.3 (2012): 26–55. Print.

Teres, Harvey. "Remaking Marxist Criticism: *Partisan Review*'s Eliotic Leftism 1934–36." *American Literature* 64.1 (Mar. 1992): 127–53. Print.

Zhdanov, Andrei A. *Essays on Literature, Philosophy, and Music.* New York: International, 1950. Print.

## Intersections with Feminist Theory and Criticism

Barrett, Michèle. *Women's Oppression Today: Problems in Marxist Feminist Analysis*. London: New Left, 1980. Rev. ed. *Women's Oppression Today: The Marxist/Feminist Encounter*. London: Verso, 1988. Print.

Boer, Roland, and Jorunn Økland, eds. *Marxist Feminist Criticism of the Bible*. Sheffield, UK: Sheffield Phoenix, 2008. Print.

Hennessey, Rosemary. *Materialist Feminism and the Politics of Discourse*. New York: Routledge, 1993. Print.

Howard, June. "Toward a 'Marxist-Feminist Cultural Analysis.'" *Minnesota Review* n.s. 20 (Spr. 1983): 77–92. Print.

Kaplan, Cora. *Sea Changes: Essays on Culture and Feminism*. London: Verso, 1986. Print. See especially Kaplan's discussion of Charlotte Brontë and *Jane Eyre*.

Landry, Donna, and Gerald Maclean. *Materialist Feminisms*. Cambridge: Blackwell, 1993. Print.

Mitchell, Juliet. "Women: The Longest Revolution." *New Left Review* 40 (1966): 11–37. Print.

Moi, Toril, and Janice Radway, eds. *Materialist Feminism*. Spec. issue of *South Atlantic Quarterly* 93.4 (1994). Print.

Newton, Judith. *Starting Over: Feminism and the Politics of Cultural Critique*. Ann Arbor: U of Michigan P, 1994. Print.

Newton, Judith Lowder, and Deborah Rosenfelt, eds. *Feminist Criticism and Social Change: Sex, Class, and Race in Literature and Culture*. New York: Methuen, 1985. Print.

Papke, Mary E. "American Marxwomen: Duelling with Historical Materialism." *Germany and German Thought in American Literature and Cultural Criticism*. Ed. Peter Freese. Essen: Blaue Eule, 1990. 454–69. Print.

Rowbotham, Sheila. *Woman's Consciousness, Man's World*. Harmondsworth: Penguin, 1973. Print.

## Intersections with Other Critical Perspectives

Ahmad, Aijaz. *In Theory: Classes, Nations, Literatures*. New York: Verso, 1992. Print. Critiques postcolonial theory.

Amuta, Chidi. *The Theory of African Literature: Implications for Practical Criticism*. Atlantic Highlands: Zed, 1989. Print.

Bartolovich, Crystal, and Neil Lazarus, eds. *Marxism, Modernity, and Postcolonial Studies*. New York: Cambridge UP, 2002. Print.

Callinicos, Alex. *Against Postmodernism: A Marxist Critique*. Cambridge: Polity, 1989. Print.

Coward, Rosalind, and John Ellis. *Language and Materialism: Developments in Semiology and the Theory of the Subject*. Boston: Routledge, 1977. Print.

Derrida, Jacques. *Specters of Marx*. Trans. Peggy Kamuf. New York: Routledge, 1994. Print. Applies deconstruction.

Eagleton, Terry. *Against the Grain: Selected Essays, 1975–1985*. London: Verso, 1986. Print.

Evans, Malcolm. *Signifying Nothing: Truth's True Contents in Shakespeare's Text*. Athens: U of Georgia P, 1986. Print. Applies deconstruction.

Floyd, Kevin. *The Reification of Desire: Toward a Queer Marxism*. Minneapolis: U of Minnesota P, 2009. Print.

Gallagher, Catherine. "Marxism and the New Historicism." *The New Historicism*. Ed. H. Aram Veeser. New York: Routledge, 1989. 37–48. Print.

Hawthorn, Jeremy. *Cunning Passages: New Historicism, Cultural Materialism, and Marxism in the Contemporary Literary Debate*. New York: Arnold, 1996. Print.

Kellner, Douglas, ed. *Postmodernism/Jameson/Critique*. Washington, DC: Maisonneuve, 1989. Print.

Nilges, Mathias. "Marxist Literary Criticism." *The Routledge Companion to Latino/a Literature*. Eds. Suzanne Bost and Frances R. Aparicio. New York: Routledge, 2012. 143–51. Print.

Parry, Benita. *Postcolonial Studies: A Materialist Critique*. New York: Routledge, 2004. Print.

Quayson, Ato. *Calibrations: Reading for the Social*. Minneapolis: U of Minnesota P, 2003. Print.

Spivak, Gayatri Chakravorty. "Can the Subaltern Speak?" *Marxism and the Interpretation of Culture*. Eds. Cary Nelson and Lawrence Grossberg. Urbana: U of Illinois P, 1988. 271–313. Print.

———. *A Critique of Postcolonial Reason: Toward a History of the Vanishing Present*. Cambridge: Harvard UP, 1999. Print.

———. *In Other Worlds: Essays in Cultural Politics*. New York: Methuen, 1987. Print. Integrates deconstruction, feminism, and Marxism.

Villarejo, Amy. *Lesbian Rule: Cultural Criticism and the Value of Desire*. Durham: Duke UP, 2003. Print.

Wang, Orrin N. C. *Romantic Sobriety: Sensation, Revolution, Commodification, History*. Baltimore: Johns Hopkins UP, 2011. Print. Applies deconstruction.

Wood, Ellen Meiksins, and John Bellamy Foster, eds. *In Defense of History: Marxism and the Postmodern Agenda*. New York: Monthly Review, 1997. Print.

Zavarzadeh, Mas'ud, Teresa L. Ebert, and Donald Morton, eds. *Marxism, Queer Theory, Gender*. Syracuse: Red Factory, 2001. Print.

Žižek, Slavoj. *The Sublime Object of Ideology*. London, New York: Verso, 1989. Print. Applies Lacanian psychoanalytic theory.

### Marxist Readings

Boer, Roland. *Marxist Criticism of the Bible: A Critical Introduction to Marxist Literary Theory and the Bible*. New York: T & T International, 2003. Print.

Bök, Christian. "The Secular Opiate: Marxism as an Ersatz Religion in Three Canadian Texts." *Canadian Literature* 147 (Win. 1995): 11–22. Print.

Booker, M. Keith. *Ulysses, Capitalism, and Colonialism: Reading Joyce After the Cold War*. Westport: Greenwood, 2000. Print.

Castellitto, George P. "Willy Loman: The Tension between Marxism and Capitalism." *"The Salesman Has a Birthday": Essays Celebrating the Fiftieth Anniversary of Arthur Miller's Death of a Salesman*. Ed. Stephen A. Marino. Lanham: UP of America, 2000. 79–86. Print.

Eagleton, Terry. *Exiles and Émigrés: Studies in Modern Literature*. London: Chatto & Windus, 1970. Print.

Egan, Gabriel. *Shakespeare and Marx*. New York: Oxford UP, 2004. Print.

Garcellano, Edel E. *Knife's Edge: Selected Essays*. Quezon City: U of the Philippines P, 2001. Print.

Hitchcock, Peter. "Answering as Authoring: Or, Marxism's Joyce." *Mosaic* 32.1 (Mar. 1999): 55–69. Print.

Howard, Jean E., and Scott Cutler Shershow, eds. *Marxist Shakespeares*. New York: Routledge, 2001. Print.

Hughes, Kenneth, ed. and trans. *Franz Kafka: An Anthology of Marxist Criticism*. Hanover: UP of New England, 1981. Print.

Jameson, Fredric. *Archaeologies of the Future: The Desire Called Utopia and Other Science Fictions*. New York: Verso, 2005. Print.

———. *The Modernist Papers*. New York: Verso, 2007. Print.

Langer, Monika. "Sartre and Marxist Existentialism." *Sartre Alive*. Eds. Ronald Aronson and Adrian van den Hoven. Detroit: Wayne State UP, 1991. 160–82. Print.

LeSeur, Geta. "Claude McKay's Marxism." *The Harlem Renaissance: Revaluations.* Eds. Amritjit Singh, William S. Shiver, and Stanley Brodwin. New York: Garland, 1989. 219–31. Print.

Markels, Julian. *The Marxian Imagination: Representing Class in Literature.* New York: Monthly Review, 2003. Print.

Martin, Loy D. *Browning's Dramatic Monologues and the Post-Romantic Subject.* Baltimore: Johns Hopkins UP, 1985. Print.

Ngara, Emmanuel. *Art and Ideology in the African Novel: A Study of the Influence of Marxism on African Writing.* London: Heinemann, 1985. Print.

Siegel, Paul N. *Shakespeare's English and Roman History Plays: A Marxist Approach.* Rutherford: Fairleigh Dickinson UP, 1986. Print.

Singh, Raman K. "Marxism in Richard Wright's Fiction." *Indian Journal of American Studies* 4 (1974): 21–35. Print.

Van Zee, Amy. "How to Apply Marxist Criticism to *Prince Caspian.*" *How to Analyze the Works of C. S. Lewis.* Minneapolis: Abdo, 2012. 48–57. Print.

Walsh, David. *The Sky between the Leaves: Film Reviews, Essays and Interviews, 1992–2012.* Oak Park, MI: Mehring, 2013. Print.

Weimann, Robert. *Shakespeare and the Popular Tradition in the Theatre: Studies in the Social Dimension of Dramatic Form and Function.* 1967. Ed. Robert Schwartz. Baltimore: Johns Hopkins UP, 1978. Print.

## Marxist Readings of *Frankenstein*

Comitini, Patricia. "The Limits of Discourse and the Ideology of Form in Mary Shelley's *Frankenstein.*" *Keats-Shelley Journal* 55 (2006): 179–98. Print.

Crafts, Stephen. "*Frankenstein*: Camp Curiosity or Premonition?" *Catalyst* 3 (Sum. 1967): 96–103. Print.

Gigante, Denise. "Facing the Ugly: The Case of *Frankenstein.*" *ELH* 67.2 (2000): 565–87. Print.

Hatlen, Burton. "Milton, Mary Shelley, and Patriarchy." *Bucknell Review* 28.2 (1983): 19–47. Print.

Jones, Jonathan. "Hidden Voices: Language and Ideology in Philosophy of Language in the Eighteenth Century and Mary Shelley's *Frankenstein.*" *Textual Practice* 19.3 (2005): 265–87. Print.

Lamb, John B. "Mary Shelley's *Frankenstein* and Milton's Monstrous Myth." *Nineteenth-Century Fiction* 47.3 (Dec. 1992): 303–19. Print.

Michie, Elsie B. "Production Replaces Creation: Market Forces and *Frankenstein* as Critique of Romanticism." *Nineteenth-Century Contexts* 12.1 (1988): 27–33. Print.

Moretti, Franco. *Signs Taken for Wonders: Essays in the Sociology of Literary Forms.* Trans. Susan Fischer, David Forgacs, and David Miller. London: Verso, 1983. Print.

O'Flinn, Paul. "Production and Reproduction: The Case of *Frankenstein.*" *Literature and History* 9.2 (Aut. 1983): 194–213. Print.

Vlasopolos, Anca. "*Frankenstein*'s Hidden Skeleton: The Psycho-Politics of Oppression." *Science-Fiction Studies* 10.2 (July 1983): 125–36. Print.

## A MARXIST PERSPECTIVE

WARREN MONTAG

### The "Workshop of Filthy Creation": A Marxist Reading of *Frankenstein*

The literary work, perhaps because of its physical appearance, presents itself as an autonomous artifact bearing within it all that is necessary to decipher the secrets that it seems to contain. A Marxist reading of a literary work begins with a refusal of this illusion of autonomy and seeks instead to restore to the work that peculiar form of dependence that its very structure is designed to mask or deny. For the literary text is in no way independent of the historical moment in which it emerged. It is not a closed, self-contained whole whose meaning would derive from itself alone. On the contrary, it is no more than a "node within a network" (Foucault 19). The work is bound both to the literary and nonliterary discourses with which it coexists (and in relation to which alone it possesses a meaning), and to the "non-discursive" social, economic, and political practices that make discourse possible.

We are thus obliged to begin our investigation of Mary Shelley's *Frankenstein* by ascertaining the character of the second decade of the nineteenth century, and more generally the period of English (and to a certain extent European) history between the French Revolution of 1789 and the period of relative social stability that set in with the passage of the Reform Bill in 1832 in England. Even the most cursory examination of this singular period reveals that its key themes are precisely those of *Frankenstein*: there is everywhere a sense of monstrous forces unwittingly conjured up in order to serve the project of progress and the Enlightenment but that have ultimately served to call that very project into question.

The French Revolution, unquestionably the major event of the period, had apparently come to a close just prior to the publication of *Frankenstein*, with the final defeat of Napoleon in 1815. Jean-Jacques Lecercle has demonstrated that although not once mentioned in *Frankenstein*, the French Revolution is nevertheless alluded to (Lecercle). Walton's letters to his sister are dated but with the decade and year omitted (for example, 28 March 17—). A passage that occurs rather late in the text, however, allows us to determine the years during which the action of the novel takes place. Victor Frankenstein, accompanied by his friend Henry Clerval, journeys to Scotland seeking a remote spot in which he can work to fulfill his promise to create a mate to relieve the monster's terrible solitude. When they stop briefly in Oxford, Frankenstein records the following sentiments:

> As we entered this city, our minds were filled with the remembrance of the events that had been transacted there more than a century and a half before. It was here that Charles I. had collected his forces. This city had remained faithful to him, after the whole nation had forsaken his cause to join the standard of parliament and liberty. (pp. 139–40 in this volume)

Frankenstein's meditation on the Revolution of 1642 in England locates the narrative in the 1790s, placing it in the midst of the French Revolution. It is indeed remarkable that the work refers to a revolution that occurred "more than a century and a half before" rather than to the most important event of contemporary history. But the absence of the French Revolution from the text is not the only surprising fact in this passage. Its tone is unexpectedly sympathetic to Charles I, a monarch typically regarded by Whigs (the moderates of the day), let alone the Radicals of Shelley's circle, as the very figure of a tyrant. His absolutist policies, his refusal to base his rule on the consent of Parliament, his abolition of religious freedom were all held to be the causes of the English civil war that began in 1642 and ended in 1649 when Charles was executed by order of Parliament.

Two discrepancies have thus appeared: (1) a substitution of the English revolution of one hundred fifty years earlier for the French; (2) a brief commentary on the English civil war that is at odds with everything we know of Mary Shelley's political sympathies. But these discrepancies are precisely what will allow us to proceed from the work to the history on which it depends and that made it possible. For the English and the French revolutions together were the most developed and elaborate social and political "experiments" in modern history and both had "failed," both were attempts to create social orders based on justice or (especially in the case of the French Revolution) reason that had collapsed into tyranny or chaos. The movements that destroyed (or attempted to destroy) absolutist monarchies were usually led by new elites (the rural or urban bourgeoisie: landowners, merchants, and financiers) whose access to political power was blocked by the old regime. In order to overthrow the old state and to create a system that more adequately represented their interests, the new elites were forced to mobilize the plebeian masses (peasants, workers, and the urban poor). But in doing so they found that they had conjured up a monster that, once unleashed, could not be controlled. It was widely felt, even by those sympathetic to such experiments, that the mass mobilizations necessary to destroy the old order effectively blocked the creation of the new. Unleashing the power of the multitude had led to anarchy, and to the proliferation of innumerable demands that went far beyond what was rational or even "just" (according to the norms of middle-class revolutionaries). The dreams of progress toward a rational state faded in the face of what appeared to be the unpredictable, seemingly "irrational" character of the activity of the masses. The Enlightenment, far from having led to the reign of reason, had unloosed elemental forces deaf to the appeals of the morality that had liberated them in the first place. Accordingly, a general demoralization followed the close of the French Revolution, creating an atmosphere in which the Enlightenment was called radically into question and with it the notion of history conceived as progress toward a world organized on the basis of reason.

And the close of the French Revolution did little to resolve this dilemma. Instead, it was displaced to England which, following the Napoleonic wars, itself entered a period of social crisis the character of which only further underscored these questions. According to historian E. P. Thompson, "it is as if the English nation entered a crucible in the 1790s and emerged after the wars in a different form" (191). This crucible, often referred to as the industrial revolution, was anything but a period of smooth evolution. First, the era was marked by the sudden emergence of new technologies whose origins seemed inexplicable to contemporaries, appearing to herald a world utterly unlike what had gone before. As a contemporary commentator, Cooke Taylor, noted in 1843: "steam engine had no precedent and the spinning-jenny is without ancestry . . . they sprang into sudden existence like Minerva from the brain of Jupiter" (qtd. in Thompson 190). Before the paradox of technologies created by human beings but whose nature seemed to defy human understanding, the mind sought refuge in the familiar language of mystery and miracle.

But these new technologies and the industrial systems they made possible were perhaps less disturbing than their effects on the lives of the laboring population. Increased unemployment, falling wages, rising prices for food and other necessities: these were the conditions that grew alongside the prosperity of the employing class. This contradictory development of capitalism meant that the peace and social harmony associated with a rural economy had been replaced by the apparently insurmountable conflict of the industrial order: "the cotton-mill is seen as the agent not only of industrial but also social revolution, producing not only more goods but also the labor movement itself" (Thompson 192). For Thompson, "the outstanding fact of the period between 1790 and 1830 is the formation of 'the working class'" (194), a social force conscious of its own interests as opposed to the interests of the dominant classes that began to act on the basis of these interests.

The English working class had entered the political stage, but in forms that could only appear monstrous to contemporary observers. The first wave of this movement, from 1811 to 1813, consisted of the mass action of workers bent on resisting the introduction of new technologies, particularly into the textile industry. By reducing the numbers of workers necessary to the production process, new industrial developments added to what was already a crisis of unemployment. This movement amounted to a clandestine army under the command of the mythical General Ludd (in fact no such leader existed). The "Luddites" sacked factories and smashed the new "labor saving machines." As their movement receded in the face of violent repression on the part of the British state, it was quickly succeeded by a wave of popular agitation against high prices and rents. Mass demonstrations were common, violent confrontations with the state only slightly less so. It was a time when talk of the threat or hope of revolution (according to one's perspective) was common. At the very moment that *Frankenstein* was first published, the British state suspended various civil rights (including that of habeas corpus) in order more effectively to counter the growing combativity of the unemployed and the working poor.

Mary Shelley's work is incontestably interwoven in this history: it bears witness to the birth of that monster, simultaneously the object of pity and fear, the industrial working class (Moretti). A dense network of resemblances appears to allow us to identify Frankenstein's monster with the emergent proletariat. The monster is monstrous by virtue of its being artificial rather than natural; lacking the unity of a natural organism, the monster is a factitious totality assembled from (the parts of) a multitude of different individuals (Goldner), in particular, the "poor," the urban mass that, because it is a multitude rather than an individual, is itself as nameless as Frankenstein's creation. It is also significant that the term *creation* is used at all to describe the origins of the monster. For the monster is a product rather than a creation, assembled and joined together not so much by a man (if such were the case the monster might be allotted a place in the order of things) as by science, technology, and industry (Lecourt), whose overarching logic subsumes and subjects even the greatest geniuses. In fact, Frankenstein the man struggles against Frankenstein the practitioner of science and servant of technological progress only finally to prove no more than an unwitting instrument of this progress. In this way the very notion of progress, a central ideological representation of the perpetual revolutionizing of the means by which goods are produced necessary to the development of capitalism, becomes problematic. Technological and industrial progress has produced a monster, an artificial being as destructive as it is powerful. The very logic of capitalism has produced the means of its own destruction: the industrial working class, that fabricated collectivity whose interests are irreconcilable with those of capital and which is thus rendered monstrous in the eyes of its creators. The development of capitalism, then, does not correspond to a logic at all, except perhaps a dialectical logic capable of grasping the manner in which the production of wealth engenders terrible poverty, and in which the greater the intelligence of the machine the more stunted the mind of the worker.

But of course, Mary Shelley is not content to denounce the "hideous progeny" (p. 25) of the first phase of industrial capitalism. For the monster is no less contradictory than the process that created it. Far from being simply the object of horror, the monster, so eloquent in describing his suffering and solitude, also elicits pity, if not exactly sympathy. Shelley thus lends her voice to the voiceless, those who, bowed and numbed by oppression and poverty, cannot speak for themselves.

The same ambivalence, the same combination of pity and fear is to be found in "The Mask of Anarchy," a poem by Percy Bysshe Shelley for which Mary Shelley wrote an explanatory note. The poem, written in response to the Peterloo massacre of 1819, describes the "slavery" of the "men of England." Starvation, poverty, injustice, and the violence of the ruling class and its state will cause the masses to "Feel revenge / Fiercely thirsting to exchange / Blood for blood—and wrong for wrong."

Shelley concludes the stanza with the admonition "Do not thus when ye are strong." Sympathy circumscribed by fear, finally conditional, an appeal to reason and law that is unconvincing even in the poem's own terms, "The Mask of Anarchy" with its refrain, "ye are many—they are few," fears nothing so much as the ever present possibility of the irrational (although objectively determined) violence of the "sleeping giant," the British working class, and a repetition of the Terror of the French Revolution. Is not *Frankenstein* this very dilemma presented as a fable?

Considered in this way, the work assumes a kind of coherence that in turn derives from the "class location" of the author. *Frankenstein* seems to center on the emergence of the industrial working class as a political and social force, seen in the light of the French and perhaps even British revolutions by the "progressive" artist: unable finally to identify with the proletariat and to adopt its point of view, even the radicals of Mary Shelley's milieu are constrained to regard it as a monster. If Marxist criticism worked this way it would resemble a kind of decoding. The critic replaces the apparent with the real and the mythological with the historical: the monster *is* the proletariat. History disguised as the novel remains only to be unmasked by the reader.

But such a reading is too simple; to stop here would be to reduce the literary work to a mere allegory structured by a set of symbolic equivalences: the monster equals the proletariat. Conceived in this way the work remains outside history, which is alluded to even as it is concealed. But a Marxist reading demands a more complex conception of the work, for Marxism is above all a materialism. All that exists, including art and culture, necessarily possesses a material existence. From a materialist point of view, the literary work cannot somehow exist outside of history and even less outside of reality. It cannot be collapsed into or reduced to something "more real" than itself, that is history. When we say that literary works are historical by their very nature we mean that history is as present in them as outside of them, that we do not leave the work in search of its historical meaning but seek the meaning of its historical existence within it.

For Marxism, history is a struggle between antagonistic social forces. Further, this struggle is inescapable: it is present in every cultural artifact, every intellectual enterprise. But the struggle is not the same throughout history, it takes many forms and involves many actors. It follows no rules and obeys no logic. Literary works are not simply expressions of some invariable, essential contradiction; they are singular, specific realizations of a struggle whose character is perpetually transformed by its own activity.

Thus, if we are to seek the signs of the historicity of the work within it, this historicity will inescapably be present in the form of a conflict. This conflict, however, is not merely or even primarily present in the content of the work, but rather in the very letter of the text. While literary works have, since Aristotle, been defined by their coherence, by their formal resolution of internal contradictions and antagonism, Marxism asks us to understand them on the basis of the specific conflicts that have generated them and that every work, no matter how apparently coherent, embodies and perhaps transforms but cannot resolve. Most often these contradictions are not what the work is about at all; instead they constitute symptomatic antagonisms that disrupt the unity that the text appears to display. From a Marxist point of view, an adequate reading of *Frankenstein* will therefore refrain from the enterprise of establishing correspondences between the apparently parallel worlds of literature and history and will instead seek to grasp the way in which history is present in the text as a force or motor ("class struggle is the motor of history," as Marx and Engels wrote in *The Communist Manifesto*). History sets the work against itself and splits it open, forcing it to reveal all that it sought to deny but cannot help revealing by the very fact of this denial. We will begin by posing the question the answer to which we have already begun to formulate: What are the contradictions, discrepancies, and inconsistencies that the work displays but does not address or attempt to resolve?

This question brings us immediately into conflict with the form of the work. For Frankenstein's life, at least as he narrates it from his deathbed, possesses an absolute coherence. His every thought, word, and deed are revealed to have been steps toward a destiny that awaited him from the beginning. He is able to see that he has always lived according to laws of whose existence he had been unaware, seeking without knowing it an end that would mean his destruction: "Destiny was too potent, and her immutable laws had decreed my utter and terrible destruction" (p. 48).

But his destiny is neither personal nor individual: Frankenstein has been the instrument of science. A seemingly chance encounter with the works of Cornelius Agrippa, his father's too casual dismissal of Agrippa, the reduction of a tree to splinters by lightning, the decision to attend the University of Ingolstadt: each of these moments was a ruse of scientific and technological progress, realizing itself through him but without his knowing it. His life as it is narrated assumes a nightmarish coherence; every experience, sensation, and feeling was a step on the road to his damnation. Although he once dreamed of creating a race that would worship him as master, he realizes as he lies dying that his relation to science ought rather to be described as a state of servitude. The ironic reversal of Frankenstein's position is perhaps clearest when his creation, far more powerful than he, calls him "slave."

Irony is natural to this dialectic of science, the essence of which is as manifest in violence as in peace, in destruction as in creation. Indifferent to human law and morality, science finally counterposes its own order to that of humankind. *Frankenstein* thus rejects one of the most fundamental myths of the Enlightenment, the notion that scientific and economic progress will continually improve the condition of humankind, the idea that once the barriers to knowledge are pushed aside, the conditions for perpetual peace and a universal harmony will have been established. Once we have stepped away from the false supports, the dogmas and formulas that prevented us from thinking on our own, once we have taken as our creed the Kantian motto *sapere aude*, "dare to know" (Kant), we will not have achieved the freedom we dreamed of but merely a new kind of servitude. For knowledge has a logic of its own, within which humankind may play only an instrumental role. There is no longer any such thing as progress in the singular; there is a plurality of progresses, some antithetical to others. No longer does the progress of science and, by extension, reason necessarily entail an improvement of the human condition. Scientific and technological progress does not strengthen human institutions by reaffirming the community of free and rational individuals but instead introduces separateness, division, and antagonism into the social world. From the moment Frankenstein surrenders to the "enticements of science" (p. 54) he is irrevocably divided from his family and friends. Even the University of Ingolstadt fails to provide anything like an academic community. It is a world of separate, solitary scientists. Krempe and Waldman seem scarcely to know each other. Upon entering the portals of science, Frankenstein experiences a solitude matched only by that of his creation.

The monster in its turn is not so much the creation that Frankenstein constantly calls it, as a product, the product of reason. In fact, the frequent recourse to theological terminology (which places Frankenstein in the position of a tragic god who is the prisoner of providence) may once again be regarded as a symptom: it masks the extent to which Frankenstein has himself been created, hailed into existence in order to hasten the realization of a reason whose ends are unknowable to him. Reason is always in the process of becoming real and its realization may well involve the production of monsters or a displacing of the human by the inhuman. For in the process, which in its largest sense is nothing other than history itself, humankind is in no way central. Humanity's greatest achievement may have been to hasten its own destruction.

Frankenstein has thus been led inescapably to the threshold represented by "the workshop of filthy creation":

> In a solitary chamber, or rather cell, at the top of the house, and separated from all the other apartments by a gallery and staircase, I kept my workshop of filthy creation: my eye-balls were starting from their sockets in attending to the details of my employment. The dissecting room and the slaughter-house furnished many of my materials; and often did my human nature turn with loathing from my occupation, whilst, still urged on by an eagerness which perpetually increased, I brought my work near to a conclusion. (p. 58)

The narrative pauses at this threshold; the reader is not conducted into the "workshop." At this point the narrative digresses into moral commentary until Frankenstein uncharacteristically refers to the presence of Walton, his listener: "your looks remind me to proceed." But his narrative does not begin again from where it left off. Instead it begins with his work completed: "It was on a dreary night of November, that I beheld the accomplishment of my toils" (p. 59). Utterly absent from the narrative is any description or explanation of the process by which the monster was created. The sequences so central to the film versions of Shelley's tale, in which the mystery of technology is reaffirmed through iconic figures of electric arcs and bubbling chemicals, have no place at this point or any other in Mary Shelley's narrative. The process of production is evoked but never described, effectively presenting us a world of effects without causes. In this sense, Victor's capacity for denial, his ability to forget after the initial shock that his creation runs amok, resembles the movement of the text itself, which "turns away" at certain key points, omitting every description of the technology so central to the tragedy of Victor Frankenstein and his creation.

In no sense can this omission be regarded as mistake or failure on Mary Shelley's part. On the contrary, the omission recurs throughout the work with a regularity that renders it integral to the work as a whole. At the same time it should not be dismissed as an authorial choice, an intentional abbreviation of the narrative for the sake of brevity or coherence. For as was evident in the sequence described above, this omission appears as a gap in the narrative that is filled in or covered over by a digression that is marked as a deviation by the narrative itself. Technology and science, so central to the novel, are present only in their effects;

their truth becomes visible only in the face of their hideous progeny and is written in the tragic lives of those who serve them.

If we now return to the passage above, we may see the way in which the systematic suppression of the scientific and the technological functions at an even more primary level. The passage begins by evoking the solitary separateness of Frankenstein's labor. He works in a "solitary chamber," a term of description that is replaced by the apparently more accurate "cell." The textual movement from chamber to cell is important. For if "cell" is a synonym for "solitary chamber," it adds certain associations that link Frankenstein's solitude to that of a monk in a monastery or a prisoner in prison. We understand the metaphor of the prison cell: Frankenstein has always been a prisoner, and perhaps most when he believed himself to be free (of familial and social obligations), forced to labor on a project of whose ultimate meaning he remained ignorant. Thus, shortly after this passage, he compares himself to "one doomed by slavery to toil in the mines" (p. 59).

But the idea of a monk's cell presents more difficulty insofar as it is incompatible with Frankenstein's scientific activity. The kind of discoveries made by monks in the closed world of their cells were precisely those of Cornelius Agrippa, the fantastic, exploded systems that were the empty creations of deluded minds. But his coupling of the religious and the scientific is far from unusual in the text as a whole. For just as the narrative cannot describe any scientific activity, so it cannot speak of the scientific without first clothing it in theological terms. The narrative thereby protects itself from the reality that it describes by casting a veil over that reality: it must continue to cover that which it reveals.

In this way, the stark heterogeneity of the phrase "workshop of filthy creation" is placed clearly in relief. Here, the incompatible worlds of industry (workshop) and theology (creation) collide. The material activity associated with the workshop, the work of manufacture, is immediately supplanted by the immateriality of creation as the text itself turns with loathing from the images that it produces. Like the dissecting room and the slaughterhouse, the "details of his employment" are too frightening to reproduce. As Victor speaks, his "eyes swim with the remembrance" (p. 57) and he frequently turns away from the reality of his own activity. Thus the technology so central to the Promethean drama is in one sense utterly absent from the work.

If we have argued that this absence is neither a fault for which the author might be reproached (for example, Mary Shelley was ignorant of scientific procedure and the technologies of her time) nor simply a stylistic choice (for example, the descriptions are in no way "essential" to the narrative and would at best be superfluous) but highly symptomatic, it is not simply because the narrative "stumbles" and digresses at the threshold of the "workshop of filthy creation." For this absence is doubled by another: the world that this "modern Prometheus" inhabits is not modern at all. Frankenstein's world is a world without industry, a rural world dominated by scenes of a sublime natural beauty in which not a single trace of Blake's "dark satanic mills" is to be found. Although Frankenstein is reared in Geneva and educated at Inglostadt, although he and Clerval visit London, Oxford, and Edinburgh, there are no significant descriptions of the urban world, none certainly to match the frequent portraits of natural vistas and rural scenes. London, at a time of explosive growth and development (cf. Wordsworth's treatment of London in the *Prelude*), is not described at all although he and Clerval passed "some months" there (p. 139). Further, there are no workers or work. The peasants who appear intermittently throughout the novel are either engaged in various forms of recreation or, as turns out to be the case with the De Lacey family, they are not peasants at all.

The effect of this suppression of the urban and the industrial is to render Frankenstein's labor as well as the product of that labor, the monster, all the more incongruous. He is the sole embodiment of the industrial in an otherwise rural world, and this is the source of his monstrousness. At one point, the monster makes explicit his identification with the working class:

> I learned that the possessions most esteemed by your fellow-creatures were high and unsullied descent united with riches. A man might be respected with only one of these advantages; but, without either, he was considered, except in very rare instances, as a vagabond and a slave, doomed to waste his powers for the profits of the chosen few! And what was I? Of my creation and creator I was absolutely ignorant; but I knew that I possessed no money, no friends, no kind of property. . . . When I looked around, I saw and heard of none like me. Was I then a monster, a blot upon the earth, from which all men fled, and whom all men disowned? (p. 109)

It is at this point that we see most clearly the associations that link the image of the monster to the industrial proletariat: an unnatural being, singular even in its collective identity, without a genealogy and belonging to no species. Its tragic fate is all the more pitiable in that it is necessary and, in the grand scheme of things, just and proper. If the proletariat speaks (like the monster always through an intermediary), the reader, like Frankenstein and Walton, must resist its eloquence: "hear him not" (p. 178). At the same time, however, Frankenstein's monster is finally not identified with the working class of Mary Shelley's time but with its absence. For the narrative precisely suppresses all that is modern in order to render this being inexplicable and unprecedented, a being for whom there is no place in the ordered world of nature. If the modern (the urban, the industrial, the proletarian) were allowed to appear, the monster would no longer be a monster; no longer alone but part of a "race of devils" (144), his disappearance would change nothing. Instead, the mass is reduced to the absolute singularity of Frankenstein's creation, which is therefore not so much the sign of the proletariat as of its unrepresentability.

Written before the notion of a postcapitalist order (a society ruled by the workers themselves) could be articulated but at a time when the oppressive and dehumanizing effects of capitalism were all too obvious, the work can do no better than to turn backward toward a time of mutual (if unequal) obligation, to a time before the creation of monsters by the industrial order, a time when the human was regulated by the natural. But if a certain historical reality is inscribed within the work as a monster to be expelled into "darkness and distance" (just as Frankenstein himself "forgets" his "hideous progeny" immediately after bringing it into this world), the act of repression can only postpone its inevitable return.

## WORKS CITED

Foucault, Michel. *The Archeology of Knowledge*. Trans. A. M. Sheridan Smith. New York: Pantheon, 1972. Print.

Goldner, Ellen J. "Monstrous Body, Tortured Soul: *Frankenstein* at the Juncture between Discourses." *Genealogy and Literature*. Ed. Lee Quinby. Minneapolis: U of Minnesota P, 1995. 28–47. Print.

Kant, Immanuel. "What Is Enlightenment?" *Political Writings*. Cambridge: Cambridge UP, 1970. 54–60. Print.

Lecercle, Jean-Jacques. *Frankenstein*. Paris: Presses Universitaires de France, 1988. Print.

Lecourt, Dominique. *Prométhée, Faust, Frankenstein: Fondment imaginaires de l'éthique*. Paris: Institut Synthélabo, 1996. Print.

Moretti, Franco. *Signs Taken for Wonders*. London: New Left, 1983. 83–90. Print.

Thompson, E. P. *The Making of the English Working Class*. New York: Vintage, 1963. Print.

# Cultural Criticism and
# *Frankenstein*

## WHAT IS CULTURAL CRITICISM?

What do you think of when you think of culture? The opera or ballet? A performance of a Mozart symphony at Lincoln Center or a Rembrandt show at the De Young Museum in San Francisco? Does the phrase "cultural event" conjure up images of young people in jeans and T-shirts— or of people in their sixties dressed formally? Most people hear "culture" and think "high culture." Consequently, when they first hear of cultural criticism, most people assume it is more formal than, well, say, formalism. They suspect it is "highbrow," in both subject and style.

Nothing could be further from the truth. Cultural critics oppose the view that culture refers exclusively to high culture, Culture with a capital *C*. Cultural critics want to make the term refer to popular, folk, urban, and mass (mass-produced, -disseminated, -mediated, and -consumed) culture, as well as to that culture we associate with the so-called classics. Raymond Williams, an early British cultural critic whose ideas will later be described at greater length, suggested that "art and culture are ordinary"; he did so not to "pull art down" but rather to point out that there is "creativity in all our living. . . . We create our human world as we have thought of art being created" (*Revolution* 37).

Cultural critics have consequently placed a great deal of emphasis on what Michel de Certeau has called "the practice of everyday life." Rather

than approaching literature in the elitist way that academic literary critics have traditionally approached it, cultural critics view it more as an
anthropologist would. They ask how it emerges from and competes with
other forms of discourse within a given culture (science, for instance, or
television). They seek to understand the social contexts in which a given
text was written, and under what conditions it was—and is—produced,
disseminated, read, and used.

Contemporary cultural critics are as willing to write about *Star Trek*
as they are to analyze James Joyce's *Ulysses*, a modern literary classic full
of allusions to Homer's *Odyssey*. And when they write about *Ulysses*,
they are likely to view it as a collage reflecting and representing cultural
forms common to Joyce's Dublin, such as advertising, journalism, film,
and pub life. Cultural critics typically show how the boundary we tend
to envision between high and low forms of culture—forms thought of
as important on one hand and relatively trivial on the other—is trans-
gressed in all sorts of exciting ways within works on both sides of the
putative cultural divide.

A cultural critic writing about a revered classic might contrast it with
a movie, or even a comic-strip version produced during a later period.
Alternatively, the literary classic might be seen in a variety of other ways:
in light of some more common form of reading material (a novel by Jane
Austen might be viewed in light of Gothic romances or ladies' conduct
manuals); as the reflection of some common cultural myths or concerns
(*Adventures of Huckleberry Finn* might be shown to reflect and shape
American myths about race and concerns about juvenile delinquency);
or as an example of how texts move back and forth across the alleged
boundary between "low" and "high" culture. For instance, one group
of cultural critics has pointed out that although Shakespeare's history
plays probably started off as popular works enjoyed by working people,
they were later considered "highbrow" plays that only the privileged
and educated could appreciate. That view of them changed, however,
due to film productions geared toward a national audience. A film version of *Henry V* produced during World War II, for example, made a
powerful, popular, patriotic statement about England's greatness during
wartime (Humm, Stigant, and Widdowson 6–7). More recently, cultural critics have analyzed the "cultural work" accomplished cooperatively by Shakespeare and Kenneth Branagh in the latter's 1992 film
production of *Henry V*.

In combating old definitions of what constitutes culture, of course,
cultural critics sometimes end up contesting old definitions of what
constitutes the literary canon, that is, the once-agreed-upon honor roll

of Great Books. They tend to do so, however, neither by adding books (and movies and television sitcoms) *to* the old list of texts that every "culturally literate" person should supposedly know nor by substituting some kind of counterculture canon. Instead, they tend to critique the very *idea* of canon.

Cultural critics want to get us away from thinking about certain works as the "best" ones produced by a given culture. They seek to be more descriptive and less evaluative, more interested in relating than in rating cultural products and events. They also aim to discover the (often political) reasons *why* a certain kind of aesthetic or cultural product is more valued than others. This is particularly true when the product in question is one produced since 1945, for most cultural critics follow Jean Baudrillard (*Simulations*, 1981) and Andreas Huyssen (*After the Great Divide*, 1986) in thinking that any distinctions that may once have existed between high, popular, and mass culture collapsed after the end of World War II. Their discoveries have led them beyond the literary canon, prompting them to interrogate many other value hierarchies. For instance, Pierre Bourdieu in *Distinction: A Social Critique of the Judgment of Taste* (1984) and Dick Hebdige in *Hiding the Light: On Images and Things* (1988) have argued that definitions of "good taste"—which are instrumental in fostering and reinforcing cultural discrimination— tell us at least as much about prevailing social, economic, and political conditions as they do about artistic quality and value.

In an article entitled "The Need for Cultural Studies," four ground-breaking cultural critics have written that "Cultural Studies should . . . abandon the goal of giving students access to that which represents a culture." A literary work, they go on to suggest, should be seen in relation to other works, to economic conditions, or to broad social discourses (about childbirth, women's education, rural decay, and so on) within whose contexts it makes sense. Perhaps most important, critics practicing cultural studies should counter the prevalent notion of culture as some preformed whole. Rather than being static or monolithic, culture is really a set of interactive *cultures,* alive and changing, and cultural critics should be present- and even future-oriented. They should be "resisting intellectuals," and cultural studies should be "an emancipatory project" (Giroux et al. 478–80).

The paragraphs above are peppered with words like *oppose, counter, deny, resist, combat, abandon,* and *emancipatory.* What such words quite accurately suggest is that a number of cultural critics view themselves in political, even oppositional, terms. Not only are they likely to take on the literary canon, they are also likely to oppose the institution of the university, for that is where the old definitions of culture as high culture (and as something formed, finished, and canonized) have been most vigorously preserved, defended, and reinforced.

Cultural critics have been especially critical of the departmental structure of universities, which, perhaps more than anything else, has kept the study of the "arts" relatively distinct from the study of history, not to mention from the study of such things as television, film, advertising, journalism, popular photography, folklore, current affairs, shoptalk, and gossip. By maintaining artificial boundaries, universities have tended to reassert the high/low culture distinction, implying that all the latter subjects are best left to historians, sociologists, anthropologists, and communication theorists. Cultural critics have taken issue with this implication, arguing that the way of thinking reinforced by the departmentalized structure of universities keeps us from seeing the aesthetics of an advertisement as well as the propagandistic elements of a work of literature. Cultural critics have consequently mixed and matched the analytical procedures developed in a variety of disciplines. They have formed—and encouraged other scholars to form—networks and centers, often outside of those enforced departmentally.

Some initially loose interdisciplinary networks have, over time, solidified to become cultural studies programs and majors. As this has happened, a significant if subtle danger has arisen. Richard Johnson, who along with Hebdige, Stuart Hall, and Richard Hoggart was instrumental in developing the Center for Contemporary Cultural Studies at Birmingham University in England, has warned that cultural studies must not be allowed to turn into yet another traditional academic discipline— one in which students encounter a canon replete with soap operas and cartoons, one in which belief in the importance of such popular forms has become an "orthodoxy" (39). The only principles that critics doing cultural studies can doctrinally espouse, Johnson suggests, are the two that have thus far been introduced: the principle that "culture" has been an "inegalitarian" concept, a "tool" of "condescension," and the belief that a new, "interdisciplinary (and even anti-disciplinary)" approach to *true* culture (that is, to the forms in which culture currently lives) is required now that history, art, and the communications media are so complex and interrelated (42).

The object of cultural study should not be a body of works assumed to comprise or reflect a given culture. Rather, it should be human consciousness, and the goal of that critical analysis should be to understand and show how that consciousness is itself forged and formed, to a great extent, by cultural forces. "Subjectivities," as Johnson has put it, are "produced, not given, and are . . . objects of inquiry" inevitably related to "social practices," whether those involve factory rules, supermarket behavior patterns, reading habits, advertisements, myths, or languages and other signs to which people are exposed (44–45).

Although the United States has probably contributed more than any other nation to the *media* through which culture is currently expressed, and although many if not most contemporary practitioners of cultural criticism are North American, the evolution of cultural criticism and, more broadly, cultural studies has to a great extent been influenced by theories developed in Great Britain and on the European continent.

Among the Continental thinkers whose work allowed for the development of cultural studies are those whose writings we associate with structuralism and poststructuralism. Using the linguistic theory of Ferdinand de Saussure, structuralists suggested that the structures of language lie behind all human organization. They attempted to create a *semiology*—a science of signs—that would give humankind at once a scientific and holistic way of studying the world and its human inhabitants. Roland Barthes, a structuralist who later shifted toward poststructuralism, attempted to recover literary language from the isolation in which it had been studied and to show that the laws that govern it govern all signs, from road signs to articles of clothing. Claude Lévi-Strauss, an anthropologist who studied the structures of everything from cuisine to villages to myths, looked for and found recurring, common elements that transcended the differences within and between cultures.

Of the structuralist and poststructuralist thinkers who have had an impact on the evolution of cultural studies, Jacques Lacan is one of three whose work has been particularly influential. A structuralist psychoanalytic theorist, Lacan posited that the human unconscious is structured like a language and treated dreams not as revealing symptoms of repression but, rather, as forms of discourse. Lacan also argued that the ego, subject, or self that we think of as being natural (our individual human nature) is in fact a product of the social order and its symbolic systems (especially, but not exclusively, language). Lacan's thought has served as the theoretical underpinning for cultural critics seeking to show the way in which subjectivities are produced by social discourses and practices.

Jacques Derrida, a French philosopher whose name has become synonymous with poststructuralism, has had an influence on cul' criticism at least as great as that of Lacan. The linguistic focus of / turalist thought has by no means been abandoned by poststructv' despite their opposition to structuralism's tendency to find universal patterns instead of textual and cultural contradictions. Indeed, Derrida has provocatively asserted that *"there is nothing outside the text"* (158), by which he means something like the following: we come to know the world through language, and even our most worldly actions and practices (the Gulf War, the wearing of condoms) are dependent upon discourses (even if they deliberately contravene those discourses). Derrida's "deconstruction" of the world/text distinction, like his deconstruction of so many of the hierarchical oppositions we habitually use to interpret and evaluate reality, has allowed cultural critics to erase the boundaries between high and low culture, classic and popular literary texts, and literature and other cultural discourses that, following Derrida, may be seen as manifestations of the same textuality.

Michel Foucault is the third Continental thinker associated with structuralism and/or poststructuralism who has had a particularly powerful impact on the evolution of cultural studies—and perhaps *the* strongest influence on American cultural criticism and the so-called new historicism, an interdisciplinary form of cultural criticism whose evolution has often paralleled that of cultural criticism. Although Foucault broke with Marxism after the French student uprisings of 1968, he was influenced enough by Marxist thought to study cultures in terms of power relationships. Unlike Marxists, however, Foucault refused to see power as something exercised by a dominant class over a subservient class. Indeed, he emphasized that power is not just repressive power, that is, a tool of conspiracy by one individual or institution against another. Power, rather, is a whole complex of forces; it is that which produces what happens.

Thus even a tyrannical aristocrat does not simply wield power but is empowered by "discourses"—accepted ways of thinking, writing, and speaking—and practices that embody, exercise, and amount to power. Foucault tried to view all things, from punishment to sexuality, in terms of the widest possible variety of discourses. As a result, he traced what he called the "genealogy" of topics he studied through texts that more traditional historians and literary critics would have overlooked, examining (in Lynn Hunt's words) "memoirs of deviants, diaries, political treatises, architectural blueprints, court records, doctors' reports—appl[ying] consistent principles of analysis in search of moments of reversal in discourse, in search of events as loci of the conflict where social practices were transformed" (39). Foucault tended not only to build interdisciplinary bridges but also, in the process, to bring into the study of culture the "histories of women, homosexuals, and minorities"—groups seldom studied by those interested in Culture with a capital *C* (Hunt 45).

Of the British influences on cultural studies and criticism, two stand out prominently. One, the Marxist historian E. P. Thompson, revolutionized the study of the industrial revolution by writing about its impact on human attitudes, even consciousness. He showed how a shared cultural view, specifically that of what constitutes a fair or just price, influenced crowd behavior and caused such things as the "food riots" of the eighteenth and nineteenth centuries (during which the women of Nottingham repriced breads in the shops of local bakers, paid for the goods they needed, and carried them away). The other, even more important early British influence on contemporary cultural criticism and cultural studies was Raymond Williams, who coined the phrase "culture is ordinary." In works like *Culture and Society, 1780–1950* (1958) and *The Long Revolution* (1961) Williams demonstrated that culture is not fixed and finished but, rather, living and evolving. One of the changes he called for was the development of a common socialist culture.

Although Williams dissociated himself from Marxism during the period 1945–58, he always followed the Marxist practice of viewing culture in relation to ideologies, which he defined as the "dominant, residual, and emergent" ways of viewing the world held by classes or individuals holding power in a given social group. He avoided dwelling on class conflict and class oppression, however, tending instead to focus on people as people, on how they experience the conditions in which they find themselves and creatively respond to those conditions through their social practices. A believer in the resiliency of the individual, Williams produced a body of criticism notable for what Stuart Hall has called its "humanism" (63).

As is clearly suggested in several of the preceding paragraphs, Marxism is the background to the background of cultural criticism. What isn't as clear is that some contemporary cultural critics consider themselves Marxist critics as well. It is important, therefore, to have some familiarity with certain Marxist concepts—those that would have been familiar to Foucault, Thompson, and Williams, plus those espoused by contemporary cultural critics who self-identify with Marxism. That familiarity can be gained from an introduction to the works of four important Marxist thinkers: Mikhail Bakhtin, Walter Benjamin, Antonio Gramsci, and Louis Althusser.

Bakhtin was a Russian, later a Soviet, critic so original in his thinking and wide-ranging in his influence that some would say he was never a Marxist at all, He viewed literary works in terms of discourses and dialogues *between* discourses. The narrative of a novel written in a society in flux, for instance, may include an official, legitimate discourse, plus others that challenge its viewpoint and even its authority. In a 1929 book on Dostoyevsky and the 1940 study *Rabelais and His World*, Bakhtin examined what he calls "polyphonic" novels, each characterized by a multiplicity of voices or discourses. In Dostoyevsky the independent status of a given character is marked by the difference of his or her language from that of the narrator. (The narrator's language may itself involve a dialogue between opposed points of view). In works by Rabelais, Bakhtin finds that the (profane) languages of Carnival and of other popular festivities play against and parody the more official discourses of the magistrates and the church. Bakhtin's relevance to cultural criticism lies in his suggestion that the dialogue involving high and low culture takes place not only between classic and popular texts but also between the "dialogic" voices that exist within all great books.

Walter Benjamin was a German Marxist who, during roughly the same period, attacked fascism and questioned the superior value placed on certain traditional literary forms that he felt conveyed a stultifying "aura" of culture. He took this position in part because so many previous Marxist critics (and, in his own day, Georg Lukács) had seemed to prefer nineteenth-century realistic novels to the modernist works of their own time. Benjamin not only praised modernist movements, such as dadaism, but also saw as promising the development of new art forms utilizing mechanical production and reproduction. These forms, including photography, radio, and film, promised that the arts would become a more democratic, less exclusive, domain. Anticipating by decades the work of those cultural critics interested in mass-produced, mass-mediated, and mass-consumed culture, Benjamin analyzed the meanings and (defensive) motivations behind words like *unique* and *authentic* when used in conjunction with mechanically reproduced art.

Antonio Gramsci, an Italian Marxist best known for his *Prison Notebooks* (first published in 1947), critiqued the very concept of literature and, beyond that, of culture in the old sense, stressing the importance of culture more broadly defined and the need for nurturing and developing proletarian, or working-class, culture. He argued that all intellectual or cultural work is fundamentally political and expressed the need for what he called "radical organic" intellectuals. Today's cultural critics urging colleagues to "legitimate the notion of writing reviews and books for the general public," to "become involved in the political reading of popular culture," and more generally to "repoliticize" scholarship have viewed Gramsci as an early precursor (Giroux et al. 482).

Gramsci related literature to the ideologies—the prevailing ideas, beliefs, values, and prejudices—of the culture in which it was produced. He developed the concept of "hegemony," which refers at once to the process of consensus formation and to the authority of the ideologies so formed, that is to say, their power to shape the way things look, what they would seem to mean, and, therefore, what reality *is* for the majority of people. But Gramsci did not see people, even poor people, as the helpless victims of hegemony, as ideology's pathetic robots. Rather, he believed that people have the freedom and power to struggle against and shape ideology, to alter hegemony, to break out of the weblike system of prevailing assumptions and to form a new consensus. As Patrick Brantlinger has suggested in *Crusoe's Footprints: Cultural Studies in Britain and America* (1990), Gramsci rejected the "intellectual arrogance that views the vast majority of people as deluded zombies, the victims or creatures of ideology" (100).

Of those Marxists who, after Gramsci, explored the complex relationship between literature and ideology, the French Marxist Louis Althusser had a significant impact on cultural criticism. Unlike Gramsci, Althusser tended to portray ideology as being in control of people, and not vice versa. He argued that the main function of ideology is to reproduce the society's existing relations of production, and that that function is even carried out in literary texts. In many ways, though, Althusser is as good an example of how Marxism and cultural criticism part company as he is of how cultural criticism is indebted to Marxists and their ideas. For although Althusser did argue that literature is relatively autonomous—more independent of ideology than, say, church, press, or state—he meant literature in the high cultural sense, certainly not the variety of works that present-day cultural critics routinely examine alongside those of Tolstoy and Joyce, Eliot and Brecht. Popular fictions, Althusser assumed, were mere packhorses designed (however unconsciously) to carry the baggage of a culture's ideology, or mere brood mares destined to reproduce it.

Thus, while a number of cultural critics would agree both with Althusser's notion that works of literature reflect certain ideological formations and with his notion that, at the same time, literary works may be relatively distant from or even resistant to ideology, they have rejected the narrow limits within which Althusser and some other Marxists (such as Georg Lukács) have defined literature. In "Marxism and Popular

Fiction" (1986), Tony Bennett uses *Monty Python's Flying Circus* and another British television show, *Not the 9 O'clock News*, to argue that the Althusserian notion that all forms of culture belong "among [all those] many material forms which ideology takes . . . under capitalism" is "simply not true." The "entire field" of "popular fiction"—which Bennett takes to include films and television shows as well as books—is said to be "replete with instances" of works that do what Bennett calls the "work" of "distancing." That is, they have the effect of separating the audience from, not rebinding the audience to, prevailing ideologies (249).

Although Marxist cultural critics exist (Bennett himself is one, carrying on through his writings what may be described as a lovers' quarrel with Marxism), most cultural critics are not Marxists in any strict sense. Anne Beezer, in writing about such things as advertisements and women's magazines, contests the "Althusserian view of ideology as the construction of the subject" (qtd. in Punter 103). That is, she gives both the media she is concerned with and their audiences more credit than Althusserian Marxists presumably would. Whereas they might argue that such media make people what they are, she points out that the same magazines that, admittedly, tell women how to please their men may, at the same time, offer liberating advice to women about how to preserve their independence by not getting too serious romantically. And, she suggests, many advertisements advertise their status as ads, just as many people who view or read them see advertising *as* advertising and interpret it accordingly.

The complex sort of analysis that Beezer has brought to bear on women's magazines and advertisements has been focused on paperback romance novels by Tania Modleski and Janice A. Radway in *Loving with a Vengeance* (1982) and *Reading the Romance* (1984) respectively. Radway, a feminist cultural critic who uses but ultimately goes beyond Marxism, points out that many women who read romances do so in order to carve out a time and space that is wholly their own, not to be intruded upon by husbands or children. Although many such novels end in marriage, the marriage is usually between a feisty and independent heroine and a powerful man she has "tamed," that is, made sensitive and caring. And why do so many of these stories involve such heroines and end as they do? Because, as Radway demonstrates through painstaking research into publishing houses, bookstores, and reading communities, their consumers *want* them to. They don't buy—or, if they buy they don't recommend—romances in which, for example, a heroine is raped: thus, in time, fewer and fewer such plots find their way onto the racks by the supermarket checkout. Radway's reading is typical of feminist cultural criticism in that it is *political*, but not exclusively about oppression. The subjectivities of women may be "produced" by romances—the thinking of romance readers may be governed by what is read—but the same women also govern, to a great extent, what gets written or produced, thus performing "cultural work" of their own. Rather than seeing all forms of popular culture as manifestations of ideology, soon to be remanifested in the minds of victimized audiences, cultural critics tend to see a sometimes disheartening but always dynamic synergy between cultural forms and the culture's consumers. Their observations have increasingly led to an analysis of consumerism, from a feminist but also from a more general point of view. This analysis owes a great deal to the work of de Certeau, Hall, and, especially, Hebdige, whose 1979 book *Subculture: The Meaning of Style* paved the way for critics like John Fiske (*Television Culture*, 1987), Greil Marcus (*Dead Elvis*, 1991), and Rachel Bowlby (*Shopping with Freud*, 1993). These latter critics have analyzed everything from the resistance tactics employed by television audiences to the influence of consumers on rock music styles to the psychology of consumer choice.

The overlap between feminist and cultural criticism is hardly surprising, especially given the recent evolution of feminism into various feminisms, some of which remain focused on "majority" women of European descent, others of which have focused instead on the lives and writings of minority women in Western culture and of women living in Third World (now preferably called postcolonial) societies. The culturalist analysis of value hierarchies within and between cultures has inevitably focused on categories that include class, race, national origin, gender, and sexualities; the terms of its critique have proved useful to contemporary feminists, many of whom differ from their predecessors insofar as they see *woman* not as a universal category but, rather, as one of several that play a role in identity- or subject-formation. The influence of cultural criticism (and, in some cases, Marxist class analysis) can be seen in the work of contemporary feminist critics such as Gayatri Spivak, Trinh T. Minh-ha, and Gloria Anzaldúa, each of whom has stressed that while all women are female, they are something else as well (such as working-class, lesbian, Native American, Muslim, Pakistani), and that that something else must be taken into account when their writings are read and studied.

The expansion of feminism and feminist literary criticism to include multicultural analysis, of course, parallels a transformation of education in general. On college campuses across North America, the field of African-American studies has grown and flourished. African-American critics have been influenced by and have contributed to the cultural approach by pointing out that the white cultural elite of North America has tended to view the oral-musical traditions of African Americans (traditions that include jazz, the blues, sermons, and folktales) as entertaining, but nonetheless inferior. Black writers, in order not to be similarly marginalized, have produced texts that, as Henry Louis Gates has pointed out, fuse the language and traditions of the white Western canon with a black vernacular and traditions derived from African and Caribbean cultures. The resulting "hybridity" (to use Homi K. Bhabha's word), although deplored by a handful of black separatist critics, has proved both rich and complex—fertile ground for many cultural critics practicing African-American criticism.

Interest in race and ethnicity at home has gone hand in hand with a new, interdisciplinary focus on colonial and postcolonial societies abroad, in which issues of race, class, and ethnicity also loom large. Edward Said's book *Orientalism* (1978) is generally said to have inaugurated postcolonial studies, which in Bhabha's words "bears witness to the unequal and uneven forces of cultural representation involved in the contest for political and social authority within the modern world order" ("Postcolonial Criticism" 437). *Orientalism* showed how Eastern and Middle Eastern peoples have for centuries been systematically stereotyped by the West, and how that stereotyping facilitated the colonization of vast areas of the East and Middle East by Westerners. Said's more recent books, along with postcolonial studies by Bhabha and Patrick Brantlinger, are among the most widely read and discussed works of literary scholarship. Brantlinger focuses on British literature of the Victorian period, examining representations of the colonies in works written during an era of imperialist expansion. Bhabha complements Brantlinger by suggesting that modern Western culture is best understood from the postcolonial perspective.

Thanks to the work of scholars like Brantlinger, Bhabha, Said, Gates, Anzaldúa, and Spivak, education in general and literary study in particular are becoming more democratic, decentered (less patriarchal and Eurocentric), and multicultural. The future of literary criticism will owe a great deal indeed to those early cultural critics who demonstrated that the boundaries between high and low culture are at once repressive and permeable, that culture is common and therefore includes all forms of popular culture, that cultural definitions are inevitably political, and that the world we see is seen through society's ideology. In a very real sense, the future of education *is* cultural studies.

A fairly recent development in cultural criticism is ecocriticism, or "green" criticism and theory. Although it may at first seem counterintuitive to link the environmentalist program to preserve nature with the postmodernist project of describing the interplay of human cultures and subcultures, the fact is the impact on nature by culture has been so pronounced, since even before the Industrial Revolution, that the boundary between the two has long been elided if not erased. (Atmospheric studies have shown that the air trapped inside well-preserved, multi-gasketed telescopes dating from the seventeenth and eighteenth centuries is, in terms of its mix of gaseous elements, quite different from the air we are accustomed to breathing.) It follows, then, that attempts to intervene in nature and to change it, whether to alter it further or to restore it to what it was, may be seen as manifestations of cultural work. Other instances would include literary works that advocate or warn against the manipulation of nature, as well as the work performed by ecocritics analyzing those texts.

The essay that follows, by Siobhan Carroll, offers an ecocritical approach to various works, including Mary Shelley's *Frankenstein*, that take positions for and against the reengineering of nature—or that display a deep-seated ambivalence toward attempts to alter the environment. "Situating *Frankenstein* in its climatological context," Carroll writes, "enables us to see the novel's exploration of the ramifications of Victor's experiment as symptomatic of a *larger cultural concern* over European's readiness to wield the nature-shaping power of imperial science" (p. 516 in this volume; emphasis added). It allows us to see Mary Shelley's work as one "positing . . . that Europeans are, as yet, not ready to accept the responsibilities of global management" (p. 516).

Carroll begins by recounting how John Barrow, an early-nineteenth-century Secretary to the British Admiralty, used articles he published anonymously in the *Quarterly Review* to build public support for Arctic exploration. The expeditions that ensued, Professor John Leslie maintained in the *Edinburgh Review*, were intended to score political points in what had become a growing debate about climate change. Thanks in part to the writings of Erasmus Darwin, "Romantic" plans for "global climate improvement" had been developed with the goal of staving off what, even before 1816 (which had been dubbed "the year without a summer"), had seemed like "the apocalyptic cooling of the globe"

(p. 504). The proposed reengineering of what was thought to be an increasingly inhospitable environment into one more hospitable to a "cosmopolitan world" was to have been accomplished, in part, by towing enormous masses of polar ice southward toward the equator. If accomplished, this feat would provide, in Darwin's words, "two great advantages to mankind, the tropic countries would be much cooled . . . and our winters in this latitude would be rendered much milder for perhaps a century or two" (p. 507).

Whereas the apparently threatening march of frigid weather southward "was often cast in imperial terms, as a spreading dominion of cold or as an empire of ice that constituted a natural check on European ambitions," what was truly imperialist was the idea that all of nature might be "subject to improvement by Europeans" and their navies. This is made eminently clear by "Darwin's poetic description of . . . 'swarthy nations' gratefully 'hail[ing]' the 'thousand sails' that signal the icebergs' destruction" and, concomitantly, "Europe's (and particularly Britain's) dominance over the seas" (p. 507). Carroll argues that *Frankenstein* takes a different view, expressing an attitude not unlike the one implicit in Samuel Taylor Coleridge's "The Rime of the Ancient Mariner."

"Among those forced to re-evaluate their belief in humans' ability to modify nature was Percy Bysshe Shelley," Mary's husband, who had once linked scientifically engineered "climate change to humanity's moral progress" (p. 510). Along with the "cessation of war," Percy had envisioned the "pursuit of environmental improvements triggering the destruction of the 'ungenial poles' . . . , the replacement of Arctic winds with 'fragrant zephyrs' . . . , and the dawn of a new age of cosmopolitan and climatic harmony" (p. 510). But in 1816 he personally observed "the relentless advance of polar-influenced glaciers," and it "forced him to rethink his earlier optimism and contemplate, however reluctantly, '[Georges] Buffons sublime but gloomy theory, that this globe which we inhabit will at some future period, be changed into a mass of frost'" (p. 510). In short, Carroll concludes, "To describe a polar expedition in 1818, as *Frankenstein* does, is . . . to engage with the highly controversial topic of ecological crisis" (p. 515).

Mary Shelley's novel, of course, not only begins by depicting just such an expedition but also abounds in descriptions of Artic weather, with Robert Walton, "the novel's poet-turned-polar-explorer," speaking of the "cold northern breeze play[ing] on [his] cheeks" "fill[ing] him with delight," and giving him "a foretaste of those icy climes'" (p. 27). Walton's intention, as expressed to his sister in a letter, is to "confer on all mankind" an "inestimable benefit" by finding a "passage near the pole" that leads to "a country of eternal light," a "land never before imprinted by the foot of man". But, in Carroll's words, "The narrative that Walton's ruminations introduce" is highly "skeptical of the projects of men like Walton and Frankenstein, men whose attempts to improve the world seem, at best, foolishly hubristic, and which stem, the novel suggests, from self-interested ambition rather than a genuine desire to benefit humanity" (p. 516).

Carroll takes pains to point out that Shelley's novel stops short of taking extreme views, arguing that "*Frankenstein* is notably less willing" than Benjamin Bragg's *Voyage to the North Pole* to "confirm the inevitability of apocalypse," and not as willing as works by other authors to insist that "limits" be "place[d]" on "humans' capacity to intervene in nature. Victor's notorious experiment, after all, serves as evidence that grand interventions in nature are possible, and if humans can reverse death's hold on the human frame, why not death's hold on the planet?" (p. 518). Although the phrase "Victor's notorious experiment" clearly refers to his attempt to create a more powerful form of human being, Carroll shows how closely Shelley aligns that experiment with Walton's expedition by focusing on the scene in which Victor shames Walton's frightened, increasingly mutinous sailors. "Victor mocks their desire to retreat back to the ostensive domestic security of 'their warm firesides,' declaring that . . . . the human race can and will overcome the empire of ice" because " '[t]his ice is not made of such stuff as your hearts might be . . . it is mutable, it cannot withstand you, if you say that it shall not' " (p. 518).

By drawing an analogy between the two experiments, however, Shelley implicitly causes readers to wonder whether Victor really imagines that the human race as we know it—an always imperfect, distracted, and conflict-riven collection of mainly ordinary folk—will overcome the figurative "empire of ice," which would include death and a host of other natural terrors. Thus, as Carroll points out, "Part of the Creature's threat . . . may be that it so neatly . . . suggests, from the moment of its creation, that the human race is in imminent danger of being supplanted. . . . Read in this context, the Creature, a product of a scientific intervention in nature, appears as a monstrous embodiment of the cosmopolitan world that Romantic 'crusades against frost' dreamed of creating" (p. 520).

In the final paragraphs of her essay, Carroll reminds the reader that she has been referring to the first (1818) edition of Shelley's novel, not the 1831 version that you have been reading. She says she made this textual choice because "As fear of an imminent climatic catastrophe faded from the public mind, Mary Shelley revised *Frankenstein* to reflect the diminished urgency of climate change. . . . Whereas in the 1818 edition . . . nature frequently appears inscrutable and menacing, in the 1831 edition, characters express their faith in a comprehensible, uniformitarian nature governed by 'immutable laws'" (p. 523).

Cultural attitudes change, toward issues like global cooling and warming, toward how imminent the threats and opportunities facing us are, and toward how aggressively artists should be bringing them to our attention. Think about 9/11—what it was then, what it is now, and what it could conceivably become. Recall that one Todd Beamer, a passenger on hijacked United Airlines Flight 93, which was deliberately crashed in rural Pennsylvania, managed to place a last-minute credit card call on one of the phones in the back of a passenger seat. He told customer service representative Lisa Jefferson that some of the plane's passengers, aware of what had happened in New York and Washington, DC, were planning to seize the plane from hijackers. His last audible words—"Are you guys ready? OK, let's roll"—became the source of four song titles: Neil Young's "Let's Roll" (2001), dc Talk's "Let's Roll" (2002), L.A. Guns' "OK, Let's Roll" (2002), and The Bellamy Brothers' "Let's Roll, America" (2002). No one is currently writing hit songs about innocent Americans responding bravely to terrorist acts. Do we dare believe that that kind of music has been preempted by positive forces of [inter]cultural [ex]change?

Ross C Murfin

## CULTURAL CRITICISM: A SELECTED BIBLIOGRAPHY

### General Introductions to Cultural Criticism, Cultural Studies

Bathrick, David. "Cultural Studies." *Introduction to Scholarship in Modern Languages and Literatures.* Ed. Joseph Gibaldi. New York: MLA, 1992. 320–40. Print.

Brantlinger, Patrick. *Crusoe's Footprints: Cultural Studies in Britain and America.* New York: Routledge, 1990. Print.

———. "Cultural Studies vs. the New Historicism." *English Studies/ Cultural Studies: Institutionalizing Dissent.* Ed. Isaiah Smithson and Nancy Ruff. Urbana: U of Illinois P, 1994. 43–58. Print.

Brantlinger, Patrick, and James Naremore, eds. *Modernity and Mass Culture*. Bloomington: Indiana UP, 1991. Print.

Brummett, Barry. *Rhetoric in Popular Culture*. New York: St. Martin's, 1994. Print.

Desan, Philippe, Priscilla Parkhurst Ferguson, and Wendy Griswold. "Editors' Introduction: Mirrors, Frames, and Demons: Reflections on the Sociology of Literature." *Literature and Social Practice*. Ed. Desan, Ferguson, and Griswold. Chicago: U of Chicago P, 1989. 1–10. Print.

During, Simon, ed. *The Cultural Studies Reader*. New York: Routledge, 1993. Print.

Eagleton, Terry. "Two Approaches in the Sociology of Literature." *Critical Inquiry* 14 (1988): 469–76. Print.

Easthope, Antony. *Literary into Cultural Studies*. New York: Routledge, 1991. Print.

Fisher, Philip. "American Literary and Cultural Studies since the Civil War." *Redrawing the Boundaries: The Transformation of English and American Literary Studies*. Ed. Stephen Greenblatt and Giles Gunn. New York: MLA, 1992. 232–50. Print.

Giroux, Henry, David Shumway, Paul Smith, and James Sosnoski. "The Need for Cultural Studies: Resisting Intellectuals and Oppositional Public Spheres." *Dalhousie Review* 64.2 (1984): 472–86. Print.

Graff, Gerald, and Bruce Robbins. "Cultural Criticism." *Redrawing the Boundaries: The Transformation of English and American Literary Studies*. Ed. Stephen Greenblatt and Giles Gunn. New York: MLA, 1992. 419–36. Print.

Grossberg, Lawrence, Cary Nelson, and Paula A. Treichler, eds. *Cultural Studies*. New York: Routledge, 1992. Print.

Gunn, Giles. *The Culture of Criticism and the Criticism of Culture*. New York: Oxford UP, 1987. Print.

Hall, Stuart. "Cultural Studies: Two Paradigms." *Media, Culture and Society* 2 (1980): 57–72. Print.

Humm, Peter, Paul Stigant, and Peter Widdowson, eds. *Popular Fictions: Essays in Literature and History*. New York: Methuen, 1986. Print.

Hunt, Lynn, ed. *The New Cultural History*. Berkeley: U of California P, 1989. Print.

Johnson, Richard. "What Is Cultural Studies Anyway?" *Social Text* 16 (1986–87): 38–80. Print.

Pfister, Joel. "The Americanization of Cultural Studies." *Yale Journal of Criticism* 4 (1991): 199–229. Print.

Punter, David, ed. *Introduction to Contemporary Critical Studies.* New York: Longman, 1986. Print. See especially Punter's "Introduction: Culture and Change," Tony Dunn's "The Evolution of Cultural Studies," and the essay "Methods for Cultural Studies Students" by Anne Beezer, Jean Grimshaw, and Martin Barker.

Storey, John. *An Introductory Guide to Cultural Theory and Popular Culture.* Athens: U of Georgia P, 1993. Print.

Turner, Graeme. *British Cultural Studies: An Introduction.* 3d ed. London: Routledge, 2002. Print.

## Cultural Studies: Some Early British Examples

Hoggart, Richard. *Speaking to Each Other.* 2 vols. London: Chatto, 1970. Print.

———. *The Uses of Literacy: Changing Patterns in English Mass Culture.* Boston: Beacon, 1961. Print.

Thompson, E. P. *The Making of the English Working Class.* New York: Harper, 1958. Print.

———. *William Morris: Romantic to Revolutionary.* New York: Pantheon, 1977. Print.

Williams, Raymond. *Culture and Society, 1780–1950.* New York: Harper, 1966. Print.

———. *The Long Revolution.* New York: Columbia UP, 1961. Print.

## Cultural Studies: Continental and Marxist Influences

Althusser, Louis. *For Marx.* Trans. Ben Brewster. New York: Pantheon, 1969. Print.

———. "Ideology and Ideological State Apparatuses." *Lenin and Philosophy.* Trans. Ben Brewster. New York: Monthly Review, 1971. 127–86. Print.

———, and Étienne Balibar. *Reading Capital.* Trans. Ben Brewster. New York: Pantheon, 1971. Print.

Bakhtin, Mikhail. *The Dialogic Imagination: Four Essays.* Ed. Michael Holquist. Trans. Caryl Emerson. Austin: U of Texas P, 1981. Print.

———. *Rabelais and His World.* Trans. Hélène Iswolsky. Cambridge: MIT, 1968. Print.

Baudrillard, Jean. *Simulations.* Trans. Paul Foss, Paul Patton, and Philip Beitchman. 1981. New York: Semiotext(e), 1983. Print.

Benjamin, Walter. *Illuminations*. Ed. Hannah Arendt. Trans. H. Zohn. New York: Harcourt, 1968. Print.

Bennett, Tony. "Marxism and Popular Fiction." Humm, Stigant, and Widdowson 237–65. Print.

Bourdieu, Pierre. *Distinction: A Social Critique of the Judgment of Taste*. Trans. Richard Nice. Cambridge: Harvard UP, 1984. Print.

de Certeau, Michel. *The Practice of Everyday Life*. Trans. Steven F. Rendall. Berkeley: U of California P, 1984. Print.

Derrida, Jacques. *Of Grammatology*. 1969. Trans. Gayatri C. Spivak. Baltimore: Johns Hopkins UP, 1976. Print.

Foucault, Michel. *Discipline and Punish: The Birth of the Prison*. Trans. Alan Sheridan. New York: Pantheon, 1978. Print.

———. *The History of Sexuality. Vol. 1*. Trans. Robert Hurley. New York: Pantheon, 1978. Print.

Gramsci, Antonio. *Selections from the Prison Notebooks*. Ed. Quintin Hoare and Geoffrey Nowell Smith. New York: International, 1971. Print.

## Modern Cultural Studies:
### Selected British and American Examples

Bagdikian, Ben H. *The Media Monopoly*. Boston: Beacon, 1983. Print.

Bowlby, Rachel. *Shopping with Freud*. New York: Routledge, 1993. Print.

Chambers, Iain. *Popular Culture: The Metropolitan Experience*. New York: Methuen, 1986. Print.

Colls, Robert, and Philip Dodd, eds. *Englishness: Politics and Culture, 1880–1920*. London: Croom Helm, 1986. Print.

Denning, Michael. *Mechanic Accents: Dime Novels and Working-Class Culture in America*. New York: Verso, 1987. Print.

Fiske, John. "British Cultural Studies and Television." *Channels of Discourse Reassembled: Television and Contemporary Criticism*. Ed. Robert C. Allen. Chapel Hill: U of North Carolina P, 1987. 214–45. Print.

———. *Television Culture*. New York: Methuen, 1987. Print.

Hebdige, Dick. *Hiding the Light: On Images and Things*. New York: Routledge, 1988. Print.

———. *Subculture: The Meaning of Style*. London: Methuen, 1979. Print.

Huyssen, Andreas. *After the Great Divide: Modernism, Mass Culture, Postmodernism*. Bloomington: Indiana UP, 1986. Print.

Marcus, Greil. *Dead Elvis: A Chronicle of a Cultural Obsession.* New York: Doubleday, 1991. Print.

———. *Lipstick Traces: A Secret History of the Twentieth Century.* Cambridge: Harvard UP, 1989. Print.

Modleski, Tania. *Loving with a Vengeance: Mass-Produced Fantasies for Women.* Hamden: Archon, 1982. Print.

Poovey, Mary. *Uneven Developments: The Ideological Work of Gender in Mid-Victorian England.* Chicago: U of Chicago P, 1988. Print.

Radway, Janice A. *Reading the Romance: Women, Patriarchy, and Popular Literature.* Chapel Hill: U of North Carolina P, 1984. Print.

Reed, T. V. *Fifteen Jugglers, Five Believers: Literary Politics and the Poetics of American Social Movements.* Berkeley: U of California P, 1992. Print.

## Race and Ethnic Readings

Anzaldúa, Gloria. *Borderlands/La Frontera: The New Mestiza.* San Francisco: Spinsters/Aunt Lute, 1987. Print.

Baker, Houston. *Blues, Ideology, and Afro-American Literature: A Vernacular Theory.* Chicago: U of Chicago P, 1984. Print.

———. *The Journey Back: Issues in Black Literature and Criticism.* Chicago: U of Chicago P, 1980. Print.

Bhabha, Homi K. *The Location of Culture.* New York: Routledge, 1994. Print.

———. "Postcolonial Criticism." *Redrawing the Boundaries: The Transformation of English and American Literary Studies.* Ed. Stephen Greenblatt and Giles Gunn. New York: MLA, 1992. 437–65. Print.

———, ed. *Nation and Narration.* New York: Routledge, 1990. Print.

Brantlinger, Patrick. *Rule of Darkness: British Literature and Imperialism, 1830–1914.* Ithaca: Cornell UP, 1988. Print.

Gates, Henry Louis, Jr. *Black Literature and Literary Theory.* New York: Methuen, 1984. Print.

———, ed. *"Race," Writing, and Difference.* Chicago: U of Chicago P, 1986. Print.

Gayle, Addison. *The Black Aesthetic.* Garden City: Doubleday, 1971.

———. *The Way of the New World: The Black Novel in America.* Garden City: Doubleday, 1975. Print.

JanMohamed, Abdul. *Manichean Aesthetics: The Politics of Literature in Colonial Africa.* Amherst: U of Massachusetts P, 1983. Print.

————, and David Lloyd, eds. *The Nature and Context of Minority Discourse.* New York: Oxford UP, 1991. Print.

Kaplan, Amy, and Donald E. Pease, eds. *Cultures of United States Imperialism.* Durham: Duke UP, 1983. Print.

Minh-ha, Trinh T. *Woman, Native, Other: Writing Postcoloniality and Feminism.* Bloomington: Indiana UP, 1989. Print.

*Neocolonialism.* Spec. issue of *Oxford Literary Review* 13 (1991). Print.

Said, Edward. *After the Last Sky: Palestinian Lives.* New York: Pantheon, 1986. Print.

————. *Culture and Imperialism.* New York: Knopf, 1993. Print.

————. *Orientalism.* New York: Pantheon, 1978. Print.

————. *The World, the Text, and the Critic.* Cambridge: Harvard UP, 1983. Print.

Spivak, Gayatri Chakravorty. *In Other Worlds: Essays in Cultural Politics.* New York: Methuen, 1987. Print.

Stepto, Robert B. *From Behind the Veil: A Study of Afro-American Narrative.* Urbana: U of Illinois P, 1979. Print.

Young, Robert. *White Mythologies: Writing, History, and the West.* London: Routledge, 1990. Print.

## Cultural Studies Readings of *Frankenstein*

Anderson, Robert. " 'Misery Made Me a Fiend': Social Reproduction in Mary Shelley's *Frankenstein* and Robert Owen's Early Writings." *Nineteenth-Century Contexts* 24.4 (2002): 417–38. Print.

Clayton, Jay. "Concealed Circuits: Frankenstein's Monster, the Medusa, and the Cyborg." *Raritan* 15.4 (Mar. 1996): 53–69. Print.

Codr, Dwight. "Arresting Monstrosity: Polio, *Frankenstein*, and the Horror Film." *PMLA* 129.2 (Mar. 2014): 171–87. Print.

Craciun, Adriana. "Writing the Disaster: Franklin and *Frankenstein*." *Nineteenth-Century Literature* 65.4 (2011): 433–80. Print.

Douthwaite, Julia V., and Daniel Richter. "The Frankenstein of the French Revolution: Nogaret's Automaton Tale of 1790." *European Romantic Review* 20.3 (2009): 381–411. Print.

Feder, Helena. " 'A Blot upon the Earth': Nature's 'Negative' and the Production of Monstrosity in *Frankenstein*." *Journal of Ecocriticism* 2.1 (2010): 55–66. Print.

Garrison, Laurie. "Imperial Vision in the Arctic: Fleeting Looks and Pleasurable Distractions in Barker's Panorama and Shelley's

*Frankenstein*." *Romanticism and Victorianism on the Net* 52 (2008): n.p. Web. 10 June 2014.

Knellwolf, Christa, and Jane Goodall, eds. *Frankenstein's Science: Experimentation and Discovery in Romantic Culture, 1780–1830.* Aldershot, UK: Ashgate, 2008. Print.

Liggins, Emma. "The Medical Gaze and the Female Corpse: Looking at Bodies in Mary Shelley's *Frankenstein*." *Studies in the Novel* 32.2 (2000): 129–46. Print.

Marshall, Tim. *Murdering to Dissect: Graverobbing,* Frankenstein, *and the Anatomy Literature.* Manchester: Manchester UP, 1996. Print.

Outka, Paul. "Posthuman/Postnatural: Ecocriticism and the Sublime in Mary Shelley's *Frankenstein*." *Environmental Criticism for the Twenty-First Century.* Eds. Stephanie LeMenager, Teresa Shewry, and Ken Hiltner. New York: Routledge, 2012. 31–48. Print.

Phillips, Bill. "*Frankenstein* and Mary Shelley's 'wet ungenial summer'." *Atlantis* 28.2 (2006): 59–68. Print.

Vincent, Patrick. "'This Wretched Mockery of Justice': Mary Shelley's *Frankenstein* and Geneva." *European Romantic Review* 18.5 (2007): 645–61. Print.

Williams, Carolyn. "'Inhumanly Brought Back to Life and Misery': Mary Wollstonecraft, *Frankenstein*, and the Royal Humane Society." *Women's Writing* 8.2 (2001): 213–34. Print.

## A CULTURAL CRITIC'S PERSPECTIVE

### SIOBHAN CARROLL

## Crusades Against Frost: *Frankenstein,* Polar Ice, and Climate Change in 1818

### 1. MR. BARROW'S "DREAMS OF ROMANCE"

John Barrow (1764–1848), Second Secretary to the British Admiralty, was adept at using the written word for political ends. As J. M. R. Cameron has observed, Barrow carefully composed over two hundred *Quarterly Review* articles to promote both the careers of his fellow civil servants and his own views on the proper policies of an expanding British Empire. Today, Barrow is perhaps best remembered for using his anonymous *Quarterly* articles to build public support for the government-financed Arctic expeditions he helped organize, offering what Kim Wheatley has called "a remarkable instance of the masking of political power with cultural power" ("The Arctic" 466). However, Barrow's "mask" was flimsy at best, and his influential Arctic articles were subject to criticism spearheaded by the *Quarterly*'s archrival, the *Edinburgh Review*. One of the most famous attacks on Barrow's articles appeared in the June 1818 edition of the *Edinburgh*. In its pages, John Leslie, Professor of Mathematics at Edinburgh University, castigated Barrow's "loose reasoning . . . wild and random conjectures, and visionary declamation," and thundered, in an oft-quoted sentence, that Barrow had formed "[g]lowing anticipations . . . of the future amelioration of climate, which would scarcely be hazarded even in the dreams of romance" (5). Leslie's reference to romance has been cited by scholars exploring the intertwined histories of literature and polar exploration.[1] But such scholarship has tended to sidestep Leslie's allusion to the "future amelioration of climate" and to omit the strongly-pronounced meteorological component of Leslie's attack on Barrow.[2] Not only does this omission reinscribe what Kim Wheatley, in a recent review, noted is Arctic scholarship's tendency to submerge the "'Green' concerns" that [had] helped fuel the resurgence in nineteenth-century polar exploration ("Review" 571), but it also distorts our understanding of the 1818 controversy surrounding Barrow's articles. For, as contemporary periodical reports make clear, the Leslie-Barrow clash was primarily presented to literate Britons not as a controversy over the practicability of polar exploration but as a debate on climate change.[3]

Modern readers may well be struck both by the discontinuities and the eerie similarities between our own era's climate debates and the discussion of "the alleged change of climate in the northern countries of Europe" ("Expedition to the North Pole" 2) that engaged more than sixteen periodicals in the wake of Barrow's statements. The questions

---

[1] In referring to the 1818 controversy, scholars have presented attacks on Barrow's climatology as attacks on the practicability of polar exploration; see, for instance, Janice Cavell and Jessica Richard. Barrow's geographical speculations did indeed draw his contemporaries' ire, but the criticism aimed at his February 1818 *Quarterly* article primarily focused on his climatology.

[2] The twenty-five pages that follow Leslie's reference to "romance" are devoted to explaining the complex science of "Meteorology" (5) and to arguing that "no material change has taken place for the last thousand years in the climate of Europe" (30). In short, the "romance" that Leslie is attacking is not Barrow's representation of polar exploration, but Barrow's assertions regarding climate change.

[3] Indeed, some of his critics followed their savaging of Barrow's climatology with declarations of support for the polar expeditions; see, for instance, Janice Cavell and Jessica Richard. Opposition to Barrow's "chimerical speculations" did not therefore entail opposition to the revival of British polar exploration.

raised over the extent and consequences of the "disappearance, or breaking up, of a large part of the enormous masses of ice, which have for some
centuries been accumulating in the different parts of the northern ocean"
("Expedition to the Northern Ocean" 306), the vehement denunciations
of the "vulgar credulity" ("Varieties, Literary and Philosophical" 543) of
climate-change supporters, and the occasional acknowledgement of the
politics underpinning the "controversy" that was dividing "the learned
world . . . into two parties" ("Edinburgh Review" 549) may all resonate
with twenty-first century readers. But the *Morning Post*'s assumption that
the disappearance of icebergs "would be an event devoutly to be wished"
("Literature" 3), and the *Times*' damning allusions to Barrow's "poetical
description" ("Expedition to the North Pole" 2), signal a gulf between
Romantic and twenty-first century conceptions of climate change. These
unfamiliar components of the climate debate of 1818 point us towards
the antagonistic role occupied by polar ice in Romantic visions of global
improvement.

   In the following essay, I explore the Romantics' climatic fears regarding polar ice and the link between these fears and "poetic" schemes for
global climate improvement. As famously articulated in Erasmus Darwin's *The Botanic Garden* (1791), humans could stave off the apocalyptic
cooling of the globe, and perhaps forge a new cosmopolitan utopia, by
uniting to destroy Arctic ice. Such radical dreams of climate modification—what Thomas De Quincey, reflecting on Romantic geoengineering
schemes in 1846, dubbed "crusades against frost" (345)[4]—represented
an outgrowth of what Alan Bewell has called the late-eighteenth-
century ideal of "cosmopolitan nature," in which the different natures
of the globe were conceptualized as mobile, exploitable, and subject to
improvement by Europeans. Visions "of the role that science and
empire might play in the global re-ordering of nature" (Bewell, "Erasmus" 37) existed in tension with theories conceptualizing nature as particular, providentially-governed, and determinant of national character,
such as eighteenth-century beliefs regarding the British national climate.[5]
Romantic discussions of climate change thus took place on a fault line
between cosmopolitanism and nativism, and carried with them controversial implications regarding humans' proper place in nature and Brit-

---

   [4]For a survey of human attempts to control the weather and their representations in
literature, see Fleming.
   [5]As Jan Golinski has argued, eighteenth-century discourse on the British climate
developed alongside, and was entangled with, a sense of British national identity. See
Golinski (57–63).

ain's proper degree of involvement in the global networks of information, trade, and empire.

In the years leading up to the 1818 polar controversy, the ethics and efficacy of human-directed climate modification came under increased scrutiny as the apparent deterioration of the climate of Britain and its colonies called into question the wisdom of human interventions in nature. This new urgency surrounding climate change is reflected, I argue, not only in Barrow's controversial rhetoric in the *Quarterly*, but also in Mary Wollstonecraft Shelley's *Frankenstein* (1818), a novel whose depiction of the poetry-loving polar explorer Captain Walton has been portrayed by scholars such as Jessica Richard as a critique of Barrow's "poetical description" (qtd. on 306). My reframing of the Leslie-Barrow clash as a climate change debate [raises] the question of whether we can continue to view *Frankenstein* as a novel that anticipates this controversy. As I argue in the final third of this paper, we can indeed read *Frankenstein* in this light, as a novel whose engagement with climate goes far beyond the thunderstorms that Jan Golinski suggests link the Creature with a vengeful nature (9), and the lightning imagery that John Clubbe argues ties the novel to the stormy weather of 1816. Whereas periodical articles tended to stake out firm, and usually politicized, positions on climate, *Frankenstein* highlights instead the flawed nature of the individuals advocating "crusades against frost." While its depiction of the negative consequences of Victor's experiment is expressive of a wider cultural concern over the improvements advocated by cosmopolitan men of science, *Frankenstein*'s response to the "year without a summer" is characterized less by a lack of faith in humans' ability to modify nature than by a suspicion of Europeans' willingness to fully embrace a supranational identity that would make global administration both practicable and ethical.

## 2. THE DOMINION OF COLD

In the late eighteenth century, polar ice, whether originating at the North or South Poles, was widely assumed to play a significant role in shaping the climate of temperate latitudes. The influence of polar ice was often cast in imperial terms, as a spreading dominion of cold or as an empire of ice that constituted a natural check on European ambitions.[6]

---

[6]See, for example, David Ramsay's remarks on the Canadian Arctic. "This vast empire of ice and snow . . . will never be colonized by Europeans or their descendents" (243).

Given the widespread belief that agricultural improvements could alter regional temperature and rainfall patterns, the "empire of ice" also tested European efficiency in administering territories vulnerable to polar influence. In *The History of America* (1777), for example, William Robertson traces the "peculiar temperature of [America's] climate" back to the continent's proximity "to the pole" (252, 253). Robertson, whose perspective on America owes much to that of Comte Georges-Louis Leclerc de Buffon, observes that the wind, in passing over the Arctic, "becomes . . . impregnated with cold." It is to "this powerful cause we may ascribe the extraordinary dominion of cold, and its violent inroads into the southern provinces in that part of the globe" (254). Just as the "martial spirit of Europeans . . . prompted them to deliver the Holy Land from the dominion of infidels" (30), so, Robertson suggests, does Europeans' understanding of climate prompt them to deliver America from the dominion of cold—a goal that necessitates the European colonization of America.[7]

Erasmus Darwin was one of the first to describe the threat posed by polar ice to Britain, and significantly for the 1818 polar controversy, he delivered his warning in a poetic form. Stanza XI of *The Botanic Garden* (1791) describes the Goddess of Botany commanding her nymphs to sail icebergs into tropical seas, ushering in a new era of climatic harmony through the destruction of polar ice.[8] A footnote to this idealistic vision of geoengineering notes that "the islands of ice in the higher northern latitudes, as well as the Glaciers on the Alps, continue perpetually to increase in bulk"—a worrisome development, given that "northern ice is the principle source of the coldness of our winters" (59). Like Robertson, Darwin assumes that Arctic winds cool lower latitudes by blowing icy evaporation into temperate climes, a process that Darwin believes is aided by the pernicious influence of drifting icebergs on southern ocean waters. "Hence," Darwin explains, "the increase of the ice in the polar regions, by increasing the cold of our climate, adds, to the same time, to the bulk of the Glaciers of Italy and Switzerland" (60).

In the next paragraph, Darwin outlines a potential cosmopolitan response to the developing crisis, exemplifying what Alan Bewell has called *The Botanic Garden*'s contribution to the late-eighteenth century concept of "cosmopolitan or globalized nature" ("Erasmus" 21). Indebted to the

---

[7] For more on Robertson's climatology, see Golinski (179–80).
[8] Part 2 of *The Botanic Garden*, *The Loves of the Plants*, was published in 1789; Part 1, *The Economy of Vegetation*, appeared as part of the complete poem in 1791.

information-gathering networks of empire and to European cosmopolitan culture, visions of "cosmopolitan nature" depicted biota detached from their local contexts and pressed into international service by European science. Such a vision underpins Darwin's admonition to European nations to transcend their petty national interests and act on their responsibilities as citizens of a world united by nature. "If the nations who inhabit this hemisphere of the globe, instead of destroying their sea-men and exhausting their wealth in unnecessary wars, could be induced to unite their labours to navigate these immense masses of ice into the more southern oceans," then, Darwin declares, "two great advantages would result to mankind, the tropic countries would be much cooled by their solution, and our winters in this latitude would be rendered much milder for perhaps a century or two" (60).

While Darwin suggests that the only "necessary war" is the one to be fought against polar ice, his vision of climatic harmony illustrates the manner in which *The Botanic Garden*'s conception of cosmopolitan nature would, as Bewell has argued, "underpin Britain's emergence as an imperial nation" ("Erasmus" 21). Darwin's poetic description of climate intervention depicts "swarthy nations" gratefully "hail[ing]" the "thousand sails" that signal the icebergs' destruction, and which, as the footnote makes clear, also signal Europe's (and particularly Britain's) dominance over the seas. In the next line, this dominance is extended into the heavens, as the atmosphere is transformed into an extension of European naval power: "[c]louds sail in squadrons o'er the darken'd heaven" (1.541, 542, 529, 546). The overlap between cosmopolitan "crusades against frost" and imperialism is thus exemplified in Darwin's call for Europeans to unilaterally exert power over the lands of "swarthy nations" in the name of global improvement, a project that Britain, by virtue of its naval power and scientific prowess, would naturally lead.[9]

Darwin's "scheme for towing Ice-Islands to the Tropics" ("Change of Climate" 226) was cited repeatedly in the nineteenth century as a quintessential example of a hubristic scientific plan to improve the world. Moreover, while pastoral poetry had long been invoked in discussions of climate, the literary mode in which Darwin's iceberg scheme was delivered forged a new link between climate change and "the poets" (Leslie

[9]While such visions of global improvement ostensibly anticipated peaceful cooperation between European powers, in practice, improvements were implemented in a field of imperial competition. For the national politics of cosmopolitan science, see Gascoigne (162–65).

22) in the British imagination. Reflecting on Darwin's legacy in 1827, William Wadd describes him as "a poetical man of science," observing that this "title . . . will readily be granted him, when we enumerate a few of his plans, by which . . . he was to control the winds, and manage the seasons." For Wadd, Darwin's status as "poet" derived not from his composition of poetry, but from his ambitions of "altering the *climate*" (292). So powerful was the association between poetry and dreams of inducing the "melting of the polar ice caps" (Gidal 75) that De Quincey, in questioning the Victorian abandonment of the geoengineering schemes he dubs "crusades against frost" in 1846, classifies these meteorological schemes according to the poetic vision to which they adhere. Plans that precisely outline climatic mechanisms are said to follow "Dr. Darwin's scheme for improving our British climate," while projects that avoid mechanics are said to resemble the vagary of "the Ancient Mariner's scheme" of destroying "frost and snow" (De Quincey 345).

By the dawn of the nineteenth century, "crusades against frost" were coming under increased scrutiny from writers expressing doubts about the wisdom of human attempts to manipulate nature. While many natural philosophers, farmers, and travel writers agreed that the "*Climate of England has been evidently changing*" (Williams 104), not everyone agreed that polar ice was the cause, or that the dominion of frost should be combated through agricultural improvements. Indeed, some commentators suggested that Britain's modification of local natures was causing the climate deterioration it was supposed to combat. In 1800, Thomas Garnett drew a connection between imperial mismanagement and the changes observed on domestic soil: "Have not our winds become more violent, and the temperature of our seasons more equable, since our forests were cleared, and the country cultivated? . . . did not the island of Bermudas, though situated so much to the southward of us, become barren of fruit in consequence of the destruction of its timber trees?" (177) In 1806, John Williams asked "May not what is termed *improvement* prove the reverse?" and attributed the cooling of the British climate to the "men who have incautiously removed . . . vegetable productions" from foreign climates and cultivated "exotic vegetables" (108, 30) in Britain. The latter remark lays responsibility for British climate change at the door of Sir Joseph Banks and his cosmopolitan botanical networks. No wonder, then, that Banks preferred Erasmus Darwin's theory of British climate change, declaring in his correspondence that "I have always attributed the increasing Coldness of our Climate to the increase in polar ice" (331).

## 3. POLAR ICE AND THE "YEAR
## WITHOUT A SUMMER"

From 1816 through 1818, discussions of climate change took on new urgency as the unusually cool weather of the "year without a summer" [lent] fresh credibility to climatic fears. In 1815, "the largest eruption of recorded history" destroyed the peak of Mount Tambora and tossed massive amounts of volcanic gas and debris into the atmosphere (Oppenheimer 231). The world-wide veil of volcanic dust diminished the amount of sunlight reaching Earth's surface and distorted the global pattern of wind circulation, triggering what H. H. Lamb calls one of the greatest "world disasters associated with climate"—a wave of famines, epidemics, and political unrest that followed in the wake of poor harvests (227).

As the depressed temperatures of 1816 seemed to validate fears of climate deterioration, Britons responded to the apparent triumph of the empire of ice with despair, denial, and, in some cases, calls for the actual implementation of geoengineering schemes such as the one described in Darwin's *Botanic Garden*. The "year without a summer" thus put unusual pressure on the question of the practicability and ethics of human interventions in nature. Not only did the crisis revive calls for Darwin's brand of natural cosmopolitanism in a Europe recently scarred by Napoleon's imperial ambitions, but it also challenged what Jan Golinski has noted was Britons' comfortable belief that "they had been blessed by a benevolent providence with a climate well adapted to sustain the nation's prosperity and well-being" (4). The widespread nature of the crisis forced many Britons to recognize that, far from being providentially insulated from the crisis, their national climate was subject to the same mysterious international forces shaping the climates of Europe and America. To contemplate climate change in the wake of 1816 was thus to contemplate a nightmare version of cosmopolitan nature, in which the previously-secure front of the domestic could be threatened by a mysterious international force that seemed beyond the understanding and control of European science.

Among those forced to re-evaluate their belief in humans' ability to modify nature was Percy Bysshe Shelley, who, touring the Alps with Mary in 1816, found himself observing firsthand one of the frontlines in the war against ice. In 1813, P. B. Shelley had published his own contribution to poetic "crusades against frost," the Darwin-influenced *Queen Mab,* in which he had confidently anticipated the melting of the ice he considered symptomatic of human moral failings.[10] Linking climate change to humanity's moral progress, Shelley had envisioned mankind's cessation of war and pursuit of environmental improvements triggering the destruction of the "ungenial poles" (6.44), the replacement of Arctic winds with "fragrant zephyrs" (8.64), and the dawn of a new age of cosmopolitan and climatic harmony. But in 1816, the sight of the relentless advance of polar-influenced glaciers forced him to rethink his earlier optimism and contemplate, however reluctantly, "Buffons sublime but gloomy theory, that this globe which we inhabit will at some future period, be changed into a mass of frost" (499). Recalling Buffon's notorious suggestion that efforts to combat the empire of ice would ultimately be overwhelmed by the inexorable cooling of the planet, Shelley experimented with a more pessimistic vision of climate change in "Mont Blanc" (1816), a poem that, as Alan Bewell has argued, "describes a world in which the human power to create temperate environments seems impotent in the face of a power that dwells apart from human control" (*Romanticism* 224). The strange weather observed across the northern hemisphere in 1816 thus caused even former improvement enthusiasts like P. B. Shelley to re-evaluate humans' ability to intervene in natural processes. Nature, far from being a benign force subject to human understanding and manipulation, increasingly appeared inscrutable and dangerously intractable.

Not all Britons shared Shelley's newfound doubts concerning improvements. Indeed, some went so far as to suggest that the time for implementing "poetic" geoengineering schemes had arrived. The *Morning Chronicle,* for example, after reviewing the evidence for a worldwide deterioration of climate, declared on 4 October 1817 that "every effort, to which human ingenuity and strength are competent, ought to be exerted for the purpose of counteracting the growing evil." To that end, the *Chronicle* proposes that the "combined force of the naval world" be dispatched to navigate "these immense masses of ice into the more southern oceans." Vowing to render the impious notion of geoengineering "more agreeable" to its readers by laying "the project before them in its poetic garb," the *Chronicle* then launches into an untitled excerpt [from] Stanza XI [of] Darwin's *Botanic Garden* ("Climate" 4). Such calls for the implementation of poetic visions were in turn criticized by other commentators, who, even as they mocked "reprehensible schemes" (L. M. U. B. 159) of climate improvement, also

---

[10]See Eric Gidal on P. B. Shelley's view of climatic extremes (80–81), and Bewell (*Romanticism* 209–14) on his views of climate change.

expressed anxiety over the consequences of such grand re-orderings of nature. Even as the apparent deterioration of the British climate caused some observers to reflect on the unanticipated consequences of improvements, in other words, the most extreme forms of improvement were again being proposed as the solution to an international crisis.

It is in the context of anxieties over improvement that polar ice emerged as the popular culprit for the "year without a summer." Aware of the public's tendency to attribute bad weather to government mismanagement, British officials tried to quell panic and divert the public from more politically-threatening theories of climate change by fingering polar ice as the cause of any deterioration in the British climate.[11] Darwinian conceptions of polar ice, after all, absolved agricultural improvers such as Joseph Banks (and with him, the landed interest) from having played any part in the bad weather plaguing Britain, while also holding out the possibility that a grand intervention in climate could be mounted if such ecological crisis management became necessary.[12]

As a representative of the British government, it was not in John Barrow's interest to acknowledge worsening weather when climatic deterioration was so often seen as a sign of poor administration. In his first Arctic article for the *Quarterly*, Barrow therefore walks a fine line in his handling of the polar-climate connection, on one hand trying to exploit the popular anxiety over Arctic ice but, on the other, reassuring his readers that the British climate was not, in fact, cooling. Thus Barrow reminds his readers that a new Arctic expedition could provide "more accurate observations on those huge mountains of ice which float on the sea," but he also declares climate change an illusion created by nostalgia and the unreliable perceptions of failing bodies: it "is not the climate that has altered, but we who feel it more severe as we advance in years" (170). A protégé of Joseph Banks, Barrow follows his mentor's lead in [claiming] polar ice [was] the only likely mechanism of climate alteration. No other possibilities are mentioned.

If Barrow does not wish to lend ammunition to those who suspect agricultural improvements have damaged the British climate, neither

---

[11] As Alan Bewell has noted, "bad weather was a sign of bad government" ("Jefferson's Thermometer" 133). While hypotheses linking climate deterioration to improvements had clear implications for British domestic policy, some Britons attributed alterations in the national climate to providential displeasure with national leadership. See, for example, Williams' scoffing response to those who blame the impiety of "our legislature" (3) for climate deterioration.

[12] Banks' association with the landed interest had led to his Soho Square house being attacked by Corn Law rioters in 1815. As political tensions over poor harvests rose in advance of the 1818 general election, Banks and his political allies had good reason to feel vulnerable. For more on Banks's relationship to state politics, see Gascoigne (34–64).

does he wish to stoke the anxieties of his readers by appearing to credit Buffon's vision of global cooling. In this respect, Barrow's argument is distinguished by what it omits. Whereas in 1799 the *Naval Chronicle* had suggested that a return to polar exploration would help "determine the progress which the ice may make towards the equator; and thus establish a proof of the ingenious theory of Buffon, that the earth is gradually losing its heat" ("Naval Anecdotes" 306), Barrow avoids mentioning such gloomy theories. Instead, his argument implicitly promises that a new polar expedition will refute pessimistic speculations regarding the future of the Arctic. Noting that the supposed decline in the British climate is thought to be "owing to the ice having permanently fixed itself to the shores of Greenland, which, in consequence . . . is now become uninhabitable and unapproachable," Barrow declares that "more attempts than one to land . . . must be made, before we can give credit to its being bound up in eternal ice" (170). A polar expedition would lay climatic fears to rest, not only by providing Britons with fresh observations of "the meteorological phenomena peculiar to these regions" (172), but also by disproving Buffon's fear that polar ice had so expanded its apocalyptic hold on the globe that "cette region du pôle est entièrement et à jamais perdue pour nous" ("the northern pole is forever lost to us" [Buffon 194, translation mine]).

Barrow's second Arctic article for the *Quarterly* provides a glimpse into the genuine concern underpinning his 1817 dismissal of climate change. In "Narrative of a Voyage to Hudson's Bay," Barrow controversially reverses his stance on climate change, inviting his readers to celebrate the strange Arctic ice melt that has not only prompted the British government to resume polar exploration but also, Barrow implies, saved Britain from disaster.[13] Whereas previously he had declared climate change the product of querulous imaginations, in . . . Barrow declares "That our climate has been . . . affected, in the course of the last three years, by the descent of the ice into the Atlantic . . . is a matter of record" (206). Citing natural philosophers who maintain that the deterioration of the British climate "could *only* be owing to the accumulation . . . of the polar ice to the southward" (201, my emphasis), Barrow reminds his readers of the depth of anxiety that had accompanied the notably cool

---

[13]Climate historians now believe that 1817's unusually warm northern winter was due to the Tambora eruption's continuing influence. I am indebted to Gillen D'Arcy Wood for this observation.

temperatures of 1816 and 1817, noting that "a prospect far more gloomy than the mere loss of wine had begun to present itself by the increasing chilliness of our summer months . . . there was not sufficient warmth in the summer of 1816 to ripen the grain; and it is generally thought, that if the ten or twelve days of hot weather at the end of June last had not occurred, most of the corn must have perished" (206). From the terrors of scarcity, starvation, and civil unrest, Britain had been rescued in 1818 by what Barrow's "present ignorance" must attribute to "the decree of Providence" (204): the destruction of polar ice. Climate change could be acknowledged, in other words, but only when it suited Barrow's political purposes.

"Narrative of a Voyage to Hudson's Bay" was controversial not only because Barrow reversed his position on climate change, but because he also was seen as cynically appropriating poetic visions of climate improvement. In the most notorious paragraph of "Narrative," the conservative Barrow allies himself with the utopian dreams of poems such as *The Botanic Garden* and *Queen Mab*, arguing that the destruction of northern ice holds "out a rational and not an unpleasing prospect, of our once again enjoying the genial warmth of the western breeze, and those soft and gentle zephyrs, which, in our time, have existed only in the imagination of the poet" (206). Given that both *Queen Mab* and *The Botanic Garden* assumed that Britain's climate would improve only following the moral and social improvement of humanity, Barrow is, in essence, denying the need for government reform or humanitarian action by declaring the Golden Age already here. As the *Scotsman* scathingly remarked, Barrow might as well "have arrived at the comfortable conclusion, that we had put an end to the dominion of frost and French principles on the same day" ("Quarterly Review" 103).

Dismayed by what they read as Barrow's cynical manipulation of scientific and poetic rhetoric, and infuriated by his propaganda, some of Barrow's critics tried to place climatic responsibility back where they felt it belonged. William Harris, for example, argues in an 1821 letter to the *Gentleman's Magazine* that some of the climate change phenomena described by Barrow are the result of detrimental government policies. Attributing disappearance of British vineyards to economic rather than [climatic] forces, Harris argues that "if due encouragement were given, they might again be established . . . but no encouragement is to be expected from Government, which would not countenance a measure so highly detrimental to the revenue" (71). Barrow and his ilk might sound like crusaders against frost, but they were not truly

dedicated to the regeneration of the earth; their self-interest would prevent them from forging the utopian world dreamed of by the poets.
The latter point is stridently made in a November 1818 letter to the
editor of *Blackwood's*. Satirizing the political paranoia underpinning the
Leslie-Barrow clash, "The Late Hot Weather" suggests with mock-
earnestness that the "ships of war, destined for the north for the ostensible purpose of discovery" are in fact engaged in a conspiracy to destroy
polar ice and improve the British climate. Far from being a humanitarian project, however, this geoengineering scheme is prompted by certain politicians' "reprehensible" desire for increased power and profit,
and would enable the government to "transfer a large portion of
national wealth from those of whom it feels jealous" to its "fashionable
and frenchified" supporters (L. M. U. B. 159). Suspicion of cosmopo-
lites translates into suspicion of cosmopolitan nature: the author looks
askance at the "alliance with the Esquimeaux and Copper Indians"
(158) that has been formed in order to destroy northern frost, and,
observing that "the quality of every national constitution depends almost
exclusively upon climate," asks "What better plan could be devised to
extinguish the last spark of freedom in this 'once happy' land, and to
prepare our minds and bodies for absolute slavery, than to spread over
this island the climate of Spain? or Otaheite? of Constantinople? or
China?" (158). Making explicit a nationalist unease with cosmopolitan
nature, this passage redeploys Barrow's invocation of the balmy future
envisioned in poetry as a sign of the Tories' most un-British despotic
ambitions. "The Late Hot Weather" thus usefully illustrates, not only the
degree to which the polar expeditions planned by Barrow had come to be
associated with Darwin's poetic plan for a cosmopolitan intervention in
nature,[14] but also that Barrow's contemporaries themselves recognized
and could exploit the xenophobic resonance of John Williams' desire to
defend the British atmosphere against the dangerous evaporations of foreign vegetables.

The "year without a summer" thus revived fears regarding the bale-
ful influence of polar ice on the British climate and gave new urgency
to the question of how human beings should respond to climate change.
Whereas conservative commentators such as Barrow resolutely denied
the need for any government action, some alarmed observers argued

---

[14]The poetic associations of geoengineering projects are driven home by *Blackwood's*
decision to follow this letter with "Inaccuracies of Poets in Natural History," in which
William Wordsworth, Robert Southey, and of course "Dr. Darwin," are criticized for
their misleading representations of nature (161).

for the actual implementation of "poetic" geoengineering schemes, while others expressed new doubts about the efficacy and wisdom of intervening in cosmopolitan nature. Literature composed in the wake of 1816 reflected a culture in which references to poetic visions of climate, projects of improvement, and Arctic ice had become highly charged. To describe a polar expedition in 1818, as *Frankenstein* does, is thus to engage with the highly controversial topic of ecological crisis.[15]

## 4. THE CREATURE AT THE END OF THE WORLD

Appropriately for a novel composed in 1816–1817, *Frankenstein*'s opening paragraphs comment on the weather.[16] "[A]s I walk in the streets of Petersburgh," Walton, the novel's poet-turned-polar-explorer, declares "I feel a cold northern breeze play upon my cheeks, which braces my nerves and fills me with delight . . . This breeze, which has travelled from the regions towards which I am advancing, gives me a foretaste of those icy climes" (5). Readers in 1818 would not have shared Walton's feelings: the Arctic wind he is describing is, after all, one of the possible culprits for the "year without a summer," the vehicle by which polar cold was transmitted to British shores. Perversely, however, Walton dubs this "foretaste of . . . icy climes" a "wind of promise" (5), as though poetic manipulation of language is enough to deny the dangerous future hinted at in Arctic winds. This is the type of rhetoric that would later arouse the ire of participants on both sides of the 1818 polar controversy. In attacking Leslie for what it argues is his premature dismissal of climate change, the *Literary Gazette* argued that its readers' experience of the British climate did not align with its representation

---

[15] Literary works depicting polar space were read as potential participants in the 1818 climate debate. Some works, such as Pleydell Wilton's poem "The Polar Ice" engaged overtly with *The Quarterly* controversy; others, like Eleanor Anne Porden's "The Arctic Expeditions" were discussed by critics in relation to "the effects which [the destruction of polar ice] may be expected to produce on the seasons of our island" ("Article XI. The Arctic Expeditions" 513).

[16] While the first forty pages of the *Frankenstein* manuscript are not extant, in the *Frankenstein Notebooks*, Charles Robinson indicates that M. W. Shelley had fixed on an Arctic setting for the novel's conclusion by April 1817 at the latest (lxxxiv). Britain's resumption of polar exploration was announced in February 1818, after the publication of *Frankenstein* and Bragg's *A Voyage to the North Pole*, the latter of which first appears in "Published this Day" notices on 29 May 1817. These novels' anticipation of the 1818 expeditions was prompted in part, I suggest, by the relevance of polar exploration to climate debates. All references to *Frankenstein* are to the 1818 edition unless otherwise noted.

by Leslie: "people will think that a North wind is cold, and a South wind warm, and if the atmosphere *should* absorb all of the cold and heat in its passage to us from the Pole and Equator, our senses bear evidence that it does not perform its duty" ("Edinburgh Review, No. 59" 549). It is precisely the empirical evidence of his senses that Walton ignores in favor of the romantic pole described by "poets" (6), a pole from which "snow and frost are banished" (5), and that he and his crew will achieve after conquering the ice that Buffon had predicted would both prevent polar exploration and doom the world.

Walton's rhetoric may invoke visions of the Hyperborean paradise of old, but in the climate of 1816 it also, crucially, stakes out a position in the debate over the future of the globe. Walton is clearly on the side of the "poets:" on the side of those who believe in the perfectibility of man and nature, and who proclaim the imminent dawn of an era in which frost will be "banished" from the world. The narrative that Walton's ruminations introduce, however, is skeptical of the projects of men like Walton and Frankenstein, men whose attempts to improve the world seem, at best, foolishly hubristic, and which stem, the novel suggests, from self-interested ambition rather than a genuine desire to benefit humanity. Situating *Frankenstein* in its climatological context enables us to see the novel's exploration of the ramifications of Victor's experiment as symptomatic of a larger cultural concern over Europeans' readiness to wield the nature-shaping power of imperial science. Influenced both by Buffon's theory of a cooling earth and by poetic visions of crusades against ice, the most famous literary product of the "year without a summer" hedges the question of whether humans should attempt to intervene in the global climate, positing instead that Europeans are . . . not yet ready to accept the responsibilities of global management.

In engaging with the crisis of 1816, *Frankenstein* captures the uncertainty of the period in its representation of phenomena that could be interpreted as signs of a cooling climate, or as the projections of observers' minds. The latter, of course, was one of the favorite arguments made by those who denied the existence of climate change. According to this line of argument, perceptions of a cooling climate were not objective, but were instead strongly influenced by the observer's age, superstitions, or credulous reading, particularly, as Leslie would later remark, one's credulous reading of the "lamentations . . . repeated by the poets" (22). In *Frankenstein*, Victor's return home from university is delayed by a harsh winter and an "uncommonly late" (50) spring; elsewhere in Europe, the Creature observes the "the heart-moving indications of impending famine" (90) in his beloved cottagers. This is a description of the climate of 1816—Mary Shelley is repeating language found in her *History of a Six Weeks' Tour*—but the weather observed by Victor and the Creature so closely mirrors their emotional states that it is difficult to separate observation from pathetic fallacy. When the Creature entertains hopes of human acceptance, he forgets the "bleak, damp, and unwholesome" environment that greeted him on his "birth," and allows himself to hope . . . that the greenery of spring, rather than the darkness of winter, prophesizes his future with the cottagers (92). When he is rejected by the De Laceys, the Creature flies straight into the grasp of winter: "Nature decayed around me, and the sun became heatless; rain and snow poured around me; mighty rivers were frozen; the surface of the earth was hard, and chill, and bare, and I found no shelter" (114). The latter description resembles that of Buffon's doomed world, but given the Creature's emotional state, his description of a world dominated by cruel and apparently lengthening winters cannot be depended upon as an accurate observation. While *Frankenstein* depicts the ominous weather-signs of 1816, in other words, the novel also draws attention to the subjectivity that colors interpretations of such ostensibly empirical phenomena as Arctic winds and snowfall, and in doing so, refuses to decisively side with those arguing that a climate crisis was underway.

On this point, *Frankenstein* is notably less willing to validate climate fears than its close contemporary, Benjamin Bragg's *A Voyage to the North Pole* (1817). The first British novel to feature an Englishman planning and carrying out a polar expedition, this little-studied children's adventure story features a Walton-like protagonist who, inspired by his reading, wants to locate the Arctic "Paradise" (157) his romantic imagination has painted for him. Unlike *Frankenstein*, however, *Voyage* wears its climatic anxieties on its sleeve: in the novel's opening, the protagonist paraphrases Buffon, observing that "very few human beings are now found beyond the 68 [degrees]," and that this indicates that "the earth is gradually cooling from the Poles, and that the vast mountains of ice and the region of perpetual frost, imperceptibly extends its dominion" (35). Haunted by visions of extinction, Bragg hopes to discover a Hyperborean paradise that will refute his climatic fears. But although he succeeds in overcoming the icy barrier Buffon had predicted would prove impenetrable, Bragg realizes on reaching the polar continent that neither art nor science [is] able to rehabilitate the "uninhabitable portion of the globe" (169) that mocks his earlier hopes of a verdant Eden. A disillusioned Bragg gives up his dream of reaching the

North Pole and pronounces the truth of Buffon's speculations regarding the Arctic: "whatever might have been the case when the world was young, it was now clear that it wanted energy and warmth to break forth into life" (158). Whereas in P. B. Shelley's *Queen Mab*, every portion of the Earth was assumed to be capable of regeneration, Bragg's 1817 novel declaims the limits of improvement, portraying the polar continent as a gloomy portent of a dying Earth. Walton's polar voyage is, in contrast, far less conclusive than Bragg's: forced to turn back by his crew, Walton concedes neither the inaccessibility of the North Pole nor humans' inability to reclaim the world.[17]

*Frankenstein* is neither as willing as *Voyage* to confirm the inevitability of apocalypse, nor as willing to place limits on humans' capacity to intervene in nature. Victor's notorious experiment, after all, serves as evidence that grand interventions in nature are possible, and if humans can reverse death's hold on the human frame, why not death's hold on the planet? But if, in *Queen Mab*, P. B. Shelley assumed that the perfection of the natural world would happen in tandem with the perfection of the human race, in *Frankenstein*, M. W. Shelley explores the danger of a world-shaping "improvement" being made by a decidedly imperfect human. In doing so, M. W. Shelley draws upon contemporary anxieties regarding the improvements advocated by cosmopolitan men of science in the name of defeating the empire of ice, of which geoengineering proposals were extreme examples.

The kinship between these ambitious schemes is highlighted in *Frankenstein*'s polar frame, when Victor, stepping in to support his Arctic doppelganger's quest, insists that human beings can triumph over polar ice. Animated by the "feverish fire" that "glimmers in his eyes" (182), Victor persuades the sailors that "these vast mountains of ice are molehills, which will vanish before the resolutions of man" (181). Claiming that the crew once dreamed of being the "benefactors of [their] species," Victor mocks their desire to retreat back into to the ostensive domestic security of "their warm firesides," declaring that to retreat from ice would be to "turn their backs on the foe." Ultimately, he insists that the human race can and will overcome the empire of ice, declaring that "[t]his ice is not made of such stuff as your hearts might be . . . it is mutable, it cannot withstand you, if you say that it shall not" (183). Victor's language here

---

[17]M. W. Shelley was well aware of the role played by polar ice in Buffon's theory: in her *History of a Six Weeks' Tour* (1817), she altered P. B. Shelley's sentence on Buffon to read "be changed into a mass of frost by the encroachments of the polar ice" (162), stepping beyond the Alpine context of P. B. Shelley's letter to remind her readers of the part played by the poles in Buffon's vision of a freezing globe.

is strongly reminiscent of "crusades against frost," both in his assurance that ice will "vanish" before the will of men—an image that evokes melting rather than bypassed icebergs—and its anti-domestic exhortation that European men look beyond their domestic duties to engage in a battle with ice that will benefit humanity.

Victor's project is connected to contemporary climate discussions in another respect. In *Des Époques de la Nature*, Buffon had invited his readers to speculate on whether "aurait-il un seul des êtres actuels capable de résister à cette chaleur mortelle" ("beings exist that are capable of resisting the fatal temperature of a freezing globe" [Buffon 149, translation mine]). This portion of Buffon's theory had been revisited along with Buffon's pronouncements on polar ice in the wake of 1816, and appears, for example, in Bragg's hasty assurance to his young readers that the extinction of the human race would not necessarily signal the end of life on Earth, for "[s]ome new order of beings will then arise, which it is impossible for human conjecture to penetrate" (126). M. W. Shelley would later recall these discussions in *The Last Man* (1826), a novel clearly influenced by the crisis of the "year without a summer." As the plague-clouded atmosphere threatens the survival of the human race, Lionel Verney listens with exasperation to Merrival's discussion of topics as useless as "the unknown and unimaginable lineaments of the creatures, who would . . . occupy the vacated dwelling of mankind" (227). The negative version of Merrival's equally irrelevant anticipation of the melting of "the poles," after which, the astronomer assures Verney, "an universal spring will be produced, and earth become a paradise" (172), these visions of futurity strike Verney as distractions from the imminent threat of human extinction. But whereas in *The Last Man*, Merrival fails to translate his natural philosophy into a plan for combating global catastrophe, in *Frankenstein*, these theories may indeed play a part in shaping the future of the world, because Victor has actually translated his philosophical speculations into action.

One of the charges levelled against improvements in the early nineteenth century is that they might be ushering in the very reign of ice they were supposed to combat. It is in this light, perhaps, that we should read Victor's concern over his creation's affinity for ice. Victor's reading of natural philosophers such as "Buffon" (25) have inspired his creation of a being immune to "the misery of cold and frost," whose ability to thrive even in the "everlasting ices of the north" (174) make it well-suited to inheriting a frozen world. Victor famously comes to fear that the Creature's propagation will endanger the human race. However, even before such propagation becomes possible, Victor's vague anxiety

over the Creature manifests in his description of the ominous Alps, whose
creeping glaciers appear to him already colonized by his dangerous creation, providing a vision of "another earth, the habitations of another
race of beings" (73). Part of the Creature's threat, in other words, may
be that it so neatly conforms to the parameters of the being anticipated
by Buffon, and thus suggests, from the moment of its creation, that the
human race is [in] imminent danger of being supplanted.

The Creature, however, insists that it is not an omen of human
extinction, and, indeed, it is possible to read Victor's creation more
positively, as the symbol of a type of identity that could survive an apocalypse of ice. For, as Shelley would remind her readers in *The Last Man*,
there are two possible responses to global crisis: the doomed retreat
into domestic isolationism and the embrace of a crisis cosmopolitanism
in which one acknowledges oneself as a citizen of a world in peril. Victor mocks the first option in his speech to Walton's crew, urging them
not to abandon their fight with the ice in the hope of retreating safely
to "their warm firesides." In his narrative, Victor describes his own useless attempts to retreat into domestic tranquillity, and associates his
father and Elizabeth's false sense of domestic security with the apparently peaceful beauty of the nature that surrounds them. Notably, in
declaring to Walton "how much happier that man is who believes his
native town to be the world, than he who aspires to become greater
than his nature will allow" (35), Victor does not declare the man who
remains within his native confines "safer," but merely suggests that he
is happier in his ignorance. As in *The Last Man*, when Verney is forced
to admit that there is no possibility of domestic retreat in the face of an
ecological menace spread by the "atmosphere, which as a cloak enwraps
all our fellow-creatures—the inhabitants of native Europe—the luxurious Asiatic—the swarthy African and free American" (332), *Frankenstein* indicates that, in facing the climate of 1816, domestic isolationism
is not a viable option.

If salvation lies anywhere, it lies in the human race's ability to truly
embrace the cosmopolitanism of global crisis and so assume responsibility for the management of global nature. Read in this context, the Creature, a product of a scientific intervention in nature, appears as a monstrous embodiment of the cosmopolitan world that Romantic "crusades
against frost" dreamed of creating. A figure literally composed of separate
bodies united into a new identity, the Creature's very form, as Deidre
Lynch has observed, "strains against the system of familial, civic, and
territorial categories that human beings have developed to identify one
another and to speak to themselves." A being that is "native nowhere"

(Lynch 207), Victor's creation owes no allegiance to a native country and ignores the borders of nations as it travels. As Maureen Noelle McLane notes, it is the "stateless" culmination of Victor's university studies, which were commenced in order to free Victor of native parochialism and acquaint him "with other customs than those of [his] native country" (qtd. on 967). Its resemblance to the Creature prophesied by Buffon, "fitted by [its] conformation for the endurance of cold" (107) and capable of easily negotiating both Alpine glaciers and polar icebergs, may thus signal, not that it is a harbinger of humanity's fall, but that it is a figure of an identity that could survive an apocalypse of global cooling.

The Creature's reception by human beings loyal to domestic and national forms of identity reveals, however, that Europeans are not yet willing to embrace the universal brotherhood that would render cosmopolitan responses to ecological crisis ethical and feasible. Victor cannot repress the fear and disgust he feels on seeing the culmination of his studies, while Felix and the various other humans who encounter the Creature are appalled by its appearance and the threat that they believe it poses to their domestic circles. The humans of *Frankenstein* might subscribe to cosmopolitan ideals, but when confronted with the living reality of a being that unites the bodies of men in a new formation, that brings together the European and the savage, and that represents a future beyond nativity, they cannot bring themselves to embrace what McLane dubs "the figure of the world irremediably transformed" (968).[18] In this respect, we can see *Frankenstein* anticipating the cynicism of Ryland in *The Last Man*, who observes of poetic visions of improvement, including visions of the destruction of "the poles," that "earth is not, nor ever can be heaven," for human beings are unwilling to embrace the universal "brotherhood" (172) necessary to bring it about. But while it shares a similar cynicism regarding Europeans' current aptitude for cosmopolitanism, *Frankenstein*, unlike *The Last Man*, holds out hope that the human race may yet mature to the point that it can combat global apocalypse: as Victor observes with his dying breath, hope remains that, where Victor's experiment has failed, "yet another may succeed" (186).

In contemplating humans' ability to reshape the natural order, but also human fear of and opposition to a vision of the world transformed,

---

[18]For more arguments concerning *Frankenstein*'s links to cosmopolitanism, see Armstrong and Benis. While I agree with Benis that the horror of the Creature's appearance seems to be generated by the disparate nature of its body parts, I suggest that the Creature's watery eyes and yellow skin do not connote failed unity so much as they emphasize the death of the old identities its body incorporates.

*Frankenstein* acknowledges what the authoritative voices of contemporary periodicals could not: readers' uncertainty regarding commentators' interpretation of the weather of 1816 and 1817; suspicion of claims to disinterested scientific authority; and growing pessimism regarding human beings' ability to successfully address the challenges posed by climate change. Far from being insulated from Romantic conversations regarding climate, *Frankenstein* goes beyond both the optimistic visions of *Queen Mab* and *The Botanic Garden* and the pessimistic vision of *Voyage* to explore the ramifications of human beings' ability to alter nature. If P. B. Shelley's and Darwin's poetic visions remind us that early inhabitants of the Carbon Age could indeed conceive of themselves as geological agents, M. W. Shelley's novel warily contemplates the dawn of our own geological epoch, unsure as to whether human beings are capable of staving off a climatic apocalypse, unsure as to whether human beings are ready to accept the responsibilities this new role would demand.

## EPILOGUE: THE VANISHING ICE

As the shadow cast by the [1815] Tambora eruption faded into memory, so did Britons' concerns about the cooling of their climate. As temperatures climbed, many Britons happily concurred with Barrow regarding the destruction of Arctic ice, predicting that now that "Polar ice has at last been persuaded to thaw . . . our future seasons will remind us of those of the olden time" ("Agricultural Intelligence" 359). However, while comments attributing variations in British weather to the behavior of "ice in the Polar region" appear as late as 1846 (Whistlecraft 22), Barrow himself would never again embrace the rhetoric of "crusades against frost" as fervently as he had done in early 1818. Chastened by the savaging he had received [from] Leslie and his peers, Barrow would from this point onwards confine his more tenuous speculations to Arctic geography, a subject only a few of his readers felt qualified to evaluate. In composing his *A Chronological History of Voyages into the Arctic Regions* (1818), Barrow therefore avoided any mention of climate change in a book that otherwise elaborated on the arguments first made in his *Quarterly* articles. It is to the influence of this book, which consolidated an ideology of polar exploration from which the rhetoric of environmental management had been deliberately excised, that we, in all likelihood, owe our perception of the 1818 controversy as a strictly geographical affair.

As fear of an imminent climatic catastrophe faded from the public mind, Mary Shelley revised *Frankenstein* to reflect the diminished urgency of climate change. As *The Last Man* indicates, the questions confronting humans on the brink of an ecological apocalypse continued to intrigue Shelley, but the apocalypse itself appeared further off in 1831 than it had during the "year without a summer." This renewed, but qualified, trust in the stability of climate is reflected M. W. Shelley's revised descriptions of the glaciers whose expansion had made such an impression on her and P. B. Shelley in 1816. In the 1831 edition, Victor observes that although it has been six years since he visited the valley of Chamounix, "nought had changed in those savage and enduring scenes" (p. 88 in this volume). This observation is a far cry from M. W. Shelley's own description of Chamounix in 1816, in which she had recorded that "This Glacier is encreasing every day a foot closing up the valley." This addition, moreover, erases the implied threat of the *Frankenstein* line adapted from M. W. Shelley's 1816 journal: "Immense glaciers approached the road" (98).[19]

Whereas in the 1818 edition of *Frankenstein*, nature frequently appears inscrutable and menacing, in the 1831 edition, characters express their faith in a comprehensible, uniformitarian nature governed by "immutable laws." The famous chapter in which Victor encounters his Creature on the summit of Montanvert now opens with Victor contemplating the regulatory powers of "imperial Nature," and reflecting on "the accumulated ice, which, through the silent working of immutable laws, was ever and anon rent and torn" (p. 90). In the 1818 edition, there is no suggestion of "immutable laws" governing the expansion of glaciers: indeed, the Alpine glaciers merely prompt Victor to quote from P. B. Shelley's "On Mutability." In 1831, in other words, glacial expansion no longer appears as a sign of imminent apocalypse.[20] This faith in a regulated nature is expressed also in Elizabeth's declaration that "The blue lake, and snow-clad mountains, they never change:— and I think our placid home, and our contented hearts are regulated by the same immutable laws" (p. 65). Crucially, however, Elizabeth is wrong in this passage: mountains do change, and the family's domestic contentment is shortly to be shattered. Apocalypse, in other words, may still lurk in the offing, but, in the 1831 edition of *Frankenstein*, it

[19] See M. W. Shelley, "the mountains assumed a more formitable appearance & the Glaciers approach nearer to the road" (115).

[20] In the 1831 edition, in other words, Victor is more inclined to view glaciers in the light of uniformitarianism, which had been popularized in 1830 by Charles Lyell. For more on the evolution of glaciology and its impact on the Shelleys, see Wilson (86–94).

is Victor's interference with the "immutable laws" of nature that is the immediate cause of catastrophe. If the 1818 version of *Frankenstein* hinted at a potentially-immanent apocalypse that science might need to combat, the 1831 edition thus shifts responsibility for the human race's possible annihilation more squarely onto Victor's shoulders.[21] It is the cosmopolitan scientist's experiment in improvement, and not the menacing operations of a swiftly-cooling planet, that poses the most immediate threat to humanity's survival.

Reviewing the climate discussions of 1816–1818 highlights the degree to which politics and climate were intertwined during the Romantic period, and reminds us that climate change controversies are not entirely new phenomena. While there is much that differs between Romantic understandings of climate and our own, in works such as *Frankenstein* we can nevertheless see an uncanny reflection of our own struggles to discern the nature of, and decide on the proper response to, alterations in the global climate. It may be true, as Eric Gidal has remarked of P. B. Shelley's endorsement of the doctrine of improvement in *Queen Mab*, that the ambitious visions of Romantic crusades against frost promise "disastrous consequences for the actual planet that has had to bear the consequences of such Promethean ambitions" (96). However, the challenge faced by modern environmentalists has tended to lie, not in convincing people that they have too much power over the Earth, but in convincing them to acknowledge that power. As Naomi Oreskes notes regarding contemporary discussions of climate change, "[t]o deny global warming is real is precisely to deny that humans have become geological agents, changing the most basic physical processes of the earth" (93). In assuming that human beings can affect the natural environment, as opposed to passively inhabiting a changeless Nature, Erasmus Darwin and the Shelleys anticipate and, in M. W. Shelley's case, look with apprehension upon, the dawning of our own era, one in which the human race is increasingly considered "a main determinant of the environment of the planet" (Chakrabarty 209).

---

[21] This interpretation gains strength when we consider that, in the 1831 edition of *Frankenstein*, Victor attributes his decision to pursue his disastrous experiment to "Destiny . . . [whose] immutable laws had decreed my utter and terrible destruction" (43). In this and other passages, the phrase "immutable laws" removes human agency as a factor to be considered when contemplating omens of future disaster, and crucially, in this passage, is used by Victor to partly absolve himself of responsibility for his subsequent actions.

# WORKS CITED

"Agricultural Intelligence—Scotland." *Farmer's Magazine* 19.75 (1818): 351–76. Print.

Armstrong, Nancy. *How Novels Think: The Limits of British Individualism from 1719–1900.* New York: Columbia UP, 2005. Print.

"Article XI. The Arctic Expeditions. A Poem." *British Critic* 9 (1818): 513–16. *British Periodicals.* Web. 9 Jan. 2011.

"Article XI. Some Remarks on the Deterioration of the Climate of Britain, with an attempt to point out its Cause." *Journal of Science and the Arts.* Vol. 4. London: John Murray, 1818. 281–87. Print.

Banks, Joseph. "Letter to Thomas Andrew Knight F. R. S." *The Letters of Sir Joseph Banks: A Selection, 1768–1820.* Ed. Neil Chambers. London: Imperial College, 2000. 331–32. Print.

Barrow, John. "Article VIII. A Sketch of the British Fur Trade in North America; with Observations relative to the North-West Company of Montreal." *Quarterly Review* 16.1 (1816: Oct.): 129–72. Print.

———. "Article XI. Narrative of a Voyage to Hudson's Bay, in His Majesty's Ship Rosamond, Containing Some Account of the North-Eastern Coast of America, and of the Tribes Inhabiting That Remote Region." *Quarterly Review* 18.35 (1817: Oct.): 199–223. Print.

———. *A Chronological History of Voyages into the Arctic Regions.* London: John Murray, 1818. Print.

Benis, Toby R. *Romantic Diasporas: French Emigrés, British Convicts, and Jews.* New York: Palgrave Macmillan, 2009. Print.

Bewell, Alan. "Erasmus Darwin's Cosmopolitan Nature." *ELH* 76.1 (2009): 19–48. Print.

———. *Romanticism and Colonial Disease.* Baltimore & London: Johns Hopkins UP, 1999. Print.

———. "Jefferson's Thermometer: Colonial Biogeographical Constructions of the Climate of America." *Romantic Science: The Literary Forms of Natural History.* Ed. Noah Heringman. Albany: State U of New York P, 2008. 111–38. Print.

Bigland, John. "Bigland on the Deterioration of the Climate of Great Britain." *The Northern Star, or, Yorkshire Magazine.* Vol. 2. London: Baldwin, Cradock and Joy, 1818. 213–21. *Google Books.* Web. 4 Apr. 2012.

Bragg, Benjamin. *A Voyage to the North Pole.* London: W. Wilson, 1817. Print.

Buffon, Georges Louis Leclerc, Comte de. *Des Époques de la Nature.* Paris: Éditions Rationalists, 1971. Print.

Cameron, J. M. R. "John Barrow, *The Quarterly's* Imperial Reviewer." *Conservatism and the Quarterly Review: A Critical Analysis.* Ed. Jonathan Cutmore. London: Pickering & Chatto, 2007. 133–49. Print.

Cavell, Janice. *Tracing the Connected Narrative: Arctic Exploration in British Print Culture, 1818–1860.* Toronto: U of Toronto P, 2008. Print.

Chakrabarty, Dipesh. "The Climate of History: Four Theses." *Critical Inquiry* 35 (2009): 197–222. Print.

"Change of Climate." *Omniana: or Horae otiosiores.* Vol. 1. Ed. Robert Southey. London: Longman, Hurst, Rees, Orme, and Brown, 1812. 222–26. Print.

"Climate." *Morning Chronicle* 4 Oct. 1817: 4. *British Newspapers 1600–1900.* Web. 21 Apr. 2008.

Clubbe, John. "The Tempest-Toss'd Summer of 1816: Mary Shelley's *Frankenstein.*" *The Byron Journal* 19 (1991): 26–40. Print.

Darwin, Erasmus. *The Economy of Vegetation.* Vol. 1 *of The Botanic Garden, a poem.* London: J. Johnson, 1799. *Eighteenth Century Collections Online.* Web. 22 Apr. 2009.

De Quincey, Thomas. "On Christianity, as an Organ of Political Movement." *Tait's Edinburgh Magazine* 13.150 (1846): 341–48. *British Periodicals.* Web. 9 Jan. 2011.

"The Edinburgh Review, No. 59." *Literary Gazette* 2.84 (1818): 547–49. *British Periodicals.* Web. 9 Jan. 2011.

"The Expedition to the North Pole." *The Times.* 15 Aug. 1818. 2F. *The Times Digital Archive 1795–1985.* Web. 30 Jun. 2011.

"Expedition to the Northern Ocean." April 1818. *Annals of Philosophy.* Vol. 11. London: Baldwin, Cradock and Joy, 1818. 306–8. Print.

Fleming, James Rodger. *Fixing the Sky: The Checkered History of Weather and Climate Control.* New York: Columbia UP, 2010. Print.

Garnett, Thomas. *Observations on a Tour through the Highlands and Part of the Western Isles of Scotland. A New Edition.* London: John Stockdale, 1811. Print.

Gascoigne, John. *Science in the Service of Empire: Joseph Banks, the British State and the Uses of Science in the Age of Revolution.* Cambridge: Cambridge UP, 1998. Print.

Gidal, Eric. " 'Oh Happy Earth! Reality of Heaven!' Melancholy and Utopia in Romantic Climatology." *The Journal for Early Modern Cultural Studies* 8.2 (2008): 74–101. Print.

Golinski, Jan. *British Weather and the Climate of the Enlightenment.* Chicago & London: Chicago UP, 2007. Print.

Harris, William. "Variation of the Seasons." *Gentleman's Magazine* 91.1 (1821): 69–71. *British Periodicals.* Web. 20 Apr. 2010.

"History of Weather." *The Times.* 19 Aug. 1818. 2F. *The Times Digital Archive 1795–1985.* Web. 30 Jun. 2011.

L. M. U. B. "The Late Hot Weather." *Blackwood's Edinburgh Magazine* 4.20 (1818): 157–59. *British Periodicals.* Web. 9 Apr. 2012.

Lamb, H. H. *Climate, History, and the Modern World.* 2nd ed. New York: Routledge, 2005. Print.

Leslie, John. "Article I. The Possibility of Approaching the North Pole Asserted." *Edinburgh Review* 30.59 (1818): 1–59. *British Periodicals.* Web. 15 Apr. 2010.

"Literature." *The Morning Post.* 13 Mar. 1818. 3. *19th Century British Library Newspapers: Part II.* Web. 30 June 2011.

Loudon, John Claudius, ed. *An Encyclopaedia of Gardening.* 3rd ed. London: Longman, Rees, Orme, Brown, Green, and Longman, 1835. *Google Books.* Web. 8 Feb. 2012.

Lynch, Deidre Shauna. "The (Dis)locations of Romantic Nationalism: Shelley, Staël, and the Home-Schooling of Monsters." *The Literary Channel: The Inter-National Invention of the Novel.* Ed. Margaret Cohen and Carolyn Dever. Princeton: Princeton UP, 2002. 194–224. Print.

McLane, Maureen Noelle. "Literate Species: Populations, 'Humanities,' and Frankenstein." *ELH* 63.4 (1996): 959–88. Print.

"Naval Anecdotes." *The Naval Chronicle. From July to December.* Vol. 2. London: Bunney & Gold, 1799. 305–11. Print.

Oppenheimer, Clive. "Climatic, Environmental, and Human Consequences of the Largest Known Historical Eruption: Tambora Volcano (Indonesia) 1815." *Progress in Physical Geography* 27.2 (2003): 230–59. Print.

Oreskes, Naomi. "The Scientific Consensus on Climate Change: How Do We Know We're Not Wrong?" *Climate Change: What it Means for Us, Our Children, and our Grandchildren.* Eds. Joseph F. C. DiMento and Pamela Doughman. Cambridge: MIT P, 2007. 65–99. Print.

"The Polar Ice and the *Quarterly Review.*" *The Yellow Dwarf: a Weekly Miscellany.* 11 Apr. 1818. 116–17. Print.

Porden, Eleanor Anne. *The Arctic Expeditions, A Poem.* London: John Murray, 1818. Print.

"Quarterly Review, No. XXXV. Polar Ice." *The Scotsman* 28 Mar. 1818. 6. *The Scotsman Digital Archive.* Web. 10 Feb. 2011.

Ramsay, David. *Universal History Americanised; or, An Historical View of the World, from the Earliest Records to the Year 1808.* Vol. 9. Philadelphia: M. Carey & Sons, 1819. Print.

Richard, Jessica. " 'Paradise of My Own Creation': *Frankenstein* and the Improbable Romance of Polar Exploration." *Nineteenth-Century Contexts* 25.4 (2003): 295–314. Print.

Robertson, William. *The History of America.* Vol. 1. London: W. Strahan; T. Cadell; J. Balfour, 1777. Print.

Robinson, Charles, ed. *The Frankenstein Notebooks, Parts One and Two.* New York and London: Garland, 1996. Print.

Shelley, Mary Wollstonecraft. *Frankenstein, or the Modern Prometheus. The 1818 Text.* Ed. Marilyn Butler. Oxford & New York: Oxford UP, 1998. Print.

———. *History of a Six Weeks' Tour Through a Part of France, Switzerland, Germany, and Holland.* London: T. Hookham, and C. and J. Ollier, 1817. Print.

———. *The Journals of Mary Shelley, 1814–1844. Vol. 1: 1814–1822.* Ed. Paula R. Feldman, and Diana Scott-Kilvert. Oxford: Clarendon P, 1987. *British and Irish Women's Letters and Diaries.* Web. 18 Nov. 2010.

———. *The Last Man.* Ed. Anne McWhir. Peterborough: Broadview P, 1996. Print.

Shelley, Percy Bysshe. "Percy Bysshe Shelley to Thomas Love Peacock," 24 Jul. 1816. *The Letters of Percy Bysshe Shelley.* Ed. Frederick L. Jones. Vol. 1. Oxford: Oxford, 1964. Print.

———. *Queen Mab; A Philosophical Poem. Shelley's Poetry and Prose.* Ed. Donald H. Reiman and Neil Fraistat. New York: Norton, 2002. 16–71. Print.

———. "Mont Blanc." *Shelley's Poetry and Prose.* Ed. Donald H. Reiman and Neil Fraistat. New York: Norton, 2002. 96–101. Print.

"This Day Is Published . . ." *The Morning Post* 29, May 1817. 2. *19th Century British Library Newspapers: Part II.* Web. 9 Apr. 2012.

"Varieties, Literary and Philosophical, Including Notices of Works in Hand, Domestic and Foreign." *Monthly Magazine, or, British Register* 45.313 (1818): 540–46. *British Periodicals.* Web. 9 Apr. 2012.

Wadd, William *Mems. Maxims, and Memoirs.* London: Callow & Wilson, 1827. Print.

Wheatley, Kim. "The Arctic in the *Quarterly Review*." *European Romantic Review* 20.4 (2009): 465–90. Print.

————. Review of Jen Hill, *White Horizon: The Arctic in the Nineteenth-Century British Imagination*; Janice Cavell, *Tracing the Connected Narrative: Arctic Exploration in British Print Culture, 1818–1860. European Romantic Review* 22.4 (2011): 571–78. Print.

Whistlecraft, Orlando. *The Magnificent and Notably Hot Summer of 1846; or, a Particular Account of the Extraordinary State of the Atmosphere in England during that Season.* London: Longman & Co., 1846. Print.

Williams, John. *The Climate of Great Britain; Or, Remarks on the Changes it has Undergone, Particularly Within the Last Fifty Years.* London: C. and R. Baldwin, 1806. Print.

Wilson, Eric G. *The Spiritual History of Ice: Romanticism, Science, and the Imagination.* New York: Palgrave, 2003. Print.

Wilton, Pleydell. "The Polar Ice." *Geology, and Other Poems.* London: Hatchard, 1818. 83–85. Print.

# Postcolonial Criticism
## and *Frankenstein*

## WHAT IS POSTCOLONIAL CRITICISM?

Postcolonial criticism typically involves the analysis of works by authors from regions of the globe subject to European colonization. Postcolonial criticism might just as easily have been referred to as *post-imperialist* criticism, since the term *imperialism* refers to the extension of rulership or authority (almost always unsought and unwanted) by a politically and economically powerful empire or nation and its culture over a weaker, less "developed" foreign country or region and its culture, thereafter referred to as a "colony" or "dependency" of the imperialist, colonizing ruler nation.

Usually, the prefix *post-* in *postcolonial* signifies the period following the end of colonization and the achievement of national independence by a former colony, but sometimes it is used to refer to any point following the establishment of colonial rule. Thus, Chinua Achebe's *Things Fall Apart* (1959), a novel which implicitly opposes the ongoing colonial oppression of the Nigerian people, is often referred to as a postcolonial work. Although in such instances the prefix *post* seems to have secondary connotations of *anti*, its meaning is usually more strictly chronological. For one thing, postcolonial criticism sometimes engages texts produced by authors hailing from the colonizing culture. (Joseph Conrad's *Heart of Darkness*, written by an author Achebe has called a "bloody racist," is a case in point.) The intent of this type of postcolonial criticism is to expose colonialist attitudes held by the author and/or literary characters and to demonstrate the role such biases play in the representation of subjugated persons and cultures.

Emerging from an extraordinary variety of critical and theoretical discourses prevalent during the last half of the twentieth century, postcolonial criticism entered the twenty-first century as the predominant form of literary study. Because it may best be thought of as a convergence of discourses, postcolonial criticism may best be understood in relation to some of its antecedents.

One of these involved the study of so-called Commonwealth literature; that is, literature produced in and about areas colonized by the British empire that at one point become part of the Commonwealth of Nations (to which, for instance, Canada still belongs). Another focused on what used to be called Third World Literature, a wider field of study since it included non-English cultures and texts (e.g., francophone studies of cultures once colonized by France). Important intellectuals associated with the development of postcolonial criticism include Achebe, mentioned above; Edward Kamau Brathwaite, a Caribbean writer from Barbados whose work will be described later; Aimé Césaire; and Frantz Fanon. Césaire, a francophone postcolonial intellectual best known for his book *Discours sur le colonialisme* (*Discourse on Colonialism*) (1950), experienced the brutality of French imperialism firsthand. He established the "Negritude" movement, the purpose of which was to increase political awareness and unite the pan-national interests among black victims of European colonization. Fanon, a French-educated black Afro-Carribean psychiatrist who immigrated to Algeria, wrote a series of essays on the needs of colonized peoples, with particular emphasis on their need for political independence from the imperialist, colonizing country.

When painting the background of contemporary postcolonial criticism with the very broadest brushstrokes, it is impossible not to mention cultural criticism, or cultural studies. Indeed, in the most general sense, postcolonial criticism may be seen as a form of cultural criticism, an approach to literature and its manifold social and economic relationships that emerged in England in the 1950s and 1960s. Cultural critics notably opposed the general tendency to hear "culture" and think "high culture"—evenings at the symphony, gallery openings, belles lettres. They strived to make the term refer at least equally to popular, folk, even "street" culture. Raymond Williams, an early British cultural critic, famously suggested in his book *The Long Revolution* (1961) that "art and culture are ordinary"; he did so not to "pull art down" but rather to point out that there is "creativity in all our living. . . . We create our human world as we have thought of art as being created" (37). The idea that culture, including literature, is produced not only by the dominant or "official" culture but also by ordinary folk enabled and encouraged an interest in authors speaking from the vantage point—and often in the native language of—a colonized people.

Early cultural critics such as Williams followed the practices of Marxist criticism in viewing culture in relation to ideologies, which Williams defined as the "residual," "dominant," and "emerging" ways of viewing the world held in common by social groups or by individuals holding power. Williams's view that even repressive ideologies can evolve was linked to his belief in the resilience of even subjugated individuals, in their ability to experience the conditions in which they find themselves and creatively respond to those conditions. These relatively hopeful views paralleled those of Michel Foucault, a mid-twentieth-century French theorist who greatly influenced the new historicism, cultural criticism, and, ultimately, postcolonial criticism.

Like Williams, Foucault had been influenced by Marxist thought to study cultures in terms of power relationships. But Foucault refused to see power as something exercised by a dominant class or group over a subservient one. Instead, he viewed it as a whole web or complex of forces involving everything from "discourses"—accepted ways of thinking, writing, and speaking—to social practices. According to Foucault, not even a tyrannical aristocrat wields power, for the aristocrat is himself formed by a network of discourses and practices that constitute power. Viewed by Foucault, power is that which produces what happens. It is "positive and productive," not "repressive" and "prohibitive" (Smart 63). Furthermore no historical event, according to Foucault, has a single cause; rather, it is intricately connected with a vast web of economic, social, and political factors. Like Williams's view that culture is not, by definition, centered in "high" culture and reflective of dominant ideologies, Foucault's radically decentered view of both power relations and history—the history that power relations engender and are engendered by—reinforced the work of early postcolonial critics and enabled its development by later practitioners.

For instance, Brathwaite, generally viewed as one of the first postcolonial critics, adopted a fluid and dynamic view of the power relations that develop between imperialist nations and colonized cultures. In *The Development of Creole Society in Jamaica 1770–1820* (1971), he used the term *creolization* to describe what he viewed as a "two-way process," "a way of seeing the society, not in terms of white and black, master and slave, in separate nuclear units, but as contributory parts of a whole. . . . Here in Jamaica, fixed within the dehumanizing institution of slavery, were two cultures of people, having to adapt themselves to a new environment and to each other. The fiction created by this confrontation was cruel, but it was also creative." Homi Bhabha, a leading contemporary cultural critic, focuses on the creative aspect of the colonial confrontation, making a Foucauldian argument that marginalized people subject to repressive power in fact wield positive and productive power of their own. In an essay entitled "Of Mimicry and Man: The Ambivalence of Colonial Discourse" (1994), he uses the term *hybridity* to refer to the process whereby subjugated people, having at first assimilated aspects of oppressor culture, eventually manage to metamorphose those elements, making them their own through a process of transformation. Bhabha, it should be noted, also adopts a decentered view of history made possible by Foucault, arguing that modern Western culture is best understood from the perspective of the postcolonial world, not vice versa as Westerners (stereo)typically assume.

The overlap between postcolonial criticism and the cultural criticism from which it emerges is perhaps most evident in the work of Bhabha, who in his seminal work *The Location of Culture* speaks cryptically of "culture's archaic undecidability" in arguing that "there can be no ethically or epistemologically commensurate subject of culture" (135). Since culture is thought to distinguish humanity from the rest of nature, to define the subject of culture generally one would have to begin with an impossibility, namely, a definition of humanity that is not derived from any particular culture's sense of values. Thus, just as there is no one set of practices that can be said definitively to constitute "culture" (as opposed to "pop culture" or "high culture"), so any larger definition of human culture is a dangerous undertaking doomed by a relativism that is inevitably myopic and potentially murderous, as when the values and practices operative within one social group (e.g., the native Africans represented in Joseph Conrad's novella *Heart of Darkness)* are viewed and represented by members of another group (e.g., Mr. Kurtz, the European manager of the Company's Inner Station) as sub- or even nonhuman. ("Exterminate the brutes!" Kurtz writes in his postscript to a report for the International Society for the Suppression of Savage Customs.)

In theory, postcolonial criticism could analyze works about or arising from any colonized culture and could be written in the language of the imperialist colonizers or the language of the colonized. In fact, however, most postcolonial criticism is written in English and tends to concern itself with the following geographic areas: Africa and the Caribbean, as have been mentioned, but also the "East" (i.e., the Middle East and Asia) and the Indian subcontinent—areas in which, during the past century, liberation movements arose that ultimately led to national independence. To be sure, some attention has been paid to Australia, Canada, and New Zealand—often referred to as English "settler colonies"—and sometimes even the thirteen "settler" colonies that became the United States are viewed from the postcolonial perspective. (However, in the latter instance, the focus is far more likely to be on African American works and works by nonblack authors about African slaves brought to America and/or their free descendants than it is to be on, say, Thomas Jefferson as leader of a postcolonial rebellion!) Additionally, an occasional postcolonial reading of Irish literature has taken into account Ireland's status as a colony in all but name—but one that, unlike other colonies, was near the center of empire with respect to matters such as location, race, and (for the most part) language.

With regard to the Middle East and East, the most powerful practitioner of postcolonial criticism is, in fact, one of its acknowledged founders: Edward Said. Said, like his cultural-critic precursor Williams, understood implicitly the role played by ideology in blinding the colonizer to the realities and conditions of the colonized. More specifically influenced by Foucault, Said laid the foundations of postcolonial criticism in *Orientalism* (1978), a book in which he analyzed European discourses concerning the exotic, arguing that stereotypes systematically projected on peoples of the East contributed to the establishment of European domination and exploitation of Eastern (Asian) and Middle Eastern cultures through colonization. Although *Orientalism* focuses on colonialist discourses, both Said and those scholars influenced by him have applied its insights to interpreting the aftermath of colonialism.

Gayatri Spivak, an Indian scholar, has examined the ways in which issues of class and especially gender pertain to the postcolonial situation, relationships that develop within it, and representations of it. In her groundbreaking essay "Can the Subaltern Speak?" (1988), Spivak uses "subalterns"—a British term used to refer to the lowest-ranking officers in the military—to refer to the colonized and, more specifically, to the most vulnerable of the groups comprising that population (e.g., women, racial minorities, immigrants, and underclass persons dominated by relatively powerful groups *within* the colonized culture). With regard to the position of women, subaltern scholars have pointed out their double oppression, both by traditional patriarchal attitudes and practices within their own culture and, beyond that, by attitudes and practices inherent in colonizing cultures that were in many cases more masculinist, sexist. Indeed, Michael Payne has said that subaltern critics in India, Ngũgĩ wa Thiong'o of Kenya, and Rey Chow of China "have read imperialism as not only actively suppressing the more feminist and egalitarian of indigenous institutions and cultural practices, but also as driving the indigenous patriarchy to increasingly reactionary excesses against women and subalterns in an effort to maintain its strength *vis-à-vis* the colonizers" (425).

Issues raised by Spivak concerning whether and how agency—the ability of postcolonial, subaltern subjects to choose and to speak independently—can survive the impact of long-term hierarchical situations are central to the understanding of individuals and groups in postcolonial context. But they also highlight the difficulties faced by postcolonial scholars whose goal is to give the voiceless a voice. Some such scholars have resorted to such things as court testimony and prison memoirs, while others have studied popular cultural forms (e.g., oral literature and street theater) through which those who have been silenced may still be heard to speak. The Subaltern Studies Group has been particularly successful in producing revisionary historical accounts of life as experienced by once-silent or silenced colonial subjects. Ranajit Guha's "The Prose of Counter-Insurgency" (1983), for example, provides a critical alternative to accepted historical narratives by contrasting official documents with personal ones, contemporary accounts with retrospective ones, and European views with indigenous perspectives.

Feminist postcolonial critics have understandably focused on recovering the cultures of postcolonial women. In doing so, they have questioned whether the universal category "woman" constructed by certain French and American predecessors is appropriate to postcolonial women or the diverse groups of women comprising that general category. They have stressed that, while all women are female, they are something else as well (such as African, Muslim, Pakistani, lesbian, working class, and so forth). This "something else" is precisely what makes them—including their problems and goals—different from other women. Some feminist postcolonial critics have focused on a particular female postcolonial experience, namely, that of women marginalized not in their own colonized culture but rather in the imperialist, colonizing culture to which they have immigrated or been forcibly taken. The so-called classics of white European novels may even speak, indirectly, of the experiences of these women. In "Three Women's Texts and a Critique of Imperialism" (1985), Spivak mines Charlotte Brontë's novel *Jane Eyre* for its numerous references to the West Indies, the slave trade, and Bertha Mason (often referred to as "the madwoman in the attic"), the insane Jamaican wife of the novel's hero, Mr. Rochester. Elsie Michie subsequently focused not on images of the colonized in *Jane Eyre* but rather on "the way the colonizers are represented in Brontë's novel because, as Edward Said and subsequent postcolonial critics have noted, images of the colonized are inextricably bound up with and determined by the attitudes of the colonizers."

For the most part, however, the postcolonial women discussed by feminist postcolonial critics are not characters in novels written by white women. Amrit Wilson has written about the challenges faced by post-colonial Asian women living in London, pointing out, for instance, that they tend to be expected by their families and communities to preserve Asian cultural traditions; thus, the expression of personal identity through clothing involves a much more serious infraction of cultural rules than it does for a Western woman. Gloria Anzaldúa spoke personally and elo-quently about the experience of women on the margins of Eurocentric North American culture. "I am a border woman," she wrote in *Border-lands/La Frontera: The New Mestiza* (1987). "I grew up between two cultures, the Mexican (with a heavy Indian influence) and the Anglo. . . . Living on the borders and in margins, keeping intact one's shifting and multiple identity and integrity is like trying to swim in a new element, an 'alien' element" (i).

Powerful though it is as a force in contemporary literary studies, post-colonial criticism has its critics. Even the name *postcolonial* has been deemed imprecise, due to the various, inconsistent ways in which the pre-fix *post-* is used and the way *postcolonial* may be used to refer to political situations, writers writing from or about those contexts, and scholars and critics writing about those writers. Others find *postcolonial* misleading if not useless as an umbrella term because the attitudes and practices of some colonizing countries differed so utterly from those of nations with dissimilar political values and economic purposes. Still others take the opposite view, arguing that postcolonial critics overstress differences and undervalue attempts (for instance by the Negritude movement) to forge a shared collective (in this case African) history of repression and revolt.

Use of *postcolonial* as an adjective to describe any and all so-called "diaspora studies" has been questioned—whether these studies concern slaves living in the American South, thriving but insular "black" com-munities in London, or Chinese-American families like the one depicted in Amy Tan's novel *The Joy Luck Club* (1989). Critics have also objected to use of the term with reference to settler colonies in which the majority of the population came quickly to consist of colonists, and to minority groups living within a colonizing culture (e.g., the Irish) whose race and language they share.

Some critics of the postcolonial approach have argued that the focus on relations between imperialists and those they have colonized leaves entirely too much out of the picture, whether the picture in question be of postcolonial society or some literary representation of a post-colonial situation. Within this group are those who would prefer to see race, class, or gender difference privileged over the opposition *colonizer/colonized*. Then there are various groups of detractors who find a misleadingly bright thread in various aspects of what has been called postcolonial studies. Some of these believe that, in so often telling the story of oppressed peoples who eventually gained independence from subjugating empires, postcolonial critics imply that oppression ends when political independence is gained. In reality, most of the above-mentioned critics of postcolonial criticism are, in almost everyone else's view, postcolonial critics themselves. This fact demonstrates the dynamic liveliness of the approach — the way in which, although we have the general rubric *postcolonial criticism*, it can mean as many different things (for the time being) as the prefix *post*.

In the postcolonial approach to *Frankenstein* that follows, Allan Lloyd Smith — after summarizing some of the ways in which the novel has recently been read — turns to contexts that have largely been overlooked, namely, race and slavery, "references" to which "echo throughout the novel" (p. 549 in this volume). Asserting the influence of Shakespeare's *The Tempest*, Smith draws a connection between Shelley's monster and Shakespeare's Caliban, called an "Abhorred slave," a "devil," and a member of a "vile race" of creatures. He goes on to point out that "The narrative shape of the Creature's account of himself is akin to that of the slave narrative" (p. 555) and that it contains many parallels with another such text, *The Interesting Narrative of Olaudah Equiano, or Gustavus Vassa the African, Written by Himself* (1789). (For instance, both works contain meditations by the slave on the responsibilities of masters.)

As were slaves, Shelley's monster, or "Creature," is "denied control and fulfilment in sexuality" and is viewed as having an insatiable desire for white women (p. 559). When the Creature finds on the body of the just-murdered William Frankenstein a medallion depicting the boy's mother, he bemoans that fact that he would be "forever deprived of the delights that such beautiful creatures could bestow" (p. 560). He has the same thoughts just after finding the sleeping Justine; he wants to awaken her with the words "Awake, fairest, thy lover is here" (the accent on "fairest" is significant), but he is stopped by his own realization that "[h]ere . . . is one of those whose smiles are bestowed on all but me" (p. 560). Smith goes on to point out that the death of Elizabeth, toward the end of the novel, "similarly arouses echoes of dominant cultural anxieties and rape fantasies about white women and black men" and that this arousal is even stronger in the second edition of the novel than in the first, because "Mary Shelley's 1831 revisions intensified Elizabeth's Saxon racial features" in such a way as to make her "the flower of white girlhood" (p. 560).

Smith sees Shelley's text as an "investigation of the limits of readerly sympathy" (p. 561) with, or the extent of "alienation" from, slaves and points to the 1791 San Domingo Slave Rebellion in Haiti as an event that created conflicting reactions. "San Domingo served as model both for abolitionists, who argued that the Haitians had but seized the same rights as had the Americans shortly before them, but also for pro-slavery forces," who saw in it "a foretaste of bloody revenge at the hands of the slaves" (p. 562). Such revenge is described in Mary Hassal's *Secret History: or, the Horrors of St Domingo* (1808), which tells what happened to one young white woman who refused the advances of a slave in revolt: "The monster gave her to his guard, who hung her by the throat on an iron hook in the market place" (p. 562). Noting that "Such were the horrors popularly linked to black insurrection," Smith points out that they are "inferentially associated with the Monster's remorseless quest for autonomy and vengeance" (p. 562). Smith does not argue that Shelley's intent is to use her novel to inflame racist anxiety and hatred but, rather, that she "might be seen to be presenting both sides of the issue: sympathetic to the Monster, but also registering shock and horror at his however justifiable excesses" (p. 562).

To conclude his essay, Smith returns to the subject of his first paragraph, namely, the highly respected critics who do not take a postcolonial approach, whose works do not foreground the issues of race and slavery. He argues that placing the novel in those contexts, and particularly those involving slavery, leads to a reading of Victor's motives and feelings that is quite different from the interpretations of certain feminist and psychoanalytic readers, who "point to the idea that the atrocities committed by the Creature are in some sense the fulfilment of Frankenstein's deepest wishes" (p. 564). Smith maintains that "there is no evidence of such deeper drives in Frankenstein." Although "Frankenstein *is* responsible for the actions of his Creature, just as a slaveholder would be held responsible for the actions of his slaves" (p. 565),

[H]e need no more be understood as wishing for those actions than a slaveholder would wish for atrocities committed against his family in an uprising . . . . The Creature's tortured sense of difference-within-resemblance similarly locates him not in relation to the individual psychology of Frankenstein but to the eighteenth-century debates over cross-racial resemblance and difference. (p. 565)

Overall Smith's essay shows the powerful effect of "repositioning the Creature and his maker within the terms of contemporaneous racial discourse" (p. 564).

Ross C Murfin

## POSTCOLONIAL CRITICISM:
## A SELECTED BIBLIOGRAPHY

### Postcolonial Criticism and Theory: General Texts

Ashcroft, Bill, Gareth Griffiths, and Helen Tiffin. *The Empire Writes Back: Theory and Practice in Postcolonial Literatures.* New York: Routledge, 1989. Print.

———. *Post-Colonial Studies: The Key Concepts.* London: Routledge, 2000. Print.

———, eds. *The Post-Colonial Studies Reader.* 2d ed. London: Routledge, 2006. Print.

Barker, Francis, Peter Hulme, and Margaret Iversen, eds. *Colonial Discourse/Postcolonial Theory.* Manchester: Manchester UP, 1994. Print.

Boehmer, Elleke. *Colonial and Postcolonial Literature.* Oxford: Oxford UP, 1995. Print.

Castle, Gregory, ed. *Postcolonial Discourses: An Anthology.* Oxford: Blackwell, 2001. Print.

Chambers, Iain, and Lidia Curti, eds. *The Post-Colonial Question: Common Skies, Divided Horizons.* London: Routledge, 1996. Print.

Chrisman, Laura. *Postcolonial Contraventions: Cultural Readings of Race, Imperialism, and Transnationalism.* Manchester: Manchester UP, 2003. Print.

Desai, Gaurav, and Supriya Nair, eds. *Postcolonialisms: An Anthology of Cultural Theory and Criticism.* Piscataway: Rutgers UP, 2005. Print.

Featherstone, Simon. *Postcolonial Cultures.* Edinburgh: Edinburgh UP, 2005. Print.

Gandhi, Leela. *Postcolonial Theory: A Critical Introduction.* New York: Columbia UP, 1998. Print.

Gilbert, Helen, and Joanne Tompkins. *Post-Colonial Drama: Theory, Practice, Politics.* London: Routledge, 1996. Print.

Goldberg, David Theo, and Ato Quayson, eds. *Relocating Postcolonialism.* Oxford: Blackwell, 2002. Print.

Harrison, Nicholas. *Postcolonial Criticism: History, Theory, and the Work of Fiction.* Cambridge: Polity, 2003. Print.

King, C. Richard, ed. *Postcolonial America.* Urbana: U of Illinois P, 2000. Print.

Loomba, Ania. *Colonialism/Postcolonialism.* 2d ed. London: Routledge, 2005. Print.

López, Alfred J. *Posts and Pasts: A Theory of Postcolonialism.* Albany: State U of New York P, 2001. Print.

McLeod, John. *Beginning Postcolonialism.* Manchester: Manchester UP, 2000. Print.

Mongia, Padmini, ed. *Contemporary Postcolonial Theory: A Reader.* London: Arnold, 1996. Print.

Moore-Gilbert, Bart. *Postcolonial Theory: Contexts, Practices, Politics.* London: Verso, 1997. Print.

———, Gareth Stanton, and Willy Maley, eds. *Post-colonial Criticism.* London: Longman, 1997. Print.

Punter, David. *Postcolonial Imaginings: Fictions of a New World Order.* Edinburgh: Edinburgh UP, 2000. Print.

Quayson, Ato. *Postcolonialism: Theory, Practice or Process?* Malden, MA: Blackwell, 2000. Print.

Rajan, Gita, and Radhika Mohanram, eds. *Postcolonial Discourse and Changing Cultural Contexts: Theory and Criticism.* Westport: Greenwood, 1995. Print.

Schwarz, Henry, and Sangeeta Ray, eds. *A Companion to Postcolonial Studies.* Malden: Blackwell, 2000. Print.

Sharp, Joanne. *Geographies of Postcolonialism.* London: Sage, 2008. Print.

Smart, Barry. *Foucault, Marxism and Critique.* New York: Routledge, 2013. Print.

Smith, Rowland. *Postcolonizing the Commonwealth: Studies in Literature and Culture.* Waterloo, ON: Wilfrid Laurier UP, 2000. Print.

Sugirtharajah, R. S. *Postcolonial Criticism and Biblical Interpretation.* Oxford: Oxford UP, 2002. Print.

Syrotinski, Michael. *Deconstruction and the Postcolonial: At the Limits of Theory.* Liverpool: Liverpool UP, 2007. Print.

Williams, Patrick, and Laura Chrisman, eds. *Colonial Discourse and Post-Colonial Theory: A Reader.* Hemel Hempstead: Harvester Wheatsheaf, 1993. Print.

Young, Robert. *Postcolonialism: An Historical Introduction.* Oxford: Blackwell, 2001. Print. See especially Part V, "Formations of Postcolonial Theory."

### Works by or about Homi K. Bhabha, Edward Said, and Gayatri Chakravorty Spivak

Ansell-Pearson, Keith, Benita Parry, and Judith Squires, eds. *Cultural Readings of Imperialism: Edward Said and the Gravity of History.* London: Lawrence & Wishart, 1997. Print.

Bhabha, Homi K. "Framing Fanon." Foreword to *The Wretched of the Earth.* By Frantz Fanon. Trans. Richard Philcox. New York: Grove, 2004. Print.

———. *The Location of Culture.* New York: Routledge, 1994. Print.

———. *Nation and Narration.* New York: Routledge, 1990. Print. See especially "DissemiNation: Time, Narrative, and the Margins of the Modern Nation."

———. "Of Mimicry and Man: The Ambivalence of Colonial Discourse." *The Location of Culture* 85–92.

———. "Postcolonial Criticism." *Redrawing the Boundaries: The Transformation of English and American Literary Studies.* Eds. Stephen Greenblatt and Giles Gunn. New York: MLA, 1992. 437–65. Print.

———, and W. J. T. Mitchell, eds. *Edward Said: Continuing the Conversation.* Chicago: U of Chicago P, 2005. Originally published as special issue of *Critical Inquiry* 31 (2005). Print.

Bové, Paul A., ed. *Edward Said and the Work of the Critic: Speaking Truth to Power.* Durham: Duke UP, 2000. Print.

Morton, Stephen. *Gayatri Chakravorty Spivak.* London: Routledge, 2003. Print.

Said, Edward. *After the Last Sky: Palestinian Lives.* New York: Pantheon, 1986. Print.

———. *Culture and Imperialism.* New York: Knopf, 1993. Print.

———. *The Edward Said Reader.* Eds. Moustafa Bayoumi and Andrew Rubin. New York: Vintage, 2000. Print.

———. *Joseph Conrad and the Fiction of Autobiography.* Cambridge: Harvard UP, 1966. Print.

————. *Orientalism*. New York: Pantheon, 1978. Print.

————. *The World, the Text, and the Critic*. Cambridge: Harvard UP, 1983. Print.

Spivak, Gayatri Chakravorty. "Can the Subaltern Speak?" *Marxism and the Interpretation of Culture*. Eds. Cary Nelson and Lawrence Grossberg. Urbana: U of Illinois P, 1988. 271–313. Print.

————. *A Critique of Postcolonial Reason: Toward a History of the Vanishing Present*. Cambridge: Harvard UP, 1999. Print.

————. *Death of a Discipline*. New York: Columbia UP, 2003. Print.

————. *In Other Worlds: Essays in Cultural Politics*. New York: Methuen, 1987. Print.

————. *Other Asias*. Malden: Blackwell, 2007. Print.

————. *Outside in the Teaching Machine*. New York: Routledge, 1993. Print.

————. *The Post-Colonial Critic: Interviews, Strategies, Dialogues*. Ed. Sarah Harasym. New York: Routledge, 1990. Print.

————. *The Spivak Reader: Selected Works of Gayatri Chakravorty Spivak*. Eds. Donna Landry and Gerald MacLean. New York: Routledge, 1996. Print.

————. "Three Women's Texts and a Critique of Imperialism." *Critical Inquiry* 12.1 (1985): 243–61. Print.

## Influential Texts in the Development of Postcolonial Criticism and Theory

Brathwaite, Edward Kamau. *The Development of Creole Society in Jamaica, 1770–1820*. Oxford: Clarendon, 1971. Print.

Césaire, Aimé. *Discours sur le colonialisme (Discourse on Colonialism)*. Paris: Réclame, 1950. Print.

Derrida, Jacques. *La Dissémination (Dissemination)*. Paris: Éditions du Seuil, 1972. Print.

Fanon, Frantz. *Les damnés de la terre (The Wretched of the Earth)*. Paris: Maspero, 1961. Print. With a preface by Jean-Paul Sartre.

————. *Peau noire, masques blancs (Black Skin/White Masks)*. Paris: Éditions du Seuil, 1972. Print.

Foucault, Michel. *Surveiller et punir: Naissance de la prison (Discipline and Punish: The Birth of the Prison)*. Paris: Gallimard, 1975. Print.

Williams, Raymond. *Culture and Society, 1780–1950*. London: Chatto & Windus, 1958. Print.

————. *The Long Revolution*. New York: Columbia UP, 1961. Print.

## Postcolonial Criticism and Theory with a Feminist or Gender Emphasis

Anzaldúa, Gloria. *Borderlands/La Frontera: The New Mestiza.* San Francisco: Spinsters/Aunt Lute, 1987. Print.

Jayawardena, Kumari. *Feminism and Nationalism in the Third World.* New Delhi: Kali for Women, 1986. Print.

Kwok, Pui-lan. *Postcolonial Imagination and Feminist Theology.* Louisville: Westminster John Knox P, 2005. Print.

Lewis, Reina, and Sara Mills, eds. *Feminist Postcolonial Theory: A Reader.* Edinburgh: Edinburgh UP, 2003. Print.

McClintock, Anne, Aamir Mufti, and Ella Shohat, eds. *Dangerous Liaisons: Gender, Nation, and Postcolonial Perspectives.* Minneapolis: U of Minnesota P, 1997. Print.

Mills, Sara. *Gender and Colonial Space.* Manchester and New York: Manchester UP, 2005. Print.

Mohanty, Chandra Talpade, et al., eds. *Third World Women and the Politics of Feminism.* Bloomington: Indiana UP, 1991. Print.

Sharpe, Jenny. *Allegories of Empire: The Figure of the Woman in the Colonial Text.* Minneapolis: U of Minnesota P, 1993. Print.

Wilson, Amrit. *Finding a Voice: Asian Women in Britain.* London: Virago, 1978, Print.

## Subalternity, Subaltern Studies

Beverley, John. *Subalternity and Representation: Arguments in Cultural Theory.* Durham: Duke UP, 1999. Print.

Chaturvedi, Vinayak, ed. *Mapping Subaltern Studies and the Postcolonial.* London: Verso, 2000. Print.

Guha, Ranajit. "The Prose of Counter-Insurgency." *Subaltern Studies No. 2: Writings on South Asian History and Society.* Delhi: Oxford UP, 1983. 1–42. Print.

hooks, bell. "Marginality as a Site of Resistance." *Out There: Marginalization and Contemporary Cultures.* Eds. Russell Ferguson et al. Cambridge: MIT, 1990. 341–43. Print.

Ludden, David, ed. *Reading Subaltern Studies: Critical History, Contested Meaning and the Globalization of South India.* Delhi: Permanent Black, 2001. Print.

Payne, Michael, and Jessica Rae Barbera, eds. *A Dictionary of Cultural and Critical Theory.* Oxford: Blackwell, 1996. Print. See entries on postcolonial studies, subaltern studies.

*Subaltern Studies: Writings on South Asian History and Society.* Delhi: Oxford UP, 1982–2005. Print. Series edited by Ranajit Guha et al., comprising of 12 numbered volumes, *Selected Subaltern Studies* (1988), and *A Subaltern Studies Reader: 1986–95* (1997). See especially Ranajit Guha's essay "On Some Aspects of the Historiography of Colonial India," vol. 1.

## Further Reading on Postcolonial Criticism and Theory

Bartolovich, Crystal, and Neil Lazarus, eds. *Marxism, Modernity, and Postcolonial Studies.* Cambridge: Cambridge UP, 2002. Print.

Bohata, Kirsti. *Postcolonialism Revisited: Welsh Writing in English.* Cardiff: U of Wales P, 2004, Print.

Centre for Contemporary Cultural Studies. *The Empire Strikes Back: Race and Racism in 70s Britain.* London: Hutchinson, 1982. Print.

Chakrabarty, Dipesh. *Provincializing Europe: Postcolonial Thought and Historical Difference.* Princeton: Princeton UP, 2000. Print.

Chow, Rey. *Writing Diaspora: Tactics of Intervention in Contemporary Cultural Studies.* Bloomington: Indiana UP, 1993. Print.

Dirlik, Arif. *Third World Criticism in the Age of Global Capitalism.* Boulder: Westview, 1997. Print.

Gilroy, Paul. *The Black Atlantic: Modernity and Double Consciousness.* London: Verso, 1993. Print.

Hawley, John C., ed. *Postcolonial, Queer: Theoretical Intersections.* Albany: State U of New York P, 2001. Print.

Huggan, Graham. *The Postcolonial Exotic: Marketing the Margins.* London: Routledge, 2001. Print.

JanMohamed, Abdul, and David Lloyd, eds. *The Nature and Context of Minority Discourse.* New York: Oxford UP, 1991. Print.

Kaplan, Amy, and Donald Pease, eds. *Cultures of United States Imperialism.* Durham: Duke UP, 1983. Print.

Kelertas, Violeta. *Baltic Postcolonialism.* Amsterdam: Editions Rodopi BV, 2006. Print.

Mbembe, Achille. *On the Postcolony.* Trans. A. M. Berrett et al. Berkeley: U of California P, 2001. Print.

McCallum, Pamela, and Wendy Faith, eds. *Linked Histories: Postcolonial Studies in a Globalized World.* Calgary: U of Calgary P, 2005. Print.

Ngũgĩ wa Thiong'o. *Decolonising the Mind: The Politics of Language in African Literature.* London: Heinemann, 1986. Print.

Parry, Benita. *Postcolonial Studies: A Materialist Critique.* London: Routledge, 2004. Print.

Pines, Jim, and Paul Willeman, eds. *Questions of Third Cinema.* London: BFI, 1989. Print.

Rajan, Gita, and Radhika Mohanram, eds. *English Postcoloniality: Literatures from Around the World.* Westport: Greenwood, 1996. Print.

Rooney, Caroline. *Decolonising Gender: Literature and a Poetics of the Real.* London: Routledge, 2007. Print.

San Juan, E. (Epifanio), Jr. *Beyond Postcolonial Theory.* New York: St. Martin's, 1998. Print.

Singh, Amritjit, and Peter Schmidt, eds. *Postcolonial Theory and the United States: Race, Ethnicity, and Literature.* Jackson: UP of Mississippi, 2000. Print.

Talib, Ismail S. *The Language of Postcolonial Literatures: An Introduction.* London: Routledge, 2002. Print.

Young, Robert, ed. "Neocolonialism." Spec. issue of *Oxford Literary Review* 13 (1991). Print.

———. *White Mythologies: Writing, History, and the West.* 2d ed. London: Routledge, 2004. Print.

## Postcolonial Readings

Arata, Stephen D. "The Occidental Tourist: Stoker and Reverse Colonialism." *Fictions of Loss in the Victorian Fin de Siécle.* Cambridge: Cambridge UP, 1996. 107–32. Print.

Bongie, Chris. *Islands and Exiles: The Creole Identities of Post/Colonial Literature.* Stanford: Stanford UP, 1998. Print.

Gorra, Michael Edward. *After Empire: Scott, Naipaul, Rushdie.* Chicago: U of Chicago P, 1997. Print.

Hogan, Patrick Colm. *Colonialism and Cultural Identity: Crises of Tradition in the Anglophone Literatures of India, Africa, and the Caribbean.* Albany: State U of New York P, 2000. Print.

Keown, Michelle. *Postcolonial Pacific Writing: Representations of the Body.* London: Routledge, 2005. Print.

Meyer, Susan. *Imperialism at Home: Race and Victorian Women's Writing.* Ithaca: Cornell UP, 1996. Print.

Michie, Elsie. "White Chimpanzees and Oriental Despots: Racial Stereotyping and Edward Rochester." In Jane Eyre: *A Case Study in Contemporary Criticism.* Ed. Beth Newman. Boston: Bedford, 1996. 584–98. Print.

Narain, Denise deCaires. *Contemporary Caribbean Women's Poetry: Making Style*. London: Routledge, 2002. Print.

Ni Loingsigh, Aedín. *Postcolonial Eyes: Intercontinental Travel in Francophone African Literature*. Liverpool: Liverpool UP, 2009. Print.

Park, You-Me, and Rajeswari Sunder Rajan, eds. *The Postcolonial Jane Austen*. London: Routledge, 2000. Print.

Plasa, Carl. "Reading 'The Geography of Hunger' in Tsitsi Dangarembga's *Nervous Conditions:* From Frantz Fanon to Charlotte Brontë." *The Journal of Commonwealth Literature* 33 (1998): 33–45.

———. *Textual Politics from Slavery to Postcolonialism: Race and Identification*. New York: St. Martin's, 2000. Print.

Sabin, Margery. *Dissenters and Mavericks: Writings about India in English, 1765–2000*. Oxford: Oxford UP, 2002. Print.

Sharrad, Paul. *Postcolonial Literary History and Indian English Fiction*. Amherst: Cambria, 2008. Print.

Thieme, John. *Postcolonial Contexts: Writing Back to the Canon*. London: Continuum, 2001. Print.

## Postcolonial Readings of *Frankenstein*

Ball, John Clement. "Imperial Monstrosities: *Frankenstein*, the West Indies, and V. S. Naipaul." *Ariel* 32.3 (2001): 31–58. Print.

Cass, Jeffrey. "The Contestatory Gothic in Mary Shelley's *Frankenstein* and J. W. Polidori's *Ernestus Berchtold*: The Spectre of a Colonialist Paradign." *JAISA* 1.2 (Spr. 1996): 33–41. Print.

Lew, Joseph W. "The Deceptive Other: Mary Shelley's Critique of Orientalism in *Frankenstein*." *Studies in Romanticism* 30.2 (Sum. 1991): 255–83. Print.

Malchow, H. R. "Frankenstein's Monster and Images of Race in Nineteenth-Century Literature." *Past and Present* 139.1 (1993): 90–130. Print.

Neff, D. S. "Hostages to Empire: The Anglo-Indian Problem in *Frankenstein, The Curse of Kehama,* and *The Missionary*." *European Romantic Review* 8.4 (Fall 1987): 386–408. Print.

———. "The 'Paradise of the Mothersons': *Frankenstein* and *The Empire of the Nairs*." *Journal of English and German Philology* 95.2 (Apr. 1996): 204–22. Print.

Piper, Karen. "Inuit Diasporas: *Frankenstein* and the Inuit in England." *Romanticism* 13.1 (2007): 63–75. Print.

Spivak, Gayatri Chakravorty. "Three Women's Texts and a Critique
   of Imperialism." *Critical Inquiry* 12.1 (1985): 243–61. Print.
Stock, Paul. "The Shelleys and the Idea of 'Europe'." *European
   Romantic Review* 19.4 (2008): 335–50. Print.

# A POSTCOLONIAL PERSPECTIVE

## ALLAN LLOYD SMITH

### "This Thing of Darkness": Racial Discourse in Mary Shelley's *Frankenstein*

> Prospero: . . . this thing of darkness I / Acknowledge mine
> —SHAKESPEARE, *The Tempest*, Act V

Frankenstein's Creature has been persuasively identified as enmeshed within a variety of contemporaneous discourses, notably feminism or the rights of women, female anxieties in authorship (and Shelley's own experience of births and deaths), or radical discourse on the Rights of Man following from William Godwin's *Political Justice*, perceptions of the condition of the working class, figurations of the unvoiced and dispossessed. Ellen Moers reads *Frankenstein* as a birth myth, lodged in the author's imagination by the fact that she was herself a mother, and containing "the motif of revulsion against newborn life, and the drama of guilt, dread, and flight surrounding birth and its consequences."[1] As Moers admits, however, Mary Shelley's [j]ournal puts emphasis not on her maternity but on her reading: her immersion in the ideas about education, society and morality professed by her father, Godwin, and her mother, Mary Wollstonecraft; but also Humphry Davy on chemistry, Erasmus Darwin on biology; and the discussions of Byron, Shelley and Polidori on mesmerism, electricity and galvanism in relation to the riddle of life. She was "herself the first to point to her fortuitous immersion in the literary and scientific revolutions of her day as the source of *Frankenstein*."[2] Reading the book as a response to Milton's *Paradise*

---

[1] Ellen Moers, *Literary Women*, (1977; London: The Women's Press, 1978), p. 93.
[2] *Ibid.*, p. 94.

*Lost*, as well as to her own motherless condition and guilt over her mother's death immediately after her own birth, Sandra Gilbert and Susan Gubar discuss it as "the fearful tale of a female fall from a lost paradise of art, speech, and autonomy into a hell of sexuality, science, and filthy materiality" in which both Victor, and his monster, play the part of Eve because "for Mary Shelley the part of Eve *is* all the parts."[3] David Punter sees the novel rather as profoundly concerned with injustice, "the society which generated and read Gothic fiction was one which was becoming aware of injustice in a variety of different areas" at the stage when "the bourgeoisie, having to all intents and purposes gained social power, began to try to understand the conditions and history of their own ascent."[4] Kari J. Winter argues that in *Frankenstein* Mary Shelley "attempts to give voice to those people in society who are traditionally removed from the centers of linguistic power, people who are defined as alien, inferior, or monstrous solely because of physical features (such as sex or race) or material conditions (such as poverty)."[5] This raises, if obliquely, the question of race inflections in Shelley's Gothicism that I wish to explore here.

Issues of race and slavery were central to the emergent English culture with which Mary Shelley eagerly engaged. As Paul Gilroy points out, in this culture

> the moral and political problem of slavery loomed large not least because it was once recognised as *internal* to the structure of western civilisation and appeared as a central political and philosophical concept in the emergent discourse of modern English cultural uniqueness. Notions of the primitive and the civilised which had been integral to pre-modern understanding of "ethnic" difference became fundamental cognitive and aesthetic markers in the processes which generated a constellation of subject positions in which Englishness, Christianity, and other ethnic and racialised attributes would finally give way to the dislocating dazzle of "whiteness."[6]

---

[3]Sandra M. Gilbert and Susan Gubar, *The Madwoman in the Attic: The Woman Writer and the Nineteenth-Century Literary Imagination* (1970; New Haven and London: Yale University Press, 1984), pp. 227, 230.

[4]David Punter, *The Literature of Terror: A History of Gothic Fictions from 1765 to the Present Day* (London and New York: Longman, 1980), p. 127.

[5]Kari J. Winter, *Subjects of Slavery, Agents of Change: Women and Power in Gothic Novels and Slave Narratives, 1790–1865* (Athens and London: University of Georgia Press, 1992), p. 51.

[6]Paul Gilroy, *The Black Atlantic: Modernity and Double Consciousness* (London and New York: Verso, 1993), p. 9.

Mary Shelley's youth, her education, and the creation and revision of *Frankenstein* coincided with the great wave of British antislavery agitation that resulted in the abolition of the slave trade in 1807, and ultimately emancipation in 1833. Although governmental suppression of popular politics in the 1790s prevented large-scale public agitations such as mass meetings and petitionings until 1814, when these re-emerged (again over slavery),[7] it is evident that so significant and pressing an issue, with all its inherent implications for the rights of man, would profoundly register in the consciousness of one with Mary Shelley's lineage and inclinations. So too, of course, would an awareness of violent slave insurrections, such as the Haitian rebellion of San Domingo in the 1790s. A small but telling pointer to this awareness is the refusal of Mary and Shelley to use sugar because it came from the West Indian plantations.[8]

In fact references to race and slavery echo throughout the novel: "if no man allowed any pursuit whatsoever to interfere with the tranquility of his domestic affections, Greece had not been enslaved" (37), without unsullied descent and riches a man was considered as "a vagabond and a slave, doomed to waste his powers for the profit of the chosen few" (99), "mine shall not be the submission of abject slavery" (123), "the whole period during which I was the slave of my creature" (132), "For an instant I dared to shake off my chains . . . but the iron had eaten into my flesh" (139), "a race of devils would be propagated upon the earth" (144), "I was the slave, not the master of an impulse" (195), "the prospect of that day when, enfranchised from my miserable slavery" (1831: p. 134).[9] Such frequent references, although usually metaphorical, indicate how far the rhetoric of control and submission permeated Shelley's literary culture and thus signal the need for a closer attention to the thematics of race and slavery in the text in order to consider how *Frankenstein* can be related to contemporary discourses on race, slavery and antislavery.

---

[7] See, e.g., James Walvin, "British Popular Sentiment for Abolition" in Christine Bolt and Seymour Drescher, eds, *Anti-Slavery, Religion and Reform* (Chatham: Dawson Archon, 1980), p. 153 and passim.

[8] About which Thomas Peacock satirised them in *Melincourt*, as Miranda Seymour points out in her biography, *Mary Shelley* (London: John Murray, Picador, 2000), p. 138.

[9] Mary Shelley, *Frankenstein*, ed. by Marilyn Butler (text of 1818 with 1831 variants; London: William Pickering, 1993). Parenthetical references in this sentence are taken from this edition. Future references are to this edition, except for those prefaced with the date 1831, which are to this Bedford edition.

## MONSTROUSNESS

Gilbert and Gubar read the novel as inflected by *Paradise Lost*, and the Creature himself as resonant of Eve (and behind her, the figure of Sin). But the hyper-masculinity of the Monster (a creature "emphatically male in gender and prowess" as William Veeder observes)[10] suggests a different originary figure, Caliban, the enslaved native of the island in *The Tempest*, a vengeful "thing of darkness" having "a certain crude tenderness and heavy grace of expression"[11] but never to be trusted. "I have used thee / Filth as thou art, with human care . . . , till thou didst seek to violate / The honour of my child," says Prospero.[12] Echoing Prospero's term the Creature says of himself: "my form is a filthy type of yours, more horrid even from the very resemblance" (109). Certainly *not* used with any human care by Frankenstein, the Creature arguably has juster cause of resentment of his creator, the magician of science, than Caliban of his master Prospero. Other echoes of *The Tempest* may be relevant. Miranda says to Caliban "Abhorred slave / Which any print of goodness wilt not take, / Being capable of all ill! . . . " (I: 354–6), and "Thy vile race / Though thou didst learn, had that in't which good natures / Could not abide to be with" (I: 359–62). Prospero calls him "A devil, a born devil, on whose nature / Nurture can never stick . . . " (IV: 188–9), just as Frankenstein says of his Creature: "He is eloquent and persuasive . . . but trust him not. His soul is as hellish as his form, full of treachery and fiend-like malice" (184). Caliban, according to Frank Kermode, represents the natural man. But this figure is not, as in pastoral, a virtuous shepherd but what the "Names of the Actors" describes as "a savage and deformed slave." His name may be a derivative of "Carib," meaning a savage inhabitant of the New World, or it may be an anagram of cannibal. It may have an echo of *cauliban*, a Romany word meaning blackness. His deformity may also be related to reports from the West Indies of "curious specimens" of humanity.[13] Whether or not Caliban is black, he is definitely of mixed origins, being

[10] William Veeder, *Mary Shelley and Frankenstein: The Fate of Androgyny* (Chicago and London: University of Chicago Press, 1986), p. 91.

[11] Leo Marx, *The Machine in the Garden* (London, Oxford and New York: Oxford University Press, 1967), pp. 59, 60.

[12] William Shakespeare, *The Tempest*, Act I, ll. 347–50. Further references to the play are given in parentheses in the text. This also resonates with Victor Frankenstein's "workshop of filthy creation," Shelley, *Frankenstein*, p. 58.

[13] Frank Kermode ed., William Shakespeare, *The Tempest*, The Arden Shakespeare (London: Methuen, 1970), pp. xxxviii, xxxix.

the offspring of a devil, possibly Setebos, and a "foul witch," the "hag"
Sycorax.

When the Creature is first animated, Frankenstein describes him
thus:

> His limbs were in proportion, and I had selected his features as
> beautiful. Beautiful!—Great God! His yellow skin scarcely
> covered the work of muscles and arteries beneath; his hair was
> of a lustrous black, and flowing; his teeth of a pearly whiteness;
> but these luxuriances only formed a more horrid contrast with
> his watery eyes, that seemed almost of the same colour as the
> dun white sockets in which they were set, his shrivelled complex-
> ion, and straight black lips. (38)

Such features are, as David A. Hedrich Hirsch points out, "commonly
encountered in colonial depictions of Asian, Indian, and African 'sav-
ages'."[14] The description positions the Creature within the relays of racial
discourse popularized in the seventeenth century and persistent throughout the eighteenth, whereby the racial other was identified as grotesque and of a lower order. In "Hostages to Empire: The Anglo-Indian
Problem in *Frankenstein, The Curse of Kehama,* and *The Missionary,*"
D. S. Neff suggests that Shelley may have been working with models of
monstrousness and racial otherness derived in some part from the colonial experience of British India. In India interracial sexual partnerships
were first approved but later denounced by the East India Company; and
the Anglo-Indian offspring of such liaisons were extensively employed
but later debarred from officer rank by the Company (1791) and subsequently, as fears regarding their loyalty increased, from all service in
the British army (1808).[15] Neff is persuasive regarding the Creature's
colonial "primal scene" of self-recognition, in which "the dark-skinned
individual's irredeemable otherness is pressed home so completely and
forcibly that identification with the dominant race is rendered impossible" (399).

David Brion Davis notes that "despite the ancient belief in the fixed
distinctiveness of species, the equally ancient belief in continuity suggested the likelihood of infinite gradations between each form of animal

---

[14]David A. Hedrich Hirsch, "Liberty, Equality, Monstrosity: Revolutionizing the
Family in Mary Shelley's *Frankenstein,*" in Jeffrey Jerome Cohen, ed., *Monster Theory:
Reading Culture* (Minneapolis and London: University of Minnesota Press, 1996), p. 118.
[15]D. S. Neff, "The Anglo-Indian Problem in *Frankenstein, The Curse of Kehama,*
and *The Missionary,*" *European Romantic Review* (Fall 1997) 8.4, 386–408. Further references to this essay are given in parentheses in the text.

life."[16] The Hottentots were seen in the late seventeenth century as being close to the apes, physically grotesque and displaying brutish customs along with their bestial appearance. Subsequent claims, by Anton Leeuwenhoek for example, held that the blood of negroes was different from that of whites. Mary Shelley's [j]ournal records that in December 1814 she read Mungo Park's *Travels in Africa*, a book that described examples of violence and savagery among African people.[17] The eighteenth- and early nineteenth-century emergence of biological science, making it clear that man was part of the animal kingdom and "structurally and functionally so like the ape that no sharp distinctions could be made,"[18] served to confirm such thinking. Shelley's monster belongs with such formulations not because he is actually black, being in fact composed of a promiscuous intermixture of Bavarian human and animal body parts,[19] but because of his grotesque ugliness, superhuman animal powers, and the animal/human taint of miscegenation involved in his creation, entirely the opposite of a pure line of descent. Shelley chose not to give her scientist the arguably more straightforward route of reanimation of a dead human body; her choice of an assemblage of various human and animal parts introduces the issues attached to cross-racial and even cross-species reproduction and thus engages with the anthropological and biological discourses outlined above:

> I was, besides, endued with a figure hideously deformed and loathsome; I was not even of the same nature as man. I was more agile than they, and could subsist upon coarser diet; I bore the extremes of heat and cold with less injury to my frame; my stature far exceeded theirs.When I looked around I saw and heard of none like me. Was I then a monster, a blot upon the earth, from which all men fled, and whom all men disowned? (99–100)

Even the Creature's ability to withstand pain is in keeping with a popular misconception of the period. The Dahomeans, for example,

---

[16]David Brion Davis, *The Problem of Slavery in Western Culture* (1966; Oxford and New York: Oxford University Press, 1988), p. 454.

[17]Frederick Jones, ed., *Mary Shelley's Journal* (Norman: University of Oklahoma Press, 1947), pp. 29, 33, 71. Mungo Park, *Travels in the Interior Districts of Africa*, 2 vols (London: 1799); *Journal of a Mission to the Interior of Africa, in the Year 1805* (London 1815), read by Mary Shelley in 1816.

[18]Davis, *The Problem of Slavery in Western Culture*, p. 455

[19]Frankenstein describes this use of animal as well as human parts: "I dabbled among the unhallowed damps of the grave, or tortured the living animal to animate the lifeless clay. . . . The dissecting room and the slaughter-house furnished many of my materials" (p. 58).

"assumed a mask of insensitivity in the face of trials, thinking that self-pity in any form would only invite further troubles. To the European, however, this cultural trait often appeared as evidence of unfeeling animality."[20] Aphra Behn's story of the noble Oroonoko, stoic even in torture and calmly smoking a pipe during his martyrdom, became a legend of the eighteenth-century stage, and even as late as 1767 it was reported in the *London Magazine* that Jamaican slaves "smiled contemptuously while being burned alive."[21] But the debate had its other side: Behn's Oroonoko was portrayed as admirable, heroic, and passionate in defence of freedom, and, in the stage version that played nearly every season for a full century, only reluctantly driven into revolt. This tradition continued in the large number of plays and poems that later celebrated Toussaint L'Ouverture, the leader of . . . Haiti's San Domingo Revolution. The nobility and sensitivity of the Creature makes it apparent which side of this debate Mary Shelley would take; he is so sympathetically presented that despite his atrocious crimes, many readers have shared the view expressed by Kari J. Winter, that although the monster may be borne away by the dark waves, his remaining alive as the novel ends "leaves us with a faint hope that at some future time he will find a voice and place in the world."[22]

## THE AUTODIDACT

The extraordinary mental capacities of the Creature enable him to learn to speak and to read, merely by his covert observation of the De Lacey family. Denied knowledge by his master he is forced to learn language and literacy in secret just as the West Indian and American slaves, denied access to knowledge because of fears of organized insurrection, were forced to find their covert education as they might, whether by help from a sympathetic mistress, from fellow slaves, or in secret religious assemblies. Like the slaves, too, he has no name of his own. Unknown to the family, the Creature eavesdrops on the language instruction of Safie: "My days were spent in close attention, that I might more speedily master the language; and I may boast that I improved more rapidly than the Arabian, who understood very little, and conversed in broken accents, whilst I comprehended and could imitate almost every

[20]Davis, *The Problem of Slavery in Western Culture*, p. 468.
[21]*London Magazine*, XXXVI (1767), 258; quoted in Davis, *The Problem of Slavery in Western Culture*, p. 477.
[22]Winter, *Subjects of Slavery, Agents of Change*, p. 145.

word that was spoken" (98). He also benefits from the Jacobinite book Felix reads to Safie, Volney's *Ruins of Empires,* which gives him an overview of the history of empires, and a revelatory understanding of humankind:

> These wonderful narrations inspired me with strange feelings. Was man, indeed, at once so powerful, so virtuous, and magnificent, yet so vicious and base? He appeared at one time as a mere scion of the evil principle, and at another as all that can be conceived of noble and godlike. . . . Of my creation and creator I was absolutely ignorant; but I knew that I possessed no money, no friends, no kind of property. (99)

The realization of his "otherness" or rather "othering" comes with the acquisition of cultural knowledge in a model of coming-to-consciousness and disproof of assumed innate incapacity that is a regular element of the slave narrative: "the correlation of freedom with literacy . . . became the central trope of the slave narratives."[23] His realization is then painfully confirmed by the revulsion of the De Lacey family when they discover him. Before this moment of catastrophe, the Creature positions himself much as a domestic slave or "house-nigger," admiring but invisible, like Caliban a provider of wood for the household who neither see him nor can afford to recognize him when he risks [asking] their assistance. Until that point, the family has mystified his gifts as those of some helpful spirit, much as slaveholders indulged in the mystification that their bound servants were loyally devoted to their own welfare. When the veil finally drops, the Creature seeks revenge, burning the house in insurrectionary fashion: "I lighted the dry branch of a tree, and danced with fury around the devoted cottage . . . I waved my brand . . . with a loud scream fired the straw, and heath, and bushes, which I had collected" (117). Still not yet fully committed to rebellion, the Creature saves a child from drowning, to be rewarded not by gratitude but by a bullet from her parent. Only then does he instigate his regime of terror, killing little William and implicating the innocent Justine in the murder. "I too, can create desolation; my enemy is not impregnable; this death will carry despair to him, and a thousand other miseries shall torment and destroy him" (121). This contrasts strongly with his initial disposition: "I am thy creature, and I will be even mild

---

[23] Henry Louis Gates, *Figures In Black: Words, Signs and the "Racial" Self* (New York and Oxford: Oxford University Press, 1987), p. 108.

and docile to my natural lord and king, if thou wilt also perform thy part, the which thou owest me" (80).[24]

The narrative shape of the Creature's account of himself is akin to that of the slave narrative. It begins with the innocence of early life: "a gentle light stole over the heavens and gave me a sensation of pleasure. I started up, and beheld a radiant form rise from among the trees. I gazed with a kind of wonder" (83). He discovers that "a pleasant sound, which often saluted my ears, proceeded from the throats of the little winged creatures who had often intercepted the light from my eyes" (83), and proceeds, through self-positioning as in effect a plantation house-slave identifying with the family ("he found his store always replenished by an invisible hand" [93]), to limited self-recognition: "I had admired the perfect forms of my cottagers—their grace, beauty, and delicate complexions: but how was I terrified, when I viewed myself in a transparent pool!" (93). Self-education leads to an increasing historical and political awareness before ill treatment develops his consciousness of personal wrong and alienation: "No father had watched my infant days, no mother had blessed me with smiles and caresses; or if they had, all my past life was now a blot, a blind vacancy in which I distinguished nothing. . . .What was I?" (100, 101). The Creature's condition at this point seems to anticipate the insights of later authors of slave narratives such as the American Frederick Douglass:

> there are special reasons why I should write my own biography . . . Not only is slavery on trial, but unfortunately, the enslaved people are also on trial. It is alleged, that they are, naturally, inferior; that they are so low in the scale of humanity, and utterly stupid, that they are unconscious of their wrongs, and do not apprehend their rights.[25]

Douglass further points out that "The white children could tell their ages, I could not" and "I do not remember ever to have met a slave who could tell of his birthday." Slaves, in Henry Louis Gates's words, "stand outside of the calendar."[26] Mary Prince, an early author of a slave autobiography (1831), provides another narrative that can be "intertextually" related to Shelley's account. In "The Two Marys (Prince and Shelley)," Helena Woodard argues that despite its predated composition,

---

[24]The slave's master, of course, was very often his natural father also.

[25]Frederick Douglass, *My Bondage and My Freedom* (1985; Urbana: University of Illinois Press, 1987), p. 4

[26]Gates, *Figures In Black*, p. 90

Shelley's artistic invention can be seen as "an ironic reading of Prince's *actual existence* as an enslaved black woman."[27]

In fact, to further pursue the analogy with later theorists of race, the Monster exists in a state of "double consciousness" like that famously described by W. E. B. Du Bois: "One ever feels his twoness, — an American, a Negro; two souls, two thoughts, two unreconciled strivings; two warring ideals in one dark body."[28] Both within and outside the culture of the De Laceys (or of his creator), the Creature necessarily develops a schizophrenic sense of himself. His fall into self-awareness leads to the recognition of a need for politicised self-assertion, revenge, and autonomy, just as the defining moment of the slave narrative is an assertion of the rights of the self against the wrongs of the slave-holding system, followed by the physical search for freedom in the trajectory of flight, running away, pursued by the Master or his agents. The Creature's flight (into the frozen North, prophetic of the nineteenth-century experience of American slaves escaping to North America and Canada) fulfils this pattern.

*The Interesting Narrative of the Life of Olaudah Equiano, or Gustavus Vassa the African, Written by Himself* was first published in 1789 in London, with an American edition in 1791. An indication of its wide influence is that within five years it went through eight more editions, and was again reprinted in the nineteenth century.[29] Mary Shelley's [j]ournal makes no mention of it but she could have read this well-known autobiography before 1814, when the [j]ournal entries begin. Kidnapped by slavers from his Ibo home in Nigeria, the child Equiano "had remarked where the sun rose in the morning, and set in the evening as I travelled along; and I had observed that my father's house was towards the rising of the sun" (17). His simplicity of mind and observation leads him to expect that he will be eaten, and to believe that the slavers' ships are worked by magic rather than simply sails and anchor: "the white men had some spell or magic they put in the water when

---

[27] Helena Woodard, "The Two Marys (Prince and Shelley) on the Textual Meeting Ground of Race, Gender, and Genre," in Dolan Hubbard, ed., *Recovered Writers/ Recovered Texts, Tennessee Studies in Literature*, Vol. 38 (Knoxville, Tennessee: University of Tennessee, 1997), pp. 15–30 at p. 16 (author's italics).

[28] W. E. B. Du Bois, *The Souls of Black Folk* (1903) in Paul Lauter, ed., *The Heath Anthology of American Literature*, Vol. 2 (Boston: Houghton Mifflin Company, 2002), p. 946.

[29] *The Interesting Narative of the Life of Olaudah Equiano, or Gustavus Vassa the African, Written by Himself*, ed. Paul Edwards (Harlow: Longman, 1992), p. 183. Subsequent quotations are taken from this edition. Page numbers will be given in parentheses in the text.

they liked, in order to stop the vessel" (24). Like the Creature he finds great sadness in having no one with whom he is able to converse, is horrified by man's inhumanity and, poignantly, is betrayed yet again into slavery by his master, after years of service in England and as a British sailor: "Thus, at the moment I expected all my toils to end, was I plunged, as I supposed, in a new slavery; in comparison of which all my service hitherto had been 'perfect freedom;' and whose horrors, always present to my mind, now rushed on it with tenfold aggravation" (60). In other respects, too, some correspondences with *Frankenstein* may be noted: his desire to learn to read and write and to understand navigation, a journey to Turkey (Safie is Turkish), and a richly described expedition to the polar regions when his ship is trapped in the ice. Equiano's descriptions of slavery atrocities became widely known and were important in the British Antislavery movement. It was a report by him, for example, that led to publicity for the infamous *Zong* affair, in which 130 manacled slaves [were] thrown overboard [so the ship's owner could] claim insurance money (Preface, x, xxxvi).

But Equiano's *Narrative* is also pertinent to *Frankenstein* in another, perhaps less easily recognized way: it amounts to a life-long meditation on the responsibilities of masters and those who serve them. Equiano refuses, for example, to gain his freedom dishonestly, as he sees it, when he has the opportunity to escape at Guadeloupe (and this even after he has been re-impressed into slavery and sold again!), insisting instead on saving up his earnings through small trade and eventually buying his freedom. But even when free, he is constantly engaged in a search for suitable masters (and just as often seems to be swindled by them). The eighteenth century world is even imaginatively a culture of masters and servants, and Equiano often reflects that freedom for a black is so perilous as to be hardly worth having, since there is no legal redress for black people in the West Indies or, it would seem, in America, at least in Georgia or at Charles Town. The best that he can hope for is to find a reliable master, and become to him an invaluable servant. Like the Creature, he feels strongly the terms of this compact and is both hurt and outraged when it is so frequently broken.

A curious parallel between *Frankenstein* and the generality of later slave narratives is structural: just as the slave narrative used dominant cultural endorsement as a framing device—usually a preface attesting that the narrative could be relied upon as the original work of its author— so does *Frankenstein* offer the attestation of Frankenstein himself as to the veracity of the Creature's narrative, and Walton performs as a surrogate for the sceptical but ultimately convinced readership. Such parallels may of course be pushed too far: the embedded narratives of *Frankenstein* doubtless have more to do with the Gothic tradition, well established before 1816, than future publishing imperatives [for] enabling the acceptance of black authors by a predominantly white audience. Similarly, the Creature's narrative may be as much explained by reference to Rousseau's *Confessions*—or even the popular genre of penny confessions by condemned criminals—as by its resonance with the slave narratives that followed shortly after. And yet, if we consider the cultural subtexts of Mary Shelley's imaginative investigation of what it might mean to be a disenfranchised, unacknowledged, and spurned member of the human race, the implication of some racially inflected dimension surely becomes inescapable. In another context Diderot uses a revealing metaphor: the writer "carries the torch to the back of the cave . . . He blows upon the glorious phantom who presents himself at the entrance of the cave; and the hideous Moor whom he was masking reveals himself."[30] For later American and West Indian slaves, the possession of a voice, and of literacy, was a disproof of Enlightenment assumptions that, as for Hegel, blacks had no history and no true self-consciousness, and lay "veiled in a shroud of silence, invisible not because they had no face, but rather because they had no voice . . . the blackness of invisibility is the blackness of this silence."[31] The Creature's assertion of his literacy, and his human sensitivity, is emblematic of the breaking down of such boundary assumptions.

## THE MASTER AND THE SLAVE

The Creature is terrifying, Hirsch asserts, "not merely in his physical otherness but more profoundly in his call for recognition as a humane, if not also human, being" becoming monstrous by "undermining determinations of membership within *le genre humain* that depend on familial status (and, by extension, racial or national membership)."[32] Frankenstein's denial of his humanity, repeated by the De Laceys and the rescued child's parents, echoes the larger cultural denial of full humanity to African slaves, a convenient and even necessary justification for their bondage and mistreatment. Again, reference to *The Tempest* is illuminating. At the end of the play, Prospero says of Caliban: "this thing of darkness I /

---

[30] Diderot, responding to Richardson's *Clarissa*, quoted by Henry Louis Gates, *Figures In Black*, p. 105.

[31] *Ibid.*, p. 104.

[32] Hirsch, "Liberty, Equality, Monstrosity," p. 118.

Acknowledge mine" (V: 275–6). The initial action of *Frankenstein* is driven by Frankenstein's determination *not* to acknowledge the Creature as his own, and its conclusion by the obsessive realisation that nevertheless he *must* do so. The intertwining of master and Creature echoes Hegel's formulation of the entanglement of mastery and slavery wherein the identity of the master is seen as bound to the consciousness of his slave or bondsman. The bondsman has power over the master by refusing him autonomy and forcing him into psychological dependence. Paradoxically, then, the slave has a greater awareness of freedom, whereas the master is only conscious of his need for control and mastery:

> The truth of the independent consciousness is accordingly the consciousness of the bondsman . . . Just as lordship showed its essential nature to be the reverse of what it wants to be, so, too, bondage will, when completed, pass into the opposite of what it immediately is: being a consciousness repressed within itself, it will enter into itself, and change round into real and true independence.[33]

Ultimately, the self-assertion of the Creature, his coming to consciousness of the power relations between himself and Frankenstein, makes him the more autonomous of the two; and it is he who enables and directs Frankenstein's pursuit of him, leaving supplies for his master: "Slave, I before reasoned with you, but you have proved yourself unworthy of my condescension," says the Creature, in a reversal of the terms of bondage that shows how the discourse of slavery in the novel is more than metaphorical, "You are my creator, but I am your master;— obey!"(145).

## THE DENIAL OF SEXUALITY

Like the slave, the Creature is denied control and fulfilment in sexuality. Slave families were routinely broken up, wives and children sold on (marriage or sustained parenting was rarely permitted as domestic relations interfered with the economic flexibility of the institution). The Creature's entirely reasonable request for a partner like himself is refused by Frankenstein: "a race of devils would be propagated upon the earth, who might make the very existence of the species of man a condition precarious and full of terror" (144).

---

[33]G.W. F. Hegel, *The Phenomenology of Mind* (1807), trans. J. B. Baille (1910; New York: Harper and Row, 1967), pp. 234–47 at p. 241.

A related theme, the supposed insatiable desire of black men for white women, is also strongly hinted. When the Creature kills the child William, he finds a medallion of Frankenstein's mother, a

> portrait of a most lovely woman. In spite of my malignity, it softened and attracted me. For a few moments I gazed with delight on her dark eyes, fringed by deep lashes, and her lovely lips; but presently my rage returned: I remembered that I was forever deprived of the delights that such beautiful creatures could bestow; and that she whose resemblance I contemplated would, in regarding me, have changed that air of divine benignity to one expressive of disgust and affright. (121)

When he encounters Justine, he reiterates this: "Here, I thought, is one of those whose smiles are bestowed on all but me; she shall not escape . . ." (122). The Creature does not rape or sexually assault Justine, although Gilbert and Gubar rightly see a "sinister rape fantasy" in the 1831 revision: "Awake, fairest, thy lover is near—he who would give his life but to obtain one look of affection from thine eyes," and, "not I, but she shall suffer: the murder I have committed because I am for ever robbed of all that she could give me, she shall atone. The crime had its source in her: be hers the punishment" (p. 127).[34] The death of Elizabeth, Frankenstein's bride, similarly arouses echoes of dominant cultural anxieties and rape fantasies about white women and black men:

> She was there, lifeless and inanimate, thrown across the bed, her head hanging down, and her pale and distorted features half covered by her hair. Everywhere I turn I see the same figure— her bloodless arms and relaxed form flung by the murderer on its bridal bier. (p. 167)

At the open window the fiend grins as he jeers and points towards the corpse. Most pertinently, Mary Shelley's 1831 revisions intensified Elizabeth's Saxon racial features as the flower of white girlhood, contrasting with the other children (the "dark-eyed, hardy little vagrants") when she is first encountered; no longer as in the first edition simply beautiful and hazel-eyed, she significantly becomes, in the 1831 version,

> very fair. Her hair was the brightest living gold, and, despite the poverty of her clothing, seemed to set a crown of distinction on her head. Her brow was clear and ample, her blue eyes cloudless, and her lips and the moulding of her face so expressive of

---

[34]Gilbert and Gubar, *The Madwoman in the Attic*, p. 244.

sensibility and sweetness, that none could behold her without
looking on her as of a distinct species, a being heaven-sent, and
bearing a celestial stamp in all her features. (p. 42)

The perfect victim then, in H. L. Malchow's terms, of "the construction of both race and a vulnerable femininity,"[35] and more than merely,
as Elizabeth Bohls describes her, exemplary of the Victorian "Angel in
the House."[36] Bohls argues that *Frankenstein* "indicts aesthetics as an
inherently imperial discourse, structured by principles of hierarchy and
exclusion," and that it "binds together a little community, a microcosm
of polite British society, marred by its subordination of women and
colonization of non-European peoples" (34); and there is undeniably a
relation between eighteenth-century aesthetics and racialist constructions of beauty or ugliness. But H. L. Malchow takes the argument in a
more productive direction by showing how *Frankenstein* is in part a
product of racialist politics and contemporary history.

## REVENGE, ATROCITY, AND INSURRECTION

The extreme violence of the Creature's revenges upon Frankenstein,
his selection of innocent child or female victims, his deep malignity in
engineering Justine's wrongful conviction and execution, his attack on
the loyal friend of his master, Clerval, presents something of a conun-
drum in assessing the reader-response position that Mary Shelley may
seem to imply. The Creature's mistreatment by the humans, his evident
grasp of intellect, his remarkable sensitivity, his ability in all this in effect
to become human, all these conflict with his willingness to institute a
reign of terror. The excesses of the French Revolution, as a mausoleum
of worthy and humane intentions, may inform these choices.

In the terms established in the above set of correspondences, however, it may be that the San Domingo Rebellion after 1791 could also
underlie Shelley's investigation of the limits of readerly sympathy or
alienation. The Haitian Revolution in effect extended the principles of
the French Revolution, and also held explicit parallels with the American

---

[35] H. L. Malchow, "Frankenstein's Monster and Images of Race in Nineteenth-
Century Britain," *Past and Present*, 139 (May 1993), p. 112. See also *Gothic Images of
Race in Nineteenth Century Britain* (Stanford: Stanford University Press, 1996), for an
extended account of these arguments.

[36] Elizabeth A. Bohls, "Standards of Taste, Discourses of 'Race', and the Aesthetic
Education of a Monster: Critique of Empire in *Frankenstein*," *Eighteenth-Century Life*,
18 (November 1994), p. 26.

Revolution, with its justification of necessary violence in pursuit of free-dom. But as Eric Sundquist says, "Haiti came to seem the fearful pre-cursor of black rebellion throughout the New World, becoming an entrenched part of master-class ideology in both Latin America and the United States."[37] The Revolution of course raised the issue of what level of violence was justifiable and necessary in the pursuit of laudable aims. San Domingo served as model both for abolitionists, who argued that the Haitians had but seized the same rights as the Americans shortly before them, but also for pro-slavery forces, who claimed that it had led to carnage and degeneration, a foretaste of bloody revenge at the hands of the slaves. "Like a prism, the trope of San Domingo reflected all con-flicting sides of the tangled question of bondage and became a prophetic simulacrum of events feared to lie on the horizon of American slavery."[38] Its initial leader, Toussaint L'Ouverture, was widely acclaimed by aboli-tonists as a dignified and noble leader of a righteous cause, becoming "a key mythic figure in the war on slavery."[39] But such were the horrors and fears unleashed by the conflict that even the well-known South American revolutionary Fransisco Miranda would write in 1798: "as much as I desire the liberty and independence of the New World, I fear the anar-chy of a revolutionary system. God forbid that these beautiful countries become, as St Domingue, a theatre of blood and crime under the pre-text of establishing liberty."[40] Toussaint's successor, the infamous Jean-Jacques Dessalines, became the model for black terror. Sundquist quotes from Mary Hassal's *Secret History: or, the Horrors of St Domingo* (1808), the story of a young white woman who refused one of Dessa-line's men: "The monster gave her to his guard, who hung her by the throat on an iron hook in the market place, where the lovely, innocent, unfortunate victim slowly expired."[41]

Such were the horrors popularly linked to black insurrection, and inferentially associated with the Monster's remorseless quest for auton-omy and vegeance. Shelley, then, might be seen to be presenting both sides of the issue: sympathetic to the Monster, but also registering shock and horror at his however justifiable excesses. Doubtless she had not read Mary Hassal's *Secret History*, but she would have been aware of similar accounts of the events; certainly her Journal records that both

---

[37] Eric J. Sundquist, *To Wake the Nations: Race in the Making of American Literature* (Cambridge and London: Harvard University Press, 1993), p. 32.
[38] *Ibid.*, p. 32.
[39] *Ibid.*, p. 34.
[40] Quoted in *Ibid.*, p. 142.
[41] Quoted in *ibid.*, p. 145.

she and Percy Shelley read Bryan Edwards'*History of the West Indies* (1793) in December 1814,[42] a book that discussed differences of race and color and the horror of the slave rebellions, and described the "Carribees" of the West Indies as unnaturally cruel and violent, however peaceful and affectionate among themselves:

> it serves in some degree to lessen the indignation which a good mind necessarily feels at the abuses of power by the Whites, to observe that the Negroes themselves, when invested with command, give full play to their revengeful passions, and exercise all the wantonness of cruelty without restraint or remorse.

He also described a slave rebellion in which they surrounded the overseer's house about four in the morning, in which eight or ten White people were in bed, every one of whom they butchered in the most savage manner, and literally drank their blood mixed with rum . . . then set fire to the buildings. In one morning they murdered between thirty and forty Whites, not sparing even infants at the breast.[43]

Henry Dundas, speaking in the House of Commons in 1796, justified the use of bloodhounds in hunting down Negroes in Jamaica, claiming that "The Maroons were accustomed to descend from their fastnesses at midnight, and commit the most dreadful ravages and cruelties upon the wives, children, and property of the inhabitants, burning and destroying every place which they attacked, and murdering all who unfortunately became the objects of their fury."[44]

## THIS THING OF DARKNESS I / ACKNOWLEDGE MINE

Shelley's novel ends among the dazzling whiteness of the arctic wastes, where, after his futile pursuit, Frankenstein dies and the Creature proposes to immolate himself at the northernmost point. At some level this white-out refers implicitly to the failure and inability of the

---

[42] Bryan Edwards, *The History, Civil and Commercial, of the British Colonies in the West Indies*, 2 vols. (Dublin: 1793), noted in Frederick Jones, ed., *Mary Shelley's Journal*, pp. 31, 32.

[43] See historian H. L. Malchow's very useful account of this context in "Frankenstein's Monster and Images of Race in Nineteenth-Century Britain," pp. 107, 110, here quoting Edwards, *The History, Civil and Commercial, of the British Colonies in the West Indies*, Vol. 1, pp. 33–36, and Vol. 2, p. 74.

[44] Quoted in Malchow, "Frankenstein's Monster and Images of Race in Nineteenth-Century Britain," p. 108

dominant culture to find a place for the other; it is literally a pyrrhic victory in which the self-delusion of the urge for dominance and control has been exposed. The chastened explorer Walton will abandon his quest for mastery and glory and set sail for domestic tranquility; but the issues entangled in Shelley's discourse of master and slave, power and freedom, and the Rights (and obligations) of Man most broadly conceived, reverberate on.

One of the implications of a repositioning of the Creature and his maker within the terms of contemporaneous racial discourse is that what amounts to a critical consensus on the relation between Creature and Creator needs to be reconsidered. Rosemary Jackson puts the prevailing view effectively when she says that

> the monster confronts Frankenstein as his own body in pieces . . . What drives the narrative . . . is a strong desire to be unified with this "other" side. The monster *is* Frankenstein's lost selves, pieces of himself from which he has been severed, and with which he seeks re-unification, hence his reluctance to kill it. Their relationship is one of love-hatred, and it becomes increasingly exclusive. They have no existence apart from one another.[45]

This reading is generated by the Creature's own description of himself as "a filthy type of yours" (109), and by Frankenstein's self-blame for the catastrophes that he has set in motion: "my own spirit let loose from the grave, and forced to destroy all that was dear to me" (57).[46] Moers' reading of the novel as a birth myth and Gilbert and Gubar's sense of the creature as a version of its female author similarly assume the appropriateness of a psychoanalytical interpretation that sees the Creature as an aspect of its creator/s. These versions all point to the idea that the atrocities committed by the Creature are in some sense the fulfilment of Frankenstein's deepest wishes. But there is no evidence of such deeper drives in Frankenstein [beyond] what has been inferred through the actions of the Monster: in effect, if he does it, and his maker feels responsible and guilty, it is argued that Frankenstein himself must have wished it. In fact, however, Frankenstein's complex feelings of guilt and responsibility are neither singular nor surprising. Elizabeth too, for example, on learning of the death of William, exclaims "Oh God! I have murdered my darling" (53). Her outcry is explained by her having allowed William to wear the valuable miniature, for which he seems to

---

[45] Rosemary Jackson, *Fantasy* (London: Methuen, 1981) p. 100.
[46] *Ibid.*, p. 99.

have been murdered. Frankenstein *is* responsible for the actions of his Creature, just as a slaveholder would be held responsible for the actions of his slaves, but he need no more be understood as wishing for those actions than a slaveholder would wish for atrocities committed against his family in an uprising. The "Other" is connected to the self here not as part of the self but in a symbiosis of power relations bearing with it responsibility. The Creature's tortured sense of difference-within-resemblance similarly locates him not in relation to the individual psychology of Frankenstein but to the eighteenth-century debates over cross-racial resemblance and difference. And Frankenstein's sense that he has loosed a vampire of his own spirit into the world is qualified with "nearly" to stress its figurative meaning:

> I considered the being whom I had cast among mankind, and endowed with the will and power to effect purposes of horror, such as the deed which he had now done, *nearly* in the light of my own vampire, my own spirit let loose from the grave, and forced to destroy all that was dear to me. (57, italics added)[47]

In that their vicious practices could and sometimes did generate a cruel revenge by the oppressed, those who maintained racial superiority and subordination of the racial "Other" *were* responsible for slave atrocities without in any sense wishing for that outcome. Frankenstein's protestations of anger, remorse, and vengefulness, like the Creature's, may be read as they are uttered, enmeshed — as so often in the Gothic — within a contemporary web of discourses on rights, justice, responsibilities, and otherness.

## WORKS CITED

Bohls, Elizabeth. "Standards of Taste, Discourses of 'Race,' and the Aesthetic Education of a Monster: Critique of Empire in *Frankenstein*." *Eighteenth-Century Life* 18.3 (Nov. 1994): 23–36. Print.

Davis, David Brion. *The Problem of Slavery in Western Culture*. 1966. Oxford: Oxford UP, 1988. Print.

Douglass, Frederick. *My Bondage and My Freedom*. 1855. Urbana: U of Illinois P, 1987.

Dubois, W. E. B. "The Souls of Black Folk." *Heath Anthology of American Literature*. Ed. Paul Lauter. 4th ed. 2 vols. Boston: Houghton Mifflin, 2002. 2:922–66. Print.

[47] It is perhaps also possible to read here an echo of West Indian voodoo practices.

Equiano, Olaudah. *The Interesting Narrative of the Life of Olaudah Equiano, or Gustavas Vassa the African, Written by Himself.* Ed. Paul Edwards. Harlow: Longman, 1992. Print.

Gates, Henry Louis. *Figures in Black: Words, Signs, and the "Racial" Self.* New York: Oxford UP, 1987.

Gilbert, Sandra M., and Susan Gubar. *The Madwoman in the Attic: The Woman Writer and the Nineteenth-Century Literary Imagination.* 1978. New Haven: Yale UP, 1984. Print.

Gilroy, Paul. *The Black Atlantic: Modernity and Double Consciousness.* London: Verso, 1993. Print.

Hegel, G. F. W. *The Phenomenology of Mind.* 1807. Trans J. B. Baille. 1910. New York: Harper & Row, 1967. Print.

Hirsch, Charles A. Hedrich. "Liberty, Equality, Monstrosity: Revolutionizing the Family in Mary Shelley's *Frankenstein.*" *Monster Theory: Reading Culture.* Ed. Jeffrey Jerome Cohen. Minneapolis: U of Minnesota P, 1996. 115–39. Print.

Jackson, Rosemary. *Fantasy.* London: Methuen, 1981. Print.

Jones, Frederick, ed. *Mary Shelley's Journal.* Norman: U of Oklahoma P, 1947. Print.

Kermode, Frank. Introduction. Shakespeare iii–xciii.

Malchow, H. R. "Frankenstein's Monster and Images of Race in Nineteenth-Century Literature." *Past and Present* 139.1 (1993): 90–130. Print.

———. *Gothic Images of Race in Nineteenth-Century Britain.* Stanford: Stanford UP, 1996. Print.

Marx, Leo. *The Machine in the Garden: Technology and the Pastoral Ideal in America.* London: Oxford UP, 1967. Print.

Moers, Ellen. *Literary Women.* London: Verso, 1978. Print.

Neff, D. S. "Hostages to Empire: The Anglo-Indian Problem in *Frankenstein, The Curse of Kehama,* and *The Missionary.*" *European Romantic Review* 8.4 (Fall 1987): 386–408. Print.

Punter, David. *The Literature of Terror: A History of Gothic Fictions from 1765 to the Present Day.* London: Longman, 1980. Print.

Seymour, Miranda. *Mary Shelley.* London: Picador, 2000. Print.

Shakespeare, William. *The Tempest.* Ed. Frank Kermode. The Arden Shakespeare. London: Methuen, 1970. Print.

Shelley, Mary. *Frankenstein or the Modern Prometheus: The 1818 Text.* Ed. Marilyn Butler. London: Pickering, 1993. Print.

Sundquist, Eric J. *To Wake the Nations: Race in the Making of American Literature.* Cambridge: Harvard UP. Print.

Veeder, William. *Mary Shelley and* Frankenstein: *The Fate of Androgyny.* Chicago: U of Chicago P, 1983. Print.

Walvin, James. "The Rise of British Popular Sentiment for Abolition, 1787–1832." *Anti-Slavery, Religion and Reform.* Ed. Christine Bolt and Seymour Drescher. Chatham: Dawson Archon, 1980. 149–62. Print.

Winter, Kari J. *Subjects of Slavery, Agents of Change: Women and Power in Gothic Novels and Slave Narratives, 1790–1865.* Athens: U of Georgia P, 1992. Print.

Woodard, Helena. "The Two Marys (Prince and Shelley) on the Textual Meeting Ground of Race, Gender, and Genre." *Recovered Writers/Recovered Texts.* Ed. Dolan Hubbard. Knoxville: U of Tennessee P, 1997. 15–30. Print.

# Glossary of Critical and Theoretical Terms

The following definitions are adapted and/or abridged versions of ones found in the third edition of *The Bedford Glossary of Critical and Literary Terms*, by Ross Murfin and Supriya M. Ray (© Bedford Books 2009).

**ABSENCE** The idea, advanced by French theorist Jacques Derrida, that authors are not present in texts and that meaning arises in the absence of any authority guaranteeing the correctness of any one interpretation. *See* **presence and absence** for a more complete discussion of those concepts.

**AFFECTIVE FALLACY** *See* **New Criticism, the; reader-response criticism.**

**BASE** *See* **Marxist criticism.**

**CANON** A term used since the fourth century to refer to those books of the Bible that the Christian church accepts as being Holy Scripture—that is, divinely inspired. Books outside the canon (noncanonical books) are referred to as *apocryphal. Canon* has also been used to refer to the Saints Canon, the group of people officially recognized by the Catholic Church as saints. More recently, it has been employed to refer to the body of works generally attributed by scholars to a particular author (for example, the Shakespearean canon is currently believed to consist of thirty-seven plays that scholars feel can be definitively attributed to him). Works sometimes attributed to an author, but whose authorship is disputed or otherwise uncertain, are called apocryphal. *Canon* may also refer more generally to those literary works that are "privileged," or given special status, by a culture. Works we tend to think of as classics or as "Great Books"—texts that are repeatedly reprinted in anthologies of literature—may be said to constitute the canon.

Contemporary **Marxist**, **feminist**, minority, and **postcolonial** critics have argued that, for political reasons, many excellent works never enter the canon. Canonized works, they claim, are those that reflect—and respect—the culture's dominant ideology, or perform some socially acceptable or even necessary form of "cultural work." Attempts have been made to broaden or redefine the canon by discovering valuable texts, or versions of texts, that were repressed or ignored for political reasons. These have been published both in traditional and in nontraditional anthologies. The most outspoken critics of the canon, especially certain critics practicing **cultural criticism**, have called into question the whole concept of canon or "canonicity." Privileging no form of artistic expression, these critics treat cartoons, comics, and soap operas with the same cogency and respect they accord novels, poems, and plays.

**CULTURAL CRITICISM, CULTURAL STUDIES** Critical approaches with roots in the British cultural studies movement of the 1960s. A movement that reflected and contributed to the unrest of that decade, it both fueled and was fueled by the challenges to tradition and authority apparent in everything from the antiwar movement to the emergence of "hard rock" music. Birmingham University's Centre for Contemporary Cultural Studies, founded by Stuart Hall and Richard Hoggart in 1964, quickly became the locus of the movement, which both critiqued elitist definitions of culture and drew upon a wide variety of disciplines and perspectives.

In Great Britain, the terms *cultural criticism* and *cultural studies* have been used more or less interchangeably, and, to add to the confusion, both terms have been used to refer to two different things. On one hand, they have been used to refer to the analysis of literature (including popular literature) and other art forms in their social, political, or economic contexts; on the other hand, they have been used to refer to the much broader interdisciplinary study of the interrelationships between a variety of cultural **discourses** and practices (such as advertising, gift giving, and racial categorization). In North America, the term *cultural studies* is usually reserved for this broader type of analysis, whereas *cultural criticism* typically refers to work with a predominantly literary or artistic focus.

Cultural critics examine how literature emerges from, influences, and competes with other forms of discourse (such as religion, science, or advertising) within a given culture. They analyze the social contexts in which a given text was written, and under what conditions it was—and is—produced, disseminated, and read. Like practitioners of cultural studies, they oppose the view that culture refers exclusively to high culture, *Culture* with a capital *C*, seeking to make the term refer to popular, folk, urban, and mass (mass-produced, -disseminated, -mediated, and -consumed) culture, as well as to that culture we associate with so-called "great literature." In other words, cultural critics argue that what we refer to as a culture is in fact a set of interactive *cultures*, alive and changing, rather than static or monolithic. They favor analyzing literary works not as aesthetic objects complete in themselves but as works to be seen in terms of their relationships to other works, to economic conditions, and to broad social discourses (about childbirth, women's education, rural decay, etc.). Critics associated with film studies practice a form of cultural criticism by analyzing movies in terms of their relationships to other movies, to literary texts on which they are closely or loosely based, and/or to cultural issues, biases, and anxieties that were prevalent at the time the film was produced. For example, Bouriana Zakharieva has viewed Kenneth Branagh's film *Mary Shelley's Frankenstein* (1994) both in light of Mary Shelley's early-nineteenth-century qualms about mechanization and industrialization and in terms of the *fin de siècle* phenomenon of great concern in the 1990s, namely, with what would happen on January 1, 2000, the first day of what came to be known as Y2K.

Several thinkers influenced by **Marxist** theory have powerfully affected the development of cultural criticism and cultural studies. The French philosophical historian Michel Foucault has perhaps had the strongest influence on cultural criticism and **the new historicism**, a type of literary criticism whose evolution has often paralleled that of North American cultural criticism. In works such as *Discipline and Punish* (1975) and *The History of Sexuality* (1976), Foucault studies cultures in terms of power relationships, a focus typical of Marxist thought. Unlike Marxists, however, Foucault did not see power as something exerted by a dominant class over a subservient one. For Foucault, power was more than repressive power: it was a complex of forces generated by the confluence — or conflict — of discourses; it was that which produces what happens. British critic Raymond Williams, best known for his book *Culture and Society: 1780–1950* (1958), influenced the development of cultural studies by arguing that culture is living and evolving rather than fixed and finished, further stating in *The Long Revolution* (1961) that "art and culture are ordinary." Although Williams did not define himself as a Marxist throughout his entire career, he always followed the Marxist practice of viewing culture in relation to **ideologies**, which he defined as the "residual," "dominant," or "emerging" ways in which individuals or social classes view the world.

Recent practitioners of cultural criticism and cultural studies have focused on issues of nationality, race, gender, and sexuality, in addition to those of power, ideology, and class. As a result, there is a significant overlap between cultural criticism and **feminist criticism**, and between cultural studies and African American studies. This overlap can be seen in the work of contemporary feminists such as Gayatri Chakravorty Spivak, Trinh T. Minh-ha, and Gloria Anzaldúa, who stress that although all women are female, they are something else as well (working-class, lesbian, Native American), a facet that must be considered in analyzing their writings. It can also be seen in the writings of Henry Louis Gates, who has shown how black American writers, to avoid being culturally marginalized, have prduced texts that fuse the language and traditions of the white Western **canon** with a black vernacular and tradition derived from African and Caribbean cultures.

Interest in race and ethnicity has accompanied a new, interdisciplinary focus on colonial and postcolonial societies, in which issues of race, class, and ethnicity loom large. Practitioners of **postcolonial studies,** another form of cultural studies inaugurated by Edward Said's book *Orientalism* (1978), have, according to Homi K. Bhabha, revealed the way in which certain cultures (mis) represent others in order to achieve and extend political and social domination in the modern world order. Thanks to the work of scholars like Bhabha and Said, education in general and literary study in particular are becoming more democratic, multicultural, and "decentered" (less patriarchal and Eurocentric) in their interests and emphases.

**DECONSTRUCTION** Deconstruction involves the close reading of texts in order to demonstrate that any given text has irreconcilably contradictory meanings, rather than being a unified, logical whole. As J. Hillis Miller, the pre-eminent American deconstructor, has explained in his essay "Stevens' Rock and Criticism as Cure" (1976), "Deconstruction is not a dismantling of the structure of a text, but a demonstration that it has already dismantled itself. Its apparently solid ground is no rock but thin air."

Deconstruction was both created and has been profoundly influenced by the French philosopher of language Jacques Derrida. Derrida, who coined the term *deconstruction*, argues that in Western culture, people tend to think and express their thoughts in terms of *binary oppositions*. Something is white but not black, masculine and therefore not feminine, a cause rather than an effect. Other common and mutually exclusive pairs include beginning/end, conscious/unconscious, **presence/absence**, and speech/writing. Derrida suggests these oppositions are hierarchies in miniature, containing one term that Western culture views as positive or superior and another considered negative or inferior, even if only slightly so. Through deconstruction, Derrida aims to erase the boundary between binary oppositions—and to do so in such a way that the hierarchy implied by the oppositions is thrown into question.

Although its ultimate aim may be to criticize Western logic, deconstruction arose as a response to **structuralism** and to **formalism.** Structuralists believe that all elements of human culture, including literature, may be understood as parts of a system of signs. Derrida did not believe that structuralists could explain the laws governing human signification and thus provide the key to understanding the form and meaning of everything from an African village to Greek myth to a literary text. He also rejected the structuralist belief that texts have identifiable "centers" of meaning, a belief structuralists shared with formalists.

Formalist critics, such as the **New Critics,** assume that a work of literature is a freestanding, self-contained object whose meaning can be found in the complex network of relations among its parts (allusions, images, rhythms, sounds, etc.). Deconstructors, by contrast, see works in terms of their **undecidability.** They reject the formalist view that a work of literary art is demonstrably unified from beginning to end, in one certain way, or that it is organized around a single center that ultimately can be identified. As a result, deconstructors see texts as more radically heterogeneous than do formalists. Formalists ultimately make sense of the ambiguities they find in a given text, arguing that every ambiguity serves a definite, meaningful—and demonstrable—literary function. Undecidability, by contrast, is never reduced, let alone mastered. Though a deconstructive reading can reveal the incompatible possibilities generated by the text, it is impossible for the reader to decide among them.

**DIALECTIC** Originally developed by Greek philosophers, mainly Socrates and Plato (in *The Republic* and *Phaedrus* [c. 360 B.C.E.]), a form and method of logical argumentation that typically addresses conflicting ideas or positions. When used in the plural, dialectics refers to any mode of argumentation that attempts to resolve the contradictions between opposing ideas.

The German philosopher G. W. F. Hegel described dialectic as a process whereby a *thesis*, when countered by an *antithesis*, leads to the *synthesis* of a new idea. Karl Marx and Friedrich Engels, adapting Hegel's idealist theory, used the phrase *dialectical materialism* to discuss the way in which a revolutionary class war might lead to the synthesis of a new socioeconomic order.

In literary criticism, *dialectic* typically refers to the oppositional ideas and/ or mediatory reasoning that pervade and unify a given work or group of works. Critics may thus speak of the dialectic of head and heart (reason and passion) in William Shakespeare's plays. The American **Marxist critic** Fredric Jameson has coined the phrase "dialectical criticism" to refer to a Marxist critical approach that synthesizes **structuralist** and **poststructuralist** methodologies.

**DIALOGIC** *See* **discourse**.

**DISABILITY STUDIES** A recent movement within literary criticism and the humanities more generally that focuses on and critiques disability as it is commonly conceived, applying cultural, historical, social, and other socio-humanistic approaches to the study of disability in society. Early practitioners of disability studies include Lennard Davis, Simi Linton, and Rosemarie Garland-Thomson.

Disability studies seeks to overturn the medicalized understanding of disability and to replace it with a social model. Its proponents define disability not as a physical, mental, or developmental defect—definitions flowing from a medical model that they believe has had the effect of segregating people with disabilities—but rather as a social construct, a way of interpreting human differences. Its practitioners examine the historical formation of the social identity "disabled," pointing out that it covers such a wide range of physical, mental, and emotional variations that it encompasses a large and diverse group of people who actually have little in common.

Literary analyses of disability sometimes focus on how disability influenced the author and operates thematically in the text. In other instances, they consider the ways in which authors represent various types of disability through literary characters, some of whom reflect but others of whom resist, challenge, and even debunk prevailing biases and stereotypes.

**DISCOURSE** Used specifically, (1) the thoughts, statements, or dialogue of individuals, especially of characters in a literary work; (2) the words in, or text of, a **narrative** as opposed to its story line; or (3) a "strand" within a given narrative that argues a certain point or defends a given value system. Discourse of the first type is sometimes categorized as *direct* or *indirect*. Direct discourse relates the thoughts and utterances of individuals and literary characters to the reader unfiltered by a third-person narrator. ("Take me home this instant!" she insisted.) Indirect discourse (also referred to as free indirect discourse) is more impersonal, involving the reportage of thoughts, statements, or dialogue by a third-person narrator. (She told him to take her home immediately.)

More generally, discourse refers to the language in which a subject or area of knowledge is discussed or a certain kind of business is transacted. Human knowledge is collected and structured in discourses. Theology and medicine are defined by their discourses, as are politics, sexuality, and literary criticism.

Contemporary literary critics have maintained that society is generally made up of a number of different discourses or *discourse communities*, one or more of which may be dominant or serve the dominant ideology. Each discourse has its own vocabulary, concepts, and rules—knowledge of which constitutes power. The psychoanalyst and **psychoanalytic critic** Jacques Lacan has treated the unconscious as a form of discourse, the patterns of which are repeated in literature. **Cultural critics**, following Soviet critic Mikhail Bakhtin, use the word *dialogic* to discuss the dialogue between discourses that takes place within language or, more specifically, a literary text. Some **poststructuralists** have used *discourse* in lieu of *text* to refer to any verbal structure, whether literary or not.

**FEMINIST CRITICISM** A type of literary criticism that became a dominant force in Western literary studies in the late 1970s, when feminist theory more broadly conceived was applied to linguistic and literary matters. Since the early 1980s, feminist literary criticism has developed and diversified in a number of ways and is now characterized by a global perspective.

French feminist criticism garnered much of its inspiration from Simone de Beauvoir's seminal book, *Le deuxième sexe* (*The Second Sex*) (1949). Beauvoir argued that associating men with humanity more generally (as many cultures do) relegates women to an inferior position in society. Subsequent French feminist critics writing during the 1970s acknowledged Beauvoir's critique but focused on language as a tool of male domination, analyzing the ways in which it represents the world from the male point of view and arguing for the development of a feminine language and writing.

Though interested in the subject of feminine language and writing, North American feminist critics of the 1970s and early 1980s began by analyzing literary texts—not by abstractly discussing language—via close textual reading and historical scholarship. One group practiced "feminist critique," examining how women characters are portrayed, exposing the patriarchal **ideology** implicit in the so-called classics, and demonstrating that attitudes and traditions reinforcing systematic masculine dominance are inscribed in the literary canon. Another group practiced what came to be called "gynocriticism," studying writings by women and examining the female literary tradition to find out how women writers across the ages have perceived themselves and imagined reality.

While it gradually became customary to refer to an Anglo-American tradition of feminist criticism, British feminist critics of the 1970s and early 1980s criticized the tendency of some North American critics to find universal or "essential" feminine attributes, arguing that differences of race, class, and culture gave rise to crucial differences among women across space and time. British feminist critics regarded their own critical practice as more political than that of North American feminists, emphasizing an engagement with historical process in order to promote social change.

By the early 1990s, the French, American, and British approaches had so thoroughly critiqued, influenced, and assimilated one another that nationality no longer automatically signaled a practitioner's approach. Today's critics seldom focus on "woman" as a relatively monolithic category; rather, they view "women" as members of different societies with different concerns. Feminists of color, Third World (preferably called **postcolonial**) feminists, and lesbian feminists stress that women are not defined solely by the fact that they are female; other attributes (such as religion, class, and sexual orientation) are also important, making the problems and goals of one group of women different from those of another.

Many commentators have argued that feminist criticism is by definition **gender criticism** because of its focus on the feminine gender. But the relationship between feminist and gender criticism is, in fact, complex; the two approaches are certainly not polar opposites but, rather, exist along a continuum of attitudes toward sex, sexuality, gender, and language.

**FIGURE, FIGURE OF SPEECH** *See* **trope.**

**FILM STUDIES** *See* **cultural criticism, cultural studies.**

**FORMALISM** A general term covering several similar types of literary criticism that arose in the 1920s and 1930s, flourished during the 1940s and 1950s, and are still in evidence today. Formalists see the literary work as an object in its own right. Thus, they tend to devote their attention to its intrinsic nature, concentrating their analyses on the interplay and relationships among the text's essential verbal elements. They study the form of the work (as opposed to its content), although form to a formalist can connote anything from **genre** (for example, one may speak of "the sonnet form") to grammatical or rhetorical structure to the "emotional imperative" that engenders the work's (more mechanical) structure. No matter which connotation of form pertains, however, formalists seek to be objective in their analysis, focusing on the work itself and eschewing external considerations. They pay particular attention to literary devices used in the work and to the patterns these devices establish.

Formalism developed largely in reaction to the practice of interpreting literary **texts** by relating them to "extrinsic" issues, such as the historical circumstances and politics of the era in which the work was written, its philosophical or theological milieu, or the experiences and frame of mind of its author. Although the term *formalism* was coined by critics to disparage the movement, it is now used simply as a descriptive term.

Formalists have generally suggested that everyday language, which serves simply to communicate information, is stale and unimaginative. They argue that "literariness" has the capacity to overturn common and expected patterns (of grammar, of story line), thereby rejuvenating language. Such novel uses of language supposedly enable readers to experience not only language but also the world in an entirely new way.

A number of schools of literary criticism have adopted a formalist orientation, or at least make use of formalist concepts. **The New Criticism**, an American approach to literature that reached its height in the 1940s and 1950s, is perhaps the most famous type of formalism. But Russian formalism was the first major formalist movement; after the Stalinist regime suppressed it in the early 1930s, the Prague Linguistic Circle adopted its analytical methods. The Chicago School has also been classified as formalist insofar as the Chicago Critics examined and analyzed works on an individual basis; their interest in historical material, on the other hand, was clearly not formalist.

**GAPS** When used by **reader-response critics** familiar with the theories of Wolfgang Iser, the term refers to "blanks" in **texts** that must be filled in by readers. A gap may be said to exist whenever and wherever a reader perceives something to be missing between words, sentences, paragraphs, stanzas, or chapters. Readers respond to gaps actively and creatively, explaining apparent inconsistencies in point of view, accounting for jumps in chronology, speculatively supplying information missing from plots, and resolving problems or issues left ambiguous or "indeterminate" in the text.

Reader-response critics sometimes speak as if a gap actually exists in a text; a gap, of course, is to some extent a product of readers' perceptions. One reader may find a given text to be riddled with gaps while another reader may view that text as comparatively consistent and complete; different readers may find different gaps in the same text. Furthermore, they may fill in the gaps they find in different ways, which is why, a reader-response critic might argue, works are interpreted in different ways.

Although the concept of the gap has been used mainly by reader-response critics, it has also been used by critics taking other theoretical approaches. Practitioners of **deconstruction** might use *gap* when explaining that every text contains opposing and even contradictory **discourses** that cannot be reconciled. **Marxist critics** have used the term *gap* to speak of everything from the gap that opens up between economic base and cultural superstructure to two kinds of conflicts or contradictions found in literary texts. The first of these conflicts or contradictions, they would argue, results from the fact that even realistic texts reflect an **ideology**, within which there are inevitably subjects and attitudes that cannot be represented or even recognized. As a result, readers at the edge or outside of that ideology perceive that something is missing. The second kind of conflict or contradiction within a text results from the fact that works do more than reflect ideology; they are also fictions that, consciously or unconsciously, distance themselves from that ideology.

**GAY AND LESBIAN CRITICISM** Sometimes referred to as *queer theory*, an approach to literature currently viewed as a form of **gender criticism**. *See* **gender criticism**.

**GENDER CRITICISM** A type of literary criticism that focuses on—and critiques—gender as it is commonly conceived, seeking to expose its insufficiency as a categorizing device. Gender critics reject the view that gender is something natural or innate, arguing instead that gender is a social construct, a learned behavior, a product of culture and its institutions. Gay and lesbian criticism is generally viewed as a major emphasis within gender criticism, although not all gay and lesbian critics would so categorize their work.

Many commentators have argued that feminist criticism is also a type of gender criticism, despite the fact that feminist criticism arose as an approach to literary criticism in the 1970s, whereas gender criticism appeared on the critical scene a decade later. Gender critics have drawn heavily upon feminist theory and practice even as they have attacked many feminist concepts and claims.

Many gender critics hold "constructionist" views and take issue with those feminists who urge an "essentialist" approach. Stated simply, the word *essentialist* refers to the view that women are essentially—that is, naturally—different from men. The most essentialist feminists write as if no amount of enculturation could alter female nature, female difference. *Constructionist*, by contrast, refers to the view that most of the differences between men and women are characteristics not of the male and female sex (nature) but, rather, of the masculine and feminine genders (nurture). Constructionist gender critics vehemently disagree with those feminists who emphasize the female body, its sexual difference, and the manifold implications of that difference, especially those

French feminist critics who argue that the female body gives rise to a special feminine language, writing, and style. Unlike these essentialist feminists, constructionist gender critics would attribute differences in language, writing, and style to cultural influences, not to sexual differences between female and male bodies.

Following the lead of French philosophical historian Michel Foucault, gay and lesbian critics have argued that the heterosexual/homosexual distinction is as much a cultural construct as is the masculine/feminine dichotomy. These critics have been especially critical of heterosexuality as a norm, arguing that it is an enforced corollary and consequence of a "sex/gender system" which presupposes that men are masculine, that masculinity carries with it an attraction to women, and that it is therefore unnatural for men to be attracted to other men. Gay and lesbian writings have produced compelling, if controversial, reinterpretations of works by authors as diverse as Herman Melville, Emily Dickinson, Henry James, Virginia Woolf, and Toni Morrison.

Gay and lesbian critics are not the only gender critics who have critiqued masculinity. An unprecedented number of gender theorists have analyzed masculinity as a complex construct that produces and reproduces a constellation of behaviors and goals such as performance and conquest, many of them destructive and injurious to women. The construct of masculinity has been studied in works by Stephen Crane, T. S. Eliot, F. Scott Fitzgerald, and Nathaniel Hawthorne.

**GENRE** From the French *genre* meaning "kind" or "type," the classification of literary works on the basis of their content, form, or technique. The term also refers to individual classifications. For centuries works have been grouped and associated according to a number of classificatory schemes and distinctions, such as prose/poem/fiction/drama/lyric, and the traditional classical divisions: comedy/tragedy/lyric/pastoral/epic/satire. More recently, Northrop Frye has suggested that all literary works may be grouped with one of four sets of archetypal myths that are in turn associated with the four seasons: comedy (spring), romance (summer), tragedy (fall), and satire (winter). Many more specific genre categories exist as well, such as autobiography, the essay, Gothic, the picaresque novel, the sentimental novel. Current usage is thus broad enough to permit varieties of a given genre (such as the novel), as well as the novel in general, to be legitimately denoted by the term *genre*.

Traditional thinking about genre has been revised and even roundly criticized by contemporary critics. For example, the prose/poem dichotomy has been largely discarded in favor of a lyric/drama/fiction (or narrative) scheme. The more general idea that works of imaginative literature can be solidly and satisfactorily classified according to set, specific categories has also come under attack in recent times.

**HEGEMONY** Most commonly, one nation's dominance or dominant influence over another. The term was adopted (and adapted) by the Italian Marxist critic Antonio Gramsci to refer to the process of consensus formation and to the pervasive system of assumptions, meanings, and values—the web of ideologies, in other words—that shapes the way things look, what they mean, and therefore what reality is for the majority of people within a given culture. Although Gramsci viewed hegemony as being powerful and persuasive, he did not believe that extant systems were immune to change; rather, he encouraged people to resist prevailing ideologies, to form a new consensus, and thereby to alter hegemony.

*Hegemony* is a term commonly used by **cultural critics** as well as by Marxist critics.

**IDEOLOGY** A set of beliefs underlying the customs, habits, and practices common to a given social group. To members of that group, the beliefs seem obviously true, natural, and even universally applicable; to those who adhere to another ideology, they may seem just as obviously arbitrary, idiosyncratic, and even false. Within a society several ideologies may coexist, and one or more of these may be dominant.

Ideologies may be forcefully imposed or willingly subscribed to, and their component beliefs may be held consciously or unconsciously. In any case, they come to form what Johanna M. Smith has called "the unexamined ground of our experience." Ideology governs our perceptions, judgments, and prejudices—our sense of what is acceptable, normal, and deviant. Ideology may cause a revolution; it may also allow discrimination and even exploitation.

Ideologies are of special interest to politically oriented critics of literature because of the way in which authors reflect or resist prevailing views in their texts. Some **Marxist critics** have argued that literary texts reflect and reproduce the ideologies that produced them; most, however, have shown how ideologies are riven with contradictions that works of literature manage to expose and widen. Other Marxist critics have focused on the way in which texts themselves are characterized by gaps, conflicts, and contradictions between their ideological and anti-ideological functions. Fredric Jameson, an American Marxist critic, argues that all thought is ideological, but that ideological thought that knows itself as such stands the chance of seeing through and transcending ideology.

Not all of the politically oriented critics interested in ideology have been Marxists. Certain non-Marxist **feminist critics** have addressed the question of ideology by seeking to expose (and thereby call into question) the patriarchal ideology mirrored or inscribed in works written by men—even men who have sought to counter sexism and break down sexual stereotypes. **New historicists** have been interested in demonstrating the ideological underpinnings not only of literary representations but also of our interpretations of them.

**IMAGINARY ORDER** *See* **psychological criticism and psychoanalytic criticism.**

**IMPLIED READER** *See* **reader-response criticism.**

**INTENTIONAL FALLACY** *See* **New Criticism, the.**

**INTERTEXTUALITY** The condition of interconnectedness among texts, or the concept that any text is an amalgam of others, either because it exhibits signs of influence or because its language inevitably contains common points of reference with other texts through such things as allusion, quotation, genre, stylistic features, and even revisions. The critic Julia Kristeva, who popularized and is often credited with coining this term, views any given work as part of a larger fabric of literary **discourse**, part of a continuum including the future as well as the past. Other critics have argued for an even broader use and understanding of the term *intertextuality*, maintaining that literary history per se is too narrow a context within which to read and understand a literary text. When understood this way, *intertextuality* could be used by a **new historicist** or **cultural critic** to refer to the significant interconnectedness between a literary text and contemporary, nonliterary discussions of the issues represented in the literary text. Or it could be used by a **poststructuralist** to suggest that a work of literature can only be recognized and read within a vast field of signs and **tropes** that is like a text and that makes any single text self-contradictory and **undecidable**.

MARXIST CRITICISM A type of criticism in which literary works are viewed as the product of work (and hence of the realm of production and consumption we call economics), and whose practitioners emphasize the role of class and ideology as they reflect, propagate, and even challenge the prevailing social order. Rather than viewing texts as repositories for hidden meanings, Marxist critics view texts as material products to be understood in broadly historical terms.

Marxism began with Karl Marx, the nineteenth-century German philosopher best known for writing *Das Kapital* (*Capital*) (1867), the seminal work of the communist movement. Marx was also the first Marxist literary critic, writing critical essays in the 1830s on writers such as Johann Wolfgang von Goethe and William Shakespeare. Even after Marx met Friedrich Engels in 1843 and began collaborating on overtly political works such as *The German Ideology* (1846) and *The Communist Manifesto* (1848), he maintained a keen interest in literature. In *The German Ideology*, Marx and Engels discussed the relationships among the arts, politics, and basic economic reality in terms of a general social theory. Economics, they argued, provides the **base**, or infrastructure, of society, from which a *superstructure* consisting of law, politics, philosophy, religion, and art emerges.

The revolution anticipated by Marx and Engels did not occur in their century, let alone in their lifetime. When it did occur, in 1917, it did so in a place unimagined by either theorist: Russia, a country long ruled by despotic czars but also enlightened by the works of powerful novelists and playwrights including Anton Chekhov, Alexander Pushkin, Leo Tolstoy, and Fyodor Dostoyevsky. Russia produced revolutionaries like Vladimir Lenin, who shared not only Marx's interest in literature but also his belief in its ultimate importance. Leon Trotsky, Lenin's comrade in revolution, took a strong interest in literary matters as well, publishing a book called *Literature and Revolution* (1924) that is still viewed as a classic of Marxist literary criticism.

Of those critics active in the USSR after the expulsion of Trotsky and the triumph of Stalin, two stand out: Mikhail Bakhtin and Georg Lukács. Bakhtin viewed language—especially literary texts—in terms of discourses and **dialogues**. A novel written in a society in flux, for instance, might include an official, legitimate discourse, as well as one infiltrated by challenging comments. Lukács, a Hungarian who converted to Marxism in 1919, appreciated prerevolutionary, realistic novels that broadly reflected cultural "totalities" and were populated with characters representing human "types" of the author's place and time.

Perhaps because Lukács was the best known of the Soviet communists writing Marxist criticism in the 1930s and 1940s, non-Soviet Marxists tended to develop their ideas by publicly opposing his. In Germany, dramatist and critic

Bertolt Brecht criticized Lukács for his attempt to enshrine realism at the expense not only of the other "isms" but also of poetry and drama, which Lukács had largely ignored. Walter Benjamin praised new art forms ushered in by the age of mechanical reproduction, and Theodor Adorno attacked Lukács for his dogmatic rejection of nonrealist modern literature and for his elevation of content over form.

In addition to opposing Lukács and his overly constrictive canon, non-Soviet Marxists took advantage of insights generated by non-Marxist critical theories being developed in post–World War II Europe. Lucien Goldmann, a Romanian critic living in Paris, combined structuralist principles with Marx's base-superstructure model in order to show how economics determines the mental structures of social groups, which are reflected in literary texts. Goldmann rejected the idea of individual human genius, choosing instead to see works as the "collective" products of "trans-individual" mental structures. French Marxist Louis Althusser drew on the ideas of the **psychoanalytic theorist** Jacques Lacan and the Italian communist Antonio Gramsci, who discussed the relationship between **ideology** and **hegemony**, the pervasive system of assumptions and values that shapes the perception of reality for people in a given culture. Althusser's followers included Pierre Macherey, who in *A Theory of Literary Production* (1966) developed Althusser's concept of the relationship between literature and ideology; Terry Eagleton, who proposes an elaborate theory about how history enters texts, which in turn may alter history; and Fredric Jameson, who has argued that form is "but the working out" of content "in the realm of superstructure."

**METAPHOR** A **figure of speech** (more specifically a **trope**) that associates two unlike things; the representation of one thing by another. The image (or activity or concept) used to represent or "figure" something else is known as the **vehicle** of the metaphor; the thing represented is called the **tenor**. For instance, in the sentence "That child is a mouse," the child is the tenor, whereas the mouse is the vehicle. The image of a mouse is being used to represent the child, perhaps to emphasize his or her timidity.

Metaphor should be distinguished from **simile**, another figure of speech with which it is sometimes confused. Similes compare two unlike things by using a connective word such as *like* or *as*. Metaphors use no connective word to make their comparison. Furthermore, critics ranging from Aristotle to I. A. Richards have argued that metaphors equate the vehicle with the tenor instead of simply comparing the two.

This identification of vehicle and tenor can provide much additional meaning. For instance, instead of saying, "Last night I read a book," we might say, "Last night I plowed through a book." "Plowed through" (or the activity of plowing) is the vehicle of our metaphor; "read" (or the act of reading) is the tenor, the thing being figured. (As this example shows, neither vehicle nor tenor need be a noun; metaphors may employ other parts of speech.) The increment in meaning through metaphor is fairly obvious. Our audience knows not only *that* we read but also *how* we read, because to read a book in the way that a plow rips through earth is surely to read in a relentless, unreflective way. Note that in the sentence above, a new metaphor — "rips through" — has been used to explain an old one. This serves (which is a metaphor) as an example of just how thick (another metaphor) language is with metaphors!

Metaphors may be classified as *direct* or *implied*. A direct metaphor, such as "That child is a mouse" (or "He is such a doormat!"), specifies both tenor and vehicle. An implied metaphor, by contrast, mentions only the vehicle; the tenor is implied by the context of the sentence or passage. For instance, in the sentence "Last night I plowed through a book" (or "She sliced through traffic"), the tenor—the act of reading (or driving)—can be inferred.

Traditionally, metaphor has been viewed as the principal trope. Other figures of speech include simile, **symbol**, personification, allegory, **metonymy**, synecdoche, and conceit. **Deconstructors** have questioned the distinction between metaphor and metonymy.

**METONYMY** **A figure of speech** (more specifically a **trope**), in which one thing is represented by another that is commonly and often physically associated with it. To refer to a writer's handwriting as his or her "hand" is to use a metonymic figure.

Like other figures of speech (such as **metaphor**), metonymy involves the replacement of one word or phrase by another; thus, a monarch might be referred to as "the crown." As narrowly defined by certain contemporary critics, particularly those associated with **deconstruction**, the **vehicle** of a metonym is arbitrarily, not intrinsically, associated with the **tenor**. (There is no special, intrinsic likeness between a crown and a monarch; it's just that crowns traditionally sit on monarchs' heads and not on the heads of university professors.)

More broadly, metonym and metonymy have been used by recent critics to refer to a wide range of figures. **Structuralists** such as Roman Jakobson, who emphasized the difference between metonymy and metaphor, have recently been challenged by deconstructors, who have further argued that *all* figuration is arbitrary. Deconstructors such as Paul de Man and J. Hillis Miller have questioned the "privilege" granted to metaphor and the metaphor/metonymy distinction or "opposition," suggesting instead that all metaphors are really metonyms.

**MODERNISM** *See* **postmodernism**.

**NARRATIVE** A story or a telling of a story, or an account of a situation or events. Narratives may be fictional or true; they may be written in prose or verse. Some critics use the term even more generally; Brook Thomas, a **new historicist**, has critiqued "narratives of human history that neglect the role human labor has played."

**NARRATOLOGY** The analysis of the **structural** components of a **narrative**, the way in which those components interrelate, and the relationship between this complex of elements and the narrative's basic story line. Narratology incorporates techniques developed by other critics, most notably Russian **formalists** and French **structuralists**, applying in addition numerous traditional methods of analyzing narrative fiction (for instance, those methods outlined in the "Showing as Telling" chapter of Wayne Booth's *The Rhetoric of Fiction* [1961]). Narratologists treat narratives as explicitly, intentionally, and meticulously constructed systems rather than as simple or natural vehicles for an author's representation of life. They seek to analyze and explain how authors transform a chronologically organized story line into a literary plot. (Story is the raw material from which plot is selectively arranged and constructed.)

Narratologists pay particular attention to such elements as point of view; the relations among story, teller, and audience; and the levels and types of

**discourse** used in narratives. Certain narratologists concentrate on the question of whether any narrative can actually be neutral (like a clear pane of glass through which some subject is objectively seen) and on how the practices of a given culture influence the shape, content, and impact of "historical" narratives. Mieke Bal's *Narratology: Introduction to the Theory of Narrative* (1980) is a standard introduction to the narratological approach.

**NEW CRITICISM, THE** A type of **formalist** literary criticism that reached its height during the 1940s and 1950s and that received its name from John Crowe Ransom's 1941 book *The New Criticism.* New Critics treat a work of literary art as if it were a self-contained, self-referential object. Rather than basing their interpretations of a **text** on the reader's response, the author's stated intentions, or parallels between the text and historical contexts (such as the author's life), New Critics perform a close reading of the text, concentrating on the internal relationships that give it its own distinctive character or form. New Critics emphasize that the structure of a work should not be divorced from meaning, viewing the two as constituting a quasi-organic unity. Special attention is paid to repetition, particularly of images or symbols, but also of sound effects and rhythms in poetry. New Critics especially appreciate the use of literary devices, such as irony and paradox, to achieve a balance or reconciliation between dissimilar, even conflicting, elements in a text.

Because of the importance placed on close textual analysis and the stress on the text as a carefully crafted, orderly object containing observable formal patterns, the New Criticism has sometimes been called an "objective" approach to literature. New Critics are more likely than certain other critics to believe and say that the meaning of a text can be known objectively. For instance, **reader-response critics** see meaning as a function either of each reader's experience or of the norms that govern a particular interpretive community, and **deconstructors** argue that texts mean opposite things at the same time.

The foundations of the New Criticism were laid in books and essays written during the 1920s and 1930s by I. A. Richards (*Practical Criticism* [1929]), William Empson (*Seven Types of Ambiguity* [1930]), and T. S. Eliot ("The Function of Criticism" [1933]). The approach was significantly developed later, however, by a group of American poets and critics, including R. P. Blackmur, Cleanth Brooks, John Crowe Ransom, Allen Tate, Robert Penn Warren, and William K. Wimsatt. Although we associate the New Criticism with certain principles and terms, such as the *affective fallacy* (the notion that the reader's response is relevant to the meaning of a work) and the *intentional fallacy* (the notion that the author's intention determines the work's meaning), the New Critics were trying to make a cultural statement rather than establish a critical dogma. Generally Southern, religious, and culturally conservative, they advocated the inherent value of literary works, particularly of literary works regarded as beautiful art objects, because they were sick of the growing ugliness of modern life and contemporary events. Some recent theorists even link the rising popularity after World War II of the New Criticism (and other types of formalist literary criticism such as the Chicago School) to American isolationism. These critics tend to view the formalist inclination to isolate literature from biography and history as symptomatic of American fatigue with wider involvements. Whatever the source of the New Criticism's popularity (or the reason for its eventual decline), its practitioners and the textbooks they wrote were so influential in American academia that the approach became standard in college and even high school curricula through the 1960s and well into the 1970s.

**NEW HISTORICISM, THE** A type of literary criticism that developed during the 1980s, largely in reaction to the text-only approach pursued by **formalist New Critics** and the critics who challenged the New Criticism in the 1970s. New historicists, like formalists and their critics, acknowledge the importance of the literary **text**, but they also analyze the text with an eye to history. In this respect, the new historicism is not "new"; the majority of critics between 1920 and 1950 focused on a work's historical content and based their interpretations on the interplay between the text and historical contexts (such as the author's life or intentions in writing the work).

In other respects, however, the new historicism differs from the historical criticism of the 1930s and 1940s. It is informed by the **poststructuralist** and **reader-response** theory of the 1970s, as well as by the thinking of **feminist**, **cultural**, and **Marxist critics** whose work was also "new" in the 1980s. They are less fact- and event-oriented than historical critics used to be, perhaps because they have come to wonder whether the truth about what really happened can ever be purely and objectively known. They are less likely to see history as linear and progressive, as something developing toward the present, and they are also less likely to think of it in terms of specific eras, each with a definite, persistent, and consistent Zeitgeist (spirit of the times). Hence, they are unlikely to suggest that a literary text has a single or easily identifiable historical context.

New historicist critics also tend to define the discipline of history more broadly than did their predecessors. They view history as a social science like anthropology and sociology, whereas older historicists tended to view history as literature's "background" and the social sciences as being properly historical. They have erased the line dividing historical and literary materials, showing not only that the production of one of William Shakespeare's historical plays was both a political act and a historical event, but also that the coronation of Elizabeth I was carried out with the same care for staging and **symbol** lavished on works of dramatic art.

New historicists remind us that it is treacherous to reconstruct the past as it really was, rather than as we have been conditioned by our own place and time to believe that it was. And they know that the job is impossible for those who are unaware of that difficulty, insensitive to the bent or bias of their own historical vantage point. Hence, when new historicist critics describe a historical change, they are highly conscious of (and even likely to discuss) the theory of historical change that informs their account.

Many new historicists have acknowledged a profound indebtedness to the writings of Michel Foucault. A French philosophical historian, Foucault brought together incidents and phenomena from areas normally seen as unconnected, encouraging new historicists and cultural historicists to redefine the boundaries of historical inquiry. Like the philosopher Friedrich Nietzsche, Foucault refused to see history as an evolutionary process, a continuous development from cause to effect, from past to present toward THE END, a moment of definite closure, a Day of Judgment. No historical event, according to Foucault, has a single cause; rather, each event is tied into a vast web of economic, social, and political factors. Like Karl Marx, Foucault saw history in terms of power, but, unlike Marx, he viewed power not simply as a repressive force or a tool of conspiracy but as a complex of forces that produces what happens. Not even a tyrannical aristocrat simply wields power, for the aristocrat is himself empowered by discourses and practices that constitute power.

Not all new historicist critics owe their greatest debt to Foucault. Some, like Stephen Greenblatt, have been most nearly influenced by the British cultural critic Raymond Williams, and others, like Brook Thomas, have been more influenced by German Marxist Walter Benjamin. Still others — Jerome McGann, for example — have followed the lead of Soviet critic Mikhail Bakhtin, who viewed literary works in terms of polyphonic **discourses** and dialogues between the official, legitimate voices of a society and other, more challenging or critical voices echoing popular culture.

**POSTCOLONIAL CRITICISM, POSTCOLONIAL STUDIES** A type of **cultural criticism**, postcolonial criticism usually involves the analysis of literary texts produced in countries and cultures that have come under the control of European colonial powers at some point in their history. Alternatively, it can refer to the analysis of texts written about colonized places by writers hailing from the colonizing culture. In *Orientalism* (1978), Edward Said, a pioneer of postcolonial criticism and studies, focused on the way in which the colonizing First World has invented false images and myths of the Third (postcolonial) World, stereotypical images and myths that have conveniently justified Western exploitation and domination of Eastern and Middle Eastern cultures and peoples. In an essay entitled "Postcolonial Criticism" (1992), Homi K. Bhabha has shown how certain cultures (mis)represent other cultures, thereby extending their political and social domination in the modern world order.

Postcolonial studies, a type of **cultural studies**, refers more broadly to the study of cultural groups, practices, and **discourses** — including but not limited to literary discourses — in the colonized world. The term *postcolonial* is usually used broadly to refer to the study of works written at any point after colonization first occurred in a given country, although it is sometimes used more specifically to refer to the analysis of texts and other cultural discourses that emerged after the end of the colonial period (after the success of liberation and independence movements). Among **feminist critics**, the postcolonial perspective has inspired an attempt to recover whole cultures of women heretofore ignored or marginalized, women who speak not only from colonized places but also from the colonizing places to which many of them fled.

Postcolonial criticism has been influenced by **Marxist** thought, by the work of Michel Foucault — whose theories about the power of discourses have influenced **the new historicism** — and by **deconstruction**, which has challenged not only hierarchical, binary oppositions such as West/East and North/South but also the notions of superiority associated with the first term of each opposition.

**POSTMODERNISM** A term referring to certain radically experimental works of literature and art produced after World War II. *Postmodernism* is distinguished from *modernism*, which generally refers to the revolution in art and literature that occurred during the period 1910–1930, particularly following the disillusioning experience of World War I. The postmodern era, with its potential for mass destruction and its shocking history of genocide, has evoked a continuing disillusionment similar to that widely experienced during the modern period. Much of postmodernist writing reveals and highlights the alienation of individuals and the meaninglessness of human existence. Postmodernists frequently stress that humans desperately (and ultimately unsuccessfully) cling to illusions of security to conceal and forget the void on which their lives are perched.

Not surprisingly, postmodernists have shared with their modernist precursors the goal of breaking away from traditions (including certain modernist traditions, which, over time, had become institutionalized and conventional to some degree) through experimentation with new literary devices, forms, and styles. While preserving the spirit and even some of the themes of modernist literature (the alienation of humanity, historical discontinuity, etc.), postmodernists have rejected the order that a number of modernists attempted to instill in their work through patterns of allusion, symbol, and myth. They have also taken some of the meanings and methods found in modernist works to extremes that most modernists would have deplored. For instance, whereas modernists such as T. S. Eliot perceived the world as fragmented and represented that fragmentation through poetic language, many also viewed art as a potentially integrating, restorative force, a hedge against the cacophony and chaos that postmodernist works often imitate (or even celebrate) but do not attempt to counter or correct.

Because postmodernist works frequently combine aspects of diverse **genres**, they can be difficult to classify—at least according to traditional schemes of classification. Postmodernists, revolting against a certain modernist tendency toward elitist "high art," have also generally made a concerted effort to appeal to popular culture. Cartoons, music, "pop art," and television have thus become acceptable and even common media for postmodernist artistic expression. Postmodernist literary developments include such genres as the Absurd, the antinovel, concrete poetry, and other forms of avant-garde poetry written in free verse and challenging the **ideological** assumptions of contemporary society. What postmodernist theater, fiction, and poetry have in common is the view (explicit or implicit) that literary language is its own reality, not a means of representing reality.

Postmodernist critical schools include **deconstruction**, whose practitioners explore the **undecidability** of texts, and **cultural criticism**, which erases the boundary between "high" and "low" culture. The foremost theorist of postmodernism is Jean-François Lyotard, best known for his book *La condition postmoderne (The Postmodern Condition)* (1979).

**POSTSTRUCTURALISM** The general attempt to contest and subvert **structuralism** and to formulate new theories regarding interpretation and meaning, initiated particularly by **deconstructors** but also associated with certain aspects and practitioners of **psychoanalytic**, **Marxist**, **cultural**, **feminist**, and **gender criticism**. Poststructuralism, which arose in the late 1960s, includes such a wide variety of perspectives that no unified poststructuralist theory can be identified. Rather, poststructuralists are distinguished from other contemporary critics by their opposition to structuralism and by certain concepts they embrace.

Structuralists typically believe that meaning(s) in a text, as well as the meaning of a text, can be determined with reference to the system of signification—

the "codes" and conventions that governed the text's production and that operate in its reception. Poststructuralists reject the possibility of such "determinate" knowledge. They believe that signification is an interminable and intricate web of associations that continually defers a determinate assessment of meaning. The numerous possible meanings of any word lead to contradictions and ultimately to the dissemination of meaning itself. Thus, poststructuralists contend that texts contradict not only structuralist accounts of them but also themselves.

To elaborate, poststructuralists have suggested that structuralism rests on a number of distinctions—between signifier and signified, self and language (or **text**), texts and other texts, and text and world—that are overly simplistic, if not patently inaccurate, and they have made a concerted effort to discredit these oppositions. For instance, poststructuralists have viewed the self as the subject, as well as the user, of language, claiming that although we may speak through and shape language, it also shapes and speaks through us. In addition, poststructuralists have demonstrated that in the grand scheme of signification, all "signifieds" are also signifiers, for each word exists in a complex web of language and has such a variety of denotations and connotations that no one meaning can be said to be final, stable, and invulnerable to reconsideration and substitution. Signification is unstable and indeterminate, and thus so is meaning. Poststructuralists, who have generally followed their structuralist predecessors in rejecting the traditional concept of the literary "work" (as the work of an individual and purposeful author) in favor of the impersonal "text," have gone structuralists one better by treating texts as "intertexts": crisscrossed strands within the infinitely larger text called language, that weblike system of denotation, connotation, and signification in which the individual text is inscribed and read and through which its myriad possible meanings are ascribed and assigned. (Poststructuralist **psychoanalytic critic** Julia Kristeva coined the term **intertextuality** to refer to the fact that a text is a "mosaic" of preexisting texts whose meanings it reworks and transforms.)

Although poststructuralism has drawn from numerous critical perspectives developed in Europe and in North America, it relies most heavily on the work of French theorists, especially Jacques Derrida, Kristeva, Jacques Lacan, Michel Foucault, and Roland Barthes. Derrida's 1966 paper "Structure, Sign and Play in the Discourse of the Human Sciences" inaugurated poststructuralism as a coherent challenge to structuralism. Derrida rejected the structuralist presupposition that texts (or other structures) have self-referential centers that govern their language (or signifying system) without being in any way determined, governed, co-opted, or problematized by that language (or signifying system). Having rejected the structuralist concept of a self-referential center, Derrida also rejected its corollary: that a text's meaning is thereby rendered determinable (capable of being determined) as well as determinate (fixed and reliably correct). Lacan, Kristeva, Foucault, and Barthes have all, in diverse ways, arrived at similarly "antifoundational" conclusions, positing that no foundation or "center" exists that can ensure correct interpretation.

Poststructuralism continues to flourish today. In fact, one might reasonably say that poststructuralism serves as the overall paradigm for many of the most prominent contemporary critical perspectives. Approaches ranging from **reader-**

**response criticism** to **the new historicism** assume the "antifoundationalist" bias of poststructuralism. Many approaches also incorporate the post-structuralist position that texts do not have clear and definite meanings, an argument pushed to the extreme by those poststructuralists identified with deconstruction. But unlike deconstructors, who argue that the process of signification itself produces irreconcilable contradictions, contemporary critics oriented toward other post-structuralist approaches (**discourse** analysis or Lacanian psychoanalytic theory, for instance) maintain that texts do have real meanings underlying their apparent or "manifest" meanings (which often contradict or cancel out one another). These underlying meanings have been distorted, disguised, or repressed for psychological or **ideological** reasons but can be discovered through poststructuralist ways of reading.

    **PRESENCE AND ABSENCE** Words given a special literary application by French theorist of **deconstruction** Jacques Derrida when he used them to make a distinction between speech and writing. An individual speaking words must actually be present at the time they are heard, Derrida pointed out, whereas an individual writing words is absent at the time they are read. Derrida, who associates presence with "logos" (the creating spoken Word of a present God who "In the beginning" said "Let there be light"), argued that the Western concept of language is *logocentric.* That is, it is grounded in "the metaphysics of presence," the belief that any linguistic system has a basic foundation (what Derrida terms an "ultimate referent"), making possible an identifiable and correct meaning or meanings for any potential statement that can be made within that system. Far from supporting this common Western view of language as logocentric, however, Derrida in fact argues that presence is not an ultimate referent and that it does not guarantee determinable (capable of being determined)—much less determinate (fixed and reliably correct)—meaning. Derrida in fact calls into question the "privileging" of speech and presence over writing and absence in Western thought.

    **PSYCHOLOGICAL CRITICISM AND PSYCHOANALYTIC CRIT-ICISM** Psychological criticism, which emerged in the first half of the nineteenth century, is a type of literary criticism that explores and analyzes literature in general and specific literary texts in terms of mental processes. Psychological critics generally focus on the mental processes of the author, analyzing works with an eye to their authors' personalities. Some psychological critics also use literary works to reconstruct and understand the personalities of authors—or to understand their individual modes of consciousness and thinking.

    Psychoanalytic criticism stands in stark contrast to psychological criticism. Although a type of psychological criticism, it is actually better known and more widely practiced than its "parent" approach. Psychoanalytic criticism originated in the work of Austrian psychoanalyst Sigmund Freud, who pioneered the technique of psychoanalysis. Freud developed a language that described, a model that explained, a theory that encompassed human psychology. His theories are directly and indirectly concerned with the nature of the unconscious mind.

    The psychoanalytic approach to literature not only rests on the theories of Freud, it may even be said to have *begun* with Freud, who wrote literary criticism as well as psychoanalytic theory. Probably because of Freud's characterization of the artist's mind as "one urged on by instincts that are too clamorous," psychoanalytic criticism written before 1950 tended to psychoanalyze the individual author. Literary works were read—sometimes unconvincingly—as fantasies that allowed authors to indulge repressed wishes, to protect themselves from deepseated anxieties, or both.

After 1950, psychoanalytic critics began to emphasize the ways in which authors create works that appeal to readers' repressed wishes and fantasies. Consequently, they shifted their focus away from the author's psyche toward the psychology of the reader and the text. Norman Holland's theories, concerned more with the reader than with the text, helped to establish **reader-response criticism**. Critics influenced by D. W. Winnicott, an object-relations theorist, have questioned the tendency to see reader/text as an either/or construct; instead, they have seen reader and text (or audience and play) in terms of a relationship taking place in what Winnicott calls a "transitional" or "potential space"—space in which binary oppositions like real/illusory and objective/subjective have little or no meaning.

Jacques Lacan, another post-Freudian psychoanalytic theorist, focused on language and language-related issues. Lacan treats the unconscious as a language; consequently, he views the dream not as Freud did (that is, as a form and symptom of repression) but rather as a form of discourse. Thus we may study dreams psychoanalytically in order to learn about literature, even as we may study literature in order to learn more about the unconscious. Lacan also revised Freud's concept of the Oedipus complex, which involves the childhood wish to displace the parent of one's own sex and take his or her place in the affections of the parent of the opposite sex, by relating it to the issue of language. He argues that the pre-oedipal stage is also a preverbal or "mirror stage," a stage he associates with the *Imaginary Order*. He associates the subsequent oedipal stage—which roughly coincides with the child's entry into language—with what he calls the *Symbolic Order*, in which words are not the things they stand for but, rather, are stand-ins or substitutes for those things. The Imaginary Order and the Symbolic Order are two of Lacan's three orders of subjectivity, the third being *The Real*, which involves intractable and substantial things or states that cannot be imagined, symbolized, or known directly (such as death).

**QUEER THEORY** A contemporary approach to literature and culture that asumes sexual identities to be flexible, not fixed, and that critiques gender and sexuality as they are commonly conceived in Western culture. Queer theorists, like **gender critics**, take the constructionist position that gender is a social artifact, that masculinity and femininity are culturally constructed and determined rather than natural or innate. A majority would further contend that sexuality, like gender, is socially constructed, arguing that the binary opposition heterosexual/homosexual is as much a product of culture and its institutions as the opposition masculinity/femininity. Most also view sexuality as performative rather than normative, as a process involving signifying acts rather than personal identity.

Queer theory is an outgrowth of gender criticism and, more specifically, **gay and lesbian criticism**. In fact, the term *queer theory* is generally credited to gender theorist Teresa de Lauretis, who in 1992 edited a special issue of the journal *differences* entitled *Queer Theory: Lesbian and Gay Sexualities*. Queer theorists also draw upon the writings of the twentieth-century philosophical historian Michel Foucault as well as on the work of three contemporary American theorists of gender: poet-critic Adrenne Rich and gender critics Judith Butler and Eve Kosofsky Sedgwick.

**READER-RESPONSE CRITICISM** A critical approach encompassing various approaches to literature that explore and seek to explain the diversity (and often divergence) of readers' responses to literary works.

Louise Rosenblatt is often credited with pioneering the approaches in *Literature as Exploration* (1938). In a 1969 essay entitled "Towards a Transactional Theory of Reading," she summed up her position as follows: "a poem is what the reader lives through under the guidance of the text and experiences as relevant to the text." Recognizing that many critics would reject this definition, Rosenblatt wrote: "The idea that a *poem* presupposes a *reader* actively involved with a *text* is particularly shocking to those seeking to emphasize the objectivity of their interpretations." Rosenblatt implicitly and generally refers to formalists (the most influential of whom are the **New Critics**) when she speaks of supposedly objective interpreters shocked by the notion that a "*poem*" is cooperatively produced by a "*reader*" and a "*text*." Formalists spoke of "the poem itself," the "concrete work of art," the "real poem." They had no interest in what a work of literature makes a reader "live through." In fact, in *The Verbal Icon* (1954), William K. Wimsatt and Monroe C. Beardsley used the term **affective fallacy** to define as erroneous the very idea that a reader's response is relevant to the meaning of a literary work.

Stanley Fish, whose early work is seen by some as marking the true beginning of contemporary reader-response criticism, also took issue with the tenets of formalism. In "Literature in the Reader: Affective Stylistics" (1970), he argued that any school of criticism that sees a literary work as an object, claiming to describe what it is and never what it does, misconstrues the very essence of literature and reading. Literature exists and signifies when it is read, Fish suggests, and its force is an affective force. Furthermore, reading is a temporal process, not a spatial one as formalists assume when they step back and survey the literary work as if it were an object spread out before them. The German critic Wolfgang Iser has described that process in his books *The Implied Reader: Patterns of Communication in Prose Fiction from Bunyan to Beckett* (1974) and *The Act of Reading: A Theory of Aesthetic Response* (1976). Iser argues that texts contain gaps (or blanks) that powerfully affect the reader, who must explain them, connect what they separate, and create in his or her mind aspects of a work that aren't *in* the text but that the text incites.

With the redefinition of literature as something that only exists meaningfully in the mind of the reader, with the redefinition of the literary work as a catalyst of mental events, comes a redefinition of the reader. No longer is the reader the passive recipient of those ideas that an author has planted in a text. "The reader is *active*," Rosenblatt had insisted. Fish makes the same point in "Literature in the Reader": "reading is . . . something you *do*." Iser, in focusing critical interest on the gaps in texts, on the blanks that readers have to fill in, similarly redefines the reader as an active maker of meaning. Other reader-response critics define the reader differently. Wayne Booth uses the phrase *the implied reader* to mean the reader "created by the work." Like Booth, Iser employs the term *the implied reader*, but he also uses "the educated reader" when he refers to what Fish calls the "intended reader." Since the mid-1970s, reader-response criticism has evolved into a variety of new forms. Subjectivists like David Bleich, Norman Holland, and Robert Crosman have viewed the reader's response not as one "guided" by the text but rather as one motivated by deep-seated, personal, psychological needs. Holland has suggested that, when we read, we find our own "identity theme" in the text using "the literary work to symbolize and finally to replicate ourselves. We work out through the text our own characteristic patterns of desire." Even Fish has moved away from reader-response criticism as he had initially helped define it, focusing on "interpretive strategies" held in common by "interpretive communities"—such as the one comprised by American college students reading a novel as a class assignment.

Fish's shift in focus is in many ways typical of changes that have taken place within the field of reader-response criticism—a field which, because of those changes, is increasingly being referred to as *reader-oriented criticism*. Recent reader-oriented critics, responding to Fish's emphasis on interpretive communities and also to the historically oriented perception theory of Hans Robert Jauss, have studied the way a given reading public's "horizons of expectations" change over time. Many of these contemporary critics view themselves as reader-oriented critics and as practitioners of some other critical approach as well. Certain **feminist** and **gender critics** with an interest in reader response have asked whether there is such a thing as "reading like a woman." Reading-oriented **new historicists** have looked at the way in which racism affects and is affected by reading and, more generally, the way in which politics can affect reading practices and outcomes. **Gay and lesbian critics**, such as Wayne Koestenbaum, have argued that sexualities have been similarly constructed within and by social **discourses** and that there may even be a homosexual way of reading.

**REAL, THE** *See* **psychoanalytic criticism and psychological criticism**.

**SEMIOLOGY** Another word for **semiotics**, created by Swiss linguist Ferdinand de Saussure in his 1915 book *Course in General Linguistics. See* **semiotics**.

**SEMIOTICS** A term coined by Charles Sanders Peirce to refer to the study of signs, sign systems, and the way meaning is derived from them. **Structuralist** anthropologists, psychoanalysts, and literary critics developed semiotics during the decades following 1950, but much of the pioneering work had been done at the turn of the century by Peirce and by the founder of modern linguistics, Ferdinand de Saussure.

To a semiotician, a sign is not simply a direct means of communication, such as a stop sign or a restaurant sign or language itself. Rather, signs encompass body language (crossed arms, slouching), ways of greeting and parting (handshakes, hugs, waves), artifacts, and even articles of clothing. A sign is anything that conveys information to others who understand it based upon a system of codes and conventions that they have consciously learned or unconsciously internalized as members of a certain culture. Semioticians have often used concepts derived specifically from linguistics, which focuses on language, to analyze all types of signs.

Although Saussure viewed linguistics as a division of semiotics (semiotics, after all, involves the study of all signs, not just linguistic ones), much semiotic theory rests on Saussure's linguistic terms, concepts, and distinctions. Semioticians subscribe to Saussure's basic concept of the linguistic sign as containing a *signifier* (a linguistic "sound image" used to represent some more abstract concept) and *signified* (the abstract concept being represented). They have also found generally useful his notion that the relationship between signifiers and signified is arbitrary; that is, no intrinsic or natural relationship exists between them, and meanings we derive from signifiers are grounded in the differences among signifiers themselves. Particularly useful are Saussure's concept of the *phoneme* (the smallest basic speech sound or unit of pronunciation) and his idea that phonemes exist in two kinds of relationships: diachronic and synchronic.

A phoneme has a diachronic, or "horizontal," relationship with those other phonemes that precede and follow it (as the words appear, left to right, on this page) in a particular usage, utterance, or **narrative**—what Saussure called *parole* (French for "word"). A phoneme has a synchronic, or "vertical," relationship with the entire system of language within which individual usages, utterances, or narratives have meaning—what Saussure called *langue* (French for "tongue," as in "native tongue," meaning language). *An* means what it means in English because those of us who speak the language are plugged into the same system (think of it as a computer network where different individuals access the same information in the same way at a given time). A principal tenet of semiotics is that signs, like words, are not significant in themselves, but instead have meaning only in relation to other signs and the entire system of signs, or *langue*. Meaning is not inherent in the signs themselves, but is derived from the differences among signs.

Given that semiotic theory underlies structuralism, it is not surprising that many semioticians have taken a broad, structuralist approach to signs, studying a variety of phenomena ranging from rites of passage to methods of preparing and consuming food in order to understand the cultural codes and conventions they reveal. Because of the broad-based applicability of semiotics, furthermore, structuralist anthropologists such as Claude Lévi-Strauss, literary critics such as Roland Barthes, and **psychoanalytic theorists** such as Jacques Lacan and Julia Kristeva, have made use of semiotic theories and practices. Kristeva, who is generally considered a pioneer of feminism although she eschews the feminist label, has argued that there is such a thing as feminine language and that it is semiotic, not **symbolic** in nature. She thus employs both terms in an unusual way, using *semiotic* to refer to language that is rhythmic, unifying, and fluid, and *symbolic* to refer to the more rigid associations redefined in the Western canon. The affinity between semiotics and structuralist literary criticism derives from the emphasis placed on *langue*, or system. Structuralist critics were reacting against **formalists** and their method of focusing on individual words as if meanings did not depend on anything external to the text. *See* also **symbol**, **structuralism**.

**SIMILE** *See* **metaphor**, **trope**.

**STRUCTURALISM** A theory of humankind whose proponents attempted to show systematically, even scientifically, that all elements of human culture, including literature, may be understood as parts of a system of signs. Critic Robert Scholes has described structuralism as a reaction to "'modernist' alienation and despair."

European structuralists such as Roman Jakobson, Claude Lévi-Strauss, and Roland Barthes (before his shift toward poststructuralism) attempted to develop a **semiology**, or **semiotics** (science of signs). Barthes, among others, sought to recover literature and even language from the isolation in which they had been studied and to show that the laws that govern them govern all signs, from road signs to articles of clothing.

Structuralism was heavily influenced by linguistics, especially by the pioneering work of linguist Ferdinand de Saussure. Particularly useful to structuralists were Saussure's concept of the phoneme (the smallest basic speech sound or unit of pronunciation) and his idea that phonemes exist in two kinds of relationships: diachronic and synchronic. A phoneme has a diachronic, or "horizontal," relationship with those other phonemes that precede and follow it (as the words appear, left to right, on this page) in a particular usage, utterance, or narrative—what Saussure called *parole* (French for "word"). A phoneme has a synchronic, or "vertical," relationship with the entire system of language within which individual usages, utterances, or narratives have meaning—what Saussure called *langue* (French for "tongue," as in "native tongue," meaning language). *An* means what it means in English because those of us who speak the language are plugged into the same system (think of it as a computer network where different individuals can access the same information in the same way at a given time.)

Following Saussure, Lévi-Strauss, an anthropologist, studied hundreds of myths, breaking them into their smallest meaningful units, which he called "mythemes." Removing each from its diachronic relations with other mythemes in a single myth (such as the myth of Oedipus and his mother), he vertically aligned those mythemes that he found to be homologous (structurally correspondent). He then studied the relationships within as well as between vertically aligned columns, in an attempt to understand scientifically, through ratios and proportions, those thoughts and processes that humankind has shared, both at one particular time and across time. Whether Lévi-Strauss was studying the structure of myths or the structure of villages, he looked for recurring, common elements that transcended the differences within and among cultures.

Structuralists followed Saussure in preferring to think about the overriding *langue*, or language of myth, in which each mytheme and mytheme-constituted myth fits meaningfully, rather than about isolated individual *paroles*, or narratives. Structuralists also followed Saussure's lead in believing that sign systems must be understood in terms of binary oppositions (a proposition later disputed by poststructuralist Jacques Derrida). In analyzing myths and texts to find basic structures, structuralists found that opposite terms modulate until they are finally resolved or reconciled by some intermediary third term. Thus a structuralist reading of Milton's *Paradise Lost* (1667) might show that the war between God and the rebellious angels becomes a rift between God and sinful, fallen man, a rift that is healed by the Son of God, the mediating third term.

Although structuralism was largely a European phenomenon in its origin and development, it was influenced by American thinkers as well. Noam Chomsky, for instance, who powerfully influenced structuralism through works such as *Reflections on Language* (1975), identified and distinguished between "surface structures" and "deep structures" in language and linguistic literatures, including **texts**.

**SYMBOL** Something that, although it is of interest in its own right, stands for or suggests something larger and more complex—often an idea or a range of interrelated ideas, attitudes, and practices. Within a given culture, some things are understood to be symbols: the flag of the United States is an example, as are the five intertwined Olympic rings. More subtle cultural symbols might be the river as a symbol of time and the journey as a symbol of life and its manifold experiences. Instead of appropriating symbols generally used and understood within their culture, writers often create their own symbols by setting up a complex but identifiable web of associations in their works. As a result, one object, image, person, place, or action suggests others, and may ultimately suggest a range of ideas.

A symbol may thus be defined as a **metaphor** in which the vehicle—the image, activity, or concept used to represent something else—represents many related things (or **tenors**), or is broadly suggestive. The urn in Keats's "Ode on a Grecian Urn" (1820) suggests many interrelated concepts, including art, truth, beauty, and timelessness.

Symbols have been of particular interest to **formalists**, who study how meanings emerge from the complex, patterned relationships among images in a work, and **psychoanalytic critics**, who are interested in how individual authors and the larger culture both disguise and reveal unconscious fears and desires through symbols. Recently, French **feminist critics** have also focused on the symbolic. They have suggested that, as wide-ranging as it seems, symbolic language is ultimately rigid and restrictive. They favor **semiotic** language and writing—writing that neither opposes nor hierarchically ranks qualities or elements of reality nor symbolizes one thing but not another in terms of a third—contending that semiotic language is at once more fluid, rhythmic, unifying, and feminine.

**SYMBOLIC ORDER** See **psychological criticism and psychoanalytic criticism, symbol.**

**TENOR** See **metaphor, metonymy, symbol.**

**TEXT** From the Latin *texere*, meaning "to weave," a term that may be defined in a number of ways. Some critics restrict its use to the written word, although they may apply the term to objects ranging from a poem to the words in a book, to a book itself, to a Biblical passage used in a sermon, to a written transcript of an oral statement or interview. Other critics include nonwritten material in the designation text, as long as that material has been isolated for analysis.

French **structuralist** critics took issue with the traditional view of literary compositions as "works" with a form intentionally imposed by the author and a meaning identifiable through analysis of the author's use of language. These critics argued that literary compositions are texts rather than works, texts being the product of a social institution they called *écriture* (writing). By identifying compositions as texts rather than works, structuralists denied them the personalized character attributed to works wrought by a particular, unique author. Structuralists believed not only that a text was essentially impersonal, the confluence of certain preexisting attributes of the social institution of writing, but that any interpretation of the text should result from an impersonal *lecture* (reading).

This *lecture* included reading with an active awareness of how the linguistic system functions.

The French writer and theorist Roland Barthes, a structuralist who later turned toward **poststructuralism**, distinguished text from work in a different way, characterizing a text as open and a work as closed. According to Barthes, works are bounded entities, conventionally classified in the canon, whereas texts engage readers in an ongoing relationship of interpretation and reinterpretation. Barthes further divided texts into two categories: *lisible* (readerly) and *scriptible* (writerly). Texts that are *lisible* depend more heavily on convention, making their interpretation easier and more predictable. Texts that are *scriptible* are generally experimental, flouting or seriously modifying traditional rules. Such texts cannot be interpreted according to standard conventions.

**TROPE** One of the two major divisions of **figures of speech** (the other being *rhetorical figures*). Trope comes from a word that literally means "turning"; to trope (with figures of speech) is, figuratively speaking, to turn or twist some word or phrase to make it mean something else. **Metaphor, metonymy, simile**, personification, and synecdoche are sometimes referred to as the principal tropes.

**UNDECIDABILITY** *See* **deconstruction**.

**VEHICLE** *See* **metaphor, metonymy, symbol**.

# About the Contributors

## THE VOLUME EDITOR

**Johanna M. Smith** is an associate professor of English at the University of Texas at Arlington, where she teaches courses in eighteenth- and nineteenth-century British literature and culture, postcolonial literatures, theater, and literature and law. She has published numerous articles on figures ranging from Jane Austen to Joseph Conrad, as well as a book on Mary Shelley and a coedited anthology of selections from eighteenth-century women's life writings.

## THE CRITICS

**Siobhan Carroll** is an assistant professor at the University of Delaware, where she teaches courses on Romanticism and contemporary science fiction. Author of *An Empire of Air and Water: Uncolonizable Space in the British Imagination, 1750–1850* (2015), she is currently working on a book on the politics of global ecology in the long nineteenth century.

**David Collings** is Professor of English at Bowdoin College. He is author of *Wordsworthian Errancies: The Poetics of Cultural Dismemberment* (1994), *Monstrous Society: Reciprocity, Discipline and the Political Uncanny, c. 1780–1848* (2009), and *Stolen Future, Broken Present: The*

*Human Significance of Climate Change* (2014) and was coeditor of *Queer Romanticisms* (2004–5) and *Romanticism and Disaster* (2012). His current project is tentatively entitled *Disastrous Subjectivities: Romanticism, Catastrophe, and the Real.*

**Warren Montag** is the Brown Family Professor of Literature at Occidental College in Los Angeles. His recent books include *Althusser and His Contemporaries* (2013) and *The Other Adam Smith* (2014). Montag is also the editor of *Décalages*, a journal on Althusser and his circle, and the translator of Etienne Balibar's *Identity and Difference: John Locke and the Invention of Consciousness* (2013).

**Grant F. Scott** is Professor of English at Muhlenberg College in Pennsylvania, author of *The Sculpted Word: Keats, Ekphrasis, and the Visual Arts* (1994) and editor of *Selected Letters of John Keats* (2002) and *Joseph Severn: Letters and Memoirs* (2005). His scholarly edition, *The Illustrated Letters of Richard Doyle to His Father, 1842–1843*, will be published in 2015.

**Allan Lloyd Smith** (1945–2010) was a leading British scholar of nineteenth-century American literature. He was a lecturer at Keele University and the University of East Anglia, where he served several times as head of American studies. He also organized the first International Gothic Conference in 1991, and became president of the International Gothic Association, founded in 1995. He is the author of *American Gothic Fiction: An Introduction, Eve Tempted: Writing and Sexuality in Hawthorne's Fiction*, and *Uncanny American Fiction: Medusa's Face*.

**Christopher Stampone** is a Ph.D. candidate at Southern Methodist University. He is currently writing a dissertation on romance and Romanticism in a transatlantic context that focuses on the proliferation of several forms of romance in the period. He recently published an essay on Frank Norris's *The Octopus* and has an essay on Charles Brockden Brown's *Edgar Huntly* forthcoming in *Early American Literature.*

## THE SERIES EDITOR

**Ross C Murfin**, general editor of the series, is E. A. Lilly Distinguished Professor of English at Southern Methodist University. He has taught literature at Yale University and the University of Virginia and has published scholarly studies on Joseph Conrad, Thomas Hardy, and D. H. Lawrence. With Supriya M. Ray, he is the author of *The Bedford Glossary of Critical and Literary Terms.*